(Continued on back endsheets)

Dictionary of Literary Biography® • Volume One Hundred Thirty-Five

British Short-Fiction Writers, 1880–1914:
The Realist Tradition

Dictionary of Literary Biography® • Volume One Hundred Thirty-Five

British Short-Fiction Writers, 1880–1914: The Realist Tradition

Edited by
William B. Thesing
University of South Carolina

A Bruccoli Clark Layman Book
Gale Research Inc.
Detroit, Washington, D.C., London

Printed in the United States of America

Published simultaneously in the United Kingdom
by Gale Research International Limited
(An affiliated company of Gale Research Inc.)

The paper used in this publication meets the minimum requirements
of American National Standard for Information Sciences–Permanence
Paper for Printed Library Materials, ANSI Z39.48-1984. ∞ ™

Library of Congress Catalog Card Number 93-35683
ISBN 0–8103–5394–6

I⟨T⟩P™

The trademark **ITP** is used under license.

10 9 8 7 6 5 4 3 2 1

For Charles, Virginia, John, Harold, and Mary Ruth Isley
— Special In-Laws

and

For Pepper and Andy
— Loyal Companions

Contents

Plan of the Series

. . . Almost the most prodigious asset of a country, and perhaps its most precious possession, is its native literary product — when that product is fine and noble and enduring.

Mark Twain*

The advisory board, the editors, and the publisher of the *Dictionary of Literary Biography* are joined in endorsing Mark Twain's declaration. The literature of a nation provides an inexhaustible resource of permanent worth. We intend to make literature and its creators better understood and more accessible to students and the reading public, while satisfying the standards of teachers and scholars.

To meet these requirements, *literary biography* has been construed in terms of the author's achievement. The most important thing about a writer is his writing. Accordingly, the entries in *DLB* are career biographies, tracing the development of the author's canon and the evolution of his reputation.

The purpose of *DLB* is not only to provide reliable information in a convenient format but also to place the figures in the larger perspective of literary history and to offer appraisals of their accomplishments by qualified scholars.

The publication plan for *DLB* resulted from two years of preparation. The project was proposed to Bruccoli Clark by Frederick C. Ruffner, president of the Gale Research Company, in November 1975. After specimen entries were prepared and typeset, an advisory board was formed to refine the entry format and develop the series rationale. In meetings held during 1976, the publisher, series editors, and advisory board approved the scheme for a comprehensive biographical dictionary of persons who contributed to North American literature. Editorial work on the first volume began in January 1977, and it was published in 1978. In order to make *DLB* more than a reference tool and to compile volumes that individually have claim to status as literary history, it was decided to organize vol-

From an unpublished section of Mark Twain's autobiography, copyright by the Mark Twain Company

umes by topic, period, or genre. Each of these free-standing volumes provides a biographical-bibliographical guide and overview for a particular area of literature. We are convinced that this organization — as opposed to a single alphabet method — constitutes a valuable innovation in the presentation of reference material. The volume plan necessarily requires many decisions for the placement and treatment of authors who might properly be included in two or three volumes. In some instances a major figure will be included in separate volumes, but with different entries emphasizing the aspect of his career appropriate to each volume. Ernest Hemingway, for example, is represented in *American Writers in Paris, 1920-1939* by an entry focusing on his expatriate apprenticeship; he is also in *American Novelists, 1910-1945* with an entry surveying his entire career. Each volume includes a cumulative index of the subject authors and articles. Comprehensive indexes to the entire series are planned.

With volume ten in 1982 it was decided to enlarge the scope of *DLB*. By the end of 1986 twenty-one volumes treating British literature had been published, and volumes for Commonwealth and Modern European literature were in progress. The series has been further augmented by the *DLB Yearbooks* (since 1981) which update published entries and add new entries to keep the *DLB* current with contemporary activity. There have also been *DLB Documentary Series* volumes which provide biographical and critical source materials for figures whose work is judged to have particular interest for students. One of these companion volumes is entirely devoted to Tennessee Williams.

We define literature as the *intellectual commerce of a nation:* not merely as belles lettres but as that ample and complex process by which ideas are generated, shaped, and transmitted. *DLB* entries are not limited to "creative writers" but extend to other figures who in their time and in their way influenced the mind of a people. Thus the series encompasses historians, journalists, publishers, and screenwriters. By this means readers of *DLB* may be aided to perceive literature not as cult scripture in the keeping of intellectual high priests but firmly positioned at the center of a nation's life.

DLB includes the major writers appropriate to each volume and those standing in the ranks immediately behind them. Scholarly and critical counsel has been sought in deciding which minor figures to include and how full their entries should be. Wherever possible, useful references are made to figures who do not warrant separate entries.

Each *DLB* volume has a volume editor responsible for planning the volume, selecting the figures for inclusion, and assigning the entries. Volume editors are also responsible for preparing, where appropriate, appendices surveying the major periodicals and literary and intellectual movements for their volumes, as well as lists of further readings. Work on the series as a whole is coordinated at the Bruccoli Clark Layman editorial center in Columbia, South Carolina, where the editorial staff is responsible for accuracy of the published volumes.

One feature that distinguishes *DLB* is the illustration policy – its concern with the iconography of literature. Just as an author is influenced by his surroundings, so is the reader's understanding of the author enhanced by a knowledge of his environment. Therefore *DLB* volumes include not only drawings, paintings, and photographs of authors, often depicting them at various stages in their careers, but also illustrations of their families and places where they lived. Title pages are regularly reproduced in facsimile along with dust jackets for modern authors. The dust jackets are a special feature of *DLB* because they often document better than anything else the way in which an author's work was perceived in its own time. Specimens of the writers' manuscripts are included when feasible.

Samuel Johnson rightly decreed that "The chief glory of every people arises from its authors." The purpose of the *Dictionary of Literary Biography* is to compile literary history in the surest way available to us – by accurate and comprehensive treatment of the lives and work of those who contributed to it.

The *DLB* Advisory Board

Introduction

The nearly three and one-half decades between 1880 and 1914 were diverse and transitional, and various labels can be applied to them. Three terms are appropriate for some of these years: the late-Victorian era, the Edwardian period, and the period of early modernism. Three monarchs occupied the British throne during these years: Queen Victoria celebrated the sixtieth anniversary of her reign in 1897 and died in 1901; Edward VII reigned from 1901 to 1910; and George V ruled from 1910 through the years of World War I and beyond. In 1880 Great Britain was at peace and was the strongest imperial power in the world; in 1914 there were great battles in Europe that would undermine forever the Victorian ideals and world power of the island nation. Not all of the lamps of literature were extinguished in 1914; however, the modernist techniques and topics in works that appeared during and after the war were so fundamentally different from the literature written before the brutalities of trench fighting that a division is required. The period 1880 to 1914, then, was a transitional phase during which the stabilities of the Victorian world gradually yielded to the turbulent flux of the twentieth century.

Some of the major historical and political events of the period deserve mentioning. The 1880s in Great Britain witnessed the formation of political movements for reform, some of which occasioned direct confrontations and violence in the streets. The Social Democratic Federation was founded by H. M. Hyndman in 1881; the Fabian Society was founded in 1884. (One writer in this volume, R. B. Cunninghame Graham, became the first avowed socialist member of Parliament in 1886.) Although political democracy was further extended with the passage of the Third Reform Bill in 1884 (giving franchise to all male householders in Great Britain), there were protests of economic ills. In 1886 there were riots in Trafalgar Square to protest unemployment, followed by more riots, injuries, and death again on "Bloody Sunday," 13 November 1887. In this day's events Graham demonstrated his support for working-class policies only to be beaten and arrested. In 1888 there was a large-scale strike by matchworkers, and thousands of workers participated in the 1889 London Dock Strike. Shopwork-

ers and miners formed unions to advance their interests.

With the Boer War in South Africa (1899–1902) came a new attention to Britain's military readiness. A popular monthly of the period, the *Idler,* heralded Britain's new attention to such concerns with the appearance in volume 13 (1898) of no less than five articles on such topics as "Britannia Armed," "Great Britain as a Military Power," "The Volunteers – and Efficiency," "Watching a Naval Death-Duel," and "Is the British Navy Invincible?" There had been no attention to such matters in the thirteen years of the periodical's issues published up to this date. From the singing of jingoist songs in music halls to the distribution of patriotic poems and short stories, Britons became increasingly interested in military might and preparedness. Some writers in this volume reacted negatively and directly to the imperialism and militarism of the period. George Moore hated the Boer War and jingoism; he moved back to Ireland in 1901 and joined organizations associated with Irish nationalism. Thomas Hardy wrote ironic poems against war, including "Drummer Hodge" (first published as "The Dead Drummer" in *Literature,* December 1899) and "Channel Firing" (*Fortnightly,* 1914).

Following decades of protest women gained new rights and opportunities during this period. By the terms of the 1882 Married Women's Property Act, women were granted the right to all property that they earned or acquired before or after marriage. Women were allowed more public visibility, which was demonstrated, for example, by the first ladies' singles championship in tennis held in 1884. The Women's Hockey Association was formed in 1895. However, the right to vote in national elections was not won until after World War I, despite many protests and petitions by women's groups between 1887 and 1914.

But, beyond the social and political turbulence of the period, the 1880s and 1890s brought modern technological changes to the urban world, as electric lights and electrified subways appeared in London. Bicycles were in fashion, and cinema became a popular part of urban entertainment at London's Empire Theatre in 1896. The first motor buses came into service on London's streets in 1899, and automobiles were on the roads by the early 1900s.

The Romantic and Realist Traditions

Fiction writers such as Oscar Wilde, William Butler Yeats, Walter Pater, Joseph Conrad, and Robert Louis Stevenson held to the prevailing doctrine of the period — art for art's sake. Those authors believed that art should not be concerned with controversial social and political issues but that it should celebrate the beautiful or the exotic in a highly polished style. The scope of the romantic tradition includes romance, sentimentalism, escapism, and exoticism as well as the fantastic mode. A manifesto of the art-for-art's-sake movement appeared in 1885 with the delivery of a lecture, "Ten O'Clock," by James McNeill Whistler. The principles of the credo were expanded and refined by such critics as Pater and Wilde in the 1880s and 1890s.

This volume on the realist tradition in British short fiction encompasses such writers as Hardy, Hubert Crackanthorpe, George Gissing, Arnold Bennett, G. R. Sims, Israel Zangwill, Sir Walter Besant, Ella D'Arcy, Sarah Grand, and Arthur Morrison. The scope of the realist tradition includes the use of naturalistic or journalistic details to describe grim situations; it also embraces social comedy. These writers sought to expose and reform society's deficiencies and injustices. Their settings are not the tropical islands of the Pacific Ocean but the slums of London's East End and the dark ghettos of the newly industrialized cities of the North, including Birmingham, Manchester, and Liverpool. These writers often describe with complete candor the baseness of human motives and conduct. The family unit is often the focus of attention, as conflict and abuse abound. Domestic violence and marital strife, especially in slum conditions, are favorite topics in the short stories of Gissing and Morrison.

It is fair to ask, What attracts and holds the reader's attention in a piece of short fiction that recreates the drabness of ordinary life? To answer this question is to explore the background of the tradition of realistic fiction. What strains of realism can be defined as these writers turned to portray grim sketches of the lives of common people?

In order to understand the tradition of realistic fiction writing in Great Britain in the nineteenth century, it is important to consider the wider European literary climate. In France practitioners of realistic fiction included Emile Zola, Gustave Flaubert, and Guy de Maupassant. As a chief representative of the French naturalist movement, Zola embodied in his fiction the scientific notions of the determination of human conduct by heredity and environment. His realistic settings and characters expose a diseased society: lust, murder, drunkenness, provincial politics, corruption, and misery are depicted in his novels. Zola's *Germinal* (1885; translated, 1885) concerns the brutalized coal miners of northern France in the 1880s. The book had its effect as a political tract, but it also captures the customs and worldview of a typical miners' village of the era. Each day the workers risk injury and death on the job site. With the publication of *Madame Bovary* (1857; translated, 1881) Flaubert and his editor were tried for offenses against public morality — adultery and suicide are committed by his tragic heroine — though they were both eventually acquitted. The shoddy, banal reality of French country life serves as the setting for the story. Many of Maupassant's short stories and novels are drawn from his experiences as a minor civil servant and his knowledge of the Norman peasant. Other stories explore odd sexual encounters, the brutalities of war, and the misfits of society. With detached observation he depicts social hypocrisy and squalor.

From Russian fiction, the examples of Count Leo Tolstoy, Ivan Turgenev, and Fyodor Dostoyevsky were available to British realists. Anguish, death, and love's pitfalls and fulfillments inform Tolstoy's best fiction; Turgenev's fiction blends politics and pessimism. Dostoyevsky wrote tales of poor, oppressed city dwellers and drew on his own prison experiences in other writings. The realistic dramas of Scandinavians Henrik Ibsen and August Strindberg influenced some British short-fiction writers, particularly George Egerton. In many cases, however, British realists avoided some of the more extreme positions and sentiments of Continental realism. Flaubert once wrote to Louise Colet (with whom he was having an affair) that one side of his artistic nature "enjoys the animal sides of man." But to be *too* realistic was considered a flaw by some writers of the movement in Great Britain. Gissing parodies such tendencies in *New Grub Street* (1891). Hardy and Florence Henniker expressed their disapproval of Zola's approach, believing that a writer who dwells on the animal side of human nature abandons his role as an artist.

Between 1880 and 1914 the realistic tradition had both its defenders and detractors in Great Britain. One spirited defense of realism was based on the achievements of Zola in France. Crackanthorpe makes a strong defense of French realism in "Realism in France and England: An Interview with M. Emile Zola" (*Albemarle,* February 1892). In this arti-

Realist writers of the 1890s were frequently criticized for focusing on the harshest aspects of life and emphasizing misfortune. These illustrations from the Idler *(October 1895) depict an exaggerated contrast between realism and idealism.*

cle he claims that Zola is part of "man's continued search after truth"; the French writer represents the "temper of the age" in its development and advance. England is condemned for its reactionary tastes owing to its remaining "under the yoke of the puritans." Writers whose works were substantially colored by pessimism wrote little that is specific or theoretical in defense of their attitudes. In his essay on the realistic short story, "Reticence in Literature" (*Yellow Book,* July 1894), Crackanthorpe hints that only so much despair and "cheerlessness" can be tolerated by readers. The ultimate goal is to look forward to the day when "a man will arise who will give us a study of human happiness, as fine, as vital as anything we owe to Guy de Maupassant or to Ibsen."

In his introduction to *Tales of Mean Streets* (1894), Morrison provides a broad, general impression of the East End: its physical features, customs, and values. However, the most earnest defense of realism – and especially of the legitimacy of the realistic portrayal of working-class life – is found in Morrison's essay "What Is A Realist?" (*New Review,* 1897), in which he defines and describes the realis-

tic writer's mandate. As a tale-teller, he presents life as he sees it. The artist is allowed to look everywhere for his subject matter: "If the community have left horrible places and horrible lives before his eyes, then the fault is that of the community; and to picture these places and these lives becomes not merely his privilege but his duty." He admits that his stories and descriptions may cause discomfort, that some "were shocked to read of low creatures."

In his defense Morrison insists on the sincerity and accuracy of the pictures in his stories: "For a good few years I have lived in the East End of London, and have been, not an occasional visitor, but a familiar and equal friend in the house of the East-Ender in all his degrees." He denies that a realist selects and rearranges reality to highlight the worst evils: "A definite accusation is that I have taken bad types from divers districts, and concentrated them in my picture of the Jago. . . . The original of my Jago was a place to which those types gravitated as by natural law from other parts. . . . Not I, but their own propensity, brought these people together." He also insists that the gritty details in his stories are in no sense irrelevant: "When I am attempting to depict the squalid surroundings of a boy in a thieves' neighbourhood, and their effect on his character, I am disposed to consider those surroundings no irrelevancies at all, but strict essentials of the picture."

Henry Woodd Nevinson's "Purgation" (*Fire of Life,* 1935) explores how commonplace settings and everyday, disadvantaged people attracted his attention, interest, and study in his realistic narratives: "I was drawn to the Black Country chiefly by repulsion, for one always likes to see things at their worst, and I had long known the Black Country as the deadliest region of England. In the same spirit, I had the previous year (1894), visited the Workhouse schools around London so as to realise what education at its worst might be." Regarding his 1893 story "The 'St. George' of Rochester," he writes, "The life on those barges was to me one of intense interest, mainly for the simple character of the men, and the exact routine of their essential work." His book of East End stories, *Neighbours of Ours* (1895), grew out of knowledge that he had gradually absorbed over a period of many years by working at the experimental Toynbee Hall in the East End and living in nearby Petticoat Lane. The "invariable smell of dirty poverty" stimulated Nevinson's creative imagination.

Because the basic tenets of realism offer a disturbing picture of men and women in society, it is no surprise that critical opposition appeared in periodical reviews in the late nineteenth and early twentieth centuries. Readers and critics objected to fiction that presented realistic pictures of everyday life that seemed too brutal and sordid. Although the emphasis on sex offended some readers, more often detractors objected to the depiction of relationships in which there was no romance but only animal desire or social-class manipulation. Others complained of an underlying spirit of morbidness in some realistic fiction. D'Arcy was criticized for creating characters who were too realistic, too similar to depressing or irritating people. In an article in the *Yellow Book,* Arthur Waugh condemns the school of realism that "sought for subject matter the discussion of passions and sensations hitherto not associated with literature." In "The Short Story" (*Nineteenth Century,* March 1898) Frederick Wedmore deplores the growing trend of depicting "the life of the gutter." He berates "that distorted 'realism' which witnesses upon the part of its practitioners to *one thing only,* a profound conviction of the ugly!" He views the staunch practitioner of realism as "the

dyspeptic pessimist" who is suffering from "a malady of the mind."

In *The Spirit of Reform: British Literature and Politics, 1832–1867* (1977) Patrick Brantlinger analyzes the various elements of realism in Victorian England. He points out that the first use of the term *realism* in English seems to have occurred in 1853. Defining the implications and tenets of realism is a difficult undertaking. As Brantlinger observes, " 'Realism' in any of its avatars is a vexing word to define. . . . It is a form of illusion that aims at disillusionment." The perspective of the realistic writer can range from Zola's scientific stance to William Makepeace Thackeray's satiric one. However, the realist writer's goal is essentially to deflate and expose. Brantlinger maintains that the aim of a realist is to "take what is lofty and grand and show how it rests upon the low. . . . Realism, then, is always reductive: the realist promises to analyze experience into its basic units, to show the animal within man and the chemical machinery within the animal. The latent message in all realistic art is the conversion of people into objects, the metaphoric equivalent of the substitution of exchange value for real value which occurs in modern commercial and industrial relations." Furthermore, "It is the nature of realism not necessarily to affirm the social status quo but to present it as inevitable, an immovable object that will change itself through slow growth but that cannot be much affected (except perhaps for the worse) either by individual effort or by legislative reform."

From his late-twentieth-century perspective Brantlinger admits that there are problems with the aesthetics of realism. He points out that a common complaint against realism is that it eschews the ideal and the theoretical and focuses too exclusively on "the unanalyzed flow of sensation and event, daily business, material surroundings, and financial interests – life on the installment plan." It is, in short, a "reductive art." Realism at its worst is equated with a vulgar literalism: in presenting the grim realities of urban/industrial life it may simply mimic the worldview of utilitarianism and the factory system. Also, realistic writing opens itself to the charge of blandness or lack of excellence: in Brantlinger's estimation, "The word 'mediocrity' captures a central problem of artistic realism." To take one case, Grand (as well as other short-story writers in this volume) was committed to the value of the realistic tradition, writing that "fiction has always been held to be at its best when it was true to life." But what are the consequences to readers of viewing the truth of life? How does the realistic writer escape the dilemma that reality is truth, but that it is also inade-

Cartoon mocking the artistic style of illustrator Aubrey Beardsley, as
represented by the fashionable lady. Beardsley was artistic editor for
the Yellow Book, *one of the best-known journals of the*
1890s (Idler, *February 1895).*

quate or despicable or mundane or tedious? Why bother to read stories that depict the reductive conversion of people into objects? What can be learned from the depiction of characters who represent human beings who have lost rational control over their circumstances and are simply pawns entrapped by the cruel forces of nature and society?

Although Edgar Allan Poe's short stories of the 1840s offer a rather neat beginning point for the art in nineteenth-century America, the origins of the genre of short fiction in Great Britain are more clouded, weaving through the forms of urban sketch, tale, and moral exemplum. Developments in the realistic technique were ongoing throughout the years covered in this volume. Some of the Victorian pioneers in the tradition of realistic fiction before

1880 include Thackeray, George Eliot, Anthony Trollope, and Charles Dickens. Gissing and Hardy carried on the tradition. Other writers were involved in various controversies over realistic art, however. For example, many critics view Moore's *Esther Waters* (1894) as one of the cornerstones in the emergence of a new realism in the English novel because of its coverage of controversial issues and its presentation of daring characters.

As far as a watershed date is concerned, the 1894 ban by Mudie's and Smith's lending libraries of the three-volume novel – or what Henry James refers to as those "large loose baggy monsters" – signaled a change in the popular tastes of readers who desired shorter, more convenient modes of fiction. An institution that had been viewed by some writers as a tyranny and condemned by others as an agent of censorship in the distribution of books had been broken at last. Writers such as Moore, who had in the past seen their works banned by the circulating libraries, now found new outlets of expression as well as a wider audience. Curiously enough, the war against the stranglehold of three-volume novels and the lending libraries has roots that go back as far as 1856. In "The Art of Story-Telling" (*Fraser's,* June 1856), a manifesto that calls for British authors and readers to turn to the short-story mode (then increasingly popular in France), the anonymous commentator views the lending libraries as a major obstacle: "The proprietor of the circulating library . . . won't encourage short stories. The librarian wont have them at any price." This attitude, the astute commentator argues, is inconsistent with the trends of the time and with the national character: "Of all countries in the world, England ought to be the country in which stories should enjoy the widest range of popularity. In no other country is time of so much value. . . . This should be the country for stories which condense into a few pages the essence of volumes; which realize in fiction the great economical maxim, by packing the largest quantity into the smallest space." Train schedules and the pace of life in the period influenced the length of reading materials.

By the 1890s, however, some general-interest magazines and newspapers thrived, including the *Strand,* the *Idler,* the *Graphic,* and *Cornhill* magazine. These periodicals and others served as important popular outlets for innovative short fiction. The publishing house of John Lane devised the Keynotes series, named after the highly successful first collection of stories by George Egerton (1893). By the time this series was completed, there were thirty-three Keynotes titles featuring the best of such short-story writers as D'Arcy, Fiona Macleod, Grant Allen, and Henry Harland.

Individual Writers: Their Topics, Themes, and Techniques

A few writers in this volume – such as Crackanthorpe, who had a short, troubled life – lived almost completely within the 1880–1914 period. The lives of other writers extend in either direction beyond the confines of this volume. The earliest birthdate of a writer included in this volume belongs to Besant, who was born in 1836, one year before Queen Victoria ascended to the throne. The most recent survivor is Eden Phillpotts, who died in 1960. In all cases the decision to include a given writer was made on the basis that he or she wrote

significant pieces of short fiction or was on the way to establishing a literary reputation within the period 1880–1914. Certainly other writers – most notably James Greenwood, H. F. B. Gilbert, Murray Gilchrist, Marion Dixon, K. Douglas King, and Rudolph Dircks – could have been included. But they were not, partly because of considerations of space but also because their works may have been so similar in theme or style to those of writers discussed here that such minor authors are no longer viewed as remarkable within the annals of literary history. A deliberate effort has been made to include woman writers (eleven in all). Their contributions have received too scant attention in the past, and their achievements are herein recognized.

Realistic writers recorded the truth as they saw it, responding to such topics as marriage and relationships, slum conditions, working-class endeavors, and women's issues. To flout conventional morality and to raise objections to Victorian ideals of marriage invited criticism, as Hardy discovered with the public outcries against his last two novels, *Tess of the d'Urbervilles* (1891) and *Jude the Obscure* (1895). Of the forty-six stories that comprise his four collections, many seem to be in the vein of traditional folktales, but the elements of irony and melodrama deepen their serious meanings.

A dark view of marriage and relationships – including thwarted passion, manipulation, and spoiled idealism – appears as well in stories by G. S. Street. Several stories by Netta Syrett depict the suffering of men and women in marital relationships. Mabel Kitcat's short fiction deals realistically (and sometimes surrealistically) with marital doubts and difficulties. Henniker's stories place tragic difficulties in marital relationships in the foreground to the extent that mental illness and suicide become consequences.

Hostility between husbands and wives is often the central point of dramatic conflict in the short stories of Lucy Lane Clifford. In several stories by Egerton drunken husbands abuse their wives violently. D'Arcy explores the difficulties of Victorian marriage in "Irremediable" (*Yellow Book,* April 1894). Hardy's stories often deal with the difficulties of love across rigid class boundaries as individuals suffer the consequences of oppressive social conventions. Gissing's "A Foolish Virgin" (*A Victim of Circumstances,* 1927) protests against the female parasite who callously seeks marriage for economic advantage.

Realist writers also expressed their unflinching vision of the lower classes: people they saw as victims of the slums and oppressive working conditions. Realistic short stories can be marked by refreshing honesty and vigor. They are well worth reading not only as documents of social history but as expressions of artistic excellence, filled with unforgettable characters and memorable situations. Slum life's violence and brutality are depicted by Morrison in "Lizerunt" (*Tales of Mean Streets*), the shocking story of a working-class girl. With his insider's perspective on East End slum life he presents the desperation of poverty. Morrison also portrays petty criminals and working-class characters. Several of his works inspired social legislation that led to slum clearance. Zangwill also wrote controversial vignettes of East End ghetto life. Besant's fiction is often set in the East End. Gissing's grim stories frequently seem to be case studies of working-class misery. Besides drawing on his own personal experiences, he was especially influenced by Zola and Honoré de Balzac.

The horrendous conditions of London's slums serve as both setting and theme in stories by Besant, Gissing, Sims, Zangwill, Nevinson, and Morrison. Some of these writers' works had a direct impact on changes in the city. For example, the unsettling details of East End slums in Besant's *All Sorts and Conditions of Men* (1882) brought about government establishment of the People's Palace, an amusement and educational center for slum dwellers, in 1887. Public opinion and government investigations were clearly influenced by several of Sims's social exposés. Housing legislation forced the clearance of some of the East End's worst slums as a result of unrelenting exposés by Morrison. Edwin Pugh and W. Pett Ridge also address social and political concerns.

Though closely related to depictions of slum life, stories about the lives of laborers sometimes focus on their work environs as well as their domestic dwellings. Barry Pain, who presents working-class figures in his short stories, actually lived in a working-class London neighborhood. Low-life (circus workers, coachmen, and servants) and criminal figures are featured in Sims's stories. Many of Graham's stories display his nonjudgmental representations of prostitutes, and his refusal to sermonize outraged some readers and critics. He contributed an essay on the evils of the factory system to the *Albemarle*. Charlotte Mew wrote stories about fishermen and sailors; W. W. Jacobs explored the lives of dockworkers. Jacobs's waterfront stories about wharf laborers interweave the humorous and the macabre.

Realist short-fiction writers also address the problems and social inequality of women, and the concept of the New Woman received much attention during the period. Egerton depicts women creating fully enriched lives for themselves and rebelling against England's divorce laws; her female characters' sexuality is often frankly represented. In her stories Syrett sought to overturn stereotypes. Especially in regard to woman's issues, the "new realism," as some disparagingly referred to it, challenged prejudice, limitations, and intolerance. Ada Nield Chew's stories were used as an important part of the woman-suffrage campaign just before World War I.

Beyond considerations of topics and content of these short stories, there is the matter of technique and approach. For example, some writers emphasize the regionalist or local-color dimension, and others use dialect forms. Nevinson employs the cockney dialect of the East Enders in several of his stories. Other writers turn to the time-honored devices of satire and comedy to expose society's foibles. The most pioneering writers, such as May Sinclair, use modernist devices that anticipate the psychological realism that was further developed, especially after World War I, by such classic practitioners as Virginia Woolf, James Joyce, and D. H. Lawrence.

Regionalist or local-color writers, some of whom use dialects, include Edith Œnone Somerville and Martin Ross as well as Eden Phillpotts. Most of Phillpotts's stories are concerned with family relationships in a rural Dartmoor (Devon) setting. Many of the humorous stories by Somerville and Ross reproduce the dialect of Irish speech. Zangwill uses Yiddish expressions and dialect; some of Sir Arthur Quiller-Couch's stories employ the Cornish dialect. Louisa Molesworth represents a new kind of realism in children's literature as she attempts to present children's speech realistically.

Social satire requires astute observation and commentary on society and its shortcomings. L. P. Jacks takes up the challenge with subtle, satiric humor in short-story critiques of academic pretension. E. F. Benson, using an acerbic admixture of social comedy and social farce, wrote stories in which characters battle ambitiously for social dominance. Zangwill's social satire and humor combine protest and entertainment. The follies, rather than the evils, of society are often the targets of these writers.

Other techniques, such as Grand's frequent use of a male narrator, are of interest to current studies in narratology. Although writers such as Grand experimented cautiously with narrative techniques, the writers of this period more often tested strategies that anticipated psychological realism. D'Arcy was such a practitioner, and Egerton depicts the inner emotional world of her characters. The psychology of relationships and subtleties of sexuality are evident in stories by Sinclair, a founder of the first psychoanalytic clinic in London. Psychological realism is also evident in Mew's "Spine" (*Collected Poems and Prose,* 1981), which deals with a starving artist. Some of these premodernist techniques now appear crude, but they resulted from new concepts of representing time and consciousness, such as Crackanthorpe's method of placing rows of asterisks on the page to indicate the passage of time.

Periodicals and the Short Story

In "Fiction in the English Experimental Periodicals of the 1890s" (*Bulletin of Bibliography,* January–April 1968) Wendell V. Harris remarks on the profusion of periodicals intended to appeal to the reader with avant-garde sympathies. He uses some commentary by H. G. Wells to link the genre of the short story to the proliferation of these periodicals:

> As H. G. Wells has pointed out in his introduction to *The Country of the Blind* (London, 1911), the experimental impulses behind the new little periodicals and the renascence of interest in the short story in the 1890's were interrelated. Each encouraged the other, and thus examination of the short stories which appeared in these periodicals becomes important in understanding the fiction of the period which Wells called the "Golden Age" of the English short story.

In her more detailed study, *The Magazines of the 1890's* (1929), E. Lenore Casford also argues for the widespread cultural impact of periodicals within a literate society:

> The literary periodicals of any period are closely related to its literature and art for they reflect tendencies in thought and attitude of contemporaneous writers and artists. They afford an opportunity for fearless expression of opinion. They encourage individuality and introduce to the reading public the work of new and untried writers and artists. Through their criticism they form the advance guard of new and radical views of life and action and are powerful factors in molding tastes.

For these reasons a brief survey of the periodicals most closely associated with writers in this volume should be given. *Black & White* published stories by Sinclair as well as by Somerville and Ross. The *Butterfly* was designed to supply readers with "light literature in an artistic setting" and featured stories by Jacobs, Morrison, and Pain. Three well-known standards of the British periodical scene published works by writers in this volume: *Cassell's* (Kitcat); the *Cornhill* (Adcock, Henniker, and Pain); and the *Graphic* (Somerville and Ross). Jerome K. Jerome was the editor of two periodicals that often published short stories, the *Idler* and *To-Day.* Stories by Ridge, Jerome, Sims, Grand, Jacobs, Henniker, Zangwill, and Pain appeared over the years in the thirty-seven volumes of the *Idler. To-Day* featured contributions from Jacobs, Henniker, Zangwill, and Pain.

Crackanthorpe served as editor of the *Albemarle* (with W. H. Wilkins) through its two-volume run in 1892. These issues included fiction by Crackanthorpe, Graham, and others, selling at a newsstand price of sixpence. *Longman's* included short fiction by Somerville and Ross, Molesworth, and Kitcat. *Macmillan's* brought readers stories by Sinclair and Morrison; his works also appeared in the *National Observer. Pall Mall* magazine was one of the periodicals in which Mew published her short stories.

Along with the *Savoy,* the *Yellow Book* was the most famous and controversial periodical of the period, lasting from April 1894 to April 1897. With Harland as its literary editor and Aubrey Beardsley as its artistic editor, the *Yellow Book* was designed to appeal to readers of advanced, cultivated tastes, and it spawned many imitators. Its publishers, Elkin Mathews and John Lane, designed a quarterly of enduring value. The *Yellow Book* also strove for popularity, as demonstrated by the deliberate choice of its color. In the 1890s yellow was associated with the affected tastes of Wilde, Whistler, and their followers in the art-for-art's-sake movement. Unlike many of its competitors, the magazine was totally devoted to art and literature; no essays on political or social issues were allowed. The *Yellow Book* featured the works of many writers covered in this volume, including Arnold Bennett, Victoria Cross, Ernest Dowson, Egerton, Street, Syrett, Kitcat, D'Arcy, Mew, Crackanthorpe, and Gissing. As an assistant editor, D'Arcy was influential in enlisting many woman writers as contributors.

The *Savoy* soon replaced the *Yellow Book* as the voice of new movements in the late 1890s. Stories by Dowson and Crackanthorpe appeared in this periodical, whose literary editor was Arthur Symons. He quickly enlisted Beardsley as its artistic editor. In the first issue Symons stated the magazine's policy as "the hope to appeal to the taste of the intelligent by not being original for originality's sake, nor audacious for the sake of advertisement, nor timid for the convenience of the elderly minded." Its fiction would have "a certain sense of what is finest in living fact." Other periodicals of the period could be mentioned, but four more will serve to round out the list: the *Strand* (Jacobs, Pain), which at its high point in the 1890s reached five hundred thousand readers a month; *Temple Bar* (Sinclair, Grand, and Mew); *Vanity Fair* (Kitcat); and, finally, *Windsor* magazine (Benson).

"Forbearance" and "cooperation" are the two key words that have made for the success of this volume. From its inception Wendell V. Harris, William F. Naufftus, and John Greenfield have offered many useful insights and suggestions for the planning of this volume. I am also grateful to the many contributors, some from Canada and Great Britain, as well as others within the United States – from Florida to Texas and from Connecticut to Oklahoma – who have completed their research and writing on schedule, who have made worthwhile corrections along the way, and who have offered valuable suggestions for illustrations to enhance this volume. I also wish to thank the graduate research assistants at the University of South Carolina who have worked with me on this volume: Becky Lewis, James Boyce, Eddy Ball, and Charles Brower.

– *William B. Thesing*

ACKNOWLEDGMENTS

This book was produced by Bruccoli Clark Layman, Inc. Karen L. Rood is senior editor for the *Dictionary of Literary Biography* series. David Marshall James was the in-house editor.

Photography editors are Edward Scott and Timothy C. Lundy. Layout and graphics supervisor is Penney L. Haughton. Copyediting supervisor is Bill Adams. Typesetting supervisor is Kathleen M. Flanagan. Darren Harris-Fain and Julie E. Frick are editorial associates. Systems manager is George F. Dodge. The production staff includes Steve Borsanyi, Joseph Matthew Bruccoli, Ann M. Cheschi, Patricia Coate, Rebecca Crawford, Denise Edwards, Sarah A. Estes, Joyce Fowler, Robert Fowler, Laurel Gladden, Angeala Harwell, Jolyon M. Helterman, Ellen McCracken, Kathy Lawler Merlette, Pamela D. Norton, Thomas J. Pickett, Patricia Salisbury, Maxine K. Smalls, William L. Thomas, Jr., and Wilma Weant.

Walter W. Ross, Deborah M. Chasteen, and Brenda Gross did library research. They were assisted by the following librarians at the Thomas Cooper Library of the University of South Carolina: Linda Holderfield and the interlibrary-loan staff; reference librarians Gwen Baxter, Daniel Boice, Faye Chadwell, Cathy Eckman, Gary Geer, Qun "Gerry" Jiao, Jean Rhyne, Carol Tobin, Carolyn Tyler, Virginia Weathers, Elizabeth Whiznant, and Connie Widney; circulation-department head Thomas Marcil; and acquisitions-searching supervisor David Haggard.

Dictionary of Literary Biography® • Volume One Hundred Thirty-Five

British Short-Fiction Writers, 1880–1914:
The Realist Tradition

Dictionary of Literary Biography

Arthur St. John Adcock
(17 January 1864 – 9 June 1930)

Barry Faulk
University of Illinois

BOOKS: *An Unfinished Martyrdom, and Other Stories* (Bristol: Arrowsmith, 1894);

Beyond Atonement: A Story of London Life (London: Bellairs, 1896);

East End Idylls (London: Bowden, 1897);

The Consecration of Hetty Fleet (London: Skeffington & Son, 1898);

In the Image of God: A Story of Lower London (London: Skeffington & Son, 1898);

The Luck of Private Foster: A Romance of Love and War (London: Hodder & Stoughton, 1900);

Songs of the War (London: Johnson, 1900);

From a London Garden (London: Nutt, 1903);

More Than Money (London: Partridge, 1903);

In Fear of Man (London: Everett, 1904);

London Etchings (London: Elkin Mathews, 1904);

Admissions and Asides about Life and Literature (London: Elkin Mathews, 1905; New York: Kennikat, 1970);

London from the Top of a 'Bus (London: Hodder & Stoughton, 1906);

Love in London (London: Griffiths, 1906);

The Shadow Show (London: Elkin Mathews, 1907);

The World That Never Was (London: Griffiths, 1908);

Billicks (London: Stanley Paul, 1909);

A Man with a Past (London: Stanley Paul, 1911);

Two to Nowhere (London: Unwin, 1911);

Famous Houses and Literary Shrines of London (London: Dent, 1912; New York: Dutton, 1912; revised edition, London: Dent, 1929);

Modern Grub Street and Other Essays (London: Herbert & Daniel, 1913);

The Booklover's London (London: Methuen, 1913; New York: Macmillan, 1913);

In the Firing Line: Stories of the War by Land and Sea (London & New York: Hodder & Stoughton, 1914);

Seeing It Through: How Britain Answered the Call (New York: Hodder & Stoughton, 1914; London: Hodder & Stoughton, 1915);

Australasia Triumphant! (London: Simpkin, Marshall, 1916);

Songs of the World-War (London: Palmer & Hayward, 1916);

For Remembrance: Soldier Poets Who Have Fallen in the War (London & New York: Hodder & Stoughton, 1918; enlarged, 1920);

The Anzac Pilgrim's Progress: Ballads of Australia's Army. By Lance-Corporal Cibber (London: Simpkin, Marshall, 1918);

Tod Macmammon Sees His Soul, and Other Satires for the New Democracy (London: Swarthmore, 1920);

Exit Homo (London: Selwyn & Blount, 1921);

The Divine Tragedy (London: Selwyn & Blount, 1922);

With the Gilt Off (London & New York: Putnam, 1923);

Gods of Modern Grub Street (London: Sampson Low, Marston, 1923; New York: Stokes, 1923);

A Book of Bohemians (London: Sampson Low, Marston, 1925);

City Songs (London: Selwyn & Blount, 1926);

The Prince of Wales' African Book: A Pictorial Record of the Journey to West Africa, South Africa, and South America (London: Hodder & Stoughton, 1926);

The Glory That Was Grub Street (London: Sampson Low, Marston, 1928; New York: Stokes, 1928);

Collected Poems (London: Hodder & Stoughton, 1929);

London Memories (London: Hodder & Stoughton, 1931).

OTHER: Walter Dixon Scott, *Men of Letters,* edited by Adcock (London: Hodder & Stoughton, 1916);

Frederick Charles Owlett, *Kultur and Anarchy,* introduction by Adcock (London: Elkin Mathews, 1917);

Charles John Beech Masefield, *Poems,* introduction by Adcock (Oxford: Blackwell, 1919);

Robert Louis Stevenson: His Work and His Personality, edited by Adcock (London: Hodder & Stoughton, 1924);

The Bookman Treasury of Living Poets, edited by Adcock (London: Hodder & Stoughton, 1925; enlarged, 1928);

Wonderful London, edited by Adcock (London: Amalgamated, 1926–1927);

John Ferguson, *Thyrea,* introduction by Adcock (London: Melrose, 1929).

After reading the obituary for Arthur St. John Adcock in the *New Statesman and Nation* (14 June 1930), a reader responded, "I hope that [the *Statesman*] will duly give us a finished study of the author . . . in all his fields and duties." The reader's request remains unanswered, and not only by the *New Statesman;* there remains no full-length biographical material or critical overview of Adcock's career as novelist, journalist, and essayist. And no wonder: a study of Adcock in "all his fields and duties" would be a prodigious task indeed. Such a project would require a wide-ranging literary and critical endeavor. It would have to take in novels and several ambitious verse projects (the London *Times* obituary speculated that Adcock would be primarily remembered as a poet after the publication of his *Collected Poems* the year before his death), a considerable amount of journalism and polemical prose for the British cause during World War I (not only *Seeing It Through: How Britain Answered the Call* [1914], but *In the Firing Line* [1914] and *Australasia Triumphant!* [1916] cover the experiences of British troops during wartime), and children's stories (*The World That Never Was* [1908]). There are also popularizing essays on literature and the profession of letters. A concern with urban life was a constant of Adcock's variegated career. Sometimes this concern took the form of the jovial, impersonal travel and touristic perspectives exemplified by *London from the Top of a 'Bus* (1906) or *Famous Houses and Literary Shrines of London* (1912) or of the nostalgic rumina-

tions on the "New Grub Street" and its domination of the literary profession during the Edwardian age.

This brief catalogue of Adcock's work omits his long-standing connection with the London *Bookman,* where he served as joint editor with the distinguished Scottish journalist, critic, and theologian W. R. Nicoll from 1908 to 1923, when he became full editor. Throughout his critical enterprise Adcock returned to the topic that haunts his short fiction and novels: life in London, its hardships and innumerable pleasures. The impressive achievement of Adcock's short fiction in presenting London life, embodied in volumes such as *East End Idylls* (1897), cannot be separated from the experience of the man who was intimately aware of the struggles and possibilities that faced the fin de siècle "bookman."

Adcock's short fiction and novels of the 1890s placed him as part of a controversial literary movement: the "Cockney" school of fiction, exemplified by the successful work of Arthur Morrison (*Tales of Mean Streets* [1895] and *A Child of the Jago* [1896]) and writers such as Edwin Pugh, W. Pett Ridge, and the young W. Somerset Maugham. These tales, which focus on the struggles and sordid conditions of working-class denizens in London's East End, were often controversial for their concern with the accurate representation of working-class culture, language (careful attention to dialect was a prominent feature of the movement), and mores. Adcock initially garnered attention as a fellow traveler in this movement; even after the Cockney school lost notoriety, Adcock remained fascinated with the subtle influences of urban environment on character. A commitment to the manifold experiences allowed by the freedom of urban environs is a prominent theme of his early fiction, and it remains a feature of his later critical ruminations on how the profession of letters interacts with the experience of city life. Adcock's literary career and short fiction can be situated against this context and commitment.

Adcock was born in London on 17 January 1864, the second son of William and Eliza Adcock. Privately educated, he went into law and married Marion Louise Taylor in 1887; six years later he resigned his post as a law clerk to take up a full-time writing career. Adcock reveals a great deal about his formative experiences as a writer in "The Literary Life," included in a later collection of essays, *Modern Grub Street* (1913). He recalls that his struggle to make a "comfortable and congenial income" in literature was "started with no points in my favor." Adcock's early career was as arduous as anything that can be found in the depiction of the struggle for subsistence amid the burgeoning book market in George Gissing's *New Grub Street* (1891).

Adcock had no "affluent family connections" or private means to lessen the burdens of authorship; as a young man he had health so frail he could receive no life insurance. Unable to maintain a living by his own work, he early turned to the kind of journeyman writing that would mark his almost-forty-year career: "the reviewing of other people's books, the writing of serials, short stories, articles, essays, topical and other verse, and contributing, largely as an outside contributor, to many of the best, and some of the worst papers, in England." He edited a technical journal and regularly turned out humorous verse while in "continual pain" and collapsed health. Adcock's obituary in the *New Statesman* carried an anecdote about his "indomitable will," noting that after he was severely burned while putting out an oil-lamp fire and "though suffering the extreme of agony, [he] insisted upon having pen and paper brought in to him between the doctor's visits, and no doubt paid the doctor's bills, among others, by writing essays conveying to his readers what an unsurpassably cheerful place the world was."

His first story was published by F. W. Robinson in *Home Chimes* (1888) and was followed by minor publications in a variety of newspapers, as well as verse and essays for *Chambers' Journal* and James Payn's *Cornhill*. During this time he kept a "minimum of twenty manuscripts constant on their rounds" and confessed to never going to bed with rejected manuscripts lying on the table. His first novel, *Beyond Atonement* (1896), was written in three months, rejected by several publishers, and accepted by one "who agreed to pay a fair royalty but would make no advance" and whose eventual bankruptcy ensured that Adcock would receive no pay for his effort.

Adcock's career as a man of letters was no doubt affected by such experiences; they encouraged a journeyman ethic and a concern for productivity that limited some of his work to the second tier. However, these experiences also precluded an attraction to the cult of sensibility, or to notions of artistic autonomy that marked both decadents and naturalists. "What ever you are asked to do, don't think it beneath you or do it half-heartedly," he counsels aspiring writers in "The Literary Life": such a statement reveals an acceptance of a profession that always threatened to keep outsiders on the margins. In Adcock's case it meant a dogged attachment to the everyday and to the sights and sounds of the London life that he knew and would later elegize.

Cover for Adcock's 1914 book supporting the British cause in World War I

Adcock's first collection of stories, *An Unfinished Martyrdom* (1894), is largely undistinguished, but its general theme sounds the keynote of his career: a focus on city dwellers presented with an air of pathos. At its weakest, however, this pathos can turn into sentiment or simple whimsy. Although the *Academy* (10 November 1894) praised the collections as well constructed "in a business-like sort of way," noting the stories recall "the quieter manner of Dickens," the reviewer concludes that "there is nothing remarkable" about the volume, although the title story is singled out for special mention. Indeed, "An Unfinished Martyrdom," which details how two elderly people make and renege on a pledge of abstinence from alcohol, has delicate characterization and a sly, unpretentious manner that make it a highlight of the volume. The tone of the piece could fit comfortably in the suburban sketches that constitute Adcock's midcareer work.

Adcock's ties to a distinct milieu and his psychological interest in character become clearly discernible in *Beyond Atonement*. While he never completely aligned himself with the naturalism of the Cockney school or even with the less fiercely deterministic fiction of Ridge and Pugh, in *Beyond Atonement* Adcock moves toward a focused observation on urban life. Although his novel is not strictly about the denizens of London's East End, some of the new realism's fatalism influences his presentation of a barrister's ambition and desire for social mobility. The *Athenaeum* (21 November 1896) noted that protagonist Charles Melville's "general surroundings . . . are well observed"; this is evident not only in the novel's presentation of Melville's legal milieu and of Dickensian characters such as Riffle the clerk but in the descriptive rendering of the workaday rhythms of London life. The protagonist's character and his lack of a moral sense are sometimes alluded to in clumsy authorial intrusions, but Adcock's catalogue of London at the commencement of the workweek in chapter 5 (titled "A Novel Experience") carries great authority: "the rush and roar and rattle in the streets, the close, monotonous toil in the huge warehouses, the crowded ships, the multitudinous dark, stifling little back offices, all going on again with undiminished energy."

From the concern with the effects of the urban milieu on the development of character in *Beyond Atonement* and the novel's gritty realism, it is no great leap to the thematic concerns of the short stories collected in *East End Idylls*. The *Saturday Review* criticized the book for expressing "what a nice well-meaning gentleman could conceive of East Enders doing in certain given circumstances, not as descriptions of what he has actually seen them doing." Yet this call for verisimilitude misses the didactic, indeed polemical, edge of the collection. The short stories in *East End Idylls* are not marked by the impersonal observation that characterizes French naturalism; instead, they are touched by the exuberance and color that remain a part of Cockney fiction even in Morrison's grim *A Child of the Jago*. The stories in *East End Idylls* tend toward the balanced representation of East End life found in the work of Ridge and Clarence Rook. Neither of these writers presents the slum dweller as either entirely miserable and brutal, or eternally good-natured. Adcock's collection searches for a middle ground in representing Cockney life; this goal appears to be the rhetorical point behind the collection.

The first edition of *East End Idylls* includes a preface by the Honorable and Reverend James Granville Adderley of Saint James Mission; it was rebuked by both the *Athenaeum* and the *Saturday Review*, the latter calling it "not very illuminative" and "abounding in . . . platitudes." However, the preface

serves to remind the reader that fin de siècle literature on the East End was rarely a detached aesthetic practice. *East End Idylls* cannot be sundered from the work of evangelicals and amateur sociologists who created the East End as an object of inquiry and public concern; in fact, Adcock's fiction should be read against such investigative work.

In the preface Adderley asserts that East Londoners have developed special practices and traditions that need to be translated to other audiences; he closes with the claim: "I do not wish to encourage the idea that these East Londoners are very peculiar. They are, after all, real human beings. And to correct this mistaken idea, is perhaps, one of the uses of a book like this." Despite the flatness of this statement, Adderley clearly elaborates here on the didactic function of Adcock's short fiction. There is a congruence between Adderley's claims and Adcock's occasional authorial intrusions in *East End Idylls* (intrusions that rarely appear in his later short fiction). For example, Adderley's comments are echoed by Adcock's call for humanist sympathy in "The Street That Was Condemned":

> Although in these enlightened days other superior persona are also assuring us they have discovered that love has become genteel, and no longer sets up his tabernacle in mean localities, some of us, who are not superior, can stop and see where his footsteps do still here and there, leave a shining track across the world's waste places, can seek humbly amidst the neglected, ignorant victims of circumstance whom the favoured of circumstance ignorantly despise, and find . . . outcast, blighted human creatures whom still some sanctifying touch of our common, kindly humanity makes nearer akin to the best of us.

Along with such narrative intrusions, *East End Idylls* contains careful, realistic catalogues of East London life, such as the detailed depiction of a condemned row of houses that opens "The Street That Was Condemned." Yet the collection is not simply a didactic project or a naturalist catalogue of the city, though Adcock's increased attention to speech patterns, dialects, and precise cityscapes sharpens the prose of this collection and often toughens the sentiment evident in *An Unfinished Martyrdom* into irony: *East End Idylls* is also an exploration of psychology. There is a Wordsworthian purpose behind many of these stories, suggested by Adcock's invocation of the idyll. The stories investigate the continuity of human feeling and sympathy that persists in the midst of everyday life among the poor.

Perhaps the most striking example of the strength of human ties in *East End Idylls* is found in the mother of "The Street That Was Condemned"; she clings to her dwelling, even after it is razed, in the expectation of a returning son. Here maternal love outlasts illness, a son's negligence, and extreme deprivation. Unexpected acts of charity play a prominent role in many of the stories. In "The Spectre of a Sin" a fallen woman unknowingly saves the child of the man who seduced her. Even when she recognizes the child's father, she remains silent after glimpsing the man's wife. In "Salvation: His Holy War" — one of many portraits of Dissenters in *East End Idylls* — a running battle between Salvation, a brawler turned Dissenter, and a "hooligan" is erased by a sudden, unforeseen act of heroism on Salvation's part. In "A Heathen in Christendom" an Indian and a belligerent Cockney are reconciled after an unexpected act of kindness. One of the most celebrated in *East End Idylls,* "At the Dock Gate," is a sharp vignette in which a jilted lover abruptly gives up his sole chance of sustenance in hard times for the husband of his former lover. In "Tilly's Sister" Adcock focuses on the incident that forces a prostitute to decide that her sister should "be surrounded by healthier influences," and in "Helen of Bow" a Cockney Helen of Troy has unexpected compassion for the weaker suitor.

In keeping with Adcock's concern for delineating how affective life survives poverty and deprivation, *East End Idylls* largely refuses both the symbolic solutions of melodrama and the panacea of happy endings. "The Soul of Penelope Sanders," with its picture of a prostitute who resumes a "tainted" life after a chance encounter with the man who first seduced her, is less than idyllic; "An Interrupted Romance" comes to a chilling close when the return of a drunken husband slams the cell door on a harried woman's only chance of happiness. There is an element of psychological Grand Guignol in "A Dead Memory," as domestic ideology takes its toll on a neglectful mother. In these stories the persistence of affective life has ineluctably tragic consequences. Certainly these stark sketches of pain and missed opportunities are preferable to the straining for coincidence that marks "A Prodigal Father," in which an ambitious son gets his comeuppance for selfishness, or the chance encounter that causes a change of heart in a social Darwinist minister who scorns the poor in "The Sermon That Was Never Preached."

East End Idylls placed Adcock's work in a discernible "school" and gave him a subject matter and purpose. His reception as an urban writer influenced the spate of novels that immediately followed

East End Idylls. For example, *In the Image of God* (1898) is a convincing portrayal of Cockney life with an eye for the connections between psychological nuance and city life. Following the picture of reluctant fathers found in *East End Idylls,* the novel elaborates on the urchin 'Melia's trials in a world where "fathers bulked as a troublesome and vicious species of human animal that went to work with more or less regularity of morning and come home very drunk at night." *The Consecration of Hetty Fleet* (1898) was praised for its portrayal of urban life and maternal duty: the *Literary World* noted its "brilliant descriptions of Dickens-like characters," and the *Sun* substantiated the connection between Adcock and the London life he took as his subject matter.

However, Adcock's commitment to representing the stark realities of East London was relinquished after his fiction on the Boer War published at the turn of the century and his renewed attention to verse (*From a London Garden,* 1903). The devotion to East London eventually faded into a concern for urban misfortune sentimentally drawn; Adcock's sense of craft turned to melodramatic effect. His next collection of short stories, *Love in London* (1906), takes up suburban life, as do most of Adcock's novels from this decade. Like many Edwardian writers interested in depicting London life, Adcock moved to a scrutiny of the suburbs; many works by authors of the Cockney school, such as Ridge's *Nine to Six-Thirty* (1910), Keble Howard's *The Smiths of Surbiton* (1906), Shan Bullock's *Robert Thorne: The Story of a London Clerk* (1907), and H. G. Wells's *Ann Veronica* (1909) evidence a similar shift. *Love in London,* like *Billicks* (1909) and *A Man with a Past* (1911), focuses on characters whose ties to the city are primarily the subject of wry, low-key humor.

"All the Difference," a tale of a middle-class woman marrying a peer, turns into a marital comedy that suggests domestic love transcends all class differences. "The Unconfessed" tells of the complications that occur when a woman who marries a peer for money actually falls in love with him. Many of the stories in *Love in London* are similar tales of suburban romance and mild satire of human foibles, lacking much of the drama of *East End Idylls.* "Waxy," for example, is a whimsical portrayal of working-class life, the tale of a wax-gallery attendant and runaway husband who masquerades as a wax dummy in order to avoid a reunion with his wife.

The exceptions to these comic tales have a gruesome element that makes Adcock's later appre-

THE GLORY THAT
WAS GRUB STREET

Impressions of Contemporary Authors

BY
ST. JOHN ADCOCK

WITH THIRTY-TWO CAMERA STUDIES
BY
E. O. HOPPÉ

LONDON
SAMPSON LOW, MARSTON & CO., LTD.

Title page for Adcock's 1928 collection of essays on authors
he knew

ciative essays on O. Henry and W. W. Jacobs come as no surprise. "Nat Peplow's Crime," a grim tale of a man who takes revenge on a philandering wife, is reminiscent of Jacobs's short fiction. "Jenny Chooses," a story of rivalry and murder in Lavender Row and a gang leader's violent death, is a taut, forceful piece. "The Making of a Star" details the tragic results when a deformed young man falls in love with a music-hall singer who is mistaken for "an incarnation of purity." "Stephen the Pharisee," in which an evangelical father tries to save his prodigal son who has "fallen" in the city, is a nuanced presentation of delusion, hypocrisy, and murder that marks one of the collection's few compelling returns to Adcock's signature urban realism.

A consideration of Adcock's short fiction should also note select pieces in *Modern Grub Street*, some originally published in the *Daily Mail*. Like *Admissions and Asides* (1905), *Modern Grub Street* includes many essays that are meant to act as a breviary for the struggling writer. Several of the pieces are fascinating and unclassifiable: "The Pampered Poor" and "Man's Rights," colloquies on poverty and wealth between the "Major" and the "Youngest Man in the Club," almost suggest the techniques of metafiction. The spirited social commentary and lively banter give the speakers in these dialogues a distinct sense of character. Also of interest in *Modern Grub Street* is the atmospheric evocation of Petticoat Lane in "The Silent Way," the detailed character sketch of a Bohemian editor in "A Gentleman of the Press," and the comic dialogue of two Cockney women inveighing "Against Modesty."

Adcock's final collection of short stories, *With the Gilt Off* (1923), reprints five stories from *East End Idylls* and several from *Love in London* ("Of Two Evils" is the same as "Nat Peplow's Crime") with little substantive change. Some of the incidental revisions in "The Soul of Penelope Sanders" move the story from taut understatement to overt, explicit declarations of intent and motive at the story's close. The new stories with a Cockney flavor are largely limited to comedy, such as the tale of thievery in a lodging house recounted in "A Cash Account." "An Extra Turn" is interesting for the way it brings together suburbia and the East End in the comic misadventures of a beggar who gets too much careful attention at the hands of a suburban couple.

The volume is largely taken up by "Don Juan of Haggerston," a tale of thwarted love between a lower-class Don Juan and his unattractive wife, Bella. This subtle story of resentment and jealousy stands out in the collection for its sustained intensity. Some of the humor in *Love in London* clearly dated Adcock and evinced a curious detachment toward his subject matter, as noted by the *Times Literary Supplement* (17 May 1923): "Mr. Adcock gives what appears to be accurate reproductions of Cockney manners on the level which he has chosen, but conveys nothing of his own reaction to the realities . . . indeed, it is difficult not to suspect him of being bored."

Short fiction does not seem to have been in the forefront of Adcock's concerns during the 1920s. In the early part of the decade he returned to poetry, marked by a turn to metaphysical concerns. Adcock delivered a speech to the Rationalist Press Association in 1920 on "The Madness of Poets"; that same year he gained an entry in Joseph McCabe's *Biographical Dictionary of Modern Rationalists*. Adcock produced *Tod Macmammon Sees His Soul* (1920), a verse satire on national service and the new democracy since World War I, *Exit Homo* (1921), and *The Divine Tragedy* (1922) while in this phase. His remaining output during the 1920s mainly includes works popularizing modern authors and works of critical evaluation, such as *Gods of Modern Grub Street* (1923) and *The Glory That Was Grub Street* (1928).

Adcock took over sole editorship of the London *Bookman* on 24 May 1923. This publication performed various services for belles lettres: less austere and discriminating than the *Times Literary Supplement* or the coterie periodicals of modernism, it provided practical advice for younger writers, trade news, and surveys of authors' careers. The *Bookman* assured Adcock's status as denizen and chronicler of Grub Street. On the occasion of Adcock's death, the *London Mercury* (August 1930) observed that "there are many good authors with no wide appeal who remember that their work was first appreciated generously, with understanding and at ample length, either by Adcock or critics under his employ." Likewise, the *New Statesman and Nation* noted Adcock's literal rescue and care of poet W. H. Davies. Adcock died 9 June 1930 in Richmond, England, after a short illness. He passed away a month after the death of his beloved daughter Marion, herself an author of children's verse and prose pieces (many published in the *Sketch*). His surviving daughter, Almey St. John Adcock, who was privately educated like her father, continued to produce novels and went on to write radio dramas.

Although remembered as a man of letters and an editor of London writers, Adcock was less known at the time of his death as a prose laureate of London's streets. However, his belief that modern letters had become inextricably bound with the urban experience lingered in his criticism. This view is evidenced in the confession that opens *The Glory That Was Grub Street*. In an aside that speaks for Adcock as much as the authors discussed in the collection, he writes that "you find the author who formerly dwelt in Grub Street, but has become prosperous and changed address, will confess that, looking back from the affluence and tame security of the present, he realizes that when living in the Street, and everything seemed possible and nothing sure, those early days were more stimulating, richer in excitement, adventure, even in happiness, than he was aware of at the time." Yet when Adcock wrote that O. Henry captured city life "in all its stolid, material commonplace realism" (*Living Age,* 25 November 1916), he described his own best short fiction as well.

References:

"Arthur St. John Adcock," *Bookman* (London), 78 (April–September 1930): 235–238;

Peter Keating, *The Haunted Study* (London: Secker & Warburg, 1989);

Keating, *The Working Classes in Victorian Fiction* (New York: Barnes & Noble, 1971).

Papers:

Adcock's papers and much of his correspondence are at the Bodleian Library, Oxford.

Arnold Bennett

(27 May 1867 – 27 March 1931)

Olga R. R. Broomfield
Mount Saint Vincent University

See also the Bennett entries in *DLB 10: Modern British Dramatists, 1900–1945; DLB 34: British Novelists, 1890–1929: Traditionalists;* and *DLB 98: Modern British Essayists, First Series.*

BOOKS: *A Man from the North* (London & New York: John Lane/Bodley Head, 1898);

Journalism for Women: A Practical Guide (London: John Lane/Bodley Head, 1898);

Polite Farces for the Drawing Room (London: Lamley, 1900 [i.e., 1899]);

Fame and Fiction: An Enquiry into Certain Popularities (London: Richards, 1901; New York: Dutton, 1901);

The Grand Babylon Hotel: A Fantasia on Modern Themes (London: Chatto & Windus, 1902); republished as *T. Racksole and Daughter: Or, the Result of an American Millionaire Ordering Steak and a Bottle of Bass at the Grand Babylon Hotel, London* (New York: New Amsterdam Book Co., 1902);

Anna of the Five Towns (London: Chatto & Windus, 1902; New York: McClure, Phillips, 1903);

The Gates of Wrath: A Melodrama (London: Chatto & Windus, 1903);

The Truth About an Author, anonymous (London: Constable, 1903; New York: Doran, 1911);

How to Become an Author: A Practical Guide (London: Pearson, 1903);

Leonora: A Novel (London: Chatto & Windus, 1903; New York: Doran, 1910);

A Great Man: A Frolic (London: Chatto & Windus, 1904; New York: Doran, 1911);

Teresa of Watling Street: A Fantasia on Modern Themes (London: Chatto & Windus, 1904);

Tales of the Five Towns (London: Chatto & Windus, 1905);

The Loot of Cities: Being Adventures of a Millionaire in Search of Joy (A Fantasia) (London: Rivers, 1905); enlarged as *The Loot of Cities: Being the Adventures of a Millionaire in Search of Joy (A Fantasia) and Other Stories* (London: Nelson, 1917);

Arnold Bennett, 1905

Sacred and Profane Love: A Novel in Three Episodes (London: Chatto & Windus, 1905); republished as *The Book of Carlotta: Being a Revised Edition (With New Preface) of Sacred and Profane Love . . .* (New York: Doran, 1911);

Hugo: A Fantasia on Modern Themes (London: Chatto & Windus, 1906; New York: Buckles, 1906);

Whom God Hath Joined (London: Nutt, 1906; New York: Doran, 1911);

The Sinews of War: A Romance of London and the Sea, by Bennett and Eden Phillpotts (London: Laurie, 1906); republished as *Doubloons* (New York: McClure, Phillips, 1906);

Things That Interested Me: Being Leaves from a Journal (Burslem: Privately printed, 1906);

The Ghost: A Fantasia on Modern Themes (London: Chatto & Windus, 1907); republished as *The Ghost* (Boston: Turner, 1907); republished as *The Ghost: A Modern Fantasy* (Boston: Small, Maynard, 1911);

The Reasonable Life: Being Hints for Men and Women (London: Fifield, 1907); revised as *Mental Efficiency, and Other Hints to Men and Women* (New York: Doran, 1911; London: Hodder & Stoughton, 1912);

The Grim Smile of the Five Towns (London: Chapman & Hall, 1907);

The City of Pleasure: A Fantasia on Modern Themes (London: Chatto & Windus, 1907; New York: Doran, 1915);

Things Which Have Interested Me: Being Leaves from a Journal, Second Series (Burslem: Privately printed, 1907);

The Statue, by Bennett and Phillpotts (London: Cassell, 1908; New York: Moffatt Yard, 1908);

Buried Alive: A Tale of These Days (London: Chapman & Hall, 1908; New York: Brentano's, 1910);

How to Live on 24 Hours a Day (London: New Age, 1908; New York: Doran, 1910);

The Old Wives' Tale: A Novel (London: Chapman & Hall, 1908; New York: Doran, 1911);

The Human Machine (London: New Age, 1908; New York: Doran, 1911);

Things Which Have Interested Me, Third Series (Burslem: Privately printed, 1908);

Literary Taste: How To Form It, with Detailed Instructions for Collecting a Complete Library of English Literature (London: New Age, 1909; New York: Doran, 1911; revised, with an American book list by John Farrar, New York: Doran, 1927; revised edition, with additional lists by Frank Swinnerton, London: Hodder & Stoughton, 1937);

Cupid and Commonsense: A Play in Four Acts (London: New Age, 1909);

What the Public Wants: (A Play in Four Acts) (London: New Age, 1909);

The Glimpse: An Adventure of the Soul (London: Chapman & Hall, 1909);

The Present Crisis (Burslem: Privately printed, 1910);

Helen with the High Hand: An Idyllic Diversion (London: Chapman & Hall, 1910; New York: Doran, 1910);

Clayhanger (London: Methuen, 1910; New York: Dutton, 1910);

The Card: A Story of Adventure in the Five Towns (London: Methuen, 1911); republished as *Denry the Audacious* (New York: Dutton, 1911);

Hilda Lessways (London: Methuen, 1911; New York: Dutton, 1911);

The Honeymoon: A Comedy in Three Acts (London: Methuen, 1911; New York: Doran, 1912);

The Feast of St. Friend (London: Hodder & Stoughton, 1911; New York: Doran, 1911); republished as *Friendship and Happiness: A Plea for the Feast of St. Friend* (London: Hodder & Stoughton, 1914);

The Matador of the Five Towns, and Other Stories (London: Methuen, 1912); republished with stories from *The Grim Smile of the Five Towns* and *Tales of the Five Towns* (New York: Doran, 1912);

Milestones: A Play in Three Acts, by Bennett and Edward Knoblock (London: Methuen, 1912; New York: Doran, 1912);

Those United States (London: Secker, 1912); republished as *Your United States: Impressions of a First Visit* (New York & London: Harper, 1912);

The Regent: A Five Towns Story of Adventure in London (London: Methuen, 1913); republished as *The Old Adam: A Story of Adventure* (New York: Doran, 1913);

The Great Adventure: A Play of Fancy in Four Acts (London: Methuen, 1913; New York: Doran, 1913);

The Plain Man and His Wife (London: Hodder & Stoughton, 1913); republished as *Married Life: The Plain Man and His Wife* (New York: Doran 1913); republished as *Marriage (The Plain Man and His Wife)* (London: Hodder & Stoughton, 1916);

Paris Nights and Other Impressions of Places and People (London: Hodder & Stoughton, 1913; New York: Doran, 1913);

The Author's Craft (New York: Doran, 1914; London, New York & Toronto: Hodder & Stoughton, 1915 [i.e., 1914]);

The Price of Love: A Tale (London: Methuen, 1914; New York & London: Harper, 1914);

Liberty! A Statement of the British Case (London: Hodder & Stoughton, 1914; New York: Doran, 1914);

From the Log of the Velsa (New York: Century, 1914; London: Chatto & Windus, 1920);

Over There: War Scenes on the Western Front (London: Methuen, 1915; New York: Doran, 1915);

These Twain (New York: Doran, 1915; London: Methuen, 1916);

The Lion's Share (London: Cassell, 1916; New York: Doran, 1916);

Books and Persons: Being Comments on a Past Epoch, 1908-1911 (London: Chatto & Windus, 1917; New York: Doran, 1917);

The Pretty Lady: A Novel (London: Cassell, 1918; New York: Doran, 1918);

The Title: A Comedy in Three Acts (London: Chatto & Windus / New York: Doran, 1918);

Self and Self-Management: Essays and Existing (London: Hodder & Stoughton, 1918; New York: Doran, 1918);

The Roll-Call (London: Hutchinson, 1919; New York: Doran, 1919);

Judith: A Play in Three Acts, Founded on the Apocryphal Book of "Judith" (London: Chatto & Windus, 1919; New York: Doran, 1919);

Sacred and Profane Love: A Play in Four Acts Founded Upon the Novel of the Same Name (London: Chatto & Windus, 1919; New York: Doran, 1920);

Our Women: Chapters on the Sex-Discord (London: Cassell, 1920; New York: Doran, 1920);

Things That Have Interested Me (London: Chatto & Windus, 1921; New York: Doran, 1921);

Body and Soul: A Play in Four Acts (New York: Doran, 1921; London: Chatto & Windus, 1922);

The Love Match: A Play in Five Scenes (London: Chatto & Windus, 1922; New York: Doran, 1922);

Mr. Prohack (London: Methuen, 1922; New York: Doran, 1922);

Lilian (London: Cassell, 1922; New York: Doran, 1922);

Things That Have Interested Me, Second Series (London: Chatto & Windus, 1923; New York: Doran, 1923);

How to Make the Best of Life (London: Hodder & Stoughton, 1923; New York: Doran, 1923);

Don Juan de Marana: A Play in Four Acts (London: Laurie, 1923);

Riceyman Steps: A Novel (London: Cassell, 1923; New York: Doran, 1923);

London Life: A Play in Three Acts and Nine Scenes, by Bennett and Knoblock (London: Chatto & Windus, 1924; New York: Doran, 1924);

The Bright Island (London: Golden Cockerel, 1924; New York: Doran, 1925);

Elsie and the Child: A Tale of Riceyman Steps and Other Stories (London: Cassell, 1924); republished as *Elsie and the Child, and Other Stories* (New York: Doran, 1924);

The Clayhanger Family. I. Clayhanger. II. Hilda Lessways. III. These Twain. (London: Methuen, 1925);

Essays of Today and Yesterday (London: Harrap, 1926);

Things That Have Interested Me, Third Series (London: Chatto & Windus, 1926; New York: Doran, 1926);

Lord Raingo (London: Cassell, 1926; New York: Doran, 1926);

The Woman Who Stole Everything and Other Stories (London: Cassell, 1927; New York: Doran, 1927);

Mr. Prohack: A Comedy in Three Acts, by Bennett and Knoblock (London: Chatto & Windus, 1927; Garden City, N.Y.: Doubleday, Doran, 1928);

The Vanguard: A Fantasia (New York: Doran, 1927); republished as *The Strange Vanguard: A Fantasia* (London: Cassell, 1928);

The Savour of Life: Essays in Gusto (London: Cassell, 1928; Garden City, N.Y.: Doubleday, Doran, 1928);

Mediterranean Scenes: Rome – Greece – Constantinople (London: Cassell, 1928);

Accident (Garden City, N.Y.: Doubleday, Doran, 1928; London: Cassell, 1929);

Short Stories of Today and Yesterday (London: Harrap, 1928);

Judith: An Opera in One Act, by Bennett and Eugene Goosens (London: J. & W. Chester, 1929);

The Religious Interregnum (London: Benn, 1929);

"Piccadilly": The Story of the Film (London: Readers Library, 1929);

Journal 1929 (London: Cassell, 1930); republished as *Journal of Things New and Old* (Garden City, N.Y.: Doubleday, Doran, 1930);

Imperial Palace (London: Cassell, 1930; Garden City, N.Y.: Doubleday, Doran, 1930);

Venus Rising from the Sea (London: Cassell, 1931);

The Night Visitor and Other Stories (London: Cassell, 1931; Garden City, N.Y.: Doubleday, Doran, 1931);

Dream of Destiny: An Unfinished Novel and Venus Rising from the Sea (London: Cassell, 1932); republished as *Stroke of Luck and Dream of Destiny: An Unfinished Novel* (Garden City, N.Y.: Doubleday, Doran, 1932).

Editions and Collections: *The Journals of Arnold Bennett, 1896-1928,* 3 volumes, edited by Newman Flower (London: Cassell, 1932-1933; revised edition, New York: Viking, 1932-1933); republished with additions from the years 1906-1907 and with the *Florentine Journal* (London: Penguin, 1971);

The Author's Craft and Other Critical Writings of Arnold Bennett, edited by Samuel Hynes (Lincoln: University of Nebraska Press, 1968);

Arnold Bennett: The Evening Standard Years. Books & Persons, 1926–1931, edited by Andrew Mylett (London: Chatto & Windus, 1974; Hamden, Conn.: Shoe String, 1974);

Sketches for Autobiography, edited by James Hepburn (London & Boston: Allen & Unwin, 1980).

SELECTED PLAY PRODUCTIONS: *Cupid and Common Sense,* London, Shaftesbury Theatre, 1 January 1908;

What the Public Wants, London, Aldwych Theatre, 5 February 1909;

The Great Adventure, adapted from Bennett's *Buried Alive,* Glasgow, Royal Theatre, 18 September 1911; London, Kingsway Theatre, 25 March 1913;

The Honeymoon: A 3 Act Comedy, London, Royalty Theatre, 6 October 1911;

Milestones: A Play in 3 Acts, by Bennett and Edward Knoblock, London, Royalty Theatre, 5 March 1912;

The Title: A Comedy in 3 Acts, London, Royalty Theatre, 20 July 1918;

Judith: A Play in 3 Acts on the Apocryphal Book of Judith, Eastbourne, Devonshire Park Theatre, 5 April 1919; London, Kingsway Theatre, 30 April 1919;

Sacred and Profane Love, adapted from Bennett's novel, Liverpool, Playhouse, 15 September 1919; London, Aldwych Theatre, 10 November 1919;

The Love Match: A Play in 5 Scenes, Folkestone, Pleasure Gardens, 30 January 1922; London, Strand Theatre, 21 March 1922;

Body and Soul, Liverpool, Playhouse, 15 February 1922; London, Regent Theatre, 11 September 1922;

London Life: A Play, by Bennett and Knoblock, London, Theatre Royal, Drury Lane, 3 June 1924;

The Bright Island, London, Aldwych Theatre, 15 February 1925;

Flora: A Play, Manchester, Rusholme Repertory, 17 October 1927;

Mr. Prohack: A Play in 3 Acts, adapted by Bennett and Knoblock from Bennett's novel, London, Court Theatre, 16 November 1927;

The Return Journey, London, Saint James's Theatre, 1 September 1928;

Don Juan de Marana: A Play in 4 Acts, London, Covent Garden Theatre, 24 June 1959.

Enoch Arnold Bennett was a multifaceted celebrity in his day – novelist, short-story writer, critic, journalist, playwright, travelogue writer, pro-digious letter writer, watercolorist, member of government, yachtsman – with diverse interests and phenomenal productivity. At the height of his popularity, in the 1920s, posters advertising his latest novel were plastered on the sides of the double-decker buses in London. One of his plays, *Milestones,* written in collaboration with Edward Knoblock, ran in London's West End theater district for six hundred performances in 1912. William Maxwell Aitken, Lord Beaverbrook, appointed Bennett deputy minister in the Ministry of Information during World War I. After the Armistice in 1918, Bennett was offered a knighthood but refused to accept it. His book reviews for the *Evening Standard* ran under the title "Books and Persons" from 1926 to 1931 and were credited by Hugh Walpole and other young writers with making the fortune of a new book in a night. More significant, these articles still represent one of the highest achievements of modern literary journalism. In 1931, as he lay dying of typhoid caught while vacationing in France, straw was spread in the streets around Chiltern Court to deaden the noise of traffic, a custom previously reserved for royalty. Nevertheless, university curricula today seldom include his masterpieces in the novel, although his writings remain popular according to library circulation reports.

His short stories are even less taught; 104 of them are available in seven volumes, the last published seven months after his death. He placed writing novels highest in his literary endeavors, but developing short stories obviously interested him as well. Although his earliest attempts at professional writing were journalistic pieces for a hometown newspaper and although he won a prize for his first London publication – a parody of the sensational serial *What's Bred in the Bone,* by the popular novelist Grant Allen – Bennett's first successful attempt to write creatively was the short story "A Letter Home," published by the avant-garde periodical *Yellow Book* in July 1895. In the following year he felt capable of quitting his job as a law clerk to accept an assistant editorship of a five-year-old penny paper, *Woman.* From this point on he devoted himself to the literary life in London and Paris. But he came from the Potteries district of England, and his birthplace was always a permeating influence in his life and literature. Many of his short stories feature characters and attitudes typical of the area.

Bennett was born on 27 May 1867 in Burslem, Staffordshire, the heart of the Potteries, so called because of the great pottery kilns that towered over all six pottery towns, belching smoke to blacken the landscape. He came from generations of potters and

Bennett at Les Sablons, France (drawing by Frederick Marriott)

ciousness of living and expansion of the spirit so in contrast to the preceding penurious years that the future author never forgot the means of the change. Many of his novels and short stories feature characters with driving determination who seek wealth and status.

High parental expectations from Enoch and Sarah Ann Bennett pressured Arnold, the oldest child, and his five siblings, Frank, Fanny Gertrude, Emily, Tertia, and Septimus, at all times. In the new home Bennett's interest in sketching, his wish to be abreast of modern trends, and his talent for organizing the group culminated in extraordinary friezes, dadoes, panels, and bright designs throughout the house, achieved to the joy of his parents and the wonder of their guests. Bennett's father expected him to study law after his schooling, during which he had always been at or near the head of his classes. But to his father's disgust and his own surprise, he failed his law examinations. However, two school interests gave him entry to the worlds of London and Paris for which he longed: his acquirements of French and the new Pitman's shorthand. The latter gained him a job in London; the former gained him his first London friendship, with John Eland, a French-speaking bibliophile. At twenty-one, then, Bennett could turn his back on his father's plans for him and follow dreams of his own.

Before publishing any creative work, Bennett had in 1893 begun to write letters to another new friend, George Sturt. In their correspondence, which lasted for thirty years, Bennett enthusiastically discussed those techniques he observed in his reading and tendencies he observed in himself. Gradually he began to clarify his concept of writing fiction. By October 1894 he wrote to Sturt:

> I may say that I have no inward assurance that I could ever do anything more than mediocre viewed strictly as art – very mediocre. On the other hand, I have a clear idea that by cultivating that "lightness of touch" to which you refer, and exercising it upon the topicalities of the hour, I could turn out things which would be read with zest. . . . I would sooner succeed as a caricaturist of passing follies than fail as a producer of "documents humains."

He was to succeed at both endeavors in his best novels, short stories, and plays. By November 1895 he could complain of his difficulties to Sturt: "It is the *arrangement* that kills one, the mere arrangement of 'sensation and event,'" but he went on to say, "I feel more sure than ever I did in my life before, that I can *write* in time, and 'make people care', too, as Hy. James says – though praps only a few people."

knew they had endured appalling conditions of considerable danger. However, his forebears considered themselves a superior group. The ambition to improve their circumstances is evident as far back as 1786, when Bennett's great-great-grandfather was literate enough to sign his own name in the marriage register. Bennett's grandfather valued education so highly that when an edict from the Methodist Conference discontinued instruction in writing for poor children in Methodist Sunday schools in 1837, he and other sympathizers founded the Hill Top Chapel, where he became a trustee and superintendent of an institution that boasted a library. Bennett's father, Enoch, determined to rise above his rank, even though he was a master potter at the age of twenty-two. When his pottery business failed, he was reduced to pawnbroking until he inherited a small portion and could article himself as a solicitor's clerk for a grinding six years of poverty that were indelibly impressed upon his son's mind. However, by Bennett's teenage years the family was lifted into relative affluence. The exciting change was symbolized for Bennett in the substantial new home his father acquired, which permitted a gra-

His early fascination with technique places him among those English writers who in the 1890s were trying to create a "New Form" for the novel and the short story, looking to France for direction. From his studies of Emile Zola, Edmund and Jules de Goncourt, Gustave Flaubert, and Guy de Maupassant, he tried to produce verisimilitude in his fiction. His short story "A Letter Home" (1895) is a Zolaesque presentation of waste and futility, quite artistically achieved with a typical Maupassant ending, and its publication in *Yellow Book* was a recognition of its trendiness. But he was also aware of reactions to factmongering. The work of the impressionist and postimpressionist painters and musicians soon influenced young English writers away from simpler forms of realism. Ford Madox Ford and Joseph Conrad are more readily seen as heralding impressionism in English fiction. Ford, who accepted the title of impressionist, recalls the excitement of the time in *The March of Literature from Confucius to Modern Times* (1939):

There was writing before Flaubert; but Flaubert and his coterie opened, as it were, a window through which one saw the literary scene from an entirely new angle. Perhaps more than anything else it was a matter of giving visibility to your pages; perhaps better than elsewhere, Conrad with his "It is above all to make you see!" expressed the aims of the New World.

Ford recognized that Bennett, from the year of his arrival in London, was abreast of the trend.

Although Bennett reveled in gallery exhibitions of the impressionist and postimpressionist schools, he soon turned from what he thought to be merely the surface interest of painters such as Alfred Sisley, Claude Monet, and Edouard Manet and looked in admiration at Paul Cézanne, who tried to catch on canvas essential forms underlying surface reality. He identifies in a *Journals* entry of 29 September 1896 his "natural instincts toward a *synthetic impressionism.*" He identifies in a *Journals* entry of 11 January 1898 that "an artist must be interested primarily in presentment, not in the thing presented. He must have a passion for technique, a deep love for form." He could say on 3 January 1899 in his *Journals* that "Superficial facts are of small importance ... they might, for the sake of more clearly disclosing the beauty, suffer a certain *distortion.*" In the same *Journals* entry he further distinguishes his literary aim:

The day of my enthusiasm for "realism," for "naturalism," has passed. I can perceive that a modern work of fiction dealing with modern life may ignore realism and

yet be great. To find beauty, which is always hidden; that is the aim.... My desire is to depict the deeper beauty while abiding by the envelope of facts.

In studying varieties of English realism in his early days in London, Bennett perceived possibilities that further freed him to follow his own bent. Because of his work on *Woman,* he had been invited in 1897 to write regularly for *Hearth and Home,* a weekly that later merged with *Vanity Fair.* In the following year Lewis Hind, editor of the *Academy,* a twenty-nine-year-old serious review of the arts and sciences then at its highest prestige, invited Bennett to contribute articles. In his July–December 1899 article on George Gissing for the *Academy,* Bennett declares:

The artists who have courage fully to exploit their own temperaments are always sufficiently infrequent to be peculiarly noticeable and welcome. Still more rare are they who, leaving it to others to sing and emphasize the ideal and obvious beauties which all can in some measure see, will exclusively exercise the artist's prerogative as an explorer of hidden and recondite beauty in unsuspected places.

He begins to define that "beauty" in the statement: "The spirit of the sublime dwells not only in the high and remote, it shines unperceived amid all the usual meannesses of our daily existence." And, in daily existence, that which had come under the dominion of man, that which was controlled for a purpose, stimulated his artistic endeavors and directed his study of his fellow human beings to those areas where their activities had created an environment wholly disparate from the haunts of nature – the Potteries, the narrow side streets of London, and the great department stores, theaters, and hotels of the inner city. In an early letter to H. G. Wells, whom he met through his work on *Woman,* he further defined "beauty" and "the sublime":

It seems to me that there are immense possibilities in the very romance of manufacture – not wonders of machinery and that sort of stuff – but in the tremendous altercation with nature that is continually going on.

That "altercation with nature" was to be variously identified in the human struggles he examined throughout his life in his novels and short stories. Some identifications pursued in his short stories include his views of the arbitrary forms and restrictive nature of all systems men have devised; of the various kinds of power/domination versus freedom/individuality possible within systems; and of the dichotomy between flesh and spirit, illusion and reality, causing wasted lives. Major themes also include a "savour of life" – a typical Bennett phrase – and the importance of overcoming egoism. Throughout his examination of his chosen human situations, he was fascinated with the psychology of attitudes, of fluctuating moods, of their causes, processes, and consequences. Most of these clarifications and concentrations were clearly established in the exciting early days of his London bachelorhood.

Within six years of his association with *Woman,* Bennett not only established the direction of his concern for serious writing but also the pattern of frenetic productivity that was to astound and dismay his friends and critics throughout his life. By September 1900 he had, besides his daily work, begun one sensational novel; published his first serious novel, *A Man from the North* (1898); begun his first successful novel, *Anna of the Five Towns* (1902); published *Journalism for Women* (1898); published three one-act plays called *Polite Farces for the Drawing Room* (1899); collaborated on another play with a new friend, Arthur Hooley; helped dramatize Eden Phillpotts's novel *Children of the Mist* (1898); and published one short story, "The Police Station" (15 September 1900). In 1901 he secured the services of agent J. B. Pinker, who successfully promoted Bennett's work for the next twenty-one years.

By 1903, after the death of his father, the diffident, woman-shy northerner moved to Paris, became fluent in French, acquired a chorus girl named Chichi as mistress, and became a close friend of Marcel Schwob, scholar, critic, and linguist, in whose circle Bennett met many Continental artists. Early in this French period he published *The Truth About an Author* (anonymous, 1903), a provocative, anti-aesthetic view of a struggling writer; *How to Become an Author* (1905), a helpful manual; and *Leonora* (1903), a serious novel of a mature married woman's love affair. He stopped writing for the *Academy* in order to begin a long series of general essays for *T.P.'s Weekly.* In 1905 he published his first daring novel, *Sacred and Profane Love,* an ambitious attempt some critics repudiated for vulgarity and lack of restraint. He also published his first two collections of short stories: *The Loot of Cities* (1905) and *Tales of the Five Towns* (1905), some of which he had been writing since 1900.

Throughout these years in London and Paris, Bennett had longed for marriage and the settled life. At thirty-nine, in a stressful eighteen months, he mistakenly planned to marry a young American, Eleanor Green, but, rebuffed after wedding invitations had been sent out, he decided to marry an experienced older Frenchwoman, Marguerite Soulié, who had recently become his secretary. The mar-

riage eventually proved disastrous for both. They were legally separated in 1921; Marguerite would never permit a divorce, and she outlived him. Nevertheless, in relative married content Bennett began the major novel he had been considering for four years. He poured his mature wisdom into *The Old Wives' Tale* (1908) and was so inspired that in ten months he completed the two-hundred-thousand-word masterpiece, handwritten in a special calligraphy on special paper (holograph copies of this manuscript can be viewed in special Bennett collections, such as the Berg Collection at the New York Public Library). Within the same ten months he composed two shorter, farcical novels, *Helen with the High Hand* (1910) and the clever *Buried Alive* (1908). Around this time he also produced essays, dramatic writings, popular "pocket" philosophies, and his next collection of short stories, *The Grim Smile of the Five Towns* (1907).

His outstanding output was distinguished by its quality. *The Old Wives' Tale* instantly brought him the enthusiastic approval of the novelists Wells and Frank Harris and won the praise of the distinguished critics Ford and Edward Garnet, who wrote in the *Nation* (21 November 1908):

> Most novelists are rarely quite one with their subject; a little above or below it. But Mr. Bennett really is his subject, the breadth of it, intellectually, in a remarkable way.

Ford asked Bennett for short stories for the *English Review,* one of the most respected literary journals of its time, which he had recently launched. Bennett had already contributed avant-garde articles promoting modern Russian and French writers to the powerful socialist paper *New Age.* His short story "The Matador of the Five Towns" (*English Review,* April 1909) became the title story of his next volume of short stories (1912). At the midpoint of his career Bennett had clearly reached literary eminence.

Throughout these years Bennett pursued his interest in the theater. In 1909 he was exhilarated by the first full-scale production of *What the Public Wants,* starring Sir Charles Hawtrey and Ben Webster. It was praised by the discriminating Max Beerbohm. Bennett immediately wrote *The Honeymoon,* which in 1911 starred the acclaimed actress Marie Tempest and was cited for its humor. He also published the important first novel of the Clayhanger trilogy. For this more closely biographical novel he revisited his birthplace, which generated an intense emotion that permeates the novel. Its greatest strength is Bennett's remarkable realization of a sensitive portrait of the growth of a lovable young man.

Following the critical success of *Clayhanger* in 1910, Bennett worked on a stage adaptation of *Buried Alive,* continued to write articles and book reviews, attended to his voluminous correspondence, worked on the second Clayhanger novel, published *The Card* (1911; made into a 1952 movie, *The Promoter,* starring Sir Alec Guinness and Petula Clark) and wrote, with Knoblock, the remarkably successful play *Milestones* (1912).

In 1911 the influential American publisher George Doran persuaded Bennett to visit the United States. He was acclaimed in New York, Washington, D.C., Chicago, Indianapolis, Philadelphia, Boston, and at universities in the New England states. Bennett noted his experiences in *Those United States* (1912). He began to think of returning to England. His affluence enabled him to buy an elegant Queen Anne house in Essex and a large yacht and to hire an excellent secretary, Winifred Nerney, who served him loyally until his death. He recorded his voyages on the yacht in *From the Log of the Velsa* (1914). His *Journals* recounts his conviviality with his many relatives and his multitude of friends, but these affluent years were less productive than usual. His mother, to whom he had written every day for twenty-five years, died, and then World War I broke out. He was not to publish another volume of short stories until 1924.

In this period of crisis Bennett was spurred to complete the third of the Clayhanger novels, which deals with the experiences in marriage of the principal figures of the first two books. Informing the strength of feeling projected in the novel were the tensions always present in his own marriage, brought to the breaking point by the war years. Bennett, drawn back to London and brought into close association with Lord Beaverbrook, found himself in 1918 forced into political activity in Beaverbrook's Ministry of Information as director of propaganda in France. He wrote a series of war articles for the *Daily News;* these appeared almost every Thursday from August 1914 to the war's end. In April 1915 he became a director of the *New Statesman;* in June he toured the western front.

Within these years he completed the Clayhanger trilogy and wrote five minor novels and three plays. By 1922 he had fallen in love with the young actress Dorothy Cheston. In 1923 she agreed to become his common-law wife and took his name by deed poll. Again in relative marital satisfaction, he produced some of his best work. *Riceyman Steps* (1923), an impressive psychological study of miser-

"The Deputy-Mayor, so soon to be Mayor, walked out of the room, crushed."

Illustration by Gunning King for "His Worship the Goosedriver"
(Windsor Magazine, *January 1904*)

liness, brought him more acclaim and the award from Edinburgh University of the James Tait Black Memorial Prize for the best novel of that year. In 1924, drawing upon the popular appeal of a character in *Riceyman Steps,* he published his first volume of short stories in ten years, *Elsie and the Child: A Tale of Riceyman Steps and Other Stories.* In 1926 his only child, Virginia, was born. *Lord Raingo,* which was published that year, is his powerful record of the British war cabinet in action and an equally powerful study of melancholia in a good man in decline.

The years of emotional and sexual fulfillment with Dorothy were attended by a rising tide of criticism from a new generation of writers. In many cases, in his series of "Books and Persons" for the

Evening Standard, Bennett provoked these attacks, thoroughly enjoying the effect of stirring up "les jeunes," believing himself well able to parry their thrusts, and showing at all times an avuncular, but discriminating, interest in their development, extending even to anonymous financial support. Some, such as D. H. Lawrence, who solicited money from Bennett, bitterly resented all he stood for; some, such as Ezra Pound, damned what they viewed as his materialism; some, such as Virginia Woolf, across class barriers, misunderstood his literature.

His final years were full of worry. Burdened by his young wife's unsatisfied theatrical ambitions, his increasing need for more money to maintain his lifestyle, and the deterioration of his never-robust health, Bennett drove himself to maintain his prodigious productivity. His final volume of short stories, *The Woman Who Stole Everything and Other Stories,* was brought out in 1927. He supervised the Court Theatre's production that year of the dramatization of his novel *Mr. Prohack* (1922), in which Cheston made her return to the stage after the baby's birth and which launched the acting career of Charles Laughton. He dashed off sensational serials, *The Strange Vanguard* and *Accident,* in 1928. He maintained the flow of his journalism and reread his correspondence with Sturt for possible publication. He planned a new play, *The Return Journey,* which opened at Saint James's Theatre in 1928, and he wrote the screenplay for the film *Piccadilly* (1929). He traveled in Germany and Russia with Beaverbrook and began work on his last completed novel, *Imperial Palace* (1930), a tour de force of the hotel world as well as a sympathetic portrait of the "new woman."

What Bennett grasped in his consideration of existence, as did Henry James and Woolf, is that in the emotional lives of individuals the degree of comedy and the degree of tragedy are relative to each person's perception of experience. In his best novels and short stories his unerring accuracy in locating the forms, courses, and effects of strain in relationships links him with earlier writers such as George Eliot and Anthony Trollope and with contemporaries such as James and helped pave the way for the fine discriminations found in younger writers such as Lawrence and Woolf. In his short stories his literary aims are generally modified. However, some of the volumes include well-wrought and distinguished tales. All of the volumes have variety and a characteristic vigor.

His wish to break with tradition in short-story writing was made clear in "A Letter Home." In his *Journals* (16 January 1899) Bennett recorded his as-

tonishment at the old-fashioned air of some short stories published in 1893, finding them "positively antique." His assiduous reading, recorded throughout the three volumes of his *Journals* and the four volumes of his letters (edited by James Hepburn), indicates that he was making himself aware of almost all of those who were producing short stories in what are termed the transition years of 1880 to 1920. Helmut E. Gerber, who in 1957 established a scholarly journal, *English Fiction in Transition,* is the author of *The English Short Story in Transition, 1880–1920* (1967). Of the nineteen authors Gerber selected as creators of "the best and most exemplary short stories" of the period (not including Bennett), fifteen were well known to Bennett as friends, club members, correspondents, protégés, or those he was particularly studying.

However, Bennett's seven volumes of short stories do not show a progression in his use of the genre. He early established the ways he wanted to use the form and then maintained them throughout his career. Primarily the stories feature expansions of anecdotes of Five Towns eccentrics or develop experiences of character types, such as the quixotic millionaire, the arrogant artist, the managing wife, the temperamental thoroughbred, and the stoic laborer. Much of the action involves domestic difficulties, business deals, or extravagant, improbable intrigue and mystery. Many of the stories have a humorous or ironic point to make about human idiosyncrasies. The rest compassionately explore attitudes.

In *Tales of the Five Towns* there are thirteen stories, including the affecting tale of "Tiddy-fol-lol," a reprint of "A Letter Home," and one of Bennett's favorites, "His Worship the Goosedriver." The last-mentioned tale opens the volume with an account of Josiah Curtenty, a wealthy, retired earthenware manufacturer and jolly deputy-mayor of Bursley. Piqued by a goosedriver's comment that there is no business in Bursley, Curtenty buys all his unsold geese. Then, nettled by his friends' mocking statements, he takes the goosedriver's staff and prepares to drive the fourteen geese to his home. As Bennett develops the consequences of Curtenty's precipitation, he captures the humor and difficulty of the walk home and the inimical attitudes of Curtenty's wife and the watching citizenry of Bursley. Bennett ends the tale with a face-saving feast for the deputy-mayor, organized by his wife and friends. The characteristic of pigheadedness fascinated Bennett, who found it a typical trait of many Potteries people. He shapes his narrator to enjoy both Curtenty's idiosyncrasies and the discomfiture they bring.

In "Tiddy-fol-lol," Bennett depicts the story of a taciturn old man striking his handicapped grandson for taunting him with other boys in the street. The boy – afflicted with a hearing impairment, stammering, and a clouded intellect – lies in a coma for a day. All fear he will die. But his recovery, with removal of his ailments, seems so miraculous to his grandfather that the old man becomes reconciled to the boy's mother, from whom he has been estranged since her disapproved marriage. The family is whole again. As in "His Worship the Goose-driver," Bennett presents the trait of stubbornness, this time featuring its potential for tragedy. The title and outline for this story first appeared in *A Man from the North,* in which Richard Larch, a literary hopeful, desperately tries to write this story but fails. In that novel Bennett gave artistic shape to his own early fears. By completing the story for *Tales of the Five Towns,* Bennett gave one more indication of his greater sense of literary assurance by 1905.

Bennett placed "A Letter Home" last in the volume. This tale depicts a young northern man who has disappointed his family, squandered his resources, neglected his health, and come to die as a vagrant in a city hospital ward. His last effort is expended in writing a letter to his mother expressing his sorrow. Another friendly vagrant comes to visit him in the ward, finds him dead, and offers to post the letter. Later, needing to light a pipe, the tramp pulls the crumpled paper from his pocket and sets fire to it. The somber presentation of waste and futility is concisely and artistically achieved in the manner of the French realists who dominated Bennett's study at the time. In 1927 Arthur Symons told Bennett that this story was equal to Maupassant's work.

Of the remaining ten stories in the volume, four had been previously published in various weeklies dating from 1902. These stories range from the ironic circumstances of an accidental death and a suicide, a love match achieved through a psychic phenomenon, jealousy and a failed murder attempt, a working girl's fairy-tale finding of a wealthy father, a young man's comically destructive attempt to show off before a girl, a couple's disturbing discovery of deception in their marriage, which is overcome with the birth of their child, to two more tales featuring other consequences of the Five Towns characteristic trait of stubbornness. Bennett obviously wanted to create variety, vitality, and brevity. His choice of central incidents, his establishment of appropriate contexts, and his conclusions shaped with impact are all competently done.

Five months later Bennett published his second volume of short stories, *The Loot of Cities.* He ex-

ulted in January 1903 that he had been commissioned to write six stories for the *Windsor* magazine and had completed them by the previous November. He reprinted these with seven others in his latest volume. The six *Windsor* stories developed the adventures of a kind of Robin Hood of the business world. Bennett wrote them in less than six months, stating in his *Journals* (27 November 1903): "I have learnt a lot about the technique of construction, while writing them" but admitting that "once or twice I have been terribly bored."

The first of the six short stories introduces the young, eccentric American millionaire Cecil Thorold, who, with his valet, Lecky, likes catching schemers and making them pay. Also introduced is Eve Fincastle, a journalist who finds Thorold's maneuvers disturbingly immoral. Over the course of the other five tales, these two inadvertently meet in Europe, on the Gold Coast, in Algiers, and in the Sahara, Eve always entangled in Cecil's intrigues. Obviously Bennett's aim is light entertainment, and he achieves this with gusto. The remaining seven stories show Bennett's ingenuity in developing surprising plots featuring political poisonings, comically bungled burglaries, attempted assassinations, superstitions, and supernatural phenomena. His estimate of the value of this work is given in purely monetary terms in his *Journals.* Nevertheless, his second volume of short stories demonstrates his fertile imagination.

Bennett's third volume of short stories, *The Grim Smile of the Five Towns,* also includes thirteen tales, one of which is his best: "The Death of Simon Fuge" is a well-wrought, subtle revelation of character. It is the penultimate tale within a collection that captures aspects of Five Towns people wryly admired by Bennett. The first story, "The Lion's Share," is a tragicomic account of a half brother's extreme sense of responsibility for his younger sibling, whom he has accidentally injured, and the outrageous advantage taken for years by that young fellow. The second, "Baby's Bath," is a comically elaborated incident in the lives of a young couple and their first baby, featuring a problem caused by the failure of the new electric power at a crucial time. Bennett's comic exaggerations do not obscure his sensitive recognition of the strains and joys caused by a baby. The third tale, "The Silent Brothers," develops the absurd lengths to which stubbornness drives two feuding brothers. The next four stories feature Vera Cheswardine's overcoming various difficulties with her husband, all comically focusing on her extravagance and flights of imagination in the business life of Bursley, one of the Five Towns. Four other tales are comic presentations of other amusing behaviors of young and old Five Towns types. One tale is an elaboration of a macabre joke. But the volume is distinguished by the inclusion of "The Death of Simon Fuge."

The first-person narrator, Loring, a British Museum expert on ceramics, approaches the Potteries for the first time, having met the Bursley artist Fuge in London years before and having just read of his death in a newspaper on a train. Slowly, but with sure strokes, Bennett suggests the interests of the controlled, sensitive aesthete who appreciates Fuge's art and who has formed a fascination for the liberated artist, particularly relishing Fuge's lack of reticence in talking of himself. While vividly remembering Fuge's flamboyant personality and his graphic account of a night spent in a boat on Ilam Lake with two beautiful Bursley sisters, Loring is titillated again with "the delicious possibility of ineffable indiscretions" on the part of the artist and is curious to enter the region of Fuge's birth.

In choosing this narrator, Bennett cleverly registers the shock of the intelligent, sensitive, cosseted outsider's first experiences of the Potteries. He believably delineates Loring's attempts to reconcile the fact that the grimy industrial region could produce an artist of Fuge's stature while Loring is forced to respond to the vigor of residents who cannot be dismissed as crude provincials lacking culture. At his train exit he is surrounded by a noisy, jostling, ill-dressed crowd and thinks patronizingly that all he sees is a violent negation of Fuge. Bennett aptly captures the biases of this timid, studious man upon meeting his host, Robert Brindley, a hearty architect dressed like a country squire.

In Brindley's company Loring sees the scale of ugliness in the singular scenery of the Five Towns area as so vast that it is sublime. His assumptions of Brindley's provincial limitations are immediately shaken, and he decides Brindley is "a very tonic dose." His experiences in Brindley's home with good food, good music – Brindley plays well – good books, and unceremonious friendliness lead him to indulge himself to the point of exclaiming, "Never before or since have I been such a buck." Loring's experiences end with his meeting the two sisters with whom Fuge had so long ago rowed on the lake. One is a superior barmaid, the other the contented wife of Brindley's friend. Loring strains to preserve his notion of Fuge's dalliance with these women, but he can find no corroboration of illicit romance in the facts the Five Towns people offer him. He leaves the area with an appreciation of its genuine hospitality, talents, and unique combination of the brusque and the sensitive in its people. Bennett's mastery of the material is evident in the care with which humor, movement, conversations, and descriptions all cohere, with no false note struck, to give the reader a satisfying sense of Bennett's honesty and insight in characterization and milieu. "The Death of Simon Fuge" should be included in any representative collection of the best short stories of the period.

In his next volume of short stories, *The Matador of the Five Towns, and Other Stories,* Bennett opens with the title story, which features Loring as narrator. This is Loring's third visit to the Potteries district and to the Brindleys and their friends. As a sequel to "The Death of Simon Fuge" it does not extend the reader's knowledge of Loring but expands his experience of life in the Five Towns. It combines the passions let loose on the football field in a crucial game for the Towns with the passions restrained that evening in a parlor/bar as the owner, the football hero, copes with the death of his wife in childbirth. Throughout these events Loring makes his typical outsider's surmises and develops corrective reflections, all indicating his growing fascination with, and deepening understanding of, Potteries people. Ford, who commissioned this story for the *English Review* in 1908, said of it in the *Outlook* (1913): "I don't know a better piece of work in the English language, or a job better executed." Nevertheless, the narrator is too much the author's tool as observer of Potteries life.

The remainder of the volume holds more short stories than any of Bennett's other volumes. Besides "The Matador" there are twenty-one tales. Most of them develop incidents emphasizing the fears, illusions, and maneuverings of both sexes in various stages of marriage. Some feature Five Towns cards and curmudgeons gaining their own ways or getting humorously caught by their own tricks. One, "The Glimpse," was commissioned by the editor of the illustrated weekly *Black & White,* then refused. It is the first-person narrative of a dying man who has an out-of-body experience and then recovers as a changed being. Bennett expanded this story into a curious novel (1909) of the same name. Both the short story and the novel show Bennett letting his imagination range over topical theosophical writings. But most of the stories in the volume are told by an avuncular narrator who is gently amused at human idiosyncrasies and recognizes in them the "savour of life." One, "Mimi," tells from a more objective point of view the story of a young child's costly and useless loyalty in keeping the secret of her aunt's elopement. Altogether, Bennett's fourth volume of short stories shows him striving for variety but depending on old formulas.

Twelve years passed before Bennett published his next volume of tales, *Elsie and the Child: A Tale of Riceyman Steps and Other Stories* (1924). Nine of the thirteen tales, including the title story, were published in weeklies from 1921 to 1924. Bennett had sent André Gide a copy of *Riceyman Steps,* telling him he thought it was better than some of Gide's novels. The great popularity of the character Elsie led Bennett to write this sequel about her; Joe, her shell-shocked husband; and Eva, the young daughter of their employers, Dr. and Mrs. Raste. It is a long short story in ten chapters, but it is simply the elaboration of one event – the decision to send Eva to boarding school.

It opens with Elsie attempting to carry out her ambition to wait on the Rastes' table as Joe contentedly spends his time in the kitchen as cook. While serving dinner she is aware of Eva's unhappiness in the presence of a guest, the headmistress of a school in Bournemouth. Eva's difficulty is that although she can leave her parents, she cannot bear to part with Elsie. Elsie's troubled response is to suggest that she and Joe should leave their employment with the Rastes because of their daughter's disloyalty. Joe's reaction is to erupt into violence, always latent in his shell-shocked state, as he considers the threat that he may have to leave his sanctuary. His angry statements to Eva convince her she will lose Elsie altogether if she does not go sensibly to school. The tale ends as she is being driven to the train station. For readers meeting these characters first in the short story, rather than in the novel, Bennett sensitively develops the instinctive responses of the inarticulate earth mother Elsie, the course of violence in the infirm Joe, the stages of egoism in the pampered child, and the difficulties of the upstairs/downstairs situation of the servants with their employers.

The story develops two separate lines of experience – the Rastes' difficulty and Elsie's difficulty – both mainly concerning the husbands but brought to turning points by the catalyst of the child's willfulness. The ending – with peace in the home, both upstairs and downstairs – is arrived at when the stress on both husbands is removed. Bennett's empathy with children is clear in his presentation of Eva. His treatment of the child includes the innocence, power, and sensuality of the child. In Elsie's relationship with Eva, Bennett develops the complications with which neither can objectively deal in order to emphasize the incalculability of daily living – a recurring Bennett theme.

Bennett in early middle age

The remaining twelve stories in the volume include four set in London theatrical circles: one involves a pretty box-office girl who chooses her working-class lover over a wealthy patron; one features a dictatorial, aging female star who capitulates to the one person on the staff who defies her; one develops the realization of an aging critic that he must give way to a rising new star; and one presents an insensitive young actor whose handsome face wins him fame in spite of his having no talent. Two other stories involve wealthy parents trying to control their daughters' choices of husbands. Three other tales develop surprising realizations that come to two aging, refined, wealthy city bachelors and a Five Towns millionaire: one realizes he does want to marry a woman who is the opposite of his dreams; one realizes how unsatisfying his organized existence is without romance; and the third realizes he has always loved his forthright Five Towns cousin. The other three tales are unalike. One is the melodramatic experience of quarreling honeymooners who are taught to avoid jealousy by an ex-convict's shocking story. One presents a spinster's awakening to a love that cannot be hers. One presents a couple's delayed honeymoon on a yacht, which provokes the young wife's rebellion against the male system. In these stories Bennett again demonstrates his competence in providing entertainment. "Elsie and the Child" offers more.

Three years later Bennett published his sixth volume of short stories, *The Woman Who Stole Everything and Other Stories*. It opens with the title story, which has ten chapters; Bennett believed it to be one of his best. He reported in his *Journals* that in one week the collection sold 548 copies. The title story features fifty-year-old bachelor Henry Kearns, who is drawn into the marital difficulties of his niece Cora and her husband, Nick. The course of events is presented from Kearns's point of view and opens with his consciousness of his age, youthful feeling, desire not to be alone any longer, and belief now that involvement with women enables one to live in three dimensions instead of two. Nevertheless, at the beginning of the tale he is critical of older women he views across the hotel dining room who try to appear young and obviously seek younger men's attentions. The common characteristic of believing oneself to be the exception becomes the central problem of the tale. At the hotel Kearns first hears Nick's side of the recent estrangement. Then, at his country estate, he is surprised to find Cora and hears her view of their problems. Finally, Nick arrives, and the eventually reconciled couple leaves their uncle, who reflects that he will still pursue a recent female interest he has formed.

The neatness and expectedness of the plot outline give little evidence of why Bennett thought the tale well done. The tale is enhanced by Kearns's struggling to be objective yet sympathetic in the unfamiliar sphere of intimate relations; his biasedness yet openness to familial intimacy, which allows him to achieve wise counseling; and his consequent sense of fear, of anticipation, yet of his ability to cope with a love of his own. In the process Bennett also develops his frank view of the modern young woman on whom much of the fiction of his later years is centered. His view is to give strong encouragement with tonic criticism – essentially Kearns's stance in the tale. Being an ornamental, pampered, restricted woman as wife is viewed as a useless life, which instinctively an intelligent woman knows and an intelligent man recognizes. Both generations are prepared to govern their future actions by this knowledge as the tale ends. Throughout the tale Bennett constructs dialogue and events with appropriate pace and appealing humor. The remaining twelve stories are applications of the usual, competent Bennett formulas.

Seven months after Bennett's death his last volume of short stories, *The Night Visitor and Other Stories* (1931), was published. There are seventeen tales, most of them showing Bennett taking his formulas to extreme, even absurd lengths. In the title story a young husband wants to take a holiday with his wife without their baby. He first pretends to be sick, then finds himself pronounced sick, and, when left alone with a fever, is so angered at the attention paid to his also ailing child that he rages at his wife while a burglar who has entered his bedroom escapes. His rage is pronounced delirium, so his wife forgives him. This is merely Bennett being overly ingenious.

Most of the other tales are equally ingenious without being quite so absurd. However, "Murder" is a well-devised story of a homicide that will never be found out; "The Hat" is a curious elaboration of the inappropriateness of snobbery. Among the rest "The Peacock" involves the transposition of an actual incident in Bennett's life concerning a superstition about peacocks, and "The Cornet Player" was cited by Bennett as perhaps his best tale. One tale, "The Wind," is an interesting attempt. Unusual for his short stories, he devotes the first paragraph to scene painting – a windswept beach with a baby approaching the waves. The situation develops from the difficulty of a young father's adjusting to his wife's engrossment with their child. He negligently lets the child be overtaken by a wave, and, later, when minding her alone he leaves her in the quiet of an old mill to sleep while he watches a cricket game nearby. But the wind blows the old structure over. Both parents rush in terror to the mill, and in their joy at finding the baby unharmed they are reconciled. Bennett competently develops this plot to space the father's disgruntlements with a series of learning shocks. But, in between, Bennett believably captures the infant's sensations as she progresses in the wind on unsteady feet toward the sea and is overwhelmed by the cold water. Temporarily abandoned inside the cavernous mill, the baby wakes and falls out of her carriage. Again Bennett imaginatively enters the baby's world. Those parts distinguish this tale, but his last collection of short stories is not artistically notable.

Bennett's forte was not short-story writing. He encouraged short-story writers such as Pauline Smith to move on to novel writing as the highest literary endeavor. Nevertheless, he obviously enjoyed writing short stories, and he mastered the form for entertainment purposes. When he wished, he could use the form for aesthetic achievement. In the transition of short fiction from Victorian aspiration to Edwardian realism to Continental impressionism, Bennett's best tales show the way he wished to go.

Letters:

Arnold Bennett's Letters to His Nephew, edited by Richard Bennett (New York & London: Harper, 1935; London & Toronto: Heinemann, 1936);

Dorothy Cheston Bennett, *Arnold Bennett: A Portrait Done at Home, together with 170 Letters from A. B.* (London: Cape, 1935; New York: Kendall & Sharp, 1935);

Arnold Bennett and H. G. Wells: A Record of a Personal and a Literary Friendship, edited by Harris Wilson (London: Hart-Davis, 1960; Urbana: University of Illinois Press, 1960);

Correspondence André Gide–Arnold Bennett: Vingt Ans D'Amitié Littéraire (1911–1931), edited by Linette F. Brugmans (Geneva: Librarie Droz, 1964);

Letters of Arnold Bennett, 4 volumes, edited by James Hepburn (London & New York: Oxford University Press, 1966–1986);

Arnold Bennett in Love, edited and translated by George and Jean Beardmore (London: Bruce & Watson, 1972).

Bibliographies:

Norman Emery, *Arnold Bennett: A Bibliography* (Stoke-on-Trent, U.K.: Central Library, Hanley, 1967);

Anita Miller, *Arnold Bennett: An Annotated Bibliography, 1887–1932* (New York: Garland, 1977).

Biographies:

Marguerite Bennett, *Arnold Bennett* (London: Philpot, 1925);

Bennett, *My Arnold Bennett* (New York: Dutton, 1932);

Margaret Locherbie-Goff, *La Jeunesse d'Arnold Bennett* (Avesne-sur-Helpe: Editions de l'Observateur, 1939);

Reginald Pound, *Arnold Bennett* (London: Heinemann, 1952; New York: Harcourt, Brace, 1953);

Dudley Barker, *Writer by Trade: A View of Arnold Bennett* (London: Allen & Unwin, 1966);

Margaret Drabble, *Arnold Bennett: A Biography* (London: Weidenfeld & Nicolson, 1974);

Frank Swinnerton, *Arnold Bennett: A Last Word* (London: Hamish Hamilton, 1978).

References:

Walter Allen, *Arnold Bennett* (Denver: Swallow, 1949);

William Bellamy, *The Novels of Wells, Bennett and Galsworthy, 1890–1910* (New York: Barnes & Noble, 1971);

F. J. Harvey Darton, *Arnold Bennett* (New York: Holt, 1915);

Helmut E. Gerber, *The English Short Story in Transition, 1880–1920* (New York: Pegasus, 1967);

James Winford Hall, *Arnold Bennett: Primitivism and Taste* (Seattle: University of Washington, 1959);

James Hepburn, *The Art of Arnold Bennett* (Bloomington: Indiana University Press, 1963);

Hepburn, ed., *Arnold Bennett: The Critical Heritage* (London & Boston: Routledge, 1981);

L. G. Johnson, *Arnold Bennett of the Five Towns* (London: Daniel, 1924);

Georges Lafourcade, *Arnold Bennett: A Study* (London: Muller, 1939);

J. B. Simons, *Arnold Bennett and His Novels* (Oxford: Blackwell, 1936);

Patrick Swinden, *Unofficial Selves: Character in the Novel from Dickens to the Present Day* (London: Macmillan, 1972);

Frank Swinnerton, *Arnold Bennett* (London: Longmans, Green, 1950);

Louis Tillier, *Studies in the Sources of Arnold Bennett's Novels* (Paris: Didier, 1949);

Geoffrey West, *The Problem of Arnold Bennett* (London: Joiner & Steele, 1932);

Virginia Woolf, *Mr. Bennett and Mrs. Brown* (London: Leonard & Virginia Woolf, 1924);

Walter F. Wright, *Arnold Bennett: Romantic Realist* (Lincoln: University of Nebraska Press, 1971).

Papers:

Major collections of Bennett's papers are located at the University of Arkansas; Bibliothèque Littéraire Jacques Doucet, Paris; Cambridge University; Harry Ransom Humanities Research Center, University of Texas at Austin; University of Illinois; Keele University; Berg Collection, New York Public Library; City Museum of Stoke-on-Trent; and University College, London.

E. F. Benson
(24 July 1867 – 29 February 1940)

Catherine Jurča
Johns Hopkins University

BOOKS: *Sketches from Marlborough,* anonymous (Marlborough: Privately printed, 1888);

Dodo: A Detail of the Day (London: Methuen, 1893; New York: Appleton, 1893);

Six Common Things (London: Osgood & McIlvaine, 1893); revised as *A Double Overture* (Chicago: Sergel, 1894);

The Rubicon (London: Methuen, 1894; New York: Appleton, 1894);

The Judgement Books (London: Osgood & McIlvaine, 1895; New York: Harper, 1895);

Notes on Excavations in Alexandrian Cemeteries, by Benson and D. G. Hogarth (London: Society for the Promotion of Hellenic Studies, 1895);

Limitations (London: Innes, 1896; New York: Harper, 1896);

The Babe, B. A. (New York: Putnam, 1896; London: Putnam, 1897);

The Money Market (Bristol: Arrowsmith, 1898; Philadelphia: Biddle, 1898);

The Vintage: A Romance of the Greek War of Independence (London: Methuen, 1898; New York: Harper, 1898);

The Capsina (London: Methuen, 1899; New York: Harper, 1899);

Mammon & Co. (London: Heinemann, 1899; New York: Appleton, 1899);

The Princess Sophia (London: Heinemann, 1900; New York: Harper, 1900);

The Luck of the Vails (London: Heinemann, 1901; New York: Appleton, 1901);

Scarlet and Hyssop (London: Heinemann, 1902; New York: Appleton, 1902);

Daily Training, by Benson and Eustace Miles (London: Hurst & Blackett, 1902; New York: Dutton, 1903);

The Valkyries: A Romance Founded on Wagner's Opera (London: Dean & Son, 1903; Boston: Page, 1903);

The Book of Months (London: Heinemann, 1903; New York: Harper, 1903);

E. F. Benson, circa 1893

The Mad Annual, by Benson and Miles (London: Hurst & Blackett, 1903; New York: Dutton, 1903);

The Cricket of Abel, Hirst and Shrewsbury, by Benson and Miles (London: Hurst & Blackett, 1903; New York: Dutton, 1903);

The Relentless City (London: Heinemann, 1903; New York: Harper, 1903);

The Challoners (London: Heinemann, 1904; Philadelphia: Lippincott, 1904);

Two Generations (London: Daily Mail, 1904);

An Act in a Backwater (London: Heinemann, 1905; New York: Appleton, 1905);

The Image in the Sand (London: Heinemann, 1905; Philadelphia: Lippincott, 1905);

Diversions Day by Day, by Benson and Miles (London: Hurst & Blackett, 1905);

The Angel of Pain (Philadelphia: Lippincott, 1905; London: Heinemann, 1906);

The House of Defence (London: Authors & Newspapers Association, 1906; revised edition, Toronto: McLeod & Allen, 1906);

Paul (London: Heinemann, 1906; Philadelphia: Lippincott, 1906);

Sheaves (London: Paul, 1907; New York: Doubleday, Page, 1907);

The Climber (London: Heinemann, 1908; New York: Grosset & Dunlap, 1908);

The Blotting Book (London: Heinemann, 1908; New York: Doubleday, Page, 1908);

English Figure Skating (London: G. Bell & Sons, 1908); republished in part as *Skating Calls* (London: G. Bell & Sons, 1909);

A Reaping (London: Heinemann, 1909; New York: Doubleday, Page, 1909);

Daisy's Aunt (London: T. Nelson & Sons, 1910); republished as *The Fascinating Mrs. Halton* (New York: Doubleday, Page, 1910);

The Osbornes (London: Smith, Elder, 1910; New York: Doubleday, Page, 1910);

Margery (New York: Doubleday, Page, 1910); republished as *Juggernaut* (London: Heinemann, 1911);

Account Rendered (London: Heinemann, 1911; New York: Doubleday, Page, 1911);

The Room in the Tower and Other Stories (London: Mills & Boon, 1912);

Mrs. Ames (London: Hodder & Stoughton, 1912; New York: Doubleday, Page, 1912);

Bensoniana (London: Humphreys, 1912);

Thorley Weir (London: Smith, Elder, 1913; Philadelphia: Lippincott, 1913);

The Weaker Vessel (London: Heinemann, 1913; New York: Dodd, Mead, 1913);

Winter Sports in Switzerland (London: Allen, 1913; New York: Dodd, Mead, 1913);

Thoughts from E. F. Benson, compiled by Elsie E. Norton (London: Harrap, 1913);

Dodo's Daughter (New York: Century, 1914); republished as *Dodo the Second* (London: Hodder & Stoughton, 1914);

Arundel (London: Unwin, 1914; New York: Doran, 1915);

The Oakleyites (London: Hodder & Stoughton, 1915; New York: Doran, 1915);

Mike (London: Cassell, 1916); republished as *Michael* (New York: Burt, Doran, 1916);

David Blaize (London: Hodder & Stoughton, 1916; New York: Doran, 1916);

The Freaks of Mayfair (London: Foulis, 1916; New York: Doran, 1917);

Thoughts from E. F. Benson, compiled by H. B. Elliot (London: Holden & Hardingham, 1916);

Mr. Teddy (London: Unwin, 1917); republished as *The Tortoise* (New York: Doran, 1917);

Deutschland über Allah (London: Hodder & Stoughton, 1917); republished in *Crescent and Iron Cross* (London: Hodder & Stoughton, 1918; New York: Doran, 1918);

An Autumn Sowing (London: Collins, 1917; New York: Doran, 1918);

David Blaize and the Blue Door (London: Hodder & Stoughton, 1918; New York: Doran, 1919);

Up and Down (London: Hutchinson, 1918; New York: Doran, 1918);

Poland and Mittel-Europa (London: Hodder & Stoughton, 1918); republished in *The White Eagle of Poland* (London: Hodder & Stoughton, 1918; New York: Doran, 1919);

Across the Stream (London: Murray, 1919; New York: Doran, 1919);

Robin Linnet (London: Hutchinson, 1919; New York: Doran, 1919);

The Social Value of Temperance (London: True Temperance Association, 1919);

Queen Lucia (London: Hutchinson, 1920; New York: Doran, 1920);

The Countess of Lowndes Square and Other Stories (London: Cassell, 1920);

Our Family Affairs, 1867–1896 (London: Cassell, 1920; New York: Doran, 1921);

Lovers and Friends (London: Unwin, 1921; New York: Doran, 1921);

Dodo Wonders (London: Hutchinson, 1921; New York: Doran, 1921);

Miss Mapp (London: Hutchinson, 1922; New York: Doran, 1923);

Peter (London: Cassell, 1922; New York: Doran, 1922);

Colin (London: Hutchinson, 1923; New York: Doran, 1923);

And the Dead Spake & The Horror Horn (New York: Doran, 1923);

Visible and Invisible (London: Hutchinson, 1923; New York: Doran, 1924);

Alan (London: Unwin, 1924; New York: Doran, 1925);

David of Kings (London: Hodder & Stoughton, 1924); republished as *David Blaize of Kings* (New York: Doran, 1924);

Spinach & Reconciliation (New York: Doran, 1924);

Expiation & Naboth's Vineyard (New York: Doran, 1924);

The Face (New York: Doran, 1924);

Colin II (London: Hutchinson, 1925; New York: Doran, 1925);

Mother (London: Hodder & Stoughton, 1925; New York: Doran, 1925);

A Tale of an Empty House & Bagnell Terrace (New York: Doran, 1925);

The Temple (New York: Doran, 1925);

Rex (London: Hodder & Stoughton, 1925; New York: Doran, 1925);

Mezzanine (London: Cassell, 1926; New York: Doran, 1926);

Pharisees and Publicans (London: Hutchinson, 1926; New York: Doran, 1927);

Lucia in London (London: Hutchinson, 1927; New York: Doubleday, Doran, 1928);

Sir Francis Drake (London: John Lane, 1927; New York: Harper, 1927);

Spook Stories (London: Hutchinson, 1928);

The Life of Alcibiades (London: Benn, 1929; New York: Appleton, 1929);

The Male Impersonator (London: Mathews & Marrot, 1929);

Paying Guests (London: Hutchinson, 1929; New York: Doubleday, Doran, 1929);

Ferdinand Magellan (London: John Lane, 1929; New York: Harper, 1930);

The Inheritor (London: Hutchinson, 1930; New York: Doubleday, Doran, 1930);

As We Were: A Victorian Peep-Show (London: Longmans, 1930; New York: Blue Ribbon, 1930);

The Step (New York: Doran, 1930; London: Marrot, 1930);

Mapp and Lucia (London: Hodder & Stoughton, 1931; New York: Doubleday, Doran, 1931);

Charlotte Brontë (London: Longmans, 1932);

Secret Lives (London: Hodder & Stoughton, 1932; New York: Doran, 1932);

As We Are: A Modern Revue (London: Longmans, 1932);

Travail of Gold (London: Hodder & Stoughton, 1933; New York: Doubleday, Doran, 1933);

King Edward VII: An Appreciation (London: Longmans, Green, 1933);

The Outbreak of War, 1914 (London: Davies, 1933; New York: Putnam, 1934);

Raven's Brood (London: Barker, 1934; New York: Doubleday, Doran, 1934);

More Spook Stories (London: Hutchinson, 1934);

Lucia's Progress (London: Hodder & Stoughton, 1935); republished as *The Worshipful Lucia* (New York: Doubleday, Doran, 1935);

Queen Victoria (London: Longmans, Green, 1935);

The Kaiser and English Relations (London: Longmans, Green, 1936);

Old London, 4 volumes: *Portrait of an English Nobleman (Georgian), Janet (Victorian), Friend of the Rich (Mid-Victorian), The Unwanted (Edwardian)* (New York & London: Appleton-Century, 1937);

Queen Victoria's Daughters (New York: Appleton-Century, 1938); republished as *The Daughters of Queen Victoria* (London: Cassell, 1939);

Trouble for Lucia (London: Hodder & Stoughton, 1939; New York: Doubleday, Doran, 1939);

Final Edition: Informal Autobiography (London: Longmans, 1940; New York: Appleton-Century, 1940).

Editions and Collections: *The Horror Horn: The Best Horror Stories of E. F. Benson,* edited by Alexis Lykiard (Saint Albans: Panther, 1974);

The Tale of an Empty House and Other Ghost Stories, edited, with a foreword, by Cynthia Reavell (London: Black Swan, 1986);

The Flint Knife: Further Spook Stories, edited, with an introduction, by Jack Adrian (Wellingborough, U.K.: Equation, 1988);

Desirable Residences and Other Stories, edited, with an introduction, by Adrian (Oxford: Oxford University Press, 1991).

PLAY PRODUCTIONS: *Dodo,* London, Scala Theatre, 25 November 1905;

The Friend in the Garden, London, Savoy Theatre, 7 March 1906;

Dinner for Eight, London, Ambassador Theatre, 23 March 1915;

The Luck of the Vails, Eastbourne, Devonshire Park Theatre, 13 February 1928.

OTHER: *A Book of Golf,* edited by Benson and Eustace Miles (London: Hurst & Blackett, 1903);

Charles Dickens, *Nicholas Nickleby,* 2 volumes, introduction by Benson (London: Waverley, 1913);

A. C. Benson, *Rambles and Reflections,* compiled, with a foreword, by Benson (London: Murray, 1926; New York: Putnam, 1926);

Henry James: Letters to A. C. Benson and Auguste Monod, edited, with an introduction, by Benson (London: Mathews & Marrot, 1930; New York: Scribners, 1930);

The Age of Walnut, introduction by Benson (London: Royal Northern Hospital, 1932).

The six Mapp and Lucia novels by Edward Frederic Benson, one of the most popular short-story writers and novelists of the Edwardian period, continue to enjoy a worldwide cult following more than seventy years after the publication of *Queen Lucia* (1920). Encouraged by the brilliant success of his first novel, *Dodo* (1893), he produced more than one hundred books in a variety of genres: novels, short-story collections, biographies, memoirs, political commentaries, and sporting and fitness manuals; he also wrote plays and poetry. Although the sheer number of his novels has obscured his contributions as a short-story writer, almost two hundred stories have been traced to such exclusive, illustrated monthlies and glossy weeklies as the *Illustrated London News, Pall Mall Magazine, Pearson's Magazine,* and *Windsor Magazine,* as well as to many of the refined middle-class and "quality" ladies' magazines: *Woman, Woman at Home,* the *Lady's Realm,* and *Eve.* Fewer than one-third of these stories were printed in the eight short-story collections published during his lifetime. Much of Benson's early writing is forgettable, sentimental romance designed to satisfy the mass-market periodical consumer, and although these pieces attracted a wide readership in England and the United States, his reputation does not rest on this kind of fiction. His efforts beginning in the years just before World War I demonstrate a talent equal to that of P. G. Wodehouse as a writer of social comedies. Best remembered for acerbic society fiction in which ambitious, determined, middle-aged women battle for social dominance, Benson is rather less well known as one of the finest ghost-story writers of the twentieth century.

"Fred" Benson was born on 24 July 1867, the fifth of six children, to Mary Sidgwick Benson and Edward White Benson, then headmaster of Wellington College and later first bishop of Truro and archbishop of Canterbury. Benson's education began at Temple Grove School at East Sheen; an indifferent scholar, he failed several times to win a scholarship to Marlborough, which he entered in 1881 and remembered fondly in the highly autobiographical school story *David Blaize* (1916). Under A. H. Beesly, Benson demonstrated his academic potential as a student of Latin and Greek. His undergraduate work at King's College, Cambridge, began in 1887, and he gained a first in the classical tripos in 1890 and took a second tripos in archaeol-

ogy the following year. He initially pursued a career as an archaeologist: first in Chester, where his excavations of Roman tombstones proved that Roman legions had penetrated farther north into England than previously believed, and then in Athens for the British School of Archaeology from 1892 to 1895, followed by a year with the Hellenic Society in Egypt, where he and his sister Maggie excavated at Karnak.

Benson always remained fascinated with the ancient world. He continued to travel extensively in Egypt and Greece, setting several short stories and novels there, but writing supplanted archaeology as hobby and then profession. He began writing seriously while at Marlborough, where he edited the school newspaper, the *Marlburian,* with his lifelong friend Eustace Miles, who later gained notoriety as a health-food proponent and fitness expert. At Cambridge, Benson started a short-lived magazine, the *Cambridge Fortnightly,* but his first real foray into the literary marketplace occurred in 1888 with the publication of *Sketches from Marlborough,* a collection of light short pieces that deal with the male world of Benson's school days. The rarest of all his books, it was privately printed.

Dodo was published to great critical and popular acclaim while Benson was in Greece in 1893. Henry James, a friend of the family, was one of the novel's few detractors. Benson's mother had sent James an early version of the manuscript, about which he wrote, as Benson recorded in his memoirs, "two or three long and kindly and brilliantly evasive letters." It is not difficult to imagine James's objections; in this novel are intertwined the best and worst elements of Benson's literary style. Although Dodo, an enchanting yet heartless young beauty in high society, utters charming nonsense that both betrays the superficiality and demonstrates the appeal of late-Victorian social intercourse, the novel reverts to purple prose and melodramatic plot contrivances. For example, the unlikely deaths of Dodo's son and husband serve as ineffective punishments for her inhumanity. The novel created a small but lucrative scandal: Benson based some of the major characters on recognizable London society figures, most notably Margot Tennant, later Lady Asquith, as Dodo and the composer Ethel Smythe as Edith Staines. He repeated this technique in future stories – the best-selling novelist Marie Corelli inspired several of Benson's characters – but never with more success than in his first novel. Despite its obvious flaws, *Dodo* went through no fewer than twelve editions in under a year and was continuously in print until the author's death in 1940. The novel's popularity generated two full-length sequels,

Benson at nineteen

Dodo's Daughter (1914; republished as *Dodo the Second,* 1914) and *Dodo Wonders* (1921), as well as a few short stories in the *Lady's Realm* and *Home Magazine.* While later stories manage more or less to redeem Dodo from melodramatic excess, never in his career would Benson entirely eliminate his tendency toward overwriting.

Late in his life Benson realized that the success of *Dodo* had been a mixed blessing. Mistaking quantity for quality, he thought "that all I had to do was to keep up my interest in life and dash off stories with ease and enjoyment." And dash them off he did; completion time for a novel averaged three weeks. Critics showed his atrocious second novel no mercy, calling *The Rubicon* (1894) "the worst-written, falsest and emptiest book of the decade." For many years thereafter his fiction, when reviewed at all, tended to inspire tepid or hostile responses from critics. Although his popularity with the reading public never wavered, not until later in his career, with his social comedies and biographies, would he enjoy a consistently strong critical reputation.

Close on the heels of *Dodo,* Benson produced a collection of original short stories, *Six Common*

Things (1893). Most of the contents are less short fiction than the kind of meditative essays for which his brother A. C. Benson would become famous. The tone is almost unbearably sentimental and moralistic as the narrator explores a variety of heart-wrenching incidents. In episodes such as "Autumn and Love," about the death of an old man's only child, and "Carrington," which treats the betrayal of an elderly housekeeper by her young charge, Benson lingers over "small and trivial disappointments," which, as he explains, convey a sublime pathos that "aching tragedies" lack. Their emotional excess makes these stories all but unreadable now, except for brief passages that reveal his potential for social comedy, as in "Poor Miss Huntingford," with its witty, careless exchanges between the narrator, champion of governesses, and the catty Miss Grantham. In later stories he returns to the themes and ideas presented in *Six Common Things.* "Like a Grammarian" concerns a gentle scholar who relentlessly devotes himself to his research, literally killing himself over a manuscript that is rejected after his death. Benson would write about other "cranks" (for example, "The Case of Bertram Porter," *Windsor Magazine,* March 1911), but he omitted the sermonizing ("Life is given us that we may live") and let the ironic outcome speak for itself. The collection's dominant theme, that "those who . . . talk of little things not mattering . . . rob life of half its deepest emotions of joy and sorrow," is a constant strain in his work. As his career developed, however, Benson focused on the humor or the horror of trivialities, substituting farce and terror for sentiment.

From 1883 to 1896 the Benson family center was at Lambeth Palace, official residence of the archbishop of Canterbury. With his appointment to the archbishopric, Edward White Benson became one of the most powerful and influential men in England and the family a significant social force. His son took advantage of the opportunities presented him. While his father's position certainly opened the right doors, Benson's good looks, wit, and charming conversation kept them open. Older duchesses and countesses in particular seemed to favor the fashionable, best-selling young writer. His memoirs record endless invitations to the country estates and London townhouses of wealthy society friends, among them Lady de Grey, the duchess of Devonshire, and Lady Beresford. He was as much in demand for his athletic abilities as for his personal charms and literary reputation. In his prime Benson enjoyed golf, cricket, tennis, rugby, mountain climbing, and ice skating, for which he held the rank of gold medalist of the National Skating Association. He collaborated with Miles on several sporting and fitness pamphlets, beginning with *Daily Training* (1902). Benson's society connections gave him firsthand experience of the late-Victorian and Edwardian social milieu that he would capture so vividly in his later fiction.

In spite of Benson's frivolity and popularity, his was a remarkably unhappy family, beset by personal tragedies quite remote from the trivial disappointments that he explored in his early short stories. In 1877 his oldest brother, Martin, died of tubercular meningitis while still in his teens, a blow from which the archbishop never fully recovered. Thirteen years later Benson's sister Eleanor died of diphtheria. The death of the archbishop while visiting William Gladstone in 1896 was similarly unexpected and left the remaining family homeless. Benson eventually moved with his mother; her companion, Lucy Tait; the old family nurse, Beth; and his sister, Maggie, into Tremans, a lovely house in Sussex. But Benson could bear the undiluted society of four women only for a month, after which he fled to London. Moreover, the family exhibited a strong history of mental illness. Acute bouts of depression had tormented the archbishop, and Benson's brother Arthur (A. C.) struggled with debilitating attacks of depression after his father's death. The youngest child, Robert Hugh, suffered more than occasional melancholia. His conversion to Roman Catholicism in 1903 – and his fame as an author of popular proselytizing novels – came as a surprise and an embarrassment to his relatives. Most serious of all, the remaining sister, Maggie, experienced fits of depression and insanity that culminated in a homicidal attack, possibly on her mother. To say that Fred Benson was comparatively normal is an understatement. He not only seemed unaffected by the mental illnesses that plagued other members of his family (although he suffered from depression in old age), but he provided them with generous financial assistance and psychological support.

Another family tendency that figured significantly in Benson's writing was an interest in the occult. A Sidgwick uncle founded the Society of Psychical Research, and in *As We Were* (1930) Benson recounts his grandfather's putative experiments with black magic. All of the Benson brothers wrote supernatural fiction, and even the archbishop could claim a literary connection with the occult; James confided to Arthur that the archbishop had provided "the germ of that most tragical and even appalling story, 'The Turn of the Screw.'" The most prolific spiritualist in the family, Benson would eventually write more than seventy ghost stories

over a forty-year period; fifty-four of them were published in four volumes: *The Room in the Tower* (1912), *Visible and Invisible* (1923), *Spook Stories* (1928), and *More Spook Stories* (1934). Four others were published in *The Countess of Lowndes Square* (1920).

An interest in all things psychic proliferated during the Edwardian period, which, in light of such practitioners as Benson, his friend M. R. James, and Algernon Blackwood, is considered the golden age of the ghost story. Benson began writing supernatural fiction in earnest between 1904 and 1906, and these half-dozen stories appeared in the *Illustrated London News* and *Pall Mall Magazine*. He wrote for a middle-class audience that enjoyed reading about wealth and titles and an upper-class audience that enjoyed reading about itself. It may surprise modern readers that mainstream fiction for this market included ghost stories. Benson's ghosts are not, for the most part, genteel, Victorian visitors; they chill the blood. In all four collections his ghosts exude an utterly malignant vitality that threatens to engulf the narrator. Many of these narrators are unmarried, middle-aged writers working while on holiday, and it is not difficult to locate Benson in them. Their circumstances, minus the hauntings, replicate his own: in his prime Benson divided his time among England, Italy, Scotland, and Switzerland, and much of his writing was done abroad.

Benson's ghost stories are remarkable for their almost loving descriptions of fear. In dissecting the subtleties of what it means to feel fear, he does more than build suspense in anticipation of the thing that frightens. Repeatedly narrators and characters indulge in, relish, and perpetuate their terror. In "The Bus-Conductor" (*Pall Mall Magazine*, December 1906; collected in *The Room in the Tower*) the narrator reflects that "fear is the most absorbing and luxurious of emotions. One forgets all else if one is afraid." Terror creates and thrives upon self-consciousness, but because Benson's ghosts are real, usually carefully explained, historically determined, and vengeful productions, they threaten to obliterate consciousness. Hester in "The Face" (*Hutchinson's Magazine*, February 1924; collected in *Spook Stories*) – one of Benson's scariest stories – one day confronts in a Van Dyck portrait an evil, leering face that has stalked her in dreams since childhood. She resists her terror at this materialization of her dream: "To give way to this ever-mastering dread would have been to allow nightmare to invade her waking life, and there, for sure, madness lay."

The temptation to give oneself up to fear is a constant threat to the haunted in Benson's grislier stories. Fear is a seductive but destructive force, and one must suppress consciousness in order to preserve it. In Benson's favorite of all his short stories, "How Fear Departed from the Long Gallery" (*Windsor Magazine*, December 1911; collected in *The Room in the Tower*), the ghosts of twin toddlers, burned to death by a greedy uncle two centuries before, haunt the Peverils' ancestral home. The unlucky witnesses of their infrequent visitations die quickly and often horribly. When the twins appear to Madge, her first instinct is to plead for her life, but as she contemplates their hapless fate, "the enlightenment of pity dawned on her, [and] her fear fell from her." Fear ceases, in this case, with the contemplation of something outside the self. Overcome by the sad spectacle of their suffering, Madge unwittingly breaks the curse by comforting the twins. Victims in this story are victimized by their self-involvement, caused by terror or other personal obsessions, and they can be saved only through a redemptive act of self-denial.

Not all Benson's ghosts are intent upon vengeance, however. Ghosts occur, so several narrators reason, because a violent emotional scene, usually a murder or suicide, has recorded itself in the material world, where the scene replays itself over and over again. These atmospheric interferences cannot harm anyone, and thus curiosity often overrides fear as the witness's dominant impression. The narrator of "Expiation" (*Hutchinson's Magazine,* December 1923; collected in *Spook Stories*) selects curiosity over hate, love, and fear as the strongest emotion, while a character in "The Thing in the Hall" (*The Room in the Tower*) admits to an "insatiable curiosity after the unknown." Benson's characters are generally too interested in ghosts to run away until they have witnessed a complete manifestation. To flee the warning sounds and sensations would leave a mystery unsolved. In their ungovernable curiosity, which often leads them to seek out hauntings, the narrators often mirror ghost-story consumers, as in "Home, Sweet Home" (*Woman,* June 1927; collected in *Spook Stories*). The narrator might well be assessing the appeal of supernatural literature when he claims to be gnawed by "that appetite for the horrible which lurks in us all." Like the rest of Benson's most appealing or vibrant characters, ghost-story protagonists desire above all to be entertained.

Benson was fascinated by the prospect that evil could lurk under the most pleasant facades. Kindly Uncle Francis in *The Luck of the Vails* (1901), the lawyer Taynton in the innovative mystery *The Blotting Book* (1908), and the body of a delightful matron that harbors a murderous vampire in "Mrs.

Amworth" (*Hutchinson's Magazine,* June 1922; collected in *Visible and Invisible*) are all the more terrifying for their attractive packaging. Haunted houses seldom resemble the dilapidated Disneyland version; the otherwise idyllic properties that ghosts choose to frequent render their trespass the more unnerving. Likewise, Benson revels in the horror revealed in simple things. After sunset the pleasant room in "How Fear Departed from the Long Gallery" assumes a different aspect; Madge bumps into furniture and recoils from "the pleasant things of ordinary life which had become so terrible." The narrator of "A Thing in the Hall" reflects on a friend's fear that "somehow it was in the extreme simplicity of her experience that the horror lay." In *Six Common Things,* Benson dwells on the pathos of trivialities; in his ghost stories the trivialities are exquisitely horrifying.

As with anyone who has ever written ghost stories, the question arises: did he believe? Although anecdotal evidence suggests that Benson did credit the existence of ghosts (he even claimed to have seen one in his garden), in his supernatural fiction he certainly maintains a critical attitude toward spiritualism in general. If spiritualism is not itself a hoax, charlatans prepared to take advantage of the credulous abound. Some of Benson's best supernatural pieces are comic séance sketches that feature fraudulent mediums and gullible participants. Dubious séances appear often in his society fiction as well, as one of a host of unlikely fads. As skeptical as his emphasis on the fakes in the business proved him, even the charlatans in his tales who revert to such clichéd subterfuges as phosphorescent paint and electronic rapping devices usually possess true psychic powers. This pattern seems to suggest, as does Benson's own participation in séances, that he believed in psychic sensitivity.

Benson's prose style aligns him with his Victorian predecessors more than his more modernist contemporaries. In "Thursday Evenings" (*Pear's Annual,* 26 November 1920; collected in *More Spook Stories*) he mocks the excessiveness of both modern trends and arch-Victorian tastes as the ghost of a fiercely proper widow bullies the avant-garde composer and cubist painter who have bought her home, but in most of his fiction and literary criticism his sympathies lie with the Victorians. Benson preferred early James to late, and any James to Virginia Woolf or James Joyce. He criticized the prose of the modernists, which "had acquired lucidity by a blank disregard of euphony: they were full of jerks." Benson wrote quickly, but never gracelessly; he had a classicist's ear for balanced, harmonious sentences. Today his ghost stories are somehow the

Illustrations by George Plank for "The Compleat Snobs" and "The Grisley Kittens," from The Freaks of Mayfair *(1916)*

more frightening for their formal style and rigid adherence to the rules of good grammar, in accord with which no narrator is ever so terrified as to leave a preposition dangling.

At the same time Benson was creating some of the finest, most chilling ghost stories of the century, he continued to churn out sentimental fiction for the same clients. Although he had aspirations to high art, aspirations that he believed toward the end of his life to have gone largely unfulfilled, he was a professional writer and produced what the market required of him. And despite the market's eagerness for his ghost stories (he wrote more than forty in the 1920s alone, mainly for *Hutchinson's Magazine,* an arty, first-class periodical), it also lapped up melodrama and sentimental romance. Benson denounced writers who sold out to the sentimental inclinations of the period, but in later years he confessed that, for all his protests, others could plausibly level the same charge at him. Before beginning to create a recognizable niche for himself as a writer of social comedies, Benson composed more short stories that dwell on minor and painfully poignant disappointments, such as those collected in *Six Common Things,* as well as fiction that explores doomed May–December romances or relates the sacrifice of the lives and scruples of handsome young men.

A typical offering in the poignant-disappointment genre is "The Puce Silk" (*Lady's Realm,* December 1907), a soppy tale of an awkward old aunt's humiliation when her presence at a country-house party embarrasses an ungrateful niece. In the novella "Red Leaves" (*London Magazine,* September 1911) a woman in her fifties reciprocates a much younger man's love, until she decides that "you can't put roses and red leaves together." Sacrificing her feelings, December bequeaths the lover to her niece. If these stories are worth reading today, it is for their witty dialogue and the clever observations of minor characters, such as Jimmie Urquehart in "Red Leaves," and not for their somewhat tedious morality lessons. Most of these sentimental tales reveal glimpses of the later, brilliant, comic writer; only when the comedy became less decorative and more central, however, and the sentimentalism abated did Benson create his lasting successes.

During the Edwardian period Benson produced novels at an average rate of two a year. *Mrs. Ames* first appeared as a serial in *Woman at Home* in 1912. The women's magazines that published his work featured both his sentimental pieces and ghost stories, and their educated readership also provided an enthusiastic market for his society fiction. *Mrs. Ames* represents a transition from melodrama to farce that leads from *Dodo* and his early short stories to *Queen Lucia* and its descendants. In *Mrs. Ames,* Benson abandons London for the infinitely more intriguing setting of an English small town, where he locates his best society fiction. Mrs. Ames is the social leader of Riseborough, but her husband, ten years her junior, has grown bored and plans to run away with her cousin Millie Evans. In Benson's later society stories, husbands are essentially conveniences – the "tame, quiet man in the background," as a woman reflects in "Music" (*Windsor Magazine,* December 1924) – who applaud their wives' social successes but do not interfere. Major Ames has more spine than most Benson husbands, but even in this novel *women's* actions are of consequence; it focuses less on his decision to act than on the question of which woman will control him. In *Mrs. Ames,* as in *Dodo,* Benson treats the marital problems of the main characters seriously, yet the fight over Major Ames yields to the more significant conflict, the battle for social dominance between two ambitious women.

The plot of *Dodo* emphasizes amorous relations: a failed strategic marriage, Dodo's true passion for Jack, and her sudden elopement with Prince Waldeneck. The main characters in Benson's society fiction beginning with *Mrs. Ames* are decidedly middle-aged. The heterosexual passion that fueled his Edwardian sentimental romances evaporated by the time he wrote the Mapp and Lucia cycle. Although Major Ames's affections wander, he desires a companion, not a lover. Both he and Millie seek "an adventure without danger" with someone who "understands them." The shift from affairs of the heart to companionate relations transfers the objects of passion from romantic to social conquests.

Again in *Mrs. Ames,* Benson explores the impact of insignificant things. Citizens of Riseborough live for gossip, and as the narrator observes about Mrs. Altham, a pretender to Mrs. Ames's social throne, "the smaller a piece of news was, the more vivid was her perception of it, and the firmer her grip of it: large questions produced but a vague impression on her." As usual the characters find little things of "tragic" importance, but no longer is the reader meant to take the characters' assessments at face value. Indeed, Mrs. Ames's attempts to rejuvenate herself with cosmetics are vaguely pathetic and wistful. They are also funny. By the time of the publication of *Queen Lucia,* Benson insists that the reader laugh at, rather than commiserate with, the characters. He upholds the importance of trivialities, but exclusively as sources of entertainment and pleasure.

Personal grief haunted Benson during the war years. Beth, the beloved family nurse, died in 1911, followed in 1914 by the unexpected death of Robert Hugh. His sister Maggie died in a private asylum in 1916; Mary died two years later. Despite these tragic distractions, he continued to write at his usual furious pace. Too old to fight in World War I, Benson served his country in the Propaganda Department. He wrote books on Turkey and Poland and had earlier reported on the Vatican's pro-German sentiment. In addition, he worked as the honorary secretary of Lady Sclater's Fund for Wounded Soldiers and Sailors. For his efforts Benson was awarded the Member of the Order of the British Empire (MBE) in 1920.

While writing propaganda for the government, Benson produced two important books in 1916, the novel *David Blaize* and a collection of short stories, *The Freaks of Mayfair.* According to biographer Brian Masters, *David Blaize* is still on the reading lists of homosexual book clubs. An affectionate tribute to his Marlborough days, the novel explores the friendship of David and Maddox, an older student and mentor. Although their relationship remains quite innocent in deed, the novel shuns none of its romantic implications, an innovative and risky treatment for the time. In much of Benson's fiction the friendship between two attractive young men is the dominant, and sometimes only, convincing relationship in the text. In the otherwise marvelous *The Luck of the Vails,* for example, the romance between Harry Vail and Evie Aylwin, while amusing, never rises above the clichéd; the friendship between Harry and Geoffrey Langham, on the other hand, is both touching and credible. The tastes of Victorian readers are perhaps partly to blame for this unrealistic and often irritating portrayal of heterosexual love, but his failing in this respect introduces one of the most debated questions about Benson – his alleged homosexuality. In the years before World War I, he shared a villa on Capri with John Ellingham Brooks, a known homosexual, and as a young man he had associated with both Alfred Douglas and Oscar Wilde, of whom Benson disapproved not merely for his indiscretion but for his violation of the Hellenic principle of moderation in all things. Throughout his life Benson enjoyed friendships with handsome young men. Francis Yeats-Brown, author of the best-seller *Bengal Lancer* (1930), which Benson helped to get published, was a close friend until Benson's death. Despite the rumors, no evidence suggests that he had affairs with anyone, male or female; in fact, all of the Benson children died unmarried and seemingly untouched. Considering that he and his brothers shared a particular aversion for physical contact of any kind, it is doubtful that Benson acted on his inclinations, whatever they may have been.

The Freaks of Mayfair, little noticed by his contemporaries, is another important transition between Benson's early social stories and the Mapp and Lucia fiction. It is less a book of short stories than a collection of character sketches, or even caricatures, as the marvelous illustrations by Benson's close friend George Plank make clear. These include the effeminate bachelor Aunt Georgie, who, with his music, embroidery, and hair dye, is clearly the ancestor of the much more sympathetically rendered Georgie Pillson, and Mrs. Weston, whose dabblings in yoga, Christian Science, spiritualism, and health food anticipate Daisy Quantock's obsession with fads. He presents types of people rather than individuals; the term "Grisley Kittens," for example, refers to a class of elderly or middle-aged people unable to adjust to their maturity and given to inappropriate bursts of youthful energy. Benson's portraits are clever and biting, but again they are tantalizing suggestions of his capabilities rather than great achievements in themselves. Not until the Mapp and Lucia saga — where these isolated caricatures become well developed, individualized characters whose frequent interaction underscores the eccentricities of each — did Benson come into his own as a writer of social comedy.

The Countess of Lowndes Square came out four years later, the only short-story collection published in his lifetime that demonstrates Benson's versatility as a writer within one volume. It features selections from several Benson categories: spook, "crank," and society stories; stories about blackmail; as well as two charming tales about his cats. Unlike *The Freaks of Mayfair,* almost all of the material had been previously published in magazines between 1910 and 1919. A few remarkable satires explore trespasses against the standards of British society. Written in 1910 for the *Pall Mall Magazine,* the title story narrates the illegal activities of a countess whose poverty reduces her to blackmail. In a world where cheating at cards is the foulest crime one can commit, blackmail is less a legal offense than a social transgression. Benson satirizes the upper class's penchant for scandal, which keeps the blackmailer in business, and yet disapproves her abuse of the social position that permits access to others' secrets. In "The False Step" (*Windsor Magazine,* December 1914), Benson mocks grasping American society women, whose aspirations inevitably reveal their innate lack of taste. Backed by her husband's money and the paid services of an impoverished but well-connected "friend," Amelie almost succeeds in entering British high society, until, in order to impress her guests with her indifference to expense, she publicly incinerates a gorgeous painting by Sir Joshua Reynolds. Amelie's ambitions are thwarted because the British aristocracy perceives only her indifference to art and culture. Class, Benson suggests, cannot be bought — at least not by Americans, who lack the faculties to appreciate the great art only they can afford. American society does not fare well in his fiction overall; it is satirized again in a novel that appeared the year after "The False Step," *The Oakleyites* (1915).

In 1919 Benson took the lease on Lamb House in the village of Rye in East Sussex, a decision that proved crucial to the writing of his best-known works. Benson had visited Lamb House when it still belonged to James, who lived there until his death in 1916. By the time Benson leased the property as a country house designed to supplement his home in Brompton Square, London, he was seriously afflicted with arthritis, which curtailed the more worldly habits and wanderings of his youth. At this point he had been writing steadily for twenty-five years and was comfortable enough to support two establishments. Lamb House also served as a refuge for his brother Arthur, who shared a lease on the house for three years while he was suffering from acute depression. Benson cheered and cared for his last remaining sibling until the latter's death in 1925.

Many of Benson's later stories and novels are set in Rye, disguised under a variety of pseudonyms: most famously, Tillingham or Tilling, so named for the river that flows through the town. *Queen Lucia* takes place in Riseholme, modeled on a village called Broadway in the Cotswolds, but in *Mapp and Lucia* (1931) Benson brings his queen, Lucia Lucas, and her loyal attendant, Georgie, to Tilling/Rye, first as summer visitors and then to stay. Thus begins the social warfare between Miss Elizabeth Mapp, leader of Tilling society, and Lucia, the usurper of that title. The series of six novels, which also includes *Miss Mapp* (1922), *Lucia in London* (1927), *Lucia's Progress* (1935), and *Trouble for Lucia* (1939), supplemented by two short stories, "The Male Impersonator" (1929) and "Desirable Residences" (*Good Housekeeping,* February 1929), represents the pinnacle of Benson's achievement as a writer of social farce. *Queen Lucia* received the most enthusiastic reception from both critics and readers that any Benson novel had earned since the publication of *Dodo* almost thirty years before. (A rare unfavorable review by Katherine Mansfield appeared anonymously in *Athenaeum.*) All six novels are in print in the United States and Great Britain; the series has even inspired two sequels by Benson admirer and imitator Tom Holt.

In *Final Edition* (1940) Benson confesses that the idea for the character of Miss Mapp came to him as he sat in the garden-room window at Lamb House, watching the "ladies of Rye doing their

Lamb House, in Rye, East Sussex, home of Henry James from 1898 until his death in 1916. In 1919 Benson leased the house, which became the model for Mallards, Elizabeth Mapp's home in the Mapp and Lucia novels.

shopping in the High Street every morning, carrying large market baskets, and bumping into each other in narrow doorways, and talking in a very animated manner . . . I outlined an atrocious spinster and established her in Lamb House. She should be the centre of social life, abhorred and dominant, and she should sit like a great spider behind the curtains in the garden-room, spying on her friends, and I knew that her name must be Elizabeth Mapp." This is a revealing passage; Benson envisions yielding to Miss Mapp his own chair in the garden room at Lamb House (named Mallards in the novels), an identification that advertises some of Benson's own Mapp-like qualities: inexhaustible curiosity and a fascination with the daily events of small-town life, but without Mapp's malicious ill humor. He captured the appeal of the Tillingites' world so successfully because he knew its charms. And so he found it increasingly difficult to leave his "country house" in Rye, and it became his principal residence for almost twenty years. Benson served his community first as a magistrate and then, from 1934 to 1937, as mayor. Upon the completion of his third and final term, the Town Council awarded him the Freedom of Rye, the privileges of which included indemnity against arrest on the streets of the town.

The Mapp and Lucia novels dissect and revel in the petty jealousies and hypocrisies that swarm among these middle-aged inhabitants. True to his inspiration, Benson starts each day with the morning shopping, English weather permitting, which is merely an excuse for Tillingites to circulate and receive any gossip that might have developed since the previous day. Afternoons and evenings comprise an endless stream of teas, bridge, dinner parties, musicales, and more bridge. The outside world frequently penetrates these novels; at one point Lucia attempts a social career in London, and both Riseholme and Tilling are unusually susceptible to fads from without, be they spiritualism, yoga, cycling, or stock-market investments, to which last Benson himself was once addicted. Nonetheless, the world of Tilling is remarkably insular, almost a prewar colony that dabbles in modernity from the safe distance that its financial security and essentially Victorian values provide. The discomfort experienced in the presence of the mannish, radical painter Irene Coles (influenced by another Rye resident, Radclyffe Hall), whom the Tillingites cultivate, disapprove of, and fear, reveals their distinctly antimodern sympathies.

The title character of *Mrs. Ames* emphatically ignores local gossip; her rival's husband, Mr. Altham, surmises that "her incuriousness on the subject of the small affairs of other people was somehow connected with her ascendancy." By contrast, Tilling's social leaders try to inspire gossip – of the right sort, of course – as eagerly as they partake of and disseminate it. Olga Bracely, an opera prima donna embraced by the cultural shams of Riseholme – where Lucia can play only the first movement of Beethoven's *Moonlight* Sonata and parlays a few words of Italian into a reputation for fluency – decides to buy a house in the town after just one visit. Any moment spent away from Riseholme, performing in the world's great capitals, is time wasted for Olga. Swept along by the currents of gossip, she exclaims to her friend Georgie, "I never knew before how terribly interesting little things were!" Olga is a figure for the reader, who finds in Lucia the power "to render the trivialities of life intense for others." Instead of a dull "backwater," Olga has discovered a place that, for its combination of self-absorption, earnestness, and vitality, thrills outsiders and residents alike.

In Benson's writing throughout his career, vitality is the single greatest asset, the one indispensable quality that a person can possess; all of his heroes and many of his villains owe their success and charm to their endless energy. Nowhere is this more apparent than in Lucia: "She aggravated and exasperated them: she was a hypocrite ... a poseuse, a sham, and a snob, but there was something about her that stirred you into violent though protesting activity, and though she might infuriate you, she prevented your being dull" (*Lucia in London*). Even the Grisley Kittens, whom he maligns in *The Freaks of Mayfair,* enjoy a "vitality, which, however misapplied, is in itself the most attractive quality in the world." Although David Blaize also pulsates with an "exuberant vitality" that captivates his friends, insofar as Benson's more mature characters are concerned this quality is peculiarly associated with women. In *Mrs. Ames* the narrator concludes that for women "happiness implies the power to want and to aspire," which keeps the "lethargy of content" at bay. Men, as Diva puts it in *Mapp and Lucia,* "don't count for much in Tilling; it's brains that do." Benson's men luxuriate in lethargy, until their wives' schemes for social prominence spur them to activity. If life is actually ideas, as the narrator observes in "The Thing in the Hall," Benson's middle-aged society males (with the possible exception of Georgie Pillson) are very nearly dead. As malicious and artificial and foolish as his female characters can be, without their energy social intercourse would be not merely dull but inconceivable.

Benson liked to wring plenty of use from his ideas, and in his writing one can trace the frequent re-appearance of old material. For example, in at least four different texts spanning a fifteen-year period – a Lucia novel, two short stories, and his memoirs – he describes séances in which the deluded participants, led by fraudulent mediums, invite Cardinal John Henry Newman's spirit to attend with a rousing chorus of "Lead, Kindly Light." The joke's humor does not diminish with repetition, but Benson's habit of borrowing so zealously from himself is a strange and prominent feature of his writing, perhaps a result of rapid composition. Whole short stories often materialize as episodes in later novels, involving different characters and details but with their plots essentially intact. He recycled ample material for the Mapp and Lucia series, lifting from *The Freaks of Mayfair* particularly, while the incidents that motivate *Lucia in London* are borrowed from his "Fine Feathers" (*Woman at Home,* March 1914), a Mrs. Ames short story. Benson's writing style was well adapted to both serialization and this appropriation of previous work; many of his novels resemble a string of short stories connected by bits of everyday activity. Each episode reads like a discrete entity, and a larger, unfolding plot is only vaguely discernible, if at all. Benson also condensed material from his novels into shorter pieces: Lucia reappears under other names in subsequent short stories, most notably the Amy Bondham tales, produced primarily for the glossy *Windsor Magazine,* which in the 1920s published some of his best society short fiction.

Reflecting on his career in *Final Edition,* Benson discounts most of his fiction but reserves a few kind words for the Mapp and Lucia books, "for there was nothing fake or sentimental about them." He qualifies this praise in the same breath, continuing, "and I was not offering them as examples of serious fiction." In the late 1920s Benson sought to redress his failure as a serious writer. He began what he called his "real work" and in 1927 produced the first of eight biographies. In researching the lives of *Sir Francis Drake* (1927), *Ferdinand Magellan* (1929), and *Queen Victoria* (1935), among others, he sought a middle ground between the biographies of the Victorians, to whom "death automatically transformed the eminent into miracles of wisdom and virtue," and those of modern writers, which are dedicated to "exposing the littleness and defects of the character." Benson's biographies are thoughtful, elegantly written, scholarly works. In his *Life of Alcibiades* (1929), for example, he harnesses his years of classical scholarship into an intelligent and invigorating portrait. In the introduction to his most famous biography, *Charlotte Brontë* (1932), which is still of interest despite more-recent scholarship, he justifies the efforts of the

Benson at his desk (sketch by Bernard Gotch)

biographer, insisting that a knowledge of an author's life is not "idle inquisitiveness" but a requirement for a full appreciation of her works. Benson's biographies established him as a well-respected scholar applauded by critics, and his reputation as a serious writer was at last assured.

Benson's memoirs guaranteed that future generations of readers would understand the cultural background of his other writings. He wrote five collections of memoirs between 1920 and 1940. The first two, *Our Family Affairs* (1920) and *Mother* (1925), were largely ignored, but *As We Were* (1930) is a brilliant document that combines family anecdotes and cultural analysis into perhaps the single finest treatment of the Edwardian period. He adopts a good-humored, anthropological tone in discussing the customs of the 1890s. Favoring "impressionistic truth" over "literal accuracy," *As We Were* paints a vivid, compelling picture of turn-of-the-century England and is Benson at his best — astute, funny, and infinitely readable. His fourth volume, *As We Are* (1932), is somewhat less successful. Half parable designed to illustrate the clash of the generations just prior to and after World War I, and half direct cri-

tique of modern habits, values, literature, and personalities, the book amuses rather less than it lectures. Still, for a man of sixty-five he managed to account very reasonably for the disillusion and frivolity of the postwar generation, even though he often sided with its parents' values and traditions. Prolific until the end, his last book of memoirs, posthumously retitled *Final Edition,* was submitted for publication ten days before his death. In it Benson altogether redeemed himself as a leading voice of the Edwardian age. This is certainly the most personal of the four volumes; here he reflects most extensively on his own successes and failures as a writer. He also devotes much space to intimate anecdotes about his family, a group at least as fascinating as any fictional family he ever devised. He fell ill shortly after the completion of this radiant finale to his career. A heavy smoker all of his adult life, he was diagnosed with inoperable throat cancer and died less than two months later, on 29 February 1940.

In 1937 the Fellows of Magdalene College, Cambridge, recognized Benson's achievements as a writer, and he accepted the Honorary Fellowship, previously held by Thomas Hardy and

Rudyard Kipling. Unlike the reputations of his brothers Hugh, who has faded into obscurity, and Arthur, who is now principally remembered for the lyrics of "Land of Hope and Glory," E. F. Benson's literary fame has persisted, albeit diminished. The Tilling Society in Rye and the E. F. Benson Society in London are devoted to his memory and works, and two volumes of his previously uncollected short fiction, edited by Jack Adrian, were published in 1988 and 1991. It is all too likely that Benson would not have been wholly pleased with his present popularity, which is grounded in the very works he dismissed. Although his biographies and portions of his memoirs certainly must have fulfilled his requirement for serious writing, he never achieved the reputation for serious fiction that he craved. In an overly critical self-evaluation, Benson discarded all but four of his novels: *The Luck of the Vails, Sheaves* (1907), *The Climber* (1908), and *David Blaize*. His choices, fortunately, are not the popular ones. Benson's ghost stories and his acerbic society fiction — his tales of terror and his satires — form the foundation upon which his modern reputation and his appeal to new generations of admirers rest.

Biographies:

Cynthia and Tony Reavell, *E. F. Benson: Mr. Benson Remembered in Rye and the World of Tilling* (Rye: Martello, 1984); republished as *E. F. Benson Remembered and the World of Tilling* (Rye: Martello, 1991);

Geoffrey Palmer and Noel Lloyd, *E. F. Benson as He Was* (Luton: Lennard, 1988);

Brian Masters, *The Life of E. F. Benson* (London: Chatto & Windus, 1991).

References:

Jack Adrian, Introduction to Benson's *Desirable Residences and Other Stories,* edited by Adrian (Oxford: Oxford University Press, 1991);

Adrian, Introduction to Benson's *The Flint Knife: Further Spook Stories,* edited by Adrian (London: Equation, 1988);

Betty Askwith, *Two Victorian Families* (London: Chatto & Windus, 1971);

Iain Finlayson, *Writers of Romney Marsh* (London: Severn House, 1986);

Susan J. Leonardi, "Recipes for Reading: Summer Pasta, Lobster á la Riseholme, and Key Lime Pie," *PMLA,* 104 (May 1989): 340–347;

Michael Roper and John Tosh, eds., *Manful Assertions* (London: Routledge, 1991);

Jack Sullivan, *Elegant Nightmares: The English Ghost Story from Le Fanu to Blackwood* (Athens: Ohio University Press, 1978);

Tilling Society, *Newsletters*, July 1983–   ;

Cynthia White, *Women's Magazines, 1693–1968* (London: Joseph, 1970);

David Williams, *Genesis and Exodus: A Portrait of the Benson Family* (London: Hamish Hamilton, 1979).

Papers:

The major repository of papers relating to the Benson family is in the Department of Western Manuscripts at the Bodleian Library, Oxford.

Sir Walter Besant

(14 August 1836 – 9 June 1901)

Clinton Machann
Texas A&M University

BOOKS: *Studies in Early French Poetry* (London & Cambridge: Macmillan, 1868; Boston: Roberts, 1877);

Jerusalem: The City of Herod and Saladin, by Besant and Edward Henry Palmer (London: Bentley, 1871; New York: Scribner & Welford, 1889);

Ready-Money Mortiboy, by Besant and James Rice (3 volumes, London: Tinsley, 1872; 1 volume, New York: Worthington, 1879);

When George the Third Was King, 2 volumes (London: Low, 1872);

The French Humourists (London: Bentley, 1873; Boston: Roberts, 1874);

My Little Girl, by Besant and Rice (3 volumes, London, 1873; 1 volume, Boston: Osgood, 1873);

Ready-Money, by Besant [as Walter Maurice] and Rice (London & New York: French, 1875);

With Harp and Crown, by Besant and Rice (3 volumes, London: Tinsley, 1875; 1 volume, Boston: Osgood, 1876);

The Case of Mr. Lucraft and Other Tales, by Besant and Rice (2 volumes, London: Low, 1876; 1 volume, New York: Dodd, Mead, 1888);

The Golden Butterfly, by Besant and Rice (3 volumes, London: Tinsley, 1876; 1 volume, New York: Allison, 1877);

This Son of Vulcan, by Besant and Rice (3 volumes, London: Low, 1876; 1 volume, New York: Dodd, Mead, 1888);

Such a Good Man!, by Besant and Rice (London, 1877);

When the Ship Comes Home, by Besant and Rice (New York: Harper, 1877);

By Celia's Arbour, by Besant and Rice (3 volumes, London: Low, 1878; 1 volume, New York: Harper, 1878);

The Monks of Thelema, by Besant and Rice (3 volumes, London: Chatto & Windus, 1878; 1 volume, New York: Dodd, Mead, 1888);

Shepherds All and Maidens Fair, by Besant and Rice (New York: Harper, 1878);

Sir Walter Besant, circa 1894

Constantinople, by Besant and William J. Brodribb (London: Seeley, 1879);

Gaspard de Coligny (London: Ward, 1879; New York: Harper, 1879);

Rabelais (Edinburgh & London: Blackwood, 1879; Philadelphia: Lippincott, 1879);

'Twas in Trafalgar's Bay, by Besant and Rice (New York: Harper, 1879);

The Seamy Side, by Besant and Rice (London: Chatto & Windus, 1880; New York: Appleton, 1880);

The Captain's Room (New York: Harper, 1881);

The Chaplain of the Fleet, by Besant and Rice (London: Chatto & Windus, 1881; New York: Harper, 1881);

Sir Richard Whittington, by Besant and Rice (London: Ward, 1881; New York: Merrill, 1881);

The Ten Years' Tenant and Other Stories, by Besant and Rice (3 volumes, London: Chatto & Windus, 1881; 1 volume, New York: Dodd, Mead, 1888);

All Sorts and Conditions of Men (3 volumes, London: Chatto & Windus, 1882; 1 volume, New York: Harper, 1882);

The Revolt of Man (Edinburgh: Blackwood, 1882; New York: Holt, 1882);

So They Were Married, by Besant and Rice (New York: Harper, 1883);

All in a Garden Fair (3 volumes, London: Chatto & Windus, 1883; 1 volume, New York: Harper, 1883);

The Captain's Room and Other Stories, 3 volumes (London: Chatto & Windus, 1883);

The Life and Achievements of Edward Henry Palmer (London: Murray, 1883; New York: Dutton, 1883);

Let Nothing You Dismay (New York: Lowell, 1883);

Life in a Hospital (London: Fisher, 1883);

The Ten Years' Tenant, by Besant and Rice (New York: Munro, 1883);

Uncle Jack (New York: Munro, 1883);

The Art of Fiction (London: Chatto & Windus, 1884; Boston: Cupples, Upham, 1884; revised and enlarged edition, London & New York: Brentano's, 1902);

Dorothy Forster (3 volumes, London: Chatto & Windus, 1884; 1 volume, New York: Munro, 1884);

A Glorious Fortune (New York: Munro, 1884);

In Luck at Last (New York: Munro, 1885);

Uncle Jack and Other Stories (London: Chatto & Windus, 1885);

Children of Gibeon (3 volumes, London: Chatto & Windus, 1886; 1 volume, New York: Harper, 1886);

Twenty-One Years' Work in the Holy Land (London: Bentley, 1886);

The World Went Very Well Then (1 volume, New York: Harper, 1886; 3 volumes, London: Chatto & Windus, 1887);

The Holy Rose (New York: Munro, 1886);

Katharine Regina (Bristol: Arrowsmith, 1887; New York: Harper, 1887);

To Call Her Mine (New York: Harper, 1887);

'Twas in Trafalgar's Bay and Other Stories, by Besant and Rice (London: Chatto & Windus, 1887; New York: Dodd, Mead, 1888);

The Eulogy of Richard Jefferies (London: Chatto & Windus, 1888; New York: Longmans, Green, 1888);

Herr Paulus (3 volumes, London: Chatto & Windus, 1888; 1 volume, New York: Harper, 1888);

Fifty Years Ago (London: Chatto & Windus, 1888; New York: Harper, 1888);

The Inner House (Bristol: Arrowsmith, 1888; New York: Harper, 1888);

The Bell of St. Paul's (3 volumes, London: Chatto & Windus, 1889; 1 volume, New York: Harper, 1889);

The Doubts of Dives (Bristol: Arrowsmith, 1889);

The Lament of Dives (New York: Munro, 1889);

For Faith and Freedom (3 volumes, London: Chatto & Windus, 1889; 1 volume, New York: Harper, 1889);

To Call Her Mine and Other Stories (London: Chatto & Windus, 1889);

Armorel of Lyonesse (3 volumes, London: Chatto & Windus, 1890; 1 volume, New York: Harper, 1890);

Captain Cook (London & New York: Macmillan, 1890);

The Demoniac (Bristol: Arrowsmith, 1890; New York: Ivers, 1890);

The Holy Rose and Other Tales (London: Chatto & Windus, 1890);

The Literary Handmaid of the Church (London: Glaisher, 1890);

St. Katherine's by the Tower (3 volumes, London: Chatto & Windus, 1891; 1 volume, New York: Harper, 1891);

The Ivory Gate (3 volumes, London: Chatto & Windus, 1892; 1 volume, New York: Harper, 1892);

London (London: Chatto & Windus, 1892; New York: Harper, 1892);

Verbena Camellia Stephanotis and Other Tales (London: Chatto & Windus, 1892; New York: Harper, 1892);

The History of London (London: Longmans, 1893);

The Rebel Queen (3 volumes, London: Chatto & Windus, 1893; 1 volume, New York: Harper, 1893);

The Society of Authors (London: Incorporated Society of Authors, 1893);

Beyond the Dreams of Avarice (London: Chatto & Windus, 1895; New York: Harper, 1895);

In Deacon's Orders and Other Tales (London: Chatto & Windus, 1895; New York: Harper, 1895);

The Master Craftsman (2 volumes, London: Chatto & Windus, 1895; 1 volume, New York: Stokes, 1895);

Westminster (London: Chatto & Windus, 1895; New York: Stokes, 1895);

The Charm and Other Drawing Room Plays, by Besant and Walter Herries Pollock (London: Chatto & Windus, 1896; New York: Stokes, 1896);

The City of Refuge (3 volumes, London: Chatto & Windus, 1896; 1 volume, New York: Stokes, 1896);

A Fountain Sealed (London: Chatto & Windus, 1897; New York: Stokes, 1897);

The Rise of the Empire (London: Marshall, 1897; New York: Mansfield, 1897);

Alfred (London: Cox, 1898);

The Changeling (London: Chapman & Hall, 1898; New York: Stokes, 1898);

South London (New York: Stokes, 1898; London: Chatto & Windus, 1899);

The Orange Girl (London: Chatto & Windus, 1899; New York: Dodd, Mead, 1899);

The Pen and the Book (London: Burleigh, 1899);

The Alabaster Box (London: Burleigh, 1900; New York: Dodd, Mead, 1900);

The Fourth Generation (London: Chatto & Windus, 1900; New York: Stokes, 1900);

East London (London: Chatto & Windus, 1901; New York: Century, 1901);

The Lady of Lynn (London: Chatto & Windus, 1901; New York: Dodd, Mead, 1901);

The Story of King Alfred (London: Newnes, 1901; New York: Appleton, 1901);

Autobiography of Sir Walter Besant (London: Hutchinson, 1902; New York: Dodd, Mead, 1902);

A Five Years' Tryst and Other Stories (London: Methuen, 1902);

No Other Way (London: Chatto & Windus, 1902; New York: Dodd, Mead, 1902);

The Strand District, by Besant and Geraldine Edith Mitton, Fascination of London Series (London: A. & C. Black, 1902);

The Survey of London, 10 volumes, by Besant and others (London: A. & C. Black, 1902-1912);

As We Are and As We May Be (London: Chatto & Windus, 1903);

Westminster, by Besant and Mitton, Fascination of London Series (London: A. & C. Black, 1903);

Essays and Historiettes (London: Chatto & Windus, 1903);

Holborn and Bloomsbury, by Besant and Mitton, Fascination of London Series (London: A. & C. Black, 1903);

The Thames, Fascination of London Series (London: A. & C. Black, 1903).

PLAY PRODUCTIONS: *Ready-Money,* by Besant [as Walter Maurice] and James Rice, London, Court Theatre, 12 March 1874;

Such a Good Man, by Besant and Rice, London, Olympic Theatre, 18 December 1879;

The Charm, by Besant and W. H. Pollock, London, Saint George's Hall, 22 July 1884;

The Ballad Monger, by Besant and Pollock, Theatre Royal, Haymarket, 15 September 1887.

OTHER: *The Literary Remains of the Late C. F. Tyrwhitt Drake,* edited, with a memoir, by Besant (London, 1877);

The New Plutarch, 10 volumes, edited by Besant and W. J. Brodribb (London: Ward, 1879-1888);

Claude R. Conder, *The Survey of Western Palestine,* 3 volumes, edited, with additions, by Besant and E. H. Palmer (London: Palestine Exploration Fund, 1881-1883);

Readings in Rabelais, selected by Besant (Edinburgh & London: Blackwood, 1883);

"How Can a Love and Appreciation of Art Be Best Developed among the Masses of People?," in William Tuckwell and C. G. Leland, *Art and Hand Work for the People* (Manchester: Cornish, 1885);

William J. Collins, *Blind Love,* 3 volumes, preface by Besant (London: Chatto & Windus, 1890);

Incorporated Society of Authors, *The Author,* 11 volumes, conducted by Besant (London, 1890-1900);

Athenian Society, *The Athenian Oracle,* edited by J. Underhill, with a prefatory letter by Besant (London: Scott Library, 1892);

Alfred E. Hake, *Suffering London,* introduction by Besant (London: Scientific Press, 1892);

Dorothy Wallis, *Dorothy Wallis,* introduction by Besant (London: Longmans, 1892);

Charles Reade, *The Cloister and the Hearth,* 4 volumes, introduction by Besant (London: Chatto & Windus, 1893);

Alfred E. Haynes, *Man-Hunting in the Desert,* introduction by Besant (London: Cox, 1894);

"Ready Money Mortiboy," in Jerome K. Jerome, *My First Book* (London: Chatto & Windus, 1894);

Alfred Bowker, *Alfred the Great,* introduction by Besant (London: A. & C. Black, 1899);

John H. Round, *The Commune of London,* prefatory letter by Besant (Westminster: Constable, 1899);

Daniel Defoe, *A Journal of the Plague Year,* introduction by Besant (New York: Century, 1900);

"The Memory Cell," in Charles J. C. W. Hyne, *For Britain's Soldiers* (London: Methuen, 1900);

"The Two Sophias," in John Charlton, *Royal Naval and Military Bazaar* (London: Dangerfield, 1900);

William G. Gates, *Illustrated History of Portsmouth,* introduction by Besant (Portsmouth: Charpentier, 1900);

Walter A. Locks, *East London Antiquities,* introduction by Besant (London: East London Advertiser, 1902);

The Fascination of London, 12 volumes, edited by Besant and others (London: A. & C. Black, 1902–1908).

SELECTED PERIODICAL PUBLICATIONS – UNCOLLECTED:

FICTION

"The Doll's House – and After," *English Illustrated Magazine,* 7 (1890): 315–325;

"One of Two Millions in East London," *Century,* 59 (1899): 225–243.

NONFICTION

"The People's Palace," *Contemporary Review,* 51 (February 1887): 226–233;

"Candour in English Fiction," *New Review,* 2 (1890): 6–21;

"The Science of Fiction," *New Review,* 4 (1891): 304–319;

"The Future of the Anglo-Saxon Race," *North American Review,* 163 (August 1896): 129–143.

Walter Besant began to publish novels in the early 1870s and by the 1880s had established himself as one of the most popular and prolific novelists in England. He was also known for the short fiction he published in literary journals and collected in several widely read books. By the time of World War I, however, his fiction was nearly forgotten: this decline in reputation is one of the most precipitous in the history of British fiction. During his lifetime Besant was also celebrated for his involvement in various social issues, including the legal rights of authors, and for his ambitious survey of London, which remained unfinished at his death. Today he is remembered chiefly for his efforts in social reform rather than for his fiction; however, his novels and short stories remain of considerable interest as "popular" if not "serious" literature of their time and deserve more study than they have received in recent years.

Besant was born in Portsea, the fifth child of William Besant, a merchant, and Sarah (Ediss) Besant. He attended grammar schools at Portsea and Stockwell before going on to King's College, London, and finally to Christ's College, Cambridge, from which he was graduated in 1859. Although his career at Cambridge was distinguished, Besant had difficulty in establishing a career. After making an unsuccessful start in journalism and then giving up plans to be ordained an Anglican minister, he accepted the position of senior professor at the Royal College on the island of Mauritius in 1861. Although Besant suffered from ill health in Mauritius, he laid the foundations of his later literary career by frequent writing and the study of French language and literature.

Soon after returning to London in 1867, he published his first book, *Studies in Early French Poetry* (1868). This initial success encouraged him to continue his literary ambitions; a position as secretary of the Palestine Exploration Fund, which he was to hold for nearly two decades, left him with ample time for writing. Although he continued to write essays on French literature and other critical and historical topics, Besant soon shifted his emphasis to fiction. After publishing stories in the journal *Once a Week,* he began to collaborate with its editor, James Rice, in the writing of novels. Their first co-authored publication was *Ready-Money Mortiboy* (1872). In 1874 Besant married Mary Forster-Barham, with whom he was to have two sons and two daughters.

By the time Rice died in 1881, he and Besant had published a dozen novels together. This longstanding collaboration is the most unusual aspect of Besant's career as a novelist. Apparently he did most of the actual writing, while Rice was chiefly responsible for plot construction and handling all business arrangements with publishers. There is evidence that Besant grew to regret the partnership four or five years before Rice's death, but he did not discuss the matter publicly. Records from the firm of Chatto and Windus, which became their chief publisher, suggest that Besant and Rice were consistently underpaid for the rights to their works. Nevertheless, Besant was either unable or unwilling to involve himself in negotiations with their publishers.

Beginning with *Ready-Money Mortiboy,* Besant and Rice established their popularity as writers of the conventional Victorian three-volume novel. Typically, after serialization in a literary magazine, the "triple-decker" would be aimed especially at the lending-library market; later it would be reprinted in cheaper editions as long as it remained

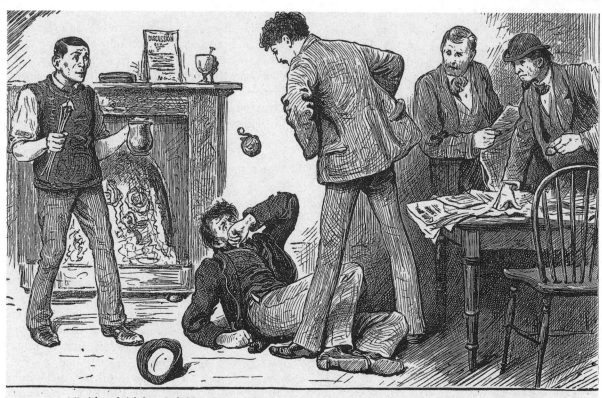

' "After he'd knocked him down, Harry invited that chap to stand up and have it out." '

Frontispiece to volume two of All Sorts and Conditions of Men *(1882)*

sufficiently in demand. But Besant and Rice did not limit themselves to this genre. They also wrote novelettes, or long short stories, about one-third the length of their novels: these were often written on commission for a journal's special Christmas or summer issue. Later a novelette might be collected with a few shorter stories, also previously published in magazines, to make a book. *'Twas in Trafalgar's Bay* (1879) is a typical example. *The Golden Butterfly* (1876), the story of a vulgar American millionaire, was their largest commercial success and established them as best-selling novelists. As late as the period 1895–1897, a sixpence paperback edition of the novel sold one hundred thousand copies.

Although the Besant/Rice novels sold well, they are uneven works. The first part of *By Celia's Arbour* (1878), which is based on Besant's childhood memories of the Portsmouth area, is sometimes singled out for critical praise, though the novel as a whole is mediocre. In general, the Besant/Rice works are marred by inconsistent characterization and improbable plots, but descriptive passages and dialogue are often handled well.

Besant went on writing after Rice's death, and among the novels he produced in the period 1882–

1886 are his most acclaimed works. *All in a Garden Fair* (1883) is a study of a young writer's development, and *Dorothy Forster* (1884), Besant's personal favorite, is his best historical novel. However, he achieved his greatest literary success with two studies of life among the poor in London's East End. Although *All Sorts and Conditions of Men* (1882) and *Children of Gibeon* (1886) contain some of the flaws that mar the collaborative novels, they convey a moral energy and conviction that not only made them widely read but made a mark on the real world that is rare in the history of fiction. In the earlier novel – which was said by a contemporary reviewer to have "shocked and aroused the conscience of all England" with its portrayal of the dismal conditions in the East End – Besant describes the planning and construction of a "Palace of Delight" for the poor. Through a public conscription organized by Sir Edmund Currie, a "Palace" serving as a "centre of organized recreation, orderly amusement, and intellectual and artistic culture," much like that in Besant's novel, was actually built and for a time was successful. Its educational facilities were eventually incorporated into the University of London. Besant's status as a reformer and philanthropist was a major reason for his being knighted in 1895.

All Sorts and Conditions of Men was, like the most popular collaborations with Rice, a best-seller, and Besant was featured, sometimes even above such authors as Anthony Trollope, Ouida, and Wilkie Collins, in advertisements by Chatto and Windus and Mudie's Library. In addition to its contemporary success, this is the one Besant novel that has been discussed at any length by modern literary scholars, though the approach taken is usually concerned more with its social and political implications than its artistry. Despite complications and subplots, the main plot of the novel is relatively simple. Angela Messenger, a graduate of Cambridge and heiress to a great brewery in London's East End, turns philanthropist and begins to develop schemes for helping the people in this part of the city. She is joined by Harry Goslet, a wealthy young gentleman who has recently discovered his hidden working-class origins. Angela converts a local sweatshop into a dressmaking cooperative that offers recreational activities and other advantages to its workers. Then Angela and Harry join forces to plan new schools, a college of art, and the Palace of Delight. After a heroic struggle they succeed.

Predictably, Besant has been scolded by modern critics for dreaming that arts and crafts and a bourgeois concept of culture could do so much to transform the lives of the East Enders. It is as though, prior to the entrance of the two slumming philanthropists, the people have had no culture of their own, and Besant seems to have little insight into how the depressing way of life in the area was tied to economic and political forces rather than simply an absence of "delight" in life. Nevertheless, Besant is sincere in his reformist vision, and he obviously was able to appeal to widespread concern (and perhaps fear) among the reading public. And, as Wim Neetens has recently pointed out, Besant's humanistic philosophy is strongly opposed to social Darwinism and any suggestion of the hereditary "degeneration" of the working class.

Although Besant was in the final analysis a conventional thinker, he had a knack for inventing unusual or bizarre situations in his fiction, especially in the novelette form. In *The Revolt of Man* (1882) the roles of the sexes are reversed, and in *The Doubts of Dives* (1889) a rich man and his poor friend exchange bodies. Among his more interesting projects in the early phase of his career as an individual writer is his science-fiction novelette *The Inner House* (1888), first published in *Arrowsmith's Christmas Annual* for 1888. The basic premise of the work anticipates Aldous Huxley's *Brave New World* (1932): in a future society technology has given

Frognal End, Besant's country estate in Hampstead

mankind the power to extend human life indefinitely, and everything has been reorganized in a "rational" manner that precludes sexual love and cultural amusements. In an unusual twist Besant chooses the villain of the story as the narrator. This device is somewhat awkward, and, in the voice of the pompous narrator, Besant's style is even more annoyingly mannered than usual — especially to a modern reader — but the book displays his powers of invention and develops his idea of culture as the center of civilized life.

A later short work, "In Deacon's Orders," shows a different side of Besant: his aversion to Calvinism and what he called Christian "religiosity," as distinguished from genuine religious faith. (This title story of a collection published in 1895 was originally syndicated by Tillotson's Fiction Bureau, while the accompanying tales had been published in the *Pall Mall Magazine, Black & White,* the *Strand,* the *Illustrated London News,* the *Humanitarian,* and the *Idler.*) The principal character in the story is a man who, from childhood, has relied on an angelic demeanor and an ability to speak in an apparently sincere, emotional manner in order to lie and cheat his way through life. Periodically his deceit is discovered, as when he is denied the office of deacon in the Anglican church. He later immigrates to America, where he experiences some success as an evangelical minister before he is once again destroyed by his own duplicity and greed. Each disgusting episode of his life is registered as another heartbreak by the woman who loves him but is fully aware of his flawed nature. That Besant's opinions about "religiosity" were second in strength only to those concerning writing and the publishing trade is made clear by their prominence in his *Autobiography* (1902).

Following the success of his "East End" novels in the early 1880s, Besant continued to publish novels at the average rate of more than one per year until his death in 1901, and several of them had large sales, but, generally speaking, his writing career suffered a gradual decline. His fiction was called "spoonmeat" and "pap" by a hostile reviewer in the *Saturday Review* (1 June 1895), and, more important, his late novels received increasingly less critical notice of any kind. Besides having the characteristic aesthetic flaws of his earlier works, the novels became more repetitive, more digressive, and less entertaining.

It is tempting to classify Besant as a kind of lesser Charles Dickens. Apart from the more superficial similarities between the two novelists – birth in the Portsmouth area; an aversion to evangelical religion; a knowledge and love of the city of London; strong opinions about authors' rights, especially international rights; and the same date of death, 9 June – Besant attempted to create a somewhat similar pantheon of outrageously eccentric characters, and, above all, he believed that his fiction could make a difference in the world, that it had the power to change human hearts. It is clear that Besant's prose lacks the poetic power of Dickens's. However, Besant – who died not only on the anniversary of Dickens's death thirty-one years earlier but also in the same year as Queen Victoria – represents the end of a certain tradition in English fiction, one in which Dickens figured prominently. Besant was a popular writer who attempted to entertain his readers and also to deal with the problems of society in an open, direct way. With more sophisticated writers such as Thomas Hardy and Henry James, a split between "serious" and "popular" literature was becoming apparent and would become even more so in the course of the twentieth century.

Whatever weaknesses he may have had as an artist, there can be little doubt that his sheer volume of work contributed to Besant's decline. Not limiting himself to fiction, he produced a steady stream of nonfiction and editions, including the series of bi-

ographies known as the "New Plutarch." Toward the end of his career he organized a massive writing project that became his primary interest: a great survey of modern London in the tradition of that published by John Stow in 1598. Besant combined his love of the city with his obsession for writing and publication, and he believed that the survey was to be among his most important contributions as a writer. At his death he had completed portions of the work, some of which were later published as collaborations with others working on the project.

In addition to his continuous output of both fiction and nonfiction, Besant's involvement in various movements and causes grew ever greater. His interests ranged from the promotion of French literature through his long-standing association with the Rabelais Club to the promotion of Anglo-American relations through the Atlantic Union late in his life. With the possible exception of his philanthropic work with the poor, however, his most significant commitment to social reform involved the improvement of copyright laws and other measures to prevent the exploitation of authors by publishers.

It is no wonder that one of Besant's areas of concern was the confused state of copyright law as it related to works by British authors published in the United States and Canada. Besant's books were extremely popular in America, just as they were in England, and many of the American editions of his works were pirated – unpaid-for and unregulated. A common practice was to lift one of Besant's novelettes or short stories from its initial publication in a British periodical and reprint it in a cheap American edition – sometimes even before the story was published in book form, either individually or in a collection, in England. Besant realized little profit from the American editions of his works, although Chatto and Windus did have a working relationship with Harper and Bros. in New York, a comparatively reputable firm that published inexpensive, authorized editions of several Besant novels that competed with the unauthorized ones.

Besant advocated a pragmatic, businesslike approach to writing and publishing, and he insisted that the author was entitled to fair payment for his product. (His tough-minded advocacy is ironic when one remembers that he left nearly all the actual negotiations involving his work to Rice during the time of their collaboration and, after Rice's death, turned to literary agents.) Besant was chiefly responsible for the formation of the Society of Authors in 1884; he also served as its first chairman, and he edited its journal until his death. Although the American piracies were a thorn in Besant's side,

Besant's study at Frognal End

their great number helped to support the claim in his *Autobiography* that his name was "known all over the English-speaking world."

As the spokesman for his fellow novelists, Besant earned his place in at least a footnote to modern literary history. In 1884 he delivered a lecture, "The Art of Fiction," at the Royal Institution in London. Besant urged the acceptance of the novel as a serious art form. Although his specific arguments are somewhat incoherent – he sees the novelist as a practical craftsman one moment and a religious visionary the next – Besant's pioneering lecture gave Henry James the opening he required to compose his own, more influential essay on the "Art of Fiction." Besant was also one of the first writers to advocate courses of instruction in creative writing. The most complete exposition of his ideas on writing and publishing is found in *The Pen and the Book* (1899), though this work, too, contains many incongruities and unsupported statements.

It has been observed that Besant the man was more significant than Besant the writer. He was a garrulous, generous person who devoted himself to good causes with great energy and zeal. Because of his popularity and goodwill, fellow writers and other contemporaries tended to conceal their low opinions of his writing until after his death. This factor – along with his machine-like production of what might be fairly termed hackwork, especially in his later career – helps to explain the rapid fall of reputation that left the works of one of the most widely read English novelists of the late nineteenth century virtually ignored only a few years after his death.

Other factors can be added. In spite of his role in practical reform, his views were generally conventional and popular rather than progressive. Aesthetically in the tradition of Dickens, Besant, it might be said, outlived his time. He supported some of the goals of socialism but rejected the movement, placing his hopes for reform in philanthropic models. Unlike Thomas Hardy and George Meredith, he tended to accept the role of general opinion in setting standards of morality for the novel. His historical works and other nonfiction do not reveal rigorous standards of scholarship. His enthusiastic support of his fellow writers against the abuses of book publishers led him to make extreme statements that left many enemies in the industry.

Besant's *Autobiography*, published posthumously, had some of the same negative effects as Trollope's (1883). His self-portrait seems to show a matter-of-fact, pedestrian sort of writer devoid of romantic inspiration, and the text (which had not been fully revised by Besant before his death) contains vitriolic attacks on publishers and critics as classes of people, as well as on organized religion. Nevertheless, the *Autobiography* remains the best source of information on Besant's life.

In spite of the critical neglect, Besant is an important, representative figure in late-Victorian literature and culture, one who made a significant impact on the society in which he lived. Because he was such a well-known and influential writer at the height of his career, both his fiction and nonfiction reveal a great deal about the prevailing ideas and values of the time, and for this reason they deserve to be studied. It is remarkable that *Victorian Britain: An Encyclopedia* (1988) not only omits a formal entry on Besant but includes only two brief mentions of him. More encouraging are recent articles that stress the enormous popularity of *All Sorts and Conditions of Men* and other novels by Besant and examine the complex publishing history of his major works.

References:

Lewis Saul Benjamin, *Victorian Novelists* (London: Constable, 1906);

Frederick Boege, "Sir Walter Besant: Novelist (Part I)," *Nineteenth-Century Fiction,* 10 (March 1956): 249–280;

Boege, "Sir Walter Besant: Novelist (Part II)," *Nineteenth-Century Fiction,* 11 (June 1956): 32–60;

Michael P. Dean, "Henry James, Walter Besant, and 'The Art of Fiction,' " *Publications of the Arkansas Philological Association,* 10 (Fall 1986): 13–24;

Simon Eliot, " 'His Generation Read His Stories': Walter Besant, Chatto & Windus, and *All Sorts and Conditions of Men," Publishing History,* 21 (1987): 25–67;

Eliot, "Unequal Partnerships: Besant, Rice, and Chatto, 1876–82," *Publishing History,* 26 (1989): 73–109;

John Goode, "The Art of Fiction: Walter Besant and Henry James," in *Tradition and Tolerance in Nineteenth-Century Fiction,* edited by David B. Howard, John Lucas, and Goode (New York: Barnes & Noble, 1967), pp. 243–281;

Wim Neetens, "Problems of a 'Democratic Text': Walter Besant's Impossible Story," *Novel,* 23 (Spring 1990): 247–264;

Mark Spilka, "Henry James and Walter Besant: 'The Art of Fiction' Controversy," *Novel,* 6 (Winter 1973): 101–119;

S. Squire Sprigge, Prefatory Note to *Autobiography of Sir Walter Besant* (London: Hutchinson, 1902; New York: Dodd, Mead, 1902), pp. vii–xxvii.

Papers:

Collections of Besant's correspondence and manuscripts are in the Huntington Library, San Marino, California; the Richmond Central Library, Surrey; Dr. Williams's Library, London; the National Library of Scotland, Edinburgh; and the Cambridge University Library. His papers as secretary of the Palestine Exploration Fund are in the private collection of that organization in London.

Ada Nield Chew

(28 January 1870 – 27 December 1945)

Ann L. Ardis
University of Delaware

BOOK: *The Life and Writings of Ada Nield Chew,* collected, with a biography, by Doris Nield Chew (London: Virago, 1982).

SELECTED PERIODICAL PUBLICATIONS – UNCOLLECTED: "The Charwoman (A True Story)," *Common Cause,* 21 September 1911;

"Making It Stretch (A True Story)," *Common Cause,* 5 & 12 October 1911;

"The Pottery Worker (A True Story)," *Common Cause,* 4 January 1912;

"All in the Day's Work: Mrs. Turpin," *Englishwoman* (July 1912);

"All in the Day's Work: Mrs. Bolt," *Englishwoman* (1912);

"The Mother's Story," *Common Cause,* 11 April 1913;

"The Separation Order," *Common Cause,* 2 May 1913;

"Mrs. Stubbs on Women's Sphere," *Common Cause,* 6 May 1913;

"A Daughter's Education," *Common Cause,* 13 June 1913;

"Mrs. Stubbs on Anti-Suffragists," *Common Cause,* 27 June 1913;

"Mrs. Stubbs on Militancy," *Common Cause,* 20 August 1913;

"As Others See Us: An Overheard Seaside Conversation: Workers and the Upper Ten (Founded on Fact)," *Cotton Factory Times,* 5 September 1913;

"Assault and Battery," *Common Cause,* 12 September 1913;

"A Woman's Work Is Never Done," *Common Cause,* 24 April 1914.

Ada Nield Chew, 1920 (Collection of Doris Nield Chew)

Ada Nield Chew was one of many turn-of-the-century British women whose fiction-writing careers were both inspired and sustained by the political controversies of their day. Prior to earning a living through her fiction, journalism, and political activism during the prewar heyday of the suffrage campaign, Chew served on the Nantwich Board of Guardians, traveled with the Clarion van (a Socialist outfit) for a year (where she met her future husband, George Chew, in 1897), and worked for more than a decade with Mary MacArthur as a women's trade union organizer. She published articles in journals such as *Common Cause* (the journal of the

National Union of Women's Suffrage Societies, the most important nonmilitant suffrage organization in the Edwardian suffrage campaign), the *Freewoman* (a radical socialist-feminist periodical that, retitled the *Egoist* in 1914, subsequently became one of the chief venues of publication for modernists such as James Joyce and Ezra Pound), and the *Englishwoman.* Her stories focus on issues she addressed while stumping on the Clarion van or writing reports for the Women's Trade Union League: the economic and physical oppressiveness of working-class domestic life, the importance of unionization as a means of recognizing the unique concerns of working-class women factory hands, the middle-class biases of woman-suffrage campaigners and social workers, and the obliviousness of both suffrage and Independent Labour party activists to the needs of working-class women.

As Wendy Mulford has argued in *Re-Reading English* (1982), the fact that most literary critics writing today concern themselves with the "appreciation and evaluation of the individual text, and the individual great writer's work" makes it easy to ignore the historical importance of the suffrage writers, whose texts are less impressive individually than they are in the aggregate. Additionally, although modernists such as Joyce originally enjoyed a much smaller readership than did the suffrage writers, it is the former rather than the latter whose work continues to be reprinted and circulated through the educational system today as representative early-twentieth-century British writing. Hence the value placed on modernist texts also contributes to the neglect of the suffrage writers, whose work differs so radically – both stylistically and ideologically – from high modernism.

Yet Mulford's point is well taken: suffrage writers such as Chew did indeed play a key role in the politicization of women in Edwardian Britain. Even though the plethora of short stories, novels, dramas, and penny pamphlets about woman suffrage produced between 1906 and 1914 typically goes unmentioned or is dismissed on aesthetic grounds in literary histories of this period, this body of work represents an important literary intervention on the national political "scene" in Britain at the turn of the century. While she is certainly not as well known today as some of her contemporaries – women such as Isabella Ford, Katharine Bruce Glasier, Elizabeth Robins, and May Sinclair – Chew's short fiction nonetheless epitomizes the literary production of the many suffrage campaigners and socialist-feminist activists. These writers saw fiction as a highly effective means of polit-

ical consciousness-raising at the turn of the century, and they conceived of their fiction writing as part and parcel of their political work in other forums. Chew's work also stands out among this body of material because her working-class status and lack of formal education make the mere fact of her career as a published writer all the more unusual.

Born on a farm in North Staffordshire to William and Jane Hammond Nield on 28 January 1870, Chew was the second of thirteen children. As the oldest and the only healthy daughter (her only sister to live past infancy, May, was an epileptic who was eventually institutionalized), Ada grew up sharing the burden of her mother's housekeeping and child-care responsibilities. As her own daughter, Doris, notes in *The Life and Writings of Ada Nield Chew* (1982), Chew chose to have only one child, and her stories attest to her familiarity with the hard physical labor involved in housekeeping in an era when stoves still had to be blacked, linens were pressed in a mangle, and front stoops were scrubbed down by hand in "respectable" working-class neighborhoods. Chew's formal education ended when she was eleven and the family moved to Worcestershire. There her father worked a small farm until Chew was seventeen, when he moved the family to Crewe and was hired on at a brickyard. (He never farmed again.)

Although it was probably not her first job in the public sector – her daughter notes that she worked in a shop at Nantwich as early as 1887 – Chew gained her first bit of national publicity when she wrote a series of letters to the local paper about her job as a tailoress in a Crewe factory that manufactured police and military uniforms. Specifically, she called attention to the factory management's policy of overcharging the government for piecework done by women, at the rates paid for that done by men (and pocketing the difference), while also objecting to various penalties and charges that the "hands" were required to pay for sewing supplies, hot water at tea time, and late arrival at the factory.

In many of these twelve letters of a "Crewe Factory Girl" to the *Crewe Chronicle* – published between 5 May and 22 September 1894 and subsequently republished in the *Clarion,* a nationally distributed Socialist weekly – Chew's opening remarks are extremely deferential toward the middle-class editorial staff and readership of the *Chronicle.* For example, her first letter opens with a request: "Sir, – Will you grant me space in your sensible and widely read paper to complain of a great grievance of the class – that of tailoresses in some of the Crewe factories – to which I belong?" (*Crewe Chron-*

icle, 5 May 1894). Highly conscious of the novelty of her position and the risks she is taking by writing these letters (she did in fact lose her job), Chew is nonetheless adamant about voicing the unique concerns of women factory workers. In spite of increased labor and union activism at the turn of the century, and in spite of increased attention among sociologists and welfare workers to the conditions of industrial labor, women are not commonly recognized as laborers, Chew observes. And this oversight stimulates her outspokenness:

> I have hoped against hope that some influential man (or woman) would take up our cause and put us in the right way to remedy – for of course there is a remedy – for the evils we are suffering from. But although one cannot open a newspaper without seeing what all sorts and conditions of men are constantly agitating for and slowly but surely obtaining – as in the miners' eight hour bill – only very vague mention is ever made of the underpaid, over-worked "Factory Girl." And I have come to the conclusion, sir, that as long as we are silent ourselves and apparently content with our lot, so long shall we be left in the enjoyment (?) of that lot.

Not only does Chew speak out; she is confident that she can offer the general public more-accurate information about the working conditions for women in the Crewe clothing industry than can any official investigators appointed by a governmental regulatory agency. Such investigators, she notes, see only what the factory owners want them to see: "a band of happy girls, apparently working in greatest ease, whose comfort is the careful consideration of their employer" (Crewe Chronicle, 9 June 1894). She goes on to describe her agenda for the whole series of twelve letters:

> The factory doors are closed on the general public, who know nothing of what takes place therein. But I, the factory girl, throw wide these doors. I invite the public, one and all, to come with me as my visitors. I will give them not the superficial view which the manager's visitors get, but a thorough good look into everything, from the factory girl's point of view. Thank God for the public press, which sheds its strong white light on all the dark corners of the earth! . . . I am thankful, too, that we have a good local paper in the Chronicle, which fearlessly publishes the opinions, however varying, of all classes of thinkers; and lends its powerful aid as willingly to the weary factory girl as to the peer of the realm.

It is worth noting Chew's characterization of the public press in this last passage. The turn of the century, particularly in America, is often thought of as the heyday of yellow journalism. Chew's reference to the press as a "strong white light" illuminat-

ing "all the dark corners of the earth" offers quite a different image of journalism's role in culture.

Perhaps in part Chew's supreme confidence in the truth-telling function of the newspaper industry is a function of her own youth and unworldliness at this point in her life. But it also begins to explain why she makes no distinction between her fiction and nonfiction. (Her daughter does so in The Life and Writings, but when these pieces are assembled in chronological order the distinction fades, particularly since the reader is as likely to find Chew writing about fictional characters in her reportage as in the sketches that are explicitly fictional.) Whether she is writing autobiographical exposés of the clothing industry or writing about fictional characters such as Mrs. Turpin and Mrs. Stubbs, Chew's narrative strategies and her intention are the same. First she graphically describes the working conditions of these real-life or fictional characters. Then, having enlisted the reader's sympathy for these people through details about their day-to-day lives, she ends her sketches with a hard-hitting punch line: change these labor conditions; give women the vote so they can have a say in the public policies that affect their lives so intimately.

In stories such as "The Pottery Worker (A True Story)" (Common Cause, 4 January 1912), "All in the Day's Work: Mrs. Turpin" (Englishwoman, July 1912), and "All in the Day's Work: Mrs. Bolt" (Englishwoman, 1912) Chew takes the reader hour by hour through two working-class women's daily routines. Mrs. Turpin's family situation is much more stable than that of the protagonist in "The Pottery Worker," who prefers to risk her health dipping pottery in a leaded glaze rather than live with an abusive husband; but the hardships of Mrs. Turpin's life are no less real. While there is bacon enough for her husband's and their oldest (and only wage-earning) son's breakfast, the rest of the children must settle for bread dipped in bacon fat. Mrs. Turpin eats dry toast "because the butter shows signs of giving out before Friday, and there's no getting any more" and drinks milkless tea "because she cannot screw more than eight pints a week out of her husband's wages, and a pint a day and a quart on Sunday (1s 2d per week) is so little among seven of them." The rest of her day consists of small emergencies: rain showers keep her rescuing clothes from the lines; yesterday's wash does not get folded because the baby demands a good deal of attention. She is relieved when her husband announces "he has another meeting on to-night" because she can "mangle and iron without irritating him"; yet ten o'clock finds her with the mending still to be done,

Chew with her husband, George, and their daughter, Doris,
circa 1903 (Collection of Doris Nield Chew)

and she will drop exhausted into bed after eleven knowing that she "will be tired to-morrow morning when she rises" as well.

Only after Chew has taken the reader through the whole of Mrs. Turpin's day does she move beyond the individual case study to argue a more general point:

> It is said that she "has no interest in public questions," and "does not want a vote."
> Every day Mrs. Turpin solves a problem by reason of her experience of life and her heroic devotion to duty, which has hitherto baffled civilised Governments. She brings up her children on a sum which housekeepers on a large scale, with their advantages of buying in bulk, find totally inadequate to such results as she produces. The whole fabric of the State rests on the work she is doing, yet she is considered incapable or unworthy of expressing an opinion on affairs in which she is expert. So long as she is excluded, the Government will continue to "muddle through somehow" in their domestic legislation.

Critics have argued that this kind of blatant demand for the reader's political support detracts from the aesthetic quality of suffrage fiction and that it turns stories such as Chew's into political tracts or propaganda. Such an argument depends on the assumption that propaganda is antithetical to art; propaganda, in this view, is something crude, institutional, and partisan, while art is complex, humane, and ideologically pure. Countering such arguments in *The Spectacle of Women: Imagery of the Suffrage Campaign, 1907–1914* (1988), Lisa Tickner suggests that "suffrage imagery is propaganda in the original sense; it meant to 'propagate' a belief, a position and a set of arguments." Fiction writing, in other words, functions for the suffragists as yet another form of political activism. Fiction can teach middle-class readers to have sympathy for people they might ignore on the street; sometimes it can even be a more effective means of consciousness-raising than a speech at a rally or a door-to-door campaign.

Norman Bentwich does not present himself as a supporter of woman suffrage in "The Novel as a Political Force" (*Nineteenth Century,* November 1906), but he makes a powerful case for the crucial interventions of literature in the British political scene at the turn of the century. Conceding that politicians "design the actual schemes of reform," Bentwich insists that the fiction writer plays an important role in the political arena because she "set[s] in motion among the people those currents of feeling which determine in the first place their political ideas, and finally the policy of the country." Where politicians have failed, the novelist can succeed:

> What Thackeray once called the lazy, novel-reading, unscientific public will not study the problems of [industrialization] in theoretical treatises or learned works of sociology; even if it did so, it would hardly be able to visualize the conditions and the problems there set out, and make them bear a real meaning. It is exactly this which the novelist can do for "the man in the street"; [she] can turn theories into people and problems into events, and by so doing bring them home to thousands who would otherwise remain ignorant or unsympathetic. The great novelist is the intermediary between different classes: by arousing sympathy for the creatures of [her] imagination [she] gains it also for ideas and ideals which [her] readers had hitherto not known or not understood.

Bentwich focuses exclusively on the novelist, not the short-story writer, in this essay, and the gender-inclusive language is not his. Nonetheless, his argument pertains to the suffragists' production of short fiction. Cheaper to publish than novels and therefore accessible to a broader readership, short stories by writers such as Chew were an important part of the suffrage campaign. For, by humanizing the political theorists' grand abstractions about class and labor, by turning "theories into people and problems into events," a writer such as Chew might hope to gain support for her most cherished political goals: universal adult suffrage and public recognition of the extent to which the national economy is built on the backs of women like Mrs. Turpin.

Chew's fiction-writing career was short-lived: her first story was published in September 1911, her last in April 1914. However, differences in publication venue and historical changes in the suffrage campaign had an impact on the thematic development of her stories. In many of the stories published between 1911 and June 1913, Chew carefully positions her first-person narrators as outsiders to the working-class communities she is describing. Much in sympathy with the women who are her protagonists (typically representing themselves as friends), her narrators are nonetheless of a different class — more "genteel," more similar to the middle-class readers of *Common Cause* and the *Englishwoman*. When working-class slang and dialect appear in these stories, they are always presented in quotation marks; terms that Chew assumed would be unfamiliar to her readers are followed by a bracketed "translation" into standard English.

Thus, in "The Pottery Worker," when Mrs. Evans gets home from the pottery factory, she has a "cup of tea to make you feel 'puti' [lively] again," and when she loses consciousness for the first time from lead colic, her coworkers deliver her to her mother's house and help her "on to the 'squab' [a rough kind of sofa bed]." Chew's narrators seek to enlist the reader's sympathy for her working-class protagonists through such detailed ethnographic studies of working-class domestic and factory life. Nevertheless, these early stories are more tentative in some respects than Chew's letters about life in the Crewe clothing industry. It is almost as if she were anxious not to shock the middle-class ladies who subscribed to *Common Cause* with the mere fact of linguistic difference, not to mention differences in sensibility.

By contrast, in stories she published after June 1913 Chew makes little if any effort to translate working-class dialect, which she uses much more extensively. Moreover, narration is notably less intrusive; and because the narrators do not function as middlemen interceding on behalf of a middle-class readership, these stories leave the reader to eavesdrop, in a sense, on conversations among working-class women. But the stories make no concessions to a middle-class audience. Chew seems to be relinquishing, or at least rethinking, her role as Virgil in this Dantean odyssey through what the late Victorians referred to as the "lower depths" of society. Thus the reader must make sense of passages such as the following from "Assault and Battery" (*Common Cause*, 12 September 1913), in which the neighbors share their views on the sounds of violence emerging from a nearby household:

"What's t'use [in calling a policeman]," asked another woman. "It's nowt fresh. It's sickenin' livin' in the same street as that pair. Never a day passes as there isn't summat to do. A nice place for childer to be browt up in! Ah'm goin' to shift as soon as Ah can get a heause — only there's no heauses to be getten i' this teawn, an' yo' hev to live next door to any sort of riff-raff, becos yo' cornd find nowheer else to gooa. Listen!"

The other striking difference between the early and late stories concerns Chew's attitude toward the possibility of cross-class relationships — either friendships or political alliances. In September 1911, when the first of her stories appeared in *Common Cause*, there was still a great deal of optimism within many suffrage societies about middle-class women's willingness to ignore class barriers and unite with working-class women to achieve the vote. This is reflected even as late as April 1913 in Chew's "The Mother's Story" (*Common Cause*, 11 April 1913), which ends with a rallying cry: "We must stand all together, and refuse to tolerate a world where women's lives are so cheap." Such optimism faded quickly, however, as the suffragists argued more and more divisively among themselves: first, about whether to support a bid for universal adult suffrage or to lobby for a more-limited woman suffrage (which would enfranchise propertied women while leaving both working-class women and men without self-representation); and, second, about the political effectiveness of the suffragists' acts of civil disobedience.

While Chew's narrators identify themselves as members of the middle class in early stories, class lines are drawn differently in a story published in the *Cotton Factory Times* in September 1913 and in the last two stories about Mrs. Stubbs that Chew published in *Common Cause* in June and August of that same year. The very title of "As Others See Us," the subtitle of which is "An Overheard Seaside Conversation: Workers and the Upper Ten (Founded on Fact)," confronts the reader with Chew's new skepticism about cross-class alliances. Rather than using her story to explain the lives of the working class to a middle-class readership, the lens of the ethnographer's narrative camera is turned around to expose the biases of the upper class, whose members object to sharing not only a seaside resort in Devon with factory workers on holiday but also the vote with people whose alleged lack of humanity they caricature brutally. And while working-class women in Chew's earlier stories never publicly refute the well-meaning but inappropriate advice of their middle-class social workers, Mrs. Stubbs does not defer to the vicar's wife when she solicits Mrs. Stubbs's support for an antisuffrage league in "Mrs. Stubbs on Anti-Suffragists" (*Common Cause*, 27 June 1913). The vicar's wife may view the suffragists as "deplorably unsexed . . . creatures," but Mrs. Stubbs refuses to follow her lead: "A dunna seigh much, shut away i' this village, but it strikes mae as other wimmin as waant a vote mun be gettin' pretty strung to mek' yo' set up another show to feight 'em. . . . If thee'r [the antisuffragists] tow idle to waant t' vote thersels, they mit let other wimmin as known better what they're woth abeigh."

The simple fact that she was writing for the *Cotton Factory Times* might begin to explain the class-based shift in narrative perspective in "As Others See Us." Mrs. Stubbs's willingness to defy the vicar's wife, however, can be interpreted as an indication of Chew's own increasing reluctance to defer to the political and intellectual authority of middle-class ladies. In this regard "Mrs. Stubbs on Militancy" (*Common Cause*, 20 August 1913) is also of interest, for here the working-class woman — the dialect speaker, not the interlocutor who uses standard English — quite literally gets the last word. When Mrs. Stubbs, the only character Chew ever sustained through more than one story, expresses with complete confidence her objections to the militant suffragists' tactics in the closing paragraph of this story, she does not need the help of a middle-class narrator to get her point across:

"What's the good o' uz wimmin treatin' men as if they wan eaur enemies? They arna. They're eaur children, an' we're responsible for 'em. If my lads an noo respect for wimmin, it'll be becos A avna respected wimmin myself. Wea'n got to bring men to that frame o' mind when they'n be ashamed o' keepin' us eaut o' votin'. Bur your methods puts their minds off votin' awtogether, an' on'y stops 'em from seighing what's reight. 'Ere am A, tellin' my lads as feightin' is on'y fur

savidges, an' as 'uman beins ought to know better than to feight; an' then wimmin must start the same game! You're behind the toimes, Mary wench; feightin's eaut o' date on'y fur young lads an' for men as dunna know no better."

The last line of Chew's story rings eerily and inversely prophetic when one looks forward to August 1914 — and beyond, to Chew's pacifist stance toward World War I. Although she lived well on into the 1940s, once the war turned the British public's attention away from domestic issues such as universal suffrage, the boom days of suffrage publishing were over. Limited suffrage (to women of property older than thirty) was granted in 1918, and universal suffrage was achieved in 1928, but by then Chew had long since given up political activism and was running a small retail business and trying to ensure herself, as her daughter notes in *The Life and Writings,* a pension for her retirement. Chew disappeared from public life as quickly as she had first appeared. But the stories remain as a record of a chapter in modern literary history that has been all but forgotten.

References:

Olive Banks, "Ada Nield Chew," in her *The Biographical Dictionary of British Feminists,* volume 1 (New York: New York University Press, 1985); pp. 49–51;

Norman Bentwich, "The Novel as a Political Force," *Nineteenth Century,* 60 (November 1906): 785–794;

Doris Nield Chew, "The Life," in *The Life and Writing of Ada Nield Chew,* collected by Doris Nield Chew (London: Virago, 1982), pp. 8–69;

Jill Liddington and Jill Norris, *One Hand Tied Behind Us* (London: Virago, 1978);

Wendy Mulford, "Socialist-Feminist Criticism: A Case Study, Women's Suffrage and Literature, 1906–14," in *Re-reading English,* edited by Peter Widdowson (London & New York: Methuen, 1982), pp. 197–192;

Lisa Tickner, *The Spectacle of Women: Imagery of the Suffrage Campaign, 1907–1914* (Chicago: University of Chicago Press, 1988).

Papers:

Chew's papers are in the private collection of her daughter.

Lucy Lane Clifford

(1853 – 21 April 1929)

Saundra Segan Wheeler
Yeshiva University

BOOKS: *Children Busy, Children Glad, Children Naughty, Children Sad* (London: Wells, Garner, 1881);

Anyhow Stories Moral and Otherwise (London, 1882);

The Dingy House at Kensington (New York: Putnam, 1882);

Mrs. Keith's Crime, anonymous (New York: Harper, 1885; London: Bentley, 1885; Leipzig: Tauchnitz, 1893; revised edition, London: Eveleigh Nash & Grayson, 1925);

Love Letters of a Worldly Woman (London: Arnold, 1891; New York: Harper, 1892; Leipzig: Tauchnitz, 1892; enlarged edition, London: Constable, 1913);

The Last Touches and Other Stories (London: Blackwood, 1892; New York & London: Macmillan, 1892; Leipzig: Tauchnitz, 1892);

Aunt Anne (New York: Harper, 1892; Leipzig: Tauchnitz, 1892);

A Wild Proxy (London: Hutchinson, 1893; New York: Cassell, 1893; Leipzig: Tauchnitz, 1893);

Marie May, or Changed Aims (London & New York: Warne, 1893);

A Grey Romance and Other Stories by H. D. Traill, W. Earl Hodgson, etc. (London: Allen, 1894);

A Flash of Summer (New York: Appleton, 1894; London: Methuen, 1895; Leipzig: Tauchnitz, 1896);

Mere Stories (London: Black, 1896; Leipzig: Tauchnitz, 1909); republished as *The Dominant Note and Other Stories* (New York: Dodd, Mead, 1897);

A Woman Alone (London & New York: Macmillan, 1898; Leipzig: Tauchnitz, 1901); republished as a play in three acts (New York: Scribners, 1915);

A Supreme Moment: A Play in One Act, in *Nineteenth Century,* volume 46 (London, 1899);

The Likeness of the Night: A Modern Play in Four Acts (London: Black, 1900; New York: Macmillan, 1900);

A Long Duel: A Serious Comedy in Four Acts (London & New York: John Lane, 1901);

Woodside Farm (London: Duckworth, 1902; Leipzig: Tauchnitz, 1902);

Margaret Vincent (New York & London: Harper, 1902);

The Searchlight: A Play in One Act, in *Nineteenth Century,* volume 53 (London, 1903); republished as a separate edition (London & New York: French, 1925);

A Honeymoon Tragedy: A Comedy in One Act (London: French, 1904);

The Modern Way (Eight Examples) (London: Chapman & Hall, 1906; Leipzig: Tauchnitz, 1907);

The Getting Well of Dorothy (Leipzig: Tauchnitz, 1907; New York: Dutton, 1917);

Proposals to Kathleen (New York: Barnes, 1908);

Plays: Hamilton's Second Marriage; Thomas and the Princess; The Modern Way (London: Duckworth, 1909; New York: Kennerley, 1910);

Sir George's Objection (London & New York: Nelson, 1910; Leipzig: Tauchnitz, 1925):

The House in Marylebone: A Chronicle (London: Duckworth, 1917);

Mr. Webster and Others (London: Collins, 1918);

Miss Fingal (Edinburgh & London: Blackwood, 1919; New York: Scribners, 1919);

Eve's Lover and Other Stories (New York: Scribners, 1924).

The work of Lucy Lane Clifford focuses on the desire of men and women to find happiness through relationships and on the courage required to cope with whatever reality follows from such aspirations. In the last four decades of her life, Clifford achieved recognition writing about these issues in popular stories, novels, and plays. Before this time her personal life dominated her activities, and until 1879 she had only the renown that comes through association with distinguished people. After her death her name appeared mostly in the biographies and letters of some of the most eminent writers of the time, and her work virtually disappeared into the oblivion assigned until recently to much of the domestic fiction and drama published at the end of the nineteenth and the beginning of the twentieth century. Before her first publications — children's stories — were produced in the 1880s, Clifford found herself in the world of prominent artists and thinkers as the wife of William Kingdon Clifford, a mathematician and scientist whose intellectual range influenced many thinkers before his death at thirty-four.

After her marriage on 7 April 1875, Mrs. W. K. Clifford — the name under which she would publish more than thirty volumes of stories, novels, and plays — was one of the few women invited to the Mary Ann Evans/George Henry Lewes Sunday afternoon salons, which included such well-known figures as Sir Leslie Stephen, Herbert Spencer, James Russell Lowell, and Henry and William James. When her husband died at Madeira of pulmonary tuberculosis on 3 March 1879, leaving his widow with two young daughters, Lucy had the comfort of such friends as Evans (George Eliot), who contributed ten pounds to a pension arranged for her, and the writer's circle. Having suffered the loss of Lewes a year earlier, the famous writer wrote to Clifford, "I understand it all." Advising the young widow to find refuge in activity, she added, "It is among my most cherished memories that I knew your husband and from the first delighted in him."

In "A Remembrance of George Eliot" (*Nineteenth Century,* July 1913), Clifford describes her experiences at the Sunday salons in the Priory, the home of Evans and Lewes, as events that marked her as someone tolerated but invisible. In this piece she comments, "They [Evans/Lewes] knew my husband, W. K. Clifford, long before I did, they loved him and delighted in his happy nature and the wild flights of his genius." When Clifford announced his engagement to Lucy Lane, daughter of John Lane of Barbados, Lewes wrote to the young scientist, congratulating him and advising how a partner would provide "a motive force" for his career and leave this "*rare* intellect free to work out its glorious destiny."

Lucy Lane Clifford writes that Lewes and Mrs. Lewes, as Evans was always addressed in her private life (even though she never married Lewes), expected Clifford to visit alone even after he married. Although he considered this expectation unreasonable, he was advised by a friend that an invitation for his wife would never be forthcoming from the Leweses, and if he wanted Mrs. Clifford to be included he would have to ask for that privilege and show that he would "consider it a great honour." After such a request the invitation was indeed granted, and Mrs. Clifford notes in her description of those afternoons that all visitors were men of intellectual distinction. "My sole claim was through my husband," she writes, "and that it covered me I felt to be yet another proof of his genius; but this did not help me to be at ease on my first visit." She calls the afternoons "a terrible ordeal for the average intelligence, if by a freak it strayed there, for inevitably at last, or at some time, eyes gravitated towards you, and you simply had to say something." Still, Lucy Lane Clifford felt that to be with Evans for only an hour, "even on one of those rather terrible Sunday afternoons, was a great achievement in your life."

If, according to Henry James, Lucy Lane was a "golden-haired, red-cheeked art student" who was spending some of her time in the British Museum sketching antique statues when she met her husband, her marriage initiated a lifetime of associations with the illustrious. After she was widowed, she remained a faithful devotee of those with literary gifts. With two young daughters to support, she not only began to write journalism, fiction, and plays but also opened her home in Saint John's Wood to many famous and rising men of letters. Leon Edel remarks that she was still wearing mourning when Henry James met her in 1880, and "he liked her from the first." Although he was nearly the same age as her husband would have been, she still treated James like one of the young protégés who visited her Sunday salon, "a hearth where one talked of old friends and met the children of the New Novel and the New Poetry over whom Aunt Lucy fussed hen-like and devoted," according to Edel.

Edel describes "Dearest Aunt Lucy," as James referred to her after the publication of her serial novel *Aunt Anne* (1892), as a woman of courage, steadfastness, and alertness. She called James her "nevvy" and helped him find a publisher for a serial he was writing during the 1890s. "By that time," writes Edel, "she had become a hearty, mothering, energetic, enveloping woman, direct in her conversation and formidable in her ability to get things done." James – who, from 1885 until his death in 1916, relied on "Aunt Lucy" as hostess, theatergoing partner, and confidante – showed his devotion by providing for her in his will. She also helped Rudyard Kipling, and when she corresponded with Lowell during his ambassadorship to England, he wrote, "Dear Mrs. Clifford, – ... How delightful it is to have women friends – they are such impartial critics." She enjoyed friendships with other distinguished men, including Thomas Henry Huxley, John Tyndall, Robert Browning, and John Morley. Even Bernard Shaw and Sir Hugh Walpole visited her salon.

Clifford presents female characters who clearly reflect the strength and independence of her own life. Her early novels anticipate her short stories in their persistent portrayal of women as morally and emotionally strong. For example, her first novel, *Mrs. Keith's Crime* (1885), which appeared anonymously and did not become identified with the author until it had gone through several editions, presents the inner struggle of a woman who, in seeking to relieve her incurably afflicted child, turns to and is tried for euthanasia. The book created a sensation among critics and the public, and while Lord John Morley thought it "revolting," Thomas Hardy admired it, and Browning called it "splendid" and wished that he had written it. In 1927, when a case of euthanasia was tried in En-

gland, the press drew a parallel with Clifford's novel.

Aunt Anne details the escapades of an elderly woman who, despite her victimization by a thoroughly unscrupulous young adventurer, remains devoted to living her life her own way. A reviewer for *Spectator* (6 August 1892) found this woman "a curious, delicate, real being ... perfectly independent ... never for a moment ridiculous even when she makes us laugh." This review also states that an elderly central character is "not generally considered an attractive object. Neither in life nor in fiction is common opinion very favorable to her." In Clifford's plays – which were produced by women and in one case starred one of the most important actresses of the day, Dame Madge Kendal – women defy the existing norms.

Clifford's writings demonstrate attitudes toward men far different from the reverence shown to the gifted set with whom she socialized, and her short stories, written largely at first for the periodical press, threatened received notions of gender. That she was herself a representative of competing realities demonstrates clearly her awareness of a changing world. The three volumes of short fiction that she published in her lifetime – *The Last Touches and Other Stories* (1892), *Mere Stories* (1896; published in the United States as *The Dominant Note and Other Stories,* 1897), and *Eve's Lover and Other Stories* (1924) – all focus on the weakness of men. A review of *The Last Touches and Other Stories* in the *Athenaeum* (19 November 1892) notes that except for the title character in the story "Thomas: Told by May's Mother," "we do not, it must be confessed, feel any great liking for Mrs. Clifford's young men ... all these specimens of modern British manhood are singularly unpleasant, with their disloyalty to the girls they pretend to love and their inordinate appreciation of their own personal attractions." The *Sewanee Review* (February 1893) found that "she has a wonderful insight into human nature – especially women. Her men are not, as a rule, pleasant creatures."

In one of the stories in *The Last Touches,* "An Interlude," Langdon meets and courts a young woman during a visit to friends in the country. After capturing her affections he announces that he is engaged to someone else. In "On the Way to the Sea," Dick Grantley, who enjoys some class advantages but has no money, falls in love with Mary Robbins, a simple country girl, while visiting the parsonage of his aunt and uncle. On another visit there, he meets a young woman of means to whom he becomes engaged. His fiancée wants to be married in the country, where they met. He agrees, but when he returns for the wedding, he has second thoughts about having abandoned his true love, Mary, and he seeks her out only to find her bereft over his engagement. He decides to throw caution to the winds and go off with Mary to New Zealand, but on the train Mary convinces him that he will be better off with his betrothed. After some resistance to the idea, he does turn back.

The stoic forbearance of women involved romantically with reprobates continues in "A Sorry Love Affair," in which May Henry cares for four young nephews after their mother dies and their father goes to New Zealand. May works as a woodcutter to support herself and her charges and has a difficult life, but she manages to meet Maurice Powers, who courts her with seeming seriousness. He convinces her that his motives are sincere and makes promises to her that turn out to be false. "A Ridiculous Tragedy" is more ridiculous than tragic as the story unfolds. A governess who has been abandoned by a lover thus becomes vulnerable to the advances of an elderly Italian widower. She marries him quickly and funds a honeymoon through France and Italy with her modest savings. En route she discovers that her Italian count has twelve children, half of whom live in the cities through which they have been traveling. In his Italian village she discovers that she will once more be a tutor in order to keep up her new family. "The Last Scene of the Play" tells the story of Harford Wilson, a character made incredible by his degree of villainy. The tale takes place in Lausanne, where he has come with his wife Charlotte as an internationally notorious fugitive being sought by the police for the murder of his first wife. Charlotte, who was already involved with Wilson when his first wife died, did not know of the murder when she married him. She does not discover the absolutely contemptible nature of her husband until they are in hiding in Lausanne. Having learned that she is married to a murderer, she suffers her husband's cruel announcement that he has never loved her, nor has he been faithful to her, and that he will escape without the burden of her if he can. Hearing the police approach the house, he offers her a gun. The story ends with the assumption that she has killed him, herself, or both as the police enter.

Not all of Clifford's stories concern women who have been turned into fools by rogues. In "On the Way to the Sea" Mary Robbins decides to give up her love, to whom she will be faithful forever, because she believes he will be happier in the mar-

riage he was planning. "A Sad Comedy" introduces Norman Luard, who appears to be a rogue for ending an eight-year romance with Madeline Dubray, a now-famous French actress, in order to marry and take a diplomatic post in Saint Petersburg; however, it soon becomes clear that ambition has contaminated this relationship from the very beginning. In its early stages both were forced to focus on the rising career of Madeleine, who would not then marry Luard as he wished. Now he tells her, "I have tasted success, and am like a tiger that has tasted blood. All things pall beside it." Still Madeleine claims that their love is stronger than anything else that has transpired in their lives, and despite his resistance Luard clearly is still attached to the actress. She extracts a promise from him that he will return with a farewell kiss just before his train leaves later that evening, and when he does so, he finds her dead.

It is unclear whether Clifford designed stories to reorganize and reform the social world, but her reviewers were attentive to the story in *The Last Touches* that explores changes in class hierarchy. One reviewer identified the title character in "Thomas: Told by May's Mother" as one who "proves to the satisfaction of everyone that the heart of a high-minded gentleman may beat beneath a page-boy's jacket." Another found the story "one of the most charming we have read for many a day, and should alone suffice to give this volume a large sale."

In this tale the orphan Thomas does odd jobs for May's mother and thereby befriends the child. Adopted by a rich South African uncle, Thomas becomes a doctor and meets May in Italy, where she has gone to winter with friends. He knows who she is, but she does not know him. They fall in love, but before they marry he comes to England to reveal himself to May's mother so that she can either approve the union or send him away before he reveals himself to his beloved. As May's mother tells the reader, she approves, and they live happily ever after. Startling though the threat of approaching social change may be in this tale, the plot still assigns to the ruling classes the authority to manage such shifts. There is also no support for the notion that Clifford consciously examined existing social hierarchies, for in her preface to the novel *A Flash of Summer* (1894), about a woman brutalized by her husband, she states that the story was conceived many years earlier and therefore made no reference to recent controversies about "marriage problems and questions."

In Clifford's short fiction, fortitude, duty, responsibility, loyalty, self-sufficiency, and undying

"SHE SAT DOWN AND NEARLY HAD HYSTERICS."

Illustration for "Powder and Paint" (English Illustrated Magazine, *December 1894*)

love represent the valorized behavior to which many of the female characters conform and from which many of the males stray, but female moral fiber does not always prevail. In the title story of her first collection, "The Last Touches," the central female character is a schemer. In this tale Carbouche, a highly visible and successful painter, avoids all human contact because of the collapse of his first and only romance many years earlier. The object of his affections reappears as the wife of an English nobleman who has convinced Carbouche to paint his former love even though he never paints portraits, particularly of women. Carbouche remains detached while painting the Comtesse until she breaks down his resistance by reconstructing the time, place, and events of their romance. While listening, Carbouche transforms the middle-aged woman, whom he has firmly decided to depict without an ounce of flattery, by painting her as the young girl he once knew. In the end she tricks him

further by leaving quickly with the painting, on the excuse of an emergency, before he has had time to realize what he has done. Thus, he is victimized twice by one woman's treachery. This story, another favorite of the critics, suggests that however admirable the behavior of many oppressed women, some seem to manage their lives by ignoble means.

Three years before her death Clifford wrote an essay for the *Saturday Review* about Maurice Hewlett – whose career as a novelist she had helped to launch – in which she shows admiration for his unconventionality. Many tales in her second collection, *Mere Stories,* anticipate this admiration. In these stories she continues to explore the conflict between the urge to follow convention through devotion to others and the need for devotion to self, but the ironic situations in some of the tales suggest that she wishes to distance herself from bourgeois behavioral norms. In "The Woman and the Philistine," for example, she presents a series of letters in which

Molly (in the last exchange) condemns her retreating lover for his choice of respectability over rapture and claims that she would have killed to spend time with him and then would have hanged for it. He burns the letter without reading it and thus never learns of these final sentiments. The story ends with an authorial "Farewell, Philistine – a safe journey to Posterity."

Julie, the fascinating title character of another tale, descends on Edouard Burmer from a former exciting Parisian life and convinces him to buy back the diamonds he has given her, since she needs only the original price of them for herself and her poor child. This respectable, well-meaning – but dim – English gentleman also has a dull-witted wife who craves diamonds. He thus ignores all the clues to Julie's ruse and learns only in a letter, delivered to him directly from her after he has bought the necklace and given it to his wife, that he has bought paste.

The other stories in this collection present contradictory attitudes toward conventional norms. In "Lady Margrave," Clifford paints an admiring portrait of Norman Byrne, a silent, suffering loner who dies for love. In "Mr. Webster," Emily Pierways engages the reader's sympathy even as she leaves her repressive husband to run off with a lover who has just returned from South Africa. "In Case of Discovery" suggests that a sinister thief has the power to use the social traps that his betters set for themselves when he accosts Eleanor on a country road and frightens her by saying, "Don't yer give us any of yer nonsense or think yer're going to git off, cus yer're not." He blackmails her into hiding the jewels he has stolen from her friend by suggesting that Eleanor could never get her friend to believe how she has come by the loot.

In "The Dominant Note" Clifford returns to her examination of unlikable men as she portrays the country meeting of four well-established young Englishmen who entertain one another at their gathering by reinforcing their smug assumptions about male superiority. When the house must be vacated because it has been promised to a woman, the four, one of whom has been recently married, decide that women are a nuisance that must be tolerated for the sake of heredity. The story ends with the suggestion that "Even Christianity couldn't find its way into the world without them." In "John Alwyn," Georgie has spent half a lifetime waiting for the return of the object of a girlish infatuation. When he finally appears, the title character has become an unattractive dullard whose wife seeks social advancement through his acquaintance with Georgie.

Despite her contact with the acknowledged greats of her day and the acclaim and encouragement from famous friends, Clifford remained a minor figure to reviewers. A critic reviewing her acclaimed early novel, *Aunt Anne,* for the *Athenaeum* (19 November 1892) wrote, "If she goes on as she has begun, and avoids certain irritating amateurishnesses, there is no reason in the nature of things why she should not attain a very high place as a novelist, below such literary queens as Charlotte Brontë and George Eliot." Reviews of *The Last Touches,* though generally favorable, included such comments as "If she would be a little less remorseless in her realism her work would be more artistic; for, to be candid, she displays on occasions a fondness for depicting the trivialities and the squalidities of life which detracts from the aim she aims at producing" (*Athenaeum,* 19 November 1892). A review of *Mere Stories* in the same periodical (1 August 1896) suggests that the very title "supplies an absence of effort on the part of their creator." It is difficult to determine whether want of "effort" meant want of skill, but this same reviewer concludes by suggesting that this collection will "not perceptibly enhance, or indeed do more than sustain, a literary reputation which is already secured by earlier triumphs."

Nonetheless, Clifford continued to write stories, and a volume of eight tales, *The Modern Way* (1906), includes four that reappear in her last collection, *Eve's Lover and Other Stories.* A *New York Times* (20 April 1924) critic found most of the characters in her last collection "fictionally inconsequential," the drama of their lives lacking the "unique," and the plots pointed toward a "too consciously premeditated conclusion." Nevertheless, the reviewer concludes that the stories in general "exhibit a skillfulness in construction" but lack "verisimilitude." Clifford's stories, even more than those in the earlier books, seem to follow a magazine formula by appealing to the largest (particularly female) audience. Some of them contain even less complexity. "Eve's Lover," for example, shows Clifford's propensity for happy endings, for here the profound hostility between husband and wife that controls the plot throughout the tale does not alter the fact that the reappearance of the wife's former lover catalyzes a marital reconciliation.

Marital happiness also concludes "Joyce," the story of a poor, uneducated, recently orphaned girl whose life is changed when an educated loner stumbles upon her and, with the help of the girl's benefactor, gives up his isolation for her. The same end comes to "Geraldine in Switzerland," a typist on her first vacation who is pursued by and eventually marries George. Other stories in this collection include situations such as another failed attempt at defiance of convention, another unfortunate case of mistaken identity, another quiet act of charity, another female rewarded for surviving under bitter circumstances, more scoundrels, and, finally, a humorous tale in which a dog becomes the rival of a young woman.

Clifford was one of Henry James's closest friends during the last thirty-five years of his life, and Edel describes him as having the kind of "passion for his friends" that reveals the "intense longing of a lonely man." He suffered keen disappointment from the response to his brief foray into drama, but in the process of converting story to play and back again, he found comfort in his relationship with "Aunt Lucy," to whom he wrote during this ordeal, "I breathe the weird tale into your ear alone" (17 February 1907). While he was still an ambassador, Lowell wrote to Clifford many times. In one letter (19 November 1884) about the ambassador being recalled, he writes that someone has told him that all the women of England "would rise as one man if he were." Lowell then asks Clifford, "I had no notion how charming I was, had you?" In another letter (16 November 1884) he seems to pick up on something Lucy has said when he comments, "I am quite willing you should prefer disagreeable men (there are quite enough of them!), provided you will tolerate me. For my part, I prefer agreeable women." It is conceivable that the side of these illustrious men encouraged by Clifford not only allowed a certain part of her own nature to flower but also gave her a glimpse of men that may have proven useful to her fiction.

In 1914 a Miss Kingston produced a play by Clifford, *A Woman Alone,* adapted from her 1898 novel of that title. The story concerns a European woman, Blanche, who enjoyed intellectual freedom and wealth before she met and married her English husband, Richard Bowden, who wishes her to live a traditional life. Blanche wants to advance a political career for her husband because she believes he has gifts in that direction. She also oversees a salon of which he disapproves. She argues that women "cannot bear the useless life any longer, unless they are stupid." He grows angry at her visitors, she at his inability to share an intellectual life with her, and eventually they separate. Neither is happy, and after several years she learns that he has anonymously published a book of enormous political influence while she has grown weary of providing the wit and charm to energize people who have little to offer except idleness. In the end, the couple reunite, each now ready to accommodate the needs of the other.

When Clifford died on 21 April 1929, her fame was such to warrant her a full-column obituary the next day in the London *Times.* Nonetheless, her literary reputation did not survive for long. She is best known as a figure in the letters of one illustrious woman and several famous men.

References:

Leon Edel, *Henry James,* 5 volumes (Philadelphia & New York: Lippincott, 1953–1972);

Edel, ed., *Henry James: Letters,* 4 volumes (Cambridge, Mass. & London: Harvard University Press, 1974–1984);

Gordon S. Haight, ed., *The George Eliot Letters,* 9 volumes (New Haven: Yale University Press, 1954–1955, 1978);

Charles E. Norton, ed., *Letters of James Russell Lowell,* 2 volumes (New York: Harper, 1894; London: Osgood, McIlvane, 1894);

Wilfrid L. Randell, "Mrs. W. K. Clifford," *Bookman* (January 1920), pp. 136–138.

Hubert Crackanthorpe
(12 May 1870 – 24 December 1896)

Benjamin Franklin Fisher IV
University of Mississippi

BOOKS: *Wreckage: Seven Studies* (London: Heinemann, 1893; New York: Cassell, 1894);

Sentimental Studies and a Set of Village Tales (London: Heinemann, 1895; New York: Putnam, 1895);

Vignettes: A Miniature Journal of Whim and Sentiment (London & New York: John Lane, 1896; New York: Bruno Chapbooks, 1915);

Last Studies (London: Heinemann, 1897);

The Light Sovereign: A Farcical Comedy in Three Acts (London: Harland, 1917).

Collection: *Collected Stories (1893–1897),* edited, with an introduction, by William Peden (Gainesville, Fla.: Scholars' Facsimiles & Reprints, 1969).

OTHER: "A Fellside Tragedy," in *Strange Assembly,* edited by John Gawsworth (London: Unicorn, 1932);

"He Wins Who Loses," in *Path and Pavement,* edited by John Rowland (London: Grant, 1937).

SELECTED PERIODICAL PUBLICATIONS – UNCOLLECTED:

FICTION

"Bread and the Circus," *Yellow Book,* 7 (October 1895): 235–257.

NONFICTION

"Mr. Henry James as a Playwright," *Albemarle,* 1 (January 1892): 34–35;

"Realism in France and England: An Interview with M. Emile Zola," *Albemarle,* 1 (February 1892): 39–43;

"Reticence in Literature," *Yellow Book,* 2 (July 1894): 259–269;

"Vignettes," *Speaker,* 10 (8 December 1894): 635–637;

"Vignettes," *Speaker,* 11 (19 January 1895): 74–75;

"Vignettes," *Speaker,* 11 (4 April 1895): 437–438;

"Vignettes," *Saturday Review* (22 June 1895): 823–824;

"Vignettes," *Saturday Review* (17 August 1895): 201–202;

Hubert Crackanthorpe, circa 1893

"Vignettes," *Speaker,* 12 (9 November 1895): 499–500;

"Notes for a Paper on Barrès and Bourget," *To-Morrow,* 3 (February 1897): 83–92.

Hubert Crackanthorpe's name seldom fails to appear in accounts of the 1890s, traditionally those that veer toward the *Yellow Book* or short fiction, most particularly the short story in England as derived from French realism. He is repeatedly cited, for better or worse, as a spearheader of the "modern" and as one who pioneered in realistic fiction that differed from the naturalism of George Moore and others. Crackanthorpe's early, mysterious death has promoted the posthumous image of a youthful artist of great promise taken untimely from the cultural scene. Thus he has been grouped with others from the 1890s who died young and left to posterity images of unfulfilled potential, such as Francis Adams, Aubrey Beardsley, Ernest Dowson, Lionel Johnson, and H. D. Lowry.

Three slender volumes of short fiction, one uncollected story, a handful of critical essays, and a negligible collaborative play constitute Crackanthorpe's literary legacy. Despite its scanty quantity his fiction testifies to efforts at the close of the nineteenth century toward liberating British fiction from a crippling moribundity fostered by the circulating library system, which promoted padding novels to tedious lengths. That clog to free artistic spirit teamed with a broader outlook of Mrs. Grundyism, or censorious morality, to impinge seriously upon literary and other arts. Crackanthorpe also adopted a Paterian impressionistic thought and expression, and his prose intermittently falls into cadences akin to those in Walter Pater's.

Opinions diverge, often extremely, over Crackanthorpe's artistic abilities. For example, William Archer and Arthur Waugh, who reviewed *Wreckage* (1893), Crackanthorpe's first book of stories, respectively in the influential *Westminster Gazette* (25 March 1893) and the *Literary World* (31 March 1893), tried to be objective in pointing out excellences and blemishes. Both submitted, and many others have concurred, that these stories derived from Guy de Maupassant. The anonymous columnist in the *Pall Mall Gazette* (27 March 1893), admittedly unsympathetic, however, objected to the new methods of the "school" that "prefers a sketch to a picture, and a scribble to a sketch." Once Crackanthorpe's stories began to circulate in the *Yellow Book,* which for many represented the depths of decadence, such hostilities intensified. An anonymous writer in the *Critic* (26 May 1894) exemplifies these animosities, saying that, in "Modern Melodrama" (*Yellow Book,* April 1984), "The gutter is celebrated in prose by Mr. Crackanthorpe, a young man who, when he writes of depravity, which he usually does, leaves nothing to the imagination. By the weak he is called 'strong,' by the strong – but what do the strong reck of Mr. Crackanthorpe?"

Reviewers of *Sentimental Studies and a Set of Village Tales* (1895) diverged widely over the worth of the volume; admiration for his growing realism in character portrayal was countered by laments over the melodrama, morbidity, and decadence found there. In *The Great Modern English Short Stories* (1919) Edward J. O'Brien comments that Crackanthorpe's "untimely end put a sudden termination to a most promising talent" and that a new edition of his writings "would be a fine public service." Contrariwise, in *Edwardians and Late Victorians* (1960) Graham Hough proposes Moore as "typical" of the 1890s because he "is discernible with the naked eye, which can hardly be said for Crackanthorpe or Dowson." Crackanthorpe's later champions, Wendell V. Harris and William Peden, see him as further removed from Maupassant and nearer Henry James in technique – and thus worth serious attention as a force in modern British fiction.

That connection seems reasonable because Crackanthorpe repeatedly presents psychologically intriguing situations embedded within rich, subtle textures. Jamesian, too, is an unmistakable and delightful irony. Many reviewers of *Sentimental Studies and a Set of Village Tales* failed to perceive the ironic drift in that title or in the harmonics played upon the term throughout his texts, setting their sights instead on surface features of pessimism, warped characters who were only sordid and nothing more – as they envisioned them – and overt sexual situations. Critics have been too content to hurry past Crackanthorpe's artistic techniques. Because just twenty-three stories make up the bulk of his total output (a figure subject to latitude if one considers "A Set of Village Tales" as a single work), his writings warrant detailed attention.

Creative quality in Crackanthorpe's stories, moreover, is unusually high – and not solely because of Jamesian attributes. He lifted the veil from sexual elements in fiction higher than had many of his predecessors, such as George Meredith, and he was at one with Thomas Hardy and Moore in desiring to free British literature from stifling censorship. Crackanthorpe takes rank with other contemporaneous fictionists, such as Ella D'Arcy, George Egerton – with whom he was repeatedly bracketed by reviewers – Arthur Morrison, and H. M. Gilbert, in presenting bleak lives in compelling guises. Thematically his fiction centers on life's reversals that cause emotional wars and pain, notably in love situations. Subtle, often-interiorized dramatizations of these disturbances constitute his usual technique. He also numbers with those whose works furthered blendings of the arts and so promoted breakdowns in generic distinctions, thereby paving the way for twentieth-century practices.

Like Beardsley, but from the opposite pathway, Crackanthorpe mingled graphic with literary techniques. Reviewers time and again singled out his word painting for favorable comment. Both men of course are heirs of the Pre-Raphaelites. Crackanthorpe also assayed the dialogue story, a form for which Anthony Hope, in *The Dolly Dialogues* (1894), gained far greater acclaim, but which rayed out as popular fare onto countless pages of magazines and newspapers during the 1890s. Linked with the dialogue as a form in itself is the impulse to intertwine stage techniques with those for fiction, reminding the reader that decades earlier Wilkie Collins called the novel and drama twins. Crackanthorpe's literary kinship with Oscar Wilde and Bernard Shaw is also likely in such ventures; moreover, he attempted to write plays, which, however, were never finished or never reached the boards and which do not survive.

Biographical information concerning Crackanthorpe has confused issues on several fronts. As late as 1966 A. Brisau lamented the absence of a biography of this important figure from the 1890s — and then left standing several myths, as had William C. Frierson and Katherine Lyon Mix. Born Hubert Montague Cookson on 12 May 1870 in London to financially comfortable parents, he had his name changed in 1888, when a legacy to his father necessitated the alteration. The eldest of three sons, Hubert grew up in an intellectual and artistic family in which semiagnostic views prevailed. Both parents, Blanche and Montague, were published writers. The father enjoyed a successful career in law; the mother's social life centered in artistic circles, and her gatherings at Rutland Gate and Newbiggin Hall (ancestral home of the Cooksons and Crackanthorpes) were enjoyed by such worthies as Hardy, James, and Marie Belloc Lowndes. Hubert's schooling included five years (1883–1888) at Eton, followed by four that remain a vague period in his life. David Crackanthorpe corrects misconceptions that during this time Hubert matriculated at Oxford or Cambridge. He spent time in France during 1889 and returned to England to study art with Selwyn Image, from whom he also acquired a Paterian outlook.

From these backgrounds Crackanthorpe emerged on the literary scene as a coeditor, with W. H. Wilkins, of the *Albemarle,* a monthly literary review that lasted from January to September 1892, financed by Montague Crackanthorpe. Hubert's first publications were a critique of James as playwright (January) and an interview with the great master of naturalism, Emile Zola (February). In the *Albemarle,* too, Crackanthorpe published his first fic-

Hubert and Dayrell Crackanthorpe on their tandem quadricycle, 1887

tion, "He Wins Who Loses" (March) and "After the Play: A Conversation" (June).

"He Wins Who Loses" (collected in *Path and Pavement,* 1937) turns on a marital mismatch between Kate, a culturally informed London spinster, and a wealthy but aesthetically limited landowner, John Hayward. An Eton classmate of John's, Lord Flamborough, visits and falls instantly in love with Kate but is rejected. Flamborough's commonplace painter's talents thereafter suddenly surge up to achieve a masterpiece (inspired, of course, by thwarted love). Crackanthorpe's ability to establish mood with economy strikes the reader in the opening sentence: "Deeper and deeper grew the twilight: longer and blacker grew the shadows." In the oncoming darkness Mrs. Hayward contemplates her married life — one, the reader soon learns, of "compression," although her "rebellious" hair and the "dreamy, far-away look" in her eyes betoken impulses to forswear such claustrophobic forces. Her husband obviously cannot empathize with her yearnings, and so Flamborough's immediate communication with those aspects in her life endear him to her. Finally, however, her timidity and long-accustomed repression reassert themselves, and she closes the proffered door to mutuality, even of the most platonic sort, with Flamborough.

The story draws toward its close by means of interchanged letters followed by a newspaper account of Flamborough's artistic success, fitting devices for diminishing directness in his appeal for and to her. Hayward's impatient reaction to Kate's dreamy response to the news and his hastening out to attend to newly purchased farm animals signal his consistent indifference and her resultant isolation. In this early story, however, many of Crackanthorpe's recurrent themes of dashed love and hopes are apparent. The kind of dramatic narrative that would attain greater forcefulness in his later tales also surfaces here in the important, if few, looks and gestures that animate the relationship between Kate and Flamborough. Their eyes are indeed windows to their souls.

"A Fellside Tragedy" (*Double Dealer,* December 1921; collected in *Strange Assembly,* 1932), a posthumous publication for which there is no date of composition, is less gripping. The circumstances of Jenny King, whose point of view the reader follows, are ironic to extremes. Stealing money from her employer, she assists the escape of her lover, "Long Joe," who in a fit of temper murdered a fellow farmworker with a pitchfork. Thereafter she is haunted by dreams of her own double until she creeps under a haystack to rest — where she is run through with pitchforks by unsuspecting haymakers. Whether this violence actually brings about her death the reader is left to ponder. The absence of dialogue makes for tediousness, although the inner drama created by Jenny's overwrought imagination is interesting. This is without question a sketch for what might have become subtler art had it been reworked.

"After the Play," the second *Albemarle* story, is also little more than a technical exercise in the dialogue form that reappears as better art elsewhere in Crackanthorpe's fiction. "After the Play," however, addresses the popular topic of art versus morality. Eustace, the philosophic speaker, opines that "morality" has been too strictly confined to issues of sexuality at the expense of other equally important concerns. Ultimately Lionel, the bluff man of action, invites his friend into his rooms for some whiskey because Eustace's disquisition has turned too gloomy for his tastes. A Shavian note of comedy in this little-known story belies notions that Crackanthorpe lacked humor. The two *Albemarle* pieces share another feature that would become "stock Crackanthorpe," so to speak — that of suggesting as much as, or more than, the stories state or define. Such suggestiveness rapidly became a hallmark in 1890s literature and infiltrated mainstreams of much twentieth-century writing.

During the *Albemarle* period Crackanthorpe also worked on the seven stories that appeared as *Wreckage* in March 1893, a volume that elicited im-

mediate if prevalently unfavorable notice and that launched him firmly in authorship. These stories — or "studies," a popular term for psychologically oriented fiction and one that may denote looseness or open-endedness — deepened the dye that had colored "He Wins Who Loses" because for many British and American readers and reviewers they seemed to be so much French realism transplanted into English. As such, themes of overt sexuality, bleak lives, and moral and physical squalor, enveloped in narratives that maintained a fairly detached point of view, were to be expected, as was the cynicism that many found in them. Writing in the *Academy* (13 May 1893) George Saintsbury comments that Crackanthorpe does not inspire sufficient delight in his art to overcome the moral and physical ugliness in the subject matter, an opinion that misses the mark as regards most of the stories. Such features might be singled out as the mainstay in *Wreckage,* although considerably more artistic substance is evident. Furthermore, one wonders whether Crackanthorpe, in youthful jeu d'esprit, deliberately insinuated more comic than tragic ironies into what passes for unmitigated stark realism in order to tweak the nose of British staidness. Like Edgar Allan Poe, who manipulated conventions of terror tales so cleverly that many missed the parodic passages within what seemed to be sober thrillers, *Wreckage* offers features that undercut sordid realism, as well as some that go beyond pastiche of French models.

The first story, "Profiles," revolves around a triangular relationship involving Maurice, Lilly, and Safford, which eventually sends Lilly spiraling downward as a prostitute. A barometer to this descent structures the story, which moves from an inviting spring afternoon when the reader first meets Maurice and Lilly, an engaged pair sporting and relaxing in the country, on through seventeen divisions — which coalesce with the shifting attitudes in the characters and reflect the disjointedness of life overall as depicted — to Maurice's last glimpse of Lilly on a rainy night, when her life is on the wane, probably from tuberculosis or venereal disease. This story is reminiscent of Maupassant in its cynical note, located principally in Safford's quick, easy discarding of Lilly once he tires of their sexual romp, but Crackanthorpe goes beyond the offhand amusement characteristic of the Frenchman's works. Far more significant here are subtly shifting psychological conflicts and reactions, especially Lilly's, which are often triggered by physical desires.

Other touches enhance these shifts. Lilly's name resonates with irony; her physical appeal rapidly fades because of feverish sexual desires, which drive her farther from the idealistic and consequently unappealing Maurice into a sexual maelstrom. The dialogue – all brief interchanges – bears razor-sharp dramatic implications, and the descriptive passages, just as brief, are likewise fraught with expanding implications. Lilly's propensities for sensuality and violence, Maurice's timidity and prudence, and Safford's obtrusive animality (symbolized in his swarthy complexion, gleaming teeth, "vermilion lips," "copper-coloured" face and massive physique, and the phallicness inherent in his first appearance standing before a pillar) are couched in terseness, as is the description of Lilly's cruel Aunt Lisbet, who undeniably resembles a witch in the "red lids to her greenish-coloured eyes ... long aquiline nose and a pointed chin." Lilly's physiognomy, too, is revealing. Her reddish, "unruly ... riotously tumbling" hair betrays a sensual being to anyone familiar with popular lore. Lilly later detects accentuations of her own resemblance to Aunt Lisbet, and like her aunt the girl does become physically and socially unattractive.

Two other stories in *Wreckage* resemble "Profiles." "When Greek Meets Greek" and "A Dead Woman" dramatize implicit power struggles between two men for one woman. Dialogue in the former imparts the chief interest, although the name Pearl adds an ironic touch because the woman's love for the successful, wealthier gambler marks her indeed as an inverted "pearl of great price." Moreover, Duncan, the loser in this story in several respects, harks back to Shakespeare's murdered king, one who remains unaware of the true nature and intents of others who work adroitly at deceiving him.

"A Dead Woman," however, was rightly held up by many of Crackanthorpe's contemporaries as the finest story in *Wreckage,* being dubbed by Bernard Muddiman, in *The Men of the Nineties* (1920), as "Crackanthorpe at last in his full stride." Emotional effects from another triangular sexual relationship hold sway, but the beloved woman has died and so is offstage except as her presence – and her physical presence is what occupies her husband and her lover – is evoked in memories. This method recalls Meredith's in *The Ordeal of Richard Feverel* (1859), wherein the character Claire gains humanity and vitality after death because her diary reveals truths about her that went unsuspected during her lifetime.

Crackanthorpe's attractive mingling of form and content permeates this story as Richard Rushout and Jonathan Hays initially discuss the sale of a white mare, which had belonged to Jane Rushout, the dead woman, and then fall naturally to discussing her death, of which this day is the first anniversary. The story at first unfolds as if supernatural phenomena will be present. Rushout's idea that Jane's ghost will appear is, however, artfully transmuted into vivid recollections of her living person, making the story a companion piece for a collaborative tale by Hardy and Florence Henniker, "The Spectre of the Real," which appeared three years later in a John Lane Keynotes series volume, *In Scarlet and Grey* (1896). Rushout and Hay's drinking to Jane's memory occasions odd glances between the two: "It was as if the one had detected the other in some secret deed." That secret, the illicit liaison, is gradually revealed. Rushout delivers a challenge, but a stroke prevents his participation. Later the men resume cordial relations, bound by their admiration for Jane. Hays eventually buys the mare because its physique and spiritedness remind him of Jane, although the horse is lamed from improper use, symbolic of the affair that had never advanced beyond rampant sex.

Mrs. Rushout is another of Crackanthorpe's women whose affections transfer from a ponderous, inactive, placid indoorsman to one whose name signifies the outdoors. Hays's gaunt physique and "bushy, red hair and untrimmed beard" mate with his rough laborer's clothes to heighten the "uncouthness of his appearance." This physiognomy also marks him out as a Judas or devil figure, that is, one who betrays his friends – often from sexual causes. The name Rushout applies with like deftness to Richard, who irrationally tries to act as his desires dictate, but whose indolence and flabby body cannot sustain such tension. The name just as deftly implies the psychological and corporeal nature of Jane, who had precipitately commenced an assignation with Hays, the more sensual being, and then abruptly left off living. The charged atmosphere that lingers about the two men, albeit pleasantly rechanneled, strikingly prefigures certain ideas of bonding that have gained currency during the later twentieth century.

Dramatic tensions in this story have fine substance. Characters move and speak with the same tragic inevitability hanging over them as one finds in a work by Hardy, and their speeches are often fraught with the psychological effects ascribed to James. Rushout's remarks to Hays about the appearance of Jane – most significantly, "Ye never knew her when that likeness was taken" – elicit surprisingly violent, yet at the time unexplained, responses from his companion. They come to make sense, however, because Hays is a superstitious countryman, and indeed he had gotten to "know"

Letter from Crackanthorpe to Selwyn Image (21 April 1893) referring to reviews by William Archer and Arthur Waugh of Crackanthorpe's Wreckage *(from David Crackanthorpe,* Hubert Crackanthorpe and English Realism in the 1890s, *1977)*

Mrs. Hays. True to life, such comments often illuminate or affect one long after they are uttered. Others, such as the "broomstick woman's" lashing out at Rushout with the truth about his wife and Hays, deliver a more immediate jolt. Both varieties deepen the tragic aura in events within the work proper while they appeal to the reader in terms of their ironies.

Variations on triangular love or on blighted marriages unify "Dissolving View," "The Struggle for Life," "A Conflict of Egoisms," and "Embers." In the first, Vivian Marston's contemplation of his approaching advantageous marriage is interrupted by his remembrances of a passionate affair with Kit, a chorus girl whose red-gold hair and yellow eyes may betray descent from alluring but volatile Pre-Raphaelite beauties. Her physical charms still fascinate him, but her lower-class status and her departure with another man pall on his inordinate self-esteem. His attempts to forget the affair are rudely jarred by Kit's note alerting him to her illness and the birth of their son. His irrational dash to find her, discovery that she and the baby have died, and subsequent relief are well handled via interior monologue. The offhand conclusion — tersely noting his and Gwynnie's "smart wedding" attended by a "fashionable crowd," and the couple's honeymooning in Italy — imparts a Maupassantian dismissive note to the events, although the glimpse into Vivian's psyche suggests much more the manner of James or Meredith than that of the French writer.

"The Struggle for Life," an episode of slum life, contains two scenes. The first, in a bar, shows a young wife begging her drunken husband, safely ensconced with his prostitute, for money to feed their child. He coarsely sends her off, and the storyteller follows her out into the unpleasant night, watches her indecision, and overhears her in a "broken voice" settle on a tryst with "a small black figure of a man [who] came slinking along under the wall." Degradation is writ large, but the brevity in what speaks volumes (for example, the man who is depersonalized or bestialized; the girl's response: "Half a crown then, and I can go home in an hour") takes it well beyond recording and into ranks with Ezra Pound's "In the Station of the Metro" (1913).

The protagonist in "A Conflict of Egoisms," Oswald Nowell, a writer who has shut out all else but work from his life, unwittingly marries Letty in the belief that love will reinvigorate his creative abilities. Just as erroneously, she envisions his giving her the great affection she has lacked. Oncoming tragedy is forecast in the opening sentence:

"The sun must have gone down some time ago, for the room was darkening rapidly." Oswald works in such close, shadowy surroundings, indicating his narrow, apathetic sensibilities. Letty's "overwrought sentimental imagination [grows] in strength and richness," to her detriment. The couple's serious misunderstandings and emotional upsets are charted so that the reader identifies with one and then the other until Oswald overhears Letty pray that he will draw closer to her. Realizing that he cannot endure these pressures, as he deems them, he sets out to commit suicide, only to drop dead as he is about to leap from a bridge. He dies from heart trouble — tensions caused by his deliberate turning from humanity; presumably she will die from the bad effects of frustrated, if misguided, love. In each case egoism, its usage undeniably Meredithean (and quite reasonably so; Letty may be Crackanthorpe's inversion of a character in *The Egoist* [1879]), is the culprit.

Companion reading may be found in "Embers," the final story in *Wreckage*. Frank Gorridge resembles Oswald in having nothing to do with mutuality. Like Oswald, too, Gorridge is introduced indirectly, as if his isolating himself since his wife's disappearance five years before has placed him at a remove from the rest of humankind. The opening sentence — "The room was small, but the twilight shadows made it appear larger" — conveys the cramped surroundings and, since the room is the man, simultaneously hints at either the potential renewal of his relationship with Mag, his quondam wife, or at his capacities for emotional breadth. Thus the title comes into play: just as embers on the hearth create shadows, Frank's emotional depths at first seem uncertain. Like Herman Melville's Bartleby, Frank might enter larger quarters and enjoy more out of life otherwise, were his "embers" fanned.

The point of view is skillfully shifted: "Outside, a drizzling rain." Amid these stormy environs Mag reappears appropriately, as she will wreak havoc in Frank's routine life and because her drunkard's existence is a kind of drizzling. After the temporary upset in both their lives because of Mag's return, her fleeting hopes of resuming a respectable life, her draining Frank of money, and their last meeting, during which he soothes her outburst — "the hysterical sobbing of a ruined nervous system; it was very painful to hear" — she vanishes again into the squalor whence she had suddenly emerged. "Embers" resonates with psychological alternations between apathetic and high-pitched moments. Mag's departure — "she stepped on to the pavement, and moved slowly away down the street" — may be flat prose to some, but it may also be the last dying ember in the tale and so holds out a final bit of well-turned art.

The year 1893 proved to be momentous for Crackanthorpe. On Valentine's Day he married Leila Macdonald, another writer, who was financially comfortable and who, because of an inheritance that soon came to her, grew even wealthier and more independent. This marriage sustained more strains than pleasures, ending disastrously in late 1896. At the outset, though, the couple seemed to enjoy each other, their social life, and writing in France, where Hubert's friend, the poet Francis Jammes, secured for them the Villa Baron close to Sallespisse, in the Orthez area. Hubert published "A Commonplace Chapter," the longest of his stories, in the *New Review* (February, March 1894). A condensation was brought out as "The Haseltons" in the *Yellow Book* (April 1895), and a full-length, revised version was included in *Sentimental Studies and a Set of Village Tales*, published in the summer of 1895.

He also came to be numbered among authors who have been traditionally associated with John Lane's venture in avant-garde publishing, the *Yellow Book*, which commenced in April 1894. Crackanthorpe contributed several stories and the critical essay "Reticence in Literature" (July 1894), a manifesto declaring for thematic and technical freedom in literary expression. "Modern Melodrama" (April 1894), a tale of mental horrors for a woman soon to die from tuberculosis, along with Ella D'Arcy's grim tale of a loveless marriage, "Irremediable," was rated by many reviewers as a specimen of the worst in decadence because of its unflinching realism — although most of the unreceptive failed to consider the fine psychological portraiture in both pieces. In the *Realm* (31 May 1895) one critic went so far as to state that D'Arcy's story "is as much Hubert Crackanthorpe as Ella D'Arcy — if not more."

Only one Crackanthorpe story from the *Yellow Book*, "Bread and the Circus" (October 1895), was never collected. This pleasant recounting of what were surely some of Crackanthorpe's own brief adventures with a circus troupe (which he joined at Dieppe in the summer of 1895), in technique a diary of sharp scenes and excellent dialogue that merge into interesting psychological revelations of the characters, brings to light a different vein from that generally thought to be representative in his fiction. Much like "The Struggle for Life," this story is told from an outsider's point of view, and therefore the attention to detail and the clear recol-

lections of events, conversations, and pictorial attractions gain plausibility. "Trevor Perkins: A Platonic Episode" ran in the *English Illustrated Magazine* (September 1896), a publication that has escaped many of Crackanthorpe's bibliographers, and reappeared in *Last Studies* (1897), assembled by his mother after his death.

Perhaps the family wished to minimize his connection with the *Yellow Book*, or perhaps "Bread and the Circus" was not deemed of a piece with the others gathered into the final volume. A hostile voice had sounded in the *Manchester Guardian* (12 November 1895), where the critic felt that Crackanthorpe had unsuccessfully managed "that extremely difficult literary form, travel notes, without any story." Conversely, another evaluator of the *Yellow Book*, in the *Glasgow Herald* (7 May 1896), lamented an absence from volume nine of "the really artistic kind of work that made the name of [the quarterly] — the work of Mr. Crackanthorpe [James, D'Arcy, and Kenneth Grahame]."

For many readers the fiction in *Sentimental Studies and a Set of Village Tales* indicates advances upon what appeared in *Wreckage*, although the contents reveal a continuing experimentation. In a preface to a 1911 collection of his own short stories, H. G. Wells wrote that in British literary history the 1890s was *the* era of excellent short-story writing and experimenting with forms. Although he does not name Crackanthorpe as one of those he recalls as "jewels" among story writers in *The Country of the Blind*, one need not look down upon Crackanthorpe's accomplishments. The "sentimental studies" include five pieces, two of them — "Battledore and Shuttlecock" and "Yew-trees and Peacocks" — published for the first time. "Modern Melodrama" and the revised full-length "A Commonplace Chapter" were not new. "In Cumberland" had come out as "A Study in Sentimentality" in the *Yellow Book* (October 1894).

All of these "studies" are "sentimental" in the context of that term's carrying sexual implications, which in Victorian parlance had been suppressed to maximize a mawkish outlook and falsity regarding morality and physical desires, as David Crackanthorpe reasonably suggests. The word and its derivatives recur throughout the book, much like certain notes or chords sound and re-sound in musical compositions. Crackanthorpe's preoccupation with "sentimentalism" in love trials aligns him with Ernest Dowson, whose short-story collection *Dilemmas: Stories and Studies in Sentiment* was also published in 1895, and with W. J. Dawson, whose *Mere Sentiment*, another volume of short stories (in Lane's

HE LET HIS EYES FOLLOW HER RETREATING FIGURE.

INSTINCTIVELY HE PASSED HIS ARM AROUND HER WAIST.

Illustrations by Dudley Hardy for "Trevor Perkins: A Platonic Episode" (English Illustrated Magazine, *September 1896*)

Keynotes series [1897]), prompted quibbles from reviewers over diction. A critic for the *Chap-Book* (15 August 1897) tellingly remarks that Dawson's "book as a whole would have been *Mere Sentimentality*." In all these books the sexual elements of love create more hindrances than enhancements. "Studies," too, is a term freighted with layered implications, as it is in *Wreckage,* and reviewers were quick to point out that fact. A writer for the *Glasgow Herald* (4 July 1895) deplored the term as too frequently covering over shoddy formlessness; conversely, John O'Hara Cosgrave wrote in the San Francisco *Wave* (28 September 1895) that form and theme in this volume are felicitously integrated. Such terminology may signal another example of Crackanthorpe's ironically testing his readers.

"Yew-trees and Peacocks" unquestionably presents such possibilities in the affair between Colonel Hallam and Constance Sheire, his best friend's wife. A grand panorama of natural scenery and the peacocks and dogs frolicking in natural animal plea-

sure on the lawn stand in bold relief juxtaposed to the stuttering, half-revealing utterances of Hallam and Mrs. Sheire's veiled replies regarding their situation. She obviously wants to have the best of circumstances, that is, to continue enjoying all the rights, privileges, and respectability of a wealthy lady, and to ensure that Hallam's homage will not weaken and that he will eventually return. The linear movement from the bright skies of a summer afternoon on to sunset, the casting of the human dilemma as little more than teatime surface conversation – with animal reminders that humans do not exist on higher planes of life than they do – and Mrs. Sheire's final "shivering a little" as she returns to the house are brilliantly cast. Nearby is "the black, burnt carcase of a tortured cloud . . . and no more sound, for the day was dead," artistic representation of the repressed feelings, which have flared up only momentarily, and more overtly on Hallam's part, only to be further tortured and to die. Emphasizing animal splendors and the natural scene as it does, the title makes the ill workings of sentimentality in the humans' lives all the more exquisitely ironic. Mrs. Sheire's name, "Constance," is at the foreground of these ironies.

A brief moment of misguided revelation also provides the mainspring for "In Cumberland." Apparently on his deathbed, Alec Burkett, clergyman of a rural parish, is visited by Ethel, his long-ago lover, who in a moment of thoughtlessness "confesses" that she has actually never loved anybody but him, despite her long-lasting marriage. Stimulated by her declaration, Alec regains his health, resolves to leave the ministry to elope with her to Australia, and causes turmoil by suddenly breaking this news to her. She watches his approach and recalls her bedside protestations "with secret, sentimental pride." Shattering his illusions makes her "sentimentally remorseful," and then, watching him depart, "she felt for him a shallow compassion, not unmingled with contempt." Thus ends another chronicle of the dashing of misguided hopes by one undeserving of such ardent affection. Balancings of feelings and actions are splendidly proportioned throughout this well-unified story, which gains strength, too, from motifs of battle between Burkett (in his attempts to stabilize his physical and emotional life) and his opponents: the church, his housekeeper, the doctor, Ethel, and marriage laws. Throughout, he and Ethel are the main combatants, of course. This story of psychological warring is close to Stephen Crane's *The Red Badge of Courage* (1895) in its inward-turning drift.

Another story of combat, "Battledore and Shuttlecock," is set in London for the most part. Young Ron has come to live with his widowed sister-in-law, Helen, who becomes emotionally attached to him. However, he grows fond of Midge, a woman of easy virtue and voluptuous good looks, and the story revolves around insights into the characters' psychological makeups, principally Ron's. Midge's mind is not limned because she appears to exist wholly in terms of sensory pleasures. Helen's mind, likewise, is not opened in detail because she is too much a product of Victorian repressive upbringing. Midge accepts her kind of life and enjoys it, such that she refuses Ron's offer of marriage because she knows that his social set will not accept her. The contrast between Midge's distancing herself from Ron and Helen's attempting anything short of an articulated declaration of love to him is painful, as are Ron's expanding understandings, and his misunderstandings, of the close ties linking fleshly and emotional planes of living. Rebounding from Midge's rejection, he unheedingly leaves Helen, too, to seek relief in India. Twelve years later he once more meets Midge, now married and the mother of three, but they betray no recognition, and he departs her husband's stableyard, probably to keep wandering, dissatisfied with his explorations of the world and his emotional morass.

"Modern Melodrama" and "A Commonplace Chapter" may be seen as tryouts with somewhat different materials. The first in many ways resembles a stage play. Its dialogue is effective, emanating understandably from the emotional oscillations caused as the full import of certain death hits Daisy, another Crackanthorpe demimondaine, and her lover, Dick. Daisy runs an emotional gamut from curiosity and self-consolation to horror and self-pity, to contemptuous responses to Dick, and on to one final attempt to delude herself into thinking she might recover. Dick's reply that the doctor who has pronounced her death sentence is reliable makes her raging and her hopes seem vain. She is in all ways a "daisy," lovely, even gaudy, but ephemeral, and subject therefore to life's buffetings. She is a creature of contrasts: "full, blue eyes, wide-set [that] contradicted the hard line of her vivid-red lips." The "air of subdued mystery" created at the beginning by a pink lampshade takes an ironic reversal in the conclusion as Dick lights his cigarette at the lamp and lamely tries to evade the brutal truth. Melodramatic qualities here are "modern" because of the inescapable realism of Daisy's fate and the overstrained reactions to the news of it, which are often signified through role-playing and masking, two favorite 1890s motifs.

"A Commonplace Chapter" stands as one of Crackanthorpe's highest artistic achievements, undoubtedly the result of thoughtful revision. Yet again the reader meets an unfaithful husband, false to a wife who had so looked forward to marrying one she envisioned as a paragon of manly ideals. Characterization is far more analytical than that in many of the other stories, doubtless because of expansiveness that attains novelette proportions. The title forecasts open-endedness; as a "chapter," what is chronicled may or may not pave the way to eventual conclusiveness. The reader comes away from the story questioning the genuineness of Hillier's repentance in the face of his repeated dissembling and role-playing. Modulations from articulations of emotions to their effects, in gesture and innuendo, are frequent. They are also plausible because rural inexperience and virginity cannot but conflict with urban latitudinarianism and sexual casualness.

Nell's revulsion from Hillier's dropped mask of idealism perhaps only deepens her tendencies to withdraw – from society, from obtrusive sexuality, and, more importantly, from the recognizable devotion of Swann, Hillier's cousin. Chance and inadvertence play no mean part in exacerbating feelings among these characters. Hillier and Nell's overhearing negative remarks about her lack of finish, Swann's happening upon Hillier and his mistress, Hillier's revealing his previous sexual conquests: all cause emotional shocks that change the courses of lives. Hillier's exhibitions of remorse in the last scenes incorporate much of the wrongheaded sentimentalism tied inextricably to sexual impulses in consistent Crackanthorpe fashion. The recurrent word painting places this as one of the poetic, and not overbrief, short stories that were making headway in literary circles of the day.

The "Set of Village Tales" that concludes *Sentimental Studies* reveals Crackanthorpe experimenting again, in this case with a cluster of tales unified by a first-person narrator, whose retelling of gossip and anecdotes and whose personal interactions with Sallespisse villagers give the "Tales" likenesses to many earlier frame collections and look ahead to twentieth-century works, such as James Joyce's *Dubliners* (1914) and Sherwood Anderson's *Winesburg, Ohio* (1919). The outsider narrator imparts a detachment reminiscent of that often found in *Wreckage*. Here, too, are human wrecks: a used-up prostitute, a priest frustrated by unrequited passion (and the taunts of the withholder), an unfaithful wife of a criminal husband, and an errant husband whose wife dies in childbirth, but whose sister-in-law will bear him another child and thus preserve his line. Crop failures, financial disasters, neighborhood tragedies, closeness of human to animal conditions: all encircle the hapless villagers, whose traumas nevertheless attain dramatic proportions in the spotlights directed by the author through his (naturally curious) narrator. The storyteller's predilections for ghastliness sides extend to include Gothic effects in "Ettienne Mattou." The grisly vignette of the man's head crushed by a train, along with the conception of Jeanne, Etienne's wife, isolated in her lonely château and then bestowing her money on a convent and immuring herself there as a "cloistered nun," harks back to the terrors and isolation in Charles Robert Maturin or Mrs. Ann Radcliffe.

Following the publication of *Sentimental Studies*, Crackanthorpe continued to bring out stories in periodicals, as well as some portions of what became *Vignettes: A Miniature Journal of Whim and Sentiment*, published by John Lane in late 1896. A nonfictional work, this publication recycled some of the columns from the *Speaker* and the *Saturday Review* dating back to 1894. The individual sections, which take the

reader from Great Britain to parts of the Continent, are kaleidoscopic in their collective effect, reinforcing the whim and sentiment in the title. Influences of Pater's impressionism are especially noticeable in this work, as are Ruskinian word painting and Meredithean lyricism, along with French influences. Ever alert to capitalizing on the popularity of his coterie of authors, Lane may have been instrumental in bringing about publication of this volume of poetic prose cast into the fragment form much admired in the 1890s, doubtless because Paterian impressionism was also greatly touted. This technique is a near relative of the free associations in stream-of-consciousness fiction. The reader must also not overlook possibilities of Crackanthorpe's intentionally using *Sentiment* in his subtitle (perhaps an echo from his previous book) for baiting Mrs. Grundys and his earlier reviewers.

The Crackanthorpe marriage began to deteriorate rapidly during late 1895. Leila had then become pregnant, miscarried sometime during early 1896 because of venereal infection, possibly contracted from Hubert, and departed alone for Italy in spring. Hubert then began an affair with Sissie Welch, Richard Le Gallienne's attractive sister. In mid August they went to Paris, where they stayed until November. Hubert actually reunited with Leila, now also in Paris with a French lover, d'Artaux, and she shortly invited Sissie to join them, creating what surely must have been an interesting, but far from placid, household. Hubert wrote to Grant Richards on 30 October, offering to resuscitate the *Savoy* after Arthur Symons and Beardsley could no longer manage that successor to the *Yellow Book*, but no such exchange transpired. Following her solicitor's counsel, Leila left Hubert on 4 November; Sissie returned to London the next day, and after a visit with his mother that night Hubert disappeared. On Christmas Eve his body was found in the Seine. Whether he was a victim of suicide, foul play, or an accident (the river was in high flood stage) has never been determined; his family seemed anxious to hush up the matter, and his biographer, David Crackanthorpe, is inconclusive.

Published posthumously in late 1897, *Last Studies* includes three stories, "Anthony Garstin's Courtship," "Trevor Perkins," and "The Turn of the Wheel." Contrary to what has long been on record, the last was the sole new piece. Blanche Crackanthorpe prepared a dedication to her son's memory, Stopford Brooke contributed a kindly poetic tribute, and James supplied an "Appreciation." The stories share what David Crackanthorpe calls "the theme of emotional mutilation, or of resistance against it." The briefest, "Trevor Perkins," is in many respects a satire on the 1890s decadent personality, on that prematurely aged, finicky aesthetic figure beset by ennui, as it is found in Perkins's personality. He is so wrapped up in himself that his affair with Emily, which for anybody else would be sexually liberating and fulfilling, is doomed to wither.

Far more zestful artistry appears in "Anthony Garstin's Courtship," which pits a long-time-dutiful son's tempestuous love against the will of a domineering elderly mother, who has grown skeptical and sour because of struggles to keep their farm free from debt. Anthony's dauntless love for pretty Rosa Blencarn has lightened what had been for him "the sluggish incrustation of monotonous years." He is middle-aged, she is young, and her initial antagonism toward him subtly mirrors his toward his mother. Gradually the reader comprehends that one of Rosa's flirtations, with a man named Luke Stock, has resulted in her becoming pregnant. Just as gradually the reader is led to see that Anthony will marry Rosa in defiance of all obstacles. Because of an unpleasant childhood, a worldliness, and expectations in love different from those of the dwellers in the rural parish where she has come to live with her old uncle, the clergyman, Rosa is not easily won to Anthony's viewpoint.

The oscillations between doubt and certainty, physical and emotional pressures, and age and youth are felicitously blended. Rosa's personality is as yet unformed, as seen in Tony's reiterated thoughts about her being a child as well as in her physical appearance — her "rosy, full-lipped, unstable mouth," a phrase that neatly catches her as-yet-unsolidified nature. This initial description brings to the fore her "coarsely fashioned" neck and hands, concluding that "her comeliness was brawny, literal, unfinished, as it were." Anthony constantly thinks of her face and the red ribbon in her hat. She is not altogether guileless as to her physical charms, though, as indicated in her escapades with a group of fast companions and in her final meeting with Luke, who thinks that his appeal to her sensual nature will make her accede to his wishes. Rosa's vitality and physical charms are also what most attract Anthony. At forty-six he is vigorous from rugged outdoor life, and his responses to the girl are strongly physical, if intermittently fatherly. The ever-so-slight brush strokes of incest or of sex with a child, which haunted the Victorian social scene, may exemplify an impish challenge to the social system from Crackanthorpe, but they also draw together the strands of changing affections that unify the story.

There is also a psychosexual rightness in Anthony's bounding-pulse responsiveness to Rosa's femininity because hitherto his only close ties to a woman have been those with his mother. The relationship binding old Mrs. Garstin to her son sustains variations between long-tested good feelings in each and a quickness to shift those allegiances in reactions to surprises or thwartings. Anthony seizes upon Rosa's pregnancy as an excuse to marry the girl and to make his mother unwittingly accept the marriage. The old lady capitulates, but her yielding carries with it a sting in that she will bypass her son and bequeath her land and money to a grandchild or grandchildren. Thus she fixes foundations for setting on edge the teeth of future generations, laying groundwork for continuing antagonisms between age and youth, a natural outcome in this story in which religion seemingly opposes, and yet furthers, very earthy sexuality. Rosa's presence as the organist in her uncle's church initiated Anthony's attraction, and the girl's quickened but still indeterminate sexuality finds outlets in both her musical endeavors and social life. Questions of whether or not she can endure the hard farm life that is to be hers are raised, and they throw light from an angle other than that of the Garstin family on the shaping of human nature by the Cumberland landscape.

"Anthony Garstin's Courtship" stands as a proper representative of the local-color movement in the late nineteenth century. Like Hardy, Lowry, or D'Arcy when they composed in that mode, Crackanthorpe does not stop short with landscape descriptions or dialect, as other local colorists were often accused of doing, but instead he integrates natural with psychological landscapes to produce a geography of the imagination. A representative vignette about Anthony typifies the technique: "He was of stubborn fibre, however, toughened by a long habit of a bleak, unruly climate." The dialect in the story is also excellent. Unlike Crackanthorpe's previous work, this story presents a tragicomedy. The continuance of life is sure, if muted, in this refashioning of farmer's daughter and May–December comedy into 1890s fare.

"The Turn of the Wheel," an exciting novelette of more than a hundred pages, is also one of the most densely textured of Crackanthorpe's studies in sentimentality. Issues of the divided self, another avid interest among many writers of the era, are thus accorded larger dimensions in interiorly picto-

Lindsey House (center) on Chelsea Embankment, London, circa 1890. Formerly the residence of James McNeill Whistler, this house was Crackanthorpe's last home.

rialized revelations and the externalizations of troubled psychological states through extended and often bitingly ironic dialogue. The story of Eardley Lingard's rise to political power at the expense of his marriage (an impulsive one at the time he wed, whence he has come a long way as to rational mental calculations), and its effects on his family, especially as it shapes the life of his daughter, Hilda, is one of egotism growing to a point at which fortune's wheel casts him down. Lingard's double standard makes him a match for many other Crackanthorpe characters, although his surprising death cuts short the enjoyment of his greatest political triumph, that of attaining M.P. status.

Unlike Gaston Lalanne, Adrian Safford, or Etienne Mattou, Lingard dies because he little thinks of any ill effects as he overstrains body and mind. Clues to his approaching demise, however, are planted from the opening sentence, "The city was disgorging," on through his anticipating "a new lease on life" and his plans for and enjoyment of assignations with women. He never imagines that his wife or daughter might discover his other side. Section 1 concludes with a descrip-

tion that emphasizes Eardley's self-destruction; arriving at his own door, "he revealed himself a little man, almost insignificant [with a] wiry, meagre mouth, well-worn, and hinting at a tale of long effort." In the end the city spews out Eardley, as it has many others, as but one more insignificant creature, although his wife and daughter suffer shocks because of his death.

As in "Anthony Garstin's Courtship," parental strategies, intentional or otherwise, seem bound to bequeath legacies of emotional distress to the next generation. Altogether her father's daughter, Hilda seems bent, as the story closes, on dominating her marriage, although the inconclusiveness allows room for speculation. She has not been wholly successful in such endeavors, as indicated by her broken engagement to Greaves Chamney. Her future husband, Stephen Walsh, moreover, appears to have concealed, although not deliberately, emotional reserves of his own that may match hers.

Such masking maintains the theme of role-playing that gives point to the story. All the major characters act, in the stage sense of that word.

Eardley's affair with an actress, Mrs. Whittingham (another transparency), in which both thoughtfully calculate their next moves – and for which he has callously discarded his previous mistress, Mrs. Mathurin – is wrought in masterstrokes of irony. When he visits Mrs. Whittingham's boudoir, she "crossed and recrossed in front of him, to attain a definite symbolization of that tense and neurotic restlessness, dubbed modern – an hysterical caging of spasmodic and inadequate motion," although the same kind of psychological imprisonment with which modernity afflicts her might be instrumental in shortening Eardley's life. His career and personal life have forced him to cross and recross, too. Both embody the dancer figure and its instabilities, so beloved by Beardsley, Symons, and William Butler Yeats. Finally such dissembling comes to an end for him, and the truth is revealed. Greaves Chamney also "acts" in suppressing his knowledge about Eardley's genuine self when Hilda questions him – a calm before her aunt's stormy tearing away of the illusions and daunting Hilda with unvarnished truth about her father.

The story then moves into a diminuendo as Eardley's illness and death preclude any recriminations. Bessie and Hilda's future will no longer be overcharged with emotional currents like those represented in the symbol of Eardley's life deftly placed by Crackanthorpe at the midpoint in the story. Walking home from visiting Mrs. Whittingham, Eardley sees the lights in Hyde Park Corner "blazing like some monster, gilded constellation . . . and across the East flared a sky-sign – a gaudy, crimson arabesque." This passage, lifted from *Vignettes,* mingles suggestions of the acme of Eardley's life and career with masking (the gilding), horror, mercurialness, and brevity; its position – at the opening of the thirteenth of twenty-five chapters – makes it a pivot toward which all that has gone before points and whence the remainder of the story subsides into an uncertain calm. That calm, expressed in Hilda's turning aside of Walsh's intended kiss, is not without its tinge of that "disgorging" mentioned in the opening sentence, and so the reader experiences repetition with variation in this effective question-mark ending. The entire piece gains in tensile artistic strength in that throughout the story the prose expression "sentimental" and its compounds greatly enhance themes of role-playing and deception.

In the main, Crackanthorpe's stories are permeated with a melancholy that many of his contemporaries interpreted as fin de siècle fare and nothing more. Many literary chroniclers have been content to follow these leads, leaving many cursory observations about him and his work but few probing analyses of the writings. The young author made his mark in the short-story form because he broke ground that others went on to cultivate. He was a first in transplanting French realism into British soil, just as George Egerton did with Scandinavian literature. The stories in *Wreckage* tower above the slice-of-life realism that rapidly turned shopworn in turn-of-the-century literature. "A Commonplace Chapter," "Anthony Garstin's Courtship," and "The Turn of the Wheel" are outstanding examples of Crackanthorpe's accomplishments and of the short story in the 1890s in general. They indicate, too, his propensities for novel writing by means of their amplitude in character creation and atmosphere.

Undeniably inspired by French examples, Crackanthorpe was also moved by the works of Meredith, Pater, Hardy, and others of British stock, and he assimilated many interesting elements from all into his works, which nonetheless bear his own stamp. He is a representative figure of the 1890s, when many writers altered identifiable models, often inverting them, to create an expression of their own. His unmistakable liking for his characters also sets him apart from many others who strove after realism. The real wonder is that he produced so much fine work within so brief a span. As befalls many others whose status declines from that of a foreground figure in their own day to neglect in the course of passing years and changing tastes, Crackanthorpe has languished over a long season. In light of canon revaluations, he may once again gain greater prominence.

Biography:

David Crackanthorpe, *Hubert Crackanthorpe and English Realism in the 1890s* (Columbia: University of Missouri Press, 1977).

References:

Karl Beckson, *Henry Harland: His Life and Work* (London: Eighteen Nineties Society, 1978);

A. Brisau, "The Yellow Book and Its Place in the Eighteen-Nineties," *Studia Germanica Gandensia,* 8 (1966): 135–172;

Osbert Burdett, *The Beardsley Period: An Essay in Perspective* (London: John Lane, 1925);

John O'Hara Cosgrave, "Sentimental Studies," *Wave* [San Francisco], 28 September 1895, p. 9;

Benjamin Franklin Fisher IV, "Ella D'Arcy: A Commentary with a Primary and Annotated Secondary Bibliography," *English Literature in*

Transition, 1880–1920, 35, no. 2 (1992): 179–211;

Fisher, "Ella D'Arcy: First Lady of the Decadents," *University of Mississippi Studies in English,* new series 10 (1992): 238–249;

Joseph M. Flora, ed., *The English Short Story, 1880–1945: A Critical History* (Boston: Twayne, 1985);

William C. Frierson, *The English Novel in Transition, 1885–1940* (Norman: University of Oklahoma Press, 1942);

Helmut E. Gerber, ed., *The English Short Story in Transition, 1880–1920* (New York: Pegasus, 1967);

Clare Hanson, *Short Stories and Short Fictions, 1880–1980* (New York: St. Martin's Press, 1985);

Wendell Harris, "Hubert Crackanthorpe as Realist," *English Literature in Transition,* 6, no. 2 (1963): 76–84;

Graham Hough, "George Moore and the Nineties," in *Edwardians and Late Victorians,* edited by Richard Ellmann (New York & London: Columbia University Press, 1960), pp. 1–27;

Holbrook Jackson, *The Eighteen Nineties: A Review of Art and Ideas at the Close of the Nineteenth Century* (London & Toronto: Cape, 1913);

Lionel Johnson, "Hubert Crackanthorpe," *Academy,* 52 (1897): 428–429;

Johnson, "Sentimental Studies and a Set of Village Tales," *Academy,* 45 (1895): 218–219;

Richard Le Gallienne, *Retrospective Reviews: A Literary Log,* 2 volumes (London: John Lane, 1896);

Le Gallienne, *The Romantic '90s* (New York: Doubleday, Page, 1925);

Mark Longaker, *Ernest Dowson* (Philadelphia: University of Pennsylvania Press, 1944);

Katherine Lyon Mix, *A Study in Yellow: "The Yellow Book" and Its Contributors* (Lawrence: University of Kansas Press, 1960);

Bernard Muddiman, *The Men of the Nineties* (London: Danielson, 1920);

Edward J. O'Brien, ed., *The Great Modern English Short Stories: An Anthology* (New York: Boni & Liveright, 1919);

William Peden, "Hubert Crackanthorpe: Forgotten Pioneer," *Studies in Short Fiction,* 7 (Fall 1970): 539–548;

Grant Richards, *Memories of a Misspent Youth, 1872–1896* (New York & London: Harper, 1933);

George Saintsbury, "New Novels," *Academy,* 13 May 1893, p. 414;

Derek Stanford, ed., *Short Stories of the 'Nineties: A Biographical Anthology* (London: Baker, 1968);

Vincent Starrett, *Buried Caesars: Essays in Literary Appreciation* (Chicago: Covici-McGee, 1923);

Margaret D. Stetz and Mark Samuels Lasner, *England in the 1890s: Literary Publishing at the Bodley Head* (Washington, D.C.: Georgetown University Press, 1990);

John Stokes, *In the Nineties* (Chicago: University of Chicago Press, 1989);

H. G. Wells, *The Country of the Blind and Other Stories* (London & New York: Nelson, 1911);

Richard Whittington-Egan and Geoffrey Smerdon, *The Quest of the Golden Boy: The Life and Letters of Richard Le Gallienne* (London: Unicorn, 1960).

Papers:

Crackanthorpe's letters are held by family members. None of his literary manuscripts appears to be extant.

Victoria Cross
(Annie Sophie Cory)
(1 October 1868 – 2 August 1952)

Shoshana Milgram Knapp
Virginia Polytechnic Institute and State University

BOOKS: *The Woman Who Didn't* (London: John Lane, 1895; Boston: Roberts, 1895); also published as *A Woman Who Did Not* (Boston: Roberts, 1895);

Paula: A Sketch from Life (London: Scott, 1896; New York: Munro, 1898);

A Girl of the Klondike (London: Scott, 1899; New York: Macaulay, n.d.);

Anna Lombard (London: Long, 1901; New York: Kensington, 1902);

Six Chapters of a Man's Life (London: Scott, 1903; New York: Kennerley, 1904);

To-morrow? (London: Scott, 1904; New York: Macaulay, 1904);

The Religion of Evelyn Hastings (London: Scott, 1905; New York: Kennerley, 1908);

Life of My Heart (London: Scott, 1905; New York: Macaulay, 1915);

Six Women (London: Laurie, 1906; New York: Kennerley, 1906);

Life's Shop-Window (London: Laurie, 1907; New York: Kennerley, 1907);

Five Nights (London: Long, 1908; New York: Kennerley, 1908);

The Eternal Fires (London: Laurie, 1910; New York: Kennerley, 1910);

The Love of Kusuma: An Eastern Love Story, as Bal Krishna (London: Laurie, 1910);

Self and the Other (London: Laurie, 1911; New York: Hewitt, 1911);

The Life Sentence (London: Long, 1912; New York: Macaulay, 1914);

The Night of Temptation (London: Laurie, 1912; New York: Macaulay, 1914);

The Greater Law (London: Long, 1914); republished as *Hilda Against the World* (New York: Macaulay, 1914);

Daughters of Heaven (London: Laurie, 1920; New York: Brentano's, 1920);

Victoria Cross (miniature by May B. Lee)

Over Life's Edge (London: Laurie, 1921; New York: Brentano's, 1921);

The Beating Heart (London: Daniel, 1924; New York: Brentano's, 1924);

Electric Love (London: Laurie, 1929; New York: Macaulay, 1929);

The Unconscious Sinner (London: Laurie, 1930; New York: Macaulay, 1930); republished as *The Innocent Sinner* (London: Pearson, 1931);

A Husband's Holiday (London: Laurie, 1932);

The Girl in the Studio: The Story of Her Strange, New Way of Loving (London: Laurie, 1934); republished as *The Girl in the Studio* (New York: Macaulay, 1934);

Martha Brown, M.P.: A Girl of Tomorrow (London: Laurie, 1935);

Jim (London: Laurie, 1937).

OTHER: "Theodora: A Fragment," in *Daughters of Decadence: Women Writers of the Fin de Siecle,* edited by Elaine Showalter (London: Virago, 1993), pp. 6–37.

Victoria Cross rose to prominence in 1895 as the author of a short story, "Theodora: A Fragment," and the novel *The Woman Who Didn't,* a response, in part, to Grant Allen's *The Woman Who Did* (1895). In novels and short stories that portray erotic events in exotic settings, she celebrated the power of sexual passion, based on the union of body and spirit, as life's chief reward. Rather than advocating permissiveness, her position amounted to a new religion, promoting love as the combination of spiritual affection and physical desire. During her forty-year career she wrote many novels and some short stories; her short fiction, apart from "Theodora," appears in three collections composed of stories that had not been previously published: *Six Women* (1906), *Daughters of Heaven* (1920), and *The Beating Heart* (1924). Although reviewers typically decried the excessive attention to sexuality, comparing her to Thomas Hardy and Emile Zola, her books sold well – from the 1890s through the early 1920s – in England, the United States, and elsewhere; many were reprinted, and several were translated into French, Italian, and Norwegian.

In the 1890s Cross was a household name. Frank Harris reported that Oscar Wilde, "always match-making when I think of British celebrities," dreamed of introducing Mrs. Humphry Ward to Algernon Charles Swinburne and speculated that "if one could only marry Thomas Hardy to Victoria Cross he might have gained some inkling of real passion with which to animate his little keepsake pictures of starched ladies." Sewell Stokes, excited by the prospect of meeting her in 1928, remembered her reputation: "Victoria Cross! The woman whose novels were read behind locked doors; who had at one time been accused of poisoning the purity of British homes with her sordid writings – a veritable

Noel Coward of the early Nineties!" Her titles remained familiar in the early decades of the twentieth century. In Katherine Mansfield's story "The Tiredness of Rosabel" (1908) a young woman's fantasies are fueled by seeing the cover of Cross's *Anna Lombard* (1901), a book carried by another passenger on a bus; Mansfield's audience did not need an explanation.

Cross's popularity declined in the 1920s and 1930s, and her works have not been reprinted since that time (with the exception of a single story reprinted in 1993). Although she continued writing until 1937 and lived until 1952, she was already seen as old-fashioned by the mid 1920s. In the modern context her portrayals of passion were less shocking and her glimpses of international settings less illuminating.

Biographical information on Cross is scarce, partly because she lived, after the 1890s, apart from public life and generally abroad. Even her name has been enigmatic. Almost all sources give Vivian Cory as her true name, but her actual name (from birth and school records, her will and those of family members, and the information provided by Anthony Griffin, a surviving cousin) was Annie Sophie Cory. To complicate matters she was also known – on some publishing contracts and on the copyright pages of several volumes – as Vivian (or Vivien) Cory Griffin or V. C. Griffin. She insisted, however, that all of her published writings bear the name Victoria Cross.

The woman who became Victoria Cross was born 1 October 1868 in Punjab, India. Her father, Arthur Cory, served as major of the Bengal Staff Corps, colonel of the Army of Karachi, and joint editor of the *Civil and Military Gazette* in Lahore. Her mother was Elizabeth Fanny (also known as Fanny Elizabeth) Griffin Cory. Her parents, who married in Calcutta in 1860 and spent much of their lives in India, retained strong ties to England, where both were born and eventually died.

Their three daughters, all literary, spent considerable time in India. The eldest, Isabel Edith, was born and died in India; for many years she edited the *Sind Gazette* in Karachi. The middle sister, Adela Florence, known to friends and family as Violet, was born in Stoke Bishop, Gloucestershire, but married, wrote, and died in India. Under the name Laurence Hope she wrote fevered, passionate, haunting love lyrics with Indian settings and figures: *The Garden of Karma* (1901; republished as *Songs from the Garden of Karma,* 1908), *Stars of the Desert* (1903), and *Indian Love* (1905). Although she committed suicide two months after the death of her husband, Lt. Gen. Malcolm Hassells Nicolson of the Bombay Army, and wrote only three volumes, her poems achieved acclaim in her time (Hardy wrote her obituary for the *Athenaeum*) and have been reprinted and set to music. W. Somerset Maugham's story "The Colonel's Lady" (1946) was based on the rumors that she chose to write under a pseudonym not only because of her sensational subject matter, but because the love poems had been inspired by her personal experiences with an Indian lover.

Cross's most important family tie was to her mother's younger brother Heneage Mackenzie Griffin, with whom she lived – in France, Italy, Switzerland, and the United States – for much of her adult life. Griffin, who had lived in Colorado since 1874 (where she visited him in 1899), earning a fortune in silver mines and real estate, left the United States permanently in 1902 and lived with or near Cross for most of the time until his death in 1939. After Arthur Cory died in 1903, Griffin traveled with his niece and her mother for many years and then, after his sister's death, with Cross alone. When Stokes met the writer on the Riviera in 1928, Griffin was with her, and he is reported to have said that her father had left her to him in his will. (The actual will shows nothing of the kind.) Griffin witnessed at least fourteen of her book contracts between 1906 and 1936. Cross often referred to herself as Vivian Cory Griffin, possibly to identify herself with her mother (instead of her father) or to ally herself with Griffin. His will, dated 1910, named her as the chief heir to his large fortune.

Outside of her dealings with publishers, booksellers, and family members, there is little information about Cross's contacts. In June 1888, at the age of nineteen, she passed the London University matriculation examination in the second division; in 1890 she passed the Intermediate Arts examination. She is recorded as studying under private tuition during these years; since her name is not in the list of graduates, it appears that she did not proceed to a degree. Her claim in a letter (3 July 1905) to hold a "B.A. in Greek, Latin, Math, Foreign Languages, Anglo-Saxon, and English Composition" is a gross exaggeration. (It was not unusual at the time for students to take the London University examination without being attached to a college or taking a formal course of instruction.) She did not, at any rate, develop a network of intellectual or artistic colleagues, and her writing reflects few specific influences of any kind.

The absence of public information about Cross reflects her isolation. Although she was in her youth part of the *Yellow Book* circle and in 1899 gave as the return address for a manuscript the home of the poet William Watson, she was not personally known to the critics who judged her work (and who sometimes speculated that she was hiding behind the pseudonym to avoid direct attack) or to contemporary writers (nor did she read their work). As Rebecca West, contemptuous of Cross's ignorance, told Stokes in 1928: "Victoria Cross once found Cunninghame Graham so interesting to talk to that she said to him, quite seriously: 'Mr. Graham, why don't you try to write? I'm sure you could.'"

Her reluctance to seek the spotlight in person may have been due to shyness or an awareness of the discrepancy between her demeanor and her fictional voice. She was apparently sedate and demure in social encounters, and was described by Stokes as "doll-like." Her French translator also stressed her reclusiveness: "She would never meet anybody. If I called on her without an appointment she would refuse to see me. She would remain in her hotel room for days, never dining in the restaurant. . . . As soon as discussions on literary collaboration were over she would say my presence was no longer necessary." Isolated from literary colleagues and critics, she was not influenced by her contemporaries, and she continued to write the same story – the spiritual survival of true passion in the face of obstacles, internal and external – again and again, in different settings.

In her business dealings, however, she was far from reserved. Her nephew Malcolm Josceline John Sinclair Nicolson (son of Laurence Hope) described her thus: "She was hard and calculating as a business woman. Once, after a disagreement with her publishers, she arrived at their office with her solicitor and a van. She took away ten tons of her books. The dispute was probably over something trifling. She used to go round the book shops, and if her novels were not displayed there was a fierce argument with the shopkeeper."

Cross began her writing career during the period of "New Woman" fiction exemplified by such figures as Sarah Grand, George Egerton, and Mona Caird and characterized by an emphasis on reform of marriage laws, promotion of women's intellectual development, and advocacy of women's emotional fulfillment.

"Theodora: A Fragment," her first published work, describes a man's passion for a woman unconventionally androgynous in her attire, speech, and sexual aggressiveness. It appeared in the fourth issue of the *Yellow Book* (January 1895), which is said to have originated at a banquet in February

1894, during which George Moore and Frank Harris commented that John Lane should start "a really first-rate, up-to-date review." With Henry Harland as literary editor and Aubrey Beardsley as art editor, the *Yellow Book* became known as an adventurous journal, new, vital, and daring: it survived the scandal of Oscar Wilde, who was arrested reportedly while carrying his copy of the publication. Early *Yellow Book* contributors included John Addington Symonds, Alice Meynell, Francis Thompson, Grant Allen, Kenneth Grahame, Max Beerbohm, Richard Le Gallienne, and Wilde.

Cross seems to have chosen her literary pseudonym as a complicated joke: she deserved the Victoria Cross for her valor, and she expected to cross Queen Victoria, or to make Victoria cross, through her candor. Her name identified her as both a hero, displaying courage and enterprise, and an outlaw, violating conventions of manners and morals. Writing a fragment, an unfinished story, with a woman's name and a man's voice, moreover, left open a variety of interpretations of her goals and attitudes. Although the male narrator is clearly fascinated by Theodora's daring and sensuality, the lack of resolution in the story makes it possible to see Theodora as a phenomenon for study and the target of social and moral criticism rather than as a moral exemplar or an object of admiration.

"Theodora: A Fragment" begins in medias res. Cecil Ray, an Egyptologist temporarily in England, is spending an afternoon with an acquaintance, a wealthy young woman, "clever" and "peculiar." He finds himself drawn to her "dash of virility, a hint at dissipation, a suggestion of a certain decorous looseness of morals and fastness of manners" and "intellectual but careless and independent spirit" – not to mention her boyish figure and her slight mustache. As they converse, walk, drink, and survey artifacts from his explorations, she tantalizes him with "a strange mingling of extremes in her. At one moment she seemed will-less, deliciously weak, a thing only made to be taken in one's arms and kissed. The next, she was full of independent uncontrollable determination and opinion." Just as their visit is ending, he yields to the "overwhelming desire to take her in my arms and hold her, control her, assert my will over hers, this exasperating object who had been pleasing and seducing every sense for the last three hours" and kisses her "in a wild, unheeding, unsparing frenzy." He returns to his rooms and opens the windows to let in the snow.

This story contains several themes that became characteristic of Cross's fiction: the unconventional woman, the bewildered and bewitched man,

the hint or presence of exotic backgrounds, and the fusion of physical attraction and mental stimulation in sexual passion. It provoked considerable controversy. Janet E. Hogarth, in a piece on "Literary Degenerates" (*Fortnightly Review,* 1 April 1895), criticizes the "sex mania" of women writers of the 1890s: "Few people are without the germs of possible diseases; but are the confused and morbid imaginings, which the sane hide deep within their breast, to be offered to the world at large as the discovery of a privileged few? To be silly and sinful is not necessarily to be singular. We commend this consideration to the authoress of *Theodora.*"

B. A. Crackanthorpe, in "Sex in Modern Literature" (*Nineteenth Century,* April 1895), targeted "Theodora" as part of the second-rate literature of the "charnel-house school" (of which the first-rate examples are Moore, Hardy, and George Meredith): "Many lesser writers are there who, without the inspirations of the giants, without their fine instincts for selection and rejection, follow them closely. . . . And hideous indeed is the result of this espionage. Instead of walking on the mountain tops, breathing the pure high atmosphere of imagination freely playing around the truths of life and of love, they force us down into the stifling charnel-house, where animal decay, with its swarm of loathsome activities, meets us at every turn." It is "revolting," in fact, "that it should be possible for a girl to project herself into the mood of a man at one of his baser moments, faithfully identifying herself with the sequence of his sensation, as was done in a recent notable instance" (a direct reference to "Theodora").

Woman commented, more positively: "*Theodora* is a brilliant and penetrating study of the beginning of a passion. It shows mature, well ordered power." The reviewer for the *Daily Chronicle* wrote: "She has possessed herself of a style brutal in its strength, and she is gifted with an eye which sees the essentials of human motive and passion in an almost disquieting manner. We shall someday see her name in a high place among modern novelists."

Cross may have already had in mind the novel to which "Theodora" most directly leads. The story includes what amounts to a sermon against the notion of love as possession, which, the character Cecil says, "tends inevitably to degrade the loved one, and to debase our own passion. . . . To love or at least to strive to love an object for the object's sake, and not our own sake, to love it in relation to *its* pleasure and not in its relation to our pleasure, is to feel the only love which is worthy of offering to a fellow human being, the one which elevates – and the only one – both giver and receiver. If we ever learn the lesson, we learn it late. I had not learnt it yet." This statement amounts to a promissory note on a story yet untold.

The rest of the narrative appeared several novels later, in *Six Chapters of a Man's Life* (1903). Cross revealed that her purpose was to write a "lasting protest against all egoism, all love of love for the sake of pleasure to the lover, instead of the all-glorious and selfless love which desires only the well-being of the loved one." The novel is part sermon against possessive love and part exploration of sexual identity. The fragment implies that Theodora is masculine in physique and habits. In the expanded version she adopts male dress as well; given that Cecil is off to Mesopotamia for his work, she burns her hair and plans to join him as his companion, passing as a man. During their sea journey they meet "on equal, easy, broad, pleasant grounds, where the companionship and comradeship and friendship of a man to a man joined and met and merged easily into passionate desire and the pleasure of sense."

Keeping a rein on themselves in public, moreover, stimulates them in private. He is, however, jealous of her interactions with both men and women. In Port Said they are threatened by a group of armed men. Cecil buys his life only at the cost of yielding Theodora for a week; although Cecil would prefer to shoot them both, Theodora says she values their lives more than her honor. When she returns to him, however, she feels a difference in him and wishes he had killed her. Back on the ship she throws herself overboard, and he is left with regrets for giving her cause to feel that exclusive possession mattered more to him than her well-being. The novel's themes – the evils of possession, the fascination of androgyny – are clearly present in the early story.

Between "Theodora" and its expansion in the 1903 novel, Cross published four other novels, the first of which solidified her notoriety, placed her within the ongoing debate on women's roles, and, because of the disparity between her style and her ostensible thesis, confused the issue of the meaning of her pseudonym. In *The Woman Who Didn't*, an account of a married woman's fidelity to her unloved husband, Cross apparently defends the sacredness of the institution of marriage, which Allen attacks in the notorious "New Woman" novel *The Woman Who Did*, published earlier that year in Lane's Keynotes series, as was her novel. Allen depicts a woman who rejects marriage, on principle, as a kind of slavery and who ultimately suffers because her daughter

Cover for the novel that is a continuation of Cross's story "Theodora" (1895)

and the world at large are unwilling to share her point of view. *The Woman Who Did*, which was denounced in the good company of Hardy's *Jude the Obscure* (1895), aroused predictable anger, outrage, and curiosity. *The Woman Who Didn't*, however, is not plausible simply as a response to *The Woman Who Did*. Allen's novel deals with the decision to live in free union without legal or religious sanction: from this perspective all married women, by definition, are women who did not do what this woman did. *The Woman Who Didn't* has as its pretext a much narrower topic: not the legitimacy of marriage itself, but the allegiance to a preexisting formal tie.

Cross may have been guided in her choice of title by the publisher John Lane, as a marketing strategy with a view toward including her novel in the Keynotes series along with *The Woman Who Did*. Lane later paired H. D. Traill's *The Barbarous Britishers* (1896) with Allen's *The British Barbarians*

(1895). Cross may have acquiesced to the title in the hope that a book in apparent contrast with Allen's scandalous novel would disarm the protests against "Theodora."

Far from a response to Allen, however, *The Woman Who Didn't* is a sly portrait of a man who would like to attribute the woman's rejection of his suit to her marital scruples. *Literary World* remarked on "the slightly coarse flippancy that one would expect from the hero's narration." *Saturday Review* commented: "The man is almost incredibly coarse and tawdry; and the book is instinct with vulgarity from cover to cover." Readers seemed to sense that this novel, while avoiding the consummation of illicit passion, was not simply advocating fidelity to marital bonds and chastity outside them.

In the ten years following her double debut with "Theodora" and *The Woman Who Didn't*, Cross published seven novels, with settings ranging from London to Burma to the Klondike and with heroines as unconventional as Theodora. The books sold well, particularly *Anna Lombard*. Although the *Athenaeum* attacked *The Religion of Evelyn Hastings* (1905) for its "repulsive realism" and the *New York Times* commented that *Anna Lombard* was a novel "which no man should read immediately before dinner unless he wishes to lose his appetite," Cross was praised by some reviewers. W. T. Stead of the *Review of Reviews* mentioned several of her novels favorably and devoted a long piece subtitled "A Novel of the Ethics of Sex" to *Anna Lombard*.

In 1905 Cross began to negotiate with T. Werner Laurie, who became her favorite British publisher and who brought out most of her remaining books. She wrote to him from Italy, France, and Egypt – from wherever she and Griffin happened to be living; Laurie worked hard to present and sell her books. Their first project was her first collection of short stories, *Six Women*; his most valuable quality was agreeing to the noninterference clause that appeared in their first and subsequent contracts: "The Publisher agrees that there shall be no alteration of any nature whatsoever in the text of the author's work, nor shall anything be added to nor omitted from it, but that it shall be printed and published exactly as written by her and this is clearly understood to apply to the matter, the sense, and also to the words, syllables, punctuation, paragraphing and spacing." The relationship proved to be happy and profitable for both, in spite of a brief rift in 1912. He agreed to leave the writing to her, and she agreed to leave the marketing and physical presentation to him. She even trusted him to negotiate for cheap reprints. Given her tough-mindedness

and general suspiciousness of agents, publishers, and booksellers, the longevity of her professional relationship with Laurie (1905–1937) is unique in her career.

Six Women consists of six stories, all involving romantic longing and frustration. They are numbered, without titles; by casual inspection *Six Women* seems to be a novel rather than a set of stories. Five of them have non-British settings and couples whose romances cross lines of race or class. In the first and longest a British soldier, married twenty years to a woman who refuses to join him permanently in India, falls in love with an innocent young dancer, Saidee, who gives him total devotion. Hamilton's wife arrives for a visit and, on the day she intends to leave, secretly stabs the dancer. Hamilton chases after his wife, chokes her, and returns to die, of a snapped nerve, in Saidee's arms. The second story features another woman whose devotion leads to her death; Stanhope loves Merla, his beautiful desert guide, and wishes to marry her. Her father, enraged, sets off to kill Stanhope; Merla sends her brother to warn her lover and dies at her father's hand, in Stanhope's coat.

Two stories are built on disguise. In one a young Christian priest falls in love, in Jerusalem, with a Jewish woman and runs off with her. When the entire monastery sets out in pursuit, the woman encourages a friend to dress as the priest and allow himself to be taken back. In the other story a father wishes his eldest daughter, Doolga, to marry the Sheik, although she is in love with Melun. The younger daughter, Silka, also loves Melun; she agrees to marry the Sheik in Doolga's place in exchange for one night, disguised as Doolga, with Melun.

In another story Dilama, a Druze woman in Ahmed's Damascus harem, meets Murad, also a Druze, in a garden before her marriage is consummated. When Ahmed sends for her, she feels physically attracted to Murad and not at liberty to mate with the noble Ahmed, who agrees to wait. On the day Ahmed is to claim Dilama, Murad kills him and carries her off. The story is, in miniature, a version of one of Cross's earliest successes, *Anna Lombard*, in which a woman's physical desire for one man interferes with her esteem for another.

In the saddest story, a return to the procrastination theme treated in the novel *To-morrow?* (1904), a young woman assumes that the man she loves does not return her love because he is unwilling to speak. Although in fact he loves her deeply, he "resents her coming to him in this way, and endeavoring to surprise from him words he has already explained to her he is unwilling to say." Before drowning herself she writes a farewell letter, which arrives in the mail with his service appointment – which would have allowed him to propose to her. The story, moreover, goes beyond the twist ending to criticize the reticence of the proper British gentleman who is found wanting because of his "nervous instinct to put off, ward off a scene in which he will be called upon to demonstrate feelings he may not satisfy."

The stories were popular, in spite of the disdain of the *Times Literary Supplement,* which sneered at the collection, describing it as "six common-place tales of passion, mostly oriental; of which the chief note is a cloying animalism." The *New York Times* reviewer, while advising the writer to be more restrained, was much more favorable: "The stories are all vivid in their coloring, and poetic and highly imaginative in their treatment. There is much beauty in the book, much to appeal to the imagination, much power and discrimination and sense of color in the use of language. But Victoria Cross has a bad case of adjectivitis and would do well to make unsparing use of the blue pencil before she publishes again."

Laurie published her next three novels – *Life's Shop-Window* (1907), one of her greatest successes; *Five Nights* (1908); and *The Eternal Fires* (1910) – and even brought out *The Love of Kusuma* (1910), a purported translation from the Indian by Bal Krishna with an introduction by Cross, but actually a typical Cross novel of romantic adventure and longing. With Laurie's cooperation Mitchell Kennerley in the United States had begun to turn a profit on her books (eventually publishing a dozen of them); he went so far as to sell the dramatic rights to *Life's Shop-Window* to an Australian playwright, who turned it into a hit play.

The public was eager for anything from her hands; the reviewers continued to carp while acknowledging her power. The *New York Times,* reviewing *Life's Shop-Window,* commented: "Another book by the author whose identity, for good reason, has been successfully concealed under the pseudonym 'Victoria Cross' carries to lengths which will amaze readers whom it does not disgust that author's habitual audacity in imitating the 'frankness' of Zola." The *Times Literary Supplement* remarked that "Victoria Cross has considerable gifts as a novelist – both descriptive and emotional; but she suffers from this fatal limitation, that for her life means love-making."

The cinematic adaptation of *Five Nights* in 1915 enhanced her notoriety. The movie was produced by William George Barker and directed by Bert Haldane, who had collaborated to present *East Lynne* (1912), the first British six-reel feature. Although the British Board of Film Censors passed *Five Nights,* and it was exhibited in such places as Liverpool, Cardiff, and Bristol, it was considered indecent by local authorities in Preston, Bath, Walsall, Brighton, and other cities, including London. The ensuing disputes led to a demand for a stronger centralized censorship of films.

Cross's writing slowed down in 1916, when her mother died; six years separate *The Greater Law* (1914) from her next work, *Daughters of Heaven.* Her readers still wanted new books; Laurie, in deference to the economy and in response to demand, brought out shilling editions of her earlier novels and her first collection of stories.

The nine stories, most of them brief, in *Daughters of Heaven* are dedicated to "my beloved and adored mother, the inspirer of all my work, whose spirit lives in my soul, and who, by reason of her glorious beauty, divine gifts, and the wonderful greatness of her character, was herself most truly a daughter of heaven." Even for Cross, the plots are preposterous. In "The Bachelor," a romance set in Yellowstone Park, a young Englishwoman jumps into a steaming geyser, drawn by what she sees as a large human figure groaning in agony (a transparent symbol of passion). Her American lover, who dismisses the vision as an illusion, burns himself rescuing her and carries her back to shelter, where he finds she has died, smiling. The heroine of "The Price of an Hour" has concealed her love from her husband (a new M.P.) because passion had interfered with his drive for political success; she has also concealed a physical attraction to a Russian artist. When she agrees to meet her artist after a two-year absence, her husband finds them together, and he impulsively shoots her. She makes the artist promise to say that she shot herself. The young British couple on "Their Honeymoon" are spending three days in the Egyptian desert; Basil, a soldier, leaves his wife on hearing that he is urgently needed to ward off a Bedouin massacre nearby, and she is killed when the Bedouins beset the honeymoon hotel.

Two stories are more affirmative. In "The Vision of Love," set in Braithwaite Abbey, a young man is about to commit suicide in despair over unpaid debts. He sees, in a vision, a seventeen-year-old girl, "the Incarnation of Love," a poor houseguest at the estate whom he has hitherto ignored (and who in fact loves him). He resolves to live, and, leaving for the abbey, he sees her in the flesh and astonishes her by asking for her hand. In "The Ride into Life" Edgar Ashley helps a young woman escape becoming a Mormon's seventh wife; they ride from Utah to Flagstaff, Arizona, from polygamy to monogamous passion, from dead religion to romantic life.

"Playing the Game" is based on a simple irony: although Ada would rather join Bertie in Egypt than keep her promise to marry Victor in Arizona, and although Victor too has formed another attachment, they keep their word to each other. Even after discovering that they have committed needless sacrifice, they decide to stay together. In another story Count Arese d'Aledo, a jaded cynic, recovers his love of life when he sees "The Butterflies' Dance" on the Umbrail Pass. He saves a young Englishwoman's life on a steep slope but is willing to allow her to assume him dead of shock (believing that nothing in life could live up to what he felt in saving her life). Assuming him dead, she takes prussic acid, apparently also believing that the rest of life will be anticlimactic. Cross appears to be attempting – to an absurd extent – to make disaster the immediate, automatic sequel to love.

"The Beast of Prey," in which a young woman, Lily, marries a British soldier and joins him in Egypt, contains a long diatribe against men, delivered by Lily's aunt: "Superficially, yes, men differ, fundamentally no. . . . Their insane jealousy, their untruthfulness, their lack of honour, their intense selfishness, their ineffable stupidity will be the same in every case." In Cairo, Lily ventures out and encounters a lioness; she is fascinated by the animal and pays her many visits. One night her husband follows her, shoots her while trying to kill the person he imagines to be her lover, and looks up, over her dead body, to see the lioness.

The most interesting story in the collection is "Triumph," a rare case of Cross showing a familiarity with another writer's work and responding to it. In "A New England Nun" (1887), by Mary E. Wilkins Freeman, a woman set in her solitude is troubled when her fiancé returns after many years' absence to marry her as promised. Although he is willing to keep his word, he is eager to marry another woman, and his fiancée is pleased to let him go for all their sakes. In Cross's version Rosa has ruined her appearance by working in a munitions factory to support herself and her younger sister. Her Jim tactlessly calls attention to her "rotten" face, and she overhears him planning to run off with her sister. The disillusionment is worse than the loss of his love, and Rosa realizes that he was not worth her devotion; she dies alone, but happy. Cross mov-

ingly describes Rosa's sense that her work ("it was for England, for her country") was more important and more lasting than the "fleeting thing" of love.

The stories in *Daughters of Heaven,* though much weaker than those in her first collection (and among the weakest pieces she ever wrote), nonetheless evoked the usual shock and fascination. The *Literary Review* called it "an almost indescribable medley of astonishing crudities and awkwardnesses, with some flashes of real imagination, some soundly dramatic situations and a few truly picturesque descriptions."

In her next novel, *Over Life's Edge* (1921), the heroine, a successful novelist named Violet Cresswell, retreats to a desert island in grief over her mother's death. The heroine experiences good luck (the man she left behind shows up, and his wife is conveniently dead). She also encounters bad luck: on discovering that the man she has rescued from shipwreck is a cheerfully unrepentant medical researcher, she has her companion kill him. After this novel Cross's output slowed again. Her following work was another collection of short stories, *The Beating Heart,* several of which deal with a subtheme of *Over Life's Edge:* her concern for animal welfare and support of the antivivisection movement. Each story in the collection expresses a different emotion of the "beating heart."

"A Novel Elopement" (expressing pity) aims its attack on a man's mistreatment of animals, not primarily at the sufferings of the animals but at the man's projected deprivation of a woman's right to a full and independent life. On the first night of a romantic elopement, before the honeymoon has actually begun, Eva discovers that Eric, her new husband, is unkind to animals, striking and reproaching a dog whose only crime is excessive affection. While Eric sleeps, Eva escapes through the farmhouse window and runs to the dog. Eva and the dog, which she names Joy, become inseparable: "He understands *her* far better than Eric ever had, and at any moment he would lay down his life joyfully for her sake." She escapes, taking the dog with her; a year later she and the dog are living happily together.

In two other stories in the same collection, Cross dispenses punishment with gruesomely poetic justice: the perpetrators suffer the fates of their victims. In "The Vengeance of Pasht" (expressing fear), a young medical student, experienced in animal experimentation, shows his insensitivity by pressing his advances on a young woman, an Egyptologist's daughter. When he pursues her to the temple of Pasht, a god with a cat's face and a woman's body, the god's statue crushes him to death.

"To Sup with the Devil" (expressing indignation) is the last and longest story in *The Beating Heart.* Jenkins, a lab assistant – horrified by experiments in starving, choking, and mutilating animals – resolves to lock a medical researcher in the "lethal chamber" designed for the animals. Knowing what he does of the medical researcher's actions, Jenkins has no qualms about killing him to save thousands of helpless animals from torture and death.

Three shorter stories display ironic reversals. In "Colour" (expressing desire) George sees a painting of a beautiful nude (from the back) model in a red room, and he arranges with the painter to be left alone with her, in that pose. He knows only that she is a discontented wife with an unremarkable face. When the model turns around, he recognizes his own wife. In "Village Passion" (expressing jealousy) Apricot, engaged to John, flirts openly with Tony, who is engaged to Bessie. One night Apricot flirts with a stranger; hearing of it, John wrongly assumes she has been flirting with Tony, and he tries to kill his presumed rival. Tony takes advantage of the situation, extorting fifty pounds blackmail, and can now afford to marry Bessie. In "The Jewel Casket" (expressing sympathy), two thieves steal a casket, expecting to find jewels; instead, they find mice. One of them walks twenty-four miles to return the pets and finds a new life as a gardener.

"The Kiss in the Wilderness" expresses love. Christine Smith, a quiet, good-natured, intellectual woman of thirty-six, is touring the Holy Land with other Britons. When Arabs kill their driver by accident and take them captive on the road between Jericho and Jerusalem, she meets Sheik Lasrali, who offers to let the rest go free if she will join him. Drawn to him when she observes his kindness and tenderness toward animals, she trembles in his embrace and agrees to marry him. Although he is willing to let her go free as well, she asks to be allowed to stay. The story features traditional Cross themes and characters: an assertive and joyously sensual woman, a mysterious and exotic lover of non-English background, the connection between kindness to animals and general kindness, and affectionate respect as a prerequisite for lasting passion.

The Beating Heart is better than *Daughters of Heaven,* but the public taste had begun to change when it was published, and books by Cross were no longer as popular. Laurie wrote to her periodically, asking to have his lease extended for her books, having on hand thousands of unsold copies. Five years went by before he published another Cross novel, and for *Electric Love* (1929) the author went

so far as to suggest a "cruel bloodthirsty picture" for the cover in order to increase sales. Two years later she allowed Laurie to negotiate for her with C. Arthur Pearson for sixpenny reprints of her novels. Although she still held out for no alterations and refused to make any cuts, she agreed to a title change from *The Unconscious Sinner* to *The Innocent Sinner.*

Her last four novels were put out by Laurie in the 1930s, but her popularity had clearly crested; three of them were published only in England. She wrote to R. A. Scott-James, pleading with him to accept a short story, "The Blush," for the *Mercury,* admitting her story was "full of faults" and offering to make several changes in response to his criticism:

> However people disagree with Victoria Cross, they *do* find her things *interesting* : and they are always asking me when they can find short stories of mine. I do not write for the ordinary magazines generally because I do not like writing a very *short* story: and they do not generally want one so long as 5,000 words which is the length I prefer. With regard to *The Blush* if you would prefer a happy ending I can cut off the last line when she tells him of her baby, and leave them happy in their little flat.

Cross had always proclaimed proudly that she knew what the public wanted and gave it to them; now her public had left her, and she was pleading for the chance to publish.

Cross had appeared to be serenely intransigent, responding to negative criticism with untarnished self-regard. In a preface to *Anna Lombard* she wrote: "I endeavoured to draw in Gerald Ethridge a character whose actions should be in accordance with the principles laid down by Christ. . . . Fearlessly, and with the Gospel of Christ in my hand, I offer this example of His teaching to the great Christian public for its verdict, confident that I shall be justified by it."

She rejected allegations of immorality, writing on 20 July 1909: "People who are jealous of me always hurl at my writings the reproach that they are immoral. From my point of view I have never written a single immoral line in my life. I am immensely proud of my books and would read them aloud to a jury of Bishops with the greatest pleasure any time." In the 1930s, however, she was unable to reach the public whose attention – favorable and unfavorable – she had been accustomed to expect.

Her last two works of fiction returned to the themes of "Theodora," her first. *Martha Brown, M.P.: A Girl of Tomorrow* (1935), a utopian fantasy set in a thirtieth-century England in which women are the dominant sex, develops the notion that masculinity is attractive in a woman. The heroine, who is responsible for major reforms in politics, education, and the arts, flies her own plane from lover to lover. At the end she flies off to the United States with an American lover, joining him over the (literally) dead body of the husband who could not bear to lose her. In *Jim* (1937) the protagonist tries to forget his grief at a lover's wish for variety and freedom by pursuing a mysterious mountain woman; he dies, at her claws, when he discovers her to be a harpy. This marks a return to the male perspective with which she began her fiction, and to the position that passionate, alluring women may be dangerous to the inadequate men who encounter their fatal fascination.

Cross's personal experience in the years after Griffin's death was far different; she appears to have been more victim than predator. During the 1940s she became close to Leonard Bradford, an American consul in Marseilles, and transferred large sums of money to him. Bradford claimed that the novelist gave him the money in gratitude for his saving her life when she intended to commit suicide in grief over her uncle's death. After her death in 1952, the administrator of her estate tried to sue Bradford for recovery of more than one hundred thousand pounds, asserting that Bradford had, during a seven-year relationship, taken advantage of her emotional vulnerability and her distaste for Britain and British taxes. He had, it was alleged, written letters characterizing himself as Perseus to her Andromeda, promising to save her assets from confiscation by the sea monster of the socialist British government if she would turn them over to him.

Cross died on 2 August 1952 at the Clinica Capitanio in Milan, Italy. Officially a resident of Switzerland (as Griffin had been at his death), she left her entire fortune — more than one hundred thousand pounds, with farm property in Northants and Shropshire — to Paolo Tosi, a Milan diamond dealer, "in consideration of the debt of gratitude I owe him." She was buried as she had directed, in a grave at L'Anzo d'Intelvi, by Griffin's side.

In recent years Cross's fiction has been mentioned, briefly but favorably, in such studies of New Woman novels and 1890s literature as Nicola Beauman's *A Very Great Profession: The Woman's Novel, 1914–39* (1983), Ann L. Ardis's *New Women, New Novels: Feminism and Early Modernism* (1991), and Daphne Patai's "When Women Rule: Defamiliarization and Sex-Role Reversal" (1982). Scattered paragraphs and pages, however, do not amount to canonical status. The most extended treatment of her fiction appears in the volume *Rediscovering Forgotten Radicals: British Women Writers, 1889–1939*

(1993). The investigation of her handling of gender roles and sexuality presents the most promising prospect for rediscovering a writer whose critical eclipse was, perhaps, facilitated by her personal reclusiveness, even during her most prolific and flamboyant creative explosion.

Cross, to be sure, long outlived her notoriety; as Stokes had predicted, a post-*Chatterley* audience was harder to shock: "Her novels, when compared with Mr. Lawrence's sexual outpourings, will then generally be ranked with the harmless fantasies of Grimm and Hans Andersen." For readers with the insight to see that Grimm and Andersen are far from harmless, however, the passionate narratives of Victoria Cross — which move from the drawing room to the desert, from the theater to the thunderstorm, from the classroom to the Klondike — will retain the power to move and fascinate.

References:

Ann L. Ardis, *New Women, New Novels: Feminism and Early Modernism* (New Brunswick, N.J.: Rutgers University Press, 1991);

Nicola Beauman, *A Very Great Profession: The Woman's Novel, 1914–39* (London: Virago, 1983);

B. A. Crackanthorpe, "Sex in Modern Literature," *Nineteenth Century,* 31 (April 1895): 607–616;

Janet E. Hogarth, "Literary Degenerates," *Fortnightly Review,* 57 (1 April 1895): 586–592;

Shoshana Milgram Knapp, "Real Passion and the Reverence for Life: Sexuality and Antivivisection in the Fiction of Victoria Cross," in *Rediscovering Forgotten Radicals: British Women Writers, 1889–1939,* edited by Angela Ingram and Daphne Patai (Chapel Hill: University of North Carolina Press, 1993), pp. 156–171;

Daphne Patai, "When Women Rule: Defamiliarization and Sex-Role Reversal," *Extrapolation,* 23 (Spring 1982): 56–69;

W. T. Stead, "*Anna Lombard:* A Novel of the Ethics of Sex," *Review of Reviews,* 23 (1901): 595–597.

Papers:

Many of Cross's publishing contracts and letters to publishers are at the library of the University of Reading (United Kingdom). Her correspondence with the Society of Authors is at the British Library. A few additional letters are in the Berg Collection, New York Public Library; at the Harry Ransom Humanities Research Center, University of Texas, Austin; and at Virginia Polytechnic Institute and State University.

Ella D'Arcy

(circa 1857 – 5 September 1937)

Anne M. Windholz
Roanoke College

BOOKS: *Monochromes* (Boston: Roberts, 1895; London: John Lane, 1895);
The Bishop's Dilemma (New York & London: John Lane, 1898);
Modern Instances (New York & London: John Lane, 1898).

TRANSLATION: André Maurois, *Ariel: The Life of Shelley* (New York: Ungar, Appleton, 1924; London: John Lane, 1924).

SELECTED PERIODICAL PUBLICATIONS – UNCOLLECTED: "Our Lady of Antibes," *Century,* 59 (November 1899): 51–57;
"Agatha Blount," *English Review,* 2 (June 1909): 435–470;
"From the Chronicles of Hildesheim," *English Review,* 3 (November 1909): 619–628;
"Every Day Brings a Ship," *English Review,* 4 (February 1910): 429–455;
"An Enchanted Princess," *English Review,* 7 (December 1910): 30–46.

During the 1890s Ella D'Arcy was regarded as one of the most promising writers to emerge from the pages of the *Yellow Book.* As subeditor of and regular contributor to that quarterly, D'Arcy participated in a literary avant-garde often influenced by the "New Realism" of naturalistic French fiction. Her own most notable short stories exhibit a psychological realism and an unsentimental treatment of character and situation that have suggested to critics affinities with Honoré de Balzac, Emile Zola, and Guy de Maupassant, as well as George Gissing and Henry James. Her harsh characterizations of women in the age of the "New Woman" have led some to oversimplify her perspective as antifemale without considering her stories' implicit indictments of male assumptions about women.

Thematically concerned with issues of courtship and marriage, art, religion, and sexuality, D'Arcy's work responded to contemporary debates on gender and relations between the sexes. Her potential to develop into one of the most distinguished and influential writers of the fin de siècle period was recognized among both her friends and reviewers; on 1 June 1895 the *Saturday Review* observed that "she will have to go very wrong to disappoint the promise of this brilliant beginning." Yet disappoint D'Arcy ultimately did – not by the caliber but by the quantity of her work. Her oeuvre is small and mainly limited to the few years she was associated with the *Yellow Book;* it is primarily for this affiliation, rather than for the stories she wrote, that D'Arcy is remembered today.

Little is known of D'Arcy's life. Always elusive, known as "Goblin Ella" to friends intrigued by her unexpected comings and goings, her personal history remains largely a patchwork of fact, conjecture, and rumor. According to the most recent and reliable sources, she was born in London around 1857 to Anthony and Sophia Anne Byrne D'Arcy, who had been married about two years. Ella's father, originally from Ireland, was part owner of a company dealing in corn and the manufacturing of malt. The D'Arcy children, raised in England, spent significant time in Hythe and the Channel Islands, the latter a locality that figures prominently in Ella's writing. Ella's early inclinations were toward art, however, rather than literature. She hoped to become a painter, and, after schooling in Germany and France, she attended London's Slade School of Art from 1880 to 1881. Deteriorating eyesight compelled her to abandon a brief painting career in favor of fiction.

D'Arcy's first efforts at publication were largely frustrated; according to an interview with the *Bookman* in 1895, she wrote book reviews to help support herself. *Yellow Book* chronicler Katherine Mix records that an early story was accepted by Charles Dickens for publication in *All the Year Round*. "The Expiation of David Scott," a conventional, melodramatic tale of jealousy, revenge, and the redeeming power of a woman's love, appeared in the December 1890 issue of *Temple Bar*. The *Athenaeum* (3 August 1895) described the story as "a rather foolish performance, the sentiment rather sentimental, and the story absurd." Alan Anderson credits D'Arcy with authorship of some similarly "commonplace stories intended for popular readership," which, under the pseudonym Gilbert H. Page, appeared in *Argosy* between 1891 and 1893: "An April Folly," "A Modern Incident," "The Smile," "In a Cathedral," "Kensington Minor," and "Unqualified Assistance." These stories, like "The Expiation of David Scott," are conventional performances that do not distinguish D'Arcy from the mass of magazine writers.

Her first real break came when *Blackwood's* published "The Elegie" in November 1891. Touching on themes that would prove prevalent in D'Arcy's work throughout the 1890s – artistic genius and self-absorption, idealized and ruined romance – this story describes young composer Emil Schoenemann's betrothal to an aristocrat's daughter, Marie, whom he idolizes. Although he grows increasingly cynical and world-weary during a seven-year banishment in Paris imposed by her father to test his fidelity, Schoenemann composes a great "Elegie" when he discovers his lover remained true to him and died rather than marry her cousin.

D'Arcy undercuts most of the story's potential sentimentality by making it clear that not grief itself but the sensation of grief provides his inspiration. Reprinted in the *Living Age* (2 January 1892) and later published in D'Arcy's first collection, *Monochromes* (1895), the story received general acclaim, winning the approval of fellow short-story writer George Egerton and praise from the *Saturday Review* (1 June 1895) for its "delicate irony": "We doubt if any other living woman-writer could have written quite so well."

Earning the attention of William Blackwood was an important step forward for D'Arcy as a writer, but the increasing influence of French naturalism on her style and, more particularly, her subject matter apparently diminished her chances for further publication in *Blackwood's*. Her story "Irremediable," about a young bank clerk's ill-begotten marriage to a seamstress who is his inferior in class and education, was rejected for not treating wedlock with proper reverence. Indeed, despite an initially positive reading of her short novel, *The Bishop's Dilemma* (1898), in manuscript, and Blackwood's general encouragement, nothing by D'Arcy ever again appeared in the pages of his magazine. "Irremediable" was turned down by other magazines as well, but when Henry Harland, editor of the newly conceived *Yellow Book,* saw the manuscript, he is said to have immediately recognized its quality and originality.

D'Arcy's realism could not affront the *Yellow Book,* which, according to an announcement preceding the first issue, was resolved to break "from the bad old traditions of periodical literature . . . [and to] have the courage of its modernness, and not tremble at the frown of Mrs. Grundy." D'Arcy's "Irremediable" joined fiction by James, Egerton, Hubert Crackanthorpe, and Harland in the quarterly's first volume (April 1894). Her story was generally well received; indeed, she and James were among the few who escaped attack in the *National Observer* review (21 April 1894) of the first *Yellow Book*. The *Saturday Review* (1 June 1895) commented that D'Arcy's "present connection with the *Yellow Book* school is an accident upon which the *Yellow Book* school is chiefly to be congratulated." Certainly Harland congratulated himself on his find; D'Arcy's stories would appear in ten of the thirteen volumes of the *Yellow Book.*

D'Arcy's formal relationship to the *Yellow Book* was that of contributor, but informally she served as Harland's subeditor. Some of her duties, indicated by a letter of 20 April 1895, included correcting proofs and arranging pictures; according to Mix she sometimes dumped Harland's drawers of manuscripts so that he was compelled to make editorial decisions. Once, during Harland's absence, D'Arcy even took the decision making into her own hands. Calling herself Harland's "Guardian Angel" in a letter to John Lane of 11 April 1896, she wrote, "I'm completely revising [Harland's] Contents-list, just according to my fancy! . . . He will, certainly, murder me when he discovers it; he is already very angry because I don't send him any revise; but of course, I shan't send him any until I've passed it for press, and so my changes have become 'Irremediable.' " Harland's response was indeed wrathful; D'Arcy explained to Lane in a 23 April 1896 letter, "but that the Channel mercifully flows between him & me, I should not now be alive to write you this tale."

Harland sent her a postcard removing her from the position of subeditor, curtly explaining that he wanted someone "less untrustworthy" in the position. D'Arcy's reaction was sarcastic: "Ah, I can see the Cromwell Road blocked with the crowd of needy females all struggling for that high salaried post!" Her comment was perhaps disloyal, since Harland had taken it upon himself to pay D'Arcy despite her unofficial status on the *Yellow Book* staff. Indeed, for the most part the two had worked together well, perhaps because they complemented each other: Harland felt that D'Arcy was "a trifle inclined to take things somewhat too seriously in this least serious of possible worlds," and D'Arcy believed that Harland "lacked a serious purpose in life." D'Arcy's meddling with the contents of the *Yellow Book* and Harland's reaction suggest, however, that D'Arcy was not too serious to make mischief if the fancy struck her, and that Harland took his position as editor of the *Yellow Book* quite seriously. Still, the spat between Harland and D'Arcy did not stop her affiliation with the quarterly, which continued to publish her fiction.

If D'Arcy occasionally questioned Harland's literary judgment, she was frankly critical of Lane's decisions when he took over as art editor after Aubrey Beardsley was dismissed from the *Yellow Book*. In the same letter in which she gleefully informed Lane that she had redone the quarterly's contents, she called his art choices for one issue "simply atrocious" and argued:

Yes; you are much too soft-hearted, you let yourself be "got at." *Why* didn't you make me Art Editor? Then, all the Celia Levetuses, the Mary Holdens, the Mildred Gastans, the Kitties, the Carries, the Annies, the Fannies; all the young Persons, in short, who send you their portraits and write you sonnets unfit for publication;

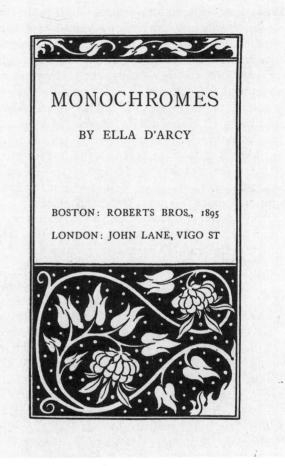

MONOCHROMES

BY ELLA D'ARCY

BOSTON: ROBERTS BROS., 1895
LONDON: JOHN LANE, VIGO ST

Title page for D'Arcy's first collection of short stories

would be kept outside of the Yellow Book . . . with a firm hand. Ah, why *didn't* you make me Art Editor?

With her artistic training D'Arcy would have been qualified for the job. Given her continual monetary crises and Lane's known munificence toward the previous art editor (in a January 1895 letter D'Arcy accused Lane of "supplying A. B. with turtle, truffles, and Pommery" while she subsisted on water), D'Arcy's interest in the position was probably even more sincere than her teasing about "the Kitties, the Carries, the Annies, the Fannies" might suggest.

Yet D'Arcy's attack on the females inundating Lane with sketches and sonnets may not be attributable to artistic outrage only. Biographer Penelope Fitzgerald suggests that D'Arcy was interested in more than a working relationship with the charming publisher. Although she never married, her history included intimate involvement with several men, including an affair in the 1880s with fantasy writer M. P. Shiel. Frederick Rolfe, in his novel *Nicholas*

Crabbe: Or the One and the Many (not published until 1958), implies (with little foundation) that she was Harland's mistress, calling her a "mouse-mannered piece of sex." Whatever her relations with other men, mouse-mannered she was not with Lane. The flirtatious tone of her letters, the musings about how she would take him in were it not for "the evil tongues of the literary world, and my own Clapham upbringing" (11 April 1896), suggest D'Arcy would have been open to any serious overtures Lane chose to make. "Petticoat" Lane generated romantic interest among more than one of his protégées – Evelyn Sharp observed that they "fell in and out of love, with or without disaster, like other people." Even if D'Arcy's interest exceeded that of the other women clustered about Lane, she was no more successful than they in forming a permanent alliance with him; in 1898 he married an American widow.

Lane did, however, promote and publish D'Arcy's work beyond the pages of the *Yellow Book*. Along with "The Elegie," "The Expiation of David Scott," and "Irremediable," three other short stories originally appearing in the *Yellow Book* – "Poor Cousin Louis," "The Pleasure Pilgrim," and "White Magic" – were published in *Monochromes,* which Lane brought out as a part of his Keynotes series in 1895. As a whole her collection received positive notice, Israel Zangwill in the *Pall Mall* magazine (September 1895) claiming it was "the cleverest volume of short stories that the year has given us." The *Athenaeum* (3 August 1895) was more guarded in its opinion, contending that "Miss Ella D'Arcy is at her best amateurish," but concluding, "Still, we can say of *Monochromes,* with a good conscience, that it is promising." "White Magic," a pleasing but undistinguished local-color sketch about superstition and romance in the Channel Islands, and "The Expiation of David Scott," dismissed by the *Saturday Review* (1 June 1895) as "juvenile" (and by D'Arcy herself in a 25 July letter to Lane), did little to enhance the author's reputation. The promise the *Athenaeum* noted, however, was particularly evident to reviewers – and to subsequent scholars – in "Irremediable," "Poor Cousin Louis," and "The Pleasure Pilgrim," all intriguing psychological studies.

"Poor Cousin Louis," which takes place in the Channel Islands, combines local color with a horrifying study of the abuse of an elderly man, Louis Renouf, by his servants and an ambitious doctor. Set against the natural beauty of the islands, their historic homesteads, and the eccentricities of their people, the story comes to a gothic close that, with little sentimentality, conveys the servants' intention to terrorize the helpless Renouf to death: "While

[Dr. Owen] watched, some one shifted the lamp . . . a woman's shadow was thrown upon the white blind . . . it wavered, grew monstrous, and spread, until the whole window was shrouded in gloom. . . . Owen put the horse into a gallop . . . and from up at Les Calais, the long-drawn, melancholy howling of the dog filled with forebodings the silent night." The *Athenaeum* (3 August 1895) called this story "a more powerful tale than any of the others"; the *Saturday Review* labeled it "a finely calculated story in culminating horror."

Though of a different sort, the horror of "The Pleasure Pilgrim" is hardly less strong than that of "Poor Cousin Louis." Picking up on the Jamesian theme of the American girl, the story tells of the flirtatious Lulie Thayer's ineffectual attempts to convince a British writer that she is truly in love with him, attempts that culminate in her shooting herself. The story leaves ambiguous whether this suicide is intentional or merely an accident of Lulie's theatricality. The *Saturday Review* called the story's characterization "masterly," an opinion later echoed in *The Beardsley Period* (1925), by Osbert Burdett, who contended that "its merit is to project without pretending to solve the heroine's character." Derek Stanford, in *Short Stories of the Nineties* (1968), sums up the story as the "cool, collected, and cogent . . . study of the psychology of the nymphomaniac." Reviewers of the 1890s and twentieth-century scholars, however, have failed to credit D'Arcy's equally masterful characterization of the neurotic, sexually repressed British writer who drives the young American girl to her death by insisting that since she has defiled the "purity" of her body by allowing others to kiss and fondle her, he will only believe she loves him if she kills herself. As it happens, not even this convinces him. Yet what is potentially most disturbing about the story is that neither its male characters nor the literary critics who have commented on it seem to acknowledge that a woman's flirtations might be less evil than a man driving a woman to kill herself – an irony unlikely to have escaped D'Arcy. Stories the caliber of "Irremediable," "Poor Cousin Louis," and "The Pleasure Pilgrim" help account for the interest D'Arcy generated in literary circles of the 1890s and for Penelope Fitzgerald's contention in *Charlotte Mew and Her Friends* (1988) that "Her *Monochromes* in Lane's Keynotes had had more quality than almost anything else in the series."

In 1898 Lane published two more books by D'Arcy: *The Bishop's Dilemma,* a short novel of thirty thousand words; and a collection of short fiction, *Modern Instances. The Bishop's Dilemma* follows the fate of an idealistic young Catholic priest who falls in love with his patron's harshly treated companion. His patron, discerning the state of things, sends the young woman away, and the depressed priest turns to drink. His bishop decides to send him out to a mission church where he will likely die, reasoning that "Life doesn't satisfy him, and he has probably discovered by this time, what I have suspected for long, that he has mistaken his vocation; or, rather, that poor silly woman, his mother, mistook it for him. She would have done much better to have made him a shopwalker in Whiteley's." Unromantic in its treatment of religion and religious calling, the book was one D'Arcy believed would appeal to a wide audience of Anglicans and Dissenters as well as Catholics. In a 13 April 1897 letter she demanded Lane double the twenty-five pounds he had offered her for the manuscript, arguing that "if you run it cleverly, I believe you could make it a success." But a review of the work in the *Bookman* (October 1898) suggests that it was less than successful with some audiences – in part because of the strength of D'Arcy's realism: "Miss D'Arcy has an admirable knack of bringing her readers into the mental atmosphere of her characters. Therefore, she should avoid writing about depressing or irritating people. She makes them too real."

Her characters also drew the attention of 1890s historian Burdett, who argued that they were stereotypical and that the work was not as original as D'Arcy's short stories. Indeed, he maintained that *The Bishop's Dilemma* is not a novel but rather "a long short-story, complete in itself, perhaps a sketch for a novel, or the kernel of a novel abandoned." *The Bishop's Dilemma* is far from a failure, but it does not have the memorable qualities of her best short fiction. In a decade when, according to H. G. Wells, "Short stories broke out everywhere," D'Arcy's talent seems to have been for the concentrated, focused effect of that genre rather than the more expansive development of the novel.

The entire contents of *Modern Instances* initially appeared in the *Yellow Book*. Unlike *Monochromes,* which contains stories of mixed quality, the short stories in D'Arcy's second collection are of a consistently high caliber and show the author at her most mature. Their naturalistic realism left the *Athenaeum* (23 July 1898) complaining about the "cheerless episodes and squalid emotions" represented but admitting that the stories were "carefully studied, vividly portrayed, and show the hand of a practised writer." Themes touched on in D'Arcy's earlier work are again apparent in *Modern Instances.* The

study of courtship and marriage begun in "Irremediable" is taken up in "At Twickenham," "A Marriage," and "An Engagement."

"At Twickenham" tells of a young woman's engagement to a doctor who breaks with her after discerning that she is interested only in his position. "A Marriage" relates how a young man's meek mistress exercises a domestic tyranny over him once they are married. Both are harsh studies of middle-class, philistine mediocrity that portray women as shallow, vapid, and potentially cruel; both contributed to critics' beliefs that D'Arcy perceived her own sex negatively and blamed women for most failed relationships.

Mix observes that "unlike many men authors of the period, who portrayed gentle femininity trampled by the male's unprincipled brutality, Miss D'Arcy showed the superior and well-intentioned man caught in the snare of a designing or stupid woman." Stanford describes D'Arcy's female characters as "trivial though terrible harpies ... who ruthlessly exploit and destroy their men"; William C. Frierson goes so far as to claim that "criticism of her sex was [D'Arcy's] only vital literary motive." Yet Burdett makes what is perhaps the most significant observation: that D'Arcy "saw all her women through masculine eyes." Certainly the perspective of male characters accounts for the most scathing indictments of women in these stories.

Critics have seldom considered the possibility that D'Arcy's point of view might deviate from that of her characters. Catterson, the hapless husband in "A Marriage," laments, "Marriage is the metamorphosis of women – the Circe wand which changes back all these smiling, gentle, tractable little girls into their true forms"; he concludes that perhaps he ought not to have married his mistress because "women require to be kept under, to be afraid of you, to live in a condition of insecurity; to know that their good fortune is dependent on their good conduct." Catterson's wife is bossy, insensitive, and cruel to their son, but clearly only Catterson's weakness keeps him from being a male tyrant every bit the equal of his wife; weakness indeed led him to marry the mistress whom he had formerly taken advantage of because "he could think of no easier way out of the dilemma." His unhappy marriage is as much his fault as hers, and his bitter perspective does not make him a disinterested judge of women in general. Doctor Matheson in "At Twickenham" provides a more just, though hardly more positive, assessment, noting that his fiancée, "like most other girls [is] a victim to her upbringing." His observation suggests that D'Arcy's purpose in portraying

Portrait of D'Arcy by P. Wilson Steer that the author called "brutal" (British Library)

the ambitious Doctor Owen, introduced in "Poor Cousin Louis," woos a Channel Islands girl whom he believes has money. He then finds a pretext under which to break his engagement when he discovers she will be an impediment rather than an aid to his success. As in "The Elegie," the heroine dies at the end of this tale. But while the portrayal of the young girl, Agnes Allez, is sympathetic, "An Engagement" avoids sentimentality and thus in many ways serves to measure D'Arcy's development as a realist.

Agnes, unlike Schoenemann's fiancée, Marie, does not die committed to and believing in her lover, but disillusioned and understanding that he has abandoned her because of her connections with trade, connections that would keep him from being received in the best circles of Island society. Furthermore, she does not die romantically of a broken heart, but prosaically of heatstroke. The narrative offers no mitigating portrait of shallow or vicious womanhood to justify Owen's treatment of the girl; Agnes is in fact the kind of sweet, highly desirable female whom Catterson thought he was marrying in "A Marriage": a woman submitting "with ready abnegation of her pleasure where it clashed with [her lover's] interests." Yet "An Engagement," far from valorizing this type of heroine, only shows how the society that has created her sets her up for victimization. The "harpies" of D'Arcy's other stories at least survive.

While the first three stories in *Modern Instances* focus on the theme of courtship and marriage, others in the collection explore the psychology of evil. "The Web of Maya," another tale set in the Channel Islands, tells of the aristocrat Le Mesurier's impulse to kill his estranged wife's mentor, whom he believes has intellectually seduced her by persuading her "to go and live in London . . . to complete her education, to develop her individuality, and a lot of damned rot of that sort." After murdering his enemy, he passes through stages of gladness, obsession, remorse, and finally despair – only to discover that the murder was a delusion, a kind of waking dream brought on by his reclusive life. Such a conclusion borders on the amateurish, but D'Arcy saves it by her chilling portrayal of Le Mesurier's revived hatred after he discovers his enemy is still alive.

The power of hatred and evil is combined with a study of fear in "The Villa Lucienne," a first-person narrative about a visit to a villa that seems to be haunted. This French local-color sketch emphasizes plot less than mood; it hints at, but does not provide, answers to account for the terror experi-

the shallowness of middle-class Englishwomen and their values was less to attack any innate deficiencies she saw in her sex than to reveal the social conditions that can turn a female into a "trivial though terrible harpy" – and that can thus victimize men as well as women.

Critics who claim D'Arcy's women are always the villains seem to have deliberately overlooked portraits such as that in "An Engagement," in which enced by the protagonist/narrator and her friends. Paradoxical relationships between evil and good, and ugliness and beauty, are explored in "The Death Mask," which describes the revelations evident in the physiognomy of a great literary artist — the Master — after his death. The narrator notes that the Master's works are evidence of his "beautiful soul"; in a certain light his death mask reflects this nobility, but viewers are shocked that a change of light reveals the artist's corrupt life in a face described as "hideously bestial." The coexistence of nobility and corruption seems partially, though not fully, explained by the Master's decadent ideology. The narrator states that the Master "never denied his vices: he recognized them, and found excuses for them, high moral reasons even, as the intellectual man can always do. To indulge them was but to follow out the dictates of Nature, who in herself is holy; cynically to expose them to the world was but to be absolutely sincere." On one level the story seems to offer D'Arcy's commentary on the Decadents of her own time, recognizing both their genius and their perversity. On another level it celebrates that art which is able to capture the paradox of a great personality — in this case the art of Peschi, the maker of the Master's death mask.

The kind of twisted morality that characterizes the Master's philosophy in "The Death Mask" is also the subject of "Sir Julian Garve," where, in order to preserve his "honor," an English aristocrat murders the naive, sympathetic American who recognizes his trick of cheating at cards. The story is a well-handled exercise in wit and understatement; the murder comes as a surprise to the reader as much as to the victim. The story also gives interesting insights into stereotypes about Jews, Englishmen, and Americans prevalent at the end of the nineteenth century. The *Athenaeum* (23 July 1898) applauded the story and its murder "as a lively and refreshing performance," the favorite in the collection.

Modern Instances and *The Bishop's Dilemma* are the last books of fiction that D'Arcy published. The end of the *Yellow Book* — whose passing she noted by observing, "We were all a little tired of it" — has also traditionally been seen as the end of D'Arcy's career. After Lane's marriage D'Arcy left England, eventually settling in Paris. She was followed there by Charlotte Mew, whom she had met in conjunction with the *Yellow Book* and to whom she had introduced French literature. Mew was in love with D'Arcy and even named the compelling heroine of her short story "Some Ways of Love" after her, but D'Arcy, described by Fitzgerald as "a warm-

blooded, clever, unreliable man's woman," was not interested in a lesbian relationship. She dismissed the unhappy Charlotte with the rather ambiguous observation, "One acts foolishly in order to write wisely — *non é vero?*"

D'Arcy continued to "write wisely" in the post-*Yellow Book* years, though her publications became rare. In November 1899 the *Century* published "Our Lady of Antibes," the tale of how Peschi, the Genoese sculptor who first appeared in "The Death Mask," woos and eventually wins the capricious French girl of his dreams. More than just a love story, "Our Lady" treats issues of domestic violence and male assumptions about what it means to be a "true woman." After the turn of the century, tracing D'Arcy's periodical publications becomes increasingly difficult; her final short stories are probably those published in the *English Review* from 1909 to 1910. Themes and scenes from her works of the 1890s reemerge in these stories: the self-absorbed artist, the unhappy marriage, the questionable religious vocation, Europe, and the Channel Islands. Yet the angle from which these subjects and places are treated is often different, the perspective new, the dimension deeper than in her earlier fiction.

D'Arcy returns to an examination of Catholicism in "Agatha Blount" (June 1909) and "From the Chronicles of Hildesheim" (November 1909). The former tells the story of Sister Marie des Agnes/Agatha Blount, who leaves the convent after twelve years, hoping to marry and realize the great joy of being a mother. A young Protestant shows an interest in marrying Agatha, partly because of her cloister-bred submissiveness, but backs out after learning the convent will not return her six-thousand-pound dowry. Upon her father's death Agatha's family is left in straitened circumstances; Agatha feels she is not wanted; and, after hearing herself described as "old" by "two or three Catholic young men of the usual type," she decides to return to the convent — a return that is clearly a defeat. In this rather brutal study of life in both cloister and high society, D'Arcy treats the latent homoeroticism and self-righteous intolerance sometimes present in religious communities, the shame of the family whose child fails in vocation, and the problem of the unmarriageable daughter. For Agatha, at least, the religious life is ultimately not a spiritual calling but an escape from a world where she is a social misfit.

"From the Chronicles of Hildesheim," which purports to be the retelling of an old legend, describes a young monk's holiness and his temptation. The narrative, full of the miracles and superstitions of medieval Germany, is fanciful, but its insights into the psychology of sexual repression and temptation are acute. The holy and innocent Brother Angelo unintentionally conjures a naked witch – in the form of the mayor's voluptuous wife – from out of the clouds. When his robe is later discovered in her bedroom, he confesses that he desired, but did not sleep with, the woman; he is nonetheless put to death at the stake.

These events are commented upon by a contemporary narrator, from the distance of "three long sad hundred years," who notes that "the citizens of Hildesheim never had a moment's doubt on the subject, nor did the cloud-witches make any severe tax on their credulity. . . . What, judging from their own hearts, they could not believe in, was the living presence of Christ, or the boy's strength to refrain." With cutting irony the narrator concludes that Frau Margaretha, the mayor's wife, "died in the odour of sanctity fifty years later, fortified by all the rites of Holy Church." With its picturesque symbolism, "The Chronicles of Hildesheim" is more successful than the naturalistic *The Bishop's Dilemma* in treating the demands of celibacy and the nature of guilt.

The themes of art and the unhappy marriage are combined in "Every Day Brings a Ship" (February 1910). In this story gender roles are reversed from what they are in D'Arcy's short stories of the 1890s: the woman, not the man, is the great artist; the woman, not the man, has married an intellectual and artistic inferior. This gender reversal changes the plot significantly: Anna von Ciriacy, a famous opera singer, must leave Vienna and give up her artistic career to marry, a sacrifice not demanded of men. This results in constant regret on Anna's part and, indeed, undermines her marriage. Bored, she tries to arrange a romance for her husband's cousin Rosa, only to discover after her husband is killed in a hunting accident that this same cousin was in love with him and carries his child.

Anna's artistic sacrifice pales before the emotional sacrifice of Rosa; only when confronted with her husband's death and Rosa's grief can Anna convince herself that she, too, actually loved him. Though not as prevalent as in "The Chronicles of Hildesheim," D'Arcy's use of symbols is again notable. The snow falling at the opening of the story seems representative of Anna's ennui and depression; its cessation and the "great and glorious Sun," which "pour[s] down, once more, life and joy upon the earth" the morning after Ciriacy's death, concludes the story on a sadly ironic note. "Every Day Brings a Ship" is a polished work of fiction, though the reader anticipates the real state of relations at the Ciriacy estate long before Anna does.

Sacrifice also determines the life of the heroine in "An Enchanted Princess" (December 1910), a local-color sketch of the Channel Islands. The work is filled with various anecdotes and descriptions of place, all childhood memories of the first-person narrator. The central episode focuses on a story told by the elderly spinster Miss Murray, whom the children liked to believe was an enchanted princess waiting for the kiss that would make her young and beautiful again. Miss Murray tells the tale of a young woman who decides she cannot run away with her sweetheart to America because of the grief and anger it will cause her family. Even as a child, the narrator suspects this is Miss Murray's own story.

Margaret D. Stetz has argued in "Turning Points: Ella D'Arcy" (1986) that the story evokes a "pathos" for the situation of the "undeservedly unhappy" heroine who sacrifices her desires for her family. Stetz claims that Miss Murray believes every "true woman" will regret having "renounced her opportunities for escape from the domestic circle." While the grandparents who raised Miss Murray do make uncompromising and perhaps unfair demands based on their beliefs about what a dutiful woman owes her family, Stetz fails to recognize that in leaving them to elope with her lover, Miss Murray would merely have stepped from one domestic circle into another. That Miss Murray never hears from her lover again suggests that his demands on her would have been no less unreasonable than those of her family. She admits to the children that the young girl in her story was later "terribly sorry" she did not go with her sweetheart – but that does not necessarily mean he was the prince who could have spared her life's wicked enchantments.

The elderly heroine, who is not afraid to "dissent from a universally accepted opinion," who passes judgment on English colonization by calling India "one vast graveyard, to which we journey with infinite toil and trouble, merely to lay our bones beneath its soil," and who has come to terms with her own fate, saves the story from an excessive sentimentality that the narrator's nostalgia tends to evoke. This story, apparently D'Arcy's last published tale, is reminiscent of American writer Sarah Orne Jewett in its quaint portraiture and local color and suggests that as D'Arcy moved further away from the 1890s her realism became less dogmatically naturalistic. With her increasing use of symbols, D'Arcy's later works show the influence of the French symbolists she so admired; in this respect they exhibit some of the tendencies of modernist fiction.

15 rue Jacob. Paris.
30th June 1930

Dear Katherine Mix,

Very glad to see your pretty writing
again, and to get so charming a letter from
you.   We must try to meet in the autumn,
though not in Paris I hope.   I am so very
tired of Paris, although I enjoy an excellent bed here which I may not find elsewhere.   Ah, the odious English beds! What
a strange thing it is that the practical Briton
has never learned the comfort of a good bed.
Any more than he has ever learned to
appreciate great poetry or fine literature.

We made a mistake you and I in our
choice of a subject. The Y.B. is abhorrent
to our Jix. ridden crowd... Rimbaud more
than anathema. That he is by far
the greatest of poets, of any age of any

Letter from D'Arcy to Katherine Mix, a friend of many Yellow Book *contributors, 30 June 1930 (Pennsylvania State University Libraries)*

How far D'Arcy would have gone in this direction is hard to say, since her output after 1900 is so small. The *Yellow Book* provided a forum and its editors a constant encouragement that D'Arcy found nowhere else; during its brief tenure D'Arcy flourished. Thereafter the literary climate and personal circumstances seemed to limit her production. Indeed, to some extent her character worked against her, even during the *Yellow Book* years. Netta Syrett, whose family D'Arcy was close to, called her "the laziest woman I ever met," recounting in her autobiography, *The Sheltering Tree* (1939), how, when D'Arcy visited her in Paris, Syrett locked her in her room to work. "Instead," writes Syrett, "she read French novels on the balcony, and when I released her, merely laughed and owned she hadn't even taken up her pen." Apparently, locking up D'Arcy was a recourse to which more than one of her friends resorted; on another occasion Harland is also said to have imprisoned her until she finished a story for the *Yellow Book*.

What those who knew her termed "laziness" may in fact be traceable to other aspects of D'Arcy's life and character. She took editorial criticism and rejection very hard. She withheld one book from publication – perhaps the life of Percy Bysshe Shelley she had long been contemplating – because, as she wrote to Lane in March 1896, Harland told her it was "a rotten book the publication of which can only damage my literary reputation." Despite Arnold Bennett's interest in seeing a manuscript of a novel by D'Arcy, she refused to let him consider it, because it had been turned down by another publisher. D'Arcy's sensitivity to rejection may have manifested itself not only in refusal to display work that had been harshly criticized or rejected, but also in a writer's block her friends and acquaintances interpreted as laziness.

D'Arcy's continual money problems also contributed to her meager output. Her letters to Lane are a constant refrain of money woes, and she asserts directly that such worries hinder her writing. With some comic exaggeration she relates in a January 1895 letter, "As I am no longer able to pay my way, the Count [her landlord] has reduced my rations to bread and water, and next week he threatens to knock off the bread. Water is a poor diet on which to write." The sense of humor that usually characterizes even her complaints fails her, however, in a 5 April 1897 letter where she haggles with Lane over a fifty-pound advance. After threatening to sell her literary wares elsewhere if Lane will not come through, she laments:

Why on earth I shouldn't have a Civil Pension £200 I don't see, just as much as W. [William] Watson. I've just as much talent as he, in my own way, and I have not his fortune of £14,000. I've an income which falls a long way short of £100. And the difficulties, the anxieties, and the worries in which I swim, are quite enough to prevent me from doing any original & good work, which always must demand a certain peace & detachment of mind.

D'Arcy's situation exemplified the dilemma of the woman writer, whom Virginia Woolf would insist needed five hundred pounds a year and a room of her own. D'Arcy certainly never got the five hundred pounds a year (there are indications she would have been happy with considerably less), and the rooms in which she settled were always temporary and always in cheap boardinghouses. Her precarious financial status haunted her throughout her life, denying her the "peace and detachment of mind" she felt necessary to do good work and resigning her, according to Fitzgerald, to a "melancholy inertia" in which she settled for small, insignificant literary jobs. She confessed in a letter to Lane (13 April 1897) that "I have none of the vanity popularly attributed to authors . . . I don't care a hang whether I'm ever published or not," but "I do care for money, having none." Had she had more money, she might have cared more about her writing career.

Yet Lane did not entirely forget her after their *Yellow Book* adventures of the 1890s. She wrote him several times about a Shelley biography she had begun – or hoped to begin – titled "Life's Great Cheat," and, remembering her enthusiastic interest, he commissioned her to do a translation of André Maurois's *Ariel* (1923), which appeared as *Ariel: The Life of Shelley* (1924). D'Arcy was further motivated to translate the works of French poet Arthur Rimbaud, but she could not find a publisher. In June 1930 she wrote Mix in frustration:

That [Rimbaud] is by far the greatest of poets, of any age of any country says nothing to them. He was a rebel, a communist, which is enough to ensure their contempt. . . . [Rimbaud] I have quite put aside for the present. It is no good running one's head against a stone wall, is it? There was not a publisher, nor an editor in London, who could hear his name without turning purple from hair roots to collar.

D'Arcy's work on Rimbaud was never published.

The philistinism that infuriated D'Arcy as she sought an English backer for her Rimbaud project was disillusioning after having worked with the Bodley Head in the 1890s. Her own generation disappointed her. In the same letter in which she lamented about Rimbaud, she complained, "Rebels once, perhaps, as well get on in years, they become tax payers, fathers of families, take tea on Sundays with Mrs. Grundy, and expiate the courage of their youth by trying to exterminate all free thought in the young people of today." D'Arcy never ceased being the rebel who had fit so well into the *Yellow Book* crowd. Mix described her in her last years as "a bright and witty talker with sharp comments about life" and hair dyed "a dreadful red orange"; she lived in Paris and spent her days at "the Cafe des Deux Magots, drinking bock and watching the young Bohemians stroll by." Her financial troubles were never relieved, and when she died at the Saint Pancras Institution in London on 5 September 1937, her situation was no better than it had been when, in the 1890s, she was writing her half-playful, half-desperate letters about money to Lane.

D'Arcy's influence as a practitioner of realism and the short story has been unquestionably mitigated by her limited output; the sketchy facts known about her life have kept her from emerging in histories of the 1890s as the vivid figure she undoubtedly was to her contemporaries. Yet the memories of those who knew her, as well as her own letters and fiction, present a warmhearted, free-spirited woman, a thoughtful writer, and a self-conscious local colorist. She was an astute student of human psychology and behavior who, like many of her *Yellow Book* colleagues, was critical of her society and some of its most sacred institutions. Those who have labeled D'Arcy primarily a denigrator of her own sex have failed to credit the diversity of her subjects and her use of point of view. Both praised for its psychological realism and criticized for its dogmatic naturalism, D'Arcy's short fiction remains representative of the time in which it was composed and the literary milieu that surrounded Lane and the *Yellow Book*. Considering the prominent role this periodical played in the 1890s, it would be wrong to underestimate the significance of a writer such as D'Arcy, who committed so much of her work and energy to its pages and thereby helped to shape literary practice at the end of the nineteenth century.

Letters:
Some Letters to John Lane, edited, with an introduction, by Alan Anderson (Edinburgh: Tragara, 1990).

Bibliography:
Benjamin Franklin Fisher IV, "Ella D'Arcy: A Commentary with an Annotated Primary and Secondary Bibliography," *English Literature in Transition,* 35, no. 2 (1992): 179–211.

References:
Karl Beckson, *Henry Harland: His Life and Work* (London: Eighteen Nineties Society, 1978);

Osbert Burdett, *The Beardsley Period: An Essay in Perspective* (London: John Lane, 1925);

Benjamin Franklin Fisher IV, "Ella D'Arcy, First Lady of the Decadents," *University of Mississippi Studies in English,* new series 10 (1992): 238–249;

Penelope Fitzgerald, *Charlotte Mew and Her Friends* (Reading, Mass.: Addison-Wesley, 1988);

William C. Frierson, *The English Novel in Transition* (Norman: University of Oklahoma Press, 1942);

Helmut Gerber, ed., *The English Short Story in Transition, 1880–1920* (New York: Western, 1967);

Katherine Mix, *A Study in Yellow: The Yellow Book and Its Contributors* (Lawrence: University of Kansas Press, 1960);

Derek Stanford, *Short Stories of the Nineties* (London: Baker, 1968);

Margaret D. Stetz, "Turning Points: Ella D'Arcy," *Turn-of-the-Century Woman,* 3 (Summer 1986): 1–14;

Netta Syrett, *The Sheltering Tree* (London: Geoffrey Bles, 1939);

H. G. Wells, Introduction to his *The Country of the Blind, and Other Stories* (London & New York: Nelson, 1911).

Papers:
D'Arcy's letters to John Lane are in the William Andrews Clark Memorial Library at the University of California; her correspondence with Katherine Mix is in the Pennsylvania State University Libraries.

Ernest Dowson

(2 August 1867 – 23 February 1900)

R. K. R. Thornton
University of Birmingham

See also the Dowson entry in *DLB 19: British Poets, 1880–1914.*

BOOKS: *A Comedy of Masks,* 3 volumes, by Dowson and Arthur Moor, (London: Heinemann, 1893);

Dilemmas: Stories and Studies in Sentiment (London: Elkin Mathews, 1895; New York: Stokes, 1895);

Verses (London: Smithers, 1896);

The Pierrot of the Minute: A Dramatic Phantasy in One Act (London: Smithers, 1897; Portland, Maine: Mosher, 1913);

Adrian Rome, by Dowson and Moore (London: Methuen, 1899; New York: Holt, 1899);

Decorations: In Verse and Prose (London: Smithers, 1899).

Editions and Collections: *The Poems of Ernest Dowson* (Portland, Maine: Mosher, 1902);

The Poems of Ernest Dowson, edited, with a memoir, by Arthur Symons (London & New York: John Lane, 1905);

Cynara: A Little Book of Verse (Portland, Maine: Mosher, 1907);

Poems and Prose of Ernest Dowson, edited, with a memoir, by Symons (New York: Boni & Liveright, 1919);

Complete Poems of Ernest Dowson (New York: Medusa Head, 1928);

The Poetical Works of Ernest Dowson, edited by Desmond Flower (London: John Lane/Cassell, 1934; Rutherford, N.J.: Fairleigh Dickinson University Press, 1970);

The Stories of Ernest Dowson, edited by Mark Longaker (Philadelphia: University of Pennsylvania Press, 1947; London: Allen, 1947);

The Poems of Ernest Dowson, edited by Longaker (Philadelphia: University of Pennsylvania Press, 1962).

TRANSLATIONS: Emile Zola, *La Terre* (London: Lutetian Society, 1894);

Ernest Dowson

Louis Couperus, *Majesty,* translated by Dowson and A. Teixeira de Mattos (London: Unwin, 1894);

Richard Muther, *The History of Modern Painting,* 3 volumes, translated by Dowson, George A. Greene, and Arthur C. Hillier (London: Henry, 1895–1896);

Honoré de Balzac, *La Fille aux yeux d'or* (London: Smithers, 1896);

Pierre Choderlos de Laclos, *Les Liaisons dangereuses* (London: Privately printed, 1898);

Dowson and a group of friends at Queen's College, Oxford. He is standing, second from right.

Voltaire, *La Pucelle,* 2 volumes (London: Lutetian
    Society, 1899);
Paul Lacroix, *Memoirs of Cardinal Dubois,* 2 volumes
    (London: Smithers, 1899);
Edmond and Jules de Goncourt, *The Confidantes of a
    King: The Mistresses of Louis XV,* 2 volumes
    (London & Edinburgh: Foulis, 1907);
The Story of Beauty and the Beast (London & New
    York: John Lane, 1908 [1907]) – probably a
    false attribution.

Ernest Dowson is frequently considered to be
the archetypal Decadent poet, the quintessence of
1890s writing, as much because of the details of his
life as for the nature of his art. He is taken to represent the self-destructive figure who writes lyrics
lamenting the loss of a virginal ideal and who is destroyed by his own self-consciousness and the realization that his ideal is both impossible and necessary. Although it ignores his capacity for hard
work, in some ways the description is not far from
the mark; but he considered his main interest to be
prose rather than poetry ("I have never done any
more than play with verse," he wrote to his friend

Charles Sayle on 1 April 1889), and he indeed put a
lot of effort into crafting stories in which ideas that
find expression in his poems also shape a distinctive, delicate, and memorable prose, until recently
unjustly ignored in favor of his poetry and personal
life.

Ernest Christopher Dowson was born on 2
August 1867 at Lee, Kent (now part of Lewisham,
southeast of London), the first child of Alfred and
Annie Swan Dowson. His family offered a cultured
background, and, at the time of Ernest's birth, it
seemed well off and leisured. Alfred had inherited
Bridge Dock in the Limehouse district of London,
and it was let to the Dry Dock Corporation of London, bringing in sufficient funds to give him social
standing and the chance to travel abroad, increasingly in pursuit of better health. The family had
connections to several literary figures. Alfred
Dommett was Alfred Dowson's uncle. The "Waring" of a poem by Robert Browning, Dommett
wrote poetry and became prime minister of New
Zealand. Alfred Dowson also knew Browning, as
well as Dante Gabriel Rossetti, George Meredith,
and Robert Louis Stevenson.

Alfred Dowson met Stevenson in 1873 at the Hotel du Pavillon in Menton, France, where they had gone because both suffered from consumption. Stevenson wrote that "I have made myself indispensable to the Dowsons' little boy (æt.6.), a popularity that brings with it its own fatigues as you may fancy; and I have been fooling about with him all afternoon, playing dominoes, and learning geography with him, and carrying him on my back a little." The Dowsons were interested in art, music, and especially literature. Alfred wrote a bit; the only known result is a translation and amplification of Frederick Fitzroy Hamilton's *Bordighera and the Western Riviera* (1883). In *Ernest Dowson* (revised version of 1967), Mark Longaker includes a letter from Alfred's brother-in-law Lewis Swan to Swan's daughter, stating that "Alfred tried to write for magazines, but his stories were always 'returned with thanks,' and did manage to get some accepted in a penny magazine eventually."

Ernest's education was probably provided by his father (who did some volunteer teaching in the East End of London from 1877 to 1878), either at home or on the European travels that took him mostly to the south of France but once to Italy. This education was sufficient to give him a distinctive familiarity with modern French literature and ideas, and it enabled him to matriculate to Queen's College, Oxford, in 1886. He left after five terms without taking a degree. His weariness with life was evident even at Queen's, but he made friendships there, particularly with Arthur Moore, with whom he was to collaborate on two published novels and others that remained unpublished and probably unfinished. He also probably got to know Lionel Johnson at Oxford. Dowson studied classical authors, particularly the poets, discussed Henry James, and read Théophile Gautier, Charles Baudelaire, Alfred de Musset, Emile Zola, Edgar Allan Poe, Arthur Schopenhauer, Olive Schreiner, and Guy de Maupassant, whom he had met. He began to write both verse and prose; his sonnet "To a Little Girl" was published by *London Society* (November 1886), which also published his poem "Moritura" (March 1887).

He reported to friends that he had prose projects under way, perhaps the early version of his never-finished "Madame de Viole," but his first prose to appear in print was "Souvenirs of an Egoist," which was published in *Temple Bar* (January 1888) and reprinted in *Dilemmas* (1895). Its plot is uninventive, being the reminiscences summoned up for a famous violinist by a barrel organ. The story recounts his journey from the gutter to his present fame and fortune, particularly his being saved by a young girl, Ninette, and his abandoning her to the orphanage of the Sœurs de la Miséricorde when offered security, education, and a Stradivarius. This tale is like a languid version of a Browning poem, concentrating the history and attitudes of an individual into a first-person account of one short period of time. Two features of the story are significant in understanding Dowson: the study of psychology and the aestheticizing of experience. Near the beginning of the story the narrator says, "I am rather an epicure of my emotions," and he remembers the comment of his patroness that "he has the true artistic sensibility. All his sensations are so much grist for his art." This is a typical blend of Victorian sentimentality moving into late-Victorian self-reflection, with its flavor of Walter Pater. The second characteristic, the tendency to value art above life, can be seen in the egoist's statement "As much as I ever cared for anything except my art, I cared for Ninette." Later he asserts that "my fiddle is my only mistress." There remains, however, the haunting sense of guilt and the suggestion that he misses Ninette, especially in the shape in which he remembers her, as a child: "I cannot conceive of her as a woman."

In a reader's report that he wrote in 1893 when the Bodley Head was considering Dowson's stories for publication, Richard Le Gallienne quite rightly commented that the "great musical composer" and another of Dowson's central figures "are very old acquaintances in fiction," adding that " 'Souvenirs of an Egoist' is a taking title, and so, I suppose, had better be left, but it suggests far more than the story fulfils." Dowson does, however, redirect the old plot to the new interest of the artist who egoistically seeks perfection of his art and whose human relationships have as their highest aim a virginal and unrealizable ideal. This is part of Dowson's pattern of thought from the beginning. In "Aesthetic Memory's Cul-de-sac: The Art of Ernest Dowson" (1992), Chris Snodgrass analyzes the effect of Schopenhauerean ideas throughout Dowson's life and work, whether in poetry or prose: "Dowson's attempts to preserve purity and 'renounce' timebound Schopenhauerian corruption take the form of the *fin-de-siède's* favourite vehicle for suspending time – the transformation of life into art, specifically turning beloveds into the equivalent of chaste and time-sequestered objects of art."

There are some overblown stories of Dowson's experiments with drink and drugs at Oxford as forms of escape from the oppressive world, but they seem founded merely on student curiosity and a morose temperament. Dowson for a while accepted the suggestion that he read for an honors degree; in March 1888 he began the examinations for Honors Moderations, then suddenly refused to proceed further, leaving Oxford that month. The reason is probably a mixture of recognition that the university life and courses did not suit him, consciousness that he was not doing well in examinations, perhaps an idea that he simply wanted to be a writer and that the university did not help him in that, and the decline in the family's fortunes. Bridge Dock had not been modernized to keep up with changes in shipbuilding and was not bringing in significant revenue. When the company renting the dock went bankrupt in 1888, the family had to take over the management, in which Ernest took his share.

At Oxford, Dowson had begun to collaborate on novels with Moore; they generally took alternate chapters. In April 1889 they finished a book called "The Passion of Dr. Ludovicus" (significantly, at one point Dowson suggested the title "The Deathly Dilemma of Dr. Ludovicus"), which was offered to several publishers but was never published. They went on to write a book called "Felix Martyr," which was probably never finished and certainly never published. Dowson continued another novel, "Madame de Viole," which was never published. The collaboration finally saw print in the novels *A Comedy of Masks* (1893) and *Adrian Rome* (1899).

Apart from the help he gave his father in the Dock, Dowson decided early on a career in literature, which he began to pursue seriously. He became for a time in 1889 the assistant editor of the *Critic,* a journal for which he reviewed plays. He also became the "special correspondent for all Music Halls" and enjoyed aspects of his editorship, though the periodical tottered toward collapse until it merged with *Society* in 1890. While Dowson was with the *Critic* he was sending his stories to magazines, and "The Diary of a Successful Man" appeared in *Macmillan's* magazine (February 1890).

Like his first story, this has a first-person singular, continuous present form, this time in the form of a diary. The story is not remarkable for its energy, though it does have a fastidious precision of phrase, as when the diarist suggests that at his time of life he had better keep out of cathedrals because "they are vault-like places, pregnant with rheumatism." The plot is crude, and the aim is obviously to create the final dilemma. The reader learns by stages that two staunch friends, in love with the same woman, each received a letter from her. The narrator's letter told him that she loved the other, so he left to marry someone else and take up a ca-

reer at the Indian bar, which has made him "disgustingly prosperous."

Now a widower, he goes back to the places associated with his early love, discovering that he and his friend each received the letter meant for the other, and that the woman they loved, in response to his unexplained leaving, has sought consolation in religion. She has become one of the Dames Rouges, a religious order of strict austerity and isolation, whose only contact with the rest of the world is that their singing can be heard in the cathedral. His conclusion that "a certain candle of hope, of promise, of pleasant possibilities, which had flickered with more or less light for so many years, had suddenly gone out and left me in utter darkness" emphasizes his view that life is rescued from the purely mechanical only by hopes that are themselves unsustainable.

Le Gallienne commented that this story was "probably the most original" of the four on which he reported, but he rather unperceptively thought that the title had "no true relation to the story." He missed its irony, which reinforces the story's examination of the true nature of success and whether it can be found at all in conventional love relationships or even in the world. Not long before the story was sent to *Macmillan's,* Dowson was conducting what he called, in a 6–7 April 1889 letter to Moore, an "episode" with a young barmaid whom he insisted on calling Lena. This was a platonic association, but he worried lest "what I am doing may not be almost as unaesthetic as a vulgar seduction." As Snodgrass notes, Dowson always tried to aestheticize relationships and memory.

Two important events for Dowson marked the early years of the 1890s, which otherwise was a period of settling down to work in the Dock, meeting friends, and writing. First, a little girl whom he found in a Polish restaurant in Soho became more and more an obsession with him. Adelaide Foltinowicz, the daughter of the proprietor, came to embody all his idealisms about innocence and purity, and his image of her remained with him and inspired him, even though she eventually married a waiter. Second, and perhaps because of disappointments in his relationship with her, he became a Roman Catholic, being received into the church on 25 September 1891. His attachment to this faith was as idealistic and aestheticizing as his love for Adelaide. In *The Trembling of the Veil* (1922), William Butler Yeats states that Dowson's religion "had certainly no dogmatic outline, being but a desire for a condition of virginal ecstasy." Arthur Symons makes a similar assessment about Dowson's devotion to Adelaide in the memoir prefaced to *The Poems of Ernest Dowson* (1905): "In the case of Dowson ... there was a sort of virginal devotion, as to a Madonna; and I think, had things gone happily, to a conventionally happy ending, he would have felt (dare I say?) that his ideal had been spoilt."

Dowson began to increase his circle of literary and artistic friends. He frequented the Rhymer's Club, formed in 1891, where he met writers such as Yeats, Symons, Le Gallienne, Oscar Wilde, Lionel Johnson, and Herbert Horne. The last of these was the editor of the *Century Guild Hobby Horse,* a magazine of small circulation but large reputation with those at the center of things, and Dowson's work profited from the confidence Horne showed in his work. In 1891 Horne published four of Dowson's poems and one story, including the poem "Non sum qualis eram bonae sub regno Cynarae" (April), which is often said to embody the essence of the period, to be *the* poem of the Decadence. Dowson felt that it was a daring thing to publish, as he wrote in a letter to Samuel Smith (March 1891): "I have seen the proofs of my 'Cynara' poem for the April Hobby. It looks less indecent in print, but I am still nervous! though I admire Horne's audacity."

Its morality appears to be at odds with his story "A Case of Conscience," published in the same issue, which agonizes over behavior, though in fact they both recount faithfulness to an ideal. The story takes a new direction in that it is a third-person narrative, but the personae are similar to those in his previous stories: Sebastian Murch, an artist past forty, and a young, simple, and innocent girl; the setting is Brittany. The artist intends to marry the girl, who loves him, but the bulk of the story consists of an argument with his friend Tregellan over whether he would be right to marry her. The first part of the argument is whether she, belonging to an ordered world, could possibly be happy in his "world without definitions, where everything is an open question." The second part of the argument is that he is divorced, and, as Tregellan tells Sebastian, Roman Catholics cannot marry a divorced man: Tregellan insists that the family must be told and the relationship terminated. Sebastian accuses Tregellan of being in love with the girl, which Tregellan realizes is true. This knowledge takes away his power to act because his motives may be suspect, so he goes away from the village, leaving Sebastian to his conscience. This lack of resolution is obviously the point of *Dilemmas,* and the story neatly provides tests of conscience for both friends in their treatment of purity.

In August 1891 *Macmillan's* published "The story of a Violin," which Dowson retitled "An Orchestral Violin" when it was reprinted in *Dilemmas.* It eschews narrative in favor of first-person singular retrospect, and, after an introduction to the place (a "dining-place" rather like the Poland where his Adelaide lived) and the central character, the narrator indicates his Paterian ancestry by commenting, "I have it in my mind to set down my impressions of him." The character is another artist, a musician, a resigned and forlorn old man "in love with his violin and with his art." After a performance of *Leonora* with Madame Romanoff, the old second violinist explains that he "invented her, the Romanoff," had made friends with her because of his violin music, had taken her over as a child when her father died, and had taught her and finally let her go into the world, where she had apparently forgotten him.

On his death his violin is left to the narrator. He uses it to confront Madame Romanoff with her past and to explore her attitude toward her old guardian, but he is left in some ambiguity about the real nature of her character as well as doubt about what exactly his own motives have been. He ends the story rather like the speaker of T. S. Eliot's "Portrait of a Lady": "Have I been pusillanimous, prudent, or merely cruel? For the life of me I cannot say!" Dowson was satisfied with only parts of the story, but he thought it modern enough to suggest that he was going to call it "Fin de Siècle." He explained to Moore in an 8 June 1890 letter that it "is simply a study of the incomplete amourette of a modern whose critical sense has rather outworn his powers of action – told in the autobiographical manner of both my printed stories." Le Gallienne thought the story conventional in idea and its first title unfortunate, but its hero's lack of action looks forward to the next century.

The *Century Guild Hobby Horse* also published Dowson's "The Statute of Limitations" (January 1893; reprinted in *Dilemmas*). This story most clearly reflects Dowson's philosophical attachment to the beauty of little girls, but it is also framed as the memory of a first-person narrator giving an account of another person – almost, as he says in the first paragraph, as "the aspect of a difficult problem in psychology." The setting of the nitrate industry in Chili [*sic*] and the voyage home derive from Dowson's peripheral familiarity with international seafaring and have no remarkable clarity. The central interest in the story is whether Michael Garth – an "enraged pessimist" who has slaved for twelve years in equatorial America to earn enough to marry the "young girl, almost a child" with whom

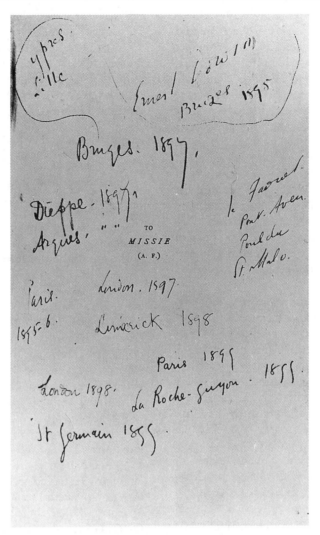

Dedication page of Dowson's copy of Dilemmas, *on which he recorded his travels*
(from Desmond Flower and Henry Maas, eds., The Letters of Ernest Dowson, *1967)*

he was in love – can face returning to the woman she has become: "The notion of the woman, which she now was, came between him and the girl whom he had loved, whom he still loved with passion, and separated them." The narrator does not know what Garth says in his last letter to his beloved, nor does he communicate to her his "private interpretation of the accident of his death," which he feels is a solution.

There are unmistakable hints of Joseph Conrad in the story; Ruth Y. Jenkins has written of this story as a source for Conrad's *Heart of Darkness* (1899). The theme of the opposition of an ideal enshrined in a little girl to the reality of the tarnished world is common in Dowson's poetry, and indeed central to his whole existence. Significantly, when five of his stories ("The Diary of a Successful Man," "A Case of Conscience," "An Orchestral Violin," "Souvenirs of an Egoist," and "The Statute of Limi-

tations") were collected and published by Elkin Mathews in 1895, this was the last one. It ends the book on a note that it is difficult to refrain from reading biographically: "May it not have been an escape for the poor devil himself, an escape too for the woman who loved him, that he chose to drop down, fathoms down, into the calm, irrecoverable depths of the Atlantic, when he did, bearing with him at least an unspoilt ideal, and leaving her a memory that experience could never tarnish, nor custom stale?" Wherever he went, Dowson took with him his copy of *Dilemmas,* which is dedicated "To *MISSIE* (A. F.)," and wrote on the dedication page the place and date.

Dowson's reputation seemed to thrive during these years, both as poet and prose writer, though he wrote to Victor Plarr in late October 1893 that he was surprised to read in the November *Bookman* that he had been "steadily making my way in literature." He published twelve poems in the 1892 and 1894 *Book of the Rhymers' Club;* finished a one-act play, *The Pierrot of the Minute,* which was performed in November 1892; and began to think of publishing a volume of poems and a volume of stories. *A Comedy of Masks,* which he wrote with Moore, was published in 1893, and Le Gallienne commented on its "success" when he was considering whether to advise publication of Dowson's stories. Dowson also began to take on the job of translation, which was to occupy a great deal of the last years of his life; his translation of Zola's *La Terre* came out in 1894. Dowson even published a story in the *Yellow Book* in October 1894, his only piece to appear in that central periodical of the decade, and one apparently out of character for the reputedly Decadent magazine.

"Apple Blossom in Brittany" returns to Dowson's invented village Ploumariel (also featured in "A Case of Conscience") and again to an older man of about forty with "a life spent in literature" and a young girl, in a religious setting (the story opens with a procession of the feast of the Assumption, in which she is involved and he is an onlooker). Marie-Ursule is Benedict Campion's ward, and her uncle the Curé suggests that Campion should marry her, which he discovers is in fact in Campion's mind. Campion puts the marriage off for a year, without telling the girl of his intentions, but before the year is up a letter from the Curé summons him back. On returning, Campion discovers that Marie-Ursule thinks she has a vocation to the Ursulines; he has not the heart to dissuade her. His dilemma can stand as an indication of the type that most interested Dowson:

> Of the two, perhaps the priest had really the more secular mind, as it certainly excelled Campion's in that practical wisdom, or commonsense, which may be of more avail than subtlety in the mere economy of life. And what to the Curé was a simple matter though, the removal of the idle fancy of a girl, might be to Campion, in his scrupulous temper, and his overweening tenderness towards just those pieties and renunciations which such a fancy implied, a task to be undertaken hardly with relish, perhaps without any real conviction, deeply as his personal wishes might be implicated in success.

Campion is the essential Dowson character "with his subtle melancholy, which made life to him almost morbidly an affair of fine shades and nice distinctions." When he finds that Marie-Ursule prefers the blossom to the apples and the cider and she asks him to decide for her between the convent and marriage, he chooses the convent, since "to lose her in that fashion was the only way in which he could keep her always." The story shares with his poem "Nuns of the Perpetual Adoration" (which in two manuscripts is called "Ursulines of the Perpetual Adoration") the notion that whatever is of value can only be preserved from life's ravages by evasion, aestheticization, or religion:

> Calm, sad, secure; with faces worn and mild:
> Surely their choice of vigil is the best?
> Yea! for our roses fade, the world is wild;
> But there, beside the altar, there, is rest.

Elements of the story – the Ursuline convent in Ploumariel, the procession of the Assumption, the name of the girl herself, and the great stone Calvary at the top of the hill from which they look down on Ploumariel – all press toward the expected end, which the beautiful impermanence of the blossom in the title adumbrates. It is likely that the story harks back to material that Dowson thought of for "Felix Martyr." In a 7 July 1889 letter to Moore, he writes of his plans for that novel: "Invitation to Madame's place in (?) Britainy [*sic*].... Other characters the village curé, charming, refined, sceptical, conforming – living with his child (niece) æt 7. (You must not blackball this character – I give you carte blanche to introduce corresponding specialities of your own)."

After the early 1890s Dowson's life began to fall apart. He failed to get jobs as librarian or secretary to a theatrical company; Adelaide's father died in April 1893; Dowson declared his intentions toward her just when the family was under great emotional strain, which made matters worse; and his first recorded tubercular attack occurred. In August 1894 his father died, and there were suspicions of suicide because of the financial state of the Dock and the advance of his tuberculosis, although the death certificate only mentions natural causes. Six months later his mother died, and this time it was suicide; she hanged herself in a fit of depression. In 1895 he left the Dock for good, with his expectation of getting money from it frustrated by legal delays (though ironically it was found after his death to be worth one thousand pounds), and his younger brother left for the United States. Dowson's life seemed more rootless than ever. He did not lack friends and acquaintances – he knew French authors such as Henry Davray, Pierre Louÿs, Jean de Tinan, and Paul Verlaine, and painters such as Henri Toulouse-Lautrec, as well as his English friends – but he needed solid friendship and found little of it. His work seemed to be reaching a wider audience: his first five stories were reprinted in *Di-*

lemmas, and the press reception was modestly encouraging, though the sales were slender. *Verses* (1896), a collection of poetry, featured a cover design by Aubrey Beardsley. It has become recognized as one of the representative books of the decade.

In 1895 Dowson met Leonard Smithers, who was to provide work, a publication outlet, and money in Dowson's later years. In 1896 Smithers started a new periodical, the *Savoy,* which replaced the *Yellow Book* as the voice of new movements in the 1890s. The *Savoy* seemed willing to accept what Dowson had to offer, and in January 1896 it published "The Eyes of Pride." The story is dedicated to Adelaide Foltinowicz and has an epigraph from Meredith's *Modern Love* (1862). In a circa 13 November 1895 letter Dowson calls it "the best I have done," with the possible exception of "Apple Blossom in Brittany." The story deals with the parting of Rosalind Lingard and Seefang, leaving him "free to his old pleasures and his old haunts, to his friends and his former wandering life, if he chose; above all, free to his art – his better passion." He considers the process of their "long quarrel" of a love, and the story quickly moves over five years during which his art is said to be better than ever and she marries the sixty-year-old Lord Dagenham. The second part of the story describes the important moment when they meet again and reexperience the passionate emotion that both brings them together and forces them apart in hostility. The story consists of two incidents of division and renunciation. The influence of Meredith is in the story as much as in the epigraph.

In April the *Savoy* published "Countess Marie of the Angels." Again a retrospective in form, its hero, Colonel Sebastian Mallory, at fifty returns to Paris and remembers particularly "a little girl, a child of fifteen, but seeming younger," and how the paths of their lives parted and she married Comte Raoul des Anges. The Count takes up bad habits and leaves Marie with her child; Mallory visits her in the family house to which she has retired. Finding how much they mean to each other, their restraint for a moment slips, but they cannot resist the power of duty: "her whole life, her education, her tradition, were stronger than his protestations, stronger than their love, their extreme sympathy, stronger than her misery." He makes the supreme gesture of leaving her. When her husband dies, Mallory leaves the army to go to Paris, and he rashly proposes to her. She explains that it is not possible and that they should be glad they have escaped from "a great madness, a certain misery": "There are some renunciations which are better

than happiness," she says, summing up much of Dowson's philosophy.

The ending lacks the studied ambiguity of the earlier stories and is less satisfactory for that, but the way the past is brought into the present reminds the reader of Dowson's earlier stories. The familiar topic is the way in which a sense of duty has blighted the lives of individuals too scrupulous to fight against it: "Had it been happier, perhaps, for him, for her, if they had been less acquiescent to circumstance, had interpreted duty, necessity – words early familiar to them – more leniently?" Mallory admits that "nature never designed me to be a man of action." Action in Dowson's stories inevitably leads to regret, and the only solution to the dilemma of the need for love while fighting the corrupting influence that that very love exerts when brought into the real world is death, a subject pursued in several of his poems.

Perhaps this philosophical yearning for death, combined with Dowson's experience of his parents' and his own fatal illness and a poetic elegance of phrasing, renders his next story so powerful. "The Dying of Francis Donne" is justifiably the most famous of Dowson's stories. It first appeared in the *Savoy* (August 1896) and takes its epigraph from the Ash Wednesday service: "*Memento homo, quia pulvis es et in pulverem reverteris*" (Remember, o man, that you are dust and will return to dust). It is called a "study," not a short story, though twentieth-century readers have no trouble with its inclusion in the genre, and deals with the thoughts of a thirty-five-year-old medical man who knows he is dying. It contrives to grasp, as so many of Dowson's stories do, the contradictory emotions and responses that make up the detail of experience:

And with his burning sense of helplessness, of a certain bitter injustice in things, a sense of shame mingled; all the merely physical dishonour of death shaping itself to his sick and morbid fancy into a violent symbol of what was, as it were, an actual *moral* or intellectual dishonour.

Francis Donne decides to meet Death in a strange land and has a brief period of almost pleasure on the coast of Finisterre. He contemplates philosophical consolations, "But what scanty consolation, in all such theories, to the poor body, racked with pain and craving peace, to the tortured spirit of self-consciousness so achingly anxious not to be lost." He contemplates Christian consolation, "a possibility like the rest"; and finally he succumbs to an "utter luxury of physical exhaustion, this calm, this release." There is a debt to Pater, both in the state-

Dowson's grave, Ladywell Cemetery, Lewisham

phrasing. Alongside the verse the book contains five prose poems, all printed for the first time.

Dowson could have been influenced by both Baudelaire and Wilde, but the pieces indicate his consciousness of the poetic possibilities of prose, which affects the stories as much as these pieces. Their topics cover familiar Dowson territory. Three of them — "The Fortunate Islands," "Markets," and "The Princess of Dreams" — set up against a fable or nursery rhyme the bitter truths of experience. There are no fortunate islands; there is no loved woman, no friend, no country to be found. The pretty maid going to market is going to sell herself; and the princess of dreams has no interest in the valiant knight who wishes to be her liberator, and she may well after all be "not even virtuous nor a princess." "Absinthia Taetra" is a pattern of hypnotic repetitions and cadences exploring a potential escape from recognition of such dismaying truths, but it repeats the disillusioned "nothing was changed." Finally "The Visit" gives a wistful account of a visit from Death, who releases the speaker from his physical and spiritual pains. Death was always for Dowson the only possible reconciler of his dilemmas:

> But all my wonder was gone when I looked again into the eyes of my guest, and I said:

> "I have wanted you all my life."

> Then said Death (and what reproachful tenderness was shadowed in his obscure smile):

> "You had only to call."

Dowson's life ended in Robert Sherard's cottage in Catford, where he was looked after for six weeks before his death on 23 February 1900.

Dowson found his theme early and did not vary substantially from it, either in verse or prose. There is no significant development in his subject or his art, but he achieved almost at once an expression of wistful, "enraged pessimism." Its manifestation in his prose works is beginning to attract an interest to balance that which is already shown in his poetry.

liness of the periods and in the quotation from the emperor Hadrian that Dowson takes (as he took other of his Latin phrases) from Pater's *Marius the Epicurean* (1885); but, as always, Dowson makes out of his limited materials a story distinctly his own.

Dowson's later years are the story of a penurious and, to some, pitiable figure moving between France and England, supported meagerly by translation work for Smithers. He did have friendships, notably for a short time with Wilde when the latter was released from prison. The response to his condition varies with the fastidiousness of the reporter, but he was at least untidy and probably disreputable. Nonetheless, he was working hard, as the number of translations testifies, and, with much help from Moore, *Adrian Rome* was finished. As if to indicate interest in both forms, in 1899 he brought out *Decorations: In Verse and Prose,* whose title he changed, while the book was in proofs, from the sentimental "Love's Aftermath" to its final aesthetic

Letters:

The Letters of Ernest Dowson, edited by Desmond Flower and Henry Maas (London: Cassell, 1967; Rutherford, N. J.: Fairleigh Dickinson University Press, 1968);

New Letters from Ernest Dowson, edited, with a preface, by Flower (Andoversford, U.K.: Whittington, 1984).

Bibliographies:

Jonathan Ramsey, "Ernest Dowson: An Annotated Bibliography of Writings About Him," *English Literature in Transition,* 14 (1971): 17–42;

G. A. Cevasco, *Three Decadent Poets, Ernest Dowson, John Gray, and Lionel Johnson: An Annotated Bibliography* (New York: Garland, 1990).

Biographies:

Victor Plarr, *Ernest Dowson, 1888–1897: Reminiscences, Unpublished Letters, and Marginalia* (London: Elkin Mathews, 1914; New York: Gomme, 1914);

Mark Longaker, *Ernest Dowson* (Philadelphia: University of Pennsylvania Press, 1944; revised, 1945, 1967).

References:

Laurence Dakin, *Ernest Dowson: The Swan of Lee* (Montreal: Warbrooke, 1972);

John Gawsworth (Terence Ian Fytton Armstrong), "The Dowson Legend," in *Essays by Divers Hands,* new series 17, edited by E. H. W. Meyerstein (London: Oxford University Press, 1938); republished as *The Dowson Legend* (London: Milford, 1939);

Wendell V. Harris, *British Short Fiction in the Nineteenth Century: A Literary and Bibliographic Guide* (Detroit: Wayne State University Press, 1979);

Ruth Y. Jenkins, "A Note on Conrad's Sources: Ernest Dowson's 'The Statute of Limitations' as Source for *Heart of Darkness,*" *English Language Notes,* 24 (March 1987): 39–42;

John R. Reed, "Bedlamite and Pierrot: Ernest Dowson's Esthetic of Futility," *ELH,* 35 (1968): 94–113;

Reed, "From Aestheticism to Decadence: Evidence from the Short Story," *Victorians Institute Journal,* 11 (1982–1983): 1–12; abridged in his *Decadent Style* (Athens: Ohio University Press, 1985);

Chris Snodgrass, "Aesthetic Memory's Cul-de-sac: The Art of Ernest Dowson," *English Literature in Transition,* 35 (1992): 26–53;

Derek Stanford, *Short Stories of the 'Nineties* (London: Baker, 1968);

Thomas Burnett Swann, *Ernest Dowson* (New York: Twayne, 1964);

W. R. Thomas, "Ernest Dowson at Oxford," *Nineteenth Century and After,* 103 (April 1928): 560–566.

Papers:

Longaker, Flower, and Maas refer to a manuscript of "The Eyes of Pride," but its present location is unknown. The *Letters* (1967) lists the many collections of Dowson's correspondence. The manuscript for an unpublished translation, "The Memoirs of the Duc de Richelieu," is at the Princeton University Library.

George Egerton
(Mary Chavelita Dunne Bright)
(1859 – July 1945)

Anita Moss
University of North Carolina at Charlotte

BOOKS: *Keynotes* (London: Elkin Mathews & John Lane, 1893; Boston: Roberts, 1894);
Discords (London: John Lane, 1894; Boston: Roberts, 1894);
Symphonies (London & New York: John Lane, 1897);
Fantasias (London & New York: John Lane, 1898);
The Wheel of God (London: Richards, 1898; New York: Putnam, 1898);
Rosa Amorosa: The Love Letters of a Woman (London: Richards, 1901; New York: Brentano's, 1901);
Flies in Amber (London: Hutchinson, 1905).
Edition: *Keynotes,* introduction by Martha Vicinus (New York: Virago, 1983).

TRANSLATIONS: Ola Hansson, *Young Ofeg's Ditties* (London: John Lane, 1895);
Knut Hamsun, *Hunger* (New York: Knopf, 1920).

"George Egerton" is the pseudonym of Mary Chavelita Dunne Bright, who took the name from her husband, George Egerton Clairmonte. Egerton's short fiction is scarcely known today, but her first volume, *Keynotes* (1893), engendered both extravagant contemporary praise and condemnation. With their ornate prose and echoes of Walter Pater's notions that art should capture exquisite moments as they pass away, *Keynotes* and Egerton's subsequent volumes, *Discords* (1894) and *Symphonies* (1897), reflect characteristic narrative practices of the fin de siècle period and the Decadents. With their attention toward the intense emotions, unconventional attitudes, and frankly sexual experiences of women characters, these collections of short fiction appealed to advocates of the "New Woman" and the woman-suffrage movement. Most late-twentieth-century critics comment on the dated quality of Egerton's fiction; Terence de Vere White goes so far as to say that "a recurring and dated archness is its most depressing feature." Other critics, notably Martha Vicinus and Wendell V. Harris, argue that her best fiction maintains its interest

George Egerton, circa 1897

for readers today, especially those interested in the history of the short story and the representations of women in late-nineteenth-century English fiction.

George Egerton was born Mary Chavelita Dunne in 1859 in Melbourne, Australia, the eldest daughter of John Joseph Dunne, an Irishman, and a mother (with the maiden name George) of Welsh descent. By all accounts Captain Dunne served in the British Army in New Zealand, but he left the army as a young man with few prospects, which soon disappeared altogether. Later Dunne fathered a large family that he supported primarily by depending on the generosity of others. Dismissed from two prison governorships for indebtedness, he nevertheless had many talents – drawing, singing, and acting among them. His supreme achievement was in angling, and he wrote a renowned book, *How and Where to Fish in Ireland* (1887) – the source, no doubt, of Egerton's precise details on the art of fly-fishing embedded in several of her short stories.

The children in Captain Dunne's family suffered a chaotic and highly insecure existence, often living with resentful relatives. In 1926 Egerton described her bitterness toward those who did nothing to help her family, even during the ordeal of her mother's death: "When she was in her coffin dead, not one came near – when she was taken to Rearey, and we six of us, I the eldest, were left in the house alone – they confessed and communicated and were good Catholics but did not come near." The family's house and goods were sold at auction, and Egerton was left to cope alone with younger siblings, one of whom died at the same time as her mother. When a landlady refused to take in Egerton and her sister, "two charming Quaker ladies next door sent out their maid and took us into their house for two nights. My first glimpse of a cultured, well-appointed, ordered house."

In 1875 Chavelita Dunne went away to school in Germany, her education apparently financed by a great-uncle, a naval admiral who resided in Chile. Even from the German school she continued to write letters on behalf of her siblings, and she urged her father not to leave her brothers. When her home broke up completely, the young woman tried to earn a living as a nurse in a London hospital and later tried to find employment in New York.

Meanwhile Captain Dunne attempted to impress friends and acquaintances by offering them introductions to celebrities, though he seemed ineffectual in changing his misfortunes or those of his children. Among his acquaintances was Henry Higginson, an unscrupulous man who had pursued many occupations, among them serving as chaplain to Mrs. Whyte Melville. Eventually Higginson divorced his American wife to marry Melville, but the union was not harmonious. For whatever reason she asked Captain Dunne to allow Chavelita to travel with her and her husband as a companion. After several melodramatic episodes Higginson deserted his wife and in 1887 took Chavelita to Norway, where he purchased a small estate, Slotnaes Park, at Langesund. Chavelita lived with Higginson until his death in 1889.

Although the immediate family forgave Chavelita for her shocking behavior, her more respectable relatives would have nothing more to do with her. Egerton provides an intimate and somewhat embellished account of her childhood and young womanhood in the novel *The Wheel of God* (1898). She describes the older man's proposal in some detail, though Higginson was in no position to propose to anyone, since he already had two wives and faced bigamy charges. The novel's character promises that he will only live two years at most, just as Higginson had. During that period, however, he was often drunk and violent with her, experiences that doubtless left her with the disturbing details featured in several of her short stories.

Despite the difficulties of life with Higginson, Chavelita found time to study while she lived in Norway. She learned Norwegian and read with avid, perceptive understanding such notable Scandinavian writers as Henrik Ibsen, August Strindberg, Bjørnstjerne Bjørnson, Knut Hamsun, and Ola Hansson, as well as the German philosopher Friedrich Nietzsche. Most especially she fell under the spell of Hamsun – first his novel *Hunger* (1890) and later the writer himself, apparently sharing a brief and somewhat disillusioning love affair, an experience described in the *Keynotes* story "Now Spring Has Come." Once Chavelita returned to London, she began translating Hamsun's novel *Hunger,* and by 1891 she had telegraphed her father of her marriage to Clairmonte, a native of Newfoundland lately returned from adventures in Africa. Clairmonte resembled her father – charming, handsome, athletic, and apparently incapable of honest employment. Eventually the Clairmontes' financial difficulties became so acute that they planned to immigrate to South Africa, but Chavelita decided to try to earn money by writing a few stories.

According to de Vere White, "She bought a penny exercise book and began." When she had completed some short stories, she sent them to T. P. Gill, who was at that time in charge of a literary column for the *Weekly Sun.* Gill took the writer of the stories to be a man and praised their originality in his column. Nevertheless, he found them far too frank in their appeals to passion and rejected them for publication in his paper. In a second letter, written after he had learned the writer's identity, he advised her to try publishing the stories as a volume. She followed Gill's advice and submitted them to William Heinemann, who returned the manuscript at once with a note indicating that the firm had no interest in "mediocre short stories." Fortunately for her, John Lane with Elkin Mathews at the Bodley Head had just embarked on a daring venture to publish new experimental literature and art. Her

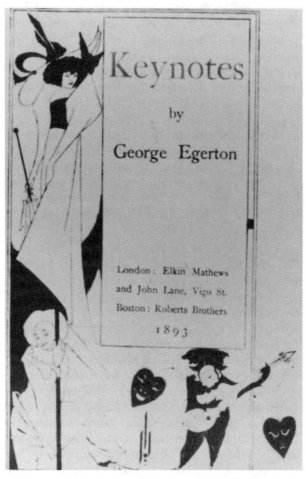

Title page, designed by Aubrey Beardsley, for Egerton's first volume of short fiction

their homes and expressed admiration for her work. She enjoyed flirtations, if not love affairs, with both Lane and Le Gallienne, yet Gill expressed some reservations about Egerton's success. In 1894 he wrote Egerton, first warning her that she should remain more aloof and reserved from celebrity scenes: "The less you emerge from the 'George Egerton' enigma – until your ground is sure – the better." Gill's second warning in the same letter was far more serious and, unfortunately, prophetic:

> Did you note the doubts – no, not doubts – the uncertainty I expressed in my review as to whether you have the large creative faculty of achieving by *imagination* independent of *experience*. Well, that is the thing you are to prove by your second book, and that is why you must be so extremely deliberate and careful. Olive Schreiner has never written a book worth reading since her *African Farm*. She put all her heart, her experience into that. The rest is bosh. Most people have one story to tell. The creative artist does not merely utter his own heart cry.

In *Keynotes* Egerton depicts intense psychological and emotional portraits of the "New Women," who rebel against the constraints of their upbringing, their lack of education, the realities of sexuality and marriage, and their limited social and economic opportunities. The women characters in *Keynotes* clearly reject conventional attitudes on virginity, religion, art, and most other social matters as well. Like the author, the characters do not value respectability or moral codes imposed by society. The best of Egerton's stories celebrate the possibilities for women to create full, enriched lives, and Gill rightly supposed that the real impetus for these stories came from Egerton's experience rather than her imagination. De Vere White similarly describes the source of her personal and literary magnetism:

> She was in love with the idea of herself – a proud and lonely being in whom sexual allure and moral earnestness were most curiously blended – an idea derived from her frustrated poverty-stricken childhood, her father's conversation larded with anecdotes of dukes, admirals and viceroys, of the grand manner of life, while reality was represented by cheap lodgings, bailiffs, and stockings without heels: an idea derived most of all, from an intense curiosity about sex in general which was unhappily wedded to a sharp, argumentative manner – the last kind of manner which is calculated to inspire a reciprocal curiosity in any particular case.

exercise-book stories made their way at last to Lane. Richard Le Gallienne, who served as a reader for the press at that time, reported enthusiastically on the stories and urged Lane to publish them at once. The author, however, had failed to include her address, and several weeks passed before she appeared at the Bodley Head in person to inquire about the status of her manuscript. Lane made immediate plans for publishing the volume, and George Egerton was born.

Keynotes was produced in a distinctive design with a cover by Aubrey Beardsley. The volume was a literary event and proved successful in England, America, Germany, and Scandinavia. Lane, quick to capitalize on public attention and commercial success, planned an entire series of books to be called the Keynotes Series, all featuring similar distinctive designs and covers by Beardsley. Hence Egerton became a celebrated literary figure almost overnight. Havelock Ellis, William Butler Yeats, and other major writers of the time invited her to

In 1894, the year after *Keynotes* created such a stir, Egerton wrote *Discords,* also published by the Bodley Head. The second volume of stories draws on similar sources of inspiration – Egerton's unconventional experiences – though some of the stories, such as "Wedlock," are much more darkly naturalistic than her previous ones. In general, however, *Discords* is a repetition of *Keynotes* and displays no real development in Egerton's literary art. *Discords* also attracted mixed reactions from reviewers, some of whom continued to be shocked that she represented the sexual feelings of women so frankly. Though the volume was not as successful as *Keynotes*, it still ran into four editions. The *Saturday Review* (26 March 1895) regretted that Egerton's second volume did not fulfill the promise of *Keynotes*. The reviewer praises the three stories that deal most naturalistically with their material – two concerning female drunkenness and the other, "Virgin Soil," depicting a seventeen-year-old girl's revulsion toward marriage, emphasizing her bitterness because her mother and society in general have kept her in ignorance as to what the facts of marriage and sexuality really are. The reviewer indicts the stories in *Discords* in which "the feminine note becomes all too evident.... The first and last of a bookful of stories are written, just as are the run of penny novelettes, about a 'She,' a wonderful heroine who goes through the tale and claims all the sympathy."

Correspondence between Lane and Egerton during this initial period suggests mutual admiration, even intimacy, but this tone and manner were to shift dramatically within a couple of years. In April 1895 Lane decided to travel to America to promote his publications. When he arrived in New York, he received the shattering news that Oscar Wilde had been arrested with a copy of the *Yellow Book*, one of Lane's key publications, under his arm. Londoners hurled stones through the windows of the Bodley Head. Lane wrote Egerton from New York that the Wilde scandal had caused him extreme worry: "I have had no peace since my arrival, nothing but cables (Oh! the expense of them!)." Eventually the scandal caused Lane to become far less adventurous as a publisher. According to one acquaintance at the time, Lane turned "morbidly suspicious and discerned a pervert behind every tree."

Egerton suffered illnesses, financial difficulties, and marital problems. A year passed before she completed her third volume of stories, *Symphonies*. By November 1896 her letters to Lane had lost their tone of coy intimacy. More seriously, Egerton seemed to have lost her earlier confidence. She wrote apologetically, even pleadingly, about Lane's comments on *Symphonies* and his insistence that she revise – his doubts in fact that he could afford to continue to publish her fiction:

> If I had only my husband and self to consider, I would not bowdlerise my poor *Symphonies*, because I would fall back on bread and tea and waiting, as I have been forced to do before now when sticking to an ideal. As I have the unfortunate little child to consider, and not a shilling in my purse, I must make a sacrifice, however resentfully I do it.

Nevertheless Egerton tried once more to please Lane. In 1898 the Bodley Head published another volume of her short stories, *Fantasias*. Dedicated to Le Gallienne, this volume lacks the vitality and originality of the first two volumes. Its five stories feature dreamers as central characters, young men and women who suffer acutely because their dreams and aspirations inevitably conflict painfully with harsh reality. In "The Star Worshipper," for example, a young lad suffers the fate of a sensitive artist trying to survive in a brutally materialistic world. Although the story is heavily allegorical rather than realistic, Egerton must have had similarly painful emotions during this time when her recent fame had begun so suddenly to diminish.

All of the stories in *Fantasias* exhibit a "once upon a time" quality, though they are not really fantasies or fairy tales. Most of the protagonists are romantics, such as the central character in "The Futile Quest," who has "a fatal quality of seeing the distant object in a halo of entrancement, whilst the next him escaped his notice altogether." The stories in *Fantasias* are essentially sentimental period pieces replete with decorative language and yearning tones. Characters do not engage in interesting dialogue but rather make pious and impassioned speeches to each other. Because of its rather obvious allegorical symbolism and its intrusive narrators characteristic of Victorian fiction, *Fantasias* offered little to interest readers of Egerton's era. *Symphonies* has similar defects, and neither volume fared well with reviewers. What had begun as an especially promising publishing venture with Lane and the Bodley Head sadly came to a close only five years later.

Egerton's most successful book in 1898 was her autobiographical novel *The Wheel of God*, which details the growth and development of an imaginative Irish girl. In the tradition of Charlotte Brontë's *Jane Eyre* (1847), *The Wheel of God* presents a kind of female bildungsroman, with a vivid picture of childhood in part 1: "The Seed in the Sheath"; of young womanhood in part 2: "The Blossom in the Bud"; and of mature womanhood in part 3: "The Ripening of the Fruit." Although the novel contributes nothing new to the already firmly established tradition of the bildungsroman in nineteenth-century British literature, it captures early childhood experience especially well. In the first chapter the reader meets the child, Mary Desmond, and learns that her favorite book is *Jane Eyre*. Much like Brontë's title character, Mary resonates to the whole world of things, beings, and particularly nature. But, perhaps like Egerton as well, Mary's senses seem to take in too much, causing an overflow of intense emotion. Presiding over this life of intense emotion and sensation is an overwhelming sense of unspeakable terror toward a powerful, vengeful God.

One of the most interesting aspects of *The Wheel of God* is the detailed, highly descriptive account of young working women in late-nineteenth-century New York. In this section Egerton conveys a compelling sense of New York's frantic pace and robust energy, as well as the young woman's loneliness in the midst of it all. Like many other female characters in the bildungsroman, Mary fails to fulfill the promise of her childhood self. In her tedious clerical job in New York, she endures poverty and boredom, conditions relieved by a mild flirtation with a law student. During her stay in New York, she also experiences fantasies or waking dreams that appear to be at once spiritual and erotic. Eventually these visions awaken a restlessness in Mary that leads her not to Dublin but to London, where she marries an emotionally immature young man, a character that George Egerton Clairmonte resented as an unfair representation of himself. Mary, again like Egerton, finds freedom and fulfillment only after the death of her irresponsible husband.

The Wheel of God ends with a vision. As Mary stands in the glow of the setting sun, she suddenly becomes aware of herself as never before, as if she knows and affirms herself for the first time. Exhilarated by this epiphany, she runs through the twilight to meet a company of women friends. Unlike *Symphonies* and *Fantasias, The Wheel of God* enjoyed splendid reviews, and it was more popular with the public, but by this time Egerton's euphoria at her success with *Keynotes* had totally diminished. Her marriage to Clairmonte had continued to deteriorate, and her financial precariousness increased. Finally, Clairmonte departed for South Africa, a venture that also failed. He returned briefly to his wife, impregnated their maid, and left for America. In 1901 Egerton divorced Clairmonte, and he died soon afterward.

After the turn of the century Egerton devoted her attention to drama, with two exceptions. She was at this time involved with a Norwegian many years her junior. In 1901 she published a version of her letters to this young lover, *Rosa Amorosa: The Love Letters of a Woman*. The letters cover a period of the writer's life (that is, the voice Egerton invents to represent her own experience) during which she explores her feelings about her distant lover and the parts they play in one another's lives. The lovers are not free to marry, and the enforced separation is a source of both pleasure and pain. The portions of the letters detailing her feelings for the lover are less interesting, however, than the woman's account of her early childhood and her views of women's emotions and their possibilities for fulfillment.

The volume presents a fairly sustained vision of childhood, one that in almost every respect resembles those of William Wordsworth and the other Romantics. Egerton records the lasting impact of sensation in childhood. The writer of the letters recalls, for example, eating a piece of apple cake in childhood, conjuring the entire ambience of the experience. Like Wordsworth, the writer of the letters apparently views growing into maturity as a loss: "I could not see a garden in the same way today, could not get that complete, perfect impression of a wondrously beautiful whole, a tender green delight, speaking to every sense and whispering of God's wonder." Also like Wordsworth, the speaker in the letters describes what Wordsworth described as "spots of time," the capacity to recover the clarity and vividness of childhood experience, a sense of being intensely alive in the present: "Sometimes now when I go to a strange place, and have thrown aside all thoughts of everyone and the responsibilities that come with human ties, I can get a sharp, clear, whole impression of a fresh scene; can throw myself into the hour and meet people with the same unquestioning trust as in the old good days! but alas! always more and more rarely." In these fictional memories Egerton represses all the unhappiness and poverty that gripped her and her siblings in childhood. Indeed the speaker omits any reference to a father at all but dwells on the perfection of the mother, invoking a kind of pre-Oedipal paradise with the mother and, by extension, with nature as mother.

In *Rosa Amorosa* as in other of Egerton's works, she rejects the narrow creed of Roman Catholicism and embraces a transcendental, Romantic view of divinity. Her remarks also suggest a close affinity with Eastern religion:

If you tell the truth to yourself, it is only in such moments of exaltation that one ever bows in actual worship – moments called up in us by beauty, joy, sorrow, or some intimate revelation in a moment of solitude, almost a turning in the lock of a universal key to open the portal of the great mystery of our cosmic being, our intimate relation to the All Spirit behind, who is never so near revealing himself as when we are alone with Nature.

Egerton also writes extensively in *Rosa Amorosa* about woman's position in society and what she believes to be woman's essential nature. She disagrees with the woman-suffrage movement on several significant issues, most particularly that devotion to work alone can bring fulfillment for women. She reserves her most scathing comments on this issue for the church:

> In the past she [woman] has been only too often a mere tool in the hands of churchmen, a lay-preacher as it were, for the propagation of their false doctrine of renunciation, their prurient teaching of chastity, and their mistaken appreciation of asceticism and the value of suppressing nature.... Under its [the church's] influence she has only accentuated the cleavage between soul and senses; and, as a result, her power has been always less than that of her coarser-fibred sister who was frankly and joyously bête-humaine. She has always been treated as an inferior by ecclesiastical authorities. Now, when she is learning to think for herself, and to see that to deprive love of all sensuousness, passion, and desire would be to emasculate and impoverish it, she will know how to assign to each of them its proper place to fashion out of them a beautiful red clay lamp to hold the flame essence of her love.

In sum, Egerton's persona in *Rosa Amorosa* envisions a Utopian transformation in the relationships between men and women, one that will bring more harmony to the relationships and perhaps transform society itself. In *Rosa Amorosa* as in her other fiction, Egerton consistently celebrates woman's possibilities for bringing inner reality to bear on the actual circumstances of her life.

In 1905 Egerton published a volume of seven short stories, *Flies in Amber*. Although this group of stories is considerably more interesting than *Fantasias*, it is not an excellent example of her work. Awkward dialogue, tedious speeches, imprecise and confusing structure, and excessive sentimentality mar the quality of her final venture into short fiction. The volume contains, however, some of Egerton's sharpest social criticism. In "How the Christ-Child Comes to the Unregenerate," for example, she includes some critical details about various religious sects – Baptists and Primitive Methodists in particular. Egerton reveals the sordid poverty in which outcast single mothers must live with their children,

and she offers a utopian vision of family and community in which divisions between husbands and wives and barriers of social class dissolve in a joyous Christmas feast.

In "Mammy" and "The Interment of Little Alice," Egerton reveals the hypocrisy of the church and society. In "A Conjugal Episode" and "The Chessboard of Guendolen," she focuses on "writing women" – their desire for independence, which often conflicts with their emotional and erotic needs. More striking than any of the other stories, "The Marriage of Mary Ascension" anticipates James Joyce's story "Eveline" in *Dubliners* (1914). Despite Mary Ascension's fine education and intelligence, she allows her father, the church, and social convention to thwart her possibilities, a process in which she participates herself. The narrator explains: "All was silent again in the girl's heart – it was numb and cold in there; and she followed passively to the sound of the triumphant church bells, dominating all sounds in the Irish town – even those that love makes in the heart of man and maid." Like flies in amber, many of the characters in these stories appear hopelessly trapped by circumstances beyond their control.

In 1901 Egerton met a young drama critic, Reginald Golding Bright, who wrote a theater column for the *Sun*. Bright was not an accomplished writer, however, and soon gave up his column to establish a drama agency. In this position he undertook to promote several of Egerton's plays. Meanwhile, she departed to Norway to visit her lover. In March 1901 she wrote to Bright from Christiania (now Oslo), explaining that her relationship with her lover had changed: "Today I am one burning pain, body, heart, and soul. I feel like a tired child alone in a boat on a big sea. Now I want you to understand. You will ask me if I go back free or bound. I can only say I came here looking upon myself as Ole's wife. I go back not that. Ole himself wishes me to leave Norway." Bright sailed for Norway shortly after receiving Egerton's sad letter, and they were married in July 1901.

Egerton's marriage to Bright was to prove enduring at least, but her career as a playwright was short-lived. Only three of her plays were ever performed, and these were not successful. In 1907 Bernard Shaw wrote to Egerton that her play *His Wife's Family* had no commercial value. He also offered her some sound advice: "You have not got the proper quality of dramatic dialogue: and you will write a practicable commercial play as soon as you condescend to study the market and the materials you have to work with." Egerton resented and ignored

Shaw's advice. Arnold Daly produced *His Wife's Family* in autumn 1908, after he had tried to adapt it for an American audience. When the play failed miserably, Egerton blamed Daly's revisions.

In 1925 her last play, *Camilla States Her Case,* was produced at the Globe Theatre. The central character resembles many of Egerton's heroines in desiring children more than a husband. Reviewers were merciless in their assessment of the play. After the failure of *Camilla,* Egerton disappeared from the literary world altogether. She declined later to list her plays on her official bibliography.

Egerton's marriage to Bright was, in the minds of many friends and relatives (such as de Vere White), essentially a mother-son relationship. Perhaps because Bright was fifteen years younger, the couple never had children together, but he lavished affection on his stepson, George Clairmonte. Egerton, too, loved the child intensely, despite the fact that he had been especially difficult to rear. In 1914 the young man was nineteen and poised to enter Cambridge when World War I intervened, as it did for so many other young men in England. On Friday, 7 August 1914, Egerton wrote in her journal that her son had to report for military service, and she expressed extreme anxiety about him: "The boy had planned out his Varsity course, loved the idea of college.... Doesn't care about War, I think. At heart he hates the idea of killing wretched people who are flung at us. Yet feels he ought to do something.... I ache for news."

The news she received was devastating. Her son was killed in action on 26 September 1915. His body was never recovered. According to de Vere White, neither Egerton nor Bright ever really got over the loss. De Vere White, in fact, believed that young George Clairmonte's death affected Bright even more deeply and permanently than it did his mother, whose interest and vitality never quite dimmed.

Egerton's liveliness and literary talent in her later years found expression entirely in letters — long letters, according to de Vere White, "written in an exquisite hand, full of opinions on politics, on Ireland, on new plays and books." Bright developed diabetes in early 1941. His condition declined, and he died on 14 April 1941, with his head on his wife's shoulder. Egerton lived until July 1945, when she died at the bottom of the stairs in a house to which she had recently moved.

Despite the brief flare of Egerton's literary light, her short fiction, especially the stories in *Keynotes* and *Discords,* holds a small but distinctive place in the literature of the period, in the history of the short story, and in fiction depicting the inner lives of women. While Egerton's emphasis on the psychological complexity of her women characters and her frankness about women's sexual feelings do not strike late-twentieth-century readers as remarkable, these emphases shocked her readers when *Keynotes* first appeared. Early reviewers either praised her originality and honesty or reprehended her "erotomania." A writer in the *Review of Reviews* (December 1893) observed that in *Keynotes* "some woman has crystallised her life's drama, has written down her soul on the page." *Punch* (1894) preferred to caricature Egerton's fiction, referring irreverently to "She Notes" by "Borgia Smudgiton." More-serious conservative critics expressed moral outrage at what they considered her obsessive interest in sexuality. In "Tommyrotics" (*Blackwood's,* 1895) Hugh Stutfield castigates a host of women writers of the period whose "chief delight seems to be in making their characters discuss matters which would not have been tolerated in the novels a decade ago. Emancipated woman in particular loves to show her independence by dealing freely with the relations of the sexes."

In "The Psychology of Feminism" (*Living Age,* 13 March 1897) Stutfield writes that Egerton was "the ablest of our women writers of the neurotic school.... The authoress of *Keynotes* ... is essentially a womanly writer. Her gifts are intuitive rather than intellectual, and she owes nothing whatever to reason or the research of man ... she personifies our modern nervousness, and her characters are quivering bundles of nerves." Stutfield adds, as other reviewers noted, that Egerton seemed to write entirely from her "own mental experience without any attempt at concealment. The mood varies in these books — sometimes tender, sometimes sorrowful, sometimes vicious, as though the authoress would like to scratch somebody; but they are always purely subjective, or else rapid generalizations from limited experience." Stutfield then dwells on the morbidity and gloom of current fiction, observing that Egerton's *Discords* and Thomas Hardy's *Jude the Obscure* (1895) were by far the worst.

More-recent critics have assessed Egerton's realistic short fiction much more favorably. All agree that her finest work appears in *Keynotes* and *Discords* and that even *Symphonies* shows a marked decline in her literary power. In "Egerton: Forgotten Realist" (1968), Wendell V. Harris argues that Egerton's work in short fiction deserves more serious critical appraisal, if only because her fiction is the most representative of the "new realism," that is, the kind of fiction that developed near the end of the nineteenth century and the beginning of the twentieth. This "new realism" drew heavily on previous movements of realism and naturalism and featured a marked emphasis on the emotional and psychological inner worlds of the characters. Egerton's realistic technique, Harris notes, owes more to Scandinavian than to French realism. Harris observes that, in addition to her unconventional treatment of love and marriage,

> To Hamsun she almost certainly owes her interest in reproducing the indirect, at times wayward, progress by which the mind assimilates thoughts and impressions. Now and again in her earlier stories she paused to analyze the succession of thoughts, images, and associations that, set in motion by some greater or lesser perception or emotion — falling in love or noticing a pebble in the path, ramify unpredictably according to the psychological idiosyncrasies of the particular person. Egerton of course shares this interest in the psychology of the individual with the majority of the other experimental realists, but in the prominence that she gives to private eccentricities of each mind she is, thanks probably to her acquaintance with Norwegian literature, alone among English writers in her time.

Harris also suggests that the hope implicit in Egerton's fiction rescues it from the grim naturalism of her contemporaries. He also credits her with being the first writer of short fiction to eliminate all background exposition of characters' situations, as well as the first to infuse realism with poetic imagination and fantasy.

In her introduction to the 1983 edition of *Keynotes,* Martha Vicinus reassesses Egerton's short fiction for its redefinitions of womanhood, its frankness in representing female sexuality, and its rebellion against conventional morality: "Even her mentors thought she might be a little more cautious in discussing sexual desire. But Egerton was never interested in guilt or punishment; rather, her works celebrate the potential in women, not the possibly debilitating consequences of living the life of a New Woman in an old world." Vicinus also stresses Egerton's difference from other feminist writers of the 1890s: "Certainly she shared with her female contemporaries a zeal (and zest) for describing the effects of sexual ignorance on women faced with venereal disease, or alcoholism or gratuitous violence on the part of a careless man. But she differed from her contemporaries in her portrayal of solutions to these situations; she advocated not restraint and meaningful work, but sexual fulfillment and power."

Vicinus concurs with other critics that Egerton's later writings show a disappointing decline from the quality of *Keynotes* and *Discords,* and she ac-

Portrait of Egerton by Edward Arthur Walton (from Yellow Book, *April 1895)*

counts for it thus: "Egerton's strength — the subtle transformation of personal experience — was also her weakness. Once she was settled into respectable marriage, she could not develop new themes with the daring and excitement of her first stories." Vicinus agrees with Harris that Egerton's originality and pioneering courage in representing internal states of consciousness remain to twentieth-century readers compelling features of her fiction and thus secure Egerton's small but significant place in the history of short fiction in England. Vicinus argues that Egerton resembles other late-nineteenth-century writers in blending realism and fantasy. Because she recognized mysterious aspects of herself that neither life nor art had taught her to express, her fiction is, according to Vicinus, utopian. Egerton's characters experience intense moments of vision and feeling that allow them to embrace their sexual power, to recognize their being, and to celebrate the possibility of mutuality among men and women. Vicinus concludes: "The real excitement of reading George Egerton comes from the discovery of self — the pushing outward of woman's potential in her stories. She refuses to accept less than the most complete life, the most complete freedom, the most complete soul for her women. Sometimes this means a traditional marriage, sometimes a free liaison, sometimes simple independence, but never does a woman deny her self without denying her soul. For Egerton the price of repression was always too high."

"A Cross Line"(*Keynotes*) demonstrates Vicinus's points effectively. The protagonist knows that her marriage does not really offer much personal fulfillment. Her husband is not a bad man; he just possesses no understanding of her inner life. The result is that she feels a profound restlessness that manifests itself in her intense pleasure of the outdoors and a rather wild fantasy life. The woman wonders whether other women experience "this restless craving for sun and love and motion." Women, she thinks to herself, are far too complex for the limited understanding of most men: "it is that the workings of our hearts are closed to them, that we are cunning enough or *great* enough to seem to be what they would have us, rather than be what we are." Men, this woman feels, "have all overlooked the eternal wildness, the untamed primitive savage temperament that lurks in the mildest, best woman . . . this primeval trait burns, an untameable quantity that may be concealed but is never eradicated by culture – the keynote of woman's witchcraft and woman's strength." The plot turns on the woman's flirtation with a fisherman, who perceives her mystery and knows that he cannot really possess her. She belongs to herself and somehow appeals to the fisherman's own buried and unexpressed desires. The fisherman needs her more than she needs him, and she gives up the flirtatious friendship as she and her maid plan the layette for her first child.

The climax of "A Cross Line" appears as a sustained fantasy, a feature characteristic of many other Egerton stories. The central character imagines herself dancing on the stage of an ancient theater in the open air, "before an audience of hundreds. Somehow through the power of her dance, she imagines that she can touch the soul of every man in the audience." The ending suggests that the kind of mutuality she desires with men is not forthcoming. In her friendship with the fisherman she encounters a line that she is unwilling to cross and thus finds her fulfillment in the more traditional role of mother.

Many of the stories in *Keynotes, Discords,* and *Symphonies* express a keen awareness of the mutual fictions men and women create to sustain their relationships. The theme appears most prominently in a *Keynotes* story, "Now Spring Has Come," more or less a dramatic account of Egerton's relationship with Hamsun. The famous writer in this story and the young woman who narrates it dream of one another for a year. When they first meet, the woman is already in love with the idea of the novelist. For his part the writer appears to be in love with the idea of the young woman's passion for his prose. After a year has passed, with many passionate letters between them, they are both disillusioned upon their second meeting. She no longer engages his imagination; neither party can sustain the fantasy. The narrator makes it clear that the writer suffers less than the young woman because he has his art. He belongs to himself, and she does not. Repeatedly in her stories, however, Egerton insists that work alone, or even art alone, will not suffice for the fulfillment of women.

When Egerton represents "writing women," these characters often seem to lack something basic to their happiness. Another *Keynotes* story, "The Spell of the White Elf," centers on a worldly woman who felt that she lacked the vocation for marriage and therefore rejected an offer to wed. The woman admits, "I have been alone now for five years, working away, though I was left enough to keep me before. Somehow I have not the same gladness in my work of late years. Working for one's-self seems a poor end even if one puts by money." The narrator of the tale expresses admiration for this intellectual woman and her achievements yet insists that there is something "manlike" about her. The woman describes her involvement with a friend who has a baby (the "white elf " of the title), and it is clear that the woman is deeply aware of a profound lack in herself. Egerton's "New Woman," however, is not simply a creature who can be happy only if she has a husband and children in her life. She is far more complex. She finds her fulfillment in various ways, but she does not find it in trying to be as much like a man as possible.

Perhaps the weakest story in *Keynotes* is "A Little Grey Glove." The narrator is a bachelor who has never quite found the woman who suits him. While on a holiday he meets a woman with a "past." Her husband has unjustly accused her of adultery and divorced her. There is no real development of character, conflict, or plot in this story. The tone is pervasively sentimental, and the happy reunion of lovers at the end is rather trite. An older Egerton was to write Bright that she felt like a "tired child" in need of rescue. Her weakest stories seem to turn on this rescue theme and in many ways contradict the utopian vision of womanhood celebrated in her best stories. Yet even "A Little Grey Glove" was daring for its time, since it openly questions society's double standard for men and women and specifically questions England's divorce laws.

At its best Egerton's fiction celebrates the beauty of varied types of women, from delicate, childlike women to those who are vigorous, grand, and statuesque, although she more often depicted petite women with penetrating eyes, physically much like herself. She strongly affirms the power of these women to regard themselves as beautiful and to ignore male standards of beauty. In some stories she suggests that women who betray themselves by trying to conform to what men wish them to be are guilty not only of bad faith but self-mutilation. In "Now Spring Has Come," for example, the narrator notes that male constraints on women have resulted in their actual deformity: "What half creatures we are, we women! Hermaphrodite by force of circumstances. Deformed results of a fight of centuries between physical suppression and natural impulse to fulfil our destiny." Despite the narrator's pain and disappointment, she also suggests that her disillusionment is necessary in order to free her to enjoy her moments as they pass. Under the spell of a powerful man whom she had admired almost to the point of worship, the woman had literally languished and sickened.

Many reviewers of *Discords* thought that it was inferior to *Keynotes*. The critics complained that the stories were morbid, that they captured only the darkest aspects of modern existence. Others remarked that the narrators were entirely too preachy and intrusive, a just criticism at least by modern standards. In this volume Egerton looks more critically and directly at harsh social reality and somewhat less at the rich inner lives of women. "Wedlock" deals with violence within marriage, the corrosive effects of alcoholism on the entire social fabric, and how such circumstances may drive poor women to tragic action – infanticide in this story. "Gone Under" reveals a pathetic woman's descent into prostitution and degradation.

Egerton's subjects and frank treatment of them led some reviewers to label her fiction lurid as well as morbid. Her purpose in portraying these naturalistic characters and circumstances stemmed apparently from her desire to change them. She seems fully conscious that such people remain in general unseen and unheard in society. By portraying them accurately, she invites the reader to see and to hear society's victims, as the central character of the first story in *Discords*, "A Psychological Moment," sees and hears the evidence of a dwarf's suffering: "His mouth gapes, and his tongue lolls from side to side, the saliva forming little bubbles as the great head wags."

Egerton's ironic intent becomes even more intense when the reader observes that this highly naturalistic scene is set amid ornately rendered fin de siècle images, as the breeze "scatters dying leaves like golden butterflies to bring no message." The young girl who views all of this feels powerless to change it and can only rail at the people around the boy who refuse to see his agony, and even at God: "She throws herself breathlessly down at the foot of a great tree, and bursts into tears, not sorrowful tears, but heaving rebellious sobs against the All-Father for His ordering of things here below." In the end she declares that she loves the "poor things of creation" more than God.

The stories in *Keynotes* and *Discords* remain valuable to students of the Edwardian period. The stories in *Discords* and *Symphonies* appeared in the *Yellow Book* before they were published in collections. They reflect aspects of both the "art for art's sake" movement and the adoption of naturalistic subjects and techniques from Continental writers. Egerton represented the inner emotions of characters in unprecedented ways and in so doing anticipated such major modernist writers as James Joyce, D. H. Lawrence, and Virginia Woolf. Egerton introduced new techniques, modes, and subjects to the short story of this period and hence deserves far more attention than her work has yet received.

Letters:

Terence de Vere White, *A Leaf from the Yellow Book: The Correspondence of George Egerton* (London: Richards, 1958).

References:

Wendell V. Harris, "Egerton: Forgotten Realist," *Victorian Newsletter,* 35 (Spring 1968): 31–35;

Harris, "John Lane's 'Keynote Series' and the Fiction of the 1890's," *PMLA,* 83 (October 1968): 1407–1413;

"Prurient Literature," *Saturday Review* (25 September 1897): 345–346;

Hugh Stutfield, "The Psychology of Feminism," *Living Age,* 212 (13 March 1897): 711–712;

Stutfield, "Tommyrotics," *Blackwood's,* 157 (June 1895): 833–845;

Martha Vicinus, "Rediscovering the 'New Woman' of the 1890s: The Stories of 'George Egerton,'" in *Feminist Re-Visions: What Has Been and Might Be,* edited by Louise A. Tilly and Vivian Patraka (Ann Arbor: Women's Studies Program, 1983), pp. 12–25.

George Gissing

(22 November 1857 – 28 December 1903)

Donald E. Hall
California State University, Northridge

See also the Gissing entry in *DLB 18: Victorian Novelists After 1885.*

BOOKS: *Workers in the Dawn: A Novel* (3 volumes, London: Remington, 1880; 2 volumes, Garden City, N.Y.: Doubleday, Doran, 1935);

The Unclassed: A Novel (3 volumes, London: Chapman & Hall, 1884; 1 volume, New York: Fenno, 1896);

Demos: A Story of English Socialism (3 volumes, London: Smith, Elder, 1886; 1 volume, New York: Harper, 1886);

Isabel Clarendon, 2 volumes (London: Chapman & Hall, 1886);

Thyrza: A Tale (3 volumes, London: Smith, Elder, 1887; 1 volume, New York: Dutton, n.d.);

A Life's Morning (3 volumes, London: Smith, Elder, 1888; 1 volume, Philadelphia: Lippincott, 1888);

The Nether World: A Novel (3 volumes, London: Smith, Elder, 1889; 1 volume, New York: Harper, 1889);

The Emancipated: A Novel (3 volumes, London: Bentley, 1890; 1 volume, Chicago: Way & Williams, 1895);

New Grub Street (3 volumes, London: Smith, Elder, 1891; 1 volume, Troy, N.Y.: Brewster, 1904);

Denzil Quarrier: A Novel (London: Lawrence & Bullen, 1892; New York: Macmillan, 1892);

Born in Exile: A Novel, 3 volumes (London: Black, 1892);

The Odd Women (3 volumes, London: Lawrence & Bullen, 1893; 1 volume, New York: Macmillan, 1894);

In the Year of Jubilee (3 volumes, London: Lawrence & Bullen, 1894; 1 volume, New York: Appleton, 1895);

Eve's Ransom (London: Lawrence & Bullen, 1895; New York: Appleton, 1895);

Sleeping Fires (London: Unwin, 1895; New York: Appleton, 1895);

George Gissing, September 1888

The Paying Guest (London: Cassell, 1895; New York: Dodd, Mead, 1895);

The Whirlpool (London: Lawrence & Bullen, 1897; New York: Stokes, 1897);

Human Odds and Ends: Stories and Sketches (London: Lawrence & Bullen, 1898);

Charles Dickens: A Critical Study (London: Blackie, 1898; New York: Dodd, Mead, 1898);

The Town Traveller (London: Methuen, 1898; New York: Stokes, 1898);

The Crown of Life (London: Methuen, 1899; New York: Stokes, 1899);

By the Ionian Sea: Notes of a Ramble in Southern Italy (London: Chapman & Hall, 1901; New York: Scribners, 1905);

Our Friend the Charlatan (London: Chapman & Hall, 1901; New York: Holt, 1901);

The Private Papers of Henry Ryecroft (London: Constable, 1903; New York: Dutton, 1903);

Veranilda: A Romance (London: Constable, 1904; New York: Dutton, 1905);

Will Warburton: A Romance of Real Life (London: Constable, 1905; New York: Dutton, 1905);

The House of Cobwebs and Other Stories (London: Constable, 1906; New York: Dutton, 1906);

An Heiress on Condition (Philadelphia: Privately printed for the Pennell Club, 1923);

Critical Studies of the Works of Charles Dickens (New York: Greenberg, 1924);

Sins of the Fathers and Other Tales (Chicago: Covici, 1924);

The Immortal Dickens (London: Palmer, 1925);

A Victim of Circumstances and Other Stories (London: Constable, 1927; New York: Houghton Mifflin, 1927);

Brownie (New York: Columbia University Press, 1931);

Notes on Social Democracy (London: Enitharmon, 1968).

Editions and Collections: *Selections Autobiographical and Imaginative from the Works of George Gissing,* edited by A. C. Gissing (London: Cape, 1929);

Stories and Sketches, edited by A. C. Gissing (London: Joseph, 1938);

George Gissing's Commonplace Book, edited by Jacob Korg (New York: New York Public Library, 1962);

George Gissing: Essays and Fiction, edited by Pierre Coustillas (Baltimore: Johns Hopkins University Press, 1970);

My First Rehearsal and My Clerical Rival, edited by Coustillas (London: Enitharmon, 1970);

London and the Life of Literature in Late Victorian England: The Diary of George Gissing, Novelist, edited by Coustillas (Hassocks, U.K.: Harvester, 1978; Lewisburg, Pa.: Bucknell University Press, 1978);

George Gissing on Fiction, edited by Jacob Korg and Cynthia Korg (London: Enitharmon, 1978);

Six Sonnets on Shakespearean Heroines (London: Eric & Joan Stevens, 1982);

George Gissing at Work: A Study of His Notebook "Extracts from My Reading," edited by Coustillas and Patrick Bridgewater (Greensboro, N.C.: ELT, 1988);

George Gissing: Lost Stories from America, edited by Robert L. Selig (Lewiston, N.Y.: Mellen, 1992).

OTHER: *The Rochester Edition of the Works of Charles Dickens,* 9 volumes, introduction by Gissing (London: Methuen, 1900–1901);

John Forster, *Forster's "Life of Dickens,"* abridged and revised by Gissing (London: Chapman & Hall, 1903).

George Robert Gissing was a thoroughly earnest and amazingly prolific writer, producing twenty-two novels, many works of nonfiction, and more than a hundred sketches and tales during his twenty-six-year career (the exact number of his stories is still unknown, since many of the early ones were published anonymously). Even so, from his day to the present, Gissing's standing among critics has remained equivocal and his following relatively small. Practically venerated by a few scholars and certainly appreciated by others, he is still untaught in many survey courses and often ignored by both Victorianists and critics of early modern British literature. Among general readers his name is barely recognized. This continuing obscurity is perhaps not surprising, for Gissing's works are clearly uneven, generally caustic, and almost unrelentingly grim, focusing obsessively on the victims and victimizers produced by a morally bankrupt society. Gissing's themes are relatively few, and his characterizations fall within a narrow range. And unlike those of his contemporaries Thomas Hardy and Joseph Conrad, Gissing's works rarely achieve a grandeur of vision or emotion and can strike a reader as claustrophobic, even when they are compelling.

To be sure, the narrow confines of Gissing's fictional worlds – often bounded by the dreary walls of a squalid lodging house or the imprisoning barriers formed by economic and familial circumstances – can be partially relieved by the ample space provided by the genre of Gissing's greatest successes: the three-volume novel. In long works such as *Thyrza* (1887), *New Grub Street* (1891), and *The Odd Women* (1893), Gissing moves between city and country, among classes and conditions, and he surveys the thoughts and emotions of many individuals. But in briefer works that freedom is generically limited; for the reader this can mean an intense, disturbing encounter with unpleasant, even if "realistic," characters and predicaments. "Gissing was no Chekhov when it came to the short story," writes one of his biographers, John Halperin. This comment rings true, for Anton Chekhov better understood the necessity and uses of texture and variety in his short fiction; even so, Gissing's tales and sketches are often powerful, even when they appear polemical or clumsy. Readers may dislike his technique, perspective, or message but will inevitably find themselves provoked out of any complacency they may bring to questions concerning social class, gender roles, and the moral nature of man.

Gissing well recognized the limitations of much of the short fiction that he wrote throughout his career in order to augment his income. In 1889 he replied to his brother Algernon's appeal for advice on fiction writing, saying that he found short stories "exceedingly difficult" and concluding bluntly, "I myself cannot write them." In 1895 he mentioned in his diary that he considered short-story writing "a great trial," and in 1898 he admitted in a letter to a friend that he had a "poor opinion" of his short fiction. Many contemporary critics shared that view. After the publication of his first collection of stories and sketches, *Human Odds and Ends* (1898), the reviews were generally unfavorable, with the London *Times* (14 February 1898) summing up the common reaction to the intense gloom of Gissing's tales:

> He looks at life through tinted spectacles from which every touch of rose-colour has been carefully excluded; all the world is drab to him, save for a black spot or two where wretchedness has led to crime. Being well acquainted with these facts we opened *Human Odds and Ends* with feelings the reverse of those one entertains in releasing the cork of a champagne bottle; and we were not what is called "pleasurably disappointed." At the same time we have known Mr Gissing in a more depressed condition. Three out of the thirty short stories of which the volume is composed end quite cheerfully; this must have cost him something, and we thank him for it.

Not even this acerbic reviewer could argue with the accuracy of many of Gissing's social observations, calling him a "most diligent student of human nature; no detail escapes him concerning the unfortunate." Several other critics were less restrained in their praise. The *Academy* (18 December 1897) argued that a few of Gissing's tales were "really fine," and the *Bookman* (December 1897) noted that there is "no waste, there are no preambles, in his straightforward, forcible narratives." These observations accurately capture the power and peculiarities of Gissing's short stories, few of which are complete failures and several of which are actually gems. Almost all remain of interest, for they reveal many of the tensions of Gissing's age and provide insights into the mind of a tortured and difficult man, whose own unhappy life was recounted time and again in his tragedy-filled novels and stories.

Careful tracing and understanding of biography is of central importance in any critical consideration of Gissing, for the personal and the political are inextricably intertwined in his fiction. Gissing's tale is as depressing as any of his works and more interesting than some. Born on 22 November 1857 in the town of Wakefield in Yorkshire, Gissing was the eldest child of a successful pharmacist, Thomas Waller Gissing, and Margaret Bedford Gissing; four other children were born after George. His early years seem to have been particularly happy; he was a smart, creative child growing up in a household filled with books. Alfred, Lord Tennyson, Charles Dickens, and classical literature were read and appreciated by Thomas Gissing, who encouraged the studious habits and artistic inclinations of his eldest son, a gifted writer from an early age, as description-filled childhood letters demonstrate.

But tragedy struck early, for in 1870 Thomas Gissing died of lung problems (to which his son also inherited a susceptibility); afterward George Gissing's education continued only through public donations. He was an overachiever in academics, seemingly nervous and ambitious from the start, but his sister Ellen remembered him as being peculiarly "over-sensitive" after the death of his father, developing a marked tendency to sneer at other boys while demonstrating an almost maniacal desire to prove himself intellectually. Certainly his academic successes continued to be remarkable as he carried off awards at his Quaker-run boarding school and later at Owens College in Manchester. But at Owens, Gissing's tendency toward both compulsive and obsessive behavior resulted in the first in a lifelong series of truly disastrous personal decisions.

After performing brilliantly on his examinations in preparation for matriculation at the University of London, Gissing became embroiled in scandal. On 31 May 1876 he was arrested for stealing money and property from fellow students. The reason for his thefts soon became apparent; for several months he had been hopelessly in love with a local prostitute, Marianne Helen Harrison, whom he called "Nell." Desperately trying to provide her with the funds that he hoped would lead to her salvation from the streets, he resorted to criminal activity. In reality his money did little to dissuade her from prostitution, and it seems to have been used only to buy the alcohol necessary to feed her lifelong dependency. Gissing, however, was obsessed with making Nell "respectable," despite her seeming disdain for the hollow designation. The results were predictable enough: Nell continued to drink and quickly returned to her old profession. Gissing spent a short time at hard labor for his crimes, was ruined academically, and was finally sent to the United States by his family and friends.

In some great ways this calamity can be seen as fortunate (at least for devotees of his work), for Gissing was forced to turn to writing to meet his needs. After first taking up residence in Massachusetts, where he taught languages, Gissing moved to Chicago and began turning out short stories. The tales that he published during his months in Illinois are painfully immature and would be wholly forgettable except for the fact that they so clearly incorporate aspects of his own life and self-perception and they begin to reveal the themes on which he would fixate for the rest of his career.

"The Sins of the Fathers" (*Chicago Tribune*, 10 March 1877; collected in *Sins of the Fathers and Other Tales*, 1924) was Gissing's first published work of fiction. It is a melodramatic tale that clearly draws on his experiences with Nell, but it also demonstrates the profound sense of doom that seemed to accompany his continued thoughts of her. In the story a Gissing-like student, Leonard Vincent, meets a poor, distressed young woman named Laura. Like many of Gissing's subsequent characters, she is an urban refugee. Abused by a stepfather and unable to make a living in her hometown, she is the first of Gissing's many victims of both economic and familial circumstances. She inevitably falls on hard times after fleeing to the city. Leonard befriends her just before she is driven to prostitution, helps her find a job, and then falls in love with her. Like parents throughout later Gissing stories, Leonard's father opposes his son's proposed alliance; Mr. Vincent represents one in a continuing series of manifestations of powerful, menacing forces that work to thwart individual happiness. He ships his son off to America and devises elaborate lies to separate the lovers permanently. Mr. Vincent is clearly a villain here; however, his skepticism about Leonard and Laura's love for one another seems at least partially justified in Gissing's mind, for Leonard does meet an American woman more economically and intellectually suited for him and marries her. Even so, a tragic outcome seems predetermined, for the malevolent hand of fate intervenes two years later; Leonard and his wife attend a play in which Laura appears as a chorus girl. He is drawn to her after the theater closes and discovers that they still desire each other. Gissing seems to view that overwhelming force of attraction, crossing all boundaries of class and property, with enormous

concern. Leonard cannot resist Laura as she leads him along the snowy streets of the New England town. Mad with thwarted, hopeless passion, she takes him to a river, clasps his neck with a wild shriek, and in a moment of frenzy throws them both through the ice covering the water.

This story suggests a myriad of anxieties and fears. To catalogue its implications and themes is to anticipate almost all of the ones that follow in Gissing's stories and novels. Here as elsewhere Gissing's fiction suggests the inescapability of the past, the malevolence of both familial and cosmic powers, the corrupting influence of the city, and even the complicity of nature in bringing about a tragic denouement. "The Sins of the Fathers" reveals Gissing's overwhelming pessimism about human life and relationships, and specifically his fascination with and terror of the power of desire, which inevitably causes disaster when it breaks strict social codes. In Gissing's imaginative world the individual exists at the mercy of a corrupt, hostile environment and powerful inner compulsions; characters seem trapped by circumstance and psychology and therefore doomed to failure, disgrace, and even untimely death.

Where these peculiar fixations and fears originated is a matter of considerable interest to Gissing scholars. One can socially contextualize Gissing's anxieties, for the second half of the nineteenth century was an era of deepening concern over the effects on the English citizenry of industrialization, urbanization, and a general loss of religious faith. This age saw the births not only of modern psychology and sociology but also of existential philosophy, as the relationships between individuals and their environments came under intense new scrutiny.

Clearly compounding such socially pervasive feelings of uneasiness and instability were Gissing's personal worries and financial troubles. Most scholars agree that the death of his father and Gissing's subsequent poverty affected him profoundly. His desperate attempts to prove himself academically and to change Nell can be viewed as futile efforts to gain a measure of control over a chaotic, even hostile, world. Gissing's financial problems persisted, for even years later, when he was at his most successful, his income was still barely sufficient to be called middle class, though his circle of friends included the wealthy and idle. Throughout his life Gissing's worries over money fed the deep-seated insecurity that he had developed in childhood. He identified with others suffering from economic woes, yet he clearly attempted to differentiate himself from them through fictionally manipulating their stories and fates.

Contributing to this gloomy worldview was Gissing's difficult relationship with his family, which helped to shape his many fictional visions of home life centering on abuse and deceit. Unlike some of his characters, Gissing was no simple victim; he bore considerable responsibility for creating his own real-life domestic hell. Therefore, his early anxieties and forebodings concerning Nell are particularly interesting and revealing. He seemed simultaneously to fear and idealize her, often killing her off fictionally, as he grappled with his own demons and desires. These potent emotions resonate through his second published story, "R.I.P." (*Chicago Tribune,* 31 March 1877; collected in *Sins of the Fathers and Other Tales*), which concerns a beautiful woman who commits suicide in a rustic inn, becoming the focus of local legend. Her background is unknown, so she is buried in a grave marked only R.I.P. Many years later a man wanders into town; when he hears the story of the strange death, he reveals that she was his wife. Again there is a doomed marriage here between a peasant girl named Marianne and a wealthy man whose father opposes the alliance. On their wedding day the groom's brother, who is the father's favorite, convinces a servant to tell Marianne that her new husband is already married. She flees and then kills herself; the heartbroken husband roams the earth aimlessly.

Marianne was, of course, Nell's first name, and it is worth noting that in "R.I.P." the female character is again given the power to set in motion the chain of events leading to the destruction of an unwitting man. Not only does Gissing indicate his own pessimism about the possibility and consequences of an alliance with her, he also reveals much of the confusion and many of the biases that he brought to his later marriages and demonstrated in some of his writings on class and gender relationships. The character Marianne is little more than a stereotype; she incarnates beauty, simplicity, and virtue, a fantasy figure that no real woman could match. The local townspeople – members of her social class to whom she returns to die – are also portrayed in a patronizing, telling way, for they are seen as bovine and vulgar. Seeing this tension between Gissing's perceptions of Nell and his reaction to her fellow members of the lower class helps in understanding the inevitable tragedy of his relationship with her. While Gissing was often attracted to women whose social standing was beneath his – and was through them able to assuage temporarily his inherent insecurity – his satisfaction was spurious and short-lived, as he always came to view the same women with contempt.

Gissing was a thorough product of his time as well as one of its severest critics; his patriarchal attitudes are those of an era that still denied voting rights to women and often vilified the poor. In each of these first two tales, as well as in later works, Gissing indicates that class boundaries are natural and acceptable, even if the grossest forms of class oppression are not. Lower-class women may be objects of short-lived desire, but their fathers, brothers, and mothers are more often than not dismissed as dull and irredeemable; tragically, Gissing came to view, treat, and dismiss his wives similarly.

Gissing was paid meagerly for these and other pieces he published in Chicago and was soon forced to return to the East Coast; from there he traveled back to England, just one year after his initial departure. His stay in the United States (his only visit there) did accomplish one of the goals that had motivated those who had sent him; he was forced both to choose a career and to take responsibility for himself. Another goal was not met, however. Friends and family hoped that the separation from Nell would lead to their permanent breakup, but Gissing continued his obsession with her and resumed their relationship; they were married on 27 October 1879.

As one might fully expect from the fears and fixations demonstrated in his fiction, Gissing's marriage was disastrous. He could not mold Nell to fit his ideals, and she could neither overcome her alcoholism nor gain the approval and acceptance of a difficult husband. Gissing was often depressed and angry, as his own fear of judgment and insecurity intensified his tendency to judge and condemn others. Even as he obsessively probed the conditions and psychologies of the poor, Gissing despised their behavior and habits, including those of a wife whom he chose freely and then came to hate for being the woman that she was.

While Gissing's general pessimism and anger are inscribed throughout the fiction of this period, he certainly continued his development as an artist. His first published story after his return to England, "Phoebe" (*Temple Bar,* March 1884), shows a striking growth in his intellectual maturity and artistic control, for he had written at least three novels by this time and had clearly fine-tuned his descriptive powers. "Phoebe" represents something of a transition between the earlier stories and the fully realized tales of Gissing's creative adulthood; certainly it reiterates many familiar themes.

A lonely, starving girl of fifteen has fled from an abusive father. She becomes an artificial-flower maker in a large city at a time when people are wearing feathers as ornaments; thus family and fashion seem to conspire against her. As she approaches homelessness and complete despair, Phoebe finds nine pounds on top of the cupboard in her garret, hidden there by a now-deceased former tenant. Determined to keep the money, she dreams fancifully of the many luxuries she can afford, but she barely summons the courage to buy a meager dinner. Tragedy then strikes with a heavy hand: after bringing a homeless beggar, Jenny, back to share her lodgings for the evening, Phoebe awakens the next morning to find that her money has been stolen and that she is again facing starvation. The story ends with the exclamation "Poor Phoebe!"

Maudlin and contrived, this tale warns simplistically that if one is not smart enough to keep one's money, then one really does not deserve it. Even though there are no nuances in the characterizations of Phoebe and Jenny (the former incarnates simplicity and the latter duplicity), Phoebe's predicament is touching because of Gissing's powerful descriptions of her miserable surroundings and physical discomfort: "The window rattled loose in its frame, through the chink beneath the door, and up through the knot-holes in the boarding, swept stinging currents of wind. Her feet were already numb, and she had to hold her hands in her bosom to warm them." Especially worth noting in this tale is the author's insight into the psychology of poverty, which renders Phoebe unable to enjoy her new wealth. She is nervous and self-conscious, much more at ease in her squalid neighborhood than in a slightly more prosperous part of town. She can look in the windows of the smarter shops but cannot bring herself to enter. In accordance with the last words of the story, Phoebe is truly defined by her poverty, making for a moving, if narrowly characterized, psychological case study and portrait of lower-class misery.

Such unswerving attention to sordid surroundings and sad histories places Gissing firmly in the realist tradition, even if his plots are often dependent on chance occurrences and one-dimensional characterizations. He freely admitted his profound debt to the great French realists Emile Zola and Honoré de Balzac, stating in a letter to his sister Margaret (31 July 1886), "The writers who help me most are French and Russian; I have not much sympathy with English points of view. And indeed that is why I scarcely think that my own writing can ever be popular." As in the case of Zola, the shock-

ing accuracy of Gissing's portrayals of the conditions of the poor resulted from his wide survey of squalid urban landscapes. In workman's clothing Gissing would prowl the streets, pubs, and haunts of the working class, making notes and accumulating the minute details that drive his social and psychological portraits.

"Letty Coe" (*Temple Bar,* August 1891) demonstrates this superb attention to detail. The protagonist, Michael Coe, is a costermonger fallen on almost unbelievably hard times. As the tale opens, his donkey has become gravely ill, he has bought a load of spoiled fish, and he has recently had to move with his daughter, Letty, into a ramshackle old washhouse behind the tenement where his wife died after falling down a broken staircase. Yet, for all the melodrama that this tale evinces, the portrait of Michael is complex and satisfying. He is brooding and introspective, even if uneducated. Basically honest at heart, he is tempted to robbery because of his extreme circumstances. The reader understands his quandary because of Gissing's careful attention to the misery of Michael and Letty's life in the vile washhouse, where rags are stuffed into broken windowpanes to keep out the frigid winds. As in the case of Phoebe, the reader is made to see and feel the thin line between barely existing and starving to death. For those whose lives exist on that edge, any small mishap can lead to tragedy.

While the story is affecting, it still does not display the full maturity of some of Gissing's later tales. The angelic little Letty is no more than a stereotype, and her death is predictable and grotesque. As the donkey thrashes about in its death throes, it pushes some straw into a fire. Letty, asleep with her arms wrapped around her pet, smothers in the smoke that fills the washhouse. Her body is discovered just as Michael returns from the robbery. Theft may be enticing, but it carries a heavy price, for Letty represents her father's purity of spirit, which dies when he commits the crime.

In "Letty Coe" as elsewhere, Gissing severely punishes crimes against property, for mixed with his revulsion at the conditions of the poor was a fear of radical social action and reform. While commenting on the misery of the underprivileged, he never fully understood his personal investment in the system responsible for it. In the words of one of his biographers, Jacob Korg, Gissing "was at heart not a rebel at all but the most conventional of Victorians, who loved good manners, pleasant surroundings, and cultivated conversation." Certainly he did not find these circumstances at home, and in letters to friends and family, he simplistically blames Nell for his inability to feel at ease with social superiors, portraying himself as a victim. Granted, they were a particularly ill-suited match, and she fell ever deeper into hopeless alcoholism, but his diffidence, biting sarcasm, and insecurity no doubt made him an unpleasant spouse as well. In 1883 they separated permanently. Gissing did not see her again until after her death in 1888, when he viewed her emaciated corpse lying in a filthy lodging house. He was moved to tears, for he discovered that she had kept many mementos of him, while he had simply attempted to forget her.

During the mid to late 1880s Gissing continued to earn money turning out stories for a few pounds apiece, but he focused his greatest creative energy on novels. These were productive and increasingly successful years for Gissing. He was finally making enough money to pull himself out of squalor, and he sent Nell a pound a week until her death. After his unsuccessful first novel, *Workers in the Dawn* (published at his own expense in 1880), Gissing met with steadily rising, if never rocketing, critical acclaim with *The Unclassed* (1884), *Demos* and *Isabel Clarendon* (both 1886), *Thyrza,* and *The Nether World* (1889).

Still suffering from bouts of depression and feelings of worthlessness, he desperately desired a change of scenery. He made a trip through Europe during late 1888 and early 1889, gathering information for future novels, rediscovering his love for antiquity, and refreshing his spirits after Nell's death. He first visited France and then fell in love with Italy; the area around Naples became one of his favorite haunts. Climbing Mount Vesuvius, lunching alfresco, and touring the ruins, he found himself spiritually revived and pulled in new artistic directions. He rushed home to correct the proofs for *The Emancipated* (1890), but by the fall of 1889 he was traveling abroad again, to both Italy and Greece. Even though ill health plagued him at times (in 1890 he was diagnosed with the lung problems that would eventually kill him), these were relatively happy days for Gissing.

With his increasing artistic and financial success, along with his legal freedom after Nell's death, Gissing began to think of another "permanent" relationship. Once again, however, he made an extraordinarily foolish and destructive choice, seeming to act out a continuing need to find a partner whom he could rescue and dominate. As the scholar Pierre Coustillas remarks in Halperin's biography, perhaps Gissing simply had a "regular genius for masochism." One might add that his actions often appeared sadistic as well. Edith Underwood was the uneducated daughter of a carpenter's assistant; Gissing hoped that she would be a willing subject whom he could mold into a careful housekeeper and passive wife. While his pedagogical skills were remembered fondly by his early pupils, his attempts to dictate to the women in his life were far less laudable or successful.

Edith and her family were thoroughly skeptical about the proposed match, unable to understand the relatively popular writer's attraction to her. But Gissing waved all objections aside and persuaded Edith that the union was to everyone's benefit. Nothing could have been further from the truth. On 25 February 1891 Gissing formalized the second of his two disastrous marriages. While he desired an angel in the house, he soon found that the dynamics of the marriage produced a demon, as the woman whom he had hoped would be a Galatea-like figure became a violent, hatred-filled opponent to his pedantry. In letter after letter he blames Edith and circumstances for his bad luck, even as one of his greatest short stories, written during this era, shows that blaming circumstances is all too often used as a means of denying one's own responsibility for one's life and actions.

Much of Gissing's mature fiction drew on and helped contribute to the late-nineteenth-century interest in psychology. "A Victim of Circumstances" (*Blackwood's,* January 1893; collected in *A Victim of Circumstances and Other Stories,* 1927) is a complex, sophisticated tale that reflects this climate of inquiry. The story concerns Horace Castledine, an aspiring painter with little talent, and his loving wife, Hilda, who can paint watercolors with adeptness. Through a series of mistakes, during which Horace remains silent, Hilda's work is assumed to be his. They continue the duplicity because it brings in needed cash, but the dishonesty and disparity in talent finally ruin their marriage and lives. In jealousy and mortification he makes her put aside her brushes, and they depend solely on his artistic output and labor as a teacher. At the tale's end, twenty-one years later, Horace is a destitute and broken man. His wife and beloved son have died in poverty, his daughter is in an abusive marriage, and he has rewritten the past so that the watercolors really were his own, representing the peak of a career that he can only look back on nostalgically while wondering at his poor fortunes. He finally attributes his decline to being shackled with a wife. Horace is a case study in insecurity, arrogance, and self-deceit.

Not only is Horace drawn with fine detail and psychological accuracy, but Hilda is also portrayed with great realism and sensitivity. When Gissing takes the reader into the consciousness of the frustrated, talented woman who is smothered under the weight of her husband's ego and pride, one feels the plight of the woman artist. Hilda is thrilled to learn she has talent and works diligently at her art; Horace, however, is lazy and impatient. She paints landscapes, carefully observing her surroundings; he attempts grand historical subjects that appear out of touch with the reality of his circumstances. Gissing's artistic beliefs are encapsulated in Hilda's fidelity to truth and her keen eye for detail.

Aware of the boundaries imposed on women by a patriarchal society, Gissing renders Hilda's tragedy faithfully. When Horace exclaims that he and his family were "victims of circumstances," he speaks truthfully, for if Hilda had been allowed to pursue her career, they would have thrived. Instead, a social system and patriarchal mindset working through her husband kill Hilda and lead to tragedy for her children. Her daughter's marriage to a violent man signifies the position of many women, including Hilda, who suffer psychological, if not physical, abuse and die unfulfilled. In Gissing's eyes the sins of the patriarchal father, indeed the patriarchs of society, are visited often on the innocent and good.

One might wonder what motivated Gissing's sporadic attention to women's issues (and sporadic it was, for he continued to create vapid, stereotypical female characters throughout his career). Gissing read and reread with relish the novels of Charlotte Brontë; perhaps he identified with some of her talented but oppressed heroines and transferred some of that empathy into certain sensitive portrayals of women. Another possibility is that a vague sense of guilt and sympathy toward Nell and Edith stirred his concern and motivated the writing of some of his fiction on women's issues, perhaps even his novel *The Odd Women*. In any case Gissing treated women's issues in the same way he treated class issues – with some sensitivity but also with considerable blind spots. He saw restless and abused women as case studies, often accurately recounting their tales but not wholly understanding their demands or concerns. As a recorder of the raw data of human life and misery, Gissing has no equal; however, he was not a social visionary. This is why Gissing's tales often end pessimistically, in stasis or unhappiness. He has few answers to profound social questions but insists on asking such questions forcefully and repeatedly.

This provocativeness is demonstrated in the fascinating tale "Lou and Liz" (*English Illustrated Magazine*, August 1893; collected in *A Victim of Cir-*

cumstances and Other Stories), about two working-class young women who live together in a small garret with Liz's baby, Jacky. Liz is unmarried, and Lou has been abandoned by her husband; the portraits of these women are compelling. They both earn meager salaries, but by pooling their resources and sharing all responsibilities they are able to make ends meet. They are ignorant, violent, slovenly, and inadequate mothers, yet they care for each other and the baby as best they can. The child often suffers from deprivation and neglect, but irresponsible men, a brutal economic system, and a general lack of education and training all share partial blame.

The complexity of such a situation is captured in Gissing's ending. When Lou runs across her husband at a fair, Liz is terrified because she knows that she and the baby cannot live on her earnings alone. Discovering that Lou's husband is really a bigamist, she exposes him to save herself and her child. Lou is furious with the man and disappears for several hours during the night; she comes back with a "strange note" in her voice. The reader never discovers where she has been. The "strange note" may signify the depth of her pain, or it may indicate that she has revenged herself on the man who has deceived her. In either case it makes the resumption of "normality" at the end of the tale a particularly masterful stroke. In circumstances such as these, one simply accepts whatever happens. Life continues at the end of the story as the two women awake to begin another week of hard labor. There is no escape for these women and no easy answer to their problems.

For such bleak tales Gissing clearly drew on his hellish daily existence with Edith during the early 1890s as she grew increasingly bitter and violent. Yet, as was the case when times were bad with Nell, difficulties spurred Gissing to action, and this was also a period of remarkable productivity for him. In 1893 he retained the services of a competent literary agent, William Morris Colles, who was able to place Gissing's short fiction widely and profitably. Consequently, Gissing wrote as many as seven stories a month, receiving fifteen pounds or more for each one. Many of these hastily written pieces are unremarkable, but a few show lasting merit.

"Our Mr. Jupp" (*English Illustrated Magazine*, March 1894; collected in *Human Odds and Ends*) is the story of a rising young businessman. Jupp displays both ability and intelligence, but he also incarnates conceit and selfishness. Gissing punishes the individual who sacrifices all human responsibility

"WITH THAT AND THE TEN SHILLINGS YOU'VE JUST STOLEN
YOU OUGHT TO MAKE A NICE START, DON'T YOU THINK?"

Illustration by R. A. Brownlie for "Our Mr. Jupp" (English
Illustrated Magazine, *March 1894)*

and kindness in the drive to get ahead. Cunning
and callous, Jupp stints his mother and sister, with
whom he lives, and spends all of his earnings on
himself. Another character, Martha Pimm, serves as
a contrast. When she inherits several thousand
pounds, she remains faithful to her family and continues to work in her mother's tobacco shop. She is
clever, industrious, and perspicacious. A friend of
Jupp's family, Pimm sees through the young man
and becomes the agent for his mortification. Jupp's
greed leads him to court her and allows her to ma-
nipulate him in order to better the lives of his sister
and mother.

After months of such machinations, he turns
surly and demands her hand in marriage, which she
angrily refuses, exposing him for the cad that he is.
He strikes her and flees, losing his job and all hopes
of immediate wealth. Through Jupp, Gissing emphasizes that personality is not simply a product of
economic circumstances. Much later, Pimm reads
about Jupp in the papers; he has married for money
but has run afoul of the law. Even so, Pimm re-

mains optimistic that he can change. When he returns humbly to ask her pardon, she grants it and
even agrees to loan him ten pounds to help him ex-
tricate himself from legal problems. When Jupp
steals an extra sovereign from her, she finally realizes that he will never improve morally. He departs
with the money and his original personality intact.

Certainly Pimm is another remarkable female
character; her only failure is her attempt to reform
Jupp. Here, however, Gissing remains true to his
life and worldview. He too was unable to change
Nell and Edith (except perhaps for the worse); even
as a writer Gissing only worked with what he found
"true" in human nature, faithfully recording the
flaws and foibles of his characters. Pimm must finally acknowledge and accept the fixed personality
that she discovers in Jupp. Her effort at redemption
is laudable, but it is nearly hopeless in the face of
petty corruptions instilled by a social system based
on selfishness and self-aggrandizement. Perhaps
Pimm remains uncorrupted by wealth because she
never actively seeks it, a particularly conservative
social message from Gissing that implicitly locks individuals within their class. But Gissing does use
the tale to indict a system. "Our" Mr. Jupp not only
refers to the interest in him shared by Pimm and
Gissing, but also to the responsibility for him
shared by all members of a capitalist society.

Gissing wrote his stories quickly, and many
are so brief that they often need to be examined in
pairs to discover a reasonably full treatment of a
particular theme or concern. He continues the
exposé begun in "Our Mr. Jupp" in his next story,
"A Capitalist" (*National Review,* April 1894; collected in *The House of Cobwebs and Other Stories,*
1906). This simple character study traces the successful career of an insecure, ambitious man named
Ireton. In this tale Gissing exposes the characteristics that lead to success at business. His character
desperately needs the security afforded by money
and is constantly afraid of how others see him, so
he strives eagerly to better himself. Ireton is neither
a saint nor a sinner. He exploits business situations
without ever breaking the law, takes offense easily
when he feels he is being slighted, and uses his free
time to acquire a veneer of polish because he knows
that it makes him more socially presentable. He neither hurts nor helps others; he simply uses the business arena to assuage his inferiority complex.

This is one of Gissing's most successful studies of an individual living a life dictated by a certain
psychology and the possession of moderate abilities.
Ireton may be seen as a realistically drawn William
Dorrit from Dickens's *Little Dorrit* (1857). Like

Dickens's character he is never able to overcome a self-image formed through years of poverty, but unlike Dorrit he is not prone to melodramatically self-defeating action. In this way Ireton anticipates Henry Wilcox in E. M. Forster's *Howards End* (1910), a typical capitalist with limited sensitivities and predictable character flaws. Certainly Ireton is the Phoebe of Gissing's artistic maturity; like his predecessor Ireton remains true to a psychology, but his tale is not hampered by Gissing's earlier histrionics. As in the case of Phoebe, Ireton demonstrates time and again that money does not truly assuage insecurity, that individuals carry deep scars no matter how their economic situations change.

This tension resonates through Gissing's life story as well. The years with Edith were stormy as both battled personal demons. She was psychologically troubled, and he considered her so far beneath him socially and intellectually that he scorned her. While the union did produce two sons (Walter Leonard, born 10 December 1891, and Alfred Charles, born 20 January 1896), their home life was violent and torturous. Gissing finally separated from Edith on 17 September 1897, and their last meeting was on 7 September of the following year. It was a sad scene in which she came to beg for a reconciliation, which Gissing refused. Alfred Charles, who was with his mother, did not even recognize his father. Gissing demanded sympathy from others regarding the marriage for the rest of his life, but the years he and Edith spent together were some of his most fruitful, while they were unrelentingly tragic for her. She was later committed to a mental asylum where she died in 1917, as unhappy and pathetic an individual as any that Gissing produced fictionally, but without the sympathetic audience that Gissing's tales found.

In marked contrast to his own relationships, Gissing did construct fictional visions of ideal pairings between men and intellectual, sensitive women; not surprisingly, these rarely end in marriage. A case in point is the fine story "Comrades in Arms" (*English Illustrated Magazine*, September 1894; collected in *Human Odds and Ends*), whose heroine, Miss Childerstone, is a successful writer around forty years old. Her longtime "comrade," Wilfrid Langley, also a successful writer, has always considered Childerstone too "mannish" for romantic interest. When Childerstone becomes ill and delicate, Langley falls in love with her. Here Gissing shows the results of his own hard lessons in the psychology of spurious forms of attraction, for Langley is an impulsive young man who does not truly love the robust woman that Childerstone is when healthy. Happily, she is far too intelligent and aware to be misled by Langley's protestations of love. She gently but firmly rejects him. Months later they meet as "comrades in arms" again, with only hearty good wishes on her part and a few doleful memories on his. Throughout Gissing's fiction relative contentment, or the wistful melancholy that must often suffice, is usually reserved for those individuals who avoid matrimony. To marry is always to court disaster.

Nowhere is Gissing's tragic life story more clearly revealed than in his grim tale "A Lodger in Maze Pond" (*National Review*, February 1895; collected in *The House of Cobwebs and Other Stories*). In fact one might read the tale as Gissing's reflections on and internal dialogue concerning his two failed marriages. The narrator is Harvey Munden, a writer who serves as the voice of reason in the story. His counterpart is Henry Shergold, a sensitive, socially principled man who makes not one but two bad marriages because he desperately needs affection and validation and is only comfortable making love to a working-class woman.

Shergold's long explanation to Munden about his reasons for proposing to his landlady's daughter (after he inherits eighty thousand pounds and might be comfortable for life) can be read as Gissing's flawed explanation to himself at the time he proposed to Edith Underwood — she was easily impressed with his intellect and posed no challenge to his shaky self-esteem. Shergold also blames the woman for plotting to "capture" him, but he does take substantial responsibility for his own complicity in a disastrous situation. While Munden convinces Shergold to flee England and his inappropriate fianceé, Shergold's self-destructive tendencies return. He marries the woman and dies under mysterious circumstances shortly thereafter. As the title indicates, Shergold is truly caught in a maze, one that he freely admits reflects a "morbid psychology" that Gissing no doubt came to recognize in himself.

In this tale one finds Shergold accurately "self-diagnosing," but more often than not Gissing allows his readers to arrive at their own conclusions. Through the mid 1890s he published many brief sketches of personalities and psychological types. He perfected the format to allow the exposure of human nature with seeming objectivity, as a scientist might report data or a social researcher recount a case history. Collectively titled *Human Odds and Ends*, these sketches examine what might be considered the margins of society, the odds and ends, but together they make a powerful case for these

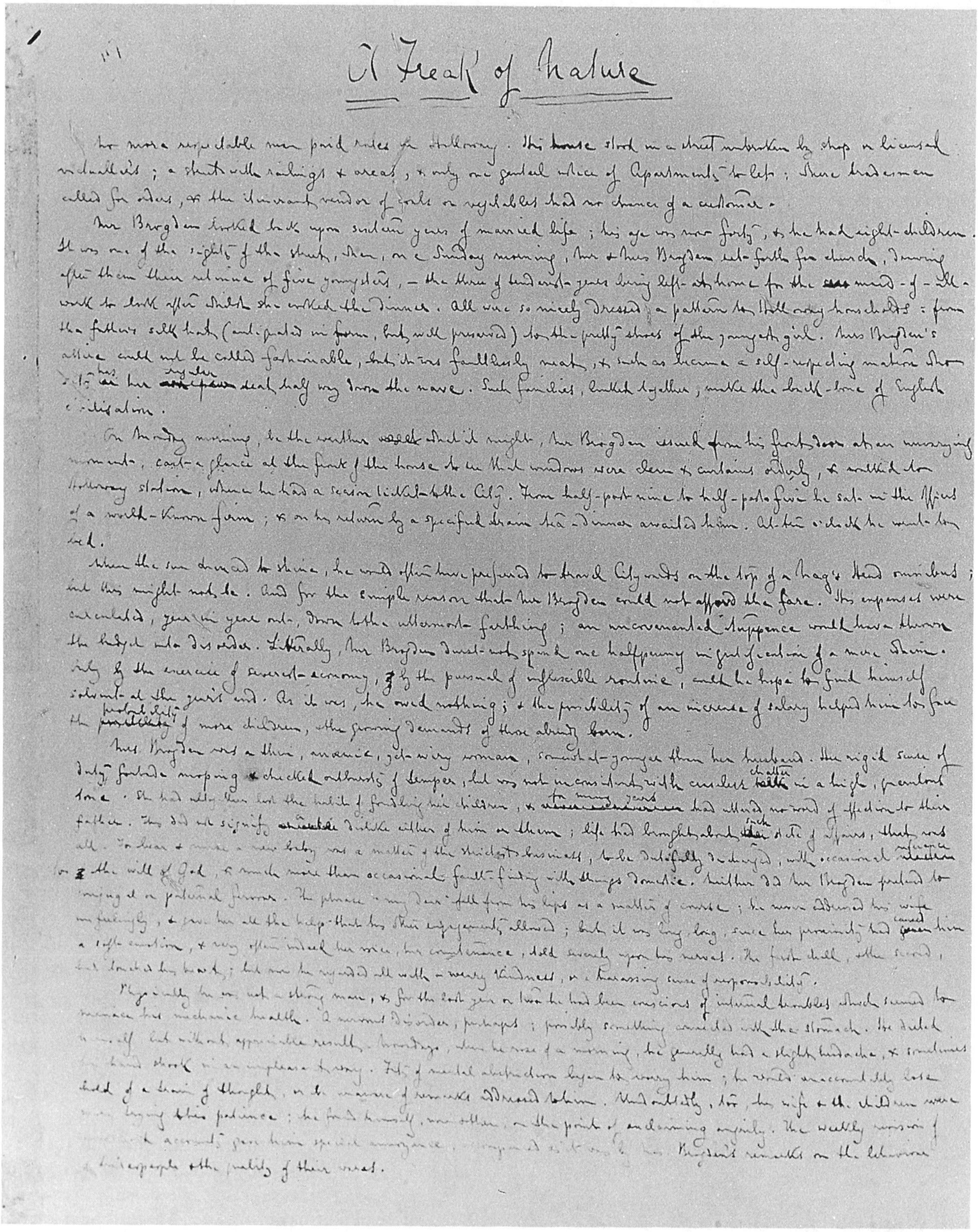

A Freak of Nature

First page of the manuscript for "A Freak of Nature," which was retitled "Mr. Brogden, City Clerk" when it was published in Harmsworth Magazine, *February 1899 (University of Kansas Libraries, MS P128A)*

HE SELECTED A CIGAR WITH FASTIDIOUS APPRECIATION.

Illustration by Fred Barnard for "An Inspiration" (English Illustrated Magazine, *December 1895*)

individuals' centrality in any understanding of society and human nature. From unqualified doctors playing on their patients' ignorance to irresponsible clergymen who skip town when their debts become overwhelming, Gissing focuses repeatedly on incarnations of negligence and corruption. He never loses sight, however, of the extraordinarily difficult economic and personal circumstances that help account for the continued replication of these types among the young.

In "The Tout of Yarmouth Bridge" (*Sketch,* 13 November 1895), he chronicles a day in the life of a conniving, wholly unscrupulous twelve-year-old girl who learns to dupe individuals into staying at a squalid lodging house and then to blackmail her corrupt employer. She is intelligent, energetic, and something of a genius at her job. One finishes the sketch with a sense of enormous but wasted potential or, rather, potential put to morally reprehensible purposes. In the face of such corruption, Gissing challenges his audience to become socially responsible, even if his vision never moves beyond a call for more benevolent paternalism by the upper classes.

Similarly, in "An Old Maid's Triumph" (*Sketch,* 30 October 1895; collected in *Human Odds and Ends*), Gissing shows the reader a few hours out of a single day in the life of a drab, hardworking governess. She has worked strenuously for many years, has denied herself all luxuries, and is modestly repaid by a tiny bonus from her last employer that allows her to purchase a small annuity — enough to buy food and lodging through her old age. Gissing foregrounds this "triumph" for his audience's inspection and education. Readers are challenged to evaluate their own lives and encouraged to take responsibility for the equitable treatment of servants, governesses, and clerks, who face problems that are as immediate and life altering as any that confront the middle or upper classes.

In this way Gissing can be considered among the most provocative short-story writers of all time. Despite his many biases he never allows readers to retain their complacency about social issues — alternately, even simultaneously, shocking, infuriating, and moving them. His exhortation to social responsibility continues powerfully in "An Inspiration"

(*English Illustrated Magazine,* December 1895; collected in *Human Odds and Ends*), which demonstrates the ability of one kind individual to change another's life for the better. On a whim Harvey Munden (the sensible, well-to-do character from "A Lodger in Maze Pond") invites a poor salesman to dine with him. The shy, nervous guest, Nangle, opens up as the meal progresses, gaining both a healthier appearance and greater self-confidence from his first good meal in ages. After confiding in his host and receiving sound advice, Nangle is able to take decisive action, finally winning the woman he loves and a better station for himself. He warmly thanks Munden, knowing that the dinner has changed his life.

While Nangle attributes the invitation to "Providence," Munden calls it simply an inspiration. Gissing's perspective seems to lie between the two. In this story he gives near-divine power to human beings, who have the ability through acts of simple kindness and sympathy to alter radically the wretched lives around them. Here and elsewhere Gissing shows the influence not only of Dickens but also of George Eliot, whose work he respected, for she also recognized well the intricate webs that connect the lives of the rich and the poor, and the responsibilities that go with such ties.

Individuals who have lived their lives quietly, nervously, and desperately populate the pages of Gissing's mature and most successful short fiction. In "The Schoolmaster's Vision" (*English Illustrated Magazine,* September 1896; collected in *A Victim of Circumstances and Other Stories*), the reader meets a drab headmaster who goes through a midlife crisis after making the acquaintance of an attractive woman. After having three dreams in which his profound fear of change and strong, "emasculating" women is revealed, he reverts to hypercomplacency at the story's end, counseling a departing student to cultivate moderation in all things and remain plodding throughout life. He justifies his unfulfilling life by articulating its rules to a young man. All melodrama has been removed from this story line; instead Gissing simply pays careful attention to the nuances distinguishing one individual's pain or happiness from another's.

Such is the case in "The Peace Bringer" (*Lady's Realm,* October 1898), perhaps Gissing's most complex and remarkable exploration of married life. Here one meets the dying poet Jaffray, who is not unhappily married but who has always looked about for another, more exciting woman than his own wife. Mrs. Jaffray is sensitive, competent, and kind but also lonely and unfulfilled. When Jaffray selfishly and insensitively hires a former girlfriend to play the piano for him, his wife allows him to enjoy the other woman's company, while she rechannels her energy and interest into socially useful projects. No longer in love with the man who ignores her, she nevertheless pities and forgives him. By the end of the tale, as he approaches death and realizes that his pianist has left him for more exciting adventures, Jaffray comes to recognize the worth of his wife, who has remained kind and generous.

This quiet, serious, and affecting story may demonstrate a coming to terms for Gissing, a recognition that marriages are always the responsibility of two parties. The approach of the "peace bringer," death, leads both characters to reevaluate their lives and expectations. Gissing extracts a profound lesson from a story with no tempestuous emotions and little real action, for the tale of the Jaffrays is finally a call for kindness, tolerance, and consideration.

Gissing finally achieved a degree in his own life. In July 1898 he met the final woman with whom he was romantically involved. Gabrielle Fleury was an intellectually gifted, sensible, and attractive Frenchwoman with wide connections to the Paris literary scene. She first contacted Gissing to inquire about doing a French translation of his successful novel *New Grub Street.* They soon fell in love, even though she was unlike any other woman with whom he had had an intimate relationship. Perhaps he perceived her as something of a conquest, for certainly much of his patriarchal arrogance was still intact. But she was clearly an intellectual match for him, and he respected her thoroughly. Gissing even went so far as to tell her that she should disregard some of his misogynous characterizations, for he "so often wrote in a bitter mood."

While they could not legally marry (Gissing was unable to get a divorce from Edith), they held a private ceremony on 7 May 1899, pledging their love for one another and quickly settling into a relatively successful partnership. Nevertheless, both individuals were strong willed and set in their ways. When Gissing inevitably tried to reshape Gabrielle to fit his preconceived notions, she was strong enough to resist him and usually patient enough to overlook his all-too-obvious faults. He was predictably querulous about the minutiae of her housekeeping and domestic arrangements. He detested French cooking and by late 1900 was complaining that his wife was starving him. In letters to friends he whined that he was emasculated by his relationship to a strong-willed woman, though, as usual, he continued to write at an amazing pace, producing four novels, a travel book, a fictional memoir, and many stories and essays in the final four years of his life.

Some of these last stories are also some of his finest. "The House of Cobwebs" (*Argosy*, May 1900; collected in *The House of Cobwebs and Other Stories*), for example, is one of Gissing's most complex tales. As Robert L. Selig notes in *George Gissing* (1983), it challenges the myth, current during Gissing's day, that young writers enjoy a comfortable, if bohemian, life while producing their first stories. Instead Gissing draws on his experiences to demonstrate the hardships and squalor endured by aspiring authors. The young hero, Goldthorpe, is a poor man trying to finish his first book. In need of a sunny place to work for three months, he moves into a run-down, cobweb-filled house occupied by a timid, kind man named Spicer. Their time is spent in labor punctuated by friendly conversation – Spicer devotes himself to his garden, while Goldthorpe writes. They are dreadfully poor but not unhappy; in fact, only rarely in Gissing's tales does one find a similarly successful marriage for one of his writer heroes.

Here Gissing's desire to portray the unhealthiness of a struggling young writer's life dovetails with certain pervasive anxieties of his era. The unwholesomeness of the house seems to register Gissing's and his society's profound discomfort with a domestic partnership between men. Much as in *Great Expectations* (1861), where Miss Havisham and Estella's diseased home signifies a social stigma attached to their relationship, so too is the house of cobwebs a symbolic manifestation of what is perceived as an unhealthy arrangement between two members of the same sex.

After finishing his work Goldthorpe falls ill and begins to dislike the crumbling abode. When his manuscript is rejected, he must return to his mother's home while he recovers from a serious illness, which his doctor attributes to living in some "unhealthy" place. Clearly this representation draws on the late-nineteenth-century medicalization of homosexuality and the homophobic climate of the years following the Oscar Wilde scandal. Only at the "natural" domestic hearth of his mother does Goldthorpe fully recover. When he is well again and his book is accepted by another publisher, he returns to visit Spicer but finds that the house has caved in and his friend is hospitalized. The chimney of the house of cobwebs, the "unnatural" domestic hearth, fell on Spicer after, significantly, he moved into the bedroom formerly inhabited by Goldthorpe. Spicer says that he will never return to live

in the house, revealing that the injury "is a chastisement for overweening desires." As was the case twenty-three years earlier in "The Sins of the Fathers," Gissing here evinces continuing anxiety over desire that transgresses social conventions.

Certainly Gissing's own unconventional domestic hearth was no place of placid bliss, for he remained querulous and Gabrielle was not without her own just complaints. She objected chiefly to Gissing's close friendship with H. G. Wells, whom she did not trust. While one might dismiss her feelings as simple jealousy, history has supported her conclusions about Wells. He was not only snide and dismissive toward Gabrielle, but also terribly disloyal to Gissing. As biographers have noted, Wells later vilified Gissing and waged a campaign to destroy the writer's posthumous reputation. Gabrielle may have simply reacted to Wells's obvious dislike for her, or she may have recognized his inherent untrustworthiness. In any event she warned her "husband" repeatedly about his supposed friend. The couple quarreled often, and they separated in 1901, though not permanently. Gissing complained about her inability to understand him; in reality, he was probably frustrated that he was yet again unable to rule his household imperiously.

Not surprisingly, strong-minded women continue to appear in Gissing's fiction from this era. His last great short story is "Miss Rodney's Leisure" (*T.P.'s Weekly*, Christmas 1903; collected in *The House of Cobwebs and Other Stories*). This funny, satisfying tale charts the war waged by a lodger, a schoolmistress named Miss Rodney, as she attempts to reform the household in which she lives. Like Gabrielle, she has strong opinions and acts decisively on them. Miss Rodney instructs her slovenly landlady in proper cooking and cleaning procedures, reforms the latter's drunken husband by teaching him Euclid, and manages to evict a debauched fellow tenant and to install a lodger of her own choosing. Throughout she remains optimistic and self-possessed. In a key scene Gissing reveals himself yet again. When Miss Rodney issues an ultimatum about her drunken neighbor (either he is evicted or she will leave), the newly reformed family chooses its taskmaster.

In 1902 Gissing and Gabrielle moved together to the south of France. He hoped to recover his health there, for he was very ill throughout his last years. His emphysema worsened while he continued to work strenuously. One might add his name to a long list of writers, which would include his beloved Dickens, whose work habits no doubt contributed to their ill health. But, like Thomas Carlyle earlier in the nineteenth century, Gissing revered work, finding it a means to structure and evaluate the successes of what he perceived as an otherwise meaningless existence – a process fictionally rendered in Gissing's last story, published a year after his death.

"The Pig and Whistle" (*Graphic,* Christmas 1904; collected in *The House of Cobwebs and Other Stories*) is an optimistic little tale about two lonely, industrious individuals who find appropriate careers and what may be a perfect marriage. Mr. Ruddiman is a teacher wholly unsuited to his profession. His daydreams center on budgets and the proper management of money, while his healthy enjoyment of the outdoors leads him to ramble far and wide in the lanes and fields surrounding his school. He finds his perfect complement in the daughter of the proprietor of a small inn that lies on one of his customary routes. Miss Fouracres is a busy, sensitive individual who loves running the small business in the countryside. Here cosmic forces conspire to bring them together. When Miss Fouracre's foolish father drowns while drunk, Ruddiman rushes to console her:

> Had it not been dark Mr. Ruddiman would hardly have ventured to make the suggestion which fell from him in a whisper. Had it not been dark Miss Fouracres would assuredly have hesitated much longer before giving her definite reply. As it was, five minutes of conversation solved what had seemed a harder problem than any the under-master set to his class at Longmeadows, and when these two turned to enter the Pig and Whistle, they went hand in hand.

As Gissing's final exploration of marriage, this is a nonsensational, optimistic, and thoroughly satisfying look at the possibility for happiness and success between well-suited individuals. It rounds out Gissing's often heavy-handed, if probing, critiques of failed relationships and perhaps indicates a new-found optimism that grew out of his final days with Gabrielle.

These days were cut tragically short, for in December 1903 Gissing caught a cold that turned into a fatal bout with pneumonia. His deathbed scene, like much of Gissing's fiction, had both comic and tragic aspects, with Gabrielle following a French doctor's advice on how to treat Gissing's illness, and English friends, including Wells, following an entirely different regimen when her back was turned. Halperin speculates that Gabrielle's caretaking was the one more likely to assuage Gissing's illness, with Wells perhaps further damaging Gissing's precarious health.

He lingered only a few days, dying on 28 December 1903, and was buried in the English cemetery at Saint Jean-de-Luz, France. There were immediate reports of a histrionic deathbed religious conversion, but this seems unlikely; Gissing no doubt remained as skeptical at the end as he had been throughout his life. His possessions were left to Edith and their sons, with no mention made of Gabrielle in his will. This may seem peculiar and negligent, but it really was quite appropriate, for Edith and the boys clearly needed financial support more than Gabrielle.

Halperin writes that "the subjects of Gissing's last works are the same as those of his first," and certainly this is true. His fiction reveals as many repetitions as it does limitations. Nevertheless, several of his novels stand out as works of lasting insight and emotional impact. *New Grub Street* and *The Odd Women* have received the bulk of the critical attention that has been paid to Gissing. Among his tales – collected in such anthologies as *The House of Cobwebs and Other Stories, Sins of the Fathers and Other Tales, A Victim of Circumstances and Other Stories, Brownie* (1931), and *Stories and Sketches* (1938) – one also finds several masterful works, but these have received relatively little notice from critics.

Certainly Gissing's biographers are helpful here, for they have placed his stories into the context of his life and times. Halperin and Jacob Korg trace the development of Gissing's craft with careful attention to factual evidence and the social currents of his day. But the best overview of Gissing's work, and one of the few to examine closely his career as a short-story writer, is Selig's *George Gissing.* Selig argues convincingly that the "inconclusive brevity [of Gissing's stories] seems particularly appropriate to his vision of human beings as fallible little creatures entangled in their petty social webs." He follows critics J. M. Mitchell and W. V. Harris in arguing that Gissing's later stories in particular remain among the most potent explorations of human misery produced during the late nineteenth century.

Gissing's contribution to the development of the short-story genre was not insignificant. His mature character studies, devoid of most sentimentality and melodrama, reveal the environmental and psychological bases for human perception and behavior. He exposes the fears and fantasies that account for human foibles, thus retaining, even in his most scathing pieces, a measure of implicit sympathy for his characters. Gissing was no hard-boiled cynic. His dense, intense tales are designed to effect positive change in readers, who are urged to self-examine as well as examine the moral failings of their society. That Gissing's articulations and representations are themselves ideologically bound and evince perceptual blindspots provides continuing grist for critical mills and a starting point for the perceptive articles that appear regularly in the *Gissing Journal*, a quarterly publication devoted to critiquing the life and art of the moody, erratic, and fascinating writer.

Certainly Gissing was a man of many contradictions and complexities, full of anger at the world and some of the people who populate it. While his stinging criticism may not always appear perfectly targeted, it remains both shocking and illuminating. Gissing's short fiction has a clear place in any consideration of English literary and social history, for it brings into focus the economic and psychological currents of an era, as well as the harsh social realities of the time. Gissing may not be the most consistent or talented writer of short fiction of his period, but he recorded its shortcomings with a directness that has lost little of its impact in the intervening years.

Letters:

Letters of George Gissing to Members of His Family, edited by Algernon Gissing and Ellen Gissing (London: Constable, 1927; Boston: Mifflin, 1927);

The Letters of George Gissing to Eduard Bertz, 1887–1903, edited by Arthur C. Young (New Brunswick, N.J.: Rutgers University Press, 1961);

Gissing and H. G. Wells: Their Friendship and Correspondence, edited by R. A. Gettmann (London: Hart-Davis, 1961; Urbana: University of Illinois Press, 1961);

The Letters of George Gissing to Gabrielle Fleury, edited by Pierre Coustillas (New York: New York Public Library, 1964);

Henry Hick's Recollections of George Gissing, Together with Gissing's Letters to Hick, edited by Coustillas (London: Enitharmon, 1973);

The Letters of George Gissing to Edward Clodd, edited by Coustillas (London: Enitharmon, 1973);

Brief Interlude: The Letters of George Gissing to Edith Sichel, edited by Coustillas (Edinburgh: Tragara, 1987);

The Collected Letters of George Gissing, 4 of 8 volumes to date, edited by Paul F. Mattheisen and others (Athens: Ohio University Press, 1990–   ).

Bibliographies:

Pierre Coustillas, "Gissing's Short Stories: A Bibliography," *English Literature in Transition,* 7, no. 2 (1964): 59–72;

Joseph J. Wolff, ed., *George Gissing: An Annotated Bibliography of Writings about Him* (De Kalb: Northern Illinois University Press, 1974);

Michael Collie, *George Gissing: A Bibliographical Study* (Winchester, U.K.: Saint Paul's Bibliographies, 1985).

Biographies:

Mabel Collins Donnelly, *George Gissing: Grave Comedian* (Cambridge, Mass.: Harvard University Press, 1954);

Jacob Korg, *George Gissing: A Critical Biography* (Seattle: University of Washington Press, 1963);

Michael Collie, *George Gissing: A Biography* (Folkestone, U.K.: Dawson, 1977);

John Halperin, *Gissing: A Life in Books* (Oxford: Oxford University Press, 1982).

References:

Pierre Coustillas, ed., *Collected Articles on George Gissing* (London: Cass, 1967);

Coustillas and Colin Partridge, eds., *Gissing: The Critical Heritage* (London & Boston: Routledge & Kegan Paul, 1972);

David Grylls, *The Paradox of Gissing* (London: Allen & Unwin, 1986);

W. V. Harris, "An Approach to Gissing's Short Stories," *Studies in Short Fiction,* 2 (1965): 137–144;

J. M. Mitchell, "Notes on George Gissing's Short Stories," *Studies in English Literature* (Tokyo), 38 (1962): 195–205;

Robert L. Selig, *George Gissing* (Boston: Twayne, 1983);

Gillian Tindall, *The Born Exile: George Gissing* (London: Temple Scott, 1974).

Papers:

Many of Gissing's papers are in the Beinecke Library, Yale University. Other significant collections are at the New York Public Library.

R. B. Cunninghame Graham

(24 May 1852 – 20 March 1936)

Dale Kramer
University of Illinois

See also the Graham entry in *DLB 98: Modern British Essayists, First Series.*

BOOKS: *The Nail and Chainmakers,* by Graham, J. L. Mahon, and C. A. V. Conybeare (London: London Press, n.d.);

Economic Evolution (Aberdeen: Leatham, 1891; London: Reeves, 1891);

Notes on the District of Menteith, for Tourists and Others (London: Black, 1895);

Father Archangel of Scotland, and Other Essays, by Graham and G. [Gabriela Marie Cunninghame Graham] (London: Black, 1896);

Mogreb-el-Acksa: A Journey in Morocco (London: Heinemann, 1898; revised edition, London: Duckworth, 1921; New York: Viking, 1930);

Aurora La Cujiñi: A Realistic Sketch in Seville (London: Smithers, 1898);

The Ipané (London: Unwin, 1899; New York: Boni, 1925);

Thirteen Stories (London: Heinemann, 1900);

A Vanished Arcadia: Being Some Account of the Jesuits in Paraguay, 1607–1767 (London: Heinemann, 1901; New York: Macmillan, 1901);

Success (London: Duckworth, 1902);

Hernando de Soto: Together with an Account of One of His Captains, Gonçalo Silvestre (London: Heinemann, 1903; New York: Dial, 1924);

Progress, and Other Sketches (London: Duckworth, 1905);

His People (London: Duckworth, 1906);

Faith (London: Duckworth, 1909);

Hope (London: Duckworth, 1910);

Charity (London: Duckworth, 1912);

A Hatchment (London: Duckworth, 1913);

Scottish Stories (London: Duckworth, 1914);

Bernal Díaz del Castillo: Being Some Account of Him, Taken from His True History of the Conquest of New Spain (London: Nash, 1915; New York: Dodd, Mead, 1915);

R. B. Cunninghame Graham in Buenos Aires, 1876

Brought Forward (London: Duckworth, 1916; New York: Stokes, 1916);

A Brazilian Mystic: Being the Life and Miracles of Antonio Conselheiro (London: Heinemann, 1920; New York: Dodd, Mead, 1920);

Cartagena and the Banks of the Sinú (London: Heinemann, 1920; New York: Doran, 1921);

The Conquest of New Granada: Being the Life of Gonzalo Jiménez de Quesada (London: Heinemann, 1922; Boston: Houghton Mifflin, 1922);

The Dream of the Magi (London: Heinemann, 1923);

The Conquest of the River Plate (London: Heinemann, 1924; Garden City, N.Y.: Doubleday, Page, 1924);

Doughty Deeds: An Account of the Life of Robert Graham of Gartmore, Poet and Politician, 1735–1797 (London: Heinemann, 1925; New York: MacVeagh, 1925);

Pedro de Valdivia, Conqueror of Chile (London: Heinemann, 1926; New York & London: Harper, 1927);

Redeemed, and Other Sketches (London: Heinemann, 1927);

José Antonio Páez (London: Heinemann, 1929; Philadelphia: Macrae-Smith, 1929);

Bibi (London: Heinemann, 1929);

The Horses of the Conquest (London: Heinemann, 1930; Norman: University of Oklahoma Press, 1949);

Writ in Sand (London: Heinemann, 1932);

Portrait of a Dictator, Francisco Solano Lopez (Paraguay, 1865–1870) (London: Heinemann, 1933);

Mirages (London: Heinemann, 1936);

Three Fugitive Pieces (Hanover, N.H.: Westholm, 1960).

Editions and Collections: *Thirty Tales and Sketches,* edited, with an introduction, by Edward Garnett (London: Duckworth, 1929; New York: Viking, 1929);

Rodeo: A Collection of the Tales and Sketches of R. B. Cunninghame Graham, edited by A. F. Tschiffely (London: Heinemann, 1936; Garden City, N.Y.: Doubleday, Doran, 1936);

The Essential R. B. Cunninghame Graham, edited by Paul Bloomfield (London: Cape, 1952);

Two Letters on an Albatross, by Graham and William Henry Hudson, edited by Herbert F. West (Hanover, N.H.: Westholm, 1955);

Selected Short Stories of R. B. Cunninghame Graham, edited by Clover Pertiñez (Madrid: Alhambra, 1959);

The South American Sketches of R. B. Cunninghame Graham, edited by John Walker (Norman: University of Oklahoma Press, 1978);

Beattock for Moffat and the Best of R. B. Cunninghame Graham (Edinburgh: Harris, 1979); republished as *Reincarnation: The Best Short Stories of R. B. Cunninghame Graham* (New Haven: Ticknor & Fields, 1980);

Selected Writings of R. B. Cunninghame Graham, edited by Cedric T. Watts (Rutherford, N.J.: Fairleigh Dickinson University Press, 1981; London: Associated University Presses, 1981);

Tales of Horsemen, edited by Alexander Maitland (Edinburgh: Canongate, 1981);

The Scottish Sketches of R. B. Cunninghame Graham, edited by Walker (Edinburgh: Scottish Academic Press, 1982);

The North American Sketches of R. B. Cunninghame Graham, edited by Walker (Edinburgh: Scottish Academic Press, 1986; Tuscaloosa: University of Alabama Press, 1986).

The most common judgment made of R. B. Cunninghame Graham is that his life was more interesting than his writing. That view is not incorrect, but then his life was to an unusual degree varied, involving an amount of travel rivaling that of such great Victorian adventurers as Sir Richard Burton and Wilfrid Scawen Blunt, along with efforts at earning a livelihood in singular and sometimes dangerous enterprises (including ranching on the pampas in South America, searching for a legendary gold mine in Spain, and selling horses in a South American civil war) before he inherited a debt-laden ancestral property. His socialist political convictions made him an exciting if frequently disruptive member of Parliament and led him to a prison term following a political demonstration. He was both the founder of the separatist National party of Scotland and a friend of the poet, interior designer, and Marxist William Morris (and of many other people with political and literary interests). From the events of his life, many of them adventitious, he developed the sketches and tales that are his principal legacy. As Cedric T. Watts and Laurence Davies state in *Cunninghame Graham: A Critical Biography* (1979): "Robert's South American exploits stocked his brain with remembered situations and remembered sensations for the rest of his life." The same observation applies to Graham's travels in Spain, North Africa, Texas, and Mexico and to memories of life in Scotland.

More than a half century after his death, Graham is best known today for his friendship with and influence on Joseph Conrad, who, despite differences in political beliefs, greatly admired Graham's generous spirit and knowledge of the world. Conrad once said that he could not imagine life without Graham, and the fame of several of Conrad's characters, such as Charles Gould (*Nostromo,* 1904), has eclipsed that of their model, Graham. Graham wrote a good deal of history and biography centered in

South America, in addition to the sketches that constitute his claim to attention as a writer of short fiction – although much of the fiction is in fact autobiography, some of it undisguised. His prose style was admired by other writers and the public despite frequent slovenly syntax and odd punctuation, qualities caused in part by his contempt for the drab work of proofreading. He was admired for his frankness and lack of cant in a time when finding a prose writer who could write directly with neither coyness nor brazenness was rare.

Many of Graham's stories involve prostitutes, most of whom have higher morals than their clients. Other stories depict the pampas culture of gauchos who stoically accept violence, both ritual (knife fights) and political (warring factions), and the stark assurance of death at the loss of one's horse, which is essential to escape predators, animal and human. Nearly all of Graham's stories employ a surplus of detail, evoking a range of experiences that envelop and sometimes overwhelm the events. The consciousness portrayed in Graham's narratives is penetratingly masculine, but imbued with idealism and tolerance.

Ford Madox Ford thought that Graham was rivaled as a prose writer only by W. H. Hudson; Leonard Woolf agreed, and such critics as V. S. Pritchett, Compton Mackenzie, Frank Harris, and H. M. Tomlinson felt his prose style ranked among the highest in the English language. D. H. Lawrence had a far lower opinion, resenting Graham for his clichés and for presenting a "bluff, manly style of soldiers who have not imagination enough to see the things that really matter." T. E. Lawrence, on the contrary, believed that Graham could write "the best 5 or 6 pages imaginable" and that although Graham had "not much brain," he had "a great heart."

An admirer of Guy de Maupassant, Graham had a deep-seated anger at privilege that exploited others, at power that harmed ordinary citizens, and at belief systems that were intolerant. He was openminded on most issues, especially sexual mores. And he was no jingoist: as Richard E. Haymaker notes in *Prince-Errant and Evocator of Horizons* (1967), Graham sarcastically rejected the Eurocentric thought process of the conquistadores that justified their repression of South American natives "by raising the charge of rebellion" (as Haymaker paraphrases Graham, whom "the Indians were to rebel against is not so clear"). He was also capable of unexamined biases, most markedly anti-Semitism. He has been criticized for stories that give the impression of fragmentariness, accidentality, and incompleteness, and in recent years there has been awareness of his own narrow vision, which often caused

him to erupt in outrage without fully considering a situation. But his outrage was directed at large forces, not personal enemies.

Robert Bontine Cunninghame Graham was born in London on 24 May 1852. His father, William Cunninghame Bontine, was an officer in the Scots Greys, a radical in politics, and the heir to vast acreage in Scotland (Gartmore, Ardoch, and Finlaystone). An entail on the Ardoch property required the eldest son to have the surname Bontine until he succeeded to the Gartmore estates. Graham's mother, Anne Elizabeth Fleeming Bontine, was half Scottish and half Spanish, the daughter of an admiral, Charles Elphinstone Fleeming, who served in South American waters and was a reformist member of Parliament, and Doña Catalina Paulina Alesandro de Jiménez. Graham and his mother remained close until her death in 1925, at age ninety-six.

Graham attended Harrow after a few years at a school in Leamington; he also studied in Brussels. The most adventurous parts of his life occurred before he began to write extensively, but his life was never sedentary, even during his most productive years. He was attracted to South America at an early age and went there for the first time shortly before his eighteenth birthday. His ostensible purpose was to learn ranching, but a civil war was under way when he arrived. He may have been captured by one of the bands, but this is uncertain. In any event he fell ill and wired his mother for money to return to Scotland in 1872. In the meantime he suffered an attack of typhus and attempted to turn a quick profit by driving and selling a small herd of horses. He soon returned to South America, however, traveling to interior ports and villages, meeting European revolutionary expatriates, and trying his hand in land developments.

Returning again to Europe in 1874, Graham was legally unable to play a role in administering the family estates despite the near incapacity of his father. Graham traveled on the Continent and in Africa, winding up in Buenos Aires in 1876. He became involved in ranching and another horse drive (described in "Cruz Alta," *Thirteen Stories,* 1900). On most of his trips Graham noticed picturesque aspects of local life, and his writings mix pastoralism and bloody violence, the sounds and odors of quiet evenings in the wild and the harsh, quick conflicts between people with no patience for verbal resolutions of disputes. He became acquainted with both gauchos and Indians.

On another trip to Europe he met in Paris an orphan from Chile, Gabrielle (Gabriela) Marie de la

Balmondière, a Catholic, and married her in London on 24 October 1878. Watts and Davies call it an "elopement"; Gabriela was never made to feel comfortable in the presence of her mother-in-law. The exact reason for this family coolness is not known. Graham resumed his traveling, taking his wife to Texas and Mexico. "A Hegira" (*Thirteen Stories*) reports their party's following, on their way to the United States, the route of a band of escaped Mescalero Apaches who were being killed off by lawmen and ranchers on their flight to refuge in the mountains.

In 1883 Graham's father died; as the eldest of three sons Graham inherited the heavily encumbered estates, which he struggled to maintain, with steadily decreasing revenues. In 1900 he sold out in order to pay off the debts; thereafter he lived on the remaining capital. (The small property Ardoch had been sold in 1887; in 1904 the Grahams bought back the house there.)

His inheritance marked the beginning of Graham's political career. Declaring himself a Liberal candidate for Parliament in 1885, he lost in the election, possibly because the Irish leader Charles Parnell had asked his followers to vote Conservative. But in 1886, following the defeat of William Gladstone's Irish Home Rule bill, Graham won a seat in the ensuing election, for North-West Lanark. From his first speech — an attack on the monarchy, capitalism, colonialism, and imperialism that a news account indicates kept the House "in [a] continuous roar for more than half-an-hour" — his argumentative stances and witty, biting orations in Parliament made him a notorious figure. His support of working-class policies culminated in his being beaten and arrested on Bloody Sunday (13 November 1887) for supporting free speech at a public assembly in Trafalgar Square, in defiance of about two thousand assembled police. (William Morris — who was also there — wrote about this historical event in *News from Nowhere* [1890].) Accused of physically assaulting a police officer, he was eventually sentenced to six weeks in jail for the lesser charge of unlawful assembly.

Always a determined fighter for the causes in which he believed, his no-compromise positions reduced his influence to the point that, as he admitted, he was a leader without a following, however well known he was and however admired for his sympathy for the oppressed. He thought that the miners of his district ought to be represented in Parliament by a miner and — according to some historians — encouraged Keir Hardie in a political career. Graham began to publish political pieces during the late 1880s in such journals as the *Labour Elector,* the *People's Press,* and the *Nineteenth Century.* In the election of 1892, standing as a Labour candidate, he lost; Graham then began to travel again and increased his efforts to salvage Gartmore and Ardoch from their steady financial deterioration.

Spain and Morocco attracted him at this time: Spain, so he could do research on South America in Spanish archives and so Gabriela could research a biography of Saint Teresa (two volumes, published in 1894); Morocco, initially as an extension of Spain's history but eventually for its own exoticism and customs. He and Gabriela thought they had uncovered in a Spanish translation of *Historia Naturalis,* by Pliny the Elder (first century A.D.), a clue to a gold mine, but after considerable effort the assay proved the site, the workings of a former mine, to be exhausted. A foiled journey in Morocco to the forbidden Muslim city Tarudant in 1897 became the subject of his classic travel book, *Mogreb-el-Acksa* (1898). He disguised himself as a Muslim holy man and was detected by the kaid of Kintafi and detained several days before being turned back.

He already had published — in addition to articles on parliamentary subjects, current events, and letters to editors — two collections of essays. *Notes on the District of Menteith* (1895), a highly personalized tourist guide to Graham's early home area, was described as "whimsical" by the London *Times* (6 September 1895), and *Father Archangel of Scotland* (1896), partially written by Gabriela, contains several fine short pieces, such as "A Jesuit." In the same year as *Mogreb-el-Acksa* he published a pamphlet, *Aurora la Cujiñi* (1898), still remarkable for its straightforward details of gore in the bullring and its depictions of powerful sexual arousal; not surprisingly, Graham had a hard time finding a publisher for this essay, which was not widely read. Reviewers were again upset when it was republished in *Charity* (1912).

The travel book established his name — he never wrote a more successful or better-received book — and encouraged a continuing stream of essays, biographies, and histories with a South American focus; reminiscences of Scotland; books of short fiction; other travel books; and sketches on sundry subjects. Throughout his life reviewers praised *Mogreb-el-Acksa* for its style and colorful presentation of an exotic scene, perhaps more than for Graham's contempt for injustice and pretentiousness. Its success had at least one unfortunate aspect: it marked him in the minds of readers and reviewers as a travel writer and may have encouraged him in the direction of excessive detail.

His later life was not without its adventures, including an assignment as honorary colonel (when he was past sixty) to travel to South America to purchase horses for the British Army in Europe (written about in "Bopicuá" [*Brought Forward*, 1916], where he sympathizes with the suffering of animals in war) and a final stand for Parliament (as a Liberal) in 1918. But all in all the last forty years of Graham's life are a tale of literary productivity (of uneven value) and friendships with a host of well-known persons, including literary figures such as Conrad, and an active engagement with the Scottish National party. The "adventures" lay in his advocacy of political reform, defense of helpless animals and violence-oppressed persons of many nations (especially Spain, Argentina, Paraguay, and Scotland), and usually gentle but unmistakable sarcasm at establishment powers of church and capitalism.

Graham's marriage was marked by common interests (travel and writing in particular) and separate individualities. They had no children, and as both were fiercely independent, Graham and Gabriela often went their own ways, frequently writing each other in complaint of loneliness. Although for years weakened by pleurisy and consumption, Gabriela was a heavy smoker. She died of tuberculosis at Hendaye (not far from Biarritz), France, in 1906 and was buried in the ruins of an Augustinian priory on the island Inchmahome in the Lake of Monteith, part of the former Graham estates.

Graham's image is circumscribed by a few quasi-anecdotal details repeated so often by biographers as to turn him into a caricature of a man of principle, adventurous spirit, and haughty demeanor. For instance, his response to the Speaker of the House, who told him to "withdraw" (remove himself from the House floor for having violated procedural rules), of "I never withdraw!" was used by Bernard Shaw as a line for Sergius Saranoff in *Arms and the Man* (1898). There are references to Graham as "the uncrowned king of Scotland" (his family was descended from Robert the Bruce) and "the modern Don Quixote" (William Strang painted Graham as the idealistic, vehement battler for the socially helpless in an illustration for Miguel de Cervantes' novel, and that image remains the standard). There is also his self-promulgated image as a Scottish dandy just as proficient at horses, lassos, and guns as a South American gaucho, transported to the British Parliament as defender of the poor, the voiceless, and the downtrodden. He is sometimes portrayed as a Scottish Nationalist with the ideas of Karl Marx.

All of these details are true, but the glitter of the figure he cut as an aristocrat still vitally concerned with his nation's life damagingly draws attention from the realism, inventiveness, and originality of his fiction. That he was often criticized for a confusing style and linguistic muddle may further explain why he has not endured as one of the major writers of the early part of the twentieth century. Nevertheless, Graham was well regarded by Conrad, Ford, and Shaw. His books usually went through more than one printing, and several had multiple editions.

There is not a significant expansion in the breadth of his vision from the 1890s to the 1930s, perhaps because his essential strategy was to interweave recollection of a personal experience with a general attitude or philosophical judgment, and he had most of the experiences on which he drew in his fiction before the turn of the century, indeed before his writing became a primary activity. By and large his feelings about humanity – the source of an author's characteristic tone – were established before he left South America for the first time. This is not to say that he was a man of little sensitivity or reflectiveness, but as the paradigmatic "man of action" he perceived quickly the critical features and shaping energies of a situation, and, having devised the important generalities, he did not have the patience to tease out ambiguities and complexities.

What Graham's intentions as a writer may have been are unclear. As an aristocrat mixing the manners and expectations of a Spanish grandee and a Scottish laird, Graham portrayed himself as one writing not for money but only to please himself. In short fiction the form he found congenial was the sketch or brief narrative – to term his characteristic writings "short stories" is to suggest a generic relationship to conventional writing that would be misleading. Graham rarely wrote stories with a shaping plot or tracing of consequence. Of first importance to him was the situation, both in the details of its surroundings that establish the uniqueness of the moment and in its bearings upon a diachronic or historical perspective. At least one of his purposes was to memorialize the ways of life in boundary situations – on the literal frontiers of South America and on the metaphoric edge between life and death, danger and safety, in everyday actions. A good Graham story is at once nostalgic and intensely immediate.

His narrative essays – another possible term for Graham's work – began to appear in the mid 1890s, gaining him a reputation as an expert on the vanishing frontiers of South America and on conditions in Spain and adding to his reputation as a perceptive, if scathing, critic of arbitrary power. Some of those published in the *Saturday Review,* the *Social-Democrat,* and the *Badminton Magazine of Sports and Pastimes* were collected in *The Ipané* (1899), the first volume of T. Fisher Unwin's "Over-Seas Library." This was the brainchild of Graham's friend Edward Garnett, who was partly inspired by Graham's short stories, which Garnett thought would be effective if brought together. The aim of the library, as defined in the back of each volume, was to print

> literature from any quarter that deals with the actual life of the English outside England, whether of Colonial life or the life of English emigrants, travellers, traders, officers, over-seas, among foreign and native races, black or white. Pictures of life in the American States will not necessarily be excluded. "The Over-Seas Library" makes no pretence at Imperial drum-beating, or putting English before Colonial opinion. It aims, instead, at getting the atmosphere and outlook of the new peoples recorded.

Graham's loathing of colonialism and British insularity gives an edge of outrage and diatribe to the library's inaugural volume. British fascination with the exotic provided a ready market for Graham's remembrances of unusual circumstances and events.

What attracts one to Graham's narratives is the economical presentation of fact, but the concomitant aspect of this is that the reader seldom develops an emotional commitment to a character before the conclusion, which almost always is presented as a capstone or illustration to the meditation on detail and contingency that has comprised most of the narrative. This emphasis on scene setting is common in late-nineteenth-century short narratives, and so in this Graham was not innovative. What sets Graham distinctly apart from his contemporaries is the nature of his presentation – relentless details of suffering and pain set out in a prosaic, seemingly offhand, unhortatory manner. The moral outrage is conveyed through the sense that "this is what life is, and if it's hard, we must manage to live through it."

The paradigmatic Graham tale in these terms is "Salvagia" (*The Ipané*), set in Scotland, where religion is of faith, not of good works: "Almost the most horrible doctrine ever enunciated by theologians is, in my opinion, the attribution of our misfortunes to Providence" – "an all-wise power, all merciful and omnipresent, enthroned somewhere in omnipotence . . . [that] sees two trains approaching on one line, and yet does nothing to avert the catastrophe or save the victims." In Graham's portrayal life is brutish in Scotland, whose populace is coarse and ignorant, as hapless as the natives of Australia to the European extirpators, or a black rat to the Norwegian rat that expels it. As if to sharpen the contrast, the narrative deals with the widow Campbell, who had religious faith and whose four sons worked hard and did not drink. She lived an exemplary life, with no woes or particular joy, then all of her sons drowned one day in a local pool:

> I asked a woman for whom the cry [the Celtic coronach, which he overhears walking through the village] was raised. She answered, "For the four sons of Lilias Campbell." In the dull way one asks a question in the face of any shock, I said, "What did she say or do when they were brought home dead?"
>
> "Say?" said the woman; "nothing; n'er a word. She just gaed out and milked the kye [cow]."

Graham's ostensible purpose in this story, as in "A Survival" (*The Ipané*), is to correct the sentimental, condescending view of Scotland given by the so-called Kailyard (cabbage patch) School that included J. M. Barrie; but the stories' portrayal of the unrelenting harshness of rural life creates a powerful impact quite independent of a revision of a stereotype. This part of Graham's manner may reflect his admiration for Maupassant. Thus in Graham's work appear graftings of nearly incompatible methods onto an imaginative perception of himself as aristocratic truth teller.

Graham's exotic events and landscapes, presented in a tone other than judgmental in conventional Victorian terms; his offhandedly presented horrificness of incidental cruelty; and his passages of sexuality and violence without conventional moral colorings sharply contrast in other ways with short stories of his times – for example, with those in one of the last of the controversial Keynotes Series, Carlton Dawe's *Kakemonos* (1897), which are prejudiced against women and most people who are not British, and with many of Rudyard Kipling's stories. Kipling, who had begun writing only a few years before Graham, was to a great extent responsible for the enthusiasm for stories of life abroad that Graham exploited in his writings.

In one respect Graham's standard narrative practice conforms to a traditional British form – the tale – more traditional than what is thought of as the "well-made story." The Victorians' love for the unusual, the foreign, and the exotic accounts at least in part for the popularity of many writers, from Kipling's knowledgeable sketches of life in India to H. G. Wells's expertise in scientific and industrial

Gabrielle Marie de la Balmondière, Graham's wife (portrait by G. P. Jacomb-Hood; private collection; from A. F. Tschiffely, Don Roberto, *1937)*

process (as in "The Cone" [1895]) and theories, to Sir Arthur Conan Doyle's sensational but frequently inaccurate employment of details of natural history, such as the use of the cowardly puma as the ferocious animal in "The Brazilian Cat" (1898). Even Wells was comparatively conscious of fiction as art; for Graham, life predominated, and so the preparations of a narrative event are not to establish motivation or mood, but to establish the factuality of the real scene against which the narrative event is perceived.

The first half of the title story in *The Ipané* presents the society and mores of the Casa Horrocks, a general meeting place for Europeans in Asunción, Paraguay, after the civil war that had depleted the population, particularly the men. Graham marks details of speech with quotation marks, presumably to certify the accuracy of his knowledge. He is also taken by details of clothing: Lieutenant Hansel, "late of the British Navy," first appears "in black merino Turkish trousers, high riding-boots, vicuña poncho, red silk handkerchief tied round the neck with the two points neatly spread out behind upon his shoulders in the same style the artist's

'contadina' was assumed to wear her headdress in the 'fifties." References to events in Paraguay and Europe are offhand, as if they would be readily accessible in the minds of his readers, although he describes situations of twenty years earlier. This characteristic is oddly effective: granted that the scenes and information are even more strange than they would have been on initial publication, had Graham emphasized their peculiarities they would seem merely forced, rather than establishing a base for the stark but unsensationalized events.

The dramatized event in the story is the death – by boiler explosion on *The Ipané* (an ancient steamer on the river Plate) – of Hartogg, a German who has married a native woman. Hartogg is an atheist who allows his wife to let a priest bless him at point of death because it will do *her* good; he ends his life with the dry, sardonic statement, "God is great, but inconsiderate." The tone throughout is unsentimentally realistic, climaxed by Hartogg's youngest daughter "smiling" as she finds a remnant of her father fallen from his clothes as he is lowered on an open bier into his grave.

Characteristic of Graham are the unembarrassed description of sexual liaisons between Europeans and local women and the straightforward, dryly offhand observation about Hartogg, buried in the Protestant cemetery "where Germans, Englishmen, atheists, and those who died outside the Christian faith in Paraguay are suffered to remain, *until the armadillos dig them up*" (emphasis added). Such statements, while pleasantly free from cant and sentiment, nevertheless create one of the difficulties in reading Graham, for it is not clear how he places his created narrator – that is, whether the narrator is supposed to be his biographical self, stating his true opinions, or an imaginary self whose views are, like those of the other characters, open to question.

In "The Ipané," for instance, the reader wonders whether the "we" who share ideas about "native" women include Graham or just the other, generic Europeans: "Somehow or other none of us liked Hartogg; perhaps it was his learning, his nationality, his way of stating what he knew was false, in such convincing fashion that it seemed more feasible than truth; it may have been his Paraguayan wife, to whom, being an atheist and violent Bible-smasher, he had been married in a church, thus losing caste according to *our* notions, for, with *us,* concubinage with 'native' women was an honourable state, but marriage carried with it something of degradation" (emphases added). There is a pleasant wit at oneself here, but whether it conveys a present or entirely former standard of conduct is not evident.

The narrative effectively intertwines the fate of the aged steamer with that of Hartogg, one of few people foolhardy enough to entrust their lives to it. Two elements of Paraguayan life held in no great respect – a rusting steamer and a European who has lowered himself by marrying a native woman – are destroyed together. Graham's sense of the importance of detail is pertinent: had the boat not been going upstream at the rapids where the river was flowing at seven knots, the boiler would not have been fired to a hundred pounds per inch (it was rated at forty and had tested at sixty), and the accident would not have happened. These numbers suggest the specificity of Graham in contrast to Conrad, whose *Heart of Darkness* (1902) seldom if ever gets into technical facts in order to explain things. These details convey the idea that it is not fate or an inconsiderate God – but facts understandable and controllable by humans – that determine life's outcome.

Also typical of Graham's strategy is "Bristol Fashion" (*The Ipané*), set along the coast of Africa. Most of the story is an illustration of the title, which refers to the European way of harshly treating Africans. The story begins with an extended description of an African tribe called the Krooboy and of a school in Accra that trains native girls to become translators and, in effect, mistresses for English captains plying the shore trade. No shock is implied by Graham at this; the job "was held to be an honourable and lucrative estate." There is, however, some fairly heavy irony in English captains' admiring native girls' dancing, and waxing tearful about their wives and daughters at home: "Men's minds are built in reason-tight compartments, and what they do but little influences them, for the real life we live is one of thought, and it is not impossible even that in a brothel the mind may still be pure."

Following many pages of such conveyance of a culture both independent of and affected by the colonial European powers, the narrative proper is but a single scene related by the captain, telling how he had deceived three Krooboys of his crew – who had stolen a canoe and gone ashore – into thinking that his ship was a Yankee bark, thus causing the Krooboys to row out and offer to join the Yankee crew. He put them in chains and sold them to a cannibal tribe farther down the coast. The similarity with Conrad's "An Outpost of Progress" is evident, but Graham's command of contingent details makes this story perhaps a more devastating critique of European conduct, although Conrad's European char-

acters are more richly developed as personalities. In *R. B. Cunningham Graham* (1983), Watts discusses the story in relation to both Kipling and Conrad: "Graham's opposition to Kipling is both explicit and implicit. The implicit opposition is evident in the exposure of civilized hypocrisy" and "becomes explicit in the opening survey (written before Conrad's *Heart of Darkness*) of white men's lives on the coast."

"Snaekoll's Saga" (*The Ipané*) is frequently declared one of Graham's best stories. Its setting in Iceland suggests that Graham's genius was not restricted to South America, Hispanic cultures, or Scotland. Indeed, the story conveys that Graham's genius is as essentially mythic and evocative as it is exotic and startling. The tale seems the most conventional one of this collection, with less arcane and detailed preparation. The information about setting is incorporated into the narrative rather than preceding the narrative in a way that makes the narrative itself only an illustrative detail (Graham's frequent tactic in his early stories).

Snaekoll is a fierce horse, a meat eater, powerful and able to go fifty miles with little food. His owner, Thorgrimur, is "a survival . . . of atavism strongly developed" who wants to cross the "great icy desert" Vatna Jokull. His friends call him mad, but the narrator thinks that Thorgrimur's resolve is a sign of strength. The scattered focus of the attack on civilized values conveys both something of Graham's energy and its potential for diffusion:

> The world is to the weak. The weak are the majority. The weak of brain, of body, the knock-kneed and flat-footed, muddle-minded, loose-jointed, ill-put-together, baboon-faced, the white-eye-lashed, slow of wit, the practical, the unimaginative, forgetful, selfish, dense, the stupid, fatuous, the "candle-moulded," give us our laws, impose their standard on us, their ethics, their philosophy, canon of art, literary style, their jingling music, vapid plays, their dock-tailed horses, coats with buttons in the middle of the back; their hideous fashion, aniline colours, their Leaders, Leightons, Logsdails; their false morality, their supplemented monogamic marriage, social injustice done to women; legal injustice that men endure, making them fearful of the law, even with a good case when the opponent is a woman; in sum, the monstrous ineptitude of modern life with all its inequalities, its meannesses, its petty miseries, contagious diseases, its drink, its gambling, Grundy, Stock Exchange, and terror of itself, we owe to those, our pug-nosed brothers in the Lord, under whose rule we live.

Only the horse returns, nearly dead and cannibalistic of other horses. He recovers, refuses to be ridden, and subsequently sires the finest "ice-eater"

Icelandic horses (those that can survive on little vegetation). The man who "owns" him, Hiötr Helagson, remarks: "How he lived amongst the ice and found his way to Beru-fjörd, I cannot tell. Up in the Vatna there is naught but ice, and yet he must have eaten something; *what* it was, God knows!" (emphasis Graham's). Conrad commented to Graham about this story: "It confirms me in my conviction that you have a fiendish gift of showing the futility – the ghastly, jocular futility of life." Graham correlates one culture with another, this time analogizing Snaekoll the horse with "camels in the desert, llamas in Peru, reindeer in Lapland, dogs in Greenland, and caiques amongst the Esquimaux." Life in Iceland is impossible without horses because they carry loads and because Icelanders do not walk anywhere.

The basic strength of this story is that it carries a mythic force. There is no conventional characterization, only a meat-eating horse, a throwback Icelander who prefers the possibility of death alone to a mundane existence, and the wise commentator (Hiötr) who, with a little experience (nearly being killed when he tries to ride Snaekoll), understands the significance of the action. Like most of Graham's fare, it is unsentimental, frank in sexuality, and honest in suggesting that familial and domestic emotions are secondary to Thorgrimur – and to his wife, who is just as glad to see him out of the house.

"Un Pelado" (*The Ipané*) illustrates Graham's anthropological manner of using detail, here to evoke the west Texas cowboy lifestyle. His distance from the scene is conveyed partly through the use of "nigger" in quotation marks, as if to indicate that it is the local word usage, not his, and in noting that José is a " 'greaser,' " a term Americans use "for reasons not explained." The narrator (whose relationship to the scene is, characteristically, never made explicit), as in so many Graham stories, simply observes in a detached, sometimes sardonic manner, as in the oblique but easily decipherable description of whorehouse row, frequented by churchgoers. His relativist perspective dominates the story: just as "mankind is ever wont to typify, making the virtues feminine, the vices (if I mistake not) male, calling the Spaniard proud, the Italian treacherous, the Frenchman fickle, and so on, and understanding best what a town, country, race, or what not, is like by summing up his, their, or its characteristics in some man, I do the same."

José Maria Mendiola and G. M. Hodges, the main characters, are posed "as prototypes, both of Chihuahua and of Encinal," the towns that Graham says are like "man and wife, never to understand each other's motives though living side by side." Graham's pithy and rudimentary domestic allusions go far to humanize all the jargon and detail, and he uses stereotypes or models to make his point about the locations he is describing: "Both [men are] rogues, but different in degree, and each unable to discover any taint of virtue in the other's life."

José shoots Hodges and is condemned to hang. Graham's culture-comparative eye places in a footnote this commentary about José's accusation against Hodges that he has been cheated out of his ivory-handled pistol: "It is the ambition of every Texan and most Mexicans to own either an ivory-handled or a mother-of-pearl handled pistol. It gratifies them just as much as a baronetcy does a successful sweater [exploiter of low-paid workers], and is more readily compassed by the poor in spirit." Graham the radical shows his contempt for British exploiters of the working class, correlating the workers to an illiterate part-Indian peasant denigrated by the white man's term *greaser*.

Graham gives further indication of sympathy for the murderer José, pointing out that the trial had been conducted in English. He also provides José with intellectual and political judgment: he had been born a Catholic but rejected that religion for Universalist beliefs, and he is contemptuous of Americans because they had torn down the original scaffold and rebuilt it because it was not level, an irrelevancy in a world of such rank inequalities: "What does it matter if it was level or not? Even the earth is not quite level, for a poor man, very poor Mexican."

The final observation of the story, as in many Graham stories, has the double edge of conveying impercipience within the society being observed. "An aged settler" notes about the execution: "No sense at all . . . just didn't have no sense at all. Like killing a goat, didn't have sense enough to be afraid." The "aged settler" (who is white) represents Encinal's inability to understand Chihuahua and thus is also like José and Hodges in typifying a general position. This is not an ironic evaluation of either Encinal or Chihuahua, but an iteration of the artist's aesthetic tactic of calling into question all conventional value systems.

Although it is not fiction, the essay "Niggers" (*The Ipané*) has special pertinence in any study of Graham. It clarifies both his views about racial status in Britain and Conrad's, who is often criticized for employing racist attitudes in *Heart of Darkness*. Graham's tone is heavily ironic, and the basic theme of the essay is that God requires "niggers" – races that his favored Aryans/whites can treat contemptuously. The essay traces the development of Europeans through the discardable groups up to the English, who are supreme: "A bold, beef-eating, generous, narrow-minded type, kindly but arrogant; the men fine specimens of well-fed animals, red in the blood and face; the women cleanly, 'upstanding' creatures, most divinely tall; both sexes slow of comprehension, but yet not wanting sense" – and so forth, at some length.

The English see nearly every other national group as "niggers":

> Hindus, as Brahmins, Bengalis, and the dwellers in Bombay; the Cingalese, Sikhs and Pathans, Rajpoots, Parsis, Afghans, Kashmiris, Beluchis, Burmese, with all the peoples from the Caspian Sea to Timur Laut, are thus described. Arabs are "niggers." So are Malays, the Malagasy, Japanese, Chinese, Red Indians, as Sioux, Comanches, Navajos, Apaches with Zapatecas, the Esquimaux, and in the south Ranqueles, Lenguas, Pampas, Pehuelches, Tobas, and Araucanos, all these are "niggers" though their hair is straight. . . . A plague of pigments, blackness is in the heart, not in the face, and poverty, no matter how it washes, still is black. Niggers are niggers, whether black or white, but the archetype is found in Africa. . . . The Ethiopian cannot change his skin, and therefore we are ready to possess his land and to uproot him for the general welfare of mankind, smiting him hip and thigh, as the Jews did the Canaanites when first they opened up the promised land. Niggers who have no cannons have no rights. Their land is ours, their cattle and their fields.

It is understandable why Edward Garnett comments, in his introduction to Graham's *Thirty Tales and Sketches* (1929), "The immortal 'Niggers' . . . and its fellow sketch 'Success' . . . would confer immortality on him if he had written nothing more." Watts observes that "what gave the piece its high reputation was the obliqueness of method and the lofty ironic tone," although to modern taste perhaps "the descriptive catalogs [are] prolix and the ironic stance inconsistently maintained."

However that may be, the essay published in *The Ipané* is a shortened, less caustic version than that published as "Bloody Niggers" in the *Social-Democrat* (April 1897). Nonetheless, reviewers were, according to Herbert Faulkner West in his 1932 biography of Graham, "uncomfortably irritated by *Niggers*. The readers of Conan Doyle, Lucas Mallet, Anthony Hope and other vendors of popular wares could not, with any stretch of the imagination, take kindly to *The Ipané*. Any writer who dares write what only a small intellectual minority feel, and who damns the hypocrisy of his fellows and his

country with such intensity and clarity, must remain unpopular."

Perhaps this explains the reviewer for the *Oxford Magazine* (8 November 1899) finding *The Ipané* an objectionable portrayal of Englishmen, or the suggestion in the *Academy* (29 April 1899) that Graham's hatred of conventionality is a pose. Greater weight was given to literary issues by the reviewer for the *Spectator* (24 June 1899), who observed that Graham's manner is evocative if occasionally too realistic and found pleasure in his strong egotism, energetic language, and original views. The reviewer for *Literature* (29 April 1899) admired Graham's descriptive skills and felt that his cynical tone would please readers; and the *Saturday Review* (29 April 1899) defined Graham's merits as those of "a literary impressionist." Graham was not entirely free of racism himself, as revealed in various slurs and denigrative allusions, such as "a negro is soon moved to tears" ("The Ipané"); but, like Conrad, he was a person of his time, and his casual, lazy racial assumptions were less central than his deliberate emphasis on the equality of all persons subject to the power of the ruling class.

Graham's collections of short narratives usually include pieces first published in periodicals, sometimes nearly ten years before the book. Like Conrad he appears to have felt that a collection should have a common thread or theme. For example, the preface to *Thirteen Stories* claims that most of the sketches

> treat of scenes seen in that magic period, youth, when things impress themselves on the imagination more sharply than in after years; and the scenes too have vanished; that is, the countries where they passed have all been changed, and now-a-days are full of barbed-wire fences, advertisements, and desolation, the desolation born of imperfect progress. The people, too, I treat of, for the most part have disappeared; being born unfit for progress, it has passed over them, and their place is occupied by worthy men who cheat to better purpose, and more scientifically.

But this description is not very exclusionary, noting only the common source of most of his writing and the common scorn for humanity. The message of the first story, "Cruz Alta," is that "failure alone is interesting," which could have placed the story equally well in Graham's next collection, *Success* (1902), in which the title essay insists, "failure alone can interest speculative minds."

In Graham's early years as a writer the reviewers tended to be friendly and admiring. The *Academy* (13 October 1900) reviewer of *Thirteen Stories,* for example, mentions Graham's wit, pathos, and the excitement and generosity engendered by tales ranging from Britain to South America. Given that Graham was a well-known opponent of the monarchy and imperialism, the review attests this journal's stature as one of the principal intellectual organs of the time. The review in *Literature* (27 October 1900) is in keeping with that periodical's emphasis on quality of writing, finding that Graham's work would be more satisfying were his style less vehemently individualistic. In 1936 Garnett noted that "in brilliance and atmospheric strength Graham never surpassed that book's original quality."

In Graham's stories the tone of the narrator is all-important. In "La Clemenza de Tito" the speaker, an engine-room worker, reads Edward Bulwer-Lytton, like Singleton in Conrad's *The Nigger of the "Narcissus"* (1897). The speaker tells about a time he went to a whorehouse and found a black girl who wore a crucifix and called herself a "Klistian girl, Johnny, me Klistian all the same you." He continues:

> That was a stopper over all, and I just reached for my hats, says, "Klistian are yer," and I gave her two of them Spanish dollars and a kiss, and quit the place. What did she say? Why, nothing, looked at me and laughed, and says, "You Klistian, Johnny, plenty much damn fool." No, I don't know what she meant, I done my duty, and that's all I am concerned about.

This story shows Graham's contempt for the moral claptrap of the engine-room man. The prostitute gets Graham's tone right in her scorn for her would-be client's hypocrisy. The narrator's attitude (the story has an "objective" first-person frame) is revealed by his refusing the tale teller's offer of another drink.

In other stories the persona employed as narrator (usually impossible to distinguish from Graham himself) sardonically notes details that in other works of the time would be sensationalized, and sometimes the narrator uses them for philosophical judgment. For example, the narrator of "In a German Tramp" (*Thirteen Stories*) is sensitive to the suffering of fish that are caught and left to gasp out their lives on the deck: "Pathetic but unwept, the tragedy of all the animals, and we but links in the same chain with them, look at it all as unconcerned as gods." Another example of narratorial presence in *Thirteen Stories* is "Calvary," set in the delta of the river Plate, where the message of the vegetation, islands, and trees is that life can pass swiftly: "A land of vegetation so intense as to bedwarf mankind almost as absolutely as we

bedwarf ourselves with our machinery in a manufacturing town."

The story involves a deal for horses, which are put on board a ship. The narrator muses which suffers more, the four-footed animal or the biped. Men may be a "higher organism," but "who shall say if animals, when suddenly removed from all that sanctifies their lives, do not pass agonies far more intense than such endured by those whose education or whose reason — what you will — still leaves them hope." The description of the shipboard agonies and terrors of the animals being taken to Europe for use as cab horses on London streets reminds one of Stevie's sympathy for the cabhorse that is being beaten in Conrad's *The Secret Agent* (1907), although Conrad makes clear that the cabdriver is as miserable in his own way as the horse and that when he leads the horse to drink he is establishing a brotherhood. If there is a distinction between the two writers in this respect, Graham is here, as nearly everywhere, more activated by social considerations than Conrad. Graham condemns the mistreatment of animals by modern society; Conrad demonstrates mistreatment by the universe.

In other stories narratorial judgment seems to be beside the point, and these can be among his most powerful. "La Pulperia" (the pub; the meeting place) is a sketch or description of activities in a saloon frequented by gauchos; the narrator indulges in some verbal posturing about how the gauchos "took a life as other men take a cigar." The sketch is climaxed by the narrator's shouting an inflammatory slogan ("Viva Urquiza") to an old Rosas supporter of whom all the gauchos are afraid. The Rosas supporter fulminates but is evidently either too feeble or too drunk to hold his knife, so the narrator goes outside and "either impelled by the strange savagery inherent in men's blood *or by some reason I cannot explain,* caught the infection, and getting on my horse, a half-wild 'redomon,' spurred him and set him plunging, and at each bound struck him with the flat edge of my facon [knife or stiletto], then shouting 'Viva Rosas,' galloped out furiously upon the plain" (emphasis added).

The conclusion is not ineffective, but just what it means is uncertain: had he just been baiting the old Rosas supporter, posturing for the benefit of the supposedly tough gauchos, or hoping to goad the Rosas supporter into a real fight so he could shoot him with his revolver? Perhaps the intention is to suggest that the narrator has been embittered by some emotional experience. The last scene, with the spurring of the horse, is like the end of James

Joyce's "Araby" (written 1905; published 1914) — an undefined epiphany. In "Cunninghame Graham's South American Sketches" (1972), Davies — referring to the way the story is typical of Graham in offering a mass of details and generic information about country stores — suggests that the conclusion is in effect a comment on Graham's literary method: "One might even say that the sketch is about the way objective memory may suddenly become personal."

Another strength of this volume is the nearness to myth of many of these stories. "The Gold Fish" tells of a messenger, Amarabat, charged with carrying a beautiful bowl with seven golden fish from one Arab leader, a Khalifa, to another, the Sultan, across varied terrains, and who dies on the way. Amarabat fails not because the task is impossible, but because he smokes hashish; two days from the end of his long trip he goes into a state between sleeping and waking and becomes lost. It is not known whether Amarabat violates his charge to the extent of drinking the water in which the fish live (thus hastening their deaths); but he clearly obeys the most pressing charge, to deliver the bowl unchanged. When his corpse is found, the bowl "still glistened beautiful as gold, in the fierce rays of the Saharan sun." This neatly arranged story produces a mythlike aura not unlike that of "Snaekoll's Saga."

A basic issue that Graham's critics need to address concerns the difference between the pieces that are most characteristic of him and those that conform to traditional expectations of short fiction. Many of Graham's most interesting short narratives only marginally meet conventional expectations; naturally, most readers feel more comfortable with pieces that have beginnings, middles, and ends and that display characters operating within cause-and-effect relationships to society and their own intentions. Graham began his career by writing about subjects that appealed to him, but as time went on, conventional tactics of presentation gained precedence over his unique vision (which of course had limitations as well as strengths).

The result was not a dilution of Graham's socialist and misanthropic vision, but by embodying his aggravation in accustomed aesthetic form he diluted its impact. His manner became less that of reportage and more that of a fictional shaping of reality — and the implication of traditional fictional form is that it imposes a mediating artistry between fact and reader. The transition seems to have occurred during the writing of the stories that were collected in *Success* and *Progress* (1905). Watts be-

lieves that Graham's proficiency increased markedly after *The Ipané;* however, "proficiency" nullifies the sense of unmediated recollection that is at the core of the power of Graham's raw directness. By the time he wrote the pieces collected in *Progress* and later volumes of short fiction, Graham had used up his most viscerally effective recollections.

None of the collections, however, is without touches that smack of Graham. Several stories in *Success* superbly represent two qualities that pervade nearly all of his fiction: disenchantment with humanity and indifference to conventional estimates of behavior. The preface sets out the book's intentions, offering a lengthy, sometimes obscurely phrased analogy between Roman gladiators — whose lives depend on thumbs-up/down of people not capable of understanding, let alone performing, the actions they judge — and a writer, whose trifling subjects (such as political economy) become antiquated within a decade. The writer who has "anything to say" has an even keener battle "with his heaven-sent readers" because once a creed is accepted "all the interest of the fight is gone." Emphasizing Graham's urbane invective against the background of late-nineteenth-century complacency and imperial arrogance, Watts states that "the preface is a humorous attack on patrons, critics and the 'respectable public' in general." Although Conrad wrote Graham that "there may be a fallacy somewhere in your view of the world," he held comparable misanthropic views.

The title essay — essentially an opinion piece with no elements of fiction other than a description of the skeleton of a fictional Spanish general sitting in a chair and looking out to sea — turns on the proposition that failure is more engrossing than success, the effect of which is to diminish the personality. Who is remembered more, Elizabeth I or Mary, Queen of Scots; Hannibal and Napoleon or their conquerors? Every success has been preceded by many failures, by other similar people. This makes success hard to bear for the sensitive person, and popular acclaim odious:

> Who with a spark of humour in his soul can bear success without some irritation in his mind? But for good luck he might have been one of the shouters who run sweating by his car.... Success is but the recognition (chiefly by yourself) that you are better than your fellows are. A paltry feeling, nearly allied to the base scheme of punishments and of rewards which has made most faith arid, and rendered actions noble in themselves mere huckstering affairs of fire insurance.... Nothing can stand against success and yet keep fresh. Nations as well as individuals feel its vulgarising power.

UP AGAINST THE MARGIN OF A STREAM

Illustration by Anthony De Bree for "The Bolas" (Badminton Magazine, *June 1898*)

The illustrations of these ideas in the stories are predictably wry and often biting, although Graham manages to mute his contempt for the arrogant classes who do not perceive human standards of success. Some of Graham's most effectively managed deployments of irony are in *Success*. "Might, Majesty, and Dominion" describes the funeral cortege of Queen Victoria through London. An encomium on her rule notes the great wealth created in sixty years, the power of the empire, and so forth. The brief final scene, presented without a change in tone, bears upon her success: an old man "grown old in the long reign of the much-mourned ruler," feeding "ravenously" on a piece of food discarded by a mourner, "which the two dogs had looked at with disdain." Victoria's "triumph" is rather modified by this final image of her rule.

"The Pyramid" proceeds as a sketch of a music-hall audience, "idealistic," susceptible to "claptrap sentiment," unashamed to see performers prostitute their talents for them. The final scene is of an Italian acrobatic group, of a human pyramid at the top of which is the youngest daughter, who "glared at the applauders with hatred and contempt," while the applauders keep on clapping, "being aware that acrobats live on its breath, and counting it as righteousness they were not stinted in their food." "The Evolution of a Village" (originally an 1891 political pamphlet) shows a village populace happy in its in-

dolence. Then an educated person decides that the town needs a mill, that the only thing needed is some capital; and so the mill is built. People become weary and consumptive; the daughters get pregnant out of wedlock; and the only people to benefit (make money) are the shareholders: "Peace and content are gone." Capital had come, and it had made the people slaves. The mill produces shoddy goods for which savages in far-off lands are forced to barter at the point of imperialism's bayonets.

Two of the collection's stories go a bit beyond the issues of the preface, and they are among the most frequently cited stories by Graham. "The Impenitent Thief," possibly his best-known story, presents the thief who while on the cross rejected the penitent thief's declaration that Jesus was king, telling the other thief to be quiet and die like a man. The narrator makes some guess as to what this thief's life must have been and suggests that whatever kind of thief or rascal he had been in life, he had died steady, unlike the whining penitent thief. The narrator also suggests that the penitent thief was just "taking out fire insurance" by telling the third person on a cross that Jesus was a god; or perhaps he was just defying the Jews "by testifying that the hated one was king." An analogy is drawn between the impenitent thief and an Indian in a canoe caught in the Niagara's current who simply lights up a pipe and smokes peacefully as the canoe draws ever nearer the precipice. He is true to himself. This meditation on a circumstance suggests that Graham had all the skills necessary to be a fine novelist/storyteller, in spite of the way his career as a whole gives evidence that he was not able to sustain a long piece of fiction.

A second frequently cited story, "Beattock for Moffat," describes the train ride that takes the consumptive Andra' back to Scotland. He hopes to stay alive until he reaches Moffat, his home. His cockney wife prates of "Pairadise" while his Calvinist brother, Jock, is angered at the idleness of this kind of afterlife. The purpose of this story seems to be to convey the specialness of Scottish life and customs and the shallowness of London life; but however that may be, the pacing of the train ride, with Andra' growing ever worse as the names of the towns and landscapes are recounted, is excellent. In "R. B. Cunninghame Graham as a Writer of Short Fiction" (1969), James Steel Smith observes that "the noting of the stops of the northbound train carrying the dying Scot back to Moffat makes very real his desperation for arrival, and its unlikelihood."

They get out at Beattock, and Andra' dies just as the train's next destination is announced, "Beattock, for Moffat." Jock, the unsentimental brother not given to cant, snorts into a handkerchief, saying that Andra' has "made a richt gude fecht o' it." He takes consolation that even if Andra' did not live to reach Moffat, at least he will have a fine ride to the graveyard in the undertaker's new hearse. Despite the potential for sentimentality that is more cleverly manipulated than avoided, toward the end of Graham's life this story was referred to in the *Glasgow Weekly Herald* (18 December 1937) as his best creative work. More substantially, Stephen Gwynn in the *Fortnightly Review* (1 February 1933) uses this story to defend his claim that Graham at his best rivals Maupassant.

To a late-twentieth-century reader not enchanted by revisions of the story of Christ or by the lachrymosity surrounding death by wasting illness, in many ways the most successful of the thirteen stories – and the least constricted by the definitions of the preface – is "Los Seguidores" (Two Horses Tied Together). It presents the story of two brothers, Cruz and Froilan, the latter (and younger) of whom is a wastrel, who are like *seguidores* in being thought of together by their mother. The tone of the narration is established by the mother's thinking uncomplainingly of violence and pain, assuming she is no better than any other animal. She realizes that both brothers have incestuous feelings toward their half sister, Luz. The narrator feels no surprise at

this, describing how "whilst the petty tragedy was brewing, so to speak, nature, serene, inimitable and pitilessly sad, but all unconscious of the puny passions of mankind, unrolled the panorama of the seasons.

Their jealous feelings go unspoken until suddenly one evening Cruz attacks Froilan with a knife but trips and stabs himself. The dead brother is strapped onto one horse of the *seguidores,* and the surviving brother mounts the other; they ride off to the cemetery. The mother says to her daughter, "The male Christian is the wildest thing which God has made." The story may be a bit stark in modern terms, and the final scene may strain credulity in its abruptness, but it is clear that Graham realizes that he is describing a neat, classical tragedy. The reviewer in the *Academy* (25 October 1902) remarked that Graham "is always relating all species and types of human life together at his will and pleasure, relating us in Fleet Street, say, with the Gauchos in this sketch, or with the Arab tribesmen in that."

Graham's career as a writer of short narratives can be partitioned into three chronological groupings. The work that most distinguishes him came early, in *The Ipané, Thirteen Stories,* and *Success.* The qualities of these stories are those that most commentators have in mind when writing about Graham, particularly in defining his method as sketching a background situation, with a sudden revelatory moment that dramatically places in perspective all the foregoing, seemingly casual information. It is difficult to schematize firmly the transitions in his career, partly because of the increasing retrospectiveness of his tone as the events about which he writes recede into the past. But it seems evident that with *Progress* and *His People* (1906) Graham has become a more conventional writer. Part of the conventionalism is in narrative technique – the background situation is integrated into a developing narrative, and more often there is a meaningful sequence of actions (although whether it resembles more a plot or a fixed history could be argued). There are fewer concluding revelatory moments, and those that are present are less abrupt and more detailed.

An instance in *Progress* of this development is "A Convert." A puritanical Scot missionary in Africa, the Reverend Archibald Macrae, is hated on all rivers and coasts: "All that is hard and self-assertive in the Scottish character, in him seemed to be multiplied a hundredfold." He is worse than a slave raider because he tries to "enslave and kill the soul." The narrative presents his long-term skirmish to convert one of the local chiefs, "Monday Flatface."

The two argue – Macrae in the spirit of true sportsmanship, refusing to work some chemical "magic" to show Flatface the power of his god.

The narrator notes that after some years Macrae appears to undergo a change: Flatface comes to him, promising to become a Christian if his ill main wife were to recover. Macrae brings medicine, but she does not seem to grow better, so Flatface sacrifices in the manner of his people, chopping off a finger. She still does not get better, so he chops off another finger. Macrae realizes that humans' feelings are the same (husbandly love), whatever their religious loyalties. Eventually the main wife recovers, but Flatface does not convert. (The narrator does not seem to realize that Macrae's god had failed, that Flatface's god had done the trick.) This is quite a polished story, and it compares well with some of Conrad's Malay short stories – for example, "The Lagoon" (1897) and its melodramatic suggestion of the extremes to which a man can be urged by heterosexual love and a culture that valorizes the authority of one's word.

That Graham had not lost his ability to shock the English is attested by laments in the *Spectator* (11 February 1905) about the shocking lapses of taste in *Progress*, which Watts attributes to a characteristically unemotional and equable Graham portrayal of a rape victim in "His Return." Subsequent volumes of short fiction – including *Faith* (1909), *Hope* (1910), and *Charity* (1912) – explore several of Graham's analyses of prostitution in different cultures. These collections predictably gained unfavorable notices, especially *Charity*, which includes "Un Autre Monsieur." There was outrage and frustration at Graham's emphasis on prostitutes and on his nonjudgmental attitudes. The *Academy* (30 March 1912) admired the style but attacked the intrusiveness of the "slum orator" and the portrayals of the police who help oppress the poor. At this time the *Academy* was a High Church and Tory journal, and it had little patience with Graham's unremitting attacks on British imperialism.

This was not as severe as two attacks in *New Age* (21 March, 25 April 1912) by A. E. Randall, who scorned Graham's style as that of an "auctioneer's clerk: his method is cumulative, his description is an inventory," calling him a "stable-yard humourist." Graham, of course, was undeterred, and he wrote on. (There was also admiration for Graham's attacks on hypocrisy, as in a review of *Hope* in the *Nation* [14 January 1911].) More-recent evaluation of Graham's writing about prostitutes deals with the tact and balance of his portrayals. Paul Bloomfield criticizes Graham for writing

"on the whole too sentimentally, about prostitutes," suggesting that Anton Chekhov in "The Chorus Girl" (1892) and Maupassant in "Maison Tellier" (1881) capture the tone of the "good-natured tart" much better.

The trajectory of Graham's career demonstrates that greater sophistication and skill are not always gains in art. Graham's stories became more polished, and he came to know the effect he wanted and went after it efficiently. But as "Sor Candida and the Bird" (*Faith*) demonstrates, something crucial was being lost. This story is quite well done, showing an advance since *The Ipané* in terms of the arrangement of a string of events and the control of imagery and connotations. James Steel Smith calls it a "deftly told, unsentimental story." It is a rather consciously artistic story, based on the premise that all animals are in essential matters of the same species. For example, the bird of the title and the nuns in the story are equally in a cage, or a prison. Some humor is developed on this idea when the provincial (male overseer of convents) eating a sweet potato makes a noise "with a sound as when a duck plunges his beak below the water of a pond to eat a weed."

The plot involves Sister Candida and a bird she saves from dying of thirst just outside the convent gate. She brings it inside, makes it a cage, and she and the other young nuns enjoy listening to it sing (she rationalizes her action by telling the prioress, who discovers the bird, that their Lord Jesus also had suffered from thirst). The prioress turns the question of whether Candida can be allowed to keep the bird over to the provincial, a pompous chap who thinks that matters of discipline and science should be left to men, that faith is the province of women. He thinks the bird will serve as a good example "to show them resignation to the conventual life," but he will ask his vicar-general.

A year passes, to the day of the celebration of Saint Avila, "who, born a simple gentlewoman, died the most human of the saints." After the day of the celebration, Candida discovers the bird has died of thirst, its water vessel upset, "rescued, as it seemed, to taste once more the bitterness of death, by an inexorable fate." Candida laments, saying Saint Avila could have reminded her during her praying to think about the bird. Weeping, she says, "This punishment perhaps has come upon me as a warning that we nuns should not attach ourselves to any one but Christ." The irony of the narrator's statement about "an inexorable fate" based on forgetfulness reinforces, in a low-key manner, Candida's blaming herself for her "sin against the Holy Ghost"; nonetheless, this story of selfish innocence is far from the hard-edged Graham of the earlier and autobiographical pieces.

"A Saint" (*Faith*) provides an exemplary contrast with Graham's earlier stories in its being well written but less engrossing, in its lacking an edge. The title character is a man whose benevolence ruins his patrimony, a factory that produces playing cards, and who thereafter remains chaste and charitable to the poor. People think he is an anarchist involved in the death of the czar. During a drought the authorities punish this man who has always opposed all governments, arrest him, and ship him in shackles to a penal colony, evidently in Morocco, where he uses what little money his mother sends him to buy tobacco to give to addicts imprisoned with him. He comes to be known as the Saint. He escapes, is rearrested, and then is pardoned. Back in Cadiz he is hailed, in time dies, and is interred with much fanfare. Then things go on as before – he may be a saint, but it makes no difference in the way humanity's existence works itself out.

Hope may be the best of Graham's collections according to conventional standards of judgment. The *Academy* (28 January 1911) ranked some of its pieces with Maupassant's and praised Graham's ability to "paint broad landscapes on a small canvas." *Charity* is the last of his books to utilize these conventional techniques with skill and a degree of freshness, thus concluding this second chronological period of his career. In the third period, beginning with *A Hatchment* (1913), much of Graham's fiction is weak. Not many contemporary reviewers recognized the falling-off, although the *Saturday Review* (27 December 1913) objected to his lax tone and overfamiliarity with the reader. Complaints about his punctuation continued, but he was still thought to have charm, and his stories were considered vivid and colorful. He was termed the "realist of romance" by the *Nation* (24 January 1914). Watts admires these stories' proficiency "within his slight and minor genres," praising their excellent management as "anecdotes." But Graham himself seemed to feel that he had drawn down the well. He suggested that with *Brought Forward* he would offer the public no more collections, although the *Nation* (21 October 1916) and the *Spectator* (18 November 1916) regretted his intention to stop writing literature. The *Saturday Review* (28 October 1916) admired Graham's wit, irony, and pity for his characters; John Ravenshaw in the *New Statesman* (11 November 1916) praised his empathy for romanticism and heroic failure that evokes the strength of an older civilization.

Graham's political activities in his later years included another run for Parliament as a Liberal in 1918 and continued efforts on behalf of Scottish nationalism and home rule. At this time he was inspiring many young Scots to political and literary work, including Hugh MacDiarmid and Mackenzie; MacDiarmid lamented in later publications their fellow Scots' lack of knowledge and appreciation of Graham. But his writings were mostly on South American history and biography: *A Brazilian Mystic* (1920), *The Conquest of the River Plate* (1924), and *Pedro de Valdivia* (1926). However, *Doughty Deeds* (1925) is the biography of an earlier Robert Graham (1735–1797) of Gartmore whose life of various pursuits rivaled the author's. Graham's writings on South American subjects were well received on publication and are occasionally cited in modern studies.

But he was not done with fiction. With the publication of *Redeemed* (1927), Graham's decade-long abstention from fiction was noted, usually with regret. The *Fortnightly Review* (February 1928) welcomed him back, praising him as a man of "genius and very rare distinction" who has produced a book of "robust melancholy." In five years *Writ in Sand* (1932) offered several narratives, but those most praised, the title piece and "Tschiffely's Ride," stretch the definition of story even more than usual with Graham.

"Writ in Sand" presents the twenty-four hours of setting up a circus, putting on a performance, and then taking it down. "Tschiffely's Ride" is the log of a fifteen-thousand-mile ride from Buenos Aires to New York, demonstrating the value of old native horse stock rather than relying entirely on thoroughbreds imported from Europe. "Fin de Race" (End of Race) illustrates the failure of technique when insight is lost. It is the lengthy account of a wealthy Spanish nobleman whose father was a gambler and who himself both gambles and wastes money, loses his estates, fails as a diplomat in Vienna, works successfully with a friend in Mozambique but fails after the friend drowns, and seems finally to benefit from all these experiences.

He returns to his wife, who has managed to restore some of his Spanish estates, but he can keep them up for only six months before returning to his old ways. The ending is most peculiar, as if Graham were not able to vary his choice of narrative method. The nobleman, Bernardino, is on an isolated estate (its history is given in too much detail, with no relevance to the narration), and he dies of bronchitis, with little preparation for the reader. In one sense the ending is characteristic of Graham; but unlike earlier stories where there is a sense of ironic foreshortening and understatement, here it just seems to be the obligatory conclusion of a story he happened to be writing. There is an amazing lack of verve for a narration comprising such rich personal adventures.

It is, unlike some of the earlier stories, definitely a narrative, but only in the way of picaro fiction – events hung on the life of a single character. There is not much development or vigor, as if Graham were bored by the many promising events and details that, had they occupied his attention, he could have made into something fascinating. On the other hand, perhaps Graham is saying that life is meaningless, so why try to make it more than it is? This is also a theme of many earlier stories, but here the flat narration is in keeping with the de-enhancing of existence. (In his earlier works the implication is that the very fact of existence engrosses the narrator even though that fact might lack meaning – an internal contradiction that stimulates reader involvement.)

Graham was one of the most-adept and well-known horsemen of his time. Many of his stories and sketches deal with the skills of the gauchos, such as throwing the bola and *lazo*. *The Horses of the Conquest* (1930) was praised in the (New York) *Bookman* (January 1931) for its "vigorous English" and considerable learning, carried lightly and mixed with personal recollections; the *Fortnightly Review* (January 1931) liked its natural, unaffected style. This volume was the success of his later years. A set of stories selected by Edward Garnett, *Thirty Tales and Sketches,* in 1929 was reviewed positively by the *New Statesman* (5 October 1929), both the New York and London versions of the *Bookman* (December 1929, October 1929), and the (New York) *Saturday Review of Literature* and the (London) *Saturday Review* (2 November 1929).

The last volume that Graham saw through the press, *Mirages* (1936), completes the downward curve of his career as a fiction writer. Most of his work after 1912 is written with varying degrees of skill, but the dominating impression of his last books, especially *Mirages,* is one of depleted intuition – which, given his age, is scarcely surprising. Graham still possessed memories from his early years promising unique insights if approached from the correct angle. But, because of weariness or distraction, he did not perceive or utilize a vision for this material that would grant him access to an evaluative moment, such as the old man's feeding ravenously on a morsel discarded by a mourner of Queen Victoria in "Might, Majesty, and Dominion." This image crystallizes the interrelationships and ultimate significance of every lush detail of Victoria's glittering but hollow custodianship of the age named after her. That story sustains political as well as aesthetic coherence. The specialness of Graham's vision – flickering but brilliant illumination – is nowhere more apparent than when it no longer operates.

The best story in *Mirages* is "Charlie the Gaucho," which begins with a description of a *pulperia* (country store) in South America. Details are presented seemingly for their own value, including a good deal of gaucho color (such as their "great iron spurs"), as if Graham were consciously counting on exotic details to stimulate interest. Two officials are seen riding up in the distance. There is a body on the premises, and they are there to investigate the death. The dead man (who had had to hold in his intestines as he staggered out of the building) was an Englishman, Carlitos el Inglés. The narration of Carlitos's death is long (even the commissary comments on it, as if Graham were mocking his own style). Carlitos was eager to fight with knives, and when he was accused by another gaucho of riding a stolen horse, they fought. He was disemboweled but kept fighting until he was stabbed deeply in the chest.

There follows an awkward flashback, with more information (redundant and general) about the life of Charlie the Gaucho (with the shift in name); then the narrator hears the story of Charlie from an English vice-consul. Charlie has been a midshipman on the river Plate. He got into an argument with a fellow midshipman, hit him with a bottle, and, thinking him dead, dived into the river. He became a gaucho and later found that he was the sole heir of his uncle. He returned to England and played country gentleman for ten years or so, then sold out to a cousin, dissipated a couple of years in London, and returned to Paraguay.

The labored conventional narrative and flashbacks convey Graham's plodding late manner – he does not trust the details anymore. The last story of *Mirages,* "Facón Grande," deals with his earliest subject, the pampas. Facón Grande is an Englishman named Hawker, whose pampas name refers to the sword bayonet he wears in his belt. His cousin, who has a smaller knife, is called Facón Chico; he has a son by an Indian woman. The cousin marries a Scottish Argentine, and the son goes to school, growing up a quiet man. There are references to other people, and the entire piece is no more than a sketch of the men.

Mirages, however, was appreciated for its charm and elegance, although some of the reviews were perhaps kinder because they were posthumous. After completing *Mirages,* Graham traveled to Argentina, where he was received as a hero, a shaper of the modern nation's consciousness — although it may be open to question whether an admirer of the gaucho existence, a chronicler of the age of conquistadores, would have been entirely pleased with the country's "advances" in technology and complexity. The trip was the suitable conclusion of a life always lived on the edge of romanticism. Graham died of pneumonia in Buenos Aires on 20 March 1936; he was buried on the island of Inchmahome beside his wife, Gabriela.

Idealism gave Graham both success and frustration in his political efforts, and travel broadened his tastes and tolerance and contributed to his writing. He seems never to have slackened in his high ideals and his sympathy for the downtrodden. He wrote in a manner that crystallized tendencies in folk knowledge and primitive tales within a context of current politics, giving an unusually immediate and visceral edge to general truths. Despite his familiarity with and admiration for writers such as Chekhov, Bret Harte, and Maupassant, their importance to him was primarily in legitimating his absorption with random events and details, in humrum as well as exotic circumstances.

Few writers have equaled his combination of raw imagery of blood lust and myth-evoking insight. As Watts points out, "he was a shrewd and humane observer of life." While he was not free of vanity, pretentiousness, and self-dramatization, he was a master of recollection, of the sharp, unpretentious detail that attained to aesthetic and political vitality in his readers' memories after he had employed it in fiction.

Letters:

Two Letters on an Albatross, by Graham and William Henry Hudson, edited by Herbert Faulkner West (Hanover, N.H.: Westholm, 1955).

Bibliographies:

Leslie Chaundy, *A Bibliography of the First Editions of the Works of Robert Bontine Cunninghame Graham* (London: Dulau, 1934);

C. T. Watts, "R. B. Cunninghame Graham (1852–1936): A List of His Contributions to Periodicals," *Bibliotheck,* 4 (1965): 186–199;

John Walker, "A Chronological Bibliography of Works on R. B. Cunninghame Graham (1852–1936)," *Bibliotheck,* 9 (1978): 47–64;

Walker, "R. B. Cunninghame Graham: An Annotated Bibliography of Writings about Him,"

English Literature in Transition, 22 (1979): 78–156;

Walker, *Cunninghame Graham and Scotland: An Annotated Bibliography* (Dollar, U.K.: Mack, 1980).

Biographies:

Herbert Faulkner West, *A Modern Conquistador: Robert Bontine Cunninghame Graham: His Life and Works* (London: Cranley & Day, 1932);

A. F. Tschiffely, *Don Roberto* (London: Heinemann, 1937); abridged as *Tornado Cavalier* (London: Harrap, 1955);

Cedric T. Watts and Laurence Davies, *Cunninghame Graham: A Critical Biography* (London: Cambridge University Press, 1979).

References:

G. Reid Anderson, "Scots Not Spanish Traits," *Glasgow Weekly Herald* (18 December 1937): 6;

Anonymous [Edward Garnett], "An Ironist's Outlook," *Academy and Literature,* 63 (25 October 1902): 436–437;

Paul Bloomfield, Introduction to *The Essential R. B. Cunninghame Graham,* edited by Bloomfield (London: Cape, 1952);

Richard Curle, *Caravansery and Conversation* (London: Cape, 1937);

Laurence Davies, "Cunninghame Graham's South American Sketches," *Comparative Literature Studies,* 9 (September 1972): 253–265;

Davies, "R. B. Cunninghame Graham: The Kailyard and After," *Studies in Scottish Literature,* 11 (January 1974): 156–157;

Ford Madox Ford, *Return to Yesterday* (London: Gollancz, 1931);

John Galsworthy, "Note on R. B. Cunninghame Graham," in his *Forsytes, Pendyces and Others* (London: Heinemann / New York: Scribners, 1935), pp. 192–194;

Edward Garnett, Introduction to *Thirty Tales and Sketches,* edited by Garnett (London: Duckworth / New York: Viking, 1929), pp. v–ix;

Garnett, "R. B. Cunninghame Graham: Man and Writer," *London Mercury,* 34 (June 1936): 126–127;

Stephen Graham, "Laird and Caballero: Cunninghame Graham," in his *The Death of Yesterday* (London: Benn, 1930), pp. 36–52;

Stephen Gwynn, "Ebb and Flow: Mr. Cunninghame Graham," *Fortnightly Review,* 133 (1 February 1933): 251–254;

Frank Harris, "Cunninghame Graham," in his *Contemporary Portraits* (New York: Harris, 1920), pp. 45–60;

Eloise Knapp Hay and Cedric T. Watts, "To Conrad from Cunninghame Graham: Reflections on Two Letters," *Conradiana,* 5, no. 2 (1973): 5–19;

Richard E. Haymaker, *Prince-Errant and Evocator of Horizons* (Kingsport, Tenn.: Privately printed, 1967);

C. Lewis Hind, "R. B. Cunninghame Graham," in his *More Authors and I* (London: John Lane/Bodley Head, 1922), pp. 71–76;

W. H. Hudson, *Letters to R. B. Cunninghame Graham,* edited by Richard Curle (London: Golden Cockerel, 1941);

John Lavery, *The Life of a Painter* (London: Cassell, 1940);

D. H. Lawrence, "*Pedro de Valdivia* by R. B. Cunninghame Graham," *Calendar,* 3 (January 1927): 322–336;

Robie Macauley, "Stranger, Tread Light," *Kenyon Review,* 16 (Spring 1955): 280–290;

Hugh MacDiarmid, *Cunninghame Graham: A Centenary Study* (Glasgow: Caledonian, 1952);

MacDiarmid, "The Significance of Cunninghame Graham," in *Selected Essays of Hugh MacDiarmid,* edited by Duncan Glen (London: Cape, 1969), pp. 121–128;

Frank MacShane, "R. B. Cunninghame Graham," *South Atlantic Quarterly,* 68 (Spring 1969): 198–207;

Malcolm Muggeridge, "Cunninghame Graham," *Time and Tide,* 17 (28 March 1936): 440–441;

A. E. Randall, "Views and Reviews," *New Age,* new series 10 (21 March 1912): 496; (25 April 1912): 616;

William Rothenstein, "A Journey to Morocco," in his *Men and Memories* (London: Faber & Faber, 1931; New York: Coward-McCann, 1935), pp. 215–225;

Bernard Shaw, "Notes to *Captain Brassbound's Conversion,*" in his *Three Plays for Puritans* (London: Richards, 1901; New York: Brentano's, 1906), pp. 295–301;

James Steel Smith, "R. B. Cunninghame Graham as a Writer of Short Fiction," *English Literature in Transition,* 12 (1969): 61–75;

R. W. Stallman, "Robert Cunninghame Graham's South American Sketches," *Hispania,* 28 (1945): 69–75;

A. F. Tschiffely, *Bohemia Junction* (London: Hodder & Stoughton, 1950);

John Walker, "R. B. Cunninghame Graham and the *Labour Elector,*" *Bibliotheck,* 7 (1974): 72–75;

Walker, "R. B. Cunninghame Graham: Gaucho Apologist and Costumbrist of the Pampa," *Hispania,* 53 (March 1970): 102–106;

Cedric T. Watts, "Conrad and Cunninghame Graham: A Discussion with Addenda to Their Correspondence," *Yearbook of English Studies,* 7 (1977): 157–165;

Watts, *R. B. Cunninghame Graham* (Boston: Twayne, 1983);

Watts, ed., *Joseph Conrad's Letters to R. B. Cunninghame Graham* (Cambridge: Cambridge University Press, 1969).

Papers:
Some of Graham's papers are in the Scottish Record Office; the National Library of Scotland; Dartmouth College; the Harry Ransom Humanities Research Center, University of Texas at Austin; the Bodleian Library; the British Library; the Berg Collection, New York Public Library; the Brotherton Collection, University of Leeds; the British Library of Political Science; the Fawcett Library; the University of Michigan; and Yale and Harvard Universities.

Sarah Grand
(Frances Elizabeth Clarke McFall)
(10 June 1854 – 12 May 1943)

Marilyn Bonnell
Susquehanna University

BOOKS: *Two Dear Little Feet,* as Frances E. McFall (London: Jarrolds, 1873);

Constance of Calais: A Dramatic Cantata, libretto by Grand, music by Francis Edward Gladstone (London: Weekes, 1884);

Ideala: A Study from Life (London: E. W. Allen, 1888; New York: Appleton, 1893);

A Domestic Experiment (Edinburgh: Blackwood, 1891);

The Heavenly Twins (3 volumes, London: Heinemann, 1893; 1 volume, New York: Cassell, 1893);

Our Manifold Nature (London: Heinemann, 1894; New York: Appleton, 1894);

The Beth Book (New York: Appleton, 1897; London: Heinemann, 1898 [1897]);

The Modern Man and Maid (London: Marshall, 1898; New York: Crowell, 1898);

Babs the Impossible (New York: Harper, 1900; London: Hutchinson, 1901);

Emotional Moments (London: Hurst & Blackett, 1908);

Adnam's Orchard (London: Heinemann, 1912; New York: Appleton, 1913);

The Winged Victory (London: Heinemann, 1916; New York: Appleton, 1916);

Variety (London: Heinemann, 1922).

OTHER: *Singularly Deluded,* serialized in *Blackwood's,* 152 (August–December 1892);

"What to Aim At," in *The New Party,* edited by Andrew Reid (London: Hodder, 1894), pp. 355–361.

SELECTED PERIODICAL PUBLICATIONS – UNCOLLECTED:

FICTION

"Mamma's Music Lessons," *Aunt Judy's,* 14 (June–July 1878): 489–495, 527–536;

Sarah Grand, circa 1897

"School Revisited," *Aunt Judy's,* 18 (June–July 1880): 473–481, 537–546;

"The Great Typhoon," *Aunt Judy's,* 19 (April 1881): 358–370;

"A Momentary Indiscretion," *Cosmopolitan,* 20 (December 1895): 169–176.

NONFICTION

"The Morals and Manners of Appearance," *Humanitarian,* 3 (August 1893): 87–94;

"The New Aspect of the Woman Question," *North American Review,* 158 (March 1894): 270–276;

"The Man of the Moment," *North American Review,* 158 (May 1894): 620–627;

"The Modern Girl," *North American Review,* 158 (June 1894): 706–714;

"Marriage Questions in Fiction: The Standpoint of the Typical Modern Woman," *Fortnightly Review,* 69 (March 1898): 378–389; reprinted in *Littel's Living Age,* 217 (9 April 1898): 67–76;

"The New Woman and the Old," *Lady's Realm,* 4 (August 1898): 466–470;

"At What Age Should Girls Marry?," *Young Woman,* 7 (February 1899): 161–164;

"Should Married Women Follow Professions?," *Young Woman,* 7 (April 1899): 257–259;

"Some Recollections of My Schooldays," *Lady's Magazine,* 1 (January 1901): 42–43;

"The Case of the Modern Spinster," *Pall Mall,* 51 (January 1913): 52–56;

"The Case of the Modern Married Woman," *Pall Mall,* 51 (February 1913): 203–209.

Sarah Grand was one of the most talked about – and certainly one of the most vilified – authors of the 1890s, not an inconsiderable distinction in a decade characterized by the plays of Henrik Ibsen, the fiction of the *Yellow Book,* and the antics of Oscar Wilde. Her scandalous novel about the effects of syphilis, *The Heavenly Twins* (1893), drew the attention of readers on both sides of the Atlantic, the editor of the *Fortnightly Review* declaring that Grand was not fit to be received by decent people. However, most male reporters, daunted by her reputation for "advanced" notions, expressed amazement when confronted with an attractive, shy, soft-spoken, conservatively dressed woman who was, as a reporter for the *Chicago Times* (5 August 1894) noted, "about the last guest in the room I should have guessed to be Sarah Grand." Although her reputation was built on her controversial "New Woman" novels, Grand wrote three collections of short stories that established her as a skillful and insightful observer of upper-middle-class society. Leading the revolt of the daughters in the 1890s, she drew the attention of such literary lions as Bernard Shaw, Thomas Hardy, George Meredith, and Mark Twain. However, by the time of her death in 1943 her works had long been forgotten, and even her publisher had for years supposed her to be dead. The resurgence of feminist activity in the 1970s launched a revival of interest in Sarah Grand.

Frances Elizabeth Clarke, who later took the nom de guerre Sarah Grand, was born at Donaghadee in County Down, Ireland, on 10 June 1854. Frances, the fourth child in a family of five, was the daughter of Edward John Bellenden Clarke, a naval coastguard officer serving in Northern Ireland, and Margaret Bell Sherwood Clarke, the well-educated daughter of a Yorkshire gentleman. As was typical of the time, her two brothers were given the best education their parents could afford while the three sisters were educated at home until the age of fourteen. When Frances was seven her father died and the family moved to Yorkshire to be near her mother's relatives. A small annuity from a great-aunt provided the means to send her to the Royal Navy School at Twickenham, near London, and afterward to a London finishing school. Then, after only two years of formal education, she returned to Yorkshire to face genteel poverty with her only surviving sister and their widowed mother. Although she was an imaginative and intelligent sixteen-year-old, few options were open to Frances.

"I married at sixteen," she confessed in "Some Recollections of My Schooldays" (*Lady's Magazine,* January 1901), "the great inducement being that I should be able to study thoroughly any subject I liked, learn languages so that I could speak them, and music so that I could play it, have the command of good books, and escape from routine." When she married Dr. David McFall, a thirty-nine-year-old widower with two sons, in early 1871, neither the chasm of a twenty-three-year age difference between them nor the meager distance of six years between herself and her oldest stepson seemed insurmountable obstacles. Later that year her own son by McFall, David Archibald Edward, was born. The family moved about a great deal, fulfilling the promise of escape and excitement that Frances sought when she married McFall, an assistant surgeon attached to the British army. The relative freedom that she enjoyed offered an opportunity to indulge in her passion for reading and writing. Born during the heyday of the three-volume novel, at which she later excelled, Frances nevertheless turned her hand to the short story. Although she wrote in a letter (14 August 1894) to William Heinemann that "the *Conte* is only a single note," for more than four decades she published short stories that offered an incisive critique of society.

In 1873, at the age of nineteen, she published *Two Dear Little Feet,* a tract on the ravages of tight boots that, perhaps because of ready access to her husband's medical texts, incorporated practical knowledge into the fictional mode. This well-intentioned tale of a young girl's indoctrination into the world of fashion marked the beginning of one of Grand's major literary themes: the socialization of women. Although she eventually produced three collections of her tales, the publication of *Two Dear Little Feet* did little to improve the salability of her short stories. Referring to her early efforts in an 1897 interview for *Woman at Home,* she remarked, "I wrote a number of stories, the majority of which were rejected of the editors, and ended up in flames."

In the first five years of their marriage, McFall was posted to Ceylon, China, Japan, Singapore, and the Straits Settlement of the Malay Peninsula. Counting, perhaps, on the growing demand for more-exotic story settings throughout the 1870s, Grand regularly sent her stories to the editor of *Temple Bar,* continuing an exercise in futility that she had practiced since she was seventeen: "I sent the first from Singapore, the next from Hong Kong, and some from Japan, and suffered agonies once they had gone." Unfortunately, her suffering was compounded by an ever-increasing pile of rejection slips. When novelist Annie Keary saw the manuscript of "Mamma's Music Lessons," she encouraged Grand to submit it for publication. *Aunt Judy's* magazine provided the first acceptance, publishing the story in June and July 1878. (Musical herself, Grand published a libretto, *Constance of Calais,* in 1884.) Looking back at her first acceptance, accompanied by a warm and sincere letter from the editor, Mrs. Alfred Gatty, Grand recalled that she never again troubled about her ultimate success.

Grand returned to England in 1879 a widely traveled twenty-five-year-old woman glad to be free from the interruptions of the previous migratory phase of army life. Gatty published two more of Grand's stories in *Aunt Judy's* magazine. "School Revisited" (June–July 1880) is a tale of the reunion of five schoolgirls, one of whom, like Grand, has written a book. "The Great Typhoon" (April 1881) recounts her experiences in Hong Kong during an 1874 typhoon. Her next book, *Ideala* (1888), describes the vicissitudes to which married women are subject, a theme for which Grand would become famous. Grand circulated the manuscript, and it struck a hopeful note at the publishing firm of George Allen, who was John Ruskin's publisher. Unfortunately for Grand, and Allen, an agreement with Ruskin precluded the publication of any book that met with the latter's disapproval. She had it published at her own expense in 1888, at which

time it attracted the notice of E. W. Allen, who also published it the same year.

Encouraged by the acceptance of her short fiction and the success of *Ideala,* in 1890 Frances left her fifty-eight-year-old husband, eventually abandoning the shires for the London literary scene. Her optimism was not unfounded. After twenty years of rejection letters publishers began accepting her stories. "Kane, A Soldier Servant" (*Temple Bar,* July 1891; *Littel's Living Age,* August 1891), "Janey, A Humble Administrator" (*Temple Bar,* October 1891; *Littel's Living Age,* December 1891), "Boomellen" (*Temple Bar,* March 1892; *Littel's Living Age,* April 1892), and "Eugenia" (*Temple Bar,* December 1893) were her first works published under the name Sarah Grand, though she still signed her correspondence Frances E. McFall. In 1891 Blackwood published *A Domestic Experiment,* another novel of marital mismatch among the gentility. In 1892 she reached back into her stock of earlier work and produced *Singularly Deluded,* a happily-ever-after cliffhanger perfect for serialization in *Blackwood's* magazine. ("But think of what it meant to a young writer in those days to be in *Blackwood,*" she later exclaimed.)

Grand still published most of her work anonymously until the publication of her best-seller *The Heavenly Twins* in 1893. After a three-year search for a publisher (it was rejected by no less than George Meredith at Chapman and Hall), Grand found William Heinemann, who published the novel and had little to regret; it was a record-breaking sensation that the firm continued to republish as late as 1923. For some this cautionary tale set a dangerous precedent. With its horrifying portrait of the effects of syphilis on a mother and her child, it lobbied strongly against a wife's sexual submission to her disease-ridden husband.

The frankness with which Grand approached the subject earned her the scorn of many critics but the undying gratitude of many women. Grand related the story of a grandmotherly Victorian who insisted that "women should put up a monument to *The Heavenly Twins.*" The monument was not erected, but the furor raised by the book ensured Grand's status on both sides of the Atlantic. She became the celebrity of the hour, her name coupled with that other infamous Sarah, the actress Bernhardt. After years of publishing in anonymity, Frances E. McFall was officially Sarah Grand – and she was famous. Mail reached her addressed to "Madame Sarah Grand, England."

Grand used her newly acquired literary credentials to settle some old scores as well as to further her beliefs in literary realism. *Our Manifold Nature,* a collection of six short stories, was published in 1894. According to Grand's preface, this collection presents in restored and revised fashion some fiction that had been published in magazines earlier in the 1890s "in a more or less unsatisfactory condition, having been mutilated for convenience of space, or in order to remove from them any idea of unusual import." More important, Grand takes a stand for realism, insisting that "fiction has always been held to be at its best when it was true to life." However, she admits to being confused because, regarding these stories from life, "it is not the embellishments, but the literal facts, which have been attacked as 'melodramatic' and 'altogether impossible.'" In "The Yellow Leaf" she insists, "there is no fiction whatever." For some readers the realism was too much. A reviewer for the *Critic* (April 1894) — recounting the story of a gentleman who wished to obtain a copy of *Our Manifold Nature* and asked for "Our Manifold Sins" — commented that "this title would fit the present volume of short stories quite as aptly as that under which it appears."

It is difficult to assess when these stories were actually composed; however, the material for the story of a rascally Chinese servant, "Ah Man" (*Woman at Home,* October 1894), was amassed during those travel-filled years from 1873 to 1878. Other characters in the collection include a former kitchen maid, a soldier-servant, a woman artist, members of the Irish gentry, and various representatives of the English upper class. The intelligent, bold, unconventional woman with advanced notions who abounds in Grand's novels is present as well, along with the attendant themes of woman's education, the reform of reprobates, and the marriage game.

Between various convalescences for nervous exhaustion — sometimes in Paris, where the forty-year-old Grand donned bloomers to cycle the boulevards — the busy author and well-known society figure continued to give interviews and charity-benefit readings and to write articles and short stories. Finding publishers for her short fiction was easier, since *The Heavenly Twins* was the talk of boudoirs and boardrooms and *Ideala* had been republished. "The Undefinable" (*New Review* and *Cosmopolitan*) was published in 1894; "The Wrong Road" (*English Illustrated Magazine,* December) and "A Momentary Indiscretion" (*Cosmopolitan,* December) in 1895; and "She Was Silent" (*Lady's Realm,* January), "The Baby's Tragedy" (*Lady's Realm,* December), and "When the Door Opened" (*Idler,* January) in 1897.

Around this time Grand joined other public figures disillusioned by the Liberal party to establish a new platform close to that of the Independent Labour party. While various titles from "Radical" to "Isocratic" were suggested, the title assigned to the collected articles of Sarah Grand, J. Keir Hardie, Lady Henry Somerset, Richard Le Gallienne, Andrew Reid, and others was *The New Party* (1894). Grand's contribution, "What to Aim At," is a plea for a social consciousness, a theme she also pursues in her stories. She urges people, especially the well-to-do, to recognize the claims that their fellow citizens have on them, chiding those who, rather than ask why poverty and deprivation exist, look the other way or even blame victims for their circumstances. Despite her busy schedule, when staying in her Kensington flat, Grand attended weekly meetings of Mrs. Frederic Harrison's Girls' Guild, an organization that provided recreation and occupation for young London working women. In her life and through her fiction, Grand was a tireless worker for women of all classes.

Capitalizing on her notoriety, Grand wrote a fictionalized autobiography, *The Beth Book* (1897). The life of the main character, Elizabeth Caldwell Maclure, "A Woman of Genius," bears more than coincidental correspondence to the life of Grand, a woman whom Bernard Shaw characterized as having "a touch of genius." The story of Elizabeth ("Beth") allows Grand an in-depth treatment of factors that affect a woman's psychological development as well as the realities of women's lives: the disparity in education and employment; the injustice of the sexual double standard as reflected in the Contagious Diseases Acts; the establishment of lock hospitals where prostitutes were held for treatment; and the institution of marriage itself.

A year after the publication of *The Beth Book,* Grand's husband died at the age of sixty-six. Grand had only a tentative relationship at best with her son Archie, now twenty-six, who had continued to live with his father until McFall's death. But she was on good terms with her older stepson, Chambers Haldane McFall, an art critic and author in his own right. Grand relocated to Tunbridge Wells in southeastern Kent in 1898; she moved into a house with Haldane in nearby Langton in 1900. This period was marked by a dearth of publication: only one short story, "A New Sensation" (*Windsor* magazine, December 1899; republished in *Emotional Moments,* 1908), and a serialized novel, *Babs the Impossible* (*Harper's Bazaar,* June–December 1900; *Lady's Realm,* June 1900–April 1901). Although it lacks the sustained controversial content of previous novels,

Babs is an unconventional, free-spirited female, the prototypical teacup anarchist who appears in such short stories as "Eugenia" and "The Yellow Leaf."

The period from the publication of *Babs the Impossible* in 1900 to the publication of her next major work, *Adnam's Orchard* (1912), was unproductive, though she published "The Man in the Scented Coat" (*Lady's World,* June 1904; republished in *Emotional Moments*) and "One of the Olden Time" (*Pall Mall,* July 1911; republished in *Variety,* 1922). *Emotional Moments,* her second collection of short fiction, contains a dozen stories, some of which were originally published as early as 1894; these are a deviation from Grand's usual fare. The title of the collection and the titles of individual stories such as "An Emotional Moment" and "A New Sensation" indicate a psychological and emotional interest in the passion of adult women, a passion that Grand treats carefully in her longer fiction.

Because of the vicissitudes of writing, Grand turned to speaking engagements for a more reliable income. In 1901 she embarked on a lecture tour of the United States, attesting later that she had been interviewed twenty-four times in twenty-four hours. Her reputation preceded her. Though one journalist noted that women's clubs were not particularly anxious to engage her services, Grand found an open-minded and appreciative audience for her lectures, "The Way to Happiness" and "Mere Man," at Barnard College in New York and Bryn Mawr College in Pennsylvania, as well as in San Francisco and Chicago. A close friend recollected that "her brilliant lecturing tours, both in England and America, contributed further to the awakening of womanhood. The yoke had been borne so long, women had been so accustomed to submit publicly while rebelling privately, that this new prophet was hailed as a Deliverer." Anxious mothers need not have feared that Grand's seditious sentiments would corrupt their daughters; onstage her ladylike appearance and demeanor, her obvious sincerity, and her wit and humor won the day. She continued to lecture on "Mere Man," "The Art of Happiness," and "Things We Forget to Remember" for a decade.

Always a crusader in her fiction, Grand took up the banner of woman suffrage during this period. She aligned herself with such activists as Millicent Garrett Fawcett, influential leader of the National Union of Women's Suffrage Societies; Florence Pomeroy, Viscountess Harberton, founder of the Rational Dress Society; and Alice Massingberd, founder of the Pioneer Club for the political and moral advancement of women, of which Grand was a member. A nonmilitant suffragist, Grand put her

Sarah Grand and "Mere Man"

Caricature of Grand delivering her 1901 lecture "Mere Man" (Harper's Weekly, 2 November 1901)

pen to work for the Women Writers' Suffrage League and used her oratorical talents in speeches before the International Women's Suffrage Alliance in London. In addition, she was vice-president of the Women's Suffrage Society, president of her local branch of the National Council of Women, and president, chairperson, and principal speaker of the Tunbridge Wells branch of the National Union of Women's Suffrage Societies. Declaring her willingness "to appear on any platform and write for any paper that is for Woman's Suffrage," Grand was a tireless worker for "The Cause." Yet at the podium, as impeccably dressed as any of her heroines, she was careful to project a pleasant, acquiescent manner. After all, she had declared, "We women would have had suffrage long ago had not, unfortunately, some of the first fighters for it — some of the strong ones — been unprepossessing women."

At the age of fifty-eight, Grand published the first novel, *Adnam's Orchard*, of a projected trilogy. This book, which the (London) *Bookman* (January 1913) compared to George Eliot's *Middlemarch* (1871–1872), is a complex and compassionate portrait of people from both the higher and lower social ranks, but it concentrates on one male character, Adnam Pratt, marking a departure from Grand's concentration on women's issues. The "New Man" rather than the New Woman marks not a shift but an extension of Grand's social commentary. While in her earlier novels women are destined to bring about a moral reformation, here the belief in women has been supplanted by a belief in socialist policies. In the second book of the projected trilogy, *The Winged Victory* (1916), she returns to women's issues. This novel, the last that Grand wrote, is the story of socialist enterprise from the point of view of Ella Banks, an angry young lacemaker introduced in *Adnam's Orchard,* whose goal is to organize lacemakers into a corporation directed by her, eliminating the middleman and securing a fair recompense for women. World War I intervened, and the trilogy was never completed. Certainly the war changed the balance of power between the sexes in a way that Grand welcomed. Suffrage for women eventually was won despite the fact that the movement was suspended for the duration of the war; arguments against enfranchisement evaporated in light of women's war work.

In 1920 Grand moved from Tunbridge Wells to Bath, where she became mayoress of that city (an honorary position) but did not abandon her literary vocation. In 1922 Heinemann, the firm that had given Grand her first big break, published *Variety,* a collection of short stories remarkable for several examples of the New Man. *Variety* marked the last chapter in the writing career of Grand, now almost seventy years old. From 1922 to 1929 (excluding the year 1923–1924), the regal, elegant, white-haired mayoress lent a ladylike air of grace and charm to public occasions in that fashionable southwestern spa city. At seventy-five she retired from the office, living quietly with her younger sister. In 1942 the blitz drove the eighty-eight-year-old Grand out of Bath. She died on 12 May 1943, less than a month before her eighty-ninth birthday. Her son Archie, who died in a London air raid, survived her by only one year.

Grand's reputation as a short-story writer was established by her three collections of stories: six in *Our Manifold Nature,* twelve in *Emotional Moments,* and eight in *Variety.* Thirteen of these twenty-six stories had been published in magazines; only four of Grand's stories were not published in collections. Her career as a published short-story writer spanned forty-four years across two centuries, from her humble beginning with *Aunt Judy's* magazine in 1878 to *Variety.* Throughout this period Grand cast a sometimes loving, sometimes scathing, but always insightful eye over the lives of the upper-middle class.

As both champion and critic she observed the gentry with the objective lens of the outsider and the privileged knowledge of the insider. But Grand did not restrict her field of vision to writing social commentary on the leisured classes. Her sympathetic outlook and socialist leanings resulted in stories that are not only realistic in their rendition of the tribulations of the lower orders but also optimistic in their belief in the almost mythic purity of the working class. Grand – adept at catching both the truncated aspirations of working-class speech and the latest slang of the nouveau noble – painted lifelike portraits of people at both ends of the social spectrum, as well as lively and engaging portraits of the "Modern Maid."

Our Manifold Nature is Grand's shortest collection, consisting of six "studies from life," as Grand calls them, brought together to capitalize on the popularity of *The Heavenly Twins.* At ninety-five pages "The Yellow Leaf" is the longest story, and the only one not previously published in a periodical. In the collection Grand evenly divides her attention between the two extremes of society, though at this point in her career her first-person narrator is firmly rooted in the upper end of the scale.

"The Yellow Leaf," "Eugenia," and "Boomellen" are tales of upper-class foibles. "The Yellow Leaf," actually a novella, is the most ambitious in scope and illustrates one of Grand's favorite juxtapositions: the independent modern woman and the conventionally feminine woman, or the New Woman versus the Old Woman. The narrator, an impressionable teenager, is thrown together with two contemporaries: Adalesa, a fifteen-year-old nascent suffragette with whom readers identify and sympathize; and Evangeline, a budding "womanly woman" who enacts the supreme betrayal, stealing the heart of the beau to whom Adalesa is secretly engaged.

Grand continues the contrast in the second half of the story, in which the trio is reunited years later. The narrator has become a celebrated author, and Adalesa is a duchess. While they have aged well, Grand paints a horrifying yet compassionate portrait of the treacherous Evangeline, who is still clinging to femininity's trump card, appearances, and affecting girlish graces and dress – all unflatteringly accentuated by the glare of the newly installed electric lights. Attempting to recapture her youth, Evangeline throws herself into planning a ball, but she only commands the interest of two fawning young men who habitually lavish attention on women of a certain age and station in life. The ending is inevitable and pitiful, a commentary on the predicament of women who have been trained to rely solely on their looks. Evangeline is found dead the next morning, having decked herself with all her jewels, struck a pose on a couch in her bedroom, and taken a fatal dose of her nerve tonic, morphia, prescribed "to relieve pain."

"Eugenia" and "Boomellen" continue the vein of commentary on upper-class dissipation, although the focus shifts from women to men. "Eugenia" is a colorful, engaging story of another New Woman. A woman artist narrates the tale of Lord Brinkhampton, a shallow, dissipated young man who solicits the narrator's assistance in finding "something nice and young and fresh, with money, for a wife, so that I may repair all my errors at once." When he meets twenty-one-year-old Eugenia, Brinkhampton thinks he has found a sheltered maiden who will mistake him for the unsullied hero of a romantic novel. The subtitle of the tale is "A Modern Maiden and A Man Amazed," and Brinkhampton's conventional notions about women are quickly put to the test by Eugenia, an educated, strong-minded descendant of a woman who drowned her spineless fiancé. Eugenia nearly repeats history. Not only does she almost drown Brinkhampton, she is "advanced" enough to reject his proposal of marriage and to propose marriage herself to a young, well-educated yeoman farmer on the estate, thus proving the expediency of women's education and independence.

"Boomellen" also concerns the marriage of a reprobate, in this case the father of Boomellen. In this tale Grand addresses an issue in which she was deeply interested: inherited dispositions. Boomellen, the last male representative of two ancient, aristocratic, though degenerating lines of West Country Irish stock, is a good-natured yet idle youth. His name, a childish corruption of *Bummeln,* an incorrigible loiterer, describes him well. He has great beauty and a generous nature, but he is infected with an almost fatal apathy combined with an inherited craving for drink. His ineffectual life ends in an ineffectual death. On the day of his coming-of-age ceremony, he tries to rescue the passengers of a storm-tossed ship in a small rowboat.

Grand looks on the "quality" classes with a sometimes acerbic eye, exposing their affectations and inherited weaknesses. In her early stories the more heroic specimens of humanity often spring from the working class, where human endurance and self-sacrifice shine even brighter than in the marble halls of the aristocracy. In "Kane, A Soldier Servant" the title character is a debauched soldier who, when he can no longer march a mile or carry a

rifle, is taken on as a servant. "He was a worthless old dog," the narrator notes, "but he was our own old dog, and for that we valued him." Because the other servants revolt at having to do his work, Kane finally gets fired. He leaves both his employment and military service without a word. Two years later the narrator is called to Kane's deathbed. He has married an abused woman in hopes of making life better for her and her children. But her husband catches up with them, and Kane is seriously injured during an ensuing altercation. He survives for three months, during which the husband dies, allowing Kane and the woman to be properly married. In the end his former employer proclaims that although Kane is an "immoral old Irish reprobate, liar, drunkard, [and] inciter to bigamy," he is also a hero, "dead for want of the bread he had given to his rival's children, dead defending them and the woman he loved."

"Ah Man" features an even more devilish hero, one who also meets a redeeming fate. The story is based on Grand's brief stay in Hong Kong during the 1870s. A man applies for a job as a butler, bringing with him a letter of reference from his previous employer certifying that "Ah Man is the wickedest old scoundrel in China." The narrator hires Ah Man, and she does not regret it. When she falls sick, Ah Man is a concerned nurse, anxiously awaiting his mistress's return to her writing, a sign that she is truly better. One night an earthquake strikes, and Ah Man rescues the narrator, only to be killed by a falling beam when he goes back to the house to rescue her writing.

Heroism is not confined to men, however. In her early works Grand manifests a great admiration for women, particularly those of the working class. While the upper orders can be vain, self-centered, and superficial, women such as the title heroine of "Janey, A Humble Administrator" are sterling examples of a true gentility that knows no class boundaries. The narrator, a young married lady stultified by her upper-middle-class lifestyle, meets Janey through her vicar. Though paralyzed from the waist down and confined to a cramped bed, Janey helps her physically run-down mother, conducts household business from her bed, writes missives, gets her siblings jobs, and even takes in a baby to mind while at the same time supervising her father, who suffers from a brain disease. Brave, energetic, and helpful, Janey is finally brought down by her father, who, because of the progressive severity of his disease, strikes her with a stool, a blow that eventually kills her. The narrator has been transformed from a "society machine" into a human being through knowing her. Janey's legacy lives on in the narrator's renewed power to care and to love. The story, a touching example of female fortitude and endurance, is an object lesson in philanthropy.

By the time her next collection was published fourteen years later, Grand's world had changed considerably. She was now a fifty-four-year-old widow, and her immense popularity was waning. *Emotional Moments* is her largest collection and demonstrates a continuing expansion in her literary repertoire. Seven of the dozen stories had been published in periodicals: "The Undefinable," "The Wrong Road," "She Was Silent," "The Baby's Tragedy," "When the Door Opened," "A New Sensation," and "The Man in the Scented Coat." While this collection continues Grand's critique of the idle upper classes and her approbation of the lower ones, she experiments with narrative point of view. *Emotional Moments* is noteworthy in three other ways. It marks a shift in Grand's opinion of women by a decrease in the sympathetic handling of female characters and an increase in narration by men. Second, some stories center on romantic entanglements, something to which she has diametrically opposed in her novels because she felt that romance was a subject that realists should not give undue consideration. Third, unlike most of the stories in her first collection (five out of six end with a death), many of the stories in *Emotional Moments* end with varying degrees of ambiguity.

"There is nothing that brutalises a lady like Society," states a nurse in "The Baby's Tragedy" who is disgusted with the conduct of a socialite mother. It is a comment that explains yet does not excuse, and it sets the tone for this volume. No longer lady bountiful or mistress of the house like the narrators of *Our Manifold Nature,* women of the upper orders come under closer scrutiny in this volume. Nowhere is the angst and ennui of the idle rich captured better than in "An Emotional Moment," "She Was Silent," "From Dusk till Daybreak," "The Wrong Road," "The Condemned Cell," and "A New Sensation." "An Emotional Moment" and "She Was Silent" are remarkable for their examinations of lovesickness and sensual longing reminiscent of George Egerton's short stories.

In "An Emotional Moment" a successful playwright recounts to a current lover the story of a previous affair in which she had discovered that love is better without the presence of the love object, that its best form is abstract, untainted by the sensuality and passion that literally burn her up, making it impossible to focus on her writing. Her present lover, who feels she has mistaken "fever-fits of passion" for real love, chides her for posing and flirting. Indeed, though her experience of love is realistic, her self-absorption makes her seem a coquette. The ending is left nicely open when her lover, hesitating outside her door, hears her hysterical laugh. Is it the laughter of pain or of pleasure?

"She Was Silent" is another account of the obsession of love. Aldah relates her infatuation with a man whose presence, though it provokes anxiety and conflict, cuts through her numbness and upper-class malaise. The plot is complicated when a woman friend to whom Aldah is close reveals that she is involved with the same man and that she believes the man is devoted to her. She confides that she suspected Aldah had taken him away from her, but now she sees that she was mistaken (she is not). Aldah, who recounts the story to a male friend, declares that she solved the problem by not seeing her lover again. Her listener asks, "And was that the end?" But Aldah is silent.

"From Dusk till Daybreak" and "The Wrong Road" are tales of repentance. "From Dusk till Daybreak" involves a woman named Olivia who, after a wretched first marriage, now lives in luxury and is loved. But her first marriage has changed her even temper to a mercurial one. The narrator, a girlhood friend of Olivia, is summoned to Olivia's seaside villa to help her find the solace that has been evading her. Peace of mind escapes her as she is beleaguered with thoughts of her own cruelty and sins of omission. She feels especially bad that she is making her second husband suffer after he has taken her away from the brutalizing old man whom she had first married. Even this morning, she tells the narrator, she has abused him with her moods. He is on his yacht when a terrible storm rolls in. Olivia and her friend think they see the yacht go down, but when the gale subsides it comes into view. Her husband is safe, and Olivia declares, "I know I am cured at last. I hope I am forgiven."

In "The Wrong Road" Lady Grace recounts her tale to a young woman, one of many who come to this single, charming, prematurely gray woman for advice about their love affairs, never bothering to wonder how she knows so much. In her youth Lady Grace had awaited her lover, Gregory, and when he did not arrive after more than an hour, she was persuaded to take a walk through the gardens of the Albert Memorial with another man. Gregory met up with them just as the other man was showing Grace a waltz step, but Grace refused to offer him any explanation. Months went by, and her pride would not allow her to make the first advance. After years of waiting for him in the garden through which he habitually walked to and from work, she finally stumbled across Gregory, who had walked the park daily but had always taken another path. Lady Grace was amazed that sordid business concerns had contracted his soul and obliterated her image from his mind: "She had taken the wrong road . . . in every sense of the word." Instead of speaking up when it could have made a difference, she preferred to play the wronged party, with sad results. After hearing this story the young woman says she will write to her lover immediately to rectify their situation before it is too late.

Two stories focus on villainous women. "The Condemned Cell" is a clever psychological study of the last hours of a woman who is about to be executed for the murder of her husband. In her cell Lady Charlotte Templemore reviews the facts of her case. One night she had seen her husband, Rupert, with another woman, followed them, and discovered that the other woman was his first wife. So stricken was she by the betrayal of her loving husband that she seized a knife and plunged it into him. After agonizing hours in her cell before her execution at dawn, she notices a letter. It turns out to be from Rupert's first wife, explaining that he truly thought she was dead. Charlotte's love for Rupert is renewed, but they can only be reunited in death. Just before she is scheduled to be executed, a messenger arrives with a reprieve, but Lady Charlotte has gone to join Rupert.

While Lady Charlotte is a murderess but not a villainess, Lady Flora de Vigne in "A New Sensation" is a true malefactor. Not since "The Yellow Leaf" had Grand drawn such a scathing portrait of the fashionable artifice and social pretension that she must have known well. Lady Flora is the quintessential society woman, her emotions dulled by romantic conquests, her senses numbed by the overabundance wealth can buy. At age thirty-three, however, she is suddenly seized with a great distaste for her jaded life. What she needs, she declares at one of her famous little dinner parties, is "a new sensation." By the next evening she is settled at a little country inn where she meets a young man to whom she is attracted, especially when her respect for him is increased by the discovery that he lives in the big house nearby. The affair is almost brought to a halt when Lady Flora discovers the man is merely a prosperous market gardener. After an initial reaction to flee, she stays on at the inn, gradually accustoming herself to his shopkeeper status. Eventually she desires to vanquish him, but he refuses to give her a chance. "You are exactly like the girl I am going to marry," he declares, "older, of

THEY BOTH STARTED AND LOOKED ROUND, THEN FELL APART IN CONSTERNATION.

Illustration by Bertha Newcombe for "The Wrong Road" (English Illustrated Magazine, *December 1895*)

course, and with a different expression; but still wonderfully alike." Lady Flora, who has always had her way, gets a new sensation.

Two other stories are remarkable for their use of the male perspective. When a woman boards a train and engages a man in conversation, his story becomes the basis for "When the Door Opened." The man is married to a woman ten years his junior, and as they have much different tastes, each often participates in activities without the other. For instance, one night he sends her to a fancy-dress ball alone, then, regretting the act, dons an old costume and follows her. His wife cannot recognize him, and he tests her faithfulness by flirting with her. Shocked at the ease with which she responds to a stranger, he invites her home. When she unmasks in their drawing room it is he who is faced with a stranger. At this moment he hears his wife's hand on the handle of the door, but the story is not continued because the train stops at a station and the man deboards.

Grand continues this narrative departure in "The Undefinable – A Fantasia." The narrator of this tale is a middle-aged artist whose works, though powerless to move him, sell well enough to earn him a fashionable following and more-than-adequate remuneration. The New Woman reappears in this story as a model who shows up unexpectedly and challenges his concepts of art and womanhood. Under her unconventional tutelage his inspiration returns. She, alas, disappears without a trace, but the reader senses that he will not return to his fraudulent ways.

Once again, Grand does not forget the working classes. In this volume, however, the lower orders often provide social commentary on the attitudes and behavior of their "betters." While Ah Man had a mistress marked by true gentility, in "The Baby's Tragedy" an old nurse tells a tale of cruel social aspiration. The mother is so obsessed with keeping her figure that her first question after delivering a feeble, underweight boy does not concern the baby's health, but rather the possibilities of regaining the nineteen-inch waist she so carefully preserved by eating dry toast and drinking black tea throughout her pregnancy. The vain, foppish father pronounces the baby unacceptable and changes doctors until he gets one who agrees to a rich formula (the mother refuses to breast-feed because it will restrict her social life) that eventually kills the baby. The father and mother then satisfy themselves by getting sympathy in laying the blame at "the shocking way the nurse and doctor slapped it [the baby] when it was born."

Similarly, "The Rector's Bane," told by an omniscient narrator, focuses on the landed gentry, as well as the clergy, by depicting the victimization of old, poverty-stricken Dicky and Martha Jordan, shown in juxtaposition to the happiness, power, and insensitivity that wealth brings. The only daughter of the rector marries the only son of the wealthiest landowner in the parish on the same day that the rector removes the Jordans to the workhouse because they cannot pay their rent to the rich landowner. As the bishop unctuously proclaims the everlasting sanctity of the marriage vows, the Jordans are being bustled off to the workhouse to live in separate quarters after decades of marriage. The following Sunday, Martha looks forward to being reunited with her partner but finds he no longer recognizes her. A blow on the head or the enormity of his situation has left her husband a shell of a man. The rectory grounds abut the workhouse property, and the rector and his wife stroll by, counting their blessings. "How very unseemly," the rector proclaims when he hears Martha curse those who are responsible for her agony.

Along with certain passages in "The Yellow Leaf," "The Butcher's Wife" provides a "Woman Question" commentary typified by Grand's novels but less so by her shorter works. An omniscient narrator tells the story of Mrs. Durham, the butcher's wife. Mr. Durham does not favor woman suffrage or any progressive notions, believing that a woman's sphere is in the home. In actuality, his wife keeps the business going while he regales his friends with antifeminist bravado at the local pub. Mr. Durham, whose favorite saying is "I should jest like to see the woman as 'ud come a-domineerin' over me," gets his corrective when his wife, fed up with his carousing, publicly whips him to within an inch of his life. In a "worm turns" scenario that was a favorite of Grand, the butcher finally meets "the woman as 'ud come a-domineerin' over me" – his own wife.

Variety is Grand's final collection of short fiction, but only "One of the Olden Time" had seen previous publication. *Variety* seems to signal a growing disenchantment with woman's goodness and her powers of restitution or salvation. Except for the head nurse in "The Commandant," women no longer hold the potential of the New Women artists and authors or the promise of the feisty Modern Maids of the previous volumes. While always particularly adept at portrayals of such devious schemers as the man-stealing or baby-sacrificing socialite, Grand balances portraits of venomous women with portrayals of exemplary women in the same story. The good nurse offsets the evil of the self-absorbed, social-climbing mother; saintly Martha Jordan offsets the selfishness of the rector's wife.

In *Variety* there is little such balance. Although Grand still mourns the fate of oppressed women, she puts to rest the man-hating rumors that plagued her during her early career by examining the fate of the henpecked man. Men are here most often the victims. In keeping with a greater focus on and sympathy for men, the stories in *Variety* frequently use a male narrator.

Among the worst of the women in *Variety* is Eustacia Jobb Fitzalbin, an American who has married an English gentleman. "Vanity and Vexation: A Pre-war Study" is a brilliant portrait of this social climber who values people, including her husband, only for what they contribute to her pleasure and social success. A blundering outsider, Eustacia gains the admiration and envy of the wrong people, and, lacking any sense of discrimination, she counts herself a success until she overhears two men discussing her in unflattering but realistic terms. Eustacia has a moment of remorse quickly swallowed up by self-absorption when her husband dies of pneumonia. Society drops her immediately, and she is left alone with her greatest enemy – herself.

"The Turning of the Worm" features a demanding mother and sister who make a shambles of the life of Oscar Wilbraham, another long-suffering hero. His ward, Beatrice, recounts how this wealthy bachelor sacrificed his life to demanding female relatives who protected their stake in his fortune by keeping eligible women at bay. However, the one woman they forgot about was twenty-year-old Beatrice, who had been living in their midst for years. She proposes to Wilbraham; he accepts — and the worm turns.

In keeping with Grand's growing disillusionment with women, a thoroughly masculine tone is evidenced in the stories of a hunter and a soldier. In "A Thorough Change" a gentleman blackguard staggers into the hunting camp of the narrator and tells a curious tale of which he is the villain. The hunter has heard the same story from another source, and he recounts a more sordid, less romantic version, expecting that the truth will shame the reprobate, but it does not. A more heroic tale is "The Saving Grace," narrated by a Boer War soldier who had been caught behind enemy lines and imprisoned. He was held with one other captive, a soldier who had previously let down his comrades. Still, this cowardly comrade engineers the narrator's escape, at the same time realizing that there is no way to get himself out. When the narrator brings back a rescue party, it is too late. The wastrel knew that both prisoners were to be shot in the morning, and the narrator's escape was the plan by which his cell mate might be shriven for his previous disgrace.

"One of the Olden Time: A Study from Life" is reminiscent of the tales in Grand's first collection, which is subtitled "Stories from Life." The narrator is a gentlewoman, and the story is an accolade to a member of the working class, Mallory, an elderly gardener. Although Mallory shares the butcher's conservative attitudes about women, he is merely narrow-minded, not mean. For better or worse, to his "missis" Mallory symbolizes "the loyalty, the endurance, the independence, the old past England of it all! the England that still had a heart, that bore itself bravely, and never whined!"

The remaining three stories represent a new genre for Grand: mysteries or stories of the supernatural. Josepha, a character introduced in *Emotional Moments,* sounds a bit like Grand herself: a society figure "well known for her talents, much loved for her charming personality, a little alarming to her friends on account of her occasional eccentricities, but always interesting." In *Emotional Moments* an omniscient narrator tells how Josepha follows "The

Grand with a bicycle, which she considered a necessity for the New Woman

Man in the Scented Coat" through a London fog and discovers a hidden den where high-ranking government officials relax and play cards. *Variety* contains two more Josepha stories, though these concern the supernatural, a phenomenon Grand became more interested in writing about later in her career. In these two stories the narrator and Josepha sit in cozy rooms, smoking and talking, while Josepha tells her tales.

In "I Can't Explain It" she remembers a house from which a spectral presence peers at people from a window. Strangely enough, when Josepha returns to the house after an absence, not only has the evil presence disappeared, but even the window from which it habitually looked out is gone. In "Josepha Recounts a Remarkable Experience," she and her brothers hear footsteps pacing the floor of the flat above. Josepha realizes with a start that she is on the top floor of the building – no one lives above her. The pacing ceases, but both Josepha and her cook feel drawn to a window in the kitchen. Fearing this suicidal impulse, Josepha consults a psychologist who urges her to get away. She leases the flat and goes abroad. She returns to discover that the new tenant has also heard the steps. A porter tells her that years ago the owner of the house and a housekeeper fell out of the window. Josepha never returns to the flat.

Although Grand's fame rests predominantly on her novels, she was skillful at crafting the short story. While she often maintained that her plots were based on facts, her talent lay in characterization. Her contributions include her honest, unsentimental representations of the class to which she belonged, her spirited renditions of the New Woman, and her sympathetic portraits of working-class people. All of these portraits are enhanced by Grand's considerable talent at capturing the nuances of spoken language and allowing the words of the speakers to sketch their characters.

With a turn of phrase Grand is able to capture the quintessence of society. At a ball an older-but-no-wiser fading beauty, Evangeline ("The Yellow Leaf") "kept glancing at herself in a mirror near. She had always loved the good points of her own anatomy; it had been a positive pleasure to her to consider them; but now there was no pleasure in her eyes, only incessant inquiry." She now lives life in rooms made "stuffily effeminate in the fashionable manner, with tambourines and ribbons, painted plaques, and things of all kinds converted from their honest use to serve as ornaments absurdly – as, for instance, a salad-oil bottle with a pink ribbon tied round its neck, filled with grasses and hung upon the wall – dusty fripperies!" Eustacia Jobb Fitzalbin ("Vanity and Vexation") fares little better:

> She was lady-like enough in her manners – her manners in society, that is to say. Manners were an important part of her stock in trade, of the wares upon which she expected to reap a large profit in social success. And perhaps it was for this reason that she economised in manners in her private life, saving the graciousness, of which it is to be presumed that she had no very large supply, for occasions when there was something to be gained by displaying it. She put on graciousness with her gloves, and doubtless had all the more to assume because of the amount she accumulated by habitually stinting her maid.

In four sentences the reader knows more about Eustacia than she does about herself.

"The Baby's Tragedy" supplies one of the best examples of both ends of the social spectrum, accruing its force from the juxtaposition. A social-climbing husband and wife have this exchange: " 'Dear, do I smell *violette*?' she exclaimed on one occasion, pronouncing it in the French way as if to make more of it. 'You know it has quite gone out.' He smelt his pocket-handkerchief. 'By Jove!' he said, 'it is *violette*. That's my man again. He must have left some in one of the bottles. It is lucky you noticed it. I'll get another handkerchief.' " But the old north-country nurse narrator gets her own in this exchange with the self-absorbed new mother:

> "Do you know, nurse," she began – "Do you know?" was their word in Society just then. They only have one at a time, and it has to serve 'em all for everything; and "Do you know?" affectedly drawled, was on duty that season – "Do you know, nurse, my waist is only nineteen inches." "Well, you can't help it, I suppose," I said, in as pitying a tone as I could command. "You might pad, though. When folks are deformed, I'd always recommend them to hide it."

Grand puts dialect to good use to enhance characterization. Old Mallory, the gardener in "One of the Olden Time," has respect for the landed gentry and conservative principles:

> One time the Union come to our village. We was gettin' two-an'-threepence a day then, an' the Union says if we'd belong we'd get two-an'-sixpence. I was slack o' work then – tho' I never bin wot ye might call out o' work i' my life, only slack at times; an' one day I met a farmer comin' down street, an' 'e ses to me: "You b'long to Union?" 'e ses, an' I ses, "No," I ses. "I don't 'old wi' no Unions," I ses. "All right," 'e ses. "You come along up to my place to-morrer, an' I'll give ye two-an'-six." An' 'e did.

In "The Butcher's Wife" the butcher's statements sum up his antifeminism: "Fur myself, I don't 'old wi' no women's rights – no, nor any on 'em new-fangled ideas. Give me a woman as stays at 'ome, and looks after 'er man and the children. That's 'er spere. And I allus ses, if she does 'er dooty there, I ses, she'll 'ave enough to do." His long-suffering wife wins the reader's sympathy when years of hard work in the shop combined with her husband's semipermanent residence at the local pub make her snap. She walks into the pub armed with a heavy hunting whip and declares to her husband:

> I gave yew fair warnin', but yew wouldn't *be* warned, and now you'll suffer the consequences. 'Ere yew air and 'ere yew is from mornin' till night, day in, day out,

drink, drink, drink – and jaw – an' if yew're not broke this minnit it isn't yer fault.... I've done all as I ought, as fur as I know, an' I've maybe done some things as I oughtn't. But be that 'ow it may, it can't be 'elped now. All I know is, I've done everything as I could think of but one thing; and that one thing I've come to do now afore it's too late.

She then proceeds to catch him by the collar and thrash him.

Grand's stock-in-trade in her novels is the liberated woman of a century ago. The New Woman, though not a monolithic figure, had views; she smoked ("like a chimney," actress Ellen Terry remarked of Grand's habit), cycled, and was educated, articulate, and headstrong – and she often worked. Grand was a pioneer of the New Woman novel, and the Modern Maid appears in her short fiction as well. In "The Yellow Leaf" fifteen-year-old Adalesa takes the reins from the coachman and arrives at her aunt's estate with a formidable-looking puppy in tow merely to exasperate her aunt. She announces to the narrator, "I want to make her believe that the outcome of Woman's Rights is bull pups." Like Adalesa, Eugenia ("Eugenia") is a skilled horsewoman with courage that surpasses that of the dissipated young man who hopes to win her hand. Eugenia is not to be swayed by conventional romantic approaches; this highly intelligent young woman proposes to the man of her choice. But perhaps the unnamed model of "The Undefinable" describes Grand's notion of the New Woman best: "I *am* a woman with all the latest improvements. The creature the world wants." Grand also utilized the image of the self-supporting working woman in her stories. The narrator of "The Yellow Leaf" is a well-known author; the narrator of "Eugenia" is a humble artist; and "An Emotional Moment" recounts the amorous adventures of a successful playwright.

The problem with the critical reception of Grand's short stories lay in her reputation as a writer of controversial novels. Her short fiction was destined to be overshadowed by her novels. Few reviewers, for example, could resist comparing *Our Manifold Nature* to her wildly successful novel *The Heavenly Twins,* published the previous year. The *Athenaeum* (5 May 1894) insisted that the collection "shows a terrible falling off from *The Heavenly Twins*" and suggested that Grand avoid the first-person narrator, a perspective she rarely used in her longer fiction. The *Literary World* (5 May 1894) commented, "The writer's success in her popular novel – a success dependent upon her theme rather than on her artistic skill – will doubtless sell these stories, but had they preceded *The Heavenly Twins* they would have found few readers."

Grand was known in her day as a woman with a purpose, a moral reformer who used controversial material in hope of shocking the world into action. But while her novels deal with the problems of syphilitic husbands infecting their wives and unborn children, vivisection, and prostitution, her short stories never match the controversial nature of her novels. Thus, it was difficult for critics to judge the short fiction on its own merits and refrain from making comparisons between it and the novels. The (London) *Bookman* (May 1894) noted that the success of *The Heavenly Twins* "had nothing to do with artistic reasons" but was owing to "popular curiosity on subjects which conventional society has hitherto turned away its face from" and Grand's "distinct capacities for stimulating and leading popular opinion." The recommendation was that Grand stick to the role of social reformer, where her power lay.

Grand had ties to two worlds. She foresaw both the passing of a world governed by class privilege and the promise of the coming order of the New Woman. With an ear for the latest high-class slang as well as the pithiest working-class turn of phrase, Grand wrote short stories that capture the essence of life at both ends of the British class system. An appreciative review in the *Spectator* (7 April 1894) assessed Grand's chief contributions to the short story, citing her "insight into, and genuine sympathy with, widely differing phases of humanity, coupled with power to reproduce what is seen with vivid, distinct strokes, that rivet the attention somewhat like flashes of lantern-light penetrating the darkness and making visible things hidden." It applauded her "humour, pathos, fidelity to life, and power to recognise in human nature the frequent occurrence of some apparently incongruous and remote trait."

Interviews:

"A Chat with Mme. Sarah Grand," *Woman* [literary supplement] (2 May 1894): i–ii;

Jane T. Stoddart, "Sarah Grand: Illustrated Interview," *Woman at Home,* 3 (1895): 247–252;

Sarah A. Tooley, "The Woman's Question: An Interview with Madame Sarah Grand," *Humanitarian,* new series 8 (March 1896): 161–169;

"Women of Note in the Cycling World – A Chat with Mdme. Sarah Grand," *Hub,* 1 (17 October 1896): 419–420;

Tooley, "Sarah Grand," *Woman at Home,* 7 (1897): 176–178;

"Sarah Grand on the Old and the New Woman," *Woman's Signal* (1 September 1898): 140;

Athol Forbes, "My Impressions of Sarah Grand," *Lady's World,* 11 (June 1900): 880–883.

Bibliography:

Joan Huddleston, *Sarah Grand,* Victorian Fiction Research Guides, no. 1 (Saint Lucia: University of Queensland, 1979).

Biography:

Gillian Kersley, *Darling Madame: Sarah Grand and Devoted Friend* (London: Virago, 1983).

References:

Gerd Bjørhovde, "Writing on a Grand Scale: Sarah Grand and *The Heavenly Twins,*" in *Rebellious Structures: Women Writers and the Crisis of the Novel, 1880–1900* (Oslo: Norwegian University Press, 1987), pp. 87–128;

Helen C. Black, *Notable Women Authors of the Day* (London: MacLaren, 1906), pp. 320–328;

Lady Mary Jeune, "The New Woman and the Old: A Reply to Sarah Grand," *Lady's Realm,* 4 (September 1898): 600–604;

Ellen Jordan, "The Christening of the New Woman: May 1894," *Victorian Newsletter,* 63 (1983): 19–21;

Coral Lansbury, *The Old Brown Dog: Women, Workers, and Vivisection in Edwardian England* (Madi-

son: University of Wisconsin Press, 1985), pp. 144–148;

Susan Navarette, "*As You Like It:* A Source for Sarah Grand's *The Heavenly Twins,*" *Turn-of-the-Century Women,* 4 (1987): 42–47;

"Ouida" and "The New Woman," *North American Review,* 158 (May 1894): 610–619;

Robert Rowlette, "Mark Twain, Sarah Grand and *The Heavenly Twins,*" *Mark Twain Journal,* 16 (Summer 1972): 17–18;

Elaine Showalter, *A Literature of Their Own: British Women Novelists from Brontë to Lessing* (Princeton: Princeton University Press, 1977), pp. 204–210;

W. T. Stead, "The Novel of the Modern Woman," *Review of Reviews* [London], 10 (July 1894): 64–74;

Stanley Weintraub, "G. B. S. Borrows from Sarah Grand: *The Heavenly Twins* and *You Never Can Tell,*" *Modern Drama,* 14 (1971): 288–297;

Harold Williams, *Modern English Writers: Being a Study of Imaginative Literature, 1890–1914* (New York: Knopf, 1919), pp. 429–432.

Papers:

The major collection of Grand's correspondence is at the Bath Reference Library, Bath, England. Other important collections of Grand's manuscripts are at the University of California, Los Angeles; the Smith College Library; the National Library of Scotland; and the British Library.

Thomas Hardy
(2 June 1840 – 11 January 1928)

Jil Larson
Western Michigan University

See also the Hardy entries in *DLB 18: Victorian Novelists After 1885* and *DLB 19: British Poets, 1880–1914.*

BOOKS: *Desperate Remedies: A Novel,* anonymous (3 volumes, London: Tinsley, 1871; 1 volume, New York: Holt, 1874);

Under the Greenwood Tree: A Rural Painting of the Dutch School, anonymous (2 volumes, London: Tinsley, 1872; 1 volume, New York: Holt & Williams, 1873);

A Pair of Blue Eyes: A Novel (3 volumes, London: Tinsley, 1873; 1 volume, New York: Holt & Williams, 1873);

Far from the Madding Crowd (2 volumes, London: Smith, Elder, 1874; 1 volume, New York: Holt, 1874);

The Hand of Ethelberta: A Comedy in Chapters (2 volumes, London: Smith, Elder, 1876; 1 volume, New York: Holt, 1876);

The Return of the Native (3 volumes, London: Smith, Elder, 1878; 1 volume, New York: Holt, 1878);

The Trumpet-Major: A Tale (3 volumes, London: Smith, Elder, 1880; 1 volume, New York: Holt, 1880);

A Laodicean: A Novel (New York: Harper, 1881; 3 volumes, London: Low, Marston, Searle & Rivington, 1881);

Two on a Tower: A Romance (3 volumes, London: Low, Marston, Searle & Rivington, 1882; 1 volume, New York: Holt, 1882);

The Mayor of Casterbridge: The Life and Death of a Man of Character (2 volumes, London: Smith, Elder, 1886; 1 volume, New York: Holt, 1886);

The Woodlanders (3 volumes, London & New York: Macmillan, 1887; 1 volume, New York: Harper, 1887);

Wessex Tales: Strange, Lively, and Commonplace (2 volumes, London & New York: Macmillan, 1888; 1 volume, New York: Harper, 1888);

Thomas Hardy, 1889

A Group of Noble Dames (London: Osgood, McIlvaine, 1891; New York: Harper, 1891);

Tess of the d'Urbervilles: A Pure Woman Faithfully Presented (3 volumes, London: Osgood, McIlvaine, 1891; 1 volume, New York: Harper, 1892);

Life's Little Ironies: A Set of Tales with Some Colloquial Sketches Entitled "A Few Crusted Characters" (London: Osgood, McIlvaine, 1894; New York: Harper, 1894);

Jude the Obscure (London: Osgood, McIlvaine, 1895; New York: Harper, 1895);

The Well-Beloved: A Sketch of a Temperament (London: Osgood, McIlvaine, 1897: New York: Harper, 1897);

Wessex Poems and Other Verses, with Thirty Illustrations by the Author (London: Harper, 1898; New York: Harper, 1899);

Poems of the Past and the Present (London & New York: Harper, 1901);

The Dynasts, Part First (London & New York: Macmillan, 1904);

The Dynasts, Part Second (London & New York: Macmillan, 1906);

The Dynasts, Part Third (London & New York: Macmillan, 1908);

Time's Laughingstocks and Other Verses (London: Macmillan, 1909);

A Changed Man, The Waiting Supper, and Other Tales (London: Macmillan, 1913; New York: Harper, 1913);

Satires of Circumstance: Lyrics and Reveries with Miscellaneous Pieces (London: Macmillan, 1914);

Selected Poems (London: Macmillan, 1916);

Moments of Vision and Miscellaneous Verses (London: Macmillan, 1917);

Collected Poems (London: Macmillan, 1919; enlarged, 1923, 1928, 1930);

Late Lyrics and Earlier with Many Other Verses (London: Macmillan, 1922);

The Famous Tragedy of the Queen of Cornwall (London & New York: Macmillan, 1923);

Human Shows, Far Phantasies, Songs and Trifles (London & New York: Macmillan, 1925);

Winter Words in Various Moods and Metres (London & New York: Macmillan, 1928);

Chosen Poems (London & New York: Macmillan, 1929).

Editions and Collections: *The Wessex Novels,* 18 volumes (London: Osgood, McIlvaine, 1895–1913);

The Works of Thomas Hardy in Prose and Verse, with Prefaces and Notes, 24 volumes, Wessex Edition (London: Macmillan, 1912–1931);

Thomas Hardy's Personal Writings: Prefaces, Literary Opinions, Reminiscences, edited by Harold Orel (Lawrence: University of Kansas Press, 1966);

The Literary Notes of Thomas Hardy, edited by Lennart A. Bjork (Göteborg, Sweden: Acta Universitatis Gothoburgensis, 1974);

The Complete Poems, edited by James Gibson (London: Macmillan, 1976; New York: Macmillan, 1978);

The Personal Notebooks of Thomas Hardy, edited by Richard H. Taylor (London: Macmillan, 1978; New York: Columbia University Press, 1979);

The Variorum Edition of the Complete Poems of Thomas Hardy, edited by Gibson (London & New York: Macmillan, 1979);

The Complete Poetical Works of Thomas Hardy, 3 volumes, edited by Samuel Hynes (Oxford: Clarendon, 1982–1985);

Collected Short Stories, edited by F. B. Pinion, with an introduction by Desmond Hawkins (London: Macmillan, 1988);

The Excluded and Collaborative Stories, edited by Pamela Dalziel (Oxford: Clarendon, 1992).

OTHER: Florence Emily Hardy, *The Early Years of Thomas Hardy, 1840–1891,* and *The Later Years of Thomas Hardy, 1892–1928,* ghostwritten by Thomas Hardy (London & New York: Macmillan, 1928, 1930); republished in one volume as *The Life of Thomas Hardy, 1840–1928* (London: Macmillan, 1962; New York: St. Martin's Press, 1962); republished under the same title in a fully edited version by Michael Millgate (Athens: University of Georgia Press, 1985).

A writer who expressed himself prolifically and successfully in both prose and verse, Thomas Hardy hoped to be remembered for his poetry. Toward the end of his life he remarked that his sole literary ambition had been to "have some poem or poems in a good anthology like the *Golden Treasury.*" His achievement vastly exceeded this modest hope. His unique reputation as both a major poet and a major novelist, already established at the time of his death, has only strengthened and developed in the course of this century.

His standing as a writer of short stories, however, is less certain, for critics tend to disagree about the nature and quality of his work in this medium. Some dismiss the majority of his stories as potboilers or elaborately contrived narratives devoid of meaningful character development and thematic depth, recognizing in only a few of his stories the imaginative power that characterizes his work in other genres. Even then, these critics often describe Hardy's best stories as merely fine examples of an older, more discursive tradition of narrative, quite unlike modern short stories, which, in Edgar Allan Poe's formulation, strive for the unity of "a single effect." Other critics – chief among them Kristin Brady, the scholar who has undertaken the most perceptive and thorough study of Hardy's short fiction – object to this assessment of Hardy's stories. While acknowledging that some of the stories are certainly failures that were hastily or even mechanically written, Brady persuasively argues that most of them reveal a fascinating double dimension in Hardy's narrative voice by developing a traditional, oral method of storytelling in conjunction with techniques and themes that are recognizably modern, literary, and subversive of conventions and the expectations of readers.

Hardy's own assessment of his short stories is difficult to gauge because of the bitterness with which he turned his back on all his fiction after the hostile reception of *Jude the Obscure* (1895). Even though he described the stories in his final collection, *A Changed Man* (1913), as "mostly bad," adding, "I heartily wish I could snuff out several of them," he took great care arranging and revising the stories in his first three collections: *Wessex Tales* (1888), *A Group of Noble Dames* (1891), and *Life's Little Ironies* (1894). Although *A Changed Man* merely draws together miscellaneous stories, each of the other three collections exhibits a satisfying sense of formal and thematic coherence.

Many of the themes and concerns of Hardy's fiction can be traced in his personal experience. Born on 2 June 1840 in Higher Bockhampton, a village in rural Dorset, Hardy was the eldest of four children born to Thomas Hardy II, a builder like his father before him, and Jemima Hand Hardy, whose forceful personality contrasted with her husband's more passive, easygoing approach to life. Telling the story of his own birth, Hardy characteristically emphasized the dark irony of "being thrown aside as dead," only to be saved minutes later by a nurse who happened to notice that he was alive after all.

The culture in which Hardy grew up accounts for the rich oral tradition so important to the narrative voice of his stories; his was a family of storytellers, and the legends and superstitions passed down to him, by his mother in particular, were later to infiltrate his fiction. He shared his father's love of music; Hardy's memory of being moved to tears while dancing to his father's violin at the age of four suggests that the mysterious power of music he describes in "The Fiddler of the Reels" (*Scribner's*, 1893) had always played an important role in his emotional life. His fascination with Napoleonic history — evident not only in *The Dynasts* (1904, 1906, 1908) and *The Trumpet-Major* (1880) but in several of his short stories as well — also originated in his early family life. His childhood reading included *A History of the Wars*, a periodical about the English wars with Napoleon to which his grandfather subscribed. What is perhaps the most pervasive concern in his fiction — love across rigid class boundaries — also undoubtedly entered his consciousness at a very young age when Julia Augusta Martin, the lady of nearby Kingston Maurward estate, became, in Hardy's words, "passionately fond" of him.

Hardy began his education at the school that Martin founded in Bockhampton, but he transferred after one year to Dorchester British School. After leaving school at the age of sixteen, he became articled to a Dorchester architect and later accepted a job as an architectural assistant. In 1862 he went to work in London as a draftsman in the office of Arthur Blomfield. During this period of his life Hardy was torn between pursuing a career as an architect and trying his luck as a writer. Although the former seemed the safer course, Hardy spent virtually all his free hours reading literature and writing poetry. His first published narrative, the sketch "How I Built Myself a House" (*Chambers's Journal*, 1865), reflects both his background in architecture and his literary bent. Written to entertain his colleagues in Blomfield's office, the story is a client's humorous, first-person account of his dealings with an architect and the practical difficulties and absurd mishaps of having a house built. Although this piece is unlike the rest of Hardy's fiction in tone and technique, Brady notes that it does "anticipate his subsequent work in its perception that life is intrinsically unsatisfactory."

By the time Hardy published what is considered to be his first real short story, he had established himself as a novelist. It is ironic that George Meredith, who read the manuscript of "The Poor Man and the Lady" (which was never published and eventually destroyed), advised Hardy to write a novel with a more complicated plot, for Hardy's short stories have been most often faulted for their overly complex plotting. Hardy felt he had taken Meredith's advice too literally in *Desperate Remedies* (1871), his first published novel. After writing two additional novels, *Under the Greenwood Tree* (1872) and *A Pair of Blue Eyes* (1873), and deciding to give up architecture for literature, Hardy achieved his greatest success to that date with *Far from the Madding Crowd* (1874), which Leslie Stephen had commissioned for the prestigious *Cornhill* magazine. Just after completing this novel and five days before his marriage to Emma Gifford (whose father is said to have referred to Hardy as a "low-born churl"), Hardy finished "Destiny and a Blue Cloak" (1874), a story he had promised to the *New York Times*.

Although the focus of this narrative is the sexual rivalry between two women in love with the same man, Hardy's biographer Michael Millgate notes that the story's hero, Oswald Winwood, is clearly based on Hooper Tolbort, a pupil of Hardy's friend and mentor Horace Moule and in some ways Hardy's professional rival. Winwood, like Tolbort, rises from an "obscure little academy" to a brilliant career in the Indian Civil Service. At the center of the story, however, are the women who fall in love with Winwood; their competitiveness and jealous maneuvering determine the structure of the story in a way that prefigures Hardy's more assured treatment of the same theme and narrative design in "Fellow-Townsmen" (1880), "The Withered Arm" (1888), "To Please His Wife" (1891), and his other stories of sexual rivals. Although "Destiny and a Blue Cloak" is characterized by the humor and energy of his early fiction, it was obviously hurriedly written and is held in low esteem by most critics. Hardy himself disliked it, calling it "an impromptu of a trivial kind" and refusing to include it in any of his collections of stories.

In between work on *The Hand of Ethelberta* (1876) and *The Return of the Native* (1878), Hardy continued to write short fiction and to gather information on the history of Dorset, which would later prove valuable to both *Wessex Tales* and *A Group of Noble Dames*. During this period he published the first of his two short stories for children, "The Thieves Who Couldn't Help Sneezing" (1877), which appeared in an annual, *Father Christmas*. This story, which concerns a plucky boy who outwits and exposes three thieves by blowing snuff into the closet they have chosen for a hiding place, is in the tradition of "Jack and the Beanstalk" and other tales of brave, resourceful children who get the best of evil adults. Hubert, the hero, is first overtaken by the thieves in the Vale of Blackmoor, a region of Dorset with which Hardy was becoming familiar at this time because he and Emma had taken a home in Sturminster Newton on the eastern edge of the Vale. Hardy was to use this setting again, most memorably as the Valley of the Little Dairies in *Tess of the d'Urbervilles* (1891).

In the late 1870s and early 1880s Hardy began writing and publishing the stories inspired by his reading of John Hutchins's *History and Antiquities of the County of Dorset* (third edition, 1861–1873). "The Impulsive Lady of Croome Castle" (1878), Hardy's first short story to be published in England, appeared in America under the title "Emmeline, or Passion vs. Principle" (1884). Although the heroines' names vary from version to version, these stories are otherwise identical to "The Duchess of Hamptonshire" in *A Group of Noble Dames*. "The Honorable Laura," the final story in that collection, was first published during this period in the *Bolton*

Weekly Journal as "The Benighted Travellers" (1881). The concern with issues of social class in these stories and *The Hand of Ethelberta* is also evident in his reworking of the portions of "The Poor Man and the Lady" that he had not already cannibalized for his novels. The product of the final revision of this material was "An Indiscretion in the Life of an Heiress" (*New Quarterly Magazine,* 1878), a novella Hardy disparaged as "a sort of patchwork of the remains" of his first novel. The story nevertheless provides an interesting early indication of the compassion for victims of the English class system (both the privileged and the "low-born") that is a salient feature of all his novels and a crucial element in his presentation of the many characters in *Noble Dames* who are frustrated or injured by oppressive social conventions.

The following year Hardy published "The Distracted Young Preacher" (1879), which is considered one of his finest short stories. It appeared in Great Britain in the *New Quarterly Magazine* and in America in *Harper's Weekly.* (Hardy dropped "Young" from the title when he included the story in *Wessex Tales.*) The *New Quarterly Magazine,* under the editorship of Charles Kegan Paul, also published "Fellow-Townsmen" (1880), another of the stories Hardy selected for his first collection. Apart from Stephen, Paul was the literary figure who did the most for Hardy's reputation during this early period, not only publishing his fiction but writing articles in praise of it as well – and at a time when Hardy's work, as Paul put it in an article in the *British Quarterly Review* (April 1881), had not yet "taken hold on the great popular mind, sometimes slow to discover when a new genius has arisen in the intellectual sky." The best of Hardy's short fiction from this phase of his career offers a fresh ethical perspective on social problems and a thematically relevant sense of place.

Besides publishing in magazines three stories that were to be collected in *Wessex Tales* – "A Tradition of Eighteen Hundred and Four" (1882), "The Three Strangers" (1883), and "Interlopers at the Knap" (1884) – during the early 1880s Hardy also wrote some short fiction that he later wished to snuff out rather than reprint. "What the Shepherd Saw" (1881), for example, does indeed fall short of the standard Hardy established with his best stories, even though it combines the pastoral and the Gothic in a manner reminiscent of his most successful work in short fiction during this period. In this story Hardy develops an elaborate plot about a shepherd boy who witnesses a jealous duke murder a man. Ironically, the victim is not in fact the duke's wife's lover but only an admirer concerned for her safety as the wife of such a violent tyrant. Instead of exploring the emotions of fear and guilt that the situation elicits from both the shepherd and the duke (as voyeur and as murderer who realizes that his crime has been witnessed), Hardy merely entangles the reader in distracting plot complications.

After living in London and its suburbs since the beginning of their marriage, Hardy and Emma returned to Dorset in 1882, residing in Wimbourne and Dorchester before the completion of Max Gate, the house that Hardy built for himself just outside Dorchester. As Millgate notes, the stories Hardy wrote in late 1882 and early 1883 mark a turning point in his career. "The Romantic Adventures of a Milkmaid" (*Graphic,* 1883), which by critical consensus is the Hardy short story most marred by unrealism, represents the culmination of a phase of Hardy's career that includes his least successful novels, *A Laodicean* (1881) and *Two on a Tower* (1882). But "Three Strangers," a tightly constructed, wryly ironic narrative published the same year as "The Romantic Adventures of a Milkmaid," indicates the direction his career was to take.

With its fairy-tale and Gothic elements, realistic depiction of rural life, and comic subplot, "The Romantic Adventures of a Milkmaid" is indeed an odd story, but at the same time it is in some ways a precursor of Hardy's more successful blending and juxtaposing of genres in *Tess of the d'Urbervilles* and *Jude the Obscure.* Hardy's note in the margin of his copy of *A Changed Man* about preferring a more radical ending for the story, one in which Margery chooses to disappear with the baron rather than be reunited with her husband, provides one of many instances of Hardy's reluctance to submit to the Grundyan strictures imposed by the editors of the periodicals in which he published. In both his novels and short stories he resisted conventional endings as much as possible. Millgate recounts the anecdote of Stephen's accusing Hardy of allowing the heroine of *The Trumpet-Major* to marry the wrong man; when Hardy objected that women usually did, Stephen retorted, "Not in magazines."

The conventional Victorian morality that Hardy sought to challenge and supplant with a more complex ethical vision in his fiction for adults remains unquestioned in the second of his two stories for young people, "Our Exploits at West Poley," which was sent in November 1883 to the *Youth's Companion,* where it was filed away for future publication. It did not appear in print until almost ten years later, when it was serialized in the *House-*

holder from November 1892 to April 1893. Unlike "The Thieves Who Couldn't Help Sneezing," this story is aimed at an audience of older children, and at least one critic has noted that, in its characterization and exciting plot, the story is reminiscent of Mark Twain's *The Adventures of Tom Sawyer* (1876). Hardy took care to establish a "healthy tone," as he put it when the piece was commissioned (just after publication of the controversial *Two on a Tower*), and the story concludes with an unambiguous moral. Leonard and Steve become acutely aware of the dire consequences their exploits in a cave have for both themselves and their community, and they learn the value of "quiet perseverence in clearly defined courses."

While living in Dorchester during the mid 1880s, Hardy was a member of the Dorset Natural History and Antiquarian Field Club and a regular visitor to the Dorset County Museum. Around this time he became acquainted with Edward Cunnington, a local antiquary of whom Hardy disapproved because of what he perceived to be the rapacious, reckless spirit Cunnington brought to his archaeological work. "A Tryst at an Ancient Earthwork" (*Detroit Post,* March 1885) tells the story ("almost libelously," according to Millgate) of one of Cunnington's excavations. When the story was printed eight years later in the *Illustrated London News,* Hardy expressed his anxiety: "A character who appears in the narrative may be said to be drawn from a local man, still living, though it is really meant for nobody in particular." "A Tryst at an Ancient Earthwork" is more a descriptive sketch than a short story, for the narrative is slight and the description of Maiden Castle the most interesting and impressive aspect of the piece.

"A Mere Interlude" (1885) is one of the best of the stories later collected in *A Changed Man.* Baptista Trewthen, the heroine, has much in common with Elizabeth-Jane Henchard in *The Mayor of Casterbridge* (1886), the novel Hardy was writing at the time. Like Elizabeth-Jane, Baptista changes from a person who is unhappy, restless, and disappointed with life and its options into someone who considers her fate philosophically, within the context of the lives around her. Of the many quintessentially Hardyesque ironies in the plot, the most surprising is the final one. Baptista — who marries an older man she does not love in order to escape teaching school, a profession she despises — discovers with dismay that her husband has four grown daughters who are illiterate and in need of her instruction. She unexpectedly grows fond of her husband, however, because of their common interest in his daughters, who come to have a positive influence over her:

> By imperceptible pulses her heart expanded in sympathy with theirs. The sentence of her tragi-comedy, her life, confused till now, became clearer daily. That in humanity, as exemplified by these girls, there was nothing to dislike, but infinitely much to pity, she learnt with the lapse of each week in their company.

These words eloquently express Hardy's somber yet deeply compassionate vision of life.

Both his tender heart and mournfulness were responsible for the pet cemetery (with tombstones that he carved himself) in the garden of Max Gate. The house was dark because, as Millgate explains, Hardy "refused to allow the trees to be cut back for fear of 'wounding' them." In 1887 the Hardys took a long-contemplated trip to Italy, and the Italian scenes described in "Alicia's Diary" (1887) were drawn from this experience. His only experiment with the diary mode of narrative, this story never lives up to its promising beginning, and, despite its sometimes interesting treatment of the ethical problems that arise when two sisters are in love with the same man, it is generally considered one of Hardy's weakest stories. A biographical source for "Alicia's Diary" might be Hardy's transfer of affection from Eliza Nicholls to her sister Mary Jane, both of whom were romantically involved with him in the 1860s.

An early version of "The Waiting Supper" titled "The Intruder: A Legend of the Chronicle Office" was published in the *Dorset County Chronicle* (1887). When this work was collected in his final volume of short stories, Hardy lengthened it considerably and made some revisions to heighten the drama of the return of the heroine's husband (who had deserted her) on the evening before her planned marriage to another man. Even though Bellston, the husband, mysteriously disappears a second time (and only much later is found drowned in a river where the water flows with a "never-ending sarcastic hiss"), Christine refuses to marry her lover: "So they grew older. The dim shape of that third one stood continually between them; they could not displace it; neither, on the other hand, could it effectively part them." The story owes something to Robert Browning's "The Statue and the Bust" (1855), which Christine quotes, but ultimately it asks the same question as Hardy's poem "Long Plighted" (1902): after so many years of loving while waiting, what difference would it make to marry?

In 1888, in addition to publishing "The Withered Arm" in *Blackwood's Magazine* (*Longman's* rejected it because it was "too grim") and "A Tragedy of Two Ambitions" in the *Universal Review,* Hardy collected five of his stories for the first edition of *Wessex Tales:* "The Three Strangers," "The Withered Arm," "Fellow-Townsmen," "Interlopers at the Knap," and "The Distracted Preacher." Eight years earlier Stephen had suggested that he write a series of "prose idylls of country life – short sketches of Hodge & his ways," and though Hardy did not take the idea seriously at the time, he came to realize that several of his best stories shared the Wessex setting (a fictional region based on real places in the Dorset that Hardy knew so well) as well as subject matter and themes related to rural life. As many critics have observed, Hardy's best work is rooted in his personal experience and background, and in all the stories that make up this volume the imaginative impulse is fueled by memory.

Although Hardy ends the preface to the 1896 edition of *Wessex Tales* by claiming that "the stories are but dreams, and not records," his respect for the role played by fact in fiction is evident. Earlier in the preface he responds to "an aged friend" (probably his mother) who reminded him that the Rhoda Brook she heard about (and whose story Hardy tells in "The Withered Arm") flung off her incubus in a dream she had while sleeping in the afternoon, not at night as his version has it:

> To my mind the occurrence of such a vision in the daytime is more impressive than if it had happened in a midnight dream. Readers are therefore asked to correct the misrelation, which affords an instance of how imperfect memories insensibly formalize the fresh originality of living fact – from whose shape they slowly depart, as machine-made castings depart by degrees from the sharp hand-work of the mould.

Paradoxically, the "living facts" for which Hardy had such respect in these stories are the details of family or local legends, which owe as much to imagination and a belief in the supernatural as they do to faithful records (which Hardy maintained in the notebooks he kept throughout his life) and close observation of nature. An important feature of Hardy's best fiction, then, is its capacity to engage readers by convincing them that the strangest stories are grounded in the real, in "fact" that lives because people believe in it. Appropriately, *Wessex Tales* is subtitled *Strange, Lively, and Commonplace.* When Stephen chided Hardy for making "The Withered Arm" neither realistic nor altogether a story of the supernatural, Hardy dismissed the comment as "a dull and unimaginative example of gratuitous criticism."

The formal innovations of the tales reflect an unconventional vision of law and social justice.

"The Three Strangers" and "The Withered Arm" – the "two stories of hangmen" to which Hardy refers in the preface – promote this vision through their focus on a profession that loomed large in local tradition. In the first volume of his autobiography (1928) Hardy tells the story of watching a hanging through a telescope: "He [Hardy] seemed alone on the heath with the hanged man, and crept homeward wishing he had not been so curious." The hangman in "The Three Strangers" is a subtly sinister figure who seeks shelter from the rain at a christening party where, ironically, the man he is to execute (but whom he does not know) has also taken temporary refuge. The unsettling quality that the hangmen in this story and "The Withered Arm" share is a matter-of-fact attitude toward their work; their profession has conditioned them to welcome the death of a fellow creature.

In "The Withered Arm," Gertrude Lodge becomes infected with a similarly self-centered view toward those who face execution after she learns that the only way to remove the curse that has withered her arm is to touch it to the neck of a man recently hanged. During her interview with the hangman, she shrinks at the possibility that the execution might not occur after all: " 'O – a reprieve – I hope not!' she said involuntarily. 'Well, – hee, hee! – as a matter of business, so do I!' " Even though the hangmen in both stories are presented with black humor, Hardy leads his readers to deplore the ethic that they represent. As Brady argues, the real victim in "The Withered Arm" is the neglected, illegitimate son of Rhoda Brook (the woman who, out of a jealous obsession with Farmer Lodge, places the curse on Gertrude). Present "by chance" when a rick (a stack of thatched hay) was fired, a young man is hanged for the act; ironically, the death Gertrude hopes for turns out to be that of her husband's son.

Two other stories in *Wessex Tales* also explore the theme of law in conflict with a deeper understanding of ethics and justice. Like the young man who is sacrificed at the end of "A Withered Arm," Timothy Summers, the man sentenced to death in "The Three Strangers," in no way deserves the punishment meted out to him. The villagers sympathetically describe Summers as "the poor clockmaker" who defiantly stole a sheep because he was out of work and his family was starving; after the thief successfully escapes the law, he wins their admiration for "his marvelous coolness and daring in hob-and-nobbing with the hangman."

Hardy presents the smugglers in "The Distracted Preacher" in a similarly sympathetic man-

ner. He had long been fascinated by those who engaged in this illegal activity; his grandfather had allowed his cottage to be used as a hiding place for contraband liquor until his wife put a stop to it in 1805. Hardy also undoubtedly learned about the exciting smuggling past of the South Dorset coast when he was romantically involved with Eliza Nicholls, who grew up in Kimmeridge Bay, where her father was a coastguardsman. In "The Distracted Preacher," Hardy portrays Mr. Stockdale, the new minister in Nether-Moynton, with gentle satire. Stockdale begins to fall in love with Lizzy Newberry before he realizes that she is passionately involved in the smuggling trade. Her deception makes him uneasy, but rather than simply wishing she would get out of the business, he wishes he were a grocer so he would not have to worry about what an unsuitable wife she would make for a minister. Her participation in this illegal enterprise, which provides a livelihood for virtually the whole community, intensifies his attraction to her, as he comes to recognize: "Perhaps it was that her experienced manner and bold indifference stirred his admiration in spite of himself."

At the end of the story the smugglers are "hunted down like rats." Years later Stockdale marries Lizzy. It seems as if the penultimate sentence of the story, which describes her rehabilitation, can be read only ironically, as an example of Hardy's subversive humor: "It is said that in after years she wrote an excellent tract called *Render unto Caesar; or, The Repentant Villagers.*" But some critics have taken the moral of this ending seriously, despite a note that Hardy appended to the story in the 1912 edition of *Wessex Tales*. This note lends support to a less moralistic interpretation and underscores the reluctance with which he submitted to the conventional expectations of editors and readers of English magazines. His preferred ending would "correspond more closely with the true incidents of which the tale is a vague and flickering shadow. Lizzy did not, in fact, marry the minister, but – much to her credit in the author's opinion – stuck to Jim the smuggler."

Hardy's conviction about the powerful role family history plays in the life of an individual is evident in all the *Wessex Tales*. Lizzy appeals to family tradition and local values, for example, when attempting to explain herself to Stockdale: "My father did it, and so did my grandfather, and almost everybody in Nether-Moynton lives by it." Encouraging readers, outsiders like Stockdale, to move beyond conventional assumptions and stereotypes to a deeper understanding of Wessex culture – and, by implication, of Hardy's family history – is an important dynamic at work in these stories. Even characters who have risen from their humble origins (or fallen from the aristocracy, as in the case of Tess) bear traces of class characteristics inherited from their ancestors. In "Fellow-Townsmen," for example, the narrator emphasizes that Mr. Barnet "was probably the first of his line who had ever passed a day without toil, and perhaps something like an inherited instinct disqualifies such men for a life of pleasant inaction, such as lies in the power of those whose leisure is not a personal accident, but a vast historical accretion which has become part of their natures."

Of all the stories in this volume, "Fellow-Townsmen" is the most layered with ironies of circumstance. It was one of Hardy's favorites, and he agreed with his friend Florence Henniker, who thought it was even better than "The Three Strangers." Some critics have speculated that one reason for this preference could be that Hardy's marriage, like Barnet's, had become unhappy. Hardy would have felt satisfied also with the story's honest presentation of the awry nature of life – the very quality that has led some readers to react against it. Barnet is a good man, but his goodness is never rewarded. The story hinges on the mistake he makes in marrying a woman who is obsessed with class distinctions rather than marrying the impoverished woman he has always loved, Lucy Savile. Once Barnet is free to marry Lucy, she has decided to marry a man she would have never met if Barnet had not wished to do a good deed by helping her. The story's final irony is that she falls in love with Barnet again when she is a widow, but only after her discouragement of his renewed suit has driven him away for the last time.

"Interlopers at the Knap" is another story about the frustrations of love, but in this narrative the heroine comes to the un-Victorian conclusion that she is content to remain single, turning down both proposals of marriage she is offered at the end of the story. "Interlopers at the Knap" is set in Melbury Osmond, the village where Hardy's mother was born, and the description of Darton's journey to this village to be married is based on the story Hardy heard about his father's long walk to Melbury Osmond the night before his wedding. As F. B. Pinion points out in his notes to Hardy's *Collected Short Stories* (1988), the Knap in this story is identical to the house in Hardy's poem "One Who Married Above Him," a ballad that, like this story, considers the destructive effects of class consciousness on love.

"An Imaginative Woman" (1893) was included in the 1896 edition of *Wessex Tales,* though in 1912 Hardy moved the story to *Life's Little Ironies,* where it is more in keeping with the tone, theme, and setting of the stories in that collection. In the 1912 edition of *Wessex Tales,* Hardy included two stories of the Napoleonic Wars, "A Tradition of Eighteen Hundred and Four" and "The Melancholy Hussar of the German Legion" (originally published in 1882 and 1890 respectively, both stories were also collected in the 1894 edition of *Life's Little Ironies* and later moved to this volume). These stories seem appropriate in *Wessex Tales* because they are set in the Napoleonic period, which was remembered so vividly by the older members of Hardy's family and community. On the first holiday he took with Emma in 1876, Hardy visited the Waterloo battlefield; a year earlier he had interviewed pensioners at Chelsea Hospital about their experiences in that battle. "A Tradition of Eighteen Hundred and Four" recounts a fictional "legend," not repeated much "thanks to the incredulity of the age," about Napoleon's visit to the Dorset coast to plan an invasion. Hardy writes in his autobiography about being "struck with the extreme improbability of such a story" and therefore seeking to use a narrative frame (which amounts to one storyteller vouching for the legitimacy of the events recounted by another) to make the fictional seem to be historical fact. He goes on to report how surprised he was to hear that his story had established a legend where none existed before: "I see you have made use of that well-known tradition of Napoleon's landing," the local people remarked.

"The Melancholy Hussar of the German Legion" also effectively employs a narrative frame, but in this case the events are a matter of historical record. The story concerns a woman who falls in love with a York Hussar who is later shot for desertion. Hardy read about the execution of two deserters in the *Morning Chronicle* (4 July 1801) in the British Museum, and a note about his interview with James Selby concerning the German soldiers is included in his autobiography. He writes in his first preface to *Life's Little Ironies* about his memory of the old woman who pointed out the men's graves to him. The ironies that unfold in Hardy's narration of his heroine's relationship with one of these men explain why he originally included the story in *Life's Little Ironies.* But, like the other Wessex tales, "The Melancholy Hussar" is rooted in local history and resonant with personal associations.

Early in 1890 Hardy published "The Lady Penelope" (*Longman's Magazine*), a story collected in *A*

First page of the manuscript for "The Melancholy Hussar / The Corporal in the German Legion," October 1889. First published as "The Melancholy Hussar" (British Times and Mirror, 4 & 11 January 1890), the story was retitled "The Melancholy Hussar of the German Legion" for the 1894 collection Life's Little Ironies (State Historical Society of Iowa, HrT 1516).

"BETTY LAY UPON THE FLOOR."

Illustration by C. S. Reinhart for "The First Countess of Wessex" (Harper's, December 1889)

Group of Noble Dames. In May of that year he completed the first version of this story sequence, which included six tales written to be published together: "Barbara of the House of Grebe," "The Marchioness of Stonehenge," "Lady Mottisfont," "The Lady Icenway," "Squire Petrick's Lady," and "Anna, Lady Baxby." The *Graphic* published *A Group of Noble Dames* in the 1890 Christmas number. However, when William Luson Thomas, the founder of the paper, read the manuscript the summer before, he was offended by the stories. His assistant editor wrote to Hardy, requesting that he make changes to four of the tales, rejecting altogether "Squire Petrick's Lady" and "Lady Mottisfont," which he described as "hopeless. Frankly, do you think it advisable to put into the hands of the Young Person stories, one of which turns upon the hysterical confession by a wife of an imaginary adultery, and the other upon the manner in which a husband foists upon his wife the offspring of a former illicit connection?"

By revising to address these objections, however, Hardy eventually managed to get all six sto-

ries accepted. At the same time as the *Graphic* publication, and in more or less unbowdlerized form, *A Group of Noble Dames* appeared in America in *Harper's Weekly*. In part because of his satisfaction with Harper for accepting the stories without changes, Hardy later took *A Group of Noble Dames* and *Tess of the d'Urbervilles* (also originally serialized in the *Graphic* in bowdlerized form) to Osgood, McIlvaine, the semi-autonomous London subsidiary of the New York house. Published in one volume in 1891, the final version of *A Group of Noble Dames* includes, in addition to the six original stories, four tales previously published in magazines: "The First Countess of Wessex," "The Lady Penelope," "The Duchess of Hamptonshire," and "The Honourable Laura."

In structure this story cycle has been compared to Geoffrey Chaucer's *Canterbury Tales* (circa 1387) and Giovanni Boccaccio's *The Decameron* (1349–1351), for the tales are unified by a frame narrative about the storytellers, members of the South-Wessex Field and Antiquarian Club who are trapped in a museum by a rainstorm and who pass the time by relating the histories of "gentle and noble dames, renowned in times past in that part of England." Most of the stories are set in the seventeenth and eighteenth centuries and, characteristically, focus on sexual alliances across class boundaries. These stories, perhaps more consistently than any of Hardy's other fictions, are also concerned with the plight of children, especially illegitimate children. Hardy and Emma remained childless, and this fact may account for the recurring theme in Hardy's work of adults who come to love children not biologically their own. (In the novels, for example, there is the love of Sue for Father Time [*Jude the Obscure*] and of Henchard for Elizabeth-Jane [*The Mayor of Casterbridge*]; the most memorable among the many instances in the stories is Ned's love for Car'line's daughter in "The Fiddler of the Reels.")

"The First Countess of Wessex," which opens the collection, tells the story of a girl manipulated and pulled in opposite directions by the plans and ambitions of her parents. In "The Marchioness of Stonehenge," Lady Caroline gives up her illegitimate baby to his father's rejected lover, Milly, a working-class woman who lovingly raises the child. Years later, when the boy has grown up to be a fine young man, in an effort to get him back the marchioness asks him to choose between his two mothers. He chooses Milly: "You see, my lady, you cared little for me when I was weak and helpless; why should I come to you now I am strong?" "Lady Mottisfont" features an illegitimate child over whom two mothers fight, but in this case the daughter is not only "doubly-desired" but also "doubly-rejected." In "The Lady Icenway" a man is separated from his son because he married the child's mother bigamously.

By far the strangest of these stories about parents and children is "Squire Petrick's Lady." The plot takes several ironic turns. On her deathbed Petrick's wife confesses that their son is not their own, and Petrick therefore persuades his grandfather to cut the child out of his will. Later, however, Petrick discovers that his illegitimate son must be of noble blood, and he commits forgery to get the boy back in the will. Finally, after talking to his wife's doctor, Petrick learns that his wife's dying words were merely hysterical, evidence of her susceptibility to delusion. He rejects the boy, dismayed by the knowledge that his son is not illegitimate after all: "To be sure, Rupert was his son physically, but that glory and halo he believed him to have inherited from the ages, outshining that of his brother's children, had departed from Rupert's brow forever; he

could no longer read history in the boy's face, and centuries of domination in his eyes."

The five other stories in the collection, though of varying quality, are interesting in their treatment of the ethics of love and desire. "Anna, Lady Baxby" is about a woman who, during the English Civil War, is divided between loyalty to her husband, a Royalist, and to her brother, who is fighting with the Parliamentarian forces. Unfortunately, this story is flawed by a weak ending. More successful in its management of theme and narrative technique, "Lady Penelope" tells the story of a woman who has three suitors, to whom she jokingly remarks, "Only bide your time quietly, and, in faith, I will marry you all in turn." Much to her embarrassment, as fate would have it, she does indeed marry each of them. By the time of her third marriage a scandal erupts insinuating that she has murdered her second husband. In this story, as in *The Mayor of Casterbridge* and *Jude the Obscure,* Hardy implicitly criticizes the victimizing power of public opinion, for the rumors torment Penelope and drive her third husband to abandon her. "The Honourable Laura," about a woman who elopes with an opera singer who later pushes her husband off a cliff to avoid a duel, is pure melodrama.

"The Duchess of Hamptonshire" and especially "Barbara of the House of Grebe" are considered by the few critics who have written about these stories to be the best in the collection. Both heroines are married to sadistic men. Emmeline, the duchess of Hamptonshire, attempts to escape her husband's cruelty by asking her former lover, Alwyn, a young curate, if she can run away with him, for he is emigrating from England that night. He loves her but is nevertheless appalled by her suggestion. Reminiscent of Angel Clare's treatment of Tess, his response to Emmeline is moralistic: "It would be sin." Years later he smugly returns to marry her when he hears of the death of the duke, only to discover that there is a new duchess of Hamptonshire. After making some inquiries, Alwyn learns that Emmeline followed him on the night of his departure from England and died aboard the ship. He is haunted by the words he keeps hearing from those who knew her: "She ran off with the curate."

"Barbara of the House of Grebe" is much more sinister in tone than any of the other tales in the volume. In *After Strange Gods* (1934) T. S. Eliot says that the story portrays "a world of pure evil," and he wonders what morbid emotion prompted Hardy to write it. Although it has been attacked by Eliot and others, the story has also been praised for its undeniably effective control of tone, character-

*Illustration by Walter Paget for "On the Western Circuit" (*English Illustrated Magazine, *December 1891)*

ization, and Gothic imagery. The story's plot is a twisted variation on the Pygmalion myth. Barbara is doomed to marry Uplandtowers, the villain of the piece, but before she does, she runs off with a handsome yet penniless man, Edmond Willowes. Her father disapproves of the match but tries to make the best of it by sending Willowes abroad with a tutor to "develop" and gain some polish.

While heroically saving his fellow theatergoers in a fire, Willowes is disfigured by burns. When he returns, Barbara is unable to hide her aversion, and, out of love and pity for her, he leaves and later dies abroad. While married to her second husband, Uplandtowers, Barbara falls in love with a statue of Willowes before his disfigurement. Annoyed by her habit of slipping away in the middle of the night, Uplandtowers follows Barbara and finds her "standing with her arms clasped tightly round the neck of her Edmond, and her mouth on his." By replacing the original statue with one that represents Willowes horribly disfigured, Uplandtowers takes malicious pleasure in shocking and coercing his wife into loving him: "The strange thing now was that

this fictitious love wrung from her by terror took on . . . a certain quality of reality." Hence, Uplandtowers – the depth of whose sadistic perversity the narrator indicates subtly and obliquely throughout the story – triumphs in the end.

In a 1987 article on *A Group of Noble Dames,* George Wing notes the "jaunty air" and "grim playfulness" of these stories and finds their strange jocularity unsettling. But as Brady argues, the distinctive narrative tone of the tales arises from a disparity between the club members who tell the stories and the implied author, who seems to endorse neither their detachment nor their easy judgments. The Old Surgeon who tells Barbara's story, for example, concludes by agreeing with the moral of the sermon preached after her death: she was guilty of "the folly of indulgence in sensuous love for a handsome form merely." Yet the narrative as a whole emphasizes not this alleged superficiality but the psychological pain her second husband so mercilessly inflicts on her.

One story originally intended for *A Group of Noble Dames,* "The Doctor's Legend" (1891), was published instead in America in the *Independent.* Critics have speculated that Hardy excluded it from his collection because of his reluctance to offend the local family associated with the legend. The story is about Milton Abbey and the wicked old squire who digs up the holy skeletons buried beneath his property. Hardy had sketched the architecture of Milton Abbey when he was young, and when writing the story he probably also drew on memories of his experience supervising the removal of bodies from graveyards in the path of planned railways, part of his work for Blomfield; in his autobiography he writes of finding a skeleton with two skulls in one of the coffins.

The late 1880s and early 1890s mark Hardy's most confident and prolific period as a writer of short fiction. With the stories that were later collected as *Life's Little Ironies,* Hardy made a transition from historical tales in the oral tradition to a more modern style of short story with a contemporary setting. In 1891 he published "For Conscience' Sake" (*Fortnightly Review*), "To Please His Wife" (*Black and White*), "On The Western Circuit" (*Harper's Weekly* and *English Illustrated Magazine*), and "The Son's Veto" (*Illustrated London News,* Christmas number). "Wessex Folk," the story cycle later retitled "A Few Crusted Characters," was serialized that year in *Harper's New Monthly Magazine.*

Life's Little Ironies – which includes all these stories as well as "The Fiddler of the Reels," "A Tragedy of Two Ambitions," and the two Napoleonic stories later moved to *Wessex Tales* — was published in February 1894. These stories are unified not only by a contemporary setting but also by the ironic and often tragic circumstances that dominate their plots. Brady rightly emphasizes the social aspect of tragedy in these stories, observing that at the end of his fiction-writing career Hardy became bolder in his questioning of both social and literary conventions: "These stories attempt to undermine the reader's respect for social advancement, his trust in the inviolability of the marriage contract, and his belief in a conventional ideal of romantic love." This subversive element in the stories — their strategies to maneuver readers away from complacent assumptions and conventional morality — is a quality that *Life's Little Ironies* shares with Hardy's novels to a greater extent than do the other three volumes of short stories.

"The Son's Veto" exposes the cruel effects of the class system in its narrative about a widow whose snobbish son forbids his mother, who married above her, to accept the proposal of a working-class man with whom she has fallen in love. Unlike many of Hardy's short stories, this one has a striking, aesthetically satisfying ending. While the son makes a successful career in the church, his mother dies alone after a life of loneliness and pathetically renewed pleas to him to relent. Hardy concludes the story with an image that underscores the contrast between the two men in her life, who both attend the funeral: "The man, whose eyes were wet, held his hat in his hand as the vehicles moved by; while from the mourning-coach a young smooth-shaven priest in a high waistcoat looked black as a cloud at the shopkeeper standing there." Hardy told his American friend Rebekah Owen that this was his best short story, a judgment in keeping with the critical assessment that its quality lies to a great extent in the personal convictions that energize its telling.

"For Conscience' Sake," another story concerned with class distinction, announces its ethical theme and central irony in the first sentence: "Whether the utilitarian or the intuitive theory of the moral sense be upheld it is beyond question that there are a few subtle-souled persons with whom the absolute gratuitousness of an act of reparation is an inducement to perform it; while exhortation as to its necessity would breed excuses for leaving it undone." The act of reparation that the protagonist attempts to make is not merely gratuitous but destructive as well. Millbourne completely changed the life of a woman whom he refused to marry because she was "beneath [his] position," even though she was pregnant with his baby; then, many years later, he persuades her to marry him "for conscience' sake."

As the story unfolds, the reader comes to see what an empty gesture this is: "Our evil actions do not remain isolated in the past, waiting only to be reversed." Once again Hardy attempts to move his readers beyond a simple, rule-bound understanding of morality. The idea for this story (and his other tales of women seduced and betrayed) could have originated as early as 1877, when one of his servants, who had been surreptitiously letting a man into her room at night, disappeared. An entry Hardy made in his notebook a few days later seems particularly relevant to "For Conscience' Sake": "The sudden disappointment of a hope leaves a scar which the ultimate fulfillment of that hope never entirely removes."

"A Tragedy of Two Ambitions" is the story of two brothers, class-conscious clergymen like the son in "A Son's Veto," who stand by and watch their alcoholic father drown rather than save him and risk his interference with their social climbing and their sister's marriage to an aristocrat. According to Hardy's autobiography, Edmund Gosse considered "A Tragedy of Two Ambitions" one of "the most thrilling and most complete stories Hardy had written — 'I walked under the moral burden of it for the remainder of the day.' " An interesting aspect of the story not present in the magazine version is Hardy's satire on the priority of the qualifications for priesthood. Without money and the university education and rank it can buy, the brothers can procure licenses to preach but not regular church appointments. Although their father thwarts their progress, they are tormented by guilt after his death. Nevertheless, Hardy's portrayal of the alcoholic father is quite negative. Coming from a family in which drinking was a problem on both sides, Hardy was a near abstainer. *The Mayor of Casterbridge*, *Tess of the d'Urbervilles*, and *Jude the Obscure* also explore the role played by alcoholism in the lives of individuals and their families.

In "To Please His Wife" social ambition has distorted the character not of a child, as in the other stories, but of a parent. The protagonist, Joanna, marries a sailor to spite her rival, who then marries a richer man. Rabid to keep up with her, Joanna encourages her husband to take their sons with him when he goes to sea — the three of them will make more money than he could possibly make on his own. They never return, and Joanna is driven mad with grief. The companion piece to this story is Hardy's poem "The Sailor's Mother" (*Late Lyrics and Earlier with Many Other Verses*, 1922).

"The Fiddler of the Reels," considered by many to be Hardy's best short story, establishes as its backdrop the Great Exhibition of 1851, an event symbolic of "a sudden bringing of ancient and modern into absolute contact." Because folklore is so resonant in this work, some have pointed out that it would be more appropriately placed in *Wessex Tales.* But, as Frank R. Giordano, Jr., argues in a 1975 article on the story, in its allusions to folk legends and Greek mythology "The Fiddler" embodies "the painful truth that modern Hebraic man ignores at his peril the demand of the human spirit for Dionysiac experience."

Wat Ollamoor, the fiddler who possesses supernatural powers as a musician and "lady's man," represents this Dionysiac force, which is in conflict with the modern rational spirit of the story's staid Victorian characters. Although Ollamoor seduces Car'line Aspent with his fiddle playing and later spirits off her daughter, Hardy never clearly encourages the reader to judge the fiddler (the judgmental narrator is obviously a screen, a representative of unthinking moralism). The story's ambiguity is one source of its continuing fascination, and its central metaphor reveals Hardy's fascination with the mysterious power of sexual attraction, a subject he treats at length in *The Pursuit of the Well-Beloved* (1892), serialized shortly before he completed "The Fiddler of the Reels."

"A Few Crusted Characters" shares the Wessex character of "The Fiddler of the Reels," but it is much less carefully crafted. Like *A Group of Noble Dames,* the story sequence "A Few Crusted Characters" is told by many narrators, in this case as they travel together in a coach with John Lackland, a native returning to Longpuddle. Unlike the tales in the longer story cycle, however, these narratives focus on the Wessex folk rather than the aristocrats. Light in tone, the stories are considered Hardy's most amusing.

Life's Little Ironies also includes two of Hardy's most erotic love stories, both of which feature women unfulfilled by their marriages. In "On the Western Circuit," Mrs. Edith Harnham falls in love with Charles Bradford Raye, the suitor of her illiterate maid, Anna. Edith becomes emotionally obsessed with Raye when ghostwriting Anna's letters to him. Charmed by the letters, Raye falls in love with her, though he marries Anna and, of course, discovers his mistake too late. Hardy's conception for this story probably owes something to his experience, when still a boy, of acting as an amanuensis for village girls lonely for their military sweethearts.

Like "On the Western Circuit," "An Imaginative Woman" was censored for periodical publication. After its appearance in this form (*Pall Mall Magazine,* 1894) and its subsequent revision for the 1896 edition of *Wessex Tales,* Hardy ultimately decided to include it in *Life's Little Ironies.* In this strange, compelling story, Ella Marchmill falls in love with the poet whose rooms she and her husband and children rent during the summer – even though she never meets him. About nine months later she dies giving birth to a boy. The father becomes convinced that the child is not his own: "By a known but inexplicable trick of Nature there were undoubtedly strong traces of resemblance to the man Ella had never seen." Critics have noted the significance of the fact that Hardy worked on the final version of this story the same year he met the novelist Florence Henniker, to whom he was strongly attracted. Moreover, "An Imaginative Woman" is set in Southsea, where the Hennikers lived; Hardy went out of his way to visit Florence there on a trip between Dorchester and London in the summer of 1893.

In the same year that *Life's Little Ironies* was published, Hardy collaborated with Henniker on a short story, "The Spectre of the Real" (*To-day,* 1894). The story is Hardyesque in its social and sexual themes, and it was probably essentially his work. Millgate points out that this story, yet another critique of marriage, could hardly not have offended Emma, who was aware of her husband's friendship with his collaborator. In the 1890s domestic relations became increasingly strained for both Hardy and Emma, and the publication of *Jude the Obscure* (which Hardy originally conceived as a short story) in 1895 coincided with what seems to have been the worst period in their marriage. The novel's bitter denunciation of the evils of marriage is a clear indication of Hardy's feelings, as is Emma's openly expressed contempt for the novel. She wrote to a friend in 1894 complaining that her husband "understands only the women he *invents* – the others not at all – & he only writes for *Art,* though ethics show up." After his wife's unexpected death in 1912, Hardy blamed himself for not responding to Emma as a fellow sufferer, for not showing her the "loving-kindness" he advocates so consistently throughout his fiction.

Just before the appearance of *Life's Little Ironies,* at the suggestion of J. M. Barrie, Hardy wrote a one-act play, "The Three Wayfarers," adapted from "The Three Strangers." By all accounts this story translated to the stage successfully. Although the play ran in London for only one week in June

1893, the *Times* reviewed it favorably, pronouncing it the "best piece of the evening." In a 1981 article on the play, Keith Wilson calls it "a small triumph of atmosphere and stagecraft." The success of this adaptation is not surprising given Hardy's skill at creating intense, dramatic moments in his fiction. In 1911 he gave his support to the production in Dorchester by amateur actors who staged the play along with A. H. Evans's dramatization of "The Distracted Preacher."

In addition to the works collected in his third volume of short stories, Hardy wrote a few other tales during the 1890s. "Master John Horsleigh, Knight" – a rather feeble story that, given its opening, Hardy probably originally intended for *A Group of Noble Dames* – was published in the *Illustrated London News* (1893). Two stories set in the Napoleonic period were published in 1896: "A Committee-Man of the Terror" (*London Illustrated Magazine*) and "The Duke's Reappearance" (*Saturday Review*). "The Grave by the Handpost," one of the most depressing Christmas stories ever written (the subject is guilt and suicide), was published the following year in the *St. James Budget*. In 1898 Hardy first considered putting these in a volume with some of his other uncollected stories, but he did not do so until 1913, with *A Changed Man, The Waiting Supper, and Other Tales*. The volume also includes "What the Shepherd Saw," "The Romantic Adventures of a Milkmaid," "A Tryst at an Ancient Earthwork," "A Mere Interlude," "Alicia's Diary," "The Waiting Supper," "A Changed Man," and "Enter a Dragoon."

Hardy considered the first title story the best in the collection. Originally published in the *Sphere* (1900), "A Changed Man," like the Wessex tales, is charged with personal associations. Through the story's account of a man who undergoes a religious conversion and devotes himself to caring for the victims of a cholera epidemic, Hardy honors the work of Horace Moule's father, vicar of Fordington during the cholera outbreaks there in 1849 and 1854.

Hardy penned his last short story, "Enter a Dragoon" (first published in *Harper's Monthly Magazine*), in 1900 and then gave up fiction, dedicating all his energy to writing poetry. "Enter a Dragoon" is an ironic story about a woman who is misguided in her dogged wish to achieve respectability after she is deserted by her lover, a sergeant major of dragoons. As Brady points out, "The quest for respectability is seen as utterly meaningless." This story's lack of freshness reflects Hardy's weariness by this point with the demands of magazine publication. In the early years of the twentieth century he delayed

Hardy late in life

fulfilling his verbal commitment to the editor Clement Shorter to provide the *Illustrated London News* with another story, and in 1914 he wrote to his literary agent, William Morris Colles, that he would not be writing any more fiction.

By the time of Emma's death in 1912, Hardy had published three volumes of poetry – *Wessex Poems* (1898), *Poems of the Past and the Present* (1901), and *Time's Laughingstocks* (1909) – as well as his three-volume verse epic based on the Napoleonic Wars, *The Dynasts* (1904–1908). Like a character in one of his stories, Hardy seemed to fall most intensely in love with his wife after her death, making a pilgrimage in 1913 to Saint Juliot, where they had met, and to Plymouth, where Emma was born. His fine *Poems of 1912–13*, published in *Satires of Circumstance* (1914), is the product of the misery of guilt and regret that he felt at her death; as Millgate observes, "What gave Hardy pain was precisely what provided the fuel for his art." He spent the remainder of his career writing the poetry collected in *Moments of Vision* (1917), *Late Lyrics and Earlier* (1922), *Human Shows, Far Phantasies, Songs and Trifles* (1925), and *Winter Words in Various Moods and Metres* (1928).

In 1914 Hardy married his second wife, Florence Dugdale, a considerably younger woman he had met nine years earlier when she was an aspiring writer. She aided Hardy in writing his autobiography (begun in 1917), which she pretended, in obedience to his request, was a biography she had authored. *The Early Years of Thomas Hardy, 1840–1891,* was published after his death in 1928, followed by *The Later Years of Thomas Hardy, 1892–1928* (1930). Florence Hardy was also responsible for the publication of one of her husband's best short stories, "Old Mrs. Chundle" (*Ladies Home Journal,* 1929), written sometime between 1888 and 1890. He probably made no effort to publish this story because of its irreverent humor, but its satire of a zealous young curate who comes to regret his efforts to get a deaf old woman to attend church is highly amusing, and the story as a whole is deeply moral in its embodiment of Hardy's love for humanity.

In the years before his death on 11 January 1928, at the age of eighty-seven, Hardy was a famous man, considered by many to be the greatest living English writer. He had risen to this prominence from rural obscurity, and despite the self-consciousness he felt about his lack of formal education, to the end he retained an affinity with the class and culture in which he was raised. As Millgate recounts, on his deathbed Hardy "asked for a rasher of bacon to be grilled for him in front of the open fire . . . as bacon had been cooked in his mother's time." Even more insistently than his novels, Hardy's stories celebrate a particular region and way of life. In their narrative technique they continue an oral tradition in which, Millgate notes, Hardy was perhaps England's "last and greatest product."

The dark vision of life as a series of absurd reversals, ironic frustrations, and tragedies of circumstance that Hardy expresses in his novels, poems, and stories was formed in his childhood and was as central to his mother's character as it was to his own. In 1870 he wrote in his notebook: "Mother's notion, & also mine: That a figure stands in our van with an arm uplifted, to knock us back from any pleasant prospect we indulge in as probable." This figure – usually a cosmic or natural force, but just as often an oppressive social convention – thwarts the desires of many of the characters in his short fiction. One of Hardy's most important contributions to the development of the short story is a particular form of irony arising from this sense of life. According to David Daiches, as quoted in Brady's *The Short Stories of Thomas Hardy,* "Hardy's irony is not directed at human egotism or at the disparity between real and assumed worth, but at the very conditions of human existence." Hence, a second, related feature of Hardy's stories is compassion for his characters. The subversive element so central to *Life's Little Ironies* serves to promote this ethic of compassion by overturning the reader's assumptions and shaking a complacent Victorian audience out of its unthinking moralism.

Critics have commonly dismissed Hardy's short stories as merely by-products of his novels. D. H. Lawrence condescendingly remarked, for example, that Hardy wrote "little tales of widows and widowers." But the erotic intensity of such stories as "On the Western Circuit" and "An Imaginative Woman" prefigures the mood that Lawrence develops in some of his own short stories, and Hardy's refusal of the conventional and the sentimental in his narrative choices makes him a precursor of many other twentieth-century short-fiction writers. Still, the critics and readers who have considered it worthwhile to turn their attention to Hardy's short stories are probably struck less by the continuity between his work and that of others and more by the uniqueness of his voice and vision. Although his stories are of uneven quality, each tale unmistakably betrays his distinctive authorial presence – and for some readers that alone makes them well worth reading.

Letters:
The Collected Letters of Thomas Hardy, edited by Richard Little Purdy and Michael Millgate, 7 volumes (Oxford: Clarendon, 1978–1990).

Bibliographies:
Richard Little Purdy, *Thomas Hardy: A Bibliographical Study* (Oxford: Clarendon, 1954; revised, 1968);
Ronald P. Draper and Martin S. Ray, *An Annotated Critical Bibliography of Thomas Hardy* (Ann Arbor: University of Michigan Press, 1989).

Biographies:
J. I. M. Stewart, *Thomas Hardy: A Critical Biography* (London: Longman, 1971);
Robert Gittings, *Young Thomas Hardy* (London: Heinemann, 1975);
Gittings, *The Older Hardy* (London: Heinemann, 1978);
Michael Millgate, *Thomas Hardy: A Biography* (New York: Random House, 1982).

References:
Kristin Brady, *The Short Stories of Thomas Hardy* (New York: St. Martin's Press, 1982);

Richard C. Carpenter, "How To Read *A Few Crusted Characters*," in *Critical Approaches to the Fiction of Thomas Hardy,* edited by Dale Kramer (London: Macmillan, 1979), pp. 155–171;

T. S. Eliot, *After Strange Gods: A Primer of Modern Heresy* (London: Faber & Faber, 1934: New York: Harcourt, Brace, 1934);

Alexander Fishler, "Theatrical Techniques in Thomas Hardy's Short Stories," *Studies in Short Fiction,* 3 (Summer 1966): 435–445;

Frank R. Giordano, Jr., "Characterization and Conflict in Hardy's 'The Fiddler of the Reels,' " *Texas Studies in Literature & Language,* 17 (Fall 1975): 617–633;

A. J. Guerard, *Thomas Hardy: The Novels and Stories* (Cambridge, Mass.: Harvard University Press, 1949);

Irving Howe, *Thomas Hardy* (New York: Macmillan, 1967);

Romney T. Keys, "Hardy's Uncanny Narrative: A Reading of 'The Withered Arm,' " *Texas Studies in Literature & Language,* 27 (Spring 1985): 106–123;

Charles Lock, *Thomas Hardy,* Criticism in Focus series (New York: St. Martin's Press, 1992);

J. Hillis Miller, *Thomas Hardy: Distance and Desire* (Cambridge, Mass.: Belknap, 1970);

Harold Orel, "Thomas Hardy: An Older Tradition of Narrative," in his *The Victorian Short Story: Development and Triumph of a Literary Genre* (Cambridge: Cambridge University Press, 1986), pp. 96–114;

Norman Page, "Hardy's Short Stories: A Reconsideration," *Studies in Short Fiction,* 11 (Winter 1974): 75–84;

Maire A. Quinn, "Thomas Hardy and the Short Story," in *Budmouth Essays on Thomas Hardy: Papers Presented at the 1975 Summer School,* edited by F. B. Pinion (Dorchester: Thomas Hardy Society, 1976), pp. 74–85;

Keith Wilson, "Hardy and the Hangman: The Dramatic Appeal of 'The Three Strangers,' " *English Literature in Transition,* 24, no. 3 (1981): 155–160;

George Wing, "*A Group of Noble Dames:* 'Statuesque Dynasties of Delightful Wessex,' " *Thomas Hardy Annual No. 5,* edited by Page (London: Macmillan, 1987), pp. 75–101.

Papers:

Of the *Wessex Tales,* only two are known to survive in manuscript: "The Three Strangers" in the Berg Collection, New York Public Library, and "The Melancholy Hussar" in the Henry E. Huntington Library and Art Gallery, San Marino, California. The manuscript of the six-story version of *A Group of Noble Dames* for the *Graphic* and that of "The Lady Penelope" were presented to the Library of Congress in 1911. The manuscript of the 1884 version of "The Duchess of Hamptonshire" is in the Pierpont Morgan Library, New York; that of "The First Countess of Wessex" was sold in New York in 1906, but its whereabouts are unknown. Manuscripts of five of the stories from *Life's Little Ironies* survive in complete form: "An Imaginative Woman," Aberdeen University Library; "For Conscience' Sake," Manchester University Library; "A Tragedy of Two Ambitions," The John Rylands Library, Manchester; "On the Western Circuit," Manchester Central Library; and "The Son's Veto," Bodmer Collection, Switzerland. An incomplete rough draft of "A Few Crusted Characters" (with the original title "Wessex Folk") is in the Berg Collection. Manuscripts of "A Changed Man," "A Committee-Man of 'the Terror,' " and "The Doctor's Legend" are also part of the Berg Collection. Those of "A Tryst at an Ancient Earthwork," "Master John Horseleigh, Knight," and "The Duke's Reappearance" are at the Harry Ransom Humanities Research Center, University of Texas at Austin. That of "The Romantic Adventures of a Milkmaid" is in the Pierpont Morgan Library. The manuscript of "What the Shepherd Saw," sold in London in 1955, remains untraced. When last traced, that of "The Grave by the Handpost" belonged to Halsted B. VanderPoel, Rome. The manuscript of "Old Mrs. Chundle" is in the Dorset County Museum.

Florence Henniker

(7 December 1855 – 4 April 1923)

Jonathan Wike
North Carolina A&T State University

BOOKS: *Sir George* (London: Bentley, 1891);
Bid Me Good-bye (London: Bentley, 1892);
Foiled (London: Hurst & Blackett, 1893);
Outlines (London: Hutchinson, 1894);
In Scarlet and Grey: Stories of Soldiers and Others (London: John Lane, 1896; Boston: Roberts, 1896);
Sowing the Sand (London & New York: Harper, 1898);
Contrasts (London: John Lane, 1903);
Our Fatal Shadows (London: Hurst & Blackett, 1907);
Second Fiddle (London: Nash, 1912).

PLAY PRODUCTION: *The Courage of Silence,* Hammersmith, King's Theatre, 22 May 1905.

OTHER: "Mrs. Livesey," in *Stories and Play Stories* (London: Chapman & Hall, 1897).

SELECTED PERIODICAL PUBLICATIONS –
UNCOLLECTED: "Unanswered," *Harper's,* 80 (March 1890): 620;
"Lines on a Stormy Petrel," *Littell's Living Age,* 194 (3 September 1892): 578;
"At the Crossing," *Speaker* (19 December 1896): 665–666;
"A Faithful Failure," *Pall Mall* (August 1900);
"A Bunch of Cowslips," *Court Journal* (2 December 1905);
"His Best Novel," *Pall Mall* (July 1906).

Florence Henniker, 1893

Florence Henniker was the daughter of a man of letters and had for her childhood companions several of the most celebrated writers of the day. She showed a natural inclination for writing at an early age and later enjoyed a productive career as a fluent, if not particularly daring, writer of fiction, with three collections of short stories and several novels to her credit. Her aristocratic background and connections, along with the gracefulness and gentility that she brought to her work, probably helped her with both publishers and readers in the rich literary culture of the 1890s, but the natural advantages that opened a career for her may also have been limitations in the long run. The inevitable impression, perhaps not an entirely fair one, given by her career is that of a pastime, a brilliant accomplishment, not a vocation to which she devoted all her energies. Her writings are now nearly forgotten, but her name remains familiar to scholars of the period through her friendship with one who became, by the time of his death, the most prominent literary figure in England, and the story of her life is now forever bound up with the story of Thomas Hardy.

"This is prodigious news you send me about a new Milnes – daughter," William Makepeace Thackeray wrote to Adelaide Anne Procter from New Orleans in early 1856. Florence Ellen Hungerford Milnes had been born 7 December 1855, the second child of Richard Monckton Milnes, later first Lord Houghton, and Annabella Hungerford Milnes, daughter of the second Baron Crewe. Milnes named her after Florence Nightingale, whom he had once wanted to marry. As a young man he had made something of a name for himself as a poet. In 1854 his edition of John Keats's poems with a biographical memoir appeared; it was republished several times.

Florence later recalled "going out for a drive with Thackeray, [who] made up some nonsense rhymes about me"; she cherished the memory of this "kind, tall, amusing, grey-haired man." She also played croquet with Algernon Charles Swinburne, who fretted at losing. After attending her seventh birthday party, Swinburne wrote her father: "I hope Florey has not forgotten her conditional engagement in ten years' time if I am rich enough to give her a trousseau of rubies. I told L[ad]y Trevelyan of the affecting ceremony, & she expressed herself 'only too thankful to hear that I have a chance of being saved by a virtuous attachment.'" The family home was Fryston Hall in Yorkshire, which Milnes once offered to Alfred, Lord Tennyson, for his honeymoon. Henry Adams described it as "one of a class of houses that no one sought for its natural beauties," surrounded at the time of his visit by "the winter mists of Yorkshire."

One of her father's letters describes seven-year-old Florence's own literary endeavors:

The second little girl has developed into a verse-writer of a very curious ability. She began theologically and wrote hymns, which I soon checked on observing that she put together words and sentences out of the sacred verse she knew; and set her to write about things she saw and observed. What she now produces is very like the verse of William Blake [whose work Milnes collected], and containing many images that she could never have read of. She cannot write, but she dictates them to her older sister, who is astonished at the phenomenon.

Possibly on the authority of Thomas Macaulay, the father believed this lyric phase would soon pass:

"We, of course, do not let her see that it is anything surprising; and the chances are that it goes off as she gets older and knows more. The lyrical faculty in men and nations seems to belong to a childish condition of mind, and to disappear with experience and knowledge."

In 1863 Richard Monckton Milnes was elevated to the peerage as Baron Houghton of Great Houghton, prompting the lines: "The Alphabet rejoiced to hear / That Monckton Milnes was made a Peer, / For in the present world of letters / But few, if any, are his betters." Milnes was notorious in his youth as a "man of society"; Thomas Carlyle described him as "a most bland-smiling, semi-quizzical, affectionate, highbred, Italianized little man of 5 feet, who has long olive-blond hair, a dimple next to [no] chin, and flings his arm round your neck when he addresses you." Milnes served in Parliament from 1837 to 1863, switching from Conservative to Liberal to support John Russell's administration in 1846. Later, like his son, Robert Crewe-Milnes, first Marquis of Crewe, he allowed public duties to supersede literary ones.

In 1872 Milnes took Florence to Paris to visit President Louis-Adolphe Thiers, an old friend. She describes their reception in a letter to her mother:

Since Papa came I have had several great pleasures. On Sunday an especial one, as he took me to Versailles to dine with M. Thiers. It was delightful, and it interested me extremely to hear him talk. I sat by him at dinner; and afterwards he was so kind, and promised to give me his photograph. We dine there on Thursday again. We were fourteen at dinner; but no ladies except Madame Thiers, her aunt, and sister. There were several officers – among others the general Ducrot, who was celebrated at Sedan. A good many gentlemen came in the evening. The house is beautiful, and guarded by soldiers in quite a royal manner. Yesterday M. Thiers lent us his *loge* in the Assembly, and it was delightful, as there was a tremendous row. It would be impossible to imagine the rage into which some of the deputies got; they looked as if they only longed to fight each other.

The details of Florence Milnes's marriage read like those of her heroines who choose principle, or love, over income. She waited until well into her twenties, and when she married Arthur Henniker-Major in 1882, the match was something of a disappointment to her then-elderly father, who lamented this propensity in his three children: "I used to say I cared only for one thing in my children's marriages – *Money*. I am well paid off for my desires." Henniker-Major, then a lieutenant in the Coldstream Guards, "an impecunious soldier," went on to serve with distinction in several overseas campaigns, eventually being promoted to major general.

The continual absence of her soldier husband, along with financial necessity, may have encouraged Henniker to pursue a literary career. Certainly his vocation lent both characters and atmosphere to her fictional works, full as they are of soldiers – old and young, and either quite virtuous or quite headstrong. Indeed, the presence of troops gives her fiction a balance against the purely aristocratic, a grounding in practical life that it might not otherwise have gotten. By 1893 Henniker had published three novels, *Sir George* (1891), *Bid Me Good-bye* (1892), and *Foiled* (1893), and had established herself as a literary hostess, continuing the tradition of friendships in the world of letters begun by her father, who had died in 1885. In 1896 she was made president of the Society of Women Journalists, then newly formed.

In the summer of 1893 Henniker was serving as hostess at the Vice-regal Lodge in Dublin where her brother served as lord lieutenant of Ireland. One of the guests was Hardy, who for some years had been a friend of her father but had never happened to meet his novelist daughter. A friendship quickly formed that lasted on cordial terms until Henniker's death in 1923. She immediately impressed Hardy as "a charming, *intuitive* woman apparently." By the end of the year Hardy was instructing Henniker in Gothic architecture, avidly discussing literary tastes with her, and taking her on tours of Wessex, that new-old country of whose existence the world had again been made aware in *Tess of the d'Urbervilles* (1891). He had also made himself her literary mentor, even going so far as to plan a collaboration on a piece of fiction. In 1894 Hardy praised her work anonymously in the *London Illustrated News,* citing its "emotional imaginativeness, lightened by a quick sense of the odd, and by touches of observation lying midway between wit and humour."

That this friendship could have taken a more earnest turn, and that Hardy wished it that way, is discussed at length in biographies of him and significantly suppressed in his autobiography. Henniker was not the only protégée of such a description whom Hardy took on: an attractive younger woman of literary interests. His eventual second wife, Florence Dugdale, fit this pattern in many ways. (Henniker had introduced them; an added note of attractiveness in Dugdale came from her admiration and emulation of her older namesake, which Hardy observed with approval.) By the 1890s Hardy's marriage to his first wife, Emma,

was becoming troublesome at the same time that he was enjoying considerable fame as a man of letters. Among other factors, Henniker's happiness in her own marriage and the maturity of herself and Hardy led her to deflect whatever romantic notions Hardy had. His letters to her show a deference and a detachment that suggest little in the way of passion or heartbreak. Hardy having accepted her refusal, their friendship continued on terms of mutual affection and interests: writing and publishing, of course, as well as her husband's career and such causes as animal protection.

Henniker's acquaintance with Hardy began during the composition of his *Jude the Obscure* (1895), and she may have served to some extent as a model for its heroine, Sue Bridehead. What is more certain is that Hardy remembered her in verse: Richard Little Purdy connects her with several poems, most notably "Wessex Heights" (1914), an almost morbid review of losses and their association with particular places and people. One often-quoted stanza provides the title for Evelyn Hardy and F. B. Pinion's collection of Hardy's letters to Henniker:

> As for one rare fair woman, I am now but a thought of hers,
> I enter her mind and another thought succeeds me that she prefers;
> Yet my love for her in its fulness she herself even did not know;
> Well, time cures hearts of tenderness, and now I can let her go.

Henniker was more prolific as a novelist than as a short-story writer. She wrote three more novels after meeting Hardy: *Sowing the Sand* (1898), *Our Fatal Shadows* (1907), and *Second Fiddle* (1912). Hardy's great project for her was to launch and promote her as a writer of short fiction for periodicals, drawing on his friendship with Clement Shorter and others to bring her name before magazine readers. Hardy's influence can be seen in all three of her story collections. The first, *Outlines* (1894), dedicated to him and containing only four stories, appeared in the year after their first meeting, suggesting some haste on both sides to get stories into print. The second and most successful, *In Scarlet and Grey: Stories of Soldiers and Others* (1896), shows the greatest intrusion by Hardy, for he lent his weight as co-author to one of the selections. In the period between this volume and the last, *Contrasts* (1903), Hardy cautioned Henniker about various problems associated with publishing fiction, especially during wartime. This was the period of the Boer War, which touched her life closely, for her husband was involved. It inspired a poetic outburst from Hardy, the eleven "War Poems" of *Poems of the Past and the Present* (1901).

A glimpse of Henniker's literary environment in the 1890s comes from *Reminiscences* (1899), by the Irish novelist Justin McCarthy, who met Bret Harte at her home:

> Mrs. Henniker is, as everyone knows, an authoress of rare gifts, a writer of delightful stories; like her brother she inherits from her father a rich poetic endowment. She is also one of the hostesses, not very common in our days who, if she had lived in Paris at a former time, would have been famous as the presiding genius of a *salon* where wit and humor, literature and art, science and statesmanship found congenial welcome.

Harte depended on Henniker's literary consolation, having once written her:

> Can you recommend anything amusing for me to read? It must be *amusing;* I am getting too old to find any pleasure in being made sad. Lately I have been trying to read serious and even scientific and philosophical books to "improve my mind." But I think I find gibbering and vacuously smiling ignorance preferable to responsible knowledge.

She complimented Harte by dedicating *Foiled,* her third novel, to him. Henniker's views on the art of fiction are revealed in her comments to Raymond Blathwayt in an interview for *Woman at Home* (April 1895). Although her stories have often struck readers as rather pessimistic, she treated life with considerable delicacy:

> In talking on how far it was possible to write a story which should depict society life with photographic accuracy, Mrs. Henniker told me that she thought it absolutely unnecessary, and certainly inartistic and unliterary, to write on only one phase, and that the most disagreeable phase of social life.
>
> "Some people think it impossible," she remarked, "to succeed in literature unless one is unconventional. I think it is too silly even to reply to."

Henniker elaborates on this sentiment, with a little more irony, in a scene from her story "A Successful Intrusion" (*In Scarlet and Grey*), where the debate is taken up by some proper English travelers in Rome:

> The Rev. Augustine was furtively fingering the outside only of a new novel by Zola.
>
> "People should not leave such books as this on the table of a respectable hotel," he remarked, with compressed lips. "One's wife or one's daughter may in all

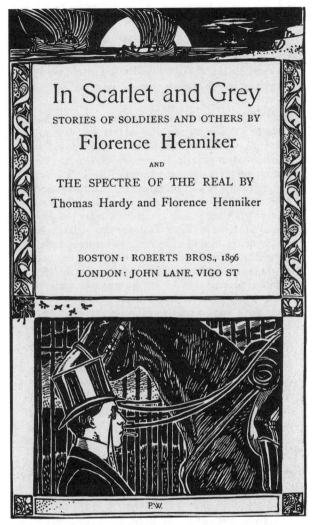

Title page for Henniker's second collection of short fiction, including a story she wrote with Thomas Hardy

innocence open it, and their eyes may drink in pollution. This realistic school – "

> "I, for one, fail to see why this branch of literature alone should be called by that epithet," said Mr. Oswald. "Must we only apply that word to all the revolting things in nature? Surely it is as realistic to describe a shining trout-stream as to dilate upon the contents of a sewer. But you are quite right. Such books ought not to be left out where ladies can see them."

With all the correct opinions aired, Mr. Oswald, the cad of the piece, takes the book away to read privately. (In an 1897 letter Hardy reassures Henniker that he too disapproves of Zola, saying, "I think him no artist, and too material. I feel that the animal side of human nature should never be dwelt on except as a contrast or foil to its spiritual side.")

If it was unladylike to read such fiction, it was naturally improper for a woman to write it.

Blathwayt asks Henniker about the "novel which a recent but more celebrated [woman] writer has given to the world within the last year." She finds it "utterly repulsive," "a distorted vision," and "false from first to last." A too-realistic female writer is only one of a too-prevalent modern type:

> But then I have the strongest objection to the shrieking woman. I dislike women who take to the platform – that is . . . I dislike women doing it. I don't mean I dislike all women who do it, for many of them are very earnest and very charming, though I think they must run a great risk of losing some of their charm when they take to venting their theories in public. Why can't women work *quietly?* they would do far more real good. It is so much the tendency of the day to talk about what one is doing, instead of working in silence. I believe myself in the truth of the old saying – where, at all events, woman's work is concerned – "silence is golden, speech is silvern." And I think the men who come forward to help these women, and who actually seem to insist that a woman is a man's superior, are simply traitors, not to their own sex only, but to the whole race. It is quite against the natural law, and I think quite against facts. As a rule men are better than women. But I confess to a strong prejudice against the emancipated female of to-day. I dislike their social views, and especially their views upon religious matter, which is perhaps natural considering that I am a very High Church person myself.

Those remarks are in line with the rest of the *Woman at Home* article, which dazzles the reader with Henniker's surroundings, both social and architectural, and presents her as a model of good looks, good breeding, and good taste, but they give some indication of her opinion of her own place as a writer.

Hardy's letters to Henniker exhibit a related delicacy about questions of appropriate "women's books." He was surprised, for example, at her interest in his *Dynasts* (1904–1908), which he attributed to her connections with the military. In some cases he may have underestimated her: she admired John Galsworthy's *The Man of Property* (1906), while Hardy reported, "I began it, but found the people too materialistic and sordid to be interesting." Earlier she had surprised him with her interest in the writings of John Stuart Mill; she may have prompted Hardy to read *The Subjection of Women* (1869). To the extent that Henniker contributed to the characterization of Sue Bridehead in *Jude the Obscure,* the lively, intelligent, sympathetic woman in her was being idealized. *Jude the Obscure* had an even more immediate impact on her literary fortunes. Her collaboration with Hardy, called "The Spectre of the Real" (*In Scarlet and Grey*), bears some resem-

blance to his novel, and its critical reception suffered as a result: attacking *Jude the Obscure* and its maker was fashionable at the time.

The evidence is strong that "The Spectre of the Real" is almost entirely Hardy's. In one letter he offers Henniker a choice of endings in about the way he would have asked her advice on his own work. This is not to say, however, that the story is untrue to her general approach to fiction. In many ways it does draw from the resources of both. The story reduces a situation that Hardy examined again and again to its barest essentials: a young couple realize that their marriage has no true foundation and agree to separate as if nothing had ever taken place between them. That this is theoretically desirable Hardy was maintaining to everyone, including Henniker, all through this period and later. That it would be tragic in practice is true to both authors' conceptions of how things work out. Finally unable to deny his connections with the woman, the husband returns to ruin the second marriage she is planning as if it were her first. The resulting suicide of her intended has either the abruptness of Hardy's haste or of Henniker's often oblique conclusions. Some of the minor touches, especially the way the natural imagery sympathetically echoes the human scene, could have come from either pen.

In Scarlet and Grey, which ends with "The Spectre of the Real," is dedicated simply "To My Husband." Perhaps Henniker's most successful collection, it is the main fruit of Hardy's assistance with her publication of short fiction. The collaborative story does not by any means overpower those written by Henniker alone. In the first piece, "The Heart of the Color Sergeant," published in *Cornhill* magazine (May 1894) as "Color Sergeant Rhodes," pretty Kitty Malone loses her heart to the title character just as he is about to join the troops bound for Egypt. Her intended, a captain, rescues the badly wounded sergeant, who had stoically bidden Kitty farewell. In the final scene the dying man is sent a bunch of forget-me-nots by the girl, whom he had first met selling carnations. This story establishes the military atmosphere of the volume (Major Henniker also served in Egypt). The flowers provide a sentimental, and ornamental, link between the frivolous flirtation of the opening and the pathos of the ending.

In "Bad and Worthless," first published in the *English Illustrated Magazine* (April 1894), a disgraced old soldier, shunned by society, in dying saves the life of an errant boy on a snowy night, inspiring the parents to greater vigilance. Though heavy-handed, the story refuses to be too idealistic: the soldier is not noble – he had been begging money for gin – and society at large does not take notice of his deed. In "A Successful Intrusion" a group of English travelers has been led by pedantic clerical guides to Rome – on a pilgrimage to the Protestant cemetery, resting place of John Keats and Percy Bysshe Shelley – when their insulated group is invaded by a charmer named Villiers Oswald. It does not come as a great shock when he leaves with most of their valuables, but the satire is handled well, and the reader is left feeling that most of the characters – even, in their different ways, the middle-aged woman and the young girl whose hearts he breaks – get what they deserve.

"A Page from a Vicar's History," about a mature clergyman whose young friend's fiancée turns out to be the clergyman's wife (who deserted him some years before), makes an interesting contrast with "The Spectre of the Real." With the return of the lost spouse, the situations are similar, though here it is handled more economically, since the character does not have to be sent offstage and then brought back, affording a little more surprise. The whole narrative serves to round out the character of the vicar, outwardly "dull," inwardly torn by regret. And the climax is no less drastic than that of the Hardy/Henniker story, with simultaneous accidental deaths, one probably a suicide.

"At the Sign of the Startled Fawn" offers a first-person framing narrative. It focuses on one event in the inn of the title: the dramatic defense of a woman against her terrorizing husband by a former lover and the resulting accident that renders her mentally ill. The story moves quickly from pastoral to rustic satire on the high and great to the brutality of the barbarous aristocrat to tragic violence, and then all of this is brought graphically up to the present. "In the Infirmary" in some ways recreates the hospital scene of "The Heart of the Color Sergeant," only this time the hoped-for act of recognition is misplaced and bitterly ill received, when only the lady's maid, not the lady herself, manages to visit a dying man. Certain reliable ideas obviously run through these tales: the virtues of the humble, the conflict of reality with passion, and the tendency of things to end badly. But they also amply demonstrate Henniker's strengths: quick evocation of character, ironic use of contrasts, and a feel for simple, connecting imagery.

Henniker's stories appeared in some of the most prominent magazines of her day, several of them almost more notable for their editors than for their contributors. The *Cornhill* magazine had begun

Illustration by C. Demain-Hammond for "Bad and Worthless" (English Illustrated Magazine, *April 1894*)

in 1859 under the editorship of her family's old friend Thackeray and was later controlled by Hardy's longtime friend Leslie Stephen; in fact Hardy achieved his first success in serial publication, *Far From the Madding Crowd,* in the *Cornhill* magazine (1874). Another of Hardy's circle, Clement Shorter, edited the *English Illustrated Magazine,* which published several of her stories. She also had stories in two of Jerome K. Jerome's magazines, the *Idler* and *To-Day,* which first brought out "The Spectre of the Real" (17 November 1894).

Critical reaction to her work was generally approving, though the qualities that appealed to one reviewer could frustrate another. The *Saturday Review* (27 June 1891) found that *Sir George,* "without being superlatively good, is clever, well written, and decidedly worth reading." *Bid Me Good-Bye,* however, struck the reviewer as careless and not up to the promise of the first two books. It saw considerable fault in her story "Mrs. Livesey," published in a collection of fiction by several authors, including Violet Hunt and Arthur Wing Pinero. The story is "fairly typical of the ineptitude of the lack of any genuine observation of life on the part of the majority of the contributors in this book" (*Saturday Review,* 7 May 1898). The magazine responded more favorably to *Sowing the Sand,* which it mistitled *Sowing the Wind,* in a review that repeats a common theme in her reputation as a writer: "There is nothing original in this tale, and no attempt, so far as we can see, to achieve originality. Perhaps it is better so; because the attempt to be extravagant or nasty – the modern equivalents of original – is usually a distinct failure, whereas this story is a moderate success" (*Saturday Review,* 23 July 1898).

Literature (21 May 1898) similarly approved this novel as "a wholly agreeable companion for an idle hour," although the *Spectator* (6 August 1898) found Henniker's book too much in the mold already established, and worn out, by Ouida (Marie Louise de la Ramée). These lukewarm words were not the final ones on her novels, however. The *Bookman* (March 1912) greeted *Second Fiddle* with a glowing and presumably gratifying appraisal, along with some notes on her career: "[it] is clearly the work of one who knows and loves nature, flowers, birds and animals, but most of all . . . who loves her fellow woman and fellow men."

This all-encompassing sympathy pervades the last of her story collections, *Contrasts,* which could have been titled "Obligations." Here the stories are if anything more gracefully performed than those in *In Scarlet and Grey.* Her landscapes are interesting and evocative, especially in "The Lonely House on the Moor," an almost Hardyesque story in which a jilted woman poses as her husband's new lover to help him flee from the law. Henniker lessens her penchant for gratuitously melancholy endings, preferring instead to make the reader aware of how specific forms of unhappiness result from ignoring or breaking specific social bonds.

Her characters, many of them old soldiers, nobly resist the degradations of institutional charity. The passed-over colonel of "The Man Who Waited" receives official recognition only after his death, while in "Ex-Trooper Tempany," in one of her most pathetic endings, the old soldier of the title is finally forced into the workhouse. Even those stories that deal with romance show this concern with social and moral duties, as she examines such favorite situations as the too-long-postponed marriage and such favorite types as the "Butterfly" who refuses too many proposals. Henniker's female char-

acters repeatedly illustrate the necessity of doing one's social and moral duties and of living with one's husband's choices as well as one's own.

Henniker's literary career occupied roughly the last decade of the nineteenth century and the first of the twentieth. The year 1912 saw the deaths of Arthur Henniker-Major and Emma Hardy. Thomas Hardy soon remarried; his literary output continued remarkably until his death in 1928. After *Second Fiddle,* Henniker spoke of writing another novel, but apparently none was completed. During the years of World War I, as earlier, she took part in various humanitarian and animal-protection efforts. Hardy's letters to her suggest that she moved about a good deal, largely as a result of deteriorating health. When she died on 4 April 1923, Hardy sadly noted in his journal: "After a friendship of 30 years!"

References:

Raymond Blathwayt, "The Hon. Mrs. Arthur Henniker," *Woman at Home,* 4 (April 1895): 52–58;

Evelyn Hardy and F. B. Pinion, eds., *One Rare Fair Woman: Thomas Hardy's Letters to Florence Henniker, 1893–1922* (London: Macmillan, 1972);

Geoffrey Bret Harte, ed., *The Letters of Bret Harte* (Boston: Houghton Mifflin, 1926);

Coulson Kernahan, "A Woman Who Expected the Impossible," *Bookman* [London], 41 (March 1912): 298–300;

Cecil Y. Lang, ed., *The Swinburne Letters,* volume 1 (New Haven: Yale University Press, 1959);

Justin McCarthy, *Reminiscences* (New York: Harper, 1899);

James Pope-Hennessy, *Lord Crewe* (London: Constable, 1955);

Pope-Hennessy, *Monckton Milnes: The Flight of Youth, 1851–1885* (New York: Farrar, Straus & Cudahy, 1955);

Gordon N. Ray, ed., *The Letters and Private Papers of William Makepeace Thackeray,* volume 3 (Cambridge, Mass.: Harvard University Press, 1946);

T. Wemyss Reid, *The Life, Letters, and Friendships of Richard Monckton Milnes, First Lord Houghton* (London: Cassell, 1890).

Papers:

Henniker's letters to Thomas Hardy are in the Dorset County Museum.

L. P. Jacks

(9 October 1860 – 17 February 1955)

Hal W. French
University of South Carolina

BOOKS: *Agnosticism from a Unitarian's Point of View*
(London: British & Foreign Unitarian Association, 1908);

Mad Shepherds (London: Williams & Norgate, 1910; New York: Holt, 1910);

The Alchemy of Thought (London: Williams & Norgate, 1910; New York: Holt, 1911);

Among the Idolmakers (London: Williams & Norgate, 1911; New York: Holt, 1912);

All Men Are Ghosts (London: Williams & Norgate, 1913; New York: Holt, 1913);

The International Crisis in Its Ethical and Psychological Aspects (London & New York: Milford, 1915);

From the Human End (London: Williams & Norgate, 1916; New York: Holt, 1916);

Philosophers in Trouble (London: Williams & Norgate, 1916);

The Life and Letters of Stopford Brooke, 2 volumes (London: Murray, 1917; New York: Scribners, 1917);

The Country Air (London: Williams & Norgate, 1917; New York: Holt, 1917);

From Authority to Freedom: The Spiritual Pilgrimage of Charles Hargrove (London: Williams & Norgate, 1920);

The Legends of Smokeover (London: Hodder & Stoughton, 1921; New York: Doran, 1921);

The Lost Radiance of the Christian Religion (London: Lindsey, 1921; New York: Doran, 1924);

Religious Perplexities (London: Hodder & Stoughton, 1922; New York: Doran, 1923);

Realities and Shams (London: Williams & Norgate, 1923; New York: Doran, 1923);

The Challenge of Life (London: Hodder & Stoughton, 1924; New York: Doran, 1925);

Responsibility and Culture (New Haven: Yale University Press, 1924);

The Faith of a Worker (London: Hodder & Stoughton, 1925; New York: Doran, 1925);

The Heroes of Smokeover (London: Hodder & Stoughton, 1926; New York: Doran, 1926);

L. P. Jacks, 1886

Constructive Citizenship (London: Hodder & Stoughton, 1927; New York: Doubleday, Doran, 1928);

The Magic Formula and Other Stories (London & New York: Harper, 1927);

The Art of Living Together (London: Hodder & Stoughton, 1928);

My Neighbour the Universe: A Study of Human Labour (London: Cassell, 1928; New York: Putnam, 1929);

The Inner Sentinel: A Study of Ourselves (New York & London: Harper, 1930);

The Education of the Whole Man (New York & London: Harper, 1931);

Education through Recreation (New York & London: Harper, 1932);

My American Friends (London: Constable, 1933; New York: Macmillan, 1933);

The Revolt Against Mechanism (London: Allen & Unwin, 1934; New York: Macmillan, 1934);

Elemental Religion (New York & London: Harper, 1934);

Ethical Factors of the Present Crisis (Baltimore: Williams & Wilkins, 1934);

Cooperation or Coercion? The League at the Crossways (London: Heinemann, 1938; New York: Dutton, 1938);

The Stolen Sword: The Tale of an Unbroken Covenant (London: Methuen, 1938);

The Last Legend of Smokeover (London: Hodder & Stoughton, 1939);

Construction Now (London: Dakers, 1940);

The Confession of an Octogenarian (London: Allen & Unwin, 1942; New York: Macmillan, 1942);

Peace by Compulsion? (London: National Peace Council, 1944);

Sir Arthur Eddington: Man of Science and Mystic (Cambridge: Cambridge University Press, 1949);

Near the Brink: Observations of a Nonagenarian (London: Allen & Unwin, 1952).

OTHER: *Hibbert Journal,* edited by Jacks (1902–1947).

TRANSLATION: Alfred T. Loisy, *The Birth of the Christian Religion* (London: Allen & Unwin, 1948).

SELECTED PERIODICAL PUBLICATIONS – UNCOLLECTED: "Oxford in Wartime," *New Republic,* 3 (26 June 1915): 194–196;

"Dramatic Dreams: An Unexplored Field for Psychic Research," *Journal of the Society for Psychical Research,* 19 (1915);

"War and the Wealth of Nations," *Atlantic,* 116 (September 1915): 419–426;

"Presidential Address: The Theory of Survival in the Light of Its Contents," *Proceedings of the Society for Psychical Research,* 29 (December 1917): 287–305;

"Good Temper in the Present Crisis," *Yale Review,* 7 (April 1918): 512–526;

"President Wilson's War Mind," *Living Age* (13 July 1918): 99–104;

"Is the War Ending in Disappointment?," *Living Age,* 303 (13 December 1919): 651–659;

"William James and His Letters," *Atlantic,* 128 (August 1921): 197–203.

Lawrence Pearsall Jacks was already a professor at Manchester College in Oxford and editor for several years of the prestigious *Hibbert Journal* when he began, at nearly age fifty, his career as a writer. From that date he wrote more than thirty books, about one-third of which are collections of short stories. His nonfiction works are predominantly on religious, social, and political themes, for he engaged many wide-ranging issues of his time. The bulk of his short fiction was composed during a four-year period before World War I and another brief period following the war. His stories mirror his general interest in the "common man," and he blends his vivid portrayals of these persons with broadly religious issues, both natural and supernatural, along with social commentary and a critique of academic pretensions. Almost all of his books were published on both sides of the Atlantic, and while, by his own acknowledgment, none was a best-seller, they earned him a respectable hearing, along with stature as a speaker and educator. His short-story collections, some of which have been republished as much as sixty years later, remain entertaining for their humor and lively character sketches.

Jacks was born in Nottingham on 9 October 1860 to Jabez and Anne Jacks, in modest circumstances. Jabez Jacks was a shopkeeper and hardware dealer, and his bankruptcy a few years before his early death left his family destitute. Lawrence Jacks recalled, however, that his father's occupation was belied by his distinguished appearance, resembling that of William Gladstone, whose liberal policies he often defended forcefully, and by his warm and cheerful manner, with a particular gift for composing and singing ballads while walking with his children. Anne Jacks, of a sterner and more practical bent, managed for her four children, of whom Lawrence, the third, was fourteen at the time of his father's death.

Given limited education until the age of nine or ten, he quickly excelled, receiving scholarship assistance to complete his secondary education at University School in Nottingham. Rather than applying for a Cambridge scholarship, however, he resolved to contribute to his family's earnings by taking a job as a schoolteacher. After several years in this occupation he began his higher education at "The Mother of Orphans," London University, which had begun to open its gates to "external students." Another reason for his educational postponement was that he did not wish to disappoint his evangelical teacher and benefactor, the Reverend George Herbert; Jacks could not reconcile orthodox teachings with Unitarian thought, which had begun to appeal to him.

To pursue a theological course at Cambridge would have seemed lacking in integrity, so Jacks chose a more independent track. In *The Confession of an Octogenarian* (1942) he identifies with Charles Hargrove, the subject of one of his two biographies, in that neither "had been born and bred in the fold." After an interlude in Göttingen, Germany, Jacks returned to London, where, in his still largely self-taught manner, he was awakened by Matthew Arnold's *Literature and Dogma* (1873), which had been loaned to him by his Unitarian friend Sam Collinson. After hearing James Martineau, Jacks determined to study theology at Manchester New College in London, of predominantly Unitarian influence and of which Martineau was principal.

Shortly before his graduation in 1886 the Hibbert trustees offered Jacks a scholarship to attend Harvard University. While at Harvard his reputation as a speaker grew so that in 1887 he was able to secure an invitation to become assistant to Stopford Brooke, distinguished minister of Bedford Chapel in London. Five months later he was engaged to one of Brooke's daughters, Olive Cecelia, and they went on to wed and have six children. Jacks also pastored Unitarian churches in Liverpool and Birmingham. In 1902 he proposed to the Hibbert trustees the creation of a journal, and they assented, naming Jacks as the first editor, a position he retained until he was eighty-seven. The following year he was appointed to Manchester College, which had relocated to Oxford. As lecturer in philosophy he was principal of that college from 1915 until his retirement in 1931.

Throughout this time Jacks made several visits to the United States and Canada, and more invitations followed after his retirement. He did several series of Hibbert lectures in England and others at Yale, Harvard, and Brown Universities; he received honorary degrees from Oxford, Harvard, and McGill Universities and the Universities of Glasgow and Liverpool. His identification with the Unitarian tradition seemed generally not to be a source of controversy for him. Perhaps his questioning of the institutional forms of that dissenting body rendered him more universalistic in his appeal and not restricted to any one religious community.

His first collection of short stories was *Mad Shepherds* (1910). While in Birmingham he had lived on a farm at Bredon Hill, and he kept that residence for some years after moving to Oxford. He felt a strong affinity for the rural characters there and was involved in the same activities as they were: tree planting, pig feeding, and dung spreading. He had a compulsion to write about them, more for his own pleasure than with publication in mind. The publisher Williams and Norgate was soon interested, however, and despite discouraging reviews the public liked the stories and clamored for more. When an early reviewer called the book a feeble imitation of Sir James Barrie's writing, Barrie found this intensely amusing and gave Jacks the supportive word that he needed.

A central character in *Mad Shepherds* is Snarley Bob, a name reflecting the selective civility that Jacks showed most persons whom he met. Snarley Bob, however, has redeeming qualities: he is a master sheep breeder, braves bad weather and declining health without complaining, and holds an affinity for the stars. He loves the song of the nightingale and is charmed one evening when a woman he admires recites John Keats's *Ode to a Nightingale* (1820). He astonishes those present when he, a rustic, continues the poem at a break. And even with his own failing energies, he seeks out and ministers to a dying shepherd friend.

The same feel for rural life is the subject of another collection, *The Country Air* (1917), about which a reviewer in the *Nation* (18 May 1918) said, "These very simple and unpretentious little studies of English rustic life and character are full of quiet humour and insight – faithful to their tiny scene and thereby faithful to the greater world of human nature." In these early writings and another, *From the Human End* (1916), Jacks stakes out his identity with the common man, identifying the values and pursuits of such persons as broadly religious in character.

In the same year that his first volume of stories appeared, Jacks also authored a volume of essays, *The Alchemy of Thought* (1910). The primary thrust of these is to affirm the universe as a "rational whole," but to demonstrate that systems of thought designed to explain this rationality inevitably fail. Other measures than rational ones, then, must be employed to account for all that is witnessed. Arnold's statement "A power not ourselves that makes for righteousness" was powerfully evocative for Jacks, but dogmatic attempts to define that power always result in partial vision. Included among these essays is an allegorical tale, "Devil's Island and the Islands of Omniscience," which indicates that contrasting islands of thought can never convince the mainland of opinion as to their general truth. These systems must blend, alchemically, with other strange ones, for each is incomplete. Jacks's title is indicative, perhaps, of another strain of investigation that had begun to interest him – parapsychology – as another way of pursuing philosophical questions. He had joined the Society for Psychical Research a few years earlier, serving as vice-president of the organization from 1909 until his death and as annual president from 1917 to 1918.

Jacks's second volume of stories, *Among the Idolmakers* (1911), engaged more specifically philosophic issues than the first. His London *Times* obituary (18 February 1955), commenting on the merciless logic, wit, and wisdom with which Jacks disposed of conventional arguments for determinism in "the Self-Deceivers," stated that he could have turned some other philosophical problems "into rollicking nonsense," had he chosen. In a review of *Among the Idolmakers,* the *Athenaeum* (6 January 1912) remarked that "though (by choice) too unconvincing wholly to subjugate healthy incredulity, he amuses, excites and moves his reader at will." The *New York Times* (10 March 1912) stated that his stories "reveal such a unique personal force, such vigor of thought, such a strong, assured hand . . . that both their literary quality and their interest are quickly felt to be exceptional. It is a welcome change to find theories rather than events endowed with dramatic form."

His next collection of stories, *All Men Are Ghosts* (1913), elaborates on his interest in paranormal matters. In the title story a memorable character, Panhandle, entertains the author at his country home, known to be haunted. Panhandle is comfortable with its ghostly inhabitants, and he acquaints his inquiring guest with them. Some, such as Micawber (from Charles Dickens's *David Copperfield,* 1849–1850), are supposed by the writer to be creations of their authors, and thus unreal. But the ghosts are astonished at this supposition, viewing "their authors," similarly, as unreal and seeing themselves, as does Micawber, not as Dickens's creation but as "a fortuitous concourse of ideas." Finally Panhandle identifies himself as a ghost, host to the others, and raiser of the question to the reader, "Who is the haunter and who the haunted?," or, as the reader might ask, "Who is the guest and who is the ghost?"

Reviews of these stories, such as the one in *Current Opinion* (March 1914), recognized Jacks as "already known as a philosophic artist of the supernatural" and "an explorer of the psychic borderland." Jacks, in the estimation of the *Boston Transcript,* "gives us a new idea of the human soul." The reviewer called the collection "an entirely original adventure into fiction," regarding genre as one of philosophical comedy, with a delightful joyousness and whimsicality. The *New York Times* (8 February 1914) observed, "If you are curious about what lies beyond the realm of the five senses, beyond the paths of logic, almost beyond even the jungles of the imagination, and do not object to venturing as far as human comprehension can go among the shadows of the jungle, you will find in his collection of short stories entertainment and stimulus and mental refreshment."

While bringing out his short-story collections, Jacks continued his editorship of the *Hibbert Journal,* which was established and thriving. W. T. Stead, who shared Jacks's interest in the supernatural, gave the journal an enthusiastic tribute in the British *Review of Reviews* (1912), crediting him with being wise and impersonal in his powers of selection and rejection. In Stead's judgment, "the most notable achievement in the domain of serious periodical literature that has occurred in the last twenty years, has been the creation of *The Hibbert Journal.*" The American *Review of Reviews* (April 1912) concurred: "In his [Jacks's] hands *The Hibbert Journal* became the arena in which all the doughty gladiators of modern thought were free to do battle in their own way for their own ideas." The journal was designed as a forum for religion, theology, and philosophy, but, by Jacks's estimation, considerably more space was given to the first of these. Clearly, a wide latitude of opinion was encouraged, with the only criteria for authorship being, "Does the man have a thought, and can he express it?" The Hibbert trustees, though somewhat skeptical of his initial proposal for the journal, thinking that it would gain a subscription of no more than three hundred, must have been astounded as it far exceeded that number almost immediately, garnering about ten thousand subscribers by the end of its first decade.

Oxford forms the background of Jacks's next volume of stories, *Philosophers in Trouble* (1916), and his title indicates the author's ambivalence toward the place of his primary professional endeavors. At one level he agreed with William James, whom he knew quite well, that there is too much "fencing and scoring of points" at Oxford. While he was to state that he loved Oxford as no place on earth, leading much of his professional life there and seeing three of his five sons through Oxford University, there is a strong sense that Jacks felt marginalized there. Manchester College, which came late to the scene, was scarcely venerable and largely maintained by Unitarians, who were not in the theological mainstream, so Jacks's academic pedigree was out of the fold.

Perhaps the most satiric story in *Philosophers in Trouble* is the final one, "A Tragedy of Parliament," in which some stodgy philosophers, in one of their club's regular sessions, decide to engage the question "Suppose Count Zeppelin were discovered in a drowning condition by a member of this Club, ought the said member to leave Count Zeppelin to drown?" Discussion of the question is delayed until all possible qualifiers are addressed: "What time of day was it?," "How deep was the water?," and "Did he really want to be rescued, and by a member of this Club?" A comparable incident from India is cited, in which a life buoy had been thrown to a drowning man, but the grease with which it had been smeared to protect it from the water attracted a crocodile, which ate both life buoy and drowning man. The vote goes against Count Zeppelin, then the circumstance is immediately duplicated in actuality, and club members have to confront what they will do for the drowning man. Faithful to their identity as philosophers, they debate the case until the count drowns. They feel gratified because any action taken before all possible ramifications were resolved would have been precipitate.

Another story, "A Psychologist Among the Saints," describes an eminent psychologist of religion (probably modeled on James) who, although he has masterfully developed the recognized "Three Laws of Conversion," was never able to experience his own. *Philosophers in Trouble* prompted the *New York Times* (8 October 1916) to remark, "Not since 'Philosophy Four' by Owen Wister have we had such a keen and amusing satire on the impracticality of moral science." For Jacks this was compounded with an anti-institutional, or at least trans-institutional, disposition, in which even the trappings of a freethinking movement such as Unitarianism seemed restrictive. Despite being principal of Manchester College for sixteen years, his vision of a ministry to the common man — beyond the confines and expectations of church, chapel, and college — was destined to be somewhat frustrated. In *The Confession of an Octogenarian* he titled a chapter that describes his Oxford years "I Overstep the Mark," recognizing that his goal, which also envisioned more of an East-West sharing, was unable to be implemented at Manchester College.

With Britain's immersion in World War I, Jacks was diverted to more-pressing concerns, such as analyzing moral and ethical issues that had become imperatives. One of Jacks's articles describes Oxford at war; another attempts a psychological study of President Woodrow Wilson's changing perspectives on the war. After writing "President Wilson's War Mind" (*Living Age*, 13 July 1918) Jacks had qualms about it, wondering whether it

Jacks with Rabindranath Tagore at Manchester College, Oxford, 1929

was unduly speculative and wide of the mark. He was immensely relieved when a 1918 letter from Wilson expressed great appreciation for the piece: "It was not only a very true interpretation of my thought, showing what . . . seems to me a very extraordinary insight and power of sympathetic interpretation, but it also seemed as I read it to reveal to me things which had not taken precise form in my mind. . . . The analysis was both true and novel and I am indebted to you for enabling me to understand myself."

The war years also occasioned Jacks's first venture into biography, his two-volume study of his late father-in-law, Stopford Brooke, to whom he had been strongly devoted. Despite good reviews for *The Life and Letters of Stopford Brooke* (1917) Jacks felt that he was too close to his subject, and he rated *From Authority to Freedom* (1920), on Charles Hargrove, as better — in fact the best book that he had written, despite its small circulation. He had found a kindred spirit in Hargrove, who had moved from being a Dominican priest to being a Unitarian minister, although one always a little at odds with his Unitarian environment.

Following the war Jacks returned to storytelling, partly basking in the optimistic mood of the time and partly satirizing some of the idealistic schemes taken by reconstructionists, such as the League of Nations. *The Legends of Smokeover* (1921), his largest collection of stories, led to *The Heroes of Smokeover* (1926) and *The Last Legend of Smokeover* (1939). Smokeover seems to have been modeled after Birmingham and other industrial cities that, in the name of progress, polluted the air and the moral environment. Here Jacks's focus is not on the common man but on the "leaders" of society. The expected leaders do not offer the most hope for reconstruction but instead an unlikely source, a betting establishment whose founder, Mr. Rumbelow, sees all of life ultimately governed by "the sportsmanlike principle." His establishment, in calculating odds of success of various enterprises and proposals, eventually displaces such institutions as the Ethical Society and even the universities.

Publishers were wary this time, however, of what was rather a hybrid enterprise, until Hodder and Stoughton picked it up. Jacks was also concerned, yet the book received a long, laudatory appraisal in the London *Times* by the eminent critic Sir Edmund Gosse. J. F. Muirhead, in the *Independent* (30 September 1923), said, "His imagination is suffused by a delightful and subtle satirical humour such as we rarely find in person or professor." C. E. Ayers, in the *New Republic* (24 January 1923), wrote, "Through all the dreamlike unreality of episode the book is a feast of reason. . . . The book is suffused with an ethereal beauty of phrase that is the natural medium of a high and fine idealism."

However, apart from the *Smokeover* trilogy, one other short-story collection, *The Magic Formula* (1927), and a novel, *The Stolen Sword* (1938), the balance of Jacks's career was occupied by his speaking activities, *Hibbert Journal* editorship, and essays on social and political themes. As had happened during World War I, his storytelling well began to dry up, in his words, "as the international horizon grew darker under the sinister apparition of Hitler." Age eighty, however, gave him occasion for retrospective musing about the long course of his life, and he did it well. *The Confession of an Octogenarian* is disarmingly modest, acknowledging doubts, failures, and limitations. It is not a brief treatise, but reviewers were left wanting more. R. E. Roberts, in the *Saturday Review* (26 September 1942), stated, "Here is a book which I would have liked more had it been ten times its length; but the reader must be grateful

for the rare quality of wine Dr. Jacks has decanted." Similarly, Ernest Baker, in the *Spectator* (26 June 1942), observed, "Its effect on a reader who has read every line can only be expressed in the words of Oliver Twist, 'Please, Sir, I want some more.'"

Readers were gratified with Jacks's continuing observations as a nonagenarian in *Near the Brink* (1952). One new subject not covered in detail in his previous autobiography is his strong belief in postmortem survival. He had long considered the subject and had sought to pursue it from all possible vantage points. It was the subject of his presidential address to the Society for Psychical Research in 1917. At this stage he engaged it with a new urgency, for he had experienced a passionate grief at his wife's death in 1945. In the opening passages of *Near the Brink,* Jacks makes the strong assertion that the life beyond must be a continuation of the mortal life, with earthly conditions still prevailing: "The departed must needs retain also the physical conditions by which speech is made audible and the command over the properties of the air which render articulation possible." The argument for survival does not sound Unitarian (though Jacks was never confined by that identity), but his need to have his conviction conform to rational laws certainly does.

Jacks continued to accept speaking invitations into his tenth decade, during which, with his still clear and alert mind, he often entertained family and friends on long walks in his orchard, with reminiscences and relevant comments on current issues. Just four months before his death the *Hibbert Journal* published his article "The Price of Our War-Making Civilization," critiquing a *Wall Street Journal* report that peace in Korea had a depressing effect on the international market. His prophetic and analytic skills were still intact.

Jacks's obituary in the London *Times* observed, "In his stories he was not a satirist, scourging the follies of his age; he was not a wit, making fun of them; he was not the philosopher, confuting them. His method was, on the whole, a kindly irony. Queer characters, queer thoughts, appealed to his sympathies without convincing his intellect. He disliked above all the conventional." A man of enormous energy and patience, Jacks possessed an appeal that crossed generations and spanned continents. It is significant that Jacks seemed more proud of being a farmer than a professor or writer, and this skepticism perhaps gave his writing more power. He remained close to his subjects, the commoners whom he knew intimately.

A telling incident is related in *The Confession of an Octogenarian,* in which he was being interviewed by Harold Begbie for a book of character sketches, *Painted Windows* (1922). Naturally self-effacing and uncomfortable with the interview process, Jacks suggested that they go out and look at some fine pigs that he was fattening for market. He took it as high tribute, then, when Begbie said of him, "This man moves like a peasant." Noting Jacks's strange resemblance to his great teacher, Martineau, Begbie states that while Jacks's face lacked Martineau's sweetness, it had a greater strength: "It does not bear witness to so sure a triumph of serenity, but shows the marks of a fiercer battle, and the scars of deeper wounds." It was an outdoor face to Martineau's indoor one. Begbie remarks that Jacks lived farther from Oxford than did any of its other academic citizens, thus retaining his identity with rural life.

Jacks enjoyed storytelling as a means of communicating with the common man. He likened his methodology with that of Jesus' telling of parables. Jacks's stories relate his insights on the human condition in a more accessible manner than formal, didactic exposition. While his initial essay in *The Alchemy of Thought* was titled "The Bitter Cry of the Plain Man," being an appeal for simplicity from the philosophers in their attempts to explicate their thoughts, he seems to have answered his own appeal best in stories, or parables. And although he was hesitant to employ the comparison with the methodology of Jesus, the response seemed to be similar: "The common people heard him gladly."

Jacks's portraits of peasants are self-portraits. Snarley Bob, rather than being a composite of shepherds, was recognized by Jacks as basically himself. His close friend J. M. Lloyd Thomas, the author of his obituary in the *Hibbert Journal,* confirmed the impression, stating that L. Leslie Brooke's drawing of Snarley Bob, which is the frontispiece to *Mad Shepherds,* bears a striking likeness to Jacks. Thomas relates how he visited Jacks at Oxford to tell him of an experience in which he broke down at the end of a sermon after quoting a passage from "The Death of Snarley Bob." Bob's final words, which his wife records while bending down to hear him, are: "He's a-blowin' again. It's the tall shepherd — 'im as wrote on the ground — and he's got no dog, and 'is sheep's scatterin'. It's me he wants. Fetch the old whistle, Polly, and blow back. I want 'im to know I'm comin'." Jacks, silent for some time but visibly moved, finally responded, "I wrote that in blood." Perhaps it is that intensity, alternating with keen insight and warm humor, which won him an early and persistent hearing.

References:

Harold Begbie, "Dr. L. P. Jacks," in his *Painted Windows: A Study in Religious Personality* (London: Mills & Boon, 1922; New York: Kennikat, 1970), pp. 70–85;

Obituary, London *Times,* 18 February 1955, p. 10;

J. M. Lloyd Thomas, "Lawrence Pearsall Jacks: Some Personal Memories," *Hibbert Journal,* 53 (March 1955): 212–221.

W. W. Jacobs

(8 September 1863 – 1 September 1943)

Glenn S. Burne
University of North Carolina at Charlotte

BOOKS: *Many Cargoes* (London: Lawrence & Bullen, 1896);

The Skipper's Wooing. The Brown Man's Servant (London: Nelson, 1897);

Sea Urchins (London: Lawrence & Bullen, 1898); published as *More Cargoes* (New York: McKinley, Stone & Mackenzie, 1898);

A Master of Craft (London: Methuen, 1900);

Light Freights (New York: Dodd, Mead, 1901);

At Sunwich Port (London: Newnes, 1902);

The Lady of the Barge (London & New York: Nelson, 1902);

Odd Craft (London: Newnes, 1903; New York: Scribners, 1903);

Dialstone Lane (London: Newnes, 1904);

Captains All (London: Hodder & Stoughton, 1905);

Short Cruises (New York: Scribners, 1907);

Salthaven (London: Methuen, 1908; New York: Scribners, 1908);

Sailor's Knots (Leipzig: Tauchnitz, 1909);

Ship's Company (London & New York: Hodder & Stoughton, 1911);

Night Watches (London: Hodder & Stoughton, 1914; New York: Scribners, 1914);

The Castaways (London & New York: Hodder & Stoughton, 1916);

Deep Waters (London & New York: Hodder & Stoughton, 1919);

Sea Whispers (London: Hodder & Stoughton, 1926);

Snug Harbour (New York: Scribners, 1931);

The Night Watchman and Other Longshoremen (London: Hodder & Stoughton, 1932).

Collection: *Selected Short Stories of W. W. Jacobs,* edited, with an introduction, by Hugh Greene (London: Bodley Head, 1975).

W. W. Jacobs, remembered today almost exclusively for his horror story "The Monkey's Paw" (*The Lady of the Barge,* 1902), was one of the most popular English humorists of the early twentieth century. His stories, many of them amusing tales of life along the London docks, were much in demand

W. W. Jacobs

by magazine publishers, as his name on the cover assured wide sales. The quality of his work was attested to by many writers and critics of his day, such as J. B. Priestley, Evelyn Waugh, G. K. Chesterton, V. S. Pritchett, Arnold Bennett, Henry Reed, and fellow humorists Jerome K. Jerome and P. G. Wodehouse, who admitted being a "disciple" of Jacobs. During his early and most productive years he wrote more stories than he acknowledged, many appearing anonymously or signed only with his initials; but then he produced, under his own name, about 158 stories, two novellas, and five full-length novels. He turned seventeen of his stories into plays (often in collaboration); one story, "The Skipper of the *Osprey*" (*Many Cargoes,* 1896), was made into a 1933 movie; and another, "The Boatswain's Mate" (*Captains All,* 1905), provided the libretto for a 1916 opera by Ethyl Smyth. Most of his stories were collected periodically and published in book form, twelve volumes in all, beginning with *Many Cargoes.*

William Wymark Jacobs was born in London on 8 September 1863, the son of a Thames wharf manager. He grew up in the dockland area of Wapping, London, and was educated in private schools. At the age of sixteen he entered the civil service as a clerk at the Post Office Savings Bank, a job he hated, referring to it as his "days of captivity." Around the age of twenty he began writing humorous stories for his own amusement, and by 1885 he was publishing in little magazines. He recalled that "it was not until I had been writing for some years for amusement and a little extra pocket money that I began to write of the waterside. . . . Then the coastwise trips that I had taken in my youth came back to me with all the illusion of the past."

Those "coastwise trips" and frequent wanderings along the Kent coast with the illustrator of his books, his friend Will Owen, provided the settings and characters, if not the plots, of his waterfront stories. "But that," Jacobs remembered, "did not happen until some years after I had left the house on the wharf at Wapping. I suppose distance lent enchantment to a view that certainly needed it." Soon Jacobs's writing came to the attention of Jerome K. Jerome – a prominent humorist and editor of two magazines, the *Idler* and *To-Day* – who published some of Jacobs's early stories. But it was the publication of his first collection of stories, *Many Cargoes,* followed by a second printing in 1897, that established Jacobs as a popular humorist in the eyes of a growing audience. From the publication of this first book of stories, Jacobs's work was treated favorably by the critics and his fellow writers. An anonymous reviewer in the *Chap-Book* (1 October 1897) set the tone: "The stories [in *Many Cargoes*] are redolent of side-lights and marlin; they bring strong whiffs of salty air. . . . In the crowded estuary of sea-tales . . . Mr. Jacobs has really taken us aboard a new craft."

Jacobs was now ready to join the illustrious rank of major writers whose works appeared regularly in the *Strand* magazine – Agatha Christie, Somerset Maugham, Graham Greene, Edgar Wallace, H. G. Wells, and Sir Arthur Conan Doyle, most of whose Sherlock Holmes adventures were first published in that magazine. The *Strand* has been called "a veritable British institution" between 1891 and 1950. At the height of its popularity, and especially when Jacobs and Doyle were featured, it reached up to five hundred thousand readers a month. After his first publication in the *Strand,* Jacobs decided to stay with it, and nearly all his subsequent writings first appeared in that magazine. He was paid well for his work, and success seemed assured; nevertheless, being of a cautious nature, Jacobs waited until the publication of his third collection of stories, *Sea Urchins* (1898), before he quit his civil-service job to devote himself to writing. He married in 1900, and not very happily, apparently: his wife, Agnes Eleanor Williams Jacobs, was a socialist and militant suffragette, whereas Jacobs was very much the conservative. It was reported that they quarreled constantly. They had two sons and two daughters.

Jacobs wrote prolifically at the beginning of his career, but his output began to diminish around 1916. During the last years of his life he wrote no new stories, preferring to spend his time converting earlier ones into short plays. At first he worked with collaborators, but as his talents in this area improved he began to make his adaptations unassisted and with considerable success. During this period his popularity remained high, and many of his earlier works were reprinted. After his death in 1943, however, Jacobs lapsed into relative obscurity, although since 1969 some of his works have been republished, and some major scholars have been reassessing his place in modern literature.

Annie Russell Marble, in *A Study of the Modern Novel: British and American Since 1900* (1928), makes an odd statement regarding Jacobs's work: "It is difficult to decide whether he should be listed among the romancers of the sea or the novelists of whimsicality and humor." Actually, Jacobs wrote almost nothing about life at sea, romance or otherwise. He depicts many ship's officers and sailors – all while the ships are in port – along with retired captains in their seaside cottages; beached sailors in dreary boardinghouses; dockworkers and barmaids; greedy landlords; conniving businessmen and their ambitious junior partners; flirtatious widows; earnest suitors pursuing pretty, pert, and often clever young women; and hard-drinking laborers and their nagging wives.

Many of the stories are narrated by the Nightwatchman, a retired sailor familiar with life

" 'Wot's this for?' ses Ginger."

Illustration by Will Owen for "The Money-Box" (from Odd Craft, *1903)*

along the docks, but only about half of Jacobs's stories deal with the misadventures of seamen on land. Many take place in the inland village of Claybury and are narrated by an old-timer who frequents the Cauliflower Inn and who, in exchange for drink and tobacco, tells amusing tales about likable scoundrels around town, especially one Bob Pretty. Priestley has called this character the "most ingenious of village rascals. . . . I am not sure that these Bob Pretty stories are not among the very best things that Mr. Jacobs has done." Other recurring characters include the sailors Ginger Dick, Peter Russet, and old Sam Small. These "friends" are usually involved in a clever project of deceit, sometimes conspiring against each other. It might be a practical joke, an effort to further someone in an amorous intrigue, or a complicated scheme to acquire money, often by less-than-honest means. The crafty plans always go awry, situations become ludicrous, and machinations backfire, usually in a surprising and unexpected way.

Most critics believed that Jacobs's characters were entirely his creations, but, according to Hugh Greene, the Nightwatchman was based on a longshoreman named Bob Osborne, himself a great storyteller; and Sam Small, Ginger Dick, and Peter Russet were based on three of Osborne's friends. Greene states that "from the same figures Will

Owen took the inspiration for his drawings in which he has left as clear an image of the Nightwatchman and his friends as Sidney Paget did of Sherlock Holmes and Watson."

Jacobs's fame and popularity derived from a type of humorous story and a recurring group of characters rather than from any single outstanding work. Critics have noted the limited range of Jacobs's plots, but they agree that he showed remarkable ingenuity in bringing freshness and variety to those plots. His readers came to anticipate the latest escapades of Ginger, Peter, Sam, and Bob Pretty, so much so that Jacobs's few ventures into other genres, such as the macabre, were not widely welcomed.

The strengths of Jacobs's stories, in addition to cleverness of plot and character, are his much-admired "felicity of style" and colorful dialogue. He was a careful craftsman, writing with precision, economy, and clarity, often relying on subtlety and suggestion rather than overt description to fill out a scene. He spent few words on setting or background, yet the reader infers an accurate picture of what is needed to enhance the action. Greene states that Jacobs wrote slowly, about a hundred words a day. With much rewriting and polishing one short story would take him about a month. Greene cites Waugh as describing Jacobs as "a writer who in his middle years developed an exquisite precision of narrative." Behind the drab facade "there lurked a pure artist."

Jacobs's technique is to tell the story, or to have it told, from a limited point of view, usually in the cockney dialect natural to the narrator. As one of his favorite narrators, the Nightwatchman, says, "Ginger Dick and Peter Russet – two men I've spoke of to you afore – tried to save their money once. They'd got so sick and tired of spending it all p'r'aps a week or ten days arter coming ashore, and 'aving to go to sea agin sooner than they'ad intended, that they determined some way or other to 'ave things different." This quote comes from "The Money-Box," which is a good example of Jacobs's art; it is both comic and typical of Jacobs's stories, which may be why it was chosen to lead off *Odd Craft* (1903).

In this story Ginger Dick and Peter Russet decide to protect themselves from spending all their money by leaving it in the hands of an old salt named Isaac, who will dole it out to them in small amounts. Surprisingly, the old man sticks to the agreement, and when, inevitably, the two thirsty sailors demand their money back in a lump sum, he refuses. Indignant, they threaten violence, but then they decide to pawn their spare clothes and to steal and pawn some of Isaac's clothes as well, thereby gaining revenge as well as additional cash.

After they have pawned the clothes and spent the money, the old man tells them that, for safekeeping, he had sewn their money into the lining of one of the coats they have pawned. In order to get their money back they agree to give him the rest of their clothes to be pawned in exchange for the coat containing the money. At the end of the story the two are left with neither clothes nor money, trapped naked in their own bedroom: "Old Isaac kept 'em there for three days, sending 'em in their clothes bit by bit and two shillings a day to live on; but they didn't set eyes on 'im agin until they all signed on aboard the *Planet,* and they didn't set eyes on their money until they was two miles below Gravesend."

When Jacobs is telling a story, before a cockney narrator takes over, he uses quite a different style, as in the introductory sentences of "The Persecution of Bob Pretty" (*Odd Craft*):

> The old man sat on his accustomed bench outside the Cauliflower. A generous measure of beer stood in a blue and white jug by his elbow, and little wisps of smoke curled slowly upward from the bowl of his churchwarden pipe. The knapsacks of two young men lay where they were flung on the table, and the owners, taking a noon-tide rest, turned a polite, if bored, ear to the reminiscences of grateful old age.
>
> Poaching, said the old man, who had tried topics ranging from early turnips to horseshoeing – poaching ain't wot it used to be in these 'ere parts.

And so, by a smooth transition, the old fellow takes over the story.

While there was, and is, general agreement among Jacobs's readers regarding his talents as a humorist, there are aspects of his work that have provoked controversy: the depiction of women in his stories; a perceived lack of substance, of ideas or significant social commentary; and the extent to which he belongs in the realist tradition. Most reviewers have found Jacobs's portrayal of women and relations between the sexes to be consistently tasteful, entertaining, and, above all, wholesome. Marble, whom one might expect to be sensitive to portrayals of female characters, emphasizes Jacobs's "wholesome humor" and "chivalrous sentiment." Yet Jacobs's female characters, young and old, have provoked the most acrimonious comments from certain male critics. This view is developed in Greene's introduction to *Selected Short Stories of W. W. Jacobs* (1975) and in Benny Green's article "Wapping Lies" in the *Spectator* (19 July 1975). Both

critics see Jacobs's male characters as essentially dishonest, greedy, conniving, and bumbling manipulators who get caught, humorously, in their own traps. All this, according to Green, is just "cheerfully callous amorality": boys will be boys. When Jacobs describes the women who are involved in the men's machinations, he chooses a different perspective, according to Green: "All the women are sadistic termagants whose intractable viciousness provokes decent men with the diversion of the only really important blood sport, which is avoiding getting married."

This judgment falters at both ends of the sentence: the reference to "all the women" reflects considerable blindness to the variety of females in the stories. Some are indeed heartless vixens, while others are attractive, saucy young ladies who reveal the men to be the fools that they often are. The sweeping "avoiding getting married" ignores the many would-be suitors engaged in inept efforts to marry women who are too smart to get involved, as in *The Skipper's Wooing* (1897).

Greene unleashes this diatribe: "Few writers in the whole of English have taken such a consistently low view of women. His older women are nagging shrews not above a bit of physical violence when their husbands misbehave themselves. His younger women are artful liars who, once they have, like carnivorous plants, got their prey in their clutches proceed to grow like their mothers." He then adds what he no doubt considers the clincher (referring to "The Interruption"): "One of his last stories . . . deals with wife murder."

While this monstrousness of some of Jacobs's female characters has not gone unnoticed by other critics, most have a much less one-sided view of the genders. Priestley, in *Figures in Modern Literature* (1924), finds many of the young ladies to be attractive enough: "pretty saucy girls with a string of admirers"; and Arthur St. John Adcock and Pritchett offer two balanced views. Adcock observes in *The Glory That Was Grub Street* (1928) that "many of the stories dispense with the love interest altogether; when they do not, the heroine is often as not a mature widow set upon marrying again, or a young girl who is hoydenish, very pretty, very self-possessed and smart at repartee . . . but his elder women and old and young men are amazingly varied in character."

Pritchett helps to put matters into perspective when he points out that Jacobs's characters, both male and female, are types, sometimes stereotypes, with deep roots in English comic tradition. Indeed, as he remarks in *Books in General* (1953), they are "traditional subjects of the English music hall":

> The mother-in-law, the knowing widow, the fulminating wife and the hen-pecked husband, the man who can't pass a pub. Fighting, black eyes, man-handling, horseplay, stealing of people's clothes, assuming disguises, changing names, spreading lying rumors, the persecution of one man by his mates for a lark, are the common coin. A man in love is fair game. Bad language is never given verbatim, but it is never let pass. (The old jokes about swearing are given a new polish. Mr. Henry Reed quotes this jewel: "The langwidge e see fit to use was a'most as much as I could answer." Only Mark Twain's Mississippi boatmen could equal that.) The laziness of the working-man is another stock joke which, in spite of political pressure, has not yet died.

Then he makes clear that Jacobs's female characters, even in their less-than-admirable traits, are not necessarily the product of misogyny but have, like the men, their predecessors in comic conventions:

> The feminine side of the mixture is conventional music-hall too. There is no sex. There is no hint of illicit love. With this goes a low opinion of married love. Young girls are pretty, tidy, heartless and always deceptively grave. They flirt. They terrorise with their caprices like any Millamant. They outwit everyone. It is their brief moment. Presently they will become mothers of ten squalling kids; and their husbands will be beating them; or they will become strong-willed monsters, the scolds of the kitchen, the touchy and jealous Grundys of the parlour.

This tendency to deal in types is especially evident in Jacobs's short stories. In his novels, while certain familiar personalities appear, there is naturally more room for development of both the characters and their comic relationships. *At Sunwich Port* (1902) and *Dialstone Lane* (1904), usually considered the best of his longer works, include attractive young ladies, such as Kate Nugent and Prudence Dewitt, who show aspects of character besides the usual cleverness and coy elusiveness in their contests with the young men who seek their favors.

In *Dialstone Lane* there are two female characters who are indeed formidable, and Jacobs gives what is perhaps his most dismal picture of the marital state. But even these "immortally awful wives," as Pritchett terms them, belong to stage farce. Pritchett comments on "the artificial, almost pastoral Jacobs of *Dialstone Lane*. The sunlight of pure malice and self-possessed sentiment gleams on this story about three gullible tradesmen who dream of going to sea." And even the presence of the two absurdly horrendous wives cannot darken the story.

Jacobs's other novels, *Salthaven* (1908) and *The Castaways* (1916), are amusing but fairly obvious in their reworking of familiar themes and characters.

In his novels Jacobs creates short episodes that are cleverly interwoven; several plots are melded into one large, seamless fabric. As Henry Reed indicates in the introduction to the 1947 edition of *Dialstone Lane,* "He knows how to make the end of one piece of confusion slyly contain the beginnings of another, and he knows how to allot to a character a remark or an act which the reader can anticipate, and *then* how to cap it with something absolutely unexpected." Reed then adds, "The book has the placid mellowness of a wine which two wars have failed to disturb."

Most critics of Jacobs's writings became aware that both his stories and his novels tend to be much the same in plot structure, but they praised the ingenuity with which he instills interest and variety into relatively few plots. This lack of growth and development did inspire one negative criticism that attracted much attention, coming as it did from a well-known writer, Arnold Bennett. In *Books and Persons* (1917), after praising Jacobs's talent for telling amusing stories, Bennett berates him for his lack of "general ideas." Bennett was "dissatisfied" because Jacobs's work showed "no signs of intellectual curiosity . . . no signs of any development whatever. . . . Mr. Jacobs seems to live apart from the movement of his age. . . . [It is] impossible to gather from Mr. Jacobs' work that he cares for anything serious at all; impossible to differentiate his intellectual outlook from that of an average reader of *The Strand Magazine*."

Bennett is on solid ground regarding the lack of development, but his comments on Jacobs's detachment from his age and his "intellectual outlook" provoked many replies. Some critics felt that Bennett was confusing Jacobs's strengths with his faults. Robert C. Whitford, writing in the *South Atlantic Quarterly* (July 1919), evaluates Bennett's last sentence: "It may be that in that sentence he has struck upon the secret of the humourist's great success. Jacobs, writing carefully and skillfully . . . with never an attempt to solve a big problem, never more than a reticent mention of sex or gender, never the impropriety of a too realistically salty oath, produces just that kind of pure humor which suits the taste of Anglo-Saxon middle classes." Priestley makes an even stronger statement: "Knowing exactly what he wanted to do, the kind of effect he wanted to make, [Jacobs] took away and refashioned the slender stock of material necessary for his settings, and boldly left out all the rest, all the darker crimes, the devastating passions, the bleak tragedies that are found everywhere in this world and that would have shattered his tiny comedies into minute fragments."

In *A Handful of Authors* (1953 edition), Chesterton is not at all concerned with Jacobs's lack of social relevance. He describes Jacobs as "in real sense a classic" – a return to the central and sane tradition of humorous literature. "He is the child of Dickens," representing that tradition in four ways: "he re-establishes humour as something violent and involuntary and outside ourselves"; "he re-establishes the old comic importance of plot . . . his short tales . . . are ingenious merely as tales." Each one is "an amplified anecdote . . . the fun is not merely in the characters, it is in the whole framework of the thing; it is structurally funny, architecturally funny." Thirdly, he is always lucid, having "no concern with that air of mystery in which so many able moderns have wrapped their amusement." And fourthly, Jacobs "touches greatness" in "his achievement as an interpreter of a great element of the democracy. He is the artistic expression of the hu-mour of the people." Jacobs exaggerates, to be sure, but "popular humour is itself in its nature an exaggeration. . . . Mr. Jacobs' labourers say better things than do most real labourers, but the same kind of thing . . . the farcical speech of Mr. Jacobs' characters is undoubtedly ingenious, and even elaborate, but in this respect more than in any other way it is the real speech of the populace."

And so the question of the extent to which, or the way in which, Jacobs's writings can be included in the realist camp remains debatable. His plots are cleverly contrived and manipulated, yet his stories retain the details that create the sense of dockside or village reality. Priestley states flatly that Jacobs "has actually been mistaken for a realist." He "is not a reporter, but an artist." Comedy demands a world of its own, and Jacobs creates one – "a world just as small, bright, and artificial as that of Jane Austen." This view is echoed by Walter Allen in *The Short Story in English* (1981): "Realism was not his aim. He was a master of artificial comedy and of his own mannered dialogue, which was based on Thames speech."

The question of realism does not arise in the case of "The Monkey's Paw," though some of his other stories involving suspense and murder could be described as psychological realism. In *Strange Tales from the Strand* (1991), Jack Adrian remarks that Jacobs's "reputation as a foremost comic writer of his day . . . too often served to obscure his other talent, as a creator of atmosphere and dread in his

stories of the macabre." "The Monkey's Paw" differs from his other "serious" stories in that it is a "horror fantasy," a rewriting of the traditional fairy tale involving the granting of three wishes, which are invariably misused – the third is needed to revoke the effects of the first two. In the story the consequences of acquiring the power to change destiny, to tamper with fate, are spelled out in nightmarish detail, with the implication that man does not have the knowledge or wisdom to control his own fate: he can only make things worse.

The father, Mr. White, makes a fatal mistake when he snatches the monkey's paw, an ugly little talisman with the power to grant wishes, from the fire where it had been thrown by the old soldier. He makes what seems like a modest, harmless wish for two hundred pounds needed to pay off the mortgage. He gets the money all right – as indemnity for the death of his son, just mangled in machinery at a factory. The distraught mother talks the father into using the second wish to bring back the dead son. The next mistake is forgetting to have the son returned in his original, preaccident condition. When he hears strange sounds at the door, Mr. White realizes that his son has returned mutilated and no doubt hideous to behold, so to protect his wife from such a spectacle he uses the third wish. Just as his frantic, heartbroken wife struggles with the door bolts, he wishes the son back in his grave. The mother opens the door on a dark and deserted street.

This powerful little drama, taut with suspense and foreboding, lent itself admirably to stage and film adaptation. It takes place entirely in the living room of a cottage, a scene lit by flickering firelight and dominated by the grotesque little paw. In the 1932 film version it clenches its fingers at the moment of granting a wish.

"The Monkey's Paw" was not Jacobs's first horror tale. It was preceded in 1897 by *The Brown Man's Servant,* a long story published in a one-volume edition with the novella *The Skipper's Wooing.* The action of *The Brown Man's Servant* centers on a stolen diamond that a Jewish pawnbroker has just purchased for five hundred pounds (a bargain, apparently) and that the original thieves want back. Despite ominous threats the pawnbroker refuses, even when confronted by a sinister "brown man," a small and wrinkled Burmese who kills people with the aid of his "servant," which turns out to be a poisonous snake. The story is full of darkness, threats, terror, and suspense, including the discovery of the Jew's dead cat (killed as a warning), leading up to a gruesome climax. The story has obvious ethnic

Mr. Chase, with his friend in his powerful grasp, was doing his best,
as he expressed it, to shake the life out of him

"And next moment I went over back'ards in
twelve foot of water."

Illustrations by Will Owen for "Fairy Gold" and "Skilled Assistance" (from Ship's Company, *1911)*

overtones, as the pawnbroker is referred to throughout as "the Jew" and the Burmese is considered particularly frightening because of his dark-skinned, alien appearance.

There are four other tales in a similar vein, and in format they are similar to the humorous stories: the protagonist tries to get away with something illicit, he fails, and his plan backfires. Jacobs also retains a grotesque humor in his macabre plots. Adrian calls "His Brother's Keeper" (*Sea Whispers,* 1926) "an artful combination of farce and terror." He remarks that while it is less well known than "The Monkey's Paw," it is "in fact even more impressive." One might question this last statement yet agree that there is an element of farce permeating Jacobs's depiction of murderers trying to escape the consequences of their deeds — trying, that is, to conceal a corpse successfully.

In "The Well" (*The Lady of the Barge*) Jem Benson is threatened with blackmail by his inept, debt-ridden cousin, who demands fifteen hundred pounds in exchange for some incriminating letters that would seriously jeopardize Jem's upcoming marriage to a desirable young lady. Jem arranges his blackmailer's disappearance down an abandoned well in the woods near Jem's home. Ironi-

cally, his fiancée insists that an evening walk take them to the old well, much to Jem's discomfiture. After a series of suspenseful moments, as the lady perches precariously on the rim of the deep well, Jem persuades her to leave with him — but only after she inadvertently drops a valuable bracelet into the dark, icy water. In his later attempt to retrieve the bracelet, Jem becomes involved, literally, in the fate of his victim.

"His Brother's Keeper" begins with these words: "Anthony Keller, white and dazed, came stumbling out into the small hall and closed the door noiselessly behind him. Only half an hour ago he had entered the room with Henry Martle, and now Martle would never leave it again until he brought him out." As in "The Well," the plot centers on the protagonist's efforts to conceal a corpse. Keller succeeds in this for a time, but only after nerve-wracking interruptions, first by the untimely arrival of a friend and then by the scheduled arrival of the charwoman. Keller's clever decision to create a rock garden on his property as a means of hiding the body is frustrated by his tendency to walk in his sleep, undoing his daytime labors. He tries to escape from his imagination and conscience, but he is ultimately trapped by his own devices.

The story is reminiscent of Edgar Allan Poe's "The Tell-Tale Heart" (1843) in that the enemy – and the source of his undoing – lies not without but within the protagonist's psyche: his own "Tell-Tale Heart" brings him to reveal himself, in this case with a "Thank God!" at the end. An added point of interest is that the reader never learns who Martle is or why Keller murders him. The reader infers that the murder was sudden and brutal because the corpse has "a white face and battered head."

One of Jacobs's later stories, "The Interruption" (*Sea Whispers*), has been reprinted in many anthologies of mystery and murder tales. This story deals with Goddard, a thirty-five-year-old man who has successfully done away with his overbearing (to hear him tell it) wife and who is now contemplating a happy life. None of the authorities suspects foul play; after all, he was a devoted husband constantly tending to his sick wife, even refusing the assistance of a nurse. All the while, apparently, he was surreptitiously poisoning her – she dies of "gastro-enteritis." Their longtime housemaid, Hannah, knows the truth, however, and uses her knowledge to gain dominance as well as greatly increased wages in return for her silence.

She is protected from Goddard's retaliation by the familiar device of a revealing letter left with her sister, to be opened in the event of her death, and much of the interest of the story lies in Jacobs's depiction of the contest between the triumphant Hannah and the enraged Goddard. While one can sympathize with his desire to eliminate the sneering, maddening female, it remains that Goddard is an unrepentant murderer. At one point he contemplates Hannah's reveling in her newfound power: "shaking with fury, he thought of her lean, ugly throat and the joy of choking her life out with his fingers." Finally, in despair, Goddard comes up with a plan: he plants incriminating evidence (poison) and contrives his own illness, which is intended to fall well short of actual death, in order to point suspicion at Hannah as attempting murder. But, as in Jacobs's other stories, the plan backfires.

Plot summaries can only partially convey the artistic merit of Jacobs's stories, for much of the quality lies in his style, a blend of directness and suggestion. As Horace Newte points out in "The Art of W. W. Jacobs" (*Bookman*, October 1926), "The Interruption" is notable for "its infinite suggestions not only of what has happened before the story opens, but the prevailing atmosphere after the murdered wife has been buried." But admiration for Jacobs's nonhumorous stories was not universal. Adcock found it necessary to defend Jacobs from an unnamed critic who had said that "he is only wearisome when he attempts to write in other veins than the humorous." Adcock replies, "I have never ceased to wonder why he has not given us more stories in this kind, since he is as fine and effective an artist in writing them as in writing those joyous comedies and farces that made him rich at first and keep him so."

Adcock made this remark in 1928, when Jacobs had about fifteen more years of life and fame, and many critics have wondered why his popular comic characters faded so quickly following Jacobs's death in 1943. In "A Jest in Season: Notes on S. J. Perelman, with a Digression on W. W. Jacobs" (*Twentieth Century*, June 1960), novelist and critic John Wain, speaking of Jacobs's humorous stories, offers some possible reasons for his slide into obscurity: "Jacobs went out because he wrote with the convention that the English working man is funny – I mean funny *per se*, funny before he does or says anything funny." But the left-wing writers of the 1930s produced "a flood of 'social realism' which usually showed proletarian life as an unending round of misery and humiliation; that tide has receded in its turn but while it lasted it did a lot to wash away the Jacobs kind of humour."

Despite the receding of the tide, Jacobs remains largely unremembered, but not because his stories are no longer worthy of attention. They are not tied to the issues and social problems of their day, and possibly because they deliberately avoid the miseries and pain of real lower-class life, they can be read and enjoyed as artfully contrived little pastorals that, despite their artificiality – or perhaps because of it – can afford pleasure to a reader of any period. One could do worse than to make the acquaintance of those genial rascals Ginger Dick, Peter Russet, Sam Small, and Bob Pretty.

Bibliography:

E. A. Osborne, "Epitome of a Bibliography of W. W. Jacobs," *Bookman* (London), 86 (May 1934): 99–101; (June 1934): 138–142; (July 1934): 204–206.

References:

Arthur St. John Adcock, "William Wymark Jacobs," in his *The Glory That Was Grub Street: Impressions of Contemporary Authors* (London: Sampson Low, Marston, 1928; New York: Stokes, 1928), pp. 147–157;

Jack Adrian, ed., *Strange Tales from the Strand* (Oxford & New York: Oxford University Press, 1991), pp. xv–xxiii, 69–70;

Walter Allen, "Jacobs, Wells, Conrad, Bennett, Saki, De la Mare," in his *The Short Story in English* (Oxford: Clarendon, 1981), pp. 76–91;

Arnold Bennett, "W. W. Jacobs and Aristophanes," in his *Books and Persons: Being Comments on a Past Epoch, 1908–1911* (London: Chatto & Windus, 1917; New York: Doran, 1917), pp. 53–56;

G. K. Chesterton, "W. W. Jacobs," in his *A Handful of Authors: Essays on Books and Writers,* edited by Dorothy Collins (London & New York: Sheed & Ward, 1953), pp. 28–35;

Benny Green, "Wapping Lies," *Spectator,* 235 (19 July 1975): 85;

Hugh Greene, Introduction to *Selected Short Stories of W. W. Jacobs,* edited by Greene (London: Bodley Head, 1975), pp. 5–9;

Joseph H. Harkey, "Foreshadowing in 'The Monkey's Paw,'" *Studies in Short Fiction,* 6 (Fall 1969): 653–654;

C. Lewis Hind, "W. W. Jacobs," in his *More Authors and I* (New York: Dodd, Mead, 1922), pp. 170–174;

Annie Russell Marble, "Whimsicality and Humor," in her *A Study of the Modern Novel: British and American Since 1900* (New York: Appleton, 1928), pp. 185–216;

Horace Newte, "The Art of W. W. Jacobs," *Bookman* (London), 71 (October 1926): 18–20;

J. B. Priestley, "Mr. W. W. Jacobs," in his *Figures in Modern Literature* (London: John Lane, 1924; New York: Dodd, Mead, 1924), pp. 103–123;

V. S. Pritchett, "W. W. Jacobs," in his *Books in General* (London: Chatto & Windus, 1953), pp. 235–241;

Henry Reed, Introduction to Jacobs's *Dialstone Lane* (London: Eyre & Spottiswoode, 1947), pp. v–viii;

John Wain, "A Jest in Season: Notes on S. J. Perelman, with a Digression on W. W. Jacobs," *Twentieth Century,* 167 (June 1960): 530–544;

Alfred C. Ward, "W. W. Jacobs: Many Cargoes," in his *Aspects of the Modern Short Story: English and American* (London: University of London Press, 1924), pp. 227–239;

Robert C. Whitford, "The Humor of W. W. Jacobs," *South Atlantic Quarterly,* 18 (July 1919): 246–251.

Papers:

Many of Jacobs's letters and manuscripts are at the Harry Ransom Humanities Research Center, University of Texas at Austin.

Jerome K. Jerome
(2 May 1859 – 14 June 1927)

Lee Baker
High Point University

See also the Jerome entries in *DLB 10: Modern British Dramatists, 1900–1945: Part One* and *DLB 34: British Novelists, 1890–1929: Traditionalists.*

BOOKS: *On the Stage – and Off* (London: Field & Tuer, 1885; New York: Holt, 1891);

The Idle Thoughts of an Idle Fellow (London: Field & Tuer / New York: Scribner & Welford, 1886; New York: Holt, 1890);

Barbara (London & New York: French, 1886);

Sunset (New York: French, 1888?);

Fennel (London & New York: French, 1888);

Stage-land (London: Chatto & Windus, 1889; New York: Holt, 1890);

Three Men in a Boat (To Say Nothing of the Dog) (Bristol: Arrowsmith / London: Simpkin, Marshall, 1889; New York: Holt, 1889);

Diary of a Pilgrimage (and Six Essays) (Bristol: Arrowsmith, 1891; New York: Holt, 1891);

Told After Supper (London: Leadenhall, 1891; New York: Holt, 1891);

Novel Notes (London: Leadenhall, 1893; New York: Holt, 1893);

John Ingerfield and Other Stories (London: McClure, 1894; New York: Holt, 1894);

The Prude's Progress, by Jerome and Eden Phillpotts (London: Chatto & Windus, 1895);

Biarritz, by Jerome and Adrian Ross, with music by F. O. Carr (London: Francis, Day & Hunter / New York: Harms, 1896);

Sketches in Lavender, Blue and Green (London: Longmans, Green, 1897; New York: Holt, 1897);

The Second Thoughts of an Idle Fellow (London: Hurst & Blackett, 1898; New York: Dodd, Mead, 1898);

Three Men on the Bummel (London: Arrowsmith, 1900); republished as *Three Men on Wheels* (New York: Dodd, Mead, 1900);

The Observations of Henry (Bristol: Arrowsmith, 1901; New York: Dodd, Mead, 1901);

Jerome K. Jerome

Paul Kelver (London: Hutchinson, 1902; New York: Dodd, Mead, 1902);

Miss Hobbs (New York & London: French, 1902);

Tea-table Talk (London: Hutchinson, 1903; New York: Dodd, Mead, 1903);

Tommy and Co. (London: Hutchinson, 1904; New York: Dodd, Mead, 1904);

Woodbarrow Farm (New York & London: French, 1904);

Idle Ideas in 1905 (London: Hurst & Blackett, 1905);

The Passing of the Third Floor Back, and Other Stories (London: Hurst & Blackett, 1907; New York: Dodd, Mead, 1908);

The Angel and the Author and Others (London: Hurst & Blackett, 1908);

Fanny and the Servant Problem (New York & London: French, 1909);

They and I (London: Hutchinson, 1909; New York: Dodd, Mead, 1909);

The Passing of the Third Floor Back: An Idle Fancy in a Prologue, a Play and an Epilogue (London: Hurst & Blackett, 1910; New York: Dodd, Mead, 1921);

When Greek Meets Greek (Philadelphia: Penn, 1910);

The Master of Mrs. Chilvers (London: Unwin, 1911; New York: Dodd, Mead, 1911);

Robina in Search of a Husband (New York: French, 1913);

Malvina of Brittany (London & New York: Cassell, 1916);

All Roads Lead to Calvary (London: Hutchinson, 1919; New York: Dodd, Mead, 1919);

Anthony John (London & New York: Cassell, 1923; New York: Dodd, Mead, 1923);

A Miscellany of Sense and Nonsense (London: Arrowsmith, 1923; New York: Dodd, Mead, 1924);

The Soul of Nicholas Snyders (London: Hodder & Stoughton, 1925);

The Celebrity (London: Hodder & Stoughton, 1926; New York & London: French, 1927);

My Life and Times (London: Hodder & Stoughton, 1926; New York & London: Harper, 1926).

PLAY PRODUCTIONS: *Barbara,* London, Globe Theatre, 19 June 1886;

Sunset, adapted from Alfred, Lord Tennyson's "The Two Sisters," London, Comedy Theatre, 13 February 1888;

Fennel, adapted from François Coppée's *Le Luthier de Crémone,* London, Novelty Theatre, 31 March 1888;

Woodbarrow Farm, London, Comedy Theatre, 18 June 1888; produced again as *The Master of Woodbarrow,* New York, Lyceum Theater, 26 August 1890;

Pity is Akin to Love, London, Olympic Theatre, 8 September 1888;

New Lamps for Old, London, Terry's Theatre, 8 February 1890;

Ruth, by Jerome and Addison Bright, Bristol, Prince's Theatre, 20 March 1890;

What Women Will Do, Birmingham, Theatre Royal, 17 September 1890;

Birth and Breeding, adapted from Hermann Sudermann's *Die Ehre,* Edinburgh, Theatre Royal, 18 September 1890;

The Councillor's Wife, by Jerome and Eden Phillpotts, New York, Empire Theater, 6 November 1892; produced again as *The Prude's Progress,* London, Comedy Theatre, 22 May 1895;

The Rise of Dick Halward, London, Garrick Theatre, 19 October 1895;

Biarritz, by Jerome and Adrian Ross, music by F. O. Carr, London, Prince of Wales's Theatre, 11 April 1896;

The MacHaggis, by Jerome and Phillpotts, London, Globe Theatre, 25 February 1897;

Miss Hobbs, New York, Lyceum Theater, 7 September 1899; London, Duke of York's Theatre, 18 December 1899;

Susan in Search of a Husband, London, Scala Theatre, 16 March 1906; produced again as *Robina in Search of a Husband,* London, Vaudeville Theatre, 16 December 1913;

Sylvia of the Letters, London, Playhouse, 15 October 1907;

The Passing of the Third Floor Back, London, St. James's Theatre, 1 September 1908;

Fanny and the Servant Problem, London, Aldwych Theatre, 14 October 1908; produced again as *The New Lady Bantock,* New York, Wallack's Theater, 8 February 1909;

The Master of Mrs. Chilvers, London, Royalty Theatre, 26 April 1911;

Esther Castways, London, Prince of Wales's Theatre, 21 January 1913;

The Great Gamble, London, Haymarket Theatre, 21 May 1914;

Poor Little Thing, adapted from Jules Lemaître's play, New York, Bandbox, 22 December 1914;

The Three Patriots, London, Queen's Theatre, 27 July 1915;

Cook, London, Kingsway Theatre, 18 August 1917; produced again as *The Celebrity,* London, Playhouse, 25 June 1928;

Man or Devil, New York, Broadhurst Theater, 21 May 1925; produced again as *The Soul of Nicholas Snyders,* London, Everyman Theatre, 13 December 1927.

Jerome K. Jerome was a popular turn-of-the-century humorist. He was a born storyteller, and his works often began as anecdotes that he developed into short stories, plays, essays, or novels. He sometimes used his short stories as the initial embodiments of themes or moral twists that he later transferred to the stage. Often the lack of character development in his short fiction can be attributed to the fact that he was writing a synopsis or abstract to be fleshed out later in another genre, usually drama. Certainly the story "The Passing of the Third Floor Back" (1907) seems slight compared to the treatment given in the play of the same name, even though critics of the day still thought the stage characters stiff and flat. In this sense Jerome is a better playwright than a short-story writer. But many of his short stories seem to be written out of a true love for the genre and are quite successful as vehicles for his purposes, sometimes serious and sometimes humorous.

Jerome was mainly regarded as a "new humorist," and his best-known work, *Three Men in a Boat (To Say Nothing of the Dog)* (1889), remains the standard by which he is judged. He also wrote serious works, but contemporary reviewers often criticized him because his fiction was not always humorous; sometimes it turned sentimental or moralistic. Jerome was also an editor for the *Idler* (1892–1897) and *To-day* (1893–1897), monthly and weekly journals, respectively, furnishing entertaining articles, fiction, and specialty features on books, theater, and politics. Two collections of his short stories, *John Ingerfield and Other Stories* (1894) and *Sketches in Lavender, Blue and Green* (1897), are drawn from pieces that he published in these two magazines. Aside from a few ghost stories collected in anthologies from 1960 to 1990 by several editors, including Alfred Hitchcock and Red Skelton, Jerome's short fiction is hardly read today.

Jerome was born in Walsall, Staffordshire, on 2 May 1859, the year of the publication of Charles Darwin's *On the Origin of Species,* an ironic fact since Jerome was raised as a Dissenter. Jerome once had the chance to become the personal secretary for Herbert Spencer, but he declined the position out of respect for his parents' faith. Jerome was caught between the new age and the old, and, although he never lost his faith in Christ, he came to a new understanding for which his religious upbringing did not prepare him. The social changes that occurred during Jerome's life, especially those involving woman's rights, often find a place in his stories. Although he was sympathetic, his depiction of women does not always echo agreement with all that the "new woman" believed.

Jerome was forced to abandon the country at an early age when his father, Jerome Clapp Jerome, lost the family fortune on mining speculations. Bankrupt, the family soon moved to the East End of London, where Jerome learned the hard lessons of cockney street life. Despite the hardships, or perhaps because of them, Jerome always remained faithful to his lower-class London background. Almost all of his stories are set in large cities, usually London; many of his stories deal with young men who manage to rise above their humble city origins because of their talents as actors or journalists. No matter how well his characters thrive, they never fully renounce the values they found in their poor urban backgrounds. This feature of Jerome's origins probably explains his sentimentality and the comparison that is often made between him and Charles Dickens.

Jerome's career as a writer was encouraged by his family. Although he was studying to become a solicitor when he married Georgina Henrietta Stanley in 1888, she supported his decision to devote himself to writing. Jerome and his wife had one child, Rowena. She later acted in two of her father's plays, *The Passing of the Third Floor Back* (performed, 1908; published, 1910) and *Esther Castways* (performed, 1913). In *My Life and Times* (1926) Jerome claims that his daughter and Gertrude Elliott "were the best Stasias I have ever seen" in *The Passing of the Third Floor Back.*

Jerome became popular for his humor, and his continued renown rests firmly on his humorous books and stories, especially *Three Men in a Boat.* But Jerome was also severely criticized by some reviewers, who used the term *New Humor* to belittle his achievement. Perhaps in reaction against this estimation, Jerome claimed to be a pensive man. In the preface to *John Ingerfield and Other Stories* he begs his readers to accept him as a writer of serious fiction. "I wish distinctly," he stresses, "to state that 'John Ingerfield,' 'The Woman of the Sæter,' and 'Silhouettes' [short stories] are not intended to be amusing." In fact, Jerome insisted that he was basically a melancholy person.

Seriousness and humor, though opposite characteristics, have a long tradition of being mixed; Jerome's humor, despite being called new humor, has a distinguished heritage. His predecessors, Miguel de Cervantes, Laurence Sterne, and Thomas Carlyle, are humorists who weave the serious side of life throughout their amazing narratives. One of the stock characters of such literature is the harmlessly eccentric character, whose depiction became a trademark of Jeromian humor. This tradition was not recognized in Jerome's day, and his humorous pieces were often seen as vulgar cockney raillery. Certainly he is not as complex a writer as Sterne or Carlyle, but as Ruth Marie Faurot notes in *Jerome K. Jerome* (1974), Jerome's humor is characterized by a freshness, a "brashness in treating ordinary subjects." Perhaps the best summary of Jeromean humor is an aphorism attributed to him in the feature "Idle Ideas" from *To-day:* "True humour notes imperfections, only to try to lighten them." Jerome is aware of people's faults, but he finds no sins. When he presents the flaws in people's characters without obvious moralizing and forced sentiment, he can be a good teller of tales.

Another typical feature of Jerome's humor is the narrative twist he often gives to his stories. In "The Surprise of Mr. Milberry" (*The Observations of Henry*, 1901) a father discovers that he has lost his baby when he inadvertently takes a basket with a dog inside. Jerome's incongruity reminds the reader of Oscar Wilde's *The Importance of Being Earnest* (1895), when Lady Bracknell chides Jack Worthing for carelessness in losing his parents since he, too, was abandoned as a baby in a handbag in a London train station. Similarly, in a story published in *Sketches in Lavender, Blue and Green,* Jerome takes an obvious gambit from Wilde. He begins "Reginald Blake, Financier and Cad" with a familiar Wildean theme: "The advantage of literature over life is that its characters are clearly defined and act consistently. Nature, always inartistic, takes pleasure in creating the impossible." Jerome turns the Wildean paradox that "life imitates art" on its head, but this is expected of Jerome. His good nature intrudes, and he finishes the story with a sentimental ending that would make Dorian Gray blanch. Reginald Blake, who begins the story as a selfish and manipulating person, ends pretending to be a cad so that he can save the reputation of his wife, who is discovered in an adulterous relationship. Reginald unexpectedly locates his conscience, since he blames himself for pushing his wife into an illicit relationship. This contrast with Wilde was recognized by Jerome's contemporary Robert Hichens, who, in *The Green Carnation* (1894), defines a philistine as one who reads Jerome.

The critical reception to *John Ingerfield and Other Stories* was mixed. The *New York Times* (25 February 1894) remarked that Jerome, "who can be delightfully comic when he is not pathetic, ought to leave the unearthly horrors, as subjects for fiction, to less gifted writers." The reference is to "The Woman of the Sæter," a holdover from Jerome's interest in ghost stories. The *Athenaeum* (3 February 1894) observed that this story is "cleverly told but gruesome and improbable." The story "John Ingerfield" was considered a success on both sides of the Atlantic, but the London *Nation* (12 April 1894) probably expressed the general view, that Jerome's "forte is in being funny, and no matter how original

his pathos is, his pathetic style is tedious." "Variety Patter" was considered "a very funny story" (*Athenaeum*). It was difficult for Jerome to change his creative direction because his first impact on the reading public was as a comic writer.

Jerome's next book of short fiction was *Sketches in Lavender, Blue and Green,* whose stories he culled, as he did those in *John Ingerfield and Other Stories,* from his contributions to the *Idler.* These pieces seem to have been written off-the-cuff, as matter needed hastily to fill the pages of a magazine with a deadline. Frank Danby, a critic for the *Saturday Review* (5 June 1897), remarked that Jerome "is known as a successful editor, perhaps because Jerome K. Jerome the editor rejected these stories by Jerome K. Jerome the author." But here, too, the reaction was mixed. The *New York Times* (29 May 1897) reviewer thought highly of the work, especially the shorter "Characterscapes." But, on the other side of the Atlantic, the critical judgment was more in line with Danby's. The *Athenaeum* (26 June 1897) noted that the stories were a mix of comic and serious pieces, "the serious ones being very slight and not very distinctive, the comic ones being a throwback to the vein of *Three Men in a Boat.*" The London *Nation* (27 January 1898) reviewer thought the stories "good, bad and indifferent, the majority being good in the Jerome style of mixing the ingenious with the commonplace, the clever with the cheap, and the fanciful with the sordid." This difference between American and British judgments became a general trend in reviews of Jerome's work, showing a British dislike of the so-called vulgar subject matter and an American approval of the same trait, which would now be called a feel for the actual nature of contemporary life.

Jerome's realism is shown not only in his contemporary city settings but also in his re-creation of characteristic west-country and London dialects. In "Silhouettes" a father hides a stranger from a lynch mob and is confronted by one of the leaders: "Coom, we've had enow chatter, master. Thee mun give un up, or thee mun get out o' th' way, an' we'll search th' house for oursel'." But Jerome is especially successful mimicking the dialects of east London. "Variety Patter" embodies a keen sense of London lower-class accents and colloquialisms. In *The Observations of Henry* the protagonist is a waiter named Henry, a kind of cockney Christopher Marlowe who has witnessed several London scenes and stories. He relates these to an unidentified person who attends his offhand conversations. In the lead

"''E threw a 'andful of shells at me.'"

" Boxed his ears, under the impression
that he was his own office-boy."

Illustrations by L. Raven-Hill for "The Beginnings of William Clodd" and "Mrs. Loveredge Receives," the second and fourth numbers of Tommy
and Co. *(*Windsor Magazine, *January and March 1904)*

story, "The Observations of Henry," Henry tells
how a young fellow, a "Young Kipper, fixes his
pitch" outside a coffee shop where Henry used to
work. Kipper finds a wastrel of a girl in need of a
good meal:

> " 'Ave an egg," he suggested, the moment the rashers
> had disappeared. "One of these eggs will just about fin-
> ish yer."
> "I don't really think as I can," says she, after consider-
> ing like.
> "Well, you know your own strength," he answers.
> "Perhaps you're best without it. Speshully if yer not
> used to 'igh living."

The two youngsters care for each other, and
Henry enjoys seeing their relationship develop. But
Kipper's regard for Carrots, as she is called because
of her red hair, is a cut above the usual, for he does
not want to stand in the way of her marrying an
upper-class gentleman:

"Why don't you marry her?" I says, "and have done
with it?"

He looked thoughtful at that. "I did think of it," he
says, "and I know, jolly well, that if I 'ad suggested it
'fore she'd found herself, she'd have agreed, but it don't
seem quite fair now."

"How d'ye mean fair?" I says.

"Well, not fair to 'er," he says. "I've got on all right, in
a small way; but she – well, she can just 'ave 'er pick of
the nobs. There's one on 'em as I've made inquiries
about. 'E'll be a dook, if a kid pegs out as is expected to,
and anyhow 'e'll be a markis, and 'e means the straight
thing – no error. It ain't fair for me to stand in 'er way."

"Well," I says, "you know your own business, but it
seems to me she wouldn't have much way to stand in if
it hadn't been for you."

"Oh, that's all right," he says, "I'm fond enough of the
gell, but I shan't clamour for a tombstone with wiolets,
even if she ain't ever Mrs. Capt'n Kit. Business is business; and I ain't going to queer 'er pitch for 'er."

Some of Jerome's best stories show the inter-
section of different classes in his depiction of the

"smart" social set. Probably the best collection of his fiction, and the least recognized in its day, is *The Observations of Henry*. This work was generally neglected by reviewers, perhaps because *Three Men on the Bummel* (1900) had only recently come out. This sequel to *Three Men in a Boat* caused considerable attention, garnering no less than eight reviews, many of them written in 1901 when *The Observations of Henry* was published. The *New York Times* (20 April 1901) did give the collection high praise, calling Jerome "a master merry-maker" and his satires "perfectly natural."

The change from one condition of life to another is a persistent theme with Jerome and can be explained by the drastic turns in his own life. He may have inherited this interest from his mother's angst-ridden questions about the family's being forced to live in inferior circumstances. This memory stands out as one of the defining moments in Jerome's autobiography, *My Life and Times*. His mother never got over the bankruptcy and the difficulties the family endured in London. Jerome's autobiography records a brief passage from his mother's diary that profiles the strain of poverty on the family: "Papa's railway is not to be proceeded with. We are overwhelmed with sorrow. Every effort my dear husband makes proves unsuccessful. We seem shut out from the blessing of God."

The interest in theosophy and spiritual matters during this period also found its way into Jerome's work, not only in the shape of ghost stories (*Told After Supper*, 1891) but also in a lively interest in the effects of potions ("The Philosopher's Joke" and "The Soul of Nicholas Snyders" in *The Passing of Third Floor Back*) and of fairies with magical powers (the title story of *Malvina of Brittany*, 1916). Some of these stories, such as "Malvina of Brittany," show the concatenation of two or more of these themes. In this story, among Jerome's best, a mischievous fairy is persuaded against her will to change the personality or station of one of the characters. Here Jerome combines a form of spirituality with his interest in how life would be for characters who undergo personality changes.

In addition, Jerome reflects his time by making the new demands of women on men and their age a common theme in many of his stories. Two stories from *The Observations of Henry* are the best examples of his sympathetic treatment of women's demands for independence and fairness in good narratives. "The Probation of James Wrench" and "The Wooing of Tom Sleight's Wife" both depict women caught in marriages in which the husbands take the wives for granted — and get a proper reward for

doing so. In "The Probation of James Wrench" a waiter comes into a fortune and convinces himself that he is better than his cockney background. He begins to believe that his wife, Susan, is keeping him back in his efforts to shine in smart society; "He grumbled [explains Henry] at her accent, which, seeing that his own was acquired in Limehouse and finished off in the Minories, was just the sort of thing a fool would do."

Wrench finally asks his wife to leave him. She does and buys a hotel cheap, makes it a success, and then sells it for a profit. She buys even better hotels and continues the cycle of her prospering management. Unfortunately, Wrench fails to find his place in high society, thus proving Henry's (and Jerome's) position that "men and women [are] just like water; sooner or later they get back to the level from which they started." When Wrench thinks about returning to Susan, he finds her running a small hotel in Brighton. She is not interested in picking up the old way and treats him coldly. Now that she has the upper hand, she decides to test him. She gives him a chance to reform himself, but under her conditions:

> "It's going to be my experiment this time, not yours. Eleven years ago I didn't give you satisfaction, so you turned me out of doors. . . . I went because there wasn't room for two of us; you know that. . . . Now I'm going to see whether you suit me."

Susan offers him the job of bootblack, which he reluctantly takes. He remains in this position until he is asked to be a waiter. He continues to advance as he obediently does what his wife requests of him. When she asks if he would like to come with her to start anew in a hotel in Dover, Wrench agrees and buys a partnership in the business with money he has saved from working for his wife. Susan relents and accepts him as her husband. The story thus combines two themes: movement from one class to another and the unexpected assertiveness of a spouse.

"The Wooing of Tom Sleight's Wife" has a similar pattern of rejection and return, except that the husband does not know that he is courting his own wife six years after their separation. After being married one hour, Tom and Mary are parted when he gets into a fight and awakes on a ship headed for Europe. Tom writes to his wife, but all the letters are returned. Finally Tom and Mary meet again in a Paris café, but he does not recognize her. She tests her husband by declining his attention and flirting with another man. Tom begins to think that he is not good enough for Marie, as she now styles herself, and resolves to return to America to find his wife. He tracks her from New Hampshire to Quebec to New York, and, with Marie's hint, to Paris, where he finally discovers her true identity. In this instance some may think that the wife is neither sufficiently independent nor strict enough with a man who apparently would have left his wife for another woman. But Susan in "The Probation of James Wrench" certainly attains an independence from her husband and extracts from him the kind of humility often reserved for obedient married women.

There is critical debate about whether Jerome developed as a writer of short fiction. Some think his stories improved as the years went by, but most believe that he continued to be a mediocre storyteller throughout his career. Perhaps the truth lies somewhere in between these two critical positions. Certainly Jerome could write some rather middling pieces, both early and late, but the stories in *The Observations of Henry* are classics in their way. And even though the stories in later collections are uneven, there are some that reveal literary merit.

No one could deny the appeal of "Malvina of Brittany," with its pranksterish fairy protagonist. Jerome's fancy connected with this story. Aside from continuing his interest in the occult and the magical, it shows a new interest in folklore. "His Evening Out" (*Malvina of Brittany*) demonstrates the care Jerome continued to lavish on cockney subjects, for here he returns to a London scene where he has a liberal politician fall in love with his cook. This piece was transformed as the play *Cook* (1917), later titled *The Celebrity* (1928).

Jerome never stopped experimenting; in *Malvina of Brittany,* his last collection of fiction, he tried his hand at the detective story in "The Street of the Blank Wall." This crime story may not match those of his friend Sir Arthur Conan Doyle, but it is superior to many of the sentimental sort for which Jerome was so famous. Because of these successes in short fiction, and because of his enormous output in other genres – chiefly the humorous essay, the novel, and the drama – Jerome established himself firmly as a writer of note at the turn of the century.

Bibliographies:
Carl Markgraf, "Jerome K. Jerome: An Annotated Bibliography of Writings about Him," *English Literature in Transition, 1889–1920,* 26 (1983): 83–132;

Markgraf, "Jerome K. Jerome: Update of a Bibliography of Writings about Him," *English Literature in Transition, 1880–1920,* 30 (1987): 180–211;

Markgraf and Russel Wiebe, "Jerome K. Jerome: Update of an Annotated Bibliography of Writings about Him – II," *English Literature in Transition, 1880–1920,* 31 (1988): 64–76.

References:
Joseph Connolly, *Jerome K. Jerome: A Critical Biography* (London: Orbis, 1982);

Ruth Marie Faurot, *Jerome K. Jerome* (New York: Twayne, 1974);

Alfred Moss, *Jerome K. Jerome* (London: Selwyn & Blount, 1928).

Mabel Greenhow Kitcat

(2 February 1859 – 12 November 1922)

Kathleen McCormack
Florida International University

BOOKS: *A Latter-Day Romance* (London: Bliss, Sands & Foster, 1893);
Concerning Teddy (London: Bowden, 1897);
Shadows of Life (London & New York: John Lane/ Bodley Head, 1898);
Chronicles of Teddy's Village (London: Ward, Lock, 1899);
Some Verses (London?, 1923?).

PLAY PRODUCTION: *The Whip Hand,* by Kitcat and Keighley Snowden, London, Royal Court Theatre, 1885.

SELECTED PERIODICAL PUBLICATIONS – UNCOLLECTED: "Henry Harland in London," *Bookman,* 29 (August 1901): 609–613;
"An Ambassador," *Living Age,* 233 (28 June 1902): 810–821.

Mabel Greenhow Kitcat chose to publish her short fiction and poetry under the name she acquired from her first marriage rather than the more distinctive one she received from her second husband in 1896. Having written a short novel, *A Latter-Day Romance* (1893), three years before her second marriage, Kitcat went on to produce stories that appeared in dozens of 1890s periodicals under the name Mrs. Murray Hickson or, occasionally, Mabel Murray Hickson. Eventually collected in volume form, they fall into two categories: the Teddy stories, which are set in a village child's world of river and cricket ground; and more serious portrayals of characters suffering through unhappy marriages. Her short fiction gains substance when she abandons the sentimentality of the Teddy stories to depict the troubled love relationships of mature people.

Mabel Greenhow was born on 2 February 1859 in the Surrey village of Esher, some fifteen miles southwest of London. Although she attended school near London as a young girl and later, as an author, participated in the urban literary circle formed by the many periodical writers of the time, she continued to make Esher her home and to draw on life there for her characters, plots, and the majority of her settings. Her poetry, collected in a posthumous volume in 1923, also centers on life in Esher.

Both Esher's traditions and the changes it went through during the decades surrounding the turn of the century helped its native daughter to create plots for the short fiction she wrote in and of the town. During the time Kitcat was living and writing there, the green that crowned the gentle rise of its High Street formed a community focal point. Overlooked by the two figures of black bears rearing against the sky from the roof of the sixteenth-century Bear Hotel, the green accommodated some of the sports activities that are among Esher's proudest traditions. Within easy reach of London, the village also experienced all the changes precipitated during the last decades of the nineteenth century by the commuter train, the bicycle, and the motor car, all of which created intrusions on its rural peace and invasions of its pleasant green.

Kitcat's writing draws on the literary background provided by the family of her mother, Marion, a niece of James and Harriet Martineau, and on the outdoor life enjoyed by her father, Judge W. T. Greenhow, also the child of a Martineau woman, James and Harriet's sister Elizabeth. When Kitcat's mother died in a mysterious railroad accident, the child focused her affections on her sportsman father, who continued to live with his daughter until his death in 1921. Despite the family's residence in Surrey, Judge Greenhow served on the bench in Leeds, where he gained a reputation for fairness, wit, longevity, and athleticism. He retired in 1916 as the Father of the Bench (its oldest member), not because of failing vitality, but only because of his increasing deafness. Indeed, having bought a new wig the previous year, he had expected, he said, to continue working long enough to wear it out. The news stories concerning his retirement and death all mentioned the closeness of his relationship with his daughter, to whom he was reputed to have written a letter every day that he spent apart from her.

Cricket, boating, swimming, boxing, wrestling, horse racing, hockey, golf, and skating all appealed to Judge Greenhow, and his daughter includes cricket in particular in the plots of such stories as "Love and Sports" (*Concerning Teddy,* 1897) and "Teddy's Second Innings" (*Chronicles of Teddy's Village,* 1899) and, more memorably if less effectively, in a 1922 poem, "To the Author of 'A Cricketer's Book'": "O! little book of cricket, / Keep safe my heart's frail wicket." Indeed, in a friendly letter (August 1901) Henry Harland makes gentle fun of Kitcat's admiration for muscular heroism; he describes the protagonist in one of his own stories as a character she would surely perceive as effeminate. His story is "one long hymn of praise to Effeminacy, one long anathema of manliness. You would think my hero a precious muff, I'm afraid. He neither shoots, nor hunts, nor fishes." As she aged, however, Kitcat became less admiring of the sporting life. Some of her poetry laments the condition of the frailer partner left behind while the athlete enjoys his luging and skating in winter, his cricket in summer.

In addition to its sports, Esher takes pride in its roses, its river, and its connections with royalty. The green boasts two monuments connected with Queen Victoria, who often visited her son and daughter-in-law Leopold and Helen, Duke and Duchess of Albany, at nearby Claremont: one a horse fountain, a gift from the queen; the other a memorial erected after her death. Both the author and her father were friends with titled and fashionable people, including the duchess of Albany, and country social relationships offered material for much of Kitcat's work, including *The Whip Hand,* the play she co-authored with Keighley Snowden for performance at the Royal Court Theatre in 1885, and *A Latter-Day Romance.*

The protagonist of *A Latter-Day Romance,* Lilian Vane, comes from a family of intellectual pessimists who believe, as her brother Horace puts it: "We are really the sport of temperament and circumstances, nothing more." Lilian expresses her agreement with such ideas on her honeymoon with Jack Dalston, who feels unworthy of his bride because of her family's cleverness. When Jack is blinded in a hunting accident, Lilian resolves to stand by him despite what the both consider a diminishment of his manhood. During the scene in which she confirms her resolution, Jack confesses his lost hope that his marriage to Lilian would have inspired him to a stellar cricket season.

Unsustained by firm principles, however, Lilian becomes increasingly exasperated with her husband's helplessness and enters into a flirtation with Graham, a callous neighbor. Shortly after she overcomes the temptation to elope, her husband drowns, and she soon receives a letter announcing Graham's death as well. The loss of both men punishes Lilian for her coldness and her near-animalistic cruelty, qualities Kitcat emphasizes through clothing metaphors. Lilian often evades her husband's affection by pulling on her gloves, and she walks out with Graham wearing her "rich furs." On her return she kneels down on "the soft fur rug," remaining as silent as possible in a perverse effort to fool her blind husband into believing she is somewhere else.

This novel depends on some themes and techniques that recur in Kitcat's short fiction, including a plot structured around flashbacks that explain current situations. Athletic, cricket-playing characters also turn up in later stories. Drownings and blindings are common catastrophes in her tales, which often feature ironic endings involving flirtatious married characters.

Well respected both by her literary associates, such as Henry Harland, and the social acquaintances who enjoyed Kitcat's "charming word pictures" and prose style of "unaffected elegance and force" (London *Times,* 14 November 1922), Kitcat had more difficulty winning the praise of professional critics. The *Athenaeum* (11 November 1893) described *A Latter-Day Romance* as "a melancholy and unwholesome little tract, the object of which is apparently to point out that young persons of either sex, but more especially of the female one, should not be brought up on the curious principle that pure and simple egotism is the only law of life." Despite such reviews Kitcat's short-story collections often went through several editions, as did her volume of poetry.

Kitcat's first marriage ended after only a few months with the death of Robert Murray Hickson from pneumonia, emphysema, and pleurisy in the spring of 1885. More than a decade after Hickson's death she married Sidney Austyn Paul Kitcat, a cricketer and hockey player nine years younger than she. In marrying Kitcat she found a husband whose athleticism matched her father's. A tall, heavily mustachioed bowler, Kitcat played cricket for Marlborough College, Gloucestershire, Middlesex, Surrey, and England. In 1888 he was elected to the Marylebone Cricket Club, the most prestigious cricket organization in Great Britain. A London stockbroker, he co-authored the book *Canadian Investments* (1926).

Kitcat family historians have engaged in efforts to account for the family's unusual name. Although any connection with the eighteenth-century Kit-Kat Club is disavowed, a 1716 verse connects the club and the name:

> Whence deathless Kit-Cat took its names
>   Few critics can unriddle,
> Some say from pastry-cook it came
>   And some from cat and fiddle.
>
> From no trim beaux its name it boasts,
>   Grey statesmen or green wits,
> But from the pell-mell pack of toasts
>   Of old cats and young kits.

Kit-Kat portraits, each of which shows only the subject's head and hand and fits into a thirty-six-by-twenty-eight-inch frame, occupy the entire Kit-Kat room in the National Portrait Gallery, London, and provide another association. A reviewer of Edmund Gosse's *Critical Kit-Kats* (1896) in the *Critic* in 1896 explains that the author of a literary kit-kat "seeks to hit off deftly certain important things . . . to succeed in kit-katery is to get very close to essentials."

After her second marriage Mabel Kitcat's literary output did not diminish, nor did she refocus her subject matter. On the one hand, her stories present women characters proud of their marriages to athletes; on the other, her autobiographical verses demonstrate the discontent of wives neglected for the bat, the golf club, and the luge. In a pair of poems in *Some Verses,* "The Man's Point of View" and "The Woman's Point of View," the male persona enjoys his sports, believing that he plays croquet and golf for his wife's sake because his energy and success make her happy. The female persona in the following poem, however, laments her loneliness and weariness:

> As things are
> One man must serve, lest others cause a slip,
> If not in thought in Scandal, reaching far.
> I am alone. With tired heart and head
> There have been times I've wished that I were dead.

Childless and excluded from the golf links and the cricket ground, Kitcat continued during her second marriage to write stories whose characters experience restlessness and disappointment with the circumscribed life of the gentlewoman; many of her tales involve fruitless flirtations. During the 1890s her short stories appeared in *Longman's, Vanity Fair, Englishwoman, Chapman's, Cassell's,* and the *Yellow Book.*

Kitcat's fond appreciation "Henry Harland in London" (*Bookman,* August 1901), which she signed with her real name, reveals that her stories did not find immediate favor at the *Yellow Book.* She gratefully describes Harland's gentleness in rejection and his detailed suggestions for revisions. But her letters to him also reveal that she remained quietly proud of her connection with the *Yellow Book* and considered the stories she published in it, such as "The Vigil" and "At the Crossroads" (both 1895), among her most serious and worthwhile.

Concerning Teddy (1897), the first volume to appear after her marriage to Kitcat, collects some stories that were first published in *Longman's,* many of them combining the point of view of Cousin Winnie with the naive point of view of Teddy himself. Adored by her young cousins, Cousin Winnie resembles her author: a childless only child herself, Kitcat sustained close relationships with younger cousins on both the Greenhow and Martineau sides of her family. Cousin Winnie lovingly guides Teddy, his brothers Aubrey and Michael, and their cousin Caroline through crises created by rebellious attempts to smoke cigarettes, through perplexities involving the differences between the sexes, and through definitions of the requirements of sportsmanship. Winnie marries H. A. M. Meredith, whose triple initials and cricketing ability match similar characteristics of S. A. P. Kitcat. The stories, like much of Kitcat's fiction, flash back to account for causes of current circumstances, divide into sections separated by numbers or asterisks, and depend on the imagery of flowers and trees to create a pastoral atmosphere.

Shadows of Life (1898) abandons Teddy and returns to meditations on relationships in which the sadness of tone proceeds from portrayals of unsatisfactory partners and potential adulteries. In "The End of a Dream," the character's fidelity to her dying husband prevents the fulfillment of her relationship with Mr. Boyle, who, instead of the sick and witless husband, is the one who dies in the end. In "A Mistaken Identity," a woman author grows disillusioned with her husband after seeing him at the theater with another woman. But her husband's friend Paul Arnoldson, the man with the fiber to fulfill the idealistic expectations of heroism embodied in her successful novel, nobly abandons their relationship so as not to sully her morally. Often in these stories the initial namelessness of Kitcat's characters establishes a sense of remoteness and identities in jeopardy.

The last two stories in *Shadows of Life* are sudden technical departures in psychological and surrealistic directions. The narrator of "The Waters of Death" evokes Charlotte Perkins Gilman's "The Yellow Wall-Paper" (1892). Her deteriorating sanity results in her own and her perceived rival's deaths by drowning in a swimming pool that, according to the news story that ends the narrative, is supposed to be empty. Unusual for Kitcat in its diary form, its increasingly brief entries reflect the character's intensifying paranoia. In "A Desert Story," Kitcat reverses her subject: not drowning but dehydration. This piece places a married couple in a wasteland setting that reduces their discontent to life-and-death urgency. Alone in a desert for unexplained reasons, the couple has agreed on a specified time for drinking their last bit of muddied water. When the husband swallows it all himself, the wife's indignant mental exclamation is of regret that she has ever loved him. But after the husband nobly conveys her nearly dead body to a British camp in the midst of the desert, she lives to discover that he drank the water not out of selfishness, but to save her from its poisonous taint.

Chronicles of Teddy's Village (1899), Kitcat's last collection, opens with a Teddy story, but he is offered only as a decoy to disguise the continuation of her subject matter. She unifies the collection by setting the stories in a village named for Warling Dean, the house she shared with her second husband and her father. Red of brick, tile, and roof, Warling Dean sits close to the Esher thoroughfare where New Road joins Martineau Close, and its diamond-paned windows look out in all directions through a thicket of holly and rhododendron. In this second volume associated with Teddy, Kitcat populates the village Warling Dean with servants, firemen, children, cricket players, and cousins, while her narrator, Miss Millicent, like the author herself, lives in a house with diamond-paned windows.

The collection begins with a tale that sets a tone of sadness. Every day Prudence Morrison makes sandwiches that she carries to the train station to meet a lover who will never arrive because he drowned thirty years ago. According to Miss Millicent, Prudence "personated the tragedy of Warling Dean [and] suits the place exactly" because she shares its air of "patient sadness which, underlying all its sunshine, one finds so often at the roots of life in a country neighborhood." Miss Millicent also narrates the second story, whose character loses her husband when he falls under the wheels of a fire truck. In the third story Kitcat becomes more daring. Unlike most people in the village, Miss Millicent fails to disapprove of Eliza Sandyman, a woman who boards (and beds) a man she refuses to marry. "It's often wisest not to wed," Eliza argues: "Maybe, if I do, Hebblethwaite'll knock me about a bit. Now I'm free; if he touches me out he goes."

"A Prophet in His Own Country" touches on autobiography, featuring a woman artist who has abandoned "little sketches of the village children" for drawings that her neighbors find not "nice," a parallel to Kitcat's abandonment of Teddy in favor of her marriage stories. In the final story, "A Postscript," Miss Millicent confesses, "Some time ago, acting upon an impulse which I can only characterize as unpardonably mischievous, I lent to my dear old friend Miss Trotwood a copy of that much-abused Quarterly known as the *Yellow Book*." Because of Miss Trotwood's shock at the sad endings to the love stories in the *Yellow Book*, the narrator decides to conclude with Eliza Sandyman's long-delayed wedding to her boarder, Hebblethwaite.

Like most of the women writers of her time, Kitcat did not escape the influence of George Eliot. In "A Tangle of Hay-Time" (*Chronicles of Teddy's Village*), Kitcat alludes to *The Mill on the Floss* (1860) in her comment that "Happy is she, they say, who has no history." Her circumscribed settings suggest Elizabeth Gaskell's *Cranford* (1853) and Jane Austen's *Emma* (1816); indeed nearby Claremont supposedly supplied the model for Highborn in the latter novel. Initially one of what Elaine Showalter later called the "feminine" writers of the nineteenth century, who adopt the values and techniques of patriarchal literature, Kitcat moved on to pessimistic portrayals of sexual transgressions, and her poems reveal a gathering feminism. In the lighthearted "Votes for Women! (A Holiday Rhyme for a Holiday Strike)," written in 1911, the persona would give women a double vote because all the men are out playing golf and tennis. In the poem "From a Suffragist to a Man" (1913), she addresses a male auditor:

> You'll learn of us, the vast familiar band,
> Who share your lives, those things you cannot know.
> Union, and not division, is our aim,
> For Man and Woman are, in truth, the same.

This conclusion differs entirely from the motto to her story "The Vigil" (1895), which tells of a wife whose husband's tardy return from town convinces her of his infidelity: "For to no man is it given to understand a woman, or to any woman understand a man." The mutual understanding possible in the later poem suggests a changed emphasis on similarities, rather than on differences, between the genders.

After the turn of the century Kitcat turned from short fiction to poetry, which she contributed to the same broad range of contemporary periodicals. Her subjects include life in a Surrey village; her travels, such as a 1902 voyage on the S.S. *Oceana*; her motor trips to Pitlochry, Scotland; and her continued reflections on relations between the sexes. With the advent of World War I she enlarged her scope in patriotic support of Great Britain and its allies in the war, during which the family Rolls Royce – described in her poetry as the magic carpet that carries the travelers through intensely colored autumn landscapes to Scotland – was used as an ambulance in France. Kitcat lived only one year following her father's death. She died at Warling Dean the same day that she spoke at the dedication of a monument to a neglected World War I casualty near the green on which life in Esher had centered.

Although the *Athenaeum* (9 July 1898) described the last stories in *Shadows of Life* as "needlessly repulsive," the reviewer also noticed, although negatively, some of their modernist aspects: "Mrs. Murray Hickson writes well; but the shortness and finality of her sentences occasionally obscure her meaning, and she leaves us almost too abruptly to work out the later crises for ourselves." In addition, the *Athenaeum* objected to Kitcat's subject matter: "They are so exclusively concerned with the shadows of woman's life, told from woman's point of view, and dealing almost exclusively with woman as the victim, that, taken together, they become monotonous." But a hundred years later the marriage stories hold more interest than Teddy and his bats and wickets, or the blind victim of *A Latter-Day Romance*, precisely because of their gloomy realism about marriage, their fin de siècle atmosphere, the premodernist remoteness of their narrators, and their modernist terseness of style. Described by Kitcat's contemporaries as the charming hobby of a leisured gentlewoman fond of motoring, gardening, and amateur theatricals, the writing is far from the amateur effort implied by some of its early critics.

References:

"Death of a Woman Novelist," London *Times*, 14 November 1922;

Elaine Showalter, *A Literature of Their Own: British Women Novelists from Brontë to Lessing* (Princeton: Princeton University Press, 1977);

Keighley Snowden, "The Father of the Bench: Character Sketch of Judge Greenhow," *Leeds Mercury* (28 March 1913): 150–151.

Charlotte Mew

(15 November 1869 – 24 March 1928)

Jill Tedford Owens
Southwestern Oklahoma State University

See also the Mew entry in *DLB 19: British Poets, 1880–1914.*

BOOKS: *The Farmer's Bride* (London: Poetry Bookshop, 1916); revised and enlarged as *Saturday Market* (New York: Macmillan, 1921).

Editions and Collections: *The Rambling Sailor,* edited by Alida Monro (London: Poetry Bookshop, 1929);

Collected Poems, edited, with a memoir, by Monro (London: Duckworth, 1953; New York: Macmillan, 1954);

Collected Poems and Prose, edited, with an introduction, by Val Warner (Manchester: Carcanet, Virago, 1981).

Charlotte Mary Mew made her contribution to short fiction with nine stories published between 1894 and 1914 and two published posthumously in the 1950s. Although her poetry is more often admired and studied today than her fiction, the stories reveal a strong voice and a distinctive perspective on life at the turn of the century. Mew's work was published in the *Yellow Book* and by Harold Monro's Poetry Bookshop press; she was taken up by the energetic Mrs. "Sappho" Dawson Scott and befriended by the eminent Sydney Cockerell. At the turn of the century her works were enthusiastically admired by Thomas Hardy, May Sinclair, Virginia Woolf, Siegfried Sassoon, and Ezra Pound.

Today, however, Mew holds a precarious place on the periphery of the literary canon. And that place is secured with her poetry, not her fiction, as the title of her obituary in the London *Times* (29 March 1928) bears witness: "Charlotte Mew: A Poet of Rare Quality." Her poems are accessible through the *Collected Poems* (1953) and such anthologies as X. J. Kennedy's *Introduction to Poetry* (1986) and Sandra Gilbert and Susan Gubar's *Norton Anthology of Literature by Women* (1985). Dissertations and scholarly essays about Mew center on the poetry. However, Mew's *Collected Poems and Prose*

Charlotte Mew

(1981), edited by Val Warner, and Penelope Fitzgerald's biography *Charlotte Mew and Her Friends* (1984) have provided easier access to and more information about the short fiction.

Mew was an eccentric, often reclusive writer whose life is a study in contrasts. Her fiery emotionalism and individualism surface in her stories, yet externally she lived the life of a conventional spinster nursing an irascible, invalid mother. Fitzgerald's biography posits a dual Charlotte whom she refers to as "Miss Lotti," the proper Victorian spinster concerned with appearances and dutifully committed to her sick mother, versus

"Charlotte," the intellectual and artist who swears freely, dresses eccentrically, and smokes constantly. This divided self may well account for the warring impulses that characterize both her life and her stories. Mew's fear of scandal and deep-seated desire for respectability came from her family. Her mother, born Anna Maria Marden Kendall, was the daughter of a successful London architect. She married Fred Mew, a junior member of her father's firm and a man perceived by her family and herself as beneath her. Fred was the son of an innkeeper in Newport on the Isle of Wight, whereas Anna Maria had been raised as the privileged granddaughter of the renowned architect H. E. Kendall, Sr. She seems to have remained a spoiled, silly woman well into her eighties and to have exerted a strong, inhibiting influence on her children's lives. She and Fred had seven children; Charlotte, born on 15 November 1869, was the third child and oldest daughter. Three siblings died in childhood, and two, Henry and Freda, were institutionalized for mental illness. The pain of these deaths and the burden of her hospitalized siblings affected Charlotte throughout her life.

Some idea of Mew's childhood can be gleaned from two of her essays, "Miss Bolt" (Temple Bar, April 1901) and "An Old Servant" (New Statesman, October 1913). The first, a delightful character sketch, describes an old woman who did sewing for the Mew household. Through her, Mew learned something of the world outside the nursery. In relating Miss Bolt's accounts of "Me-brother" and his family, Mew demonstrates her fascination with dialect and life among the lower classes. In the latter essay the title servant is Ellen Goodman, who remained with the Mew family for thirty years, beginning with the marriage of Anna Maria and Fred. Ellen ruled the nursery and certainly had an impact on Mew's development. A religious woman, she imbued in Mew a keen sense of guilt that seems never to have left her, even when she had more or less abandoned religion as an adult. Ellen never approved of Charlotte's writing; the servant believed that the child was wasting her time with reading and scribbling.

Mew often spent holidays on the Isle of Wight with her father's family and particularly enjoyed her uncle's farm, Newfairlee. Certain impressions of that landscape and her experiences there appear in her stories and poems, particularly the Newport market days and the fishermen, sailors, and seaports. Her first experience beyond the family was at the Gower Street School, where she was enrolled as a day student. Her strong will was obvious during these early years, and she exerted herself to learn only what interested her. She particularly liked music and became an accomplished pianist known for her delicate touch.

Most of all she wanted to please her headmistress, Lucy Harrison. Mew's strong emotional attachment to Harrison was evident when Harrison decided to retire; Mew literally banged her head on a wall on hearing the news. When Harrison decided to take a few boarders into her home, Fred Mew begged her to include Charlotte, for he knew the strength of his daughter's attachment. For two years she boarded with Miss Harrison, taking lessons in English literature with her at night after attending Gower Street School during the day.

Harrison influenced Mew intellectually and personally. From this time on Mew affected Harrison's dress style — tailor-made suits and close-cropped hair. And like Harrison, who lived happily with her fellow teacher Amy Greener for nearly thirty years, Mew was to develop strong attachments for women rather than men. On two other occasions she became obsessed with a woman friend.

During these school years Mew made lifelong friends, including Ethel Oliver, Maggie Browne, and the three Chick sisters. These sober, hardworking girls from quiet homes were often amazed by Mew's emotional intensity. She was unpredictable and passionate, and she made her friends laugh. They corresponded and vacationed together long after their school days ended. Mew's essay "Notes in a Brittany Convent" (Temple Bar, October 1901) tells of a holiday that the six "unmated females" took.

Her friends recorded several of Mew's distinctive physical characteristics. She was small-boned and tiny, about four feet ten inches tall as an adult. With her oval face and distinctly dark, arched eyebrows, she looked unusual. She rarely varied her dress style, usually wearing a masculine-looking tailored suit and always carrying a black, horn-handled umbrella. All her friends commented on Mew's distinctive head-tossing mannerism.

In 1888 the family moved to 9 Gordon Street, where Mew spent most of her adult life. She was a child of the 1890s in her love for London's busy streets and vibrant life. Although she writes of the virtues of country air and markets in the essay "The Country Sunday" (Temple Bar, November 1905), she loved the city. The family's finances were strained by the move to this larger house and by the hospital expenses for Henry, the oldest son, who was diagnosed with what is now labeled schizophrenia. In the early 1890s Freda, the beloved baby of the family, was similarly diagnosed. For sixty years she resided in Whiteland Hospital, Carisbrook, never recovering her sanity. Charlotte and her sister Anne were influenced by the contemporary literature outlining the hereditary nature of such illnesses, and they determined never to have children. With these shared family tragedies and the responsibility for their mother, Anne and Charlotte were totally committed to one another.

During the 1890s Fred Mew seems to have withdrawn from his family and work. Anna Maria's family legacies kept the household going. Anne enrolled at the Royal Female School of Art; Charlotte was a talented musician and needleworker skilled at embroidery, but she never applied herself conscientiously to any moneymaking craft other than writing. Anne took on sweatshoplike jobs painting antique furniture, and Charlotte suffered the guilt of witnessing Anne's thwarted talent. The family had financial problems but managed to maintain a home at a "decent" address in Bloomsbury.

Charlotte, however, often felt they could not afford to return hospitality, and if she could not reciprocate an invitation, she did not want to accept it. She was completely tied to the conventional values of her day and worried about being genteel and respectable. The bulk of her energy and time was taken with domestic chores and household concerns. Outwardly Mew appeared timorous and maddeningly tied to a stultifying late-Victorian conventionality. She remained apart from the exciting currents of her day that created the New Woman and freer thinking about sexuality. But inwardly the other Charlotte was feeling, thinking, processing her experiences, and formulating a vision that found its outlet in her writing.

Her independent, intellectual side reveals itself in stories, poems, and essays. In her early efforts Mew demonstrates several traits she would continue to develop: an attraction to humble scenes and characters, a knack for realistic detail, and an affinity for themes of isolation, loneliness, and rejection. The essay "The Minnow Fishers" and the story "A Wedding Day," both unpublished during her lifetime, are among the earliest samples of her work.

"The Minnow Fishers" is a short, two-page piece outlining an unusual event that Mew witnessed. The narrator's friend tells of an incident when a carpenter walking in front of him suddenly ran frantically to the side of a canal, dived in, and retrieved a young boy floating in the water. Three young boys were placidly fishing nearby but re-

mained oblivious to the rescue. Once the child was brought around, the carpenter left and the narrator interrogated the three youths about the almost-drowned boy. Finally, one youth said he was the boy's brother, and the narrator forced this one to lead the boy home. The narrative frame is awkward, but the striking incident is presented realistically, clearly contrasting the incipient violence with the shocking calm of the boys.

"A Wedding Day" is an overwritten, effusive epithalamium. Mew fills the story with eighteenth-century personifications of Love, the Bride, Union, Terror, and Death, emphasizing the dawn-to-night time frame of a wedding day. The plot focuses on the old woman who has raised the bride and is pained at losing the girl. A note of melancholy and sadness prevails; the old woman dies quietly in a chair in her humble cottage on the wedding night, all dressed for her special visitor, Death.

Mew's first publication was the story "Passed," in the second issue of the *Yellow Book* (July 1894). In 1894 this periodical created quite a stir on the literary scene with its startling yellow hardcover, illustrations by Aubrey Beardsley, decadent poetry, and realistic stories. The editor, Henry Harland, liked Mew's story, in which a young woman confronts the darker truths of life in the London streets. The female narrator leaves her warm fireside to visit a church said to be of some architectural interest. There a frantic girl grabs her and leads her through a destitute part of the city to the bedside of a dead woman. The girl collapses on the narrator and falls asleep. The narrator stays until all the lights burn out and then pushes the girl aside and flees in terror to her own safe world.

Some months later, while shopping in a disreputable part of town, she sees the girl of that night wearing crimson, accompanied by a man sporting the same crest she had seen on a letter in the dead woman's room. The narrator reacts violently to the scene, possibly losing her sanity. She has tried to push aside speculations about pain, poverty, and prostitution but ultimately must confront them.

The prose is highly overwrought and diffuse, but certain elements of this story appealed to the *Yellow Book* editor, particularly the seamy London streets, the poverty, the fallen nobility, and the prostitute. These fit the fin de siècle mood that characterized the publication, and for a while Mew became a part of the *Yellow Book* world. In the summer of 1894 she attended Harland's famous Saturday evenings in Cromwell Road and became friends with the strong women of the *Yellow Book* circle: Evelyn Sharp, Netta Syrett, and Ella D'Arcy.

Mew next submitted to Harland a piece written predominantly in Cornish dialect, "The China Bowl." A five-part story of a fisherman, his doting mother, and his domineering wife, it treats the conflict between the mother and daughter-in-law and ends with the deaths of the son and mother. When Harland said it was too long, she put it aside for several years. When the Oscar Wilde scandal broke in 1895, she retreated speedily from the *Yellow Book*, thus leaving friends who could have helped her art.

When Charlotte's father died in 1898, household finances became a serious problem. She, Anne, and their mother had to rent out the top floor of the home. To Charlotte this was a shameful proceeding that had to be hidden from friends and never alluded to around her mother. In September 1899 *Temple Bar* published "The China Bowl." Compared to the innovative, mildly shocking *Yellow Book*, the unillustrated *Temple Bar* seemed a dull, tedious journal. But Mew continued to send material there, becoming one of its regular contributors. Five essays and six of her nine short stories appeared in *Temple Bar* between 1899 and 1905.

These *Temple Bar* stories show Mew experimenting with various techniques and themes. Most of the pieces are highly realistic, employing varied dialects and voices and treating diverse social classes. Narrators are sometimes male, sometimes female. "Mademoiselle" (January 1904) and "Mark Stafford's Wife" (January 1905) both deal with the frustrated lives and dreams of women and demonstrate Mew's major strength, characterization.

"Mademoiselle" is the sad story of an intelligent forty-year-old woman who makes her living as a tutor in writing and literature. She is in love with a worthless artist, Monsieur de St. Pierre, who is the epitome of egotism. When St. Pierre supposedly leaves for New York to find work, Mademoiselle keeps waiting for him and starts sending money to his poor mother in Paris. When the narrator, a former pupil who has kept in touch with Mademoiselle, goes to Paris, he runs into St. Pierre in the streets and discovers that the cad has never gone to New York but is taking the money sent by Mademoiselle each month. The narrator threatens to tell her the truth if he does not call a stop to the payments. Mademoiselle never learns the truth. She keeps waiting, working hard, and slipping into greater poverty and begins to lose the battle with age. Although the prose remains overwrought, the characterization is striking. The pervasive use of gray shows Mew developing the color imagery that characterizes her poetry and stories.

In "Mark Stafford's Wife," the most Jamesian of Mew's stories, the female narrator is the guardian of Katharine (Kate) Relton, the charming, elusive, and mysterious child of an old friend, now dead. Kate first becomes engaged to a down-to-earth young man, Charlie Darch. While he is in Spain working for a year, she breaks off the engagement because she has fallen in love with Mark Stafford. He is a writer of some acclaim, but the narrator, a conventional Victorian lady, does not like his psychological, realistic novels. She describes him as a "vivisectionist at work."

Kate marries Mark and becomes a brilliant and beautiful hostess, her life filled with entertainments and new dresses. Charlie returns and perceives that Kate is not well. The narrator warns Charlie not to make trouble by befriending Kate and discounts his concern that something is seriously wrong with the young woman. Kate elopes with Charlie, leaving a note for the guardian. The guardian fears the scandal, but Kate is "saved" because she dies on the train. Her flight and death are somehow related to the observer husband.

The story is an interesting psychological study of the loss of personality in marriage. Kate admits that she has to maintain her individuality: "Well, I can't to anyone open every door; whoever owns the poor little house, there must be rooms of which, to the end, I keep the key." When her individuality becomes submerged, she dies. There is a supernatural element in this story, something rare for Mew. In a photograph taken when Mark is out of town, his face appears behind Kate, watching her.

Two other *Temple Bar* pieces, "In the Curé's Garden" (June 1902) and "An Open Door" (January 1903), relate the life stories of young women who turn to religion for direction and purpose. "In the Curé's Garden" focuses on the Catholic religious vocation. Anita is an illegitimate child who has been promised to God as atonement for her "lost" mother and unknown father. Father Laurent has taken care of her until she is old enough to enter the neighboring convent. The narrator proposes marriage, finding it a tremendous waste for this vital, lovely girl to go into the convent. He is wealthy enough to provide her with funds for her charities and will not interfere with her religion, but her choice is the convent: she seeks peace and has a clear sense of her destiny.

One of the most realistic features of Mew's fiction is the lack of certitude about right and wrong in a situation. Here the young girl obviously has a limited background. The only people she has ever known are the priest, the housekeeper, and this

Mew with her nurse, Ellen Goodman, who exerted a strong influence in Mew's early life

young man. With such slight experience she, not surprisingly, picks the known. Mew sees the tragedy of this life, yet she paints the girl as having a certain spiritual superiority. She exists on a peaceful, spiritual plane and has a clear sense of destiny that seems desirable and admirable.

In "An Open Door," Laurence (Laurie) Armitage is a beautiful, aristocratic young woman who gives up her social life and position to be a missionary in China. Her mother and sister, Stella, are angry with her, and her fiancé is deeply hurt. But she has seen the "open door" and feels she must choose this destiny. By the time she has completed the three restrictive years of training, her ardor has cooled considerably – she finds the other girls dull and the life drab. She seeks for renewal of spirit and is torn.

Her fiancé, Anthony, has the ability to win her back at his farewell visit, but he misreads her and lets her go. Within the year she is killed in a massacre while helping a sick child. Her death has a significant effect on Stella. This unmarried woman finds life interminably long: "Life was not thrilling, it never had been that; but it was no longer mildly entertaining; and she surveyed the prospective length of it; it seemed so long, she thought, before one might reasonably expect to die." Stella, influenced more by Laurie's death than her life, may well turn to mission work in her unhappiness.

Mew's attitude toward religion, as these two stories indicate, is ambivalent. She seems drawn to the serenity of the convent and admires the truly devout, but she sees the tight-lipped priests as divorced from the real world and the life of a nunnery as sterile. In "An Open Door" she paints the Protestants as colorless and dull-witted, clearly suggesting that Laurie has wasted her life. Although Mew was drawn to the traditional Anglo-Catholic services, she never was religious. In the essay "Men and Trees II" (*Englishwoman,* March 1913), she writes, "Religion is like music, one must have an ear for it; some people have none at all; but given the ear it is all significant and wonderful, from the old plainsong to a rhapsodie of Brahms."

"A White Night" (*Temple Bar,* May 1903) is a bizarre horror tale. Again Catholicism is central; it is handled rather ambivalently, with a sense of awe jarring with a sense of distaste. The narrative frame is somewhat shaky; the narrator is told this story by his friend Cameron and "thanks to a trick of accuracy" relates it word for word. Cameron, a young man in Spain on mining business in 1876, tells of escorting his sister and her new husband to a remote village. They visit a convent near this isolated town and, in their rambles, enter the church just at sunset.

They are locked in accidentally, and, despite their screams and calls, no one comes. They settle down to pass the night in absolute dark in this ancient Romanesque church. Hours later they witness a bizarre spectacle. Thirty or forty monks solemnly file into the church by candlelight, chanting. A woman in white linen ends the procession. She is screaming, but her lovely face reveals a set purpose and total acquiescence. After the chanting and ritual go on for more than two hours, the monks conclude by lowering her alive into a grave in the floor of the church and replacing the stone. The brother-in-law wants to intercede with his gun, but fear of personal harm to the three of them quells him.

After the monks' procession out of the church, the two men try unsuccessfully to find the stone in total darkness. There is no noise from the tomb to help them. When morning comes they know it is too late, and they flee from the scene. They get back to "civilization" and report their experience to the British consul. He says he has heard many strange tales in his career; this is just another one, and he cannot take any action. To the narrator, who had actually become caught up in the ritual before him, it was "an acquiescence in a rather splendid crime."

Mew uses color imagery effectively throughout this story, with the white road, white night, and white linen against the absolute darkness of the church. The exaggerated language and convoluted syntax detract from the tale, but the woman as sacrifice raises interesting questions about the symbolism. The images of sacrifice and death are powerful and negative.

During these years, aside from the stories for *Temple Bar,* Mew published "Some Ways of Love" in *Pall Mall Magazine* (September 1901) and "The Smile" in the *Theosophist* (May 1914). "Some Ways of Love" is a romantic story about growing up and the conflict between love and duty. When Capt. Henley asks a young widow, Lady Hopedene, to marry him, she puts him off for a year, knowing he is too immature to know his own mind. When he

returns he has fallen in love with another woman. He is dismayed to find Lady Hopedene overjoyed to see him. She reveals that she has only one year to live, and he then must decide between his newfound love and this old friend who is dying. His new paramour cannot understand that there "are many ways of love" and will not wait.

"The Smile" is a strange fairy tale or allegory unlike anything else Mew wrote. It features a magic tower in a wood where an ageless, sirenlike old woman lives. People forsake all to climb up to her in response to her song. In a cottage in the wood a woman lives with her naughty baby. The mother wants to join the climbers, but "women with babies cannot always do what they would." She sits below the tower and often looks up. The old woman happens to look down, sees the naughty baby, and immediately loves it. She sings, hoping to lure the child to her.

The child grows into a lazy, ill-natured young girl. She is drawn to the tower but never thinks of climbing it until she spends the night with her lover. Then "with a liberated cry" she sets off to the tower. After great difficulty she gets to the top. When she arrives, the old woman is looking the other way, and the maid "sinks lifeless with a desolate cry." The old woman turns, sees the dead girl, and ceases to smile. Travelers tell of spotting the old woman, a figure "forever speechless, desolate, striving to waken a burden in its arms." The story has a nightmarish, associational quality and creates a vivid impression of loneliness, loss, and injustice. Yearnings and desires, often for the unworthy, drive this rather violent story, and the symbols remain puzzling and disturbing.

The years 1898–1905 were Mew's most productive as a fiction writer. Whether she had a body of unpublished manuscripts is unknown. There are copies of seven other stories that she never published, two of which were published posthumously in the 1950s. But there is no clear indication of when any of these was written.

Of the stories unpublished until Warner's 1981 collection of her prose and poetry, "The Bridegroom's Friend" and "White World" appear to be early efforts. They suffer from emotional effusiveness and much overwriting. "The Bridegroom's Friend" studies the problems of contemporary marriages, but the narrator, the "friend," comes across as weak, ineffective, and irresolute, which undercuts the supposed tragedy of the marriage he could have prevented. "White World" is a highly incredible, overwrought tale of frustrated lovers who come together in a snowstorm but then die of exposure.

The striking color imagery and metaphors are all that redeem the story.

"Spine" seems a more mature piece, for it is less effusive and more objectively written than those two stories. The narrator, a starving artist who lacks "spine," leads a sordid, meaningless life. He lives meanly and cheaply, owes for rent and tailors, and blames everyone but himself for his failure. The psychological realism of this piece is depressing.

In Mew's short fiction the pervasive themes are depression, loneliness, and isolation. Again and again the characters say that life is long, particularly her frustrated women. In her realistic treatment of troubled and depressed characters, there are no happy endings. The contradictions and conflicts that characterize her stories are reflected in Mew's favorite rhetorical scheme, the oxymoron. Her tales are full of such juxtapositions as "tumultuous peace," "tempestuous calm," "formidably frail," "sentient death," and "perceptive sleep." A sense of conflict, pain, and alienation permeates this relatively small body of short fiction.

During this productive seven-year period Mew had serious personal problems, particularly trying to understand and deal with her feelings for D'Arcy, the only friend from the *Yellow Book* circle with whom she kept in touch. A small inheritance from an aunt in 1902 enabled Mew to take a trip to Paris, where D'Arcy was living at the time. Evidence suggests that Mew revealed the intensity of her feelings for D'Arcy and was rebuffed and badly hurt.

She returned home to domestic drudgery and depression. She worked on her short fiction, taking the advice of friends to avoid the novel form. She longed to do an edition of Emily Brontë's poetry, but others had started the project before her, so she wound up publishing an essay on Brontë in *Temple Bar* (August 1904). One story, "Elinor" (unpublished until 1981), clearly reflects her fascination with the Brontës. The isolation of its setting and the private world of its two sisters are distinctively Brontëesque.

Elinor and the narrator, Jean, live in an isolated manor house with one old servant, Agatha. Elinor is completely independent. An atheist, she shuns society and delights in nature, especially storms. But her intense individualism and intellectual efforts lead to her destruction. She rejects an intelligent, loving man; she burns the manuscript of her life's work on the day she dies. Again Mew's message is mixed. Conformity brings happiness to the younger sister, while the intelligent, indepen-

dent woman who is presented as gifted and admirable dies.

After this rather active period writing fiction, Mew concentrated more on her poetry and published no other stories after 1915. The two stories that were published during the 1950s may have been composed during this same period, but their objectivity and lack of effusiveness suggest that they are later efforts. "A Fatal Fidelity" appeared in *Cornhill* (Autumn 1953) and "The Wheat" in *Time and Tide* (February 1954). They are among her best stories, without the overwrought quality of much of her work, and are strong examples of realistic fiction, dealing with common, ordinary men and women who wrestle with life's problems.

"A Fatal Fidelity" is the only story in which Mew's sense of humor is displayed. A widow and a widower meet as they tend their spouses' graves. After a rather unconventional courtship – first in the cemetery and then in her apartment, where they discuss such issues as the inscriptions to be put on the tombstones – they decide to marry. Both are delightfully simple people who reveal the shortcomings of their first marriages while paying homage to their spouses' memories.

"The Wheat" is a strikingly poetic story reminiscent of Count Lev Nikolayevich Tolstoy's "The Death of Ivan Illich" (1886). A dying man confounds his grieving family by shouting out, "Don't let them cut the Wheat!" This strange utterance shows a truth about him that no one knows. The dying banker recognizes that he has wasted his life and never been happy. The image of wheat remembered from his childhood comes to represent lost beauty and life.

The years 1905–1911 were quiet for Mew, with occasional, hard-won holidays to France. Finding someone to care for her mother and Wek, her mother's irascible parrot, always presented a problem. She and Anne took their only trip together in 1911. In 1912 Mew entered a new era of her life. Mrs. Amy Dawson Scott read Mew's poem "The Farmer's Bride" in the *Nation* and contacted the author. Scott, known to her friends as "Sappho," was an enthusiastic patron of the arts who held readings in her home and provided encouragement for writers. A skilled organizer, she was the moving force in establishing International P.E.N., a worldwide organization for authors. Under her influence Mew was forced to come out, meet others, and give readings. Propelled by "Sappho," by the end of 1912 she was becoming one of the known, primarily distinguished for her strange, disturbing poetry.

While enjoying a broadened social life, she worried about problems at home. Money was again tight, and Anne was painting furniture under sweatshop conditions. Charlotte felt guilty about things going well for her, seemingly at Anne's expense. Repair bills and domestic cares plagued her. She rewrote "The China Bowl" for the stage but was sorely disappointed when nothing came of it.

She then became associated with a journal called the *Englishwoman,* in which she published three essays, one on "Mary Stuart in Fiction" (April 1912) and a two-part essay on "Men and Trees" (February and March 1913). She met new friends whom she entertained at Anne's studio for tea. These pieces for the *Englishwoman* bear evidence of wide reading and serious research in the British Library.

Her association with Sappho Scott and her circle initiated a productive period for Mew. She wrote more poetry than at any other time of her life. "Madeleine in Church" was written in 1913, and Pound published "The Fête" in the *Egoist* (1914); both poems were collected in *The Farmer's Bride* (1916). Professionally Mew was making advances and becoming known in important circles. Most significantly, she met Sinclair. The two were good friends, although Sinclair found Mew odd. As in the case of D'Arcy, Mew developed a strong attachment to Sinclair and agonized over the relationship until she was rebuffed. Sinclair told friends of Mew's proclamation of love and referred to her as a "lesbian Poetess."

Sinclair's story "The Pinprick" (*Harper's,* February 1915) may well have been based on Mew's life. It tells of a sad, shy woman who is furiously anxious not to be "in the way." Sinclair, who was active in organizing the Medico-Psychological Clinic of London and was a serious student of psychoanalysis, believed Charlotte's behavior to be a transference of love to a sympathetic friend. If Mew did have lesbian tendencies, there is no indication that she ever had a sexual relationship with anyone.

In 1915, when Mew's confidence was at its lowest, she made a new friend, again an admirer of "The Farmer's Bride," Alida Klementaski. She and Harold Monro contacted Mew to find out whether she would compile a small book of poetry for their Poetry Bookshop press. Through this association Mew met some of the most important writers of her day. At his bookshop Monro held readings and published works by Pound and Robert Graves, along with Edward Marsh's *Georgian Poets* series. To Klementaski, who married Monro in 1916, Mew was a good friend with whom she could exchange confidences over daily household affairs and concerns.

In her introductory memoir of Mew in the *Collected Poems,* Alida Monro recalls Mew's oddness, old-fashioned clothes, and quantities of white hair. To her, Charlotte remained eccentric "Aunty Mew," and Mew seems to have encouraged that image. She never revealed to Monro the madness in the family or the reason she and Sinclair were no longer friends. Monro did perceive the contradictions in Mew's personality, noting the contrast between Mew's strict moral code, which led her to flee from scandal, and her ability to create such poems as "The Fête" and "Madeleine in Church," in which characters struggle with overwhelming emotions. Monro knew of two trunks supposedly full of papers that Mew's friends speculated might be stories and poems, but when she inherited one of the trunks from Mew, it was empty.

Monro prevailed upon Mew to do readings at the Poetry Bookshop, and she was a marked success. *The Farmer's Bride* came out in May 1916, but it did not do particularly well (only 150 copies sold of the 1,000 printed). Marsh considered "The Farmer's Bride" for *Georgian Poetry IV* but was discouraged by Walter de la Mare, who considered the meter too irregular. However, Mew's poetry led to another important friendship and new contacts.

Monro sent a copy of Mew's book to Sydney Cockerell, the director of the Fitzwilliam Museum in Cambridge. Cockerell sent copies of her book to friends, including W. S. Blunt, Sassoon, A. E. Housman, and, most important, Hardy. Hardy wanted to meet her, and in December 1918 she spent a weekend at his home, Max Gate. Hardy pronounced her "far and away the best living woman poet, who will be read when others are forgotten."

A new circle of friends evolved, composed of Cockerell, his wife, Kate, Florence Hardy, and Dorothy Hawksley. Sydney Cockerell escorted Mew to the theater, and she dined out much more frequently. She began to go to Cambridge for weekend visits with the Cockerells. In 1921 a new edition of *The Farmer's Bride* was published to much greater success. Edith Sitwell reviewed it favorably; *Punch* chose to parody Mew among other well-known poets; and Woolf pronounced, "I think her very good and interesting and unlike anyone else."

Although things were going relatively well professionally for Mew, matters at home continued to be strained. The lease on the Gordon Street house was up in 1922, and Charlotte and Anne found two upper floors at 86 Delancey Street and settled in there. Their mother broke her leg, and a long period of nursing her ensued. She died on 12 May 1923. While most of Charlotte's friends saw the death as a blessing, she felt shock, disorientation, and severe loss. Financial problems worsened, for now there was no family trust on which to depend. Freda was still in the mental hospital, and rent at 86 Delancey was high. Cockerell came to her aid by secretly requesting a Civil List pension of seventy-five pounds a year. Letters of recommendation from Hardy, John Masefield, and de la Mare led to governmental approval, and Mew's financial problems were lightened.

The years 1924–1926 were relatively serene; her volume of poetry was doing well, and her reputation was spreading. She had friends who needed her, and finances were less worrisome. Anne returned to her painting, but she became ill and was diagnosed with liver cancer. In 1927 Charlotte spent all spring with Anne at a nursing home; Anne died on 18 June. The sisters had been parted for only a few weeks in fifty years, so Anne's death was a terrible blow to Charlotte. Hardy died in January 1928, and she grieved for him. Cockerell found a copy that Hardy had made of her poem "Fin de Fête," which he presented to Mew.

The Poetry Bookshop was failing, and Mew saw little of the Monros in 1928. Her behavior became more and more eccentric. She tormented herself that Anne might have been buried alive or that the little black specks in the studio might have been the cause of Anne's death. A specialist said that Charlotte could not be certified mentally incompetent, but her doctor did recommend a nursing home. She isolated herself in the miserably furnished back room of the nursing home for days. On 24 March she went out to buy a bottle of Lysol, the cheapest poison available, and killed herself. She had asked to be buried in the same grave as Anne. Beneath the inscription in memory of Anne, there is another: "Here also lies her sister, Charlotte Mary Mew." The self-effacement and insecurities of Charlotte's life are poignantly captured in these lines.

Mew's contribution to short fiction is small but distinctive. Little critical attention has been paid to her stories, but there are gems among the eighteen extant works. The same traits that have made her a well-known poet — realistic detail, striking poetic language, and memorable characterization — make her stories worth reading.

Biography:

Penelope Fitzgerald, *Charlotte Mew and Her Friends* (London: Collins, 1984; Reading, Mass.: Addison-Wesley, 1988).

References:

Theophilus Boll, "The Mystery of Charlotte Mew and May Sinclair: An Inquiry," *New York Public Library Bulletin,* 74 (September 1970): 445–453;

Shelley Jean Crisp, "The Woman Poet Emerges: The Literary Tradition of Mary Coleridge, Alice Meynell, and Charlotte Mew," Ph.D. dissertation, University of Massachusetts, 1987;

Mary C. Davidow, "Charlotte Mew and the Shadow of Thomas Hardy," *Bulletin of Research in the Humanities,* 81 (Winter 1978): 437–447;

Davidow, "The Charlotte Mew–May Sinclair Relationship: A Reply," *New York Public Library Bulletin,* 75 (March 1971): 295–300;

Linda Mizejewski, "Charlotte Mew and the Unrepentant Magdalene: A Myth in Transition," *Texas Studies in Literature,* 26 (Fall 1984): 282–302;

Alida Monro, "Charlotte Mew – A Memoir," in Mew's *Collected Poems* (London: Duckworth, 1953; New York: Macmillan, 1954);

Val Warner, "Mary Magdalene and the Bride: The Work of Charlotte Mew," *Poetry Nation,* 4 (1975): 92–106.

Papers:

Mew's papers are in the British Library, the Lockwood Memorial Library at the University of Buffalo, and the Berg Collection at the New York Public Library.

Louisa Molesworth

(29 May 1839 – 20 July 1921)

Linda Anne Julian
Furman University

BOOKS: *Lover and Husband,* as Ennis Graham, 3 volumes (London: Skeet, 1870);

She Was Young and He Was Old, as Graham, 3 volumes (London: Tinsley, 1872);

Not Without Thorns, as Graham (3 volumes, London: Tinsley, 1873; 1 volume, Boston: Osgood, 1873);

Cicely: A Story of Three Years, as Graham, 3 volumes (London: Tinsley, 1874);

Tell Me a Story, as Graham (London: Macmillan, 1875; New York: Macmillan, 1893);

"Carrots": Just a Little Boy, as Graham (London: Macmillan, 1876); as Mary Louisa Molesworth (London: Macmillan, 1879; New York: Burt, 1890?);

The Cuckoo Clock, as Graham (London: Macmillan, 1877); as Mary Louisa Molesworth (New York: Caldwell, 1877?; London: Macmillan, 1882);

Hathercourt Rectory, 3 volumes (London: Hurst & Blackett, 1878); republished as *Hathercourt* (New York: Holt, 1878);

Grandmother Dear: A Book for Boys and Girls (New York: Burt, n.d.; London: Macmillan, 1878);

The Tapestry Room: A Child's Romance (London: Macmillan, 1879; New York: Burt, 1879);

Miss Bouverie, 3 volumes (London: Hurst & Blackett, 1880);

A Christmas Child: A Sketch of a Boy-Life (London: Macmillan, 1880);

Hermy: The Story of a Little Girl (London: Routledge, 1881);

The Adventures of Herr Baby (London: Macmillan, 1881; New York: Macmillan, 1886);

Hoodie (London: Routledge, 1882);

Summer Stories for Boys and Girls (London: Macmillan, 1882);

Rosy (London: Macmillan, 1882; New York: Macmillan, 1896);

Two Little Waifs (London: Macmillan, 1883; New York: Macmillan, 1890);

Louisa Molesworth

Lettice (London: Society for Promoting Christian Knowledge, 1884; New York: Young, 1884);

The Little Old Portrait (London: Society for Promoting Christian Knowledge, 1884); republished as *Edmée: A Tale of the French Revolution* (London: Macmillan, 1916);

Christmas-tree Land (London: Macmillan, 1884); republished in *Christmas-tree Land and A Christmas Posy* (New York & London: Macmillan, 1893);

Us: An Old-Fashioned Story (London: Macmillan, 1885; New York: Harper, 1885);

A Charge Fulfilled (London: Society for Promoting Christian Knowledge, 1886);

Silverthorns (London: Hatchards, 1886; New York: Dutton, 1900?);

The Abbey by the Sea (London: Society for Promoting Christian Knowledge, 1886);

Four Winds Farm (London: Macmillan, 1887);

Marrying and Giving in Marriage (New York: Hurst, n.d.; London: Longmans, 1887);

The Palace in the Garden (London: Hatchards, 1887; New York: Whittaker, 1887);

Little Miss Peggy: Only a Nursery Story (London: Macmillan, 1887; New York: Burt, 1891?);

Four Ghost Stories (London: Macmillan, 1888);

Five Minutes' Stories (London: Society for Promoting Christian Knowledge, 1888);

The Third Miss St. Quentin (New York: Whittaker, 1888; London: Hatchards, 1889);

A Christmas Posy (London: Macmillan, 1888); republished in *Christmas-tree Land and A Christmas Posy*;

French Life in Letters (London & New York: Macmillan, 1889);

That Girl in Black, and Bronzie (London: Chatto & Windus, 1889; New York: Lovell, 1889);

Nesta: Or Fragments of a Little Life (London: Chambers, 1889);

Neighbours (London: Hatchards, 1889; New York: Whittaker, 1890);

Great Uncle Hoot-Toot (London: Society for Promoting Christian Knowledge, 1889);

The Old Pincushion, or Aunt Clotilda's Guests (London: Farran, 1889; New York: Dutton, 1890);

A House to Let (London: Society for Promoting Christian Knowledge, 1889);

The Rectory Children (London: Macmillan, 1889);

Little Mother Bunch (London: Cassell, 1890);

The Green Casket, and Other Stories (London: Chambers, 1890);

Family Troubles (London: Society for Promoting Christian Knowledge, 1890; New York: Young, 1890);

The Story of a Spring Morning, and Other Tales (London & New York: Longmans, Green, 1890);

The Children of the Castle (London: Macmillan, 1890);

Twelve Tiny Tales (London: Society for Promoting Christian Knowledge, 1890?);

The Red Grange (London: Methuen, 1891; New York: Whittaker, 1891);

Sweet Content (London: Farran, 1891; New York: Dutton, 1891?);

The Bewitched Lamp (London: Chambers, 1891);

The Lucky Ducks, and Other Stories (London: Society for Promoting Christian Knowledge, 1891);

Nurse Heatherdale's Story (London: Macmillan, 1891); republished in *Nurse Heatherdale's Story and Little Miss Peggy* (New York & London: Macmillan, 1893);

The Man with the Pan Pipes, and Other Stories (London: Society for Promoting Christian Knowledge, 1892);

Leona (London & New York: Cassell, 1892);

An Enchanted Garden: Fairy Stories (London: Unwin, 1892; New York: Cassell, 1892);

Imogen, or Only Eighteen (London: Chambers, 1892; New York: Whittaker, 1892);

Stories of the Saints for Children (London: Longmans, 1892);

Farthings: The Story of a Stray and a Waif (London: Gardner, Darton, 1892; New York: Young, 1892);

Robin Redbreast: A Story for Girls (London: Chambers, 1892; New York: Burt, 1892);

The Girls and I: A Veracious History (London: Macmillan, 1892);

Studies and Stories (London: Innes, 1893);

The Next-Door House (London: Chambers, 1893; New York: Cassell, 1893);

The Thirteen Little Black Pigs, and Other Stories (London: Society for Promoting Christian Knowledge, 1893; New York: Burt, 1901);

Mary: A Nursery Story for Very Little Children (New York & London: Macmillan, 1893);

Blanche: A Story for Girls (London: Chambers, 1894);

My New Home (London: Macmillan, 1894; New York: Macmillan, 1898);

Olivia: A Story for Girls (London: Chambers, 1894; Philadelphia: Lippincott, 1895);

Opposite Neighbours, and Other Stories (London: Society for Promoting Christian Knowledge, 1895);

The Carved Lions (London: Macmillan, 1895);

White Turrets (London: Chambers, 1895; New York: Whittaker, 1895);

Friendly Joey, and Other Stories (London: Society for Promoting Christian Knowledge, 1896);

Uncanny Tales (London: Hutchinson, 1896; New York: Longmans, Green, 1896);

The Oriel Window (London & New York: Macmillan, 1896);

Phillipa (London: Chambers, 1896; Philadelphia: Lippincott, 1896);

Stories for Children in Illustration of the Lord's Prayer (London: Gardner, Darton, 1897);

Meg Langhome, or The Day After Tomorrow (London: Chambers / Philadelphia: Lippincott, 1897);

Miss Mouse and Her Boys (London & New York: Macmillan, 1897);

The Laurel Walk (London: Isbister, 1898; Philadelphia: Biddle, 1898);

Greyling Towers: A Story for the Young (London: Chambers, 1898);

The Magic Nuts (London: Macmillan, 1898; Philadelphia: Altemus, 1899?);

The Grim House (London: Nisbet, 1899);

This and That: A Tale of Two Tinies (London: Macmillan, 1899);

The Children's Hour (London: Nelson, 1899);

The Three Witches (London: Chambers, 1900);

The House That Grew (London: Macmillan, 1900);

My Pretty and Her Little Brother Too, and Other Stories (London: Chambers, 1901; New York: Dutton, 1901);

The Blue Baby, and Other Stories (London: Unwin, 1901);

The Wood-Pigeons and Mary (London & New York: Macmillan, 1901);

Peterkin (London & New York: Macmillan, 1902);

The Mystery of the Pinewood and Hollow Tree House (London: Nister, 1903);

The Ruby Ring (London: Macmillan, 1904);

The Bolted Door, and Other Stories (London: Chambers, 1906);

The Wrong Envelope, and Other Stories (London: Macmillan, 1906);

Jasper: A Story for Children (London: Macmillan, 1906);

The Little Guest: A Story for Children (London: Macmillan, 1907);

Fairies – Of Sorts (London: Macmillan, 1908);

The February Boys: A Story for Children (London: Chambers, 1909; New York: Dutton, 1909?);

The Story of a Year (London: Macmillan, 1910);

Fairies Afield (London: Macmillan, 1911).

OTHER: Contribution, in *The Art of Authorship: Literary Reminiscences, Methods of Work, and Advice to Young Beginners,* edited by George Bainton (London: Clarke, 1890), pp. 93-96;

"For the Little Ones – 'Food, Fun, and Fresh Air,'" in *Women's Mission: Papers on the Philanthropic Work of Women,* edited by Baroness Burdett-Coutts (New York: Scribners, 1893), pp. 13-34.

SELECTED PERIODICAL PUBLICATIONS – UNCOLLECTED:
FICTION
"The Sealskin Purse," *Longman's,* 19 (February 1892): 389-406;

"The Man with the Cough," *Longman's,* 23 (March 1894): 506-520;

"Halfway Between the Stiles," *Longman's,* 25 (February 1895): 374-387.

NONFICTION
"Juliana Horatia Ewing," *Contemporary Review,* 49 (May 1886): 675-686;

"Story Reading and Story Writing," *Chambers Journal* (5 November 1898).

As a writer of short fiction for adults, Louisa Molesworth is little known, her accomplishments in this genre greatly overshadowed by her fame as a writer for children. Of the 101 books she published, only a handful are for adults: several novels and collections of stories. At the zenith of her success, she received letters from children around the world, including the crown prince of Naples (the future Victor Emmanuel III), who wrote to say that her *"Carrots": Just a Little Boy* (1876) had enabled him to survive the period of mourning for the death of his grandfather Victor Emmanuel II. The *Westminster Budget* (20 December 1893) reported that Alexandra, Princess of Wales, had read six of Molesworth's books to her children. Yet today even her children's stories are not well known, perhaps because the didactic tone is not palatable a century later and because her kind of fairy tales has been supplanted by stories whose characters are products of toy manufacturers and animation. An understanding of what has come to be called the golden age of children's literature, however, demands attention to her work; and her adult fiction, while less skillful than her children's books, comments in interesting ways on the middle-class view of the late-Victorian and Edwardian world.

Mary Louisa Stewart was born in Rotterdam, where she lived until about age two. Her parents, Agnes Janet Wilson Stewart and Charles Augustus Stewart were from Scotland. They settled in Manchester, where her father was involved in the shipping business, eventually becoming a senior partner in the firm of Robert Barbour Brothers. The family, including three sons and three daughters, lived in Manchester for twelve years and then in one of its suburbs for the next eight years.

Details of Molesworth's early life are sketchy. She began to write and tell stories at a young age, and in her teens she published some stories in periodicals. During Molesworth's yearly visits to Scotland, her grandmother Wilson filled her mind with stories; Molesworth credited her grandmother's talents as a storyteller with awakening her own. Other early influences on her fiction were her voracious reading and her experiences in school in Switzerland, which followed schooling at home by her mother and perhaps at a school in Manchester. She may have been tutored by the Reverend William Gaskell, husband of the novelist Elizabeth Gaskell. The stifling Calvinistic environment of her youth was a negative influence, leading her to resolve that she would work to avoid teaching children a religion based on fear. All of these factors contributed to a style that helped create a new kind of children's literature, one that considered the problems which middle-class children confronted.

In 1861, when she was twenty-two, Louisa married Maj. Richard Molesworth of the Royal Dragoons. After being stationed in Dublin, Birmingham, and Aldershot before 1864, they lived at Tabley Grange, near Knutsford in Cheshire, for five years. Six years before their marriage Major Molesworth had received a severe head wound during a battle in Crimea. This injury, from which all of the shrapnel was not removed, was later considered the cause of the temper flashes that contributed to the disintegration of the marriage and the couple's separation in 1879. Of their seven children, five survived to adulthood: Cicely, born in 1863; Juliet, born in 1865; Olive, born in 1867; Richard Bevil, born in 1870; and Lionel Charles, born in 1873. Their first son, Richard Walter Stewart, died in 1869 at the age of thirteen weeks; their first child, Violet, died in 1869 of scarlet fever.

Roger Lancelyn Green, whose 1961 monograph on Molesworth is still the most substantial source of information about her life and work, suggests that her grief over the deaths of Violet and Charles drew her into writing her first novel, *Lover and Husband* (1870), a three-volume work published under the pseudonym Ennis Graham. (Graham, the daughter of an explorer, was a friend who had died in Africa.) Neither this novel nor the three that followed – *She Was Young and He Was Old* (1872), *Not Without Thorns* (1873), and *Cicely: A Story of Three Years* (1874), each in three volumes – attracted much attention. These novels share the theme of unhappiness in marriage.

Molesworth likely would have continued to write novels except for the surprising reception of *Tell Me a Story* (1875), her first book for children. "I don't know that I should have thought of publishing the stories I wrote for my children if it had not been for a suggestion of my friend Sir Noel Paton," she remarked in the *Westminster Budget* (20 October 1893). "He seemed to think I had a power of making children interested and happy, and by his advice I sent something to one of the publishers, not really at that time caring much whether it was accepted or not. It was 'Tell Me a Story,' and it *was* accepted by Macmillan. Since then, for the last 18 years, this firm have had one every year." Molesworth had been telling stories to her children for years. She began writing them down and reading to her children from her manuscripts, which she carefully hid between the covers of a book so that the children would not know the stories were hers and would thus give honest criticism.

Tell Me a Story – illustrated by Walter Crane, who was to work on many of her books – contains six stories. The first two, "The Reel Fairies" and "Good-night, Winny," seem autobiographical. "Good-night, Winny" bears a striking resemblance to the circumstances surrounding the death of Molesworth's daughter Violet. "The Reel Fairies," whose main character is named Louisa, describes an introverted, serious child whose favorite playthings are the spools that hold the thread in her mother's workbox. The spools become fairies, who take Louisa away in the workbox to fairyland. She is at first delighted, as she is dressed like a queen and set on a throne, but she quickly becomes bored and tired and wants to go home "to my mamma." The fairies resist, she calls them "horrid little things," and she awakes crying out for her mother, who learns from her dream that Louisa has felt ugly and in need of attention. This story teaches Louisa a lesson when her mother reassures her that her appearance has nothing to do with the great love her mother has for her. The lesson here, however, is subordinate to an imaginative story that has touches of humor. Molesworth's didacticism becomes more dominant in later stories, in spite of her view that moral instruction should be subtle.

Molesworth's second children's book, *"Carrots": Just a Little Boy,* signaled a new kind of realism in children's literature. Rather than presenting magical adventures or fantasy, it invites the reader to share the day-to-day happenings in a middle-class family. One of her most famous books, *"Carrots"* had sold more than fourteen thousand copies by the early 1880s. Its central character, Fabian, called "Carrots" because of his red hair, is the youngest of six children, a baby at the beginning of the story and six and seven years old for most of it. Cared for by his loving older sister, Floss, Carrots struggles to learn about money, the serious consequences when one does not fully understand words, and the illness of his mother.

Interspersed in the episodes that Floss and Carrots experience are stories that they are read or told by their nurse, their older sister, or their aunt

Sybil. These stories within the story likely would be disruptive to a child interested in the problems of Carrots and Floss. Another technique that some critics have seen as a weakness in *"Carrots"* and other of Molesworth's children's books is her attempt to reproduce the speech of children realistically. For example, in *"Carrots"* Floss says, "Hair somesing like my hairs"; Carrots asks, "When will you have thinkened enough, Floss?"; and Carrots says, "I didn't touch nurse's drawer, nor nucken in it." Molesworth does not write down to children; on the contrary, she believed that the careful use of big words was worthwhile because children could figure out their meaning from the context and thus increase their vocabularies.

Another technique in *"Carrots"* that recurs in Molesworth's children's books is her habit of having the narrator directly address the child listeners, obviously reminding them of the difference between reality and story and frequently giving moral instruction. For example, in describing Carrots, the narrator says:

> It was all *there* — the root of all goodness, cleverness, and manliness — just as in the acorn there is the oak; but of course it had a great deal of *growing* before it, and, more than mere growing, it would need all the care and watchful tenderness and wise directing that could be given it, just as the acorn needs all the rain and sunshine and good nourishing soil it can get, to become a fine oak, straight and strong and beautiful. For what do I mean by "it," children? I mean the "own self" of Carrots, the wonderful "something" in the little childish frame which the wisest of all the wise men of either long ago or now-a-days have never yet been able to describe — the "soul," children, which is in you all, which may grow into so beautiful, so lovely and perfect a thing; which may, alas! be twisted and stunted and starved out of all likeness to the "image" in which it was created.

"Carrots" also includes several allusions to the Bible, at least one of them identified as such by Carrots and Floss. Molesworth, a moderate Anglican, attempted to teach Christian values through her stories, many of which were published by the Society for Promoting Christian Knowledge.

Molesworth's most famous children's book, *The Cuckoo Clock,* was published in 1877, the year after *"Carrots",* and it went through many printings up to 1945. A charming, lively story, its moral lessons are subordinate to the bizarre adventures that befall Griselda, a little girl who has gone to live with her two great-aunts in a strange house. Her adventures are orchestrated by the cuckoo from the clock that presides over the room where Griselda does her lessons with her tutor, Mr. Kneebreeches. The cuckoo comes to life, a curmudgeonly taskmaster who takes Griselda to Butterfly-Land, the land of the Mandarians, and the Other Side of the Moon, all the while muttering to her the words she hates to hear: "You have a *very* great deal to learn!" The solitary acquaintance of the motherless Griselda, whose father and brothers are "across the sea," the cuckoo leaves her once she has become friends with Phil, a little boy from a nearby estate.

"Carrots", The Cuckoo Clock, and many other books by Molesworth represent a distinctly new kind of writing. Children's literature, although not a new genre, underwent a major transformation in the mid to late nineteenth century as childhood itself was validated as a time when children should in fact *be* children, not careworn miniature adults. Fairy tales continued to play a large role in children's literature: from 1823 to 1826 the stories of Jacob and Wilhelm Grimm were published in English and illustrated by George Cruikshank; the tales of Hans Christian Andersen were translated from midcentury on. Such English writers as John Ruskin, William Makepeace Thackeray, Andrew Lang, and George Macdonald wrote fairy tales, as did Molesworth.

Bible stories and didactic stories, many intended to indoctrinate children with the views of particular religious groups, were still written, but these types were less in vogue than in the seventeenth and eighteenth centuries. Molesworth wrote some of these (*Stories for Children in Illustration of the Lord's Prayer,* 1897 and *Stories of the Saints for Children,* 1892, for example) although she approved of the movement away from overly didactic literature. For the first time authors began to write stories directed especially either to boys or girls. Fantasy and adventure stories flourished. Lewis Carroll, Juliana Horatia Ewing, Charlotte Yonge, W. H. G. Kingston, R. M. Ballantyne, Kenneth Grahame, Edith Nesbit, and Robert Louis Stevenson were some of the many writers who, along with Molesworth, flooded the market with stories for children, an audience newly encouraged to indulge in the *pleasure* of reading instead of reading for the sake of the information that could be absorbed from it.

So many writers were producing children's books that Molesworth commented in an essay, "Story Reading and Story Writing" (*Chambers Journal,* 5 November 1898), that "there are far too many children's books nowadays." She goes on to say that the quality of children's books has been declining because too many are plot-centered to the exclusion of creating real sympathy for the characters. She states that creating characters whom children can really love reveals an author whose sympathies are in tune with the development of children. She also says that children's books should not make children unduly sad; however, they should not deceive children about the sober concerns of the world. She advises against using fright to advance the plot or interest in a story.

One of Molesworth's major concerns about children's literature was that people confused writing *for* children with writing *about* them. She also bristled at the frequency with which her contemporaries viewed writing for children as a dress rehearsal for producing adult works. The *Westminster Budget* (20 October 1893) quotes her as saying, "I don't think that a child under eight or ten years gets much harm from anything it reads ... but I do think too much care and selection cannot be made in the reading of young people between the ages of 10 and 18." In the essay "Juliana Horatia Ewing" (*Contemporary Review,* May 1886), she points out that careless writing for children is a serious matter because "the evil such may do can *never* be undone." It is ironic that Molesworth complained about the surfeit of children's books when she turned out several a year. The declining quality of her books from about 1885 to 1895 seems to be related to the speed with which they were written.

Molesworth's habits as a writer reveal a surprising rigidity. As a contributor to *The Art of Authorship: Literary Reminiscences, Methods of Work, and Advice to Young Beginners* (1890), Molesworth writes that she began to develop her style by translating French and German, writing essays on narrowly focused topics, and reading aloud to friends and family to test her success. She says that she learned never to rewrite, though she realized that many writers would disagree with this method. Instead, she believed that formulating sentences once and for all in the mind leads to more careful thought and a more energetic style — and less physical exertion — than rewriting. She forced herself to write at least two pages daily, whether or not she felt inspired.

Until the early 1880s Molesworth continued to write novels for adults. Following *The Cuckoo Clock,* which was published while the Molesworths were living in Edinburgh, was her fifth three-volume novel, *Hathercourt Rectory* (1878), the sentimental story of Mary and Lilias Western, daughters of a poor rector, and their affairs of the heart. Molesworth then produced two children's books, *Grandmother Dear: A Book for Boys and Girls* (1878) and *The Tapestry Room: A Child's Romance*

(1879), the latter set in Normandy. These are among her most widely read books. Another three-volume novel, *Miss Bouverie* (1880), was followed the same year by *A Christmas Child: A Sketch of a Boy-Life.* During the next five years some of her most popular works were published, including *The Adventures of Herr Baby* (1881) and *Hoodie* (1882), which are about her own children. By 1879, when she and Major Molesworth separated, she and the children and her mother were residing in Caen. She continued to live in France and in Germany for several years, settling permanently in England in 1883. Several of her children's stories and adult stories are set in France and Germany.

After returning to England she wrote only a few more novels, including *Marrying and Giving in Marriage* (1887). Like her earlier novels, these are sentimental, and *Marrying and Giving in Marriage* is typical of her work in this genre. It relates the fortunes of Aveline Verney, a young Englishwoman living in Paris with her family. She is manipulated by her social-climbing mother into accepting the proposal of Wilfred Ayrton, the rich son of her mother's close friend, in order to save the family from financial ruin. Wilfred, a womanizer with a drinking problem, is coarse and brutish. Finally Aveline marries Nigel Hereward, a poor but worthy suitor, and Wilfred elopes with a wealthy American. The book's mawkishness makes it unpalatable today.

More enjoyable, though thoroughly predictable, is *That Girl in Black* (1889), a novella first published with the short story "Bronzie" and seventeen years later included with "Bronzie" in *The Wrong Envelope, and Other Stories* (1906). In *That Girl in Black* the arrogant bachelor Despard Norreys attends many parties at which he keeps running into the same woman, Maisie Ford, who always wears black. At the first party she overhears his brutally condescending appraisal of her appearance and conversational ability. The story's charm results from the verbal fencing of the two in subsequent meetings, and his patronizing attitude toward her begins to melt into warmth and admiration. Eventually, Maisie, who is really Lady Margaret, daughter of Lord Southwold, marries him. The story attacks pretentiousness and snobbishness, subjects of several other stories by Molesworth.

"Bronzie," a more juvenile story, is similar in plot to *That Girl in Black.* A schoolboy seated at the back of a church focuses on the beautiful reddish-gold hair of a young woman near the front, never seeing her face. Later, haunted by the beauty of the hair — and, by extension, the girl — he begins to call

Title page for Molesworth's 1896 collection of ghost stories

her "Bronzie" in his dreams. He sees her from afar on another occasion. Several years later, as the houseguest of an old school friend, he finally meets "Bronzie," but not without first being mistakenly led to believe that his friend has married her.

These stories, along with her three other tales in *The Wrong Envelope,* show Molesworth's penchant for the surprise ending and the use of coincidence, although she employs them with varying degrees of success. The surprise ending to the title story is delightful. A mix-up in envelopes allows John Alured to read unflattering remarks about himself written by Irene Brandon, with whom he has fallen in love. Months after the two have been distanced by escalating misunderstandings following on the heels of the first one, Alured discovers that the *he* referred to in "the wrong envelope" is a dachshund.

Juxtaposed to this lighthearted story is "Wanted – A Hero," which turns on the irony that the man whom Hermione perceives as dull and unheroic ultimately dies while saving a child from an accident. The final story in this collection, "A

Strange Messenger," is one of Molesworth's many ghost stories. The "strange messenger" is the ghost of Brough, a dead Welsh miner, which appears at the doctor's door to summon him to the aid of Mr. Heald, a mining manager who showed unusual kindness to Brough as he lay dying months before.

Two collections of Molesworth's ghost stories for adults are *Four Ghost Stories* (1888) and *Uncanny Tales* (1896). Never macabre, these stories skillfully create great suspense but then flatten it by introducing ambiguity. This ambiguity is suggested by the title of one of her best ghost stories, "Unexplained," first published in *Macmillan's* in 1885 and then included in *Four Ghost Stories.* This story, which may be based on a trip Molesworth took in Thuringia with two of her children, traces the walking tour of a woman named Nora and her two children. The three travelers go to the remote village of Silberbach, Germany, where the daughter sees the ghost of a pale young man. Many months later they learn that it was probably the spirit of a young man who was killed by lightning in the forest near

Silberbach, but why the ghost appears to Nora on the second anniversary of the young man's death remains unexplained. Molesworth carefully builds suspense by suggesting that the residents of Silberbach are implicated in his death. She suggests a connection between a rare china teacup the young man bought shortly before his death and a matching one purchased by the narrator. The lack of resolution adds to the power of the story.

This same sort of ambiguity undergirds one of Molesworth's most interesting stories, "The Man with the Cough" (*Longman's,* March 1894) – not a ghost story, though it is tinged with the eerie. Here Molesworth writes convincingly from a man's first-person point of view as she tells the story of a patent engineer who is nearly the victim of theft as he struggles to deliver valuable documents from Germany to England. Followed by a sinister man with a cough, the narrator, Schmidt, finds it difficult to distinguish between his dream of being waylaid and robbed and the reality that his documents are intact and he is on time.

Molesworth treats the theme of social pretense in several stories, but never better than in "The Sealskin Purse" (*Longman's,* February 1892). Here Nora Mallory, whose recent marriage has enabled her to move from the lower- to the upper-middle class, accuses a dowdy young woman who appears to be her social inferior of stealing her purse on the train. Her despicable behavior toward the accused ultimately humiliates her when she learns that the young woman is Cecil Wode, daughter of Lord Mavor, and it causes her to lose favor with her husband and her aristocratic cousin. Molesworth realistically depicts both the pretentious Nora and the abused Cecil.

Although Molesworth occasionally produced stories for adults during the 1880s and 1890s, children's books remained her major interest. Her final six books were for children; the last one, *Fairies Afield,* was published in 1911. She died of heart failure ten years later. The obituary in the London *Times* (22 July 1921) commemorated her as one who gave "happy hours to childhood" for half a century, remarking that "though now children's books come yearly in hundreds, Mrs. Molesworth's have not yet been superseded and very likely never will be." As the twentieth century progressed, however, her children's books were superseded and her novels and adult stories generally forgotten. It is unlikely that any of her work, except for five or six of her best children's stories, will regain an audience.

References:

Roger Lancelyn Green, *Mrs. Molesworth* (London: Bodley Head, 1961; New York: Walck, 1964);

Green, *Tellers of Tales* (London: Ward, 1946);

Marghanita Laski, *Mrs. Ewing , Mrs. Molesworth, and Mrs. Hodgson Burnett* (New York: Oxford University Press, 1951);

"A Popular Writer for Children: Mrs. Molesworth," *Westminster Budget* (20 October 1893): 24;

Sarah A. Tooley, "Mrs. Molesworth," in *Some Women Novelists* (London: Warwick Magazine, 1897);

Bella Sydney Woolf, "Mrs. Molesworth and 'Carrots'," *Quiver,* 41 (June 1906): 674–676.

Papers:

Some of Molesworth's letters are in the British Library.

George Moore

(24 February 1852 – 21 January 1933)

Jack W. Weaver
Winthrop University

See also the Moore entries in *DLB 10: Modern British Dramatists, 1900–1945; DLB 18: Victorian Novelists After 1885;* and *DLB 57: Victorian Prose Writers After 1867.*

SELECTED BOOKS: *A Modern Lover* (3 volumes, London: Tinsley, 1883; 1 volume, Chicago: Laird & Lee, 1890);

A Mummer's Wife (London: Vizetelly, 1885); republished as *An Actor's Wife* (Chicago: Laird & Lee, 1889);

Literature at Nurse, or Circulating Morals (London: Vizetelly, 1885);

A Drama in Muslin: A Realistic Novel (London: Vizetelly, 1886);

Parnell and His Island (London: Sonnenschein, Lowrey, 1887);

A Mere Accident (London: Vizetelly, 1887; New York: Brentano's, 1887);

Confessions of a Young Man (London: Sonnenschein, Lowrey, 1888; New York: Brentano's, 1888);

Mike Fletcher: A Novel (London: Ward & Downey, 1889; New York: Minerva, 1889);

Impressions and Opinions (London: Nutt, 1891; New York: Brentano's, 1913);

Modern Painting (London: Scott, 1893; New York: Scribners, 1893);

Esther Waters: A Novel (London: Scott, 1894; Chicago & New York: Stone, 1894);

Celibates (London: Scott, 1895; New York: Macmillan, 1895);

Evelyn Innes (London: Unwin, 1898; New York: Appleton, 1898);

Sister Teresa (London: Unwin, 1901; Philadelphia: Lippincott, 1901);

An T-Ur-Gort (Dublin: Sealy, Bryers & Walker, 1902); republished in English as *The Untilled Field* (London: Unwin, 1903; Philadelphia: Lippincott, 1903);

The Lake (London: Heinemann, 1905; New York: Appleton, 1906);

George Moore, circa 1887

Memoirs of My Dead Life (London: Heinemann, 1906; New York: Appleton, 1907);

Reminiscences of the Impressionist Painters (Dublin: Maunsel, 1906);

Hail and Farewell: A Trilogy, 3 volumes (London: Heinemann, 1911–1914; New York: Appleton, 1911–1914);

The Brook Kerith: A Syrian Story (Edinburgh: Laurie, 1916; New York: Macmillan, 1916);

234

A Story-Teller's Holiday (London & New York: Cumann Sean-eolais na h-Eireann, 1918; revised edition, 2 volumes, London: Heinemann, 1928);

Avowals (London: Cumann Sean-eolais na h-Eireann, 1919; New York: Boni & Liveright, 1919);

Héloise and Abélard (2 volumes, London: Cumann Sean-eolais na h-Eireann, 1921; 1 volume, New York: Boni & Liveright, 1921);

In Single Strictness (London: Heinemann, 1922; New York: Boni & Liveright, 1922); republished as *Celibate Lives* (London: Heinemann, 1927; New York: Boni & Liveright, 1927);

Conversations in Ebury Street (London: Heinemann, 1924; New York: Boni & Liveright, 1924);

Peronnik the Fool (New York: Boni & Liveright, 1924; London: Heinemann, 1933);

Pure Poetry: An Anthology (London: Nonesuch, 1924; New York: Boni & Liveright, 1924);

Ulick and Soracha (London: Nonesuch, 1926; New York: Boni & Liveright, 1926);

A Flood (New York: Harbor Press, 1930);

Aphrodite in Aulis (London: Heinemann, 1930; New York: Fountain Press, 1930).

Collections: *The Collected Works of George Moore,* Carra Edition, 21 volumes (New York: Boni & Liveright, 1922-1924);

Works of George Moore, Uniform Edition, 20 volumes (London: Heinemann, 1924-1933; New York: Brentano's, 1924-1933);

In Minor Keys: The Uncollected Stories of George Moore, edited, with an introduction, by Helmut E. Gerber and David B. Eakin (Syracuse: Syracuse University Press, 1985).

TRANSLATION: *The Pastoral Loves of Daphnis and Chloe: Done in English,* translated by Moore from the story by Longus and based on the 1559 translation by Jacques Amyot (London: Heinemann, 1924).

George Moore's writing holds an important place between Victorian and modernist literature. While scholars recognize that 1880-1920 was a period of transition, some are still uncomfortable with Moore. A man of letters who worked in many literary genres, he should be remembered for his achievements as an art and theater critic, a novelist, and a writer of short fiction and memoirs. Since he had opinions on most topics, one can argue that he is at his best as a memorialist, in such works as *Confessions of a Young Man* (1888), *Memoirs of My Dead Life* (1906), *Hail and Farewell* (1911-1914), and *Conversations in Ebury Street* (1924). Many of these use the "imaginary conversation" device popularized by William Hazlitt and Thomas De Quincey, mix reverie and narration, and freely fictionalize to make events and people more interesting.

Self-conscious attempts at art rather than truth, these memoirs introduce a host of literary figures – William Butler Yeats, Lady Augusta Gregory, Douglas Hyde, John Millington Synge, and AE (George William Russell), to name a few. James Joyce was at least partially inspired by *Confessions of a Young Man* to write *A Portrait of the Artist as a Young Man* (1916) and may have used details from *Hail and Farewell* in *Ulysses* (1922). Moore's example also inspired Oliver St. John Gogarty's *As I Was Going Down Sackville Street* (1937) and Sean O'Casey's autobiographical trilogy (1939-1954). Moore's parodies of Yeats in many of the memoirs led to Yeats's equally satiric pictures of Moore in *Dramatis Personae* (1935) and portions of the *Autobiographies* (1955). As AE is supposed to have remarked, "A renaissance is a literary movement in which you hate each other cordially."

Other problems for critics include Moore's long, productive career (1882-1933), which spans the late-Victorian and early-modern periods, and his refusal to be limited to a single form or style. Known for his novels as well as his memoirs, Moore began as a practitioner of the Zolaesque naturalist tradition in *A Modern Lover* (1883) and perfected it in *A Mummer's Wife* (1885). He adopted the realism of Honoré de Balzac in *A Drama in Muslin* (1886) and emulated the detached viewpoint and careful craftsmanship of another realist, Gustave Flaubert, in *Esther Waters* (1894). While *Esther Waters* was favorably compared to Thomas Hardy's greater but more sentimental *Tess of the d'Urbervilles* (1891), Moore continued to experiment with style.

In keeping with his interest in symbolism and the symbolist movement in France, he began to blend narrative and reverie in a musical way. Beginning with *Evelyn Innes* (1898), a novel about an opera singer, and its sequel, *Sister Teresa* (1901), Moore began to experiment with musical modulations in fiction. In *The Lake* (1905), *The Brook Kerith* (1916), *Héloise and Abélard* (1921), *The Pastoral Loves of Daphnis and Chloe* (1924), and *Aphrodite in Aulis* (1930), he moves easily from action to narration to description, achieving a fluidity of expression, a blend of style and subject matter that he called his "melodic line." In his use of stream of consciousness, which the melodic line often necessitated, Moore anticipated both Joyce and Virginia Woolf, and his use of melodic structures served as an example for E. M. Forster. For these accomplishments

Helmut E. Gerber places Moore on Parnassus and admires the rich tapestry of the writings, stating, "Moore is better than the critics say." That betterness deserves to be measured.

George Augustus Moore was born on 24 February 1852 to George Henry Moore and Mary Blake Moore in Moore Hall, County Mayo, Ireland. As heir to a considerable estate, he was given private tutoring until 1861, when he was placed in Oscott, a Jesuit school. In *Confessions of a Young Man* he describes conflicts with his teachers and his removal at the suggestion of the headmaster. In "Salve," the second volume of *Hail and Farewell,* he remembers being pandied by the Jesuits, an anticipation of Stephen Dedalus's plight in *A Portrait of the Artist as a Young Man.*

Moore does not describe the self-education, the desultory reading, that followed his expulsion, but he alludes to it in various works and probably makes it seem more disorganized than it actually was. George Henry Moore was bookish and had a good library. He was elected to Parliament in 1868, which necessitated the family's move to London and provided additional cultural advantages for George, especially the theater. His father died in 1870, which assured George of a sizable annual income – about five hundred pounds upon his majority. After turning twenty-one in 1873, he set out for Paris to study painting.

The Paris years are described fully, if somewhat fancifully, in *Confessions of a Young Man,* which should be read with Joseph Hone's biography (1936). Moore managed to meet many important people in Paris, including Stéphane Mallarmé, Edouard Manet, Claude Monet, Edgar Degas, Georges Seurat, Ivan Turgenev, and Emile Zola. Moore discussed aesthetic theory in the cafés and discovered that he was not destined to be a successful painter. Perhaps because he was adept at talking, he turned to writing, cultivated the outstanding French writers, and resumed his education by reading works they suggested. The study of art gave Moore subject matter for his early novels, and the practice of painting taught him design, selection of details, and the necessity of sharp focus.

Because of the pressures from the Irish Land League, which threatened to seize his estates, Moore returned to London in 1880 and began his career as a writer. He remained there until 1901, when he moved to Dublin and helped to establish the Irish Literary Theatre, the forerunner of the Abbey Theatre. While there he also gathered material for additional books and managed to quarrel with many of his friends. In 1911, to coincide with the appearance of "Ave," the first volume of *Hail and Farewell,* he moved back to London, settling on Ebury Street. Except for occasional visits to Ireland to take care of business, to Paris to visit old friends, or to the Wagner festival at Bayreuth, Germany, he remained in London for the remainder of his life. His ashes, however, were returned to Castle Island, Lough Carra, at Moore Hall in County Mayo.

In *Confessions of a Young Man,* Moore describes himself as a "man of wax," a person whose mind was unformed until he came into contact with the people of Paris. Since he had had a tutor, had spent some time at Oscott, and had had the advantage of a good home library, this is purposeful exaggeration. As with the preface of Charles Baudelaire's *Les Fleurs du mal* (1857; translated as *Flowers of Evil,* 1909), which he seems to be emulating, Moore's immediate purpose in the work was to get the attention of the public in any way he could. Still, it may be that lack of a formal education led to a lack of confidence in himself and his works. This might explain the many revisions he made in most of his works. This practice was first noted by Oscar Wilde, who quipped to James McNeill Whistler that "Moore conducted his education in public." While there is some truth to Wilde's stricture, Whistler's reply is equally appropriate: "Well, Oscar, the public's paying for it and deserves to see what it's getting for its money."

Royal Gettmann, the first critic to study Moore's revisions seriously, notes that, although some of the revisions amount to no more than corrections of grammar or punctuation, Moore often improved his style and structure or sharpened his characters. The revisions may be studied in his novels and his four collections of short fiction: *Celibates* (1895), *An T-Ur-Gort* (1902; published in English as *The Untilled Field,* 1903), *A Story-Teller's Holiday* (1918), and *In Single Strictness* (1922; republished as *Celibate Lives,* 1927). A fifth volume, which spans Moore's career, was assembled by Gerber and David B. Eakin. *In Minor Keys* (1985) reflects Moore's interest in the musicality of fiction and develops his theory that stories that end anticlimactically are written in minor key.

In his later practice of blending reverie with narrative, one may question Moore's claim to being a realist. Such a blend suggests a symbolic romanticism at least. If realism is defined as a selection of middle-class material truthfully depicted, then before 1914 Moore was the quintessential naturalist-become-realist, as John Wilson Foster argues. This judgment is true whether one analyzes Moore's use of French, English, or Irish data for his fiction.

Since the publication of *In Minor Keys,* it has been possible to study many of Moore's stories in the order of their composition and in their first versions. The reader can trace Moore's development as a writer by examining his early short fiction. For example, he divides "Under the Fan" (1882) into three chapters, substituting chapter breaks for fictional transitions. The material, essentially a Maupassant-esque anecdote, is too slim to warrant such lengthy treatment. Miss St. Vincent, a young actress, is being pursued by Lord Wedmore. He is desired by the financially needy Mrs. White, who is nearer his age. Since the actress is more interested in a young actor, she persuades Mrs. White to sign a contract to pay twenty thousand pounds to her after Mrs. White has married Wedmore. The actress discourages the lord, and he marries Mrs. White on the rebound. The payment allows the actress and her beloved to set up housekeeping and stage their own plays. Despite the creaky plot, Moore handles the theatrical environment knowledgeably. At this stage, however, he has not yet learned how to select important details and to focus them sharply.

In "A Russian Husband" (1883) he has more of a story to tell and is more in control of its Chekhovian tone. A Russian general observes that his youthful wife and a young Polish soldier have fallen in love. The general has the soldier broken in rank and orders him publicly whipped, forcing his wife and the soldier's brother to watch. The whipping is so severe that the soldier will die from it, so the brother commits suicide rather than watch it, and the wife lapses into a catatonic state rather than endure the pain of her lover's suffering. The use of violence is repulsive; however, Moore narrates the tale from the general's viewpoint, which makes the act sadistic but less dramatic.

The only other violent story in *In Minor Keys* is "Two Men: A Railway Story" (1887), which also features a love triangle. Two Englishmen, an engineer with an ill wife and an unmarried fireman, both desire the affections of a widow publican and constantly quarrel about her. She seems more interested in the engineer and makes this clear to the fireman. While on the moving train one day the two fight, wreck the train, and are killed, to the horror of the now-contrite widow. Despite the melodramatic plot, Moore faithfully describes the characters and manages to make the dialogue interesting. He is able to do the same in "Dried Fruit" (1885), where a rejected lover and his now-wilted rose meet anew and arrange to share a friendship for the remainder of their lives. The tight plot is, however, rather slight.

Because of Moore's return to the chapter structure, the plot of "A Strange Death" (1889) is stretched thin; nevertheless, he experiments with two different points of view. Each chapter chronicles the visit of Edwin Harrington to the ugly, isolated village of Charmandeon. Chapter 1 is told from the viewpoint of the suspicious villagers, who watch him arrive and help him find lodgings in a farmhouse. Because his luggage shows signs of extensive travel, however, they suspect him of some sinister purpose and begin to dog his steps. They follow him to the farmhouse and start to break down his door. In chapter 2 the same story is told from Harrington's viewpoint. In poor health, he selects this village because of its name on a map, and he hopes to settle there in some quiet country lodging. Noting the villagers' suspicious actions, however, he quickly becomes disillusioned with the setting. Suspicion turns into anxiety and then terror, and he barricades himself in his room. When the villagers begin to break down the door, he dies of a heart attack. As Gerber and Eakin note, the story's "macabre flavor" may derive from Philippe-Auguste, Comte de Villiers de l'Isle-Adam's *Contes Cruels* (1883; translated as *Cruel Tales,* 1966) or from tales by Edgar Allan Poe, whose works Moore read between 1873 and 1880. While psychologically believable, this is not the sort of story Moore attempted again.

"A Faithful Heart" (1892) is a good Balzacian study of a selfish male and a sacrificing female. Major Shepherd has a "secret" wife and daughter he maintains poorly and keeps away from his landed family because its members had objected to what they regarded as a mésalliance. When the story opens, he prepares to move his wife and daughter from the village to London because he fears their discovery. Before they leave, however, the wife asks for permission to see the grounds of the family house. She and the daughter sneak in and are observed by a sister, who tries to make friends with them. They leave, still pretending they have no relationship with the family, grateful for having experienced a moment of calm and beauty.

In "Parted" (1893) Moore focuses on a working-class couple with marital problems. Whatever the husband earns the wife wastes on alcohol; her alcoholic rages disturb the neighborhood and embarrass the husband. One day, in a subconscious wish for her to kill herself, he leaves his razors where she can find them. He feels guilty about his action and dreads going home to her certain death. When he arrives, however, he finds her dead drunk. She has seized the opportunity to pawn the razors and buy

She stood now watching Mr. Bryant eat his breakfast.

Illustration by W. D. Almond for "An Episode in Bachelor Life" (Sketch, *24 January 1894*)

even more alcohol. The neighbors laugh at the husband, who must still contend with his besotted wife. In detachment and understatement this is Moore's best early story. Its almost clinical study of the alcoholic wife compares favorably with that of Kate Ede in *A Mummer's Wife*.

According to Gerber and Eakin, the expression "a novel in a nutshell" served as a descriptive heading for "An Episode in Bachelor Life" and its companion story, "An Episode in Married Life," when the two were published in *Sketch* (January and February 1884). The first story offers another example of the theme of the downtrodden woman, best exemplified in *Esther Waters*. The story's study of unrequited love also anticipates the longer pieces in *Celibates*. In "An Episode in Bachelor Life," Clara the maid falls in love with her employer, who is having an affair with a woman of his own rank. Knowing that nothing can come of her yearning, Clara gives notice and is accused of ingratitude by her self-centered boss. The tale ends with her dull realization of her future unhappiness. Its brevity and tight focus suggest the understated stories of Ernest Hemingway and Joyce.

"An Episode in Married Life" is less compelling in content and psychology. Novelist James Mason decides to meet a potential mistress in the garb of a French clown, complete with whitened face. Madame de Beausac, having expected a sophisticated lover, flees in disgust and returns to her husband and baby. The author concludes the piece with mock moralism: "And so did a powder-puff save a woman, when other remedies had failed, from the calamity of a great passion."

According to Gerber and Eakin, this story may have been inspired by Balzac's *La Femme de trente ans* (1842; translated as *A Woman of Thirty,* 1901). Joseph Hone assigns it to an affair the youthful Moore either had or planned during his first years in Paris. Moore experimented with this theme in various memoirs and in at least two plays. He also used it in another story, "Euphorion in Texas" (*English Review,* July 1914; collected in *Memoirs of My Dead Life,* 1915 edition). In "Euphorion in Texas," which is indebted to Johann Wolfgang von Goethe's *Faust* (1808–1832) for character name and the concept of the miraculous child, an even older novelist sends his maid/secretary to the Shelbourne Hotel to find out about an ardent American correspondent. When the maid returns and reports on the attractiveness of the woman, the novelist invites the American to tea. In his apartments she confesses she has traveled to Europe especially to meet him and to become pregnant by him, in hopes of producing an extraordinary child. The reader gathers her wish is granted, for he receives a letter from Texas announcing the birth of a son. The reader assumes great art will follow.

"Euphorion in Texas," long thought to be an example of the author's wishful thinking, has a more interesting explanation, as Adrian Frazier shows. A Texas woman named Honor Woulfe corresponded with Moore, visited him on Ely Place in 1907, and told him the story of a Chicago acquaintance who had sought pregnancy by a European composer. Moore adopted the material for his story. In a memoir of her own Woulfe tells the story of her relationship with Moore and expresses her dislike for "Euphorion in Texas."

Whatever one feels about the quality of these uneven stories, they did help Moore learn how to write, and they helped him to gain the public's attention. Before *Celibates* appeared in 1895, he had published stories in the *Court and Society Review,* the *Daily Chronicle,* the *Hawk,* the *Speaker,* and the *Sketch.* In the twentieth century he also published in *Lippincott's* magazine, the *Gael,* the *Irish Review,* the *Living Age,* the *Smart Set, Cosmopolitan, Nash's* magazine, and the *Dial.* Writers with greater reputations would be hard-pressed to equal Moore's record in both quality of journal and variety of story.

Celibates was Moore's first volume of stories; to call them "short," though, one must contrast them with Victorian novels. If word count is used as a basis for judgment, the first, "Mildred Lawson," is a novel, and the other two, "John Norton" and "Agnes Lahens," are novellas. In structure, however, they are closer to tales than novels, being more like psychological studies than stories with plots. Perhaps Moore was too close to the material to work well with it. Hone suggests that "Mildred Lawson" is based on Moore's affair with Pearl Craigie, a minor writer of stories, plays, and novels. Craigie deserted Moore in hopes of marrying Lord George Curzon and was herself jilted for a younger woman. In the story Mildred kills herself with an overdose of sleeping pills, whereas Craigie apparently tried to return to Moore. Although Joyce liked the story well enough to translate it into Italian, its episodic nature tries the reader's interest.

Moore used the same material again in "Henrietta Marr" (*In Single Strictness*).

The material for "John Norton" was first used in the novel *A Mere Accident* (1887), and the character appears briefly in *Mike Fletcher* (1889). The character is at least partly modeled on Moore's cousin Edward Martyn, a confirmed bachelor devoted to the arts and his Catholic faith. John Norton may also be partly modeled on the character Des Eissentes in Joris-Karl Huysmans's novel *A Rebours* (1884; translated as *Against the Grain,* 1922). In either case the psychology of a man who dislikes women is what interested Moore. In *A Mere Accident* and "John Norton," the protagonist is the only heir to a considerable estate and is put under pressure from his mother to marry and produce children. A local minister's daughter, who frequently visits Mrs. Norton, is less repulsive to him than most women, so John proposes to her and is accepted. Before the marriage can take place, however, the girl is raped by a tramp. Rather than tell anyone or submit to a relationship with another man in marriage, the girl commits suicide. This is the "mere accident" of the novel's title and is what made John celibate for life. Not content with his story, Moore used the same material in "Hugh Monfret" (*In Single Strictness*), where he drops the rape and explains Hugh's problem as homosexuality.

"Agnes Lahens" is less ambitious yet more successful than either of the other stories in *Celibates.* Before taking her final vows as a nun, Agnes returns to visit her parents. She is immediately disappointed with her mother, Olive Lahens, who controls the family purse strings; openly entertains Lord Chadwick, her lover; and just as openly ridicules her husband, Major Lahens, who lives on the odd pound note he can earn as a copyist and exists in an unheated, spartan room in the attic. While Agnes is sympathetic with her father and his plight, she soon realizes that he can do nothing to change things in the family. The story ends with her on the way back to the cloister, a final escape from the worldliness that her mother represents. Perhaps content with his achievement, or recognizing the limitations inherent in this plot, Moore chose not to treat the Agnes Lahens story in any further work.

As if in testament to his continued commitment to realism, Moore published a story called "Emma Bovary" in *Lippincott's* magazine (May 1902). Set in both Ireland and France, it presents the apparently uneventful lives of Ismena and Letitia O'Hara, who have shared everything until they leave Dublin to study art in France. While in Paris, Letitia finds a French novel behind the wardrobe in her bedroom and, without telling her sister, begins to read it. When the two return to Dublin, she continues to read it in the privacy of their summerhouse. On her deathbed she tells her sister of a "brown-paper parcel in the summerhouse." Ismena finds it, remembers having read it long ago in France, and wonders what has happened to the man who gave it to her. She can only speculate about Letitia's interest in it and how she acquired it. Moore tells this story more economically in "Priscilla and Emily Lofft" (*In Single Strictness*).

During the late 1880s and early 1890s Moore published four other stories that he retitled and included in *An T-Ur-Gort* and its English-language version, *The Untilled Field*. These were "Grandmother's Wedding Gown" (*Lady's Pictorial,* December 1887; reprinted as "The Wedding Gown" in *English Illustrated Magazine,* June 1902), "Mr. Dumpty's Ideal" (*St. James Gazette,* 3 September 1890; retitled "The Clerk's Quest"), "Charity" (*Sketch,* 13 September 1893; reprinted in *Speaker,* 6 July 1895; retitled "Almsgiving" in *New Ireland Review,* December 1902), and "The Golden Apples" (*English Illustrated Magazine,* April 1902; retitled "Julia Cahill's Curse"). The stories are individually interesting, but the fact that they could be retitled and inserted in a later volume presumably inspired by Moore's return to Ireland might arouse questions about the integrity of that volume. However, Moore confessed that he had difficulty finding new subjects, so he felt free to use his material over and over again. His consistent interest was in producing works of art, whatever that demanded, and *The Untilled Field* is certainly artful. From its initial publication in 1903, *The Untilled Field* was one of the most heavily and frequently revised of Moore's books. The first edition contains thirteen stories: "In the Clay" (previously unpublished), "Some Parishioners," "The Exile," "Home Sickness," "A Letter to Rome" (previously unpublished), "Julia Cahill's Curse," "A Playhouse in the Waste" (written for the Gaelic version), "The Wedding Gown," "The Clerk's Quest," "Almsgiving," "So On He Fares" (previously unpublished), "The Wild Goose," and "The Way Back." The volume is framed by the concept of arrivals and departures in the first and last stories. These elements and the themes of enchantment and disillusionment are present in all versions of the volume.

The Tauchnitz edition (1903) drops "In the Clay" and "The Way Back," divides "Some Parishioners" into four stories – "Some Parishioners," "Patchwork," "The Marriage Feast" (retitled "The Wedding Feast" in the 1914 Heinemann edition and

subsequent editions), and "The Window" – and reorders some of the stories retained from the first edition. This version, now with fourteen stories, begins with "The Exile," follows with "Home Sickness," and continues with "Some Parishioners" and the three new stories in the order cited. "A Letter to Rome" follows, and the sequence continues as in the first edition but concludes with "The Wild Goose." For the 1931 edition Moore added a fifteenth story, "The Fugitives," based on subject matter from the canceled "In the Clay" and "The Way Back."

According to Hone, *The Untilled Field* originated from the suggestion of William Kirkpatrick McGee, an assistant librarian at the National Library, to Moore that he produce a volume of stories about Ireland comparable to Ivan Turgenev's *A Hunter's Notes* (1847–1851) about Russia. As Gerber shows in *George Moore in Transition* (1968), however, Moore had previously written an essay about Turgenev for the *Fortnightly Review* (1888) and had previously met the Russian in Paris during the 1870s. In the *Fortnightly Review* article, Moore focuses on *Terres Vierges* (1877; translated as *Virgin Soil,* 1877), which comes closer to approximating the concept of *The Untilled Field* and even looks ahead to his musical style. Turgenev, however, is much more objective in looking at his country than Moore is in reflecting on Ireland. In varying degrees all the stories in *The Untilled Field* suffer from anticlericalism.

The opening story in the first edition, "In the Clay," focuses on a sculptor, Rodney, who suffers from the religious bigotry around him. While he personally lacks religion, he earns a living by designing altar decorations. For a sculpture of the Madonna and Child, he employs a village girl, Lucy, as model. Father McCabe sees the work in its early stages, recognizes the girl, and tells her family. Her brothers decide to destroy the models, so the sculptor is left with only a bitter memory of his experience. He prepares to leave for the Continent, where he expects to receive more tolerance.

"Some Parishioners" treats the effect of a meddlesome young priest who wants to dictate social conduct in his parish. For example, he forces Kate Kavanagh to marry someone she scarcely likes. Since she loves someone else, the priest's action makes three people unhappy. Kate, however, escapes to America, leaving this would-be saint to continue suffering from pride, anger, and self-righteousness. A peasant woman, Biddy McHale, does approach sainthood, driving the young priest to distraction. Another priest, Father Maguire, makes exiles out of his own parishioners. Father Madden does the same in "Julia Cahill's Curse" when he drives the title character from the community. She wishes bad luck on him and the community and kills his easy living.

The theme of exile also dominates the volume. In "The Exile" James Phelan leaves for America, even though he has inherited the family farm, because the woman he loves, a released novice nun, loves his brother, a released novice priest. In "Homesickness," James Bryden returns to Ireland from America. Observing the ways a priest browbeats his parishioners, he becomes homesick for America, goes back, and marries there. In old age, however, he remembers Ireland and wants to return there to die.

Not all of the stories' priests are repressive. In "A Letter to Rome," Father MacTurnan is disturbed by the emigration from his parish. In order to increase the population, he first suggests that priests and nuns be urged to marry each other. When that idea is rejected, he writes a letter to the pope, requesting money to help needy young couples marry. His bishop intercepts the letter and sends him five pounds. In "Playhouse in the Waste" the same priest tries to bring tourists to the rural section he serves in a vain attempt to save the church's collapsing walls. Moore is certainly a realist in focusing on the ruins that are part of Ireland.

In stories reminiscent of those by other turn-of-the-century writers, Moore makes effective use of the theme of doubles. In "The Wedding Gown" an old woman relives her life by lending her gown to her niece. In "So On He Fares" middle-aged Ulick, who had run away from home years earlier to escape his domineering mother, returns to discover he has a younger brother also named Ulick, and he flees a second time.

Two of the stories in *The Untilled Field* are little more than anecdotes, but they are well told. In "The Clerk's Quest" the protagonist, a bank clerk, leads a dull, drab life until a check scented with heliotrope crosses his desk. Fantasizing, he pursues the illusion of its signer, Henrietta Brown, and he dies on his way to find her in Edinburgh. "Almsgiving" is the story of a wealthy person's response to a blind man who sells pencils. Having heard the man's story and admired his constant cheerfulness, the protagonist promises to help pay for the man's vacation.

The volume's longest and most complex story, "The Wild Goose," unites many of the volume's themes and serves as a good conclusion to its later editions. Ned Carmody, a journalist, returns to Ire-

land, marries Ellen Cronin, and quickly develops a distaste for the church. The couple have a son, and Ellen begins to consult a priest about issues that Ned feels are their private concern. She continues this until finally, in exasperation, Ned begins a book about Ireland and religion. When Ellen discusses his subject with her priest, Ned decides he must leave Ireland, Ellen, and his child in order to keep a modicum of sanity.

The thirteenth story, "The Way Back," which completes the frame of the first edition, returns the reader to "The Clay." The sculptor Rodney, on his way to Italy, talks to the novelist Harding, who is on his way to Ireland, and learns that Lucy has married an American. Ned Carmody joins the two and announces that he will go to Africa to fight in the Boer War. In the words of the narrator, "One seeks a country with a past, one a country with a future, and one goes to a place with neither past nor future."

While Jean C. Noel regards the stories in *The Untilled Field* as "five-finger exercises," Moore's revisions of individual stories and the volume as a whole show his growing mastery of his craft. The book influenced some of the best twentieth-century writers, including Joyce. In fact, the chief difference between Moore's Irish country people and Joyce's Dubliners is that some of Moore's escape. Moore also influenced the next group of Irish writers – Frank O'Connor, Sean O'Faolain, Liam O'Flaherty, and Mary Lavin. While most of Moore's stories are not as compressed as most of theirs, he attempted compression, blended fantasy with realism, made good use of locale, and centered the stories on Ireland and its problems. As John Wilson Foster has noted, "The close observation, the interweaving of theme and character, and the master themes of the volume – the bafflement of self-realization, anticlericalism, ruination – were later emulated in *Dubliners*." This makes Moore the teacher of the masters of the short story, as James F. Carens has also noted.

After *The Untilled Field* Moore returned to writing novels, memoirs, and plays. The memoirs and novels share fictionalizing techniques, an increased blend of fantasy and narration, and a commitment to musicality of form and language. The same can be said for his short stories written and published between 1903 and 1915. Gerber and Eakin include two of these in *In Minor Keys* – "The Voice of the Mountain" (*Gael,* July 1904) and "A Flood" (*Irish Review,* March 1911). "Euphorion in Texas" also belongs to this grouping. "A Flood," which may have been inspired by Zola's story of the

A tall white Pierrot, incredibly hideous, stood beside her.

Illustration by W. D. Almond for "An Episode in Married Life"
(Sketch, *21 February 1894*)

same title, is more in the tradition of bleak realism if not naturalism. In fact, it is dominated by the psychology of fatalism. Victims of continuously rising waters are stranded on the roof of a house; one by one members of this family drop off the roof and are swept away by the flood. The only survivor is the grandfather, who enjoys suffering with his rheumatism; he is sustained by a belief in an earlier prophesy that he would never drown.

"The Voice of the Mountain" combines Moore's distaste for British conquest in Africa with his rekindled affection for Ireland. In almost a parody of the "Cathleen Ni Houlihan" myth, young Dan hears a voice from a mountain telling him to go to Africa and fight in the Boer War. Mary, his betrothed, objects to his going but becomes reconciled by what the mountain tells her. She will go on visiting and talking with it during Dan's absence. Knowledge of the Boer War came to Moore from his brother, Col. Maurice Moore, who com-

manded a British troop in Africa. Moore did not approve of his brother's mission.

Moore's final original volume of short fiction, *A Story-Teller's Holiday,* was published in 1918 and followed the familiar pattern of changes and revisions. All editions make use of a framing device: Moore's persona returns to Ireland for a visit, stops in Dublin to see his friends and to examine the destruction left by the Easter Rising, and then sets out by train to Mayo. He thinks of priests, recalls sex in *Evelyn Innes,* and sees a nun near Westport. This unlikely trio of topics controls the rest of the volume, in all its editions. Near Moore Hall the persona sees Alec Trusselby, a fern gatherer famed for his storytelling skills. The narrator seeks him out, wins his friendship, and gets him started telling stories.

Trusselby begins with an anecdote about his blackthorn walking stick, which he has named "the Murrigan" (in Irish myth Murrigu was one of three sisters approximating the Greek Fates or Germanic

Norns). Alec's stories include "Liadin and Curithir," "Marban and Luachet," "Father Scothine," and "Father Moling and the Three Hermits." These are followed in contrastive style by the persona's story of Adam and Eve and how they learned to make love; by "Albert Nobbes" (reprinted in *Celibate Lives*), the story of a woman who pretends to be a man and is discovered by another woman disguised as a man; and bits from Balzac, Fyodor Dostoyevsky, and Turgenev. The 1928 edition adds, in chapters 45–57, an abbreviated story of *Ulick and Soracha* (1926) and, in chapter 58, "Dinoll and Crede" (first published as "The Hermit's Love Story" in *Cosmopolitan* and *Nash's* magazine, 1927). All editions end with the narrator retracing his way across Ireland to Dublin and back to England.

Moore's main source for the stories was Kuno Meyer, who had translated the poem "A Chrinoc, Cubaid De Cheol," in which the author tells of past years of sleeping with Chrinoc, becoming separated from he/she/it, and now delighting in the fact that the two are back together again. In *Selections from Ancient Irish Poetry* (1911), Meyer concludes that the poem describes a spiritual marriage between a monk and a nun, that the custom was intended to mortify the flesh since temptation would constantly be present, and that the custom was recognized by Irish bishops and called "virgo subintroducta." Meyer's translation and interpretation have since been challenged by Irish scholar James Carney, who reads the poem as a sustained metaphor about a priest getting back his favorite psalmbook. Harvard Celticist John V. Kelleher agrees with Carney [letter to author, 22 August 1977] and concludes: "I think there is one thing we can both be sure of – that if Moore had ever seen Carney's article he would (a) have found it very disappointing, and (b) would then have completely ignored it."

By creating a fictive friend, even one with the unlikely Irish name of Alec Trusselby, Moore works in Irish themes and stories and achieves the flavor of oral narration. By also telling stories in his own voice, he offers variations on the same themes, achieves a contrastive style, and approximates musical counterpoint in the placement of stories and the volume's structure. As Robert Langenfeld suggests, he also achieves a comic irony unlike that of his other "memoirs." There is also a vigor – a Rabelaisian gusto – that makes the volume appealing.

Trusselby's story of "Liadin and Curithir" is expanded from Meyer's 1902 translation of a seven-page poem (A.D. 1100) ascribed to Curithir. In Moore's version the two poets have been lovers, but one is forced to become a nun and the other a monk. Each flees the confinement, and they meet in Mayo, only to be disciplined by Saint Cumine: the lovers are forced to see each other but not to speak, speak but not to see each other, and then to lie in silence in the same bed. Not surprisingly, the flesh wins. In punishment Curithir is sent on a pilgrimage to Rome. When he returns, he finds both Liadin and Cumine buried on Church Island in the middle of Lake Carra. He dies too and is buried beside Liadin. As in the ballad "Barbry Allen," trees are planted by the lovers' graves and later entwine over them.

The story "Marban and Luachet" (from Meyer's *Colloquy Between King Guaire and His Brother Prince Marbhan,* 1901) duplicates the temptations described in "Liadin and Curithir." Forced to lie with a series of nuns, Marban finally gives in to the wiles of Luachet, the youngest and prettiest. "Father Scothine" concerns a monk who does not give in to temptation. Father Scothine arranges for a friend, Father Brenainn, to be tempted by a dancing nun. In order to preserve his vow of chastity, in a parody of the Cuchulain legend, Brenainn must dunk himself several times in ice water. In "Father Moling and the Three Hermits" the title cleric discovers that a nun wishes to be the bride of Christ, poses his nude body on a cross, and steps down to impregnate her. She and the nuns regard her swelling abdomen as the sign of another virgin birth, but Father Moling confesses his sin to the three hermits of the title. As an additional part of his penance, the hermits tell his bishop of the sin. Martin, the male child, grows up to become a scholar and priest. He moves to Germany, however, marries an escaped nun, and founds a new religion.

Stories told by the Moore persona are equally titillating. In his account of Eden, Adam and Eve do not know how to make love, so they try various ways learned from observing the animals in the Garden. In "Albert Nobbes" a woman pretends to be a man in order to get a job at the Shelbourne Hotel in Dublin. When the hotel becomes overcrowded, the manager forces Nobbes to share a bed with a male traveler. Her identity is discovered by Mr. Page, another woman in disguise. Anthony Farrow suggests that Moore was not tolerant of sexual aberrations and that this is revealed in *A Story-Teller's Holiday* as well as *Celibates*. Certainly Moore was intolerant of what he thought to be the church's emasculating effect on Ireland. As he states in *Hail and Farewell,* "In Ireland only the neuters survive: the nun, the priest, and the ox." Whether this was true or not, the "neuters" made good material for his writings.

Near the end of his life Yeats, in "The Circus Animals' Desertion" (*Last Poems,* 1938–1939), lamented that he could only repeat old themes. Moore did this throughout his life. His interest in history and theology kindled *The Brook Kerith* as well as *A Story-Teller's Holiday,* and he made additional use of the two sources in *Héloise and Abélard.* Theology becomes Greek myth in *The Pastoral Loves of Daphnis and Chloe* and *Aphrodite in Aulis,* two novels as sexually suggestive as *A Story-Teller's Holiday.* He returned briefly to Irish medieval history in *Ulick and Soracha,* another story of tragic lovers, which he abbreviated and included in later volumes of *A Story-Teller's Holiday.*

In focusing on the past, whether that of France, Ireland, Greece, or Palestine, Moore moved even further away from the realist tradition he had helped to popularize in England and Ireland. In choosing to rewrite and reorder stories he tried to make new works out of old ones, but his stylistic interests and philosophical focus were not the same. The stories of *In Single Strictness,* while somewhat indebted to those of *Celibates,* are offered in a fresh style and an attempt to achieve a new unity. The volume begins with "Wilfrid Holmes," a study of a would-be composer who is destined always to be mediocre and who must live off the bounty of his aunt. In being a person of limited talent, he clearly parallels Moore's earlier characters Ned Carmody, the journalist; Rodney, the sculptor; and Harding, the novelist. This parallel is clearest, however, when one examines "The Fugitives," which may owe some of its irony to this version of "Wilfrid Holmes."

"Priscilla and Emily Lofft" links to "Wilfrid Holmes" by an interest in the song of a blackbird. The story begins with Priscilla dead and Emily recalling their life together. She remembers their twinness, a trip to Aix, and Priscilla's secretiveness. At this point she discovers a book that belonged to Priscilla, about a woman unfaithful to her lover. Emily reads parts of it, burns it, and is at last free of her sister.

"Hugh Monfret" is told in part through the title character's thoughts but is too often a mere summary of events in his life. Pushed by his mother to marry and produce the necessary heir, Hugh invites a priest to mediate, whereas John Norton's mother invites a minister. The priest is on his way to bring his daughter back from France, but he leaves his son, Percy, to visit with Hugh. The two young men take a walking tour of Wales (described in too much detail) before Hugh must settle down with some woman of his mother's choosing. When

Percy's sister, Beatrice, appears, Hugh is attracted to her, proposes, and marries her, but he discovers on the honeymoon that he has loved her resemblance to her brother. Accordingly, he asks her to have the marriage annulled. Beatrice remarries, Percy dies, and Hugh is left to a life of bitterness.

Even though "Hugh Monfret" could have benefited from careful cutting, it is realistic and less tedious than "Henrietta Marr," a revision of "Mildred Lawson." Henrietta, a would-be painter in Paris, returns to her English country home and is bored. She goes to London, flirts, and leaves a man who dies for her love. In this respect she is like Mildred Lawson (or Pearl Craigie). She becomes the mistress of a French nobleman, expecting him to marry her when his ailing wife dies. After his wife's death, however, the nobleman rejects her, so she commits suicide. The best that can be said for this story is that it is competent and adequately traces the psychology of a certain type of person.

"Sarah Gwynn" is more compressed and artistically successful than the other stories of *In Single Strictness.* It is set in Ely Place, the street of Moore's residence in Dublin for ten years, and concerns a doctor – perhaps modeled on Moore's friend Sir Thornley Stoker (Bram Stoker's brother) – who hires a lapsed nun as a parlor maid. On observing her nightly rambles through the red-light district, the doctor asks for her story. She tells of a time before she was a nun, when she was befriended by a woman who worked in a biscuit factory by day and supplemented her slender earnings by prostitution at night. She is searching for this person in hopes of repaying her.

In Single Strictness was revised as *Celibate Lives,* which omits "Hugh Monfret" and adds "Albert Nobbes." In the reworked "Wilfrid Holmes" the title character finds a lady to add accompaniment to his lyric line. Moore's interest in the life of renunciation obviously continued, but the stories are not appreciably different from earlier versions.

The remainder of Moore's short fiction appeared separately. After publication in the *Dial* (November 1921), *Peronnik the Fool* was brought out by Boni and Liveright in book form in 1924. The story is derived from Breton folklore, and Moore mentions it in *Héloise and Abélard.* As Gareth W. Dunleavy suggests, this allegorical tale deals with the "innocent knight," a "half-wit resident of the friendly forest, who strays away from it only to prove that he can become a pure knight." Peronnik shares some of these qualities with Parsifal and with Mad Sweeney (from Irish saga literature). The story earned its greatest American recognition when Edward J. O'Brien listed it in "The Honor Roll of Foreign Stories for 1922" in his collection *The Best Short Stories of 1922*.

Two other stories had serial publication but were not republished until Gerber and Eakin used them in *In Minor Keys*. "At the Turn of the Road: An Irish Girl's Love Story" appeared in *Cosmopolitan* (July 1927) and was republished in *Nash's* magazine (February 1928) with a new subtitle: "A Tragedy of the New Forest." This seems more appropriate, since the story deals with the effect of a young woman's suicide on her parents and fiancé. No explanation for the suicide is given, but lack of love for the man is implied. The family cannot bear to remain in the community, so the fiancé is left to try to take care of things. The second story, "The Strange Story of the Three Golden Fishes: A Comedy of a Man Who Was Always Lucky — Especially in Marriage," also appeared in *Cosmopolitan* (September 1927) and *Nash's* magazine (February 1928). In the mode of *A Story-Teller's Holiday,* the narrator, on vacation in the Sandwich Islands, learns the story of Mr. Cather, who has caught three fish worth sixty thousand pounds. Cather's story begins with Mr. Trout — a butler for three sisters, the Pettigues — who plans to retire. The sisters, knowing that they cannot survive without him, propose marriage to him. He selects Charlotte, the eldest, and the other two continue to live in the household. In time all the sisters die, leaving Trout with an income of five thousand pounds a year. He buys racing stables and prospers. At the end, childless and infirm, he seeks his solicitor's advice as to whom he should bequeath his money. The attorney suggests Mr. Cather, explaining that he is one of many to whom he has given permission to fish in his streams, but the only one who has ever given him any fish in return. As the story's title demonstrates, each of these fish was worth a considerable amount of money.

Summing up Moore's career is not an easy task for the literary historian, critic, or bibliographer. Because republication and revision were his usual procedures, he is the beloved son of bibliographers. Literary historians have taken to him, too. A. C. Baugh, for example, in his single-volume *Literary History of England,* gives Moore some five double-column pages chronicling his life and achievements. Apostles of modernism, such as William York Tindall in his *Forces in Modern British Literature,* are pleased to cite him as the forerunner of many more experimental modern writers. Joyce, Arnold Bennett, and D. H. Lawrence acknowledged their indebtedness to him. Virginia Woolf admired his innovations in feeling and narrative style, but

she claimed to like his memoirs better than his novels. Either is better than his short fiction, though not necessarily more influential.

While recent critics continue to write most about Moore as novelist and memorialist, his short fiction and his pronouncements about painting and music are also of interest. He produced some first-rate works in almost every genre of writing (except drama) and was highly respected in his own time for his achievements. One of these was making realism palatable to English and Irish audiences. Another was moving the Victorian tale nearer the epiphanous moment of the best twentieth-century stylists. In some works Moore competes favorably with Joyce, O'Connor, O'Faolain, O'Flaherty, and Lavin. Moore stands alone in progressing from naturalism to realism to symbolism while producing excellent memoirs, novels, and short stories.

Letters:

George Moore in Transition: Letters to T. Fisher Unwin and Lena Milman, 1894–1910, edited by Helmut E. Gerber (Detroit: Wayne State University Press, 1968);

George Moore on Parnassus: Letters (1900–1933) to Secretaries, Publishers, Printers, Agents, Literati, Friends, and Acquaintances, edited by Gerber (Newark: University of Delaware Press, 1988).

Bibliographies:

Edwin Gilcher, *A Bibliography of George Moore* (De Kalb: Northern Illinois University Press, 1970);

Robert Langenfeld, *George Moore: An Annotated Secondary Bibliography of Writings About Him* (New York: AMS, 1987);

Gilcher, with Robert S. Becker and Clinton K. Krauss, *Supplement to a Bibliography of George Moore* (Westport, Conn.: Mechler, 1988).

Biographies:

Joseph Hone, *The Life of George Moore* (London: Gollancz, 1936; New York: Macmillan, 1936);

A. Norman Jeffares, *George Moore,* Writers and Their Work, pamphlet no. 180 (London: Longmans, Green, 1965);

Jean C. Noel, *George Moore: l'homme et l'œuvre* (Paris: Didier, 1966);

Janet Egleson Dunleavy, *George Moore: The Artist's Vision, the Storyteller's Art* (Lewisburg, Pa.: Bucknell University Press, 1973).

References:

Malcolm Brown, *George Moore: A Reconsideration* (Seattle: University of Washington Press, 1955);

Charles J. Burkhart, "The Short Stories of George Moore," *Studies in Short Fiction,* 6 (Winter 1969): 165–174;

James F. Carens, "In Quest of a New Impulse: George Moore's *The Untilled Field* and James Joyce's *Dubliners,*" in *The Irish Short Story: A Critical History,* edited by James F. Kilroy (Boston: G. K. Hall, 1984), pp. 45–69;

James Carney, "A Chrinoc, Cubaid Do Cheol," *Eigse,* 4 (Winter 1944): 280–283;

Richard Allen Cave, *A Study of the Novels of George Moore* (New York: Barnes & Noble, 1978);

Gareth W. Dunleavy, "George Moore's Mediaevalism: A Modern Triptych," in *George Moore in Perspective,* edited by Janet Egleson Dunleavy (Totowa, N.J.: Barnes & Noble, 1983);

Anthony Farrow, *George Moore* (Boston: Twayne, 1978);

John Firth, "George Moore and Modern Irish Autobiography," *Wisconsin Studies in Literature,* no. 5 (1968): 64–72;

John Wilson Foster, *Fictions of the Irish Literary Revival: A Changeling Art* (Syracuse, N.Y.: Syracuse University Press, 1987);

Adrian Frazier, "On His Honor: George Moore and Some Women," *English Literature in Transition,* 35, no. 4 (1992): 423–445;

Helmut E. Gerber, "George Moore: From Pure Poetry to Pure Criticism," *Journal of Aesthetics and Art Criticism,* 25 (Spring 1967): 281–291;

Royal Gettmann, "George Moore's Revisions of *The Lake,* 'The Wild Goose,' and *Esther Waters,*" PMLA, 69 (June 1944): 540–545;

Frank Harris, *Oscar Wilde: His Life and Confessions,* 2 volumes (New York, 1916);

Douglas A. Hughes, ed., *The Man of Wax* (New York: New York University Press, 1971);

Robert Langenfeld, "George Moore's *A Story-Teller's Holiday*: Irish Theme Expressed Through Comic Irony," *Cahiers du Centre d'Etudes Anglo-Irlandaises,* no. 9 (1984): 15–29;

Kenneth B. Newell, "The 'Artist' Stories in *The Untilled Field,*" *English Literature in Transition,* 14 (1971): 123–136;

Jean C. Noel, "George Moore's Five-Finger Exercises," *Cahiers du Centre d'Etudes Anglo-Irlandaises,* no. 1 (1976): 5–19;

Edward J. O'Brien, ed., *The Best Short Stories of 1922* (Boston: Houghton Mifflin, 1922);

Jack W. Weaver, "George Moore's Use of Celtic Materials: What and How," *English Literature in Transition,* 22 (1979): 38–49;

Robert Welch, *Moore's Way Back: "The Untilled Field" and "The Lake"* (Totowa, N.J.: Barnes & Noble, 1982);

Virginia Woolf, *The Death of the Moth and Other Essays* (London: Hogarth, 1942);

Honor E. Woulfe, "George Moore and the Amenities," *English Literature in Transition,* 35, no. 4 (1992): 447–461.

Papers:

Collections of Moore's papers can be found in the British Library, the National Library of Ireland, the Brotherton Library at the University of Leeds, the University of London Library, the Fitzwilliam Museum (Cambridge), the Bibliothèque Nationale (Paris), the University of Washington Library, the Academic Center Library (University of Texas at Austin), the Beinecke Rare Book and Manuscript Library (Yale University), the Boston Public Library, the Houghton Library (Harvard University), the Library of the State University of New York at Buffalo, Princeton University Library, and the New York Public Library.

Arthur Morrison

(1 November 1863 – 4 December 1945)

John R. Greenfield
McKendree College

See also the Morrison entry in *DLB 70: British Mystery Writers, 1860–1919.*

BOOKS: *The Shadows around Us* (London: Simpkin & Marshall, 1891);

Tales of Mean Streets (London: Methuen, 1894; Boston: Little, Brown, 1895);

Martin Hewitt, Investigator (London: Ward, Lock & Bowden, 1894; New York: Harper, 1894);

Zig-Zags at the Zoo (London: Newnes, 1895);

Chronicles of Martin Hewitt (London & New York: Ward, Lock & Bowden, 1895; New York: Appleton, 1896);

Adventures of Martin Hewitt (London & New York: Ward, Lock, 1896);

A Child of the Jago (London: Methuen, 1896; Chicago: Stone, 1896);

The Dorrington Deed-Box (London: Ward, Lock, 1897);

To London Town (London: Methuen, 1899; Chicago & New York: Stone, 1899);

Cunning Murrell (London: Methuen, 1900; New York: Doubleday, Page, 1900);

The Hole in the Wall (London: Methuen, 1902; New York: McClure, Phillips, 1902);

The Red Triangle: Being Some Further Chronicles of Martin Hewitt, Investigator (London: Nash, 1903; Boston: Page, 1903);

The Green Eye of Goona (London: Nash, 1904); republished as *The Green Diamond* (Boston: Page, 1904);

Divers Vanities (London: Methuen, 1905);

That Brute Simmons, by Morrison and Herbert C. Sargent (New York & London: French, 1906);

The Dumb-Cake: A Play in One Act, by Morrison and Richard Pryce (London, 1907);

Green Ginger (London: Hutchinson, 1909; New York: Stokes, 1909);

Exhibition of Japanese Screens Painted by the Old Masters (London: Yamanaka, 1910);

Arthur Morrison

The Painters of Japan, 2 volumes (London & Edinburgh: T. C. & E. C. Jack, 1911; New York: Stokes, 1911);

Guide to an Exhibition of Japanese and Chinese Paintings (London: British Museum, 1914);

Fiddle O'Dreams (London: Hutchinson, 1933).

Collection: *Short Stories of Today and Yesterday* (London: Harrap, 1929).

During the 1890s the last vestiges of Victorianism were giving way grudgingly to a new morality

247

and a more experimental, daring cultural milieu. The literary battles over what constituted realism and naturalism were being waged, and Dickensian sentimentality toward the poor was losing ground to more "objective" depictions of urban decay and slum life. Thomas Hardy and George Gissing were establishing themselves as leading novelists, while Bernard Shaw, H. G. Wells, Oscar Wilde, and Rudyard Kipling were bursting upon the literary scene. This was also the decade in which Arthur Morrison reached the peak of his talent as a writer of short stories and short novels with the publication of *Tales of Mean Streets* (1894), *A Child of the Jago* (1896), and the various Martin Hewitt stories. Although literary history has judged Morrison to have been a greater craftsman than he was an artist, he is still praised for his capacity to portray life in East London's slums from the perspective of an insider.

Morrison had four careers, not all distinct from one another: minor official, man of letters, journalist, and art collector and historian. Little is known about his life or his various careers aside from the literary one, and even that which is "known" appears sometimes contradictory. He was born 1 November 1863 on one of the two John streets in London's East End, to Richard Morrison, an engine fitter, and Jane Cooper Morrison. Because Arthur said that he was born in Kent and because his father was an engineer, he and his parents may have wanted to escape the onus of being from the East End. It is possible that the family lived in either Kent or Essex during Morrison's childhood. Little is known of his formal schooling, but it is safe to say that, like most of the better-educated persons of his class, he was largely self-taught. Judging from the content of his earliest stories, he evidently was knowledgeable about boxing, cycling, and perhaps other sports, and he was also a sharp observer of slum life.

As early as 1886 he was working as a clerk for the People's Palace, Walter Besant's charitable institution designed for the purpose of upgrading conditions in the East End. By 1889 he had the opportunity to practice journalism in his capacity as subeditor of the *Palace Journal.* He was also on the editorial staff of the *Globe* for a brief period. In 1892 he married Elizabeth Adelaide Thatcher, the daughter of Frederick Thatcher, of Dover. They had one son, Guy, born in 1893; he died in 1921 of complications from wounds received during his service in World War I.

During the late 1880s and early 1890s, Morrison began writing and publishing in magazines short, poignant tales of East End life; these were col-

lected in *Tales of Mean Streets.* W. E. Henley, editor of the *National Observer,* invited Morrison to join the other writers on his staff, including Hardy, Kipling, J. M. Barrie, Robert Louis Stevenson, and Charles Whibling. Morrison was also among the writers who contributed to Henley's *New Review,* along with W. B. Yeats, Kenneth Grahame, Maurice Hewlett, and Edwin Pugh. Morrison and Henley became friends, sharing an interest in boxing and Japanese art in addition to their literary endeavors. Morrison would sometimes call on the Henley household after midnight to share his excitement over his latest find of an inexpensive Japanese print. Morrison dedicated *Tales of Mean Streets* to Henley, who responded with gratitude and caution:

> You do me proud and I'm very much obliged to you. My opinion as to the virtues of the work has been high from the first, and the association gives me sincere pleasure. But I warn you seriously. . . . I don't bring luck to any man but a sword. We held our heads too high, we Observers . . . and now that daring costs the beggars nothing, there are not a few that will take it out of all they know.

Although "A Street" – the collection's first story, which sets the scene and atmosphere for the others – first appeared in *Macmillan's Magazine* (October 1891), most of the stories in *Tales of Mean Streets* originally appeared in the *National Observer.* Indeed, Morrison came to Henley's attention via "A Street." This piece has no plot or developed characters, but Morrison skillfully creates an oppressive, closed, even claustrophobic atmosphere that stresses the unyielding environment of the East End and the unrelenting monotony its inhabitants suffer.

The story in *Tales of Mean Streets* that achieved the most notoriety is "Lizerunt," the rather shocking study of a working-class girl who out of desperation marries a worthless, drunken lout. He first lives off his mother and then off Liza. The story ends with his sending her out to make money any way she can, which suggests that she will become a prostitute. Morrison's Liza became the model for W. Somerset Maugham's title character in *Liza of Lambeth* (1897).

The characters in *Tales of Mean Streets* form a cross section of East End types, both honest and dishonest, all victims trapped in slum life. Morrison's long-standing interest in boxing is reflected in "Three Rounds," the story of a pathetic boy trapped into repeated beatings in the boxing ring simply because he knows nothing else. Although most of the stories portray the grimness of East End life, some have a touch of humor, such as "That

Brute Simmons," in which a remarried woman's long-lost husband returns, apparently to reclaim her. The story concludes with the woman's two husbands both leaving. Morrison and Herbert C. Sargent transformed "That Brute Simmons" into a one-act play in 1904.

Tales of Mean Streets received relatively positive reviews, especially for the first effort of a virtually unknown author. The *Athenaeum* (24 November 1894) found the combination of detail, restraint, humor, and pathos "absolutely convincing." The (London) *Bookman* (January 1895) remarked that Morrison was "an unusually vigorous writer" whose vision of the streets is "scrupulously truthful." The *Spectator* (9 March 1895), while acknowledging Morrison's "great power," nonetheless took him to task for portraying only the worst aspects of East End slum life. Morrison responded to the last review, beginning a pattern of defending himself against charges of exaggeration or of portraying only the darker side of the working class.

Morrison's vitality and diversity, as well as his humorous side, are suggested by a project as whimsical as Tales of Mean Streets is serious. *Zig-Zags at the Zoo* (1895), profusely and humorously illustrated by J. A. Shepherd, is a delightful introduction to the variety of wildlife at the London Zoo. The short essays – each featuring a different animal – that comprise the volume originally appeared in the *Strand* from July 1892 to July 1894. Designed primarily to appeal to children but with charm for adult readers as well, the book takes the reader on a carefree, "zig-zag" journey through the zoo, entertaining child and adult alike with witty commentary and amusing illustrations. For example, the chapter "Zigzag Ursine" begins

> A BEAR is an adaptable creature, a philosopher every inch. He takes everything just as it comes – and doesn't readily part with it. . . . He will eat honey – when he can get it; when he can't, he consoles himself with the reflection that it is bad for the teeth.

Adorning the page are bears in various merry poses, including several climbing a pole with one holding a hat out as if to catch money from the onlookers. The book continues in this way, stopping to observe familiar animals such as dogs and cows, as well as those less common, such as giraffes, crocodiles, and exotic birds. Each chapter begins with the type set in a large *Z*.

Tales of Mean Streets brought Morrison to the attention of the Reverend A. Osborne Jay, who ministered to one of the worst East End slums, the area

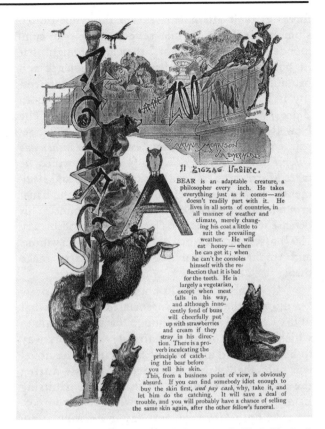

Page from "Zigzag Ursine," with an illustration by J. A. Shepherd (Strand, August 1892)

around Bethnal Green that Morrison immortalized as the Jago in his most successful novel, *A Child of the Jago*. It concerns the overwhelming struggle for survival of a young boy, Dicky Perrott, and his father, Josh. Father Sturt, the only force for good in the novel, is clearly modeled on Jay. Although he is working with Dickensian material of the urban poor and using a child as the focal point, Morrison strives, mostly successfully, to avoid lapsing into sentimentality. Like *Tales of Mean Streets, A Child of the Jago* is hard-edged and gives readers the feeling that they are being provided a privileged, inside view of the forbidden, mysterious jungle of the East End.

A Child of the Jago was much discussed and reviewed, making Morrison a controversial literary figure. This response to the novel was part of the general debate over realism during the 1890s. Although Morrison always claimed that he was simply presenting slum life as he had observed it and denied being part of a literary school, this novel in particular shares some of the literary assumptions of the naturalists, such as Gissing, Stephen Crane, and Emile Zola. The novel presents a slice of life in which the characters appear to be overwhelmed by social forces as their attempts to escape the crime-ridden slum prove futile. While several reviewers commended Morrison's "vigor," they also thought that he had gone too far in depicting the violence and brutality associated with slum life. Most noteworthy is H. D. Traill's extended discussion of both *Tales of Mean Streets* and *A Child of the Jago* in "The New Realism" (*Fortnightly Review,* January 1897; reprinted as "The New Fiction" in *The New Fiction and Other Essays on Literary Subjects* [1897]), in which he takes Morrison to task for his exaggerations and sentimentality. Morrison defended himself on the usual grounds of observed experience, and Jay came to his defense with a letter to the *Fortnightly Review* (February 1897) asserting the truth of Morrison's observations and emphasizing Morrison's credentials to make them.

Certainly the novel's notoriety helped to draw attention to the problems associated with the worst of the East End slums. Although the specific slum to which Morrison refers was already well under way to being cleared and rebuilt by the time the novel was published, Edward, Prince of Wales – during the dedication ceremony for the L. C. C. Housing Estate in March 1900 – acknowledged the importance of both Morrison and Jay in drawing attention to the problems of the slums: "Few indeed, will forget this site who have read Mr. Morrison's pathetic tale of 'A Child of the Jago,' and all of us are familiar with the labours of that most excellent philanthropist, Mr. Jay, in this neighbourhood."

During the 1890s Morrison also became a writer of detective fiction, creating Martin Hewitt, a character clearly modeled on Sherlock Holmes. Morrison sought to fill the void left by Sir Arthur Conan Doyle's decision to kill off his popular detective. Morrison wrote nineteen Martin Hewitt stories for the *Strand,* whose readers felt the loss of Holmes most keenly, and for the *Windsor Magazine.* The Hewitt stories were collected in three volumes: *Martin Hewitt, Investigator* (1894), *Chronicles of Martin Hewitt* (1895), and *Adventures of Martin Hewitt* (1896). Morrison also wrote a fourth book featuring Hewitt, *The Red Triangle* (1903). The Hewitt stories were generally well received, and Morrison was admired for his ability to make them believable and realistic, but the inevitable comparisons to Doyle's famous sleuth made Hewitt seem somewhat flat and mundane.

Morrison's success with detective fiction led him to write two more books in the genre, both without Hewitt: *The Dorrington Deed-Box* (1897) and *The Green Eye of Goona* (1904), published in America as *The Green Diamond. The Green Eye of Goona,*

heavily indebted to Wilkie Collins's *The Moonstone* (1868), revolves around Harvey Crook's attempt to trace a green diamond originally stolen from an Indian raja. Reviewers received the novel well, praising Morrison for his ability to create an intricate, exciting plot.

The Dorrington Deed-Box is a collection of stories featuring Horace Dorrington, a detective who also happens to be a criminal. Morrison's creation of a character who has it both ways suggests an effort to diversify, so that he was not typecast as a one-note writer with Hewitt. Some of the stories, such as "The Affair of the Avalanche Bicycle and Tyre Co., Limited," reflect his continuing penchant for incorporating his interest in sports and hobbies into his writing. The few reviews that *The Dorrington Deed-Box* attracted were generally positive; the *Athenaeum* (13 November 1897) praised the stories for their interest and illustrations.

Morrison wrote two more novels in the realistic vein after the diversion of the detective stories. The setting for the first of these, *To London Town* (1899), is the East End, but instead of the shocking slums of *Tales of Mean Streets* and *A Child of the Jago,* he chose the outskirts, including Epping Forest and the areas around Leytonstone, northeast London, Blackwall Cross, and Harbour Lane. Morrison's note at the beginning of the novel indicates that he intended it to be read in conjunction with *Tales of Mean Streets* and *A Child of the Jago,* the three together giving a fuller picture of East End life. Accordingly, the characters represent a class in straits not as dire as the "Jago rats." The plot revolves around a widowed shopkeeper and her son, an apprentice to an engineer. The general consensus about this novel is that Morrison is not as successful in portraying the problems of the petite bourgeoisie as he is with the desperate characters and dramatic situations of the slums. Certainly he is not up to H. G. Wells's inside portrayals of the petite bourgeoisie in such novels as *Tono-Bungay* (1908) and *The History of Mr. Polly* (1910).

Morrison's next novel, *Cunning Murrell* (1900), marks a turn in still another direction. The backdrop of this novel is the continuing practice of witchcraft in rural England – specifically Essex, around the coast of Leigh and Hadleigh – into the mid nineteenth century. Morrison bases the plot on the real James Murrell, a shoemaker who lived in Hadleigh and made additional income by telling fortunes, casting spells, practicing herbalism, and administering potions. Morrison had read various records and accounts of Murrell's activities, and the author focuses on Murrell's casting out of an innocent old woman as a witch. Morrison demonstrates considerable skill in creating a sinister tone and building up suspense. The reviewers treated *Cunning Murrell* favorably, praising Morrison especially for his characterizations of Dorrily Thorn, the heroine, and Murrell (*Bookman* [London], October 1900, and *Bookman* [New York], February 1901).

Morrison moved to Loughton, Essex, sometime between 1892 and 1896, even though he was still working in London. After his association with the People's Palace ended in 1902, he devoted much of his energies to journalism, contributing many unsigned articles to magazines and newspapers, including pieces that reflected his increasing interest in Eastern art. Morrison's last full-length novel in the realist tradition, *The Hole in the Wall* (1902), is considered by some to be his best work in terms of sheer craftsmanship. V. S. Pritchett, for example, declared it "one of the minor masterpieces of this century." Morrison was able to combine the best of his mystery-writing skills in creating atmosphere and constructing a suspenseful plot with his unflinching adherence to the realistic, informed portrayal of the desperation of East End life so skillfully set out in *Tales of Mean Streets* and *A Child of the Jago*.

The title of *The Hole in the Wall* refers to a public house owned by tough, salty Captain Nathaniel Kemp and situated on the crime-infested Radliffe Highway during the mid nineteenth century. Morrison adapts the technique of alternating narratives, which Dickens employs to good purpose in *Bleak House* (1853). The narrators are Captain Nat's grandson Stephen, who like Dickens's Esther Summerson is orphaned, and a third-person speaker. The plot involves murder, mystery, violence, and swindling, but the main interest is the change toward virtue that Stephen brings about in his grandfather.

Morrison's skill in creating vivid criminal and low-life characters – such as Dan Ogle, the murderer, and Blind George, who blinds Dan Ogle – nearly equals that of *A Child of the Jago*. Reviewers generally favored *The Hole in the Wall*, especially praising Morrison for taking a more hopeful attitude toward life in the East End than he had in his earlier realistic novels. The *Athenaeum* (27 September 1902), for example, found the novel "studiously workmanlike and artistic," and *Harper's Weekly* (4 October 1902) admired its economy, honesty, and perceptiveness, while claiming that in its uplifting portrayal of purification through pity it reached toward the heights of classical tragedy.

Many critics have been puzzled and disappointed that after the success of *The Hole in the Wall* Morrison did not go on to reach greater heights as a novelist. For whatever reasons – the demands on his time and energy from his career as a journalist, his increasing interest in Oriental art, or the possibility that he had used up his best ideas for novels – he did not produce another full-length work of fiction after *The Hole in the Wall*. It is likely that, as P. J. Keating and Jocelyn Bell suggest, he had always regarded himself as only a part-time novelist. Perhaps he found working in the short-fiction genre more compatible with his other interests. At any rate he continued writing short stories, several of which were published in the *Strand*, and collected three additional volumes of his short fiction during his lifetime: *Divers Vanities* (1905), *Green Ginger* (1909), and *Fiddle O'Dreams* (1933).

While his later efforts in short fiction may not reach the level of his two most famous novels or *Tales of Mean Streets*, many of these reveal a more playful, humorous side to Morrison's skills in fiction writing. The stories in *Divers Vanities* play on several of his familiar themes and methods – the psychology of criminality, the poverty and desperation of the working class, and the innocent point of view – but generally display a lighter touch than his other work in the realistic vein. For example, the opening pair of stories, both concerning the adventures of a small-time thief and pickpocket, Spotto Bird, are written to amuse.

In the first, "Chance of the Game," the somewhat dull-witted Spotto encounters a strange girl in his attempt to commit a theft. The girl's innocence and goodness prompt him to return her locket. In the following story, "Spotto's Reclamation," he has just gotten out of prison and is ready to resume stealing watches when he is saved from a constable known simply as "Ears" by Samuel Bullwinkle, a theorist on the criminal mind. However, Spotto has to pay a dear price for being saved: he becomes the guinea pig for Bullwinkle's experiment on how to reclaim criminals. Just when Bullwinkle believes he has succeeded in reclaiming Spotto, Spotto decides he has had enough; he fights with Bullwinkle and takes his watch.

Morrison's sympathies lie with Spotto, whose refusal to become a mere experiment appears to be a victory for individuality, perhaps foreshadowing the similar message of Anthony Burgess's *A Clockwork Orange* (1962), in which the criminal Alex becomes an experiment until his true personality is restored. One of the stories in *Divers Vanities* that first appeared in the *Strand* (September 1902), accompa-

"WITH A GASP AND A BOUNCE SHE LET GO UMBRELLA AND LUNCH-BAG TOGETHER."

Illustration by Tom Browne for "Lost Tommy Jepps" (Strand, September 1902)

nied by illustrations, is "Lost Tommy Jepps," the story of a bored, mischievous little boy who gets separated from his family at a train station and has some amusing adventures. In the end Tommy recovers his father's stolen watch and is restored to the good graces of his family.

The quotation on the title page of *Green Ginger* suggests the whimsical tone that characterizes most of the stories in the volume: "So hey with a whim-wham from the lande of green ginger." About half of the stories in the collection appeared first in the *Strand,* and several of these reuse characters Morrison had introduced earlier, such as the mendacious storyteller Dan Fisk, the clever burglar Snorkey Timms, and the mysterious Cunning Murrell.

In "The Absent Three," Fisk is introduced as one of the most popular men in Essex, "whom I have heard called the biggest liar in the county." Fisk tells the yarn of the three absentminded Brewitt brothers and their homely sister, Jane, who had "a face o' vinegar" that "'twould ha' kep' a regiment out o' gunshot; and there's no guessing how her brothers lived in the same house with it, 'cept they were too absent-minded to notice." The upshot of the story is that the ne'er-do-well Jim Bates is willing to court Jane because of her brothers' cashbox — "the more he heard of the cashbox, the

deeper in love he got." In a slapstick ending Bates attempts to elope with Jane and the cashbox until he discovers he can leave with only the latter. Jane inadvertently trips over one of her brothers, and Bates is caught and brought to justice.

"Snorkey Timms, His Marks" and "A Lucifo Match," both of which appeared in the *Strand* (March 1908, January 1909), display Morrison's skill in ending his stories with a surprise twist and eliciting sympathy for small-time criminals. Timms breaks into Mr. Marks's fancy-goods store in order to rob his safe. However, he discovers that all the valuables have been removed and that the premises have been prepared for a fire to start. He waits for Marks to come and light the fire, and when he appears, Timms offers to give himself up to the police, knowing that Marks has a strong desire not to involve them. Timms bargains with Marks, extracting twenty quid for not turning himself in, and then pulls the fire alarm on his way home.

In "A Lucifo Match" the mild-mannered pickpocket Johnson is caught by a mysterious, dark stranger who threatens to turn him in unless he comes with him. He briefly imprisons Johnson in order to have him appear on stage as part of a magic act, claiming that he can track Johnson down with several items taken from the audience. But Johnson lies low, eludes capture, and has a good laugh reading the papers about how an angry audience assaulted the great Lucifo.

Green Ginger was well received – with only a few caveats and quibbles – by the *Spectator* (20 February 1909), the *New York Times* (18 September 1909), the *Athenaeum* (10 April 1909), and the *Times Literary Supplement* (11 February 1909). Somewhat ironically – at least in light of the fact that readers respect Morrison most today for his unflinching portrayals of the grimmer aspects of East End slum life in *Tales of Mean Streets* and *A Child of the Jago* – nearly all of his contemporary reviewers expressed relief and approval that Morrison's later short stories are mostly in a much more lighthearted vein.

Morrison's next three books illustrate his capacity to channel his energies in widely divergent fields. *Exhibition of Japanese Screens Painted by the Old Masters* (1910), *The Painters of Japan* (1911), and *Guide to an Exhibition of Japanese and Chinese Paintings* (1914) represent the culmination of his admiration and study – as well as his rather extensive collection – of Eastern art. Although the exhibition books are slight, containing brief introductions and commentaries, *The Painters of Japan* – two folio-size volumes containing history, commentary, and plates – was regarded as an important contribution to Western understanding of Eastern art.

Morrison had already established his credentials as an expert on Japanese painting with a series of articles in the *Monthly Review*, and *The Painters of Japan* is, at least in part, a republication of these articles. The book was generally well received, with George Somes Layard, the reviewer for the (London) *Bookman* (January 1912), proclaiming Morrison the foremost authority on the subject. The *Times Literary Supplement* (27 July 1911) concurred with this judgment, praising his knowledge and keen observation. The *Athenaeum* (19 August 1911) and the *Saturday Review* (30 September 1911) praised his conscientious research, but both suggested that too many of the plates came from his own collection.

Morrison retired from his career as a journalist in 1913, moving to High Beech, Essex, near Epping Forest. After World War I he returned to London, moving his family to Cavendish Square, but by this time he had faded into near obscurity, and even less is known about the latter part of his life than about his early years. However, in 1924 his contributions to literature earned him membership in the Royal Society of Literature; he became a member of its council in 1935. He was also an honorary member of the Japanese Art Association. He

and his wife, Elizabeth, moved to High Barn, Chalfont Saint Peter, Buckinghamshire, in 1930 and remained there until his death on 4 December 1945.

Short Stories of Today and Yesterday – a collection of some of the more popular stories from *Tales of Mean Streets*, *Divers Vanities*, and *Green Ginger*, but with no new stories – was published in 1929. Morrison's last known book publication is *Fiddle O'Dreams*, a collection of short stories, some of which had appeared more than twenty years earlier in the *Strand*. Several of the stories, as the title suggests, are in the humorous vein of *Green Ginger*. Others are blatantly sentimental, and a few, such as "A Professional Episode" and "The Thing in the Upper Room," reveal Morrison's skill in subtly evoking horror.

The title story is a fantasy featuring Golden Lea, an old man who hears a fiddler who might be only a dream. In "The Sports of Mugby," Mr. Potter, a cheesemonger, defies local prejudice against the nearby Mugby horseraces and goes to bet on them. In a twist nearly worthy of Mark Twain, he discovers that others in the town have been betting secretly on the races and that the town's sanctimoniousness is mere hypocrisy. "Billy Blenkin's Radium" shows Morrison's soft spot for clever but harmless crooks, as Billy sells fake radium to his friends under the guise that he is doing them a favor by offering it so cheaply.

Perhaps because Morrison had been out of the literary scene for some time, *Fiddle O'Dreams* did not attract the number of reviews that his earlier collections did. The *Times Literary Supplement* (30 November 1933) pronounced "the stories in many moods . . . [to be] delightfully written." But it recalled that Morrison had his vogue in the 1890s with *Tales of Mean Streets*, adding that "our modern young realists may denounce [his] method as antiquated."

Morrison lived the last years of his life comfortably but quietly, devoting most of his energies to his impressive art collection, which by then included not only Oriental pieces but also many paintings by the English masters, including William Hogarth, Thomas Gainsborough, Sir Joshua Reynolds, John Constable, Benjamin Wilson, and J. M. W. Turner. Although he had come a long way from his humble origins in the East End, his death provoked no more than a ripple on the literary scene, with a few short notices. The London *Times* (5 December 1945) praised him especially for the way in which *Tales of Mean Streets* and *The Hole in the Wall* portray East End life with fidelity and objectivity and for having through such books inspired social legislation that led to slum clearance. Adhering to her husband's wishes, Elizabeth Morrison sold his library and art collection and, unfortunately for literary historians and biographers, burned his personal notebooks and papers.

P. J. Keating – who has assembled most of the known facts of Morrison's biography in the "Biographical Study" in his 1969 edition of *A Child of the Jago* – laments that, because of the lack of materials, it is unlikely that a full-length biography of Morrison can ever be written. Morrison will be remembered and studied for his three best portrayals of East End life – *Tales of Mean Streets*, *A Child of the Jago*, and *The Hole in the Wall* – which have gone in and out of print since his death. These works are a valuable asset to cultural historians in any attempt to understand East End life during the 1890s.

Bibliography:

Robert Calder, "Arthur Morrison: A Commentary with an Annotated Bibliography of Writings About Him," *English Literature in Transition,* 28 (1985): 276–297.

Biography:

P. J. Keating, "Biographical Study," in Morrison's *A Child of the Jago,* edited by Keating (London: MacGibbon & Kee, 1969), pp. 11–36.

References:

"Arthur Morrison," *Scholastic,* 24 (26 March 1934): 5;

Jocelyn Bell, "A Study of Arthur Morrison," in *Essays and Studies for the English Association* (London: John Murray, 1952), pp. 77–88;

Richard Benvenuto, "The Criminal and the Community: Defining Tragic Structure in *A Child of the Jago,*" *English Literature in Transition,* 31, no. 2 (1988): 152–161;

E. F. Bleiler, Introduction to Morrison's *Best Martin Hewitt Detective Stories* (New York: Dover, 1976), pp. vii–xiv;

Vincent Brome, "Arthur Morrison," in his *Four Realist Novelists* (London: Longmans, Green, 1965), pp. 7–20;

William C. Frierson, *The English Novel in Transition, 1885–1940* (Norman: University of Oklahoma Press, 1942), pp. 88–93;

P. J. Keating, *The Working Classes in Victorian Fiction* (London: Routledge & Kegan Paul, 1971);

Michael Krzak, "Arthur Morrison's East End of London," in *Victorian Writers and the City,* edited by Jean-Paul Hulin and Pierre Coustillas (Lille: University of Lille, 1979), pp. 147–182;

Krzak, Preface to Morrison's *Tales of Mean Streets* (Woodbridge, U.K.: Boydell, 1983), pp. 7–17;

V. S. Pritchett, "An East End Novelist," in his *The Living Novel and Later Appreciations* (New York: Random House, 1964), pp. 206–212;

H. D. Traill, "The New Fiction," in his *The New Fiction and Other Essays on Literary Subjects* (London: Hurst & Blackett, 1897), pp. 8–26.

Henry Woodd Nevinson

(11 October 1856 – 9 November 1941)

Becky W. Lewis
University of South Carolina

BOOKS: *A Sketch of Herder and His Times* (London: Chapman, 1884);

Life of Friedrich Schiller (London: Scott, 1889; New York: Whittaker, 1889);

Neighbours of Ours: Slum Stories of London (Bristol: Arrowsmith, 1895; New York: Holt, 1895);

In the Valley of Tophet (London: Dent, 1896; New York: Holt, 1896);

Pictures of Classic Greek Landscape and Architecture, by Nevinson and John Fulleylove (London: Dent, 1897);

Scenes in the Thirty Days War Between Greece and Turkey, 1897 (London: Dent, 1898);

Ladysmith: The Diary of a Siege (London: Methuen, 1900; New York: New Amsterdam, 1900);

The Plea of Pan (London: Murray, 1901; New York: Dutton, 1901);

Between the Acts (London: Murray, 1904; New York: Dutton, 1904);

Sketches on the Old Road through France to Florence, by Nevinson, Montgomery Carmichael, and A. H. Hallam (London: Murray, 1904; New York: Dutton, 1904);

Books and Personalities (London & New York: John Lane, 1905);

A Modern Slavery (London & New York: Harper, 1906);

The Dawn in Russia: Or, Scenes in the Russian Revolution (London & New York: Harper, 1906);

The New Spirit in India (London & New York: Harper, 1908);

Essays in Freedom (London: Duckworth, 1909; New Haven: Yale University Press, 1921);

Peace and War in the Balance (London: Watts, 1911);

The Growth of Freedom (London: Jack, 1912; New York: Dodge, 1912);

Essays in Rebellion (London: Nisbet, 1913);

Women's Vote and Men (London: Women's Freedom League, 1913);

The Dardanelles Campaign (London: Nisbet, 1918; New York: Holt, 1919);

Henry Woodd Nevinson, 1914

Original Sinners (London: Christophers, 1920; New York: Huebsch, 1921);

Lines of Life (London: Allen, 1920; New York: Boni & Liveright, 1920);

Essays in Freedom and Rebellion (New Haven: Yale University Press, 1921);

Farewell to America (New York: Huebsch, 1922; London: Bumpus, 1926);

Changes and Chances (London: Nisbet, 1923; New York: Harcourt, Brace, 1923);

More Changes, More Chances (London: Nisbet, 1925);

Last Changes, Last Chances (London: Nisbet, 1928; New York: Harcourt, Brace, 1929);

The English (London: Routledge, 1929; New York: Knopf, 1931);

Rough Islanders; Or the Natives of England (London: Routledge, 1930; New York: Knopf, 1931);

John Masefield (London: Heinemann, 1931);

Goethe: Man and Poet (London: Nisbet, 1931; New York: Harcourt, Brace, 1932);

In the Dark Backward (London: Routledge, 1934; New York: Harcourt, Brace, 1934);

Fire of Life (London: Nisbet, Gollancz, 1935; New York: Harcourt, Brace, 1935);

Running Accompaniments (London: Routledge, 1936);

Between the Wars (London: Hutchinson, 1936);

Films of Time: Twelve Fantasies (London: Routledge, 1939);

Thomas Hardy (London: P.E.N.-Allen, 1941);

Words and Deeds (Harmondsworth, U.K. & New York: Penguin, 1942).

Editions and Collections: *Henry Nevinson. The Augustan Books of Modern Poetry,* edited by Edward Thompson (London: Benn, 1926);

Visions and Memories, edited by Evelyn Sharp, with an introduction by Gilbert Murray (London & New York: Oxford University Press, 1944);

Essays, Poems and Tales of Henry Nevinson, edited, with an introduction, by H. N. Brailsford (London: Gollancz, 1948).

OTHER: "Some Memories of Ruskin," in *Ruskin the Prophet, and Other Centenary Studies,* edited by John Howard Whitehouse (New York: Dutton, 1920);

The Voice of Freedom, edited, with an introduction, by Nevinson (New York: Dutton, 1929).

Henry Woodd Nevinson was a poet, short-story writer, journalist, essayist, reformer, and autobiographer. When he died in 1941 his death notice led the obituary columns in both the London *Times* and the *New York Times*. A journalist known primarily as a war reporter and champion of human rights, he was also acknowledged as a writer of great distinction. However, Nevinson's great variety of activities obscured his literary reputation during his lifetime. In his introduction to *Essays, Poems and Tales of Henry Nevinson* (1948), H. N. Brailsford remarks that if Nevinson "had been a sedentary writer of correct opinions, everyone would have recognized his masterly prose style." Wendell V. Harris, in

British Short Fiction in the Nineteenth Century (1979), calls Nevinson's volume of short stories about the working-class poor in the East End, *Neighbours of Ours* (1895), a "masterpiece of storytelling." His contribution to British short fiction at the turn of the century consists of three volumes of stories written before he embarked on the journalistic career for which he would become most famous.

Nevinson was born in Leicester on 11 October 1856 to George and Mary Basil Woodd Nevinson. His evangelical parents were strict in his upbringing and considered immoral such secular readings as *Arabian Nights Entertainments* and plays by William Shakespeare. George Nevinson, a solicitor, hated the Papists, causing the family to attend "the most hideous church of England," according to his son. Nevertheless, Nevinson considered his childhood happy, writing that "the very strictness provided moments of excitement." He received a traditional classical education at Shrewsbury School, which he calls upon in an autobiographical sketch, "Sabrina Fair" (*Between the Acts,* 1904).

Nevinson was a timid scholarship student at Christ Church College, Oxford, where for the most part he spent a lonely three years. He later regretted that he had not made more of an effort to get to know the great men all around him there, such as John Ruskin, Henry Scott Holland, and Charles Dodgson (Lewis Carroll). Nevinson describes many of his Oxford experiences in essays and sketches. In "A Master" (*Running Accompaniments,* 1936) he poignantly describes the day when his exam grades were posted, instilling what was to become the lifelong feeling of inadequacy at producing only "a Second in Mods."

After Oxford, Nevinson traveled to Germany. His literary mentor was Thomas Carlyle, who, in rebellion against the materialism of the period, had found spiritual consolation among German intellectuals. Nevinson hoped to find the same solace and studied German literature, mainly at Jena University. After two years, however, he became disillusioned by the German submission to authority and suppression of personality. He left Germany with fodder for books about Johann Gottfried Herder, Friedrich Schiller, and Johann Wolfgang von Goethe, and a lifelong love for Friedrich Nietzsche. While in Germany in 1884 he married Margaret Wynne Jones, whom he had known since childhood.

Nevinson returned to London in 1885 with his wife and a young daughter. He and his wife began to work at Toynbee Hall, which was founded by Canon Samuel Barnett in the East End of London "to educate citizens in the knowledge of one another, to provide teaching for those willing to learn and recreation to those who are weary." A steady stream of lecturers, artists, and cultivated workers who wanted to improve the world made Toynbee Hall an extremely stimulating place during the 1880s, far more so than Oxford had been for Nevinson. He moved nearby into Petticoat Lane, where he lived "among bugs, fleas, old clothes, slippery cods' heads and other garbage," and he threw himself into helping his economically depressed neighbors. An enthusiast for military training who hoped to improve the youth of Whitechapel and Shadwell, Nevinson started the Cadet Company, which was the first military training group ever formed for the working class.

With another child to support, Nevinson attempted to earn more money by various means. He acted as secretary of the London Playing Fields Society, wrote *Life of Friedrich Schiller* (1889), taught history at Bedford College and German literature for the University Extension Society, and submitted sketches and articles to newspapers such as the *Contemporary Review,* the *St. James's Gazette,* and *Freedom.* J. W. Arrowsmith, a Bristol publisher, noticed a sketch that Nevinson had written about his Cadet Company for the *St. James's Gazette.* Arrowsmith asked Nevinson to do a book of similar sketches based on his experiences in the East End.

These sketches became *Neighbours of Ours,* which Arrowsmith held back for eleven months before publication in January 1895; meanwhile, Arthur Morrison's *Tales of Mean Streets* (1895) was published first. Both treat life in the East End slums, but Nevinson claimed that his book was praised while Morrison's was bought. The London *Bookman* (March 1895) pointed out that Nevinson's stories indicate that humor, spirit, and kindness can be found in the grimmest of settings. The American *Bookman* (March 1895) compared it favorably with a similar collection, Edward W. Townsend's *Chimmie Fadden, Major Max, and Other Stories* (1895), about the New York slums. Both authors demonstrate that these "low" characters are "neighbors of ours," but Nevinson's treatment is marked by the literary skill that "imparts that touch of wonder, or the thrill . . . which transforms the ordinary into the extraordinary."

Neighbours of Ours comprises ten stories set in Shadwell and Mile End, London slums that Nevinson knew well. An optimistic, cockney-speaking narrator holds the stories together as he interprets the world. Reminiscent of Huckleberry Finn, Jacko recognizes harsh reality but understands the human need to romanticize the world. He is tolerant, does not judge, and respects his neighbors. For example, in "An Aristocrat of Labour" Spotter Bateman is economically dependent on two disrespectful daughters for food and his room in the Millennium Buildings. When Spotter brings Jacko to one daughter's home for Sunday dinner, the daughter insults Jacko, calling him an "off-scourin' of the streets," and confines her father to eating in the kitchen. Spotter explains his philosophical outlook on life:

> "Jacko," 'e says again, "I was brought up to foller the tex' as says, 'Be 'appy and yer'll be good.' But it don't pay in the long run. If yer rides that tex' my son, yer'll get beat on the 'ome reach. I ain't 'appy now, let alone bein' good, as 'ad ought to be the natural consequence. I've been a classy casual all my time, Jacko, but the glory of casuals is vanishin' like a bloomin' 'alf-pint."

Spotter maintains his dignity and retains Jacko's respect as the "aristocrat of labour" in spite of his down-and-out condition. In "Old Parky," Jacko earns the title character's respect when he accords Parky's retarded sister dignity by calling her the "Innercent," while others make fun and call her the "Imbercycle."

Nevinson often draws his marginal characters with heroic dimension. In "Little Scotty," Mrs. Macrae raises her grandson Scotty in the strictest Christian tradition, and the neighborhood recognizes "there was always somethink queer about 'im." He is an idiot savant with a talent for mimicry. Through a series of adventures and misadventures Scotty ends up a star in the music halls in the West End. The most heroic (and sacrificial) character is Amy Morrison in "A Man of Genius." She is so in awe and enamored of her husband, "the genius," that she stuffs her coat with insurance coupons and attempts suicide by jumping into the Thames. She fails and is disappointed because she knows that money is the only thing that will enable her brutish husband to finish his absurd musical invention. She is prepared to die to make him happy.

Nevinson's stories can be romantic, as in "The 'St. George' of Rochester," which relates the story of a fallen woman who makes a home for herself and her baby on the *St. George,* a red-sailed barge that travels up and down the Thames. The captain falls in love with her and the child, and it seems as if they will live happily ever after. The child falls overboard, however, and the heartbroken woman disappears from the barge as mysteriously as she appeared. Nevinson claimed that a beautiful woman once said to him about this story, "We ought to be

Nevinson, 1875

very grateful to Mr. Nevinson for showing us what to do when we get into a scrape."

But more often than not, Nevinson's romance is cut by irony. In "In the Spring" a simpleminded old man, an " 'armless lunatic," is overcome with the memory of his first love when he smells the spring May (hawthorn blossom). He carries a bouquet of the "sweetsmelling May" to her, but she is horrified at the old man and his unwitting reference to her early lovemaking. She calls the police to arrest him, claiming, "Me a widder of three 'usbands as 'as always kep' 'erself respectable."

The biggest irony of all concerns the fate of the romantic heroine of *Neighbours of Ours,* a sensuously beautiful and talented young woman named Lina. All the young men are interested in her, and at one point Jacko appears to be courting her. In "Only An Accident" Ned, an enthusiast of the Shadwell Cadet Company, is blinded after an accident during a Cadet Camp. Lina visits his family, who points out that a blind man's only option for a livelihood is to go begging in the West End. His family deserts him, but Lina offers him both her hand and her earnings: "I always did say as the man

for me must be 'ard as pavin'-stones. Ned, a pavin'-stone's no 'arder nor a feather bed alongside of you." Ned accepts, but with a disclaimer: "Yer a good girl, there ain't no question. . . . But, O Lina, yer ain't just the same thing as the British Army."

Other stories in the collection include "Mrs. Simon's Baby," "Sissero's Return," and "Father Chris'mus." Nevinson's tales stand out for their dramatic timing, sensitive characterization, and balance of tone. Sentimentalism is missing; rather, a humorous and amiable cynicism runs throughout the stories, making them believable and enduring.

Nevinson's second volume of short stories, *In the Valley of Tophet* (1896), is based on a period he spent in 1895 in the coal-mining area between Birmingham and Wolverhampton known as the Black Country. He wrote the stories for Robertson Nicoll, editor of the *British Weekly;* however, Nicoll objected to Nevinson's brutally cynical point of view, believing that the public did not want to read about such unrelieved ugliness. In *Changes and Chances* (1923) Nevinson claims the stories were doomed because the comfortable classes did not like to hear the truth about the working class.

Nevinson's "hell on earth," a "land of iron and fire . . . where nature and man seemed to have combined to make a desolation and call it wealth," is the fictional town Wenley-on-the-Hill. As in *Neighbours of Ours,* the characters and community unify the stories. While Nevinson toured the Black Country, he lodged in Cradley Heath with a woman who made nails all day. She became the model for the grim Mother Gough, a "woman-machine of life and blood."

In "A Vicarious Sacrifice," praised in the London *Bookman* (September 1896) as a "unique conception . . . powerfully portrayed," Mother Gough's madness comes about after the disappearance of a beloved daughter. The community censures Mother Gough, believing that the old woman has sold herself to the Devil. The paradox is that Mother Gough believes this too. The daughter comes back, having attained both success in the London theater and a good husband; Mother Gough is assured that her "vicarious sacrifice" is working. When the daughter says, "I don't feel particularly wicked," the mother knows why: "I've took the wickedness on myself so as she shouldn't. And now I know as them who agreed to reckon my old body and soul in place of hern is keepin' their contrack fine."

The stories also demonstrate Nevinson's engagement in the socialist debate of the time. For example, Doctor Maguire, a socialist reformer from London, hopes to inspire the people of Wenley with his ideals. In several stories, however, Nevinson suggests that the human dimension is not always accommodated by the socialist ideal. In "An Undesired Victory" the doctor hopes to educate the community with Sunday-evening lectures. He carefully plans his "Ethical Culture" programs, but the participants understand only the Christian elements and symbols in his lectures. In "An Old Red Rag" the community mistakes a Communist flag for a sign of the Salvation Army. Nevinson recognizes the powerful consolation that religion becomes for people without power.

In "An Anti-Social Offender" a doctor and his London guest commiserate about the future. The visitor believes:

> The people here ... are scattered over the land like sheep with the rot. Unorganized, disunited, they are helpless in the hands of the capitalist. The local industries are dying out. Yet the people increase without pause.

He sees no hope "as long as the working classes continue to offer their children to the Moloch of industrial slavery." His proposal is to stop their "anti-social" reproduction. However, the doctor realizes how simplistic this solution is, stating, "If only reason ruled the world." He illustrates this point with the story of a criminal neighbor whose baby gives focus to his life. In "An Autumn Crocus" the doctor falls in love with the vision of a young woman forging a chain, standing, "glowing in the orange of sunlight and the crimson of the furnace." He comes to a realization of the full meaning of the proposition that "the world belongs not to reason, but to passion."

Nevinson seems determined not to take the socialist position, and "His Ewe Lamb" depicts individual enterprise succeeding even in a colliery town. Treacle Tim learns to work the system by secretly opening his personal property onto a company mine. Ironically, the success of Treacle Tim's "fairy tale palace of a mine" is gained at the expense of Mrs. Treacle Tim's labor as she mines the coal at night.

Nevinson's imagery is often spectacular, dramatizing the wretched life of the colliers. In "His Ewe Lamb" the pits "devour widows' houses." As the pits get bigger, "the Houses of the poor begin their dance of death. Some bow forward; some curtsey back; some raise, as it were, one foot to heaven, whilst the other plunges into the grave." "Geordie's Marrow" invokes the terror and drama of being closed up in a pit filled with "greenish smoke, eerie

sounds that the creeping of the coal" makes, and the "fire stink." In the colliery homes wives hear "the great pit panting out the exhaust air from the engine, like a beast disappointed of its prey."

Nevinson's imagery reflects his acquaintance with the naturalism of Emile Zola, portraying workers as "dumb driven cattle" with "heavy, labouring brains." But Nevinson's characters also exert free will; some, such as Mother Gough's daughter, escape from the working-class world. In "On the Road to Parnassus" a young couple tours colliery villages, singing songs and expressing passion for nobler things. Even the brutes who work in the pits have a thirst for knowledge that raises them above the animalism of Zola's naturalistic world.

These stories are powerful and rich with the resonance of the British colliery towns. The reverberations of Christian thought commingled with socialistic ideals permeate and link stories. If the unrelenting gloom of these stories doomed them at the time of their publication, what Nevinson refers to as the "attraction of repulsion" and a desire to know about the past makes them intriguing today. While there does not appear to be any more wretched place in the world than Wenley, the characters who inhabit it are memorable because they are human; they are not caricatured or sentimentalized.

In 1897 Nevinson was having difficulty eking out a living for his family; he was restless and tired of London. During a meeting with John Massingham, editor of the *Daily Chronicle,* Nevinson poured out his impassioned view concerning the Greek revolution against Turkish rule. Massingham, pro-Greek himself, hired Nevinson to cover the war for the *Daily Chronicle,* and several days later Nevinson was on his way to Greece. Two books resulted from his experiences there: *Scenes in the Thirty Days War Between Greece and Turkey, 1897* (1898) comprises the essays he wrote for the *Daily Chronicle,* and *The Plea of Pan* (1901) includes a sequence of four imaginative essays based on his travels in Greece and fortified with classical allusions.

In "An Attendant Lord: H. W. Nevinson's Friendship with W. B. Yeats" (1991), Ronald Schuchard claims that Nevinson wished to be a literary man. During his early years in London he read voraciously, writing poems and stories at night. However, by the age of forty-one, his study of literature had made him realize his limitations as a literary talent. He was therefore ready for the adventure that Massingham offered. After the war in Greece, Nevinson became the literary editor for the *Daily Chronicle* and discovered Yeats's work. An "inexplicable passion" developed for all things Irish, leading him to Ireland, a veneration of Yeats, and sympathy and work for the Irish cause against English rule.

In 1898 the *Daily Chronicle* sent Nevinson to Madrid to cover the Spanish-American War. In 1899 he was sent to South Africa to cover the Boer War, and he spent almost a year witnessing the Boer onslaught in Ladysmith. This experience resulted in *Ladysmith: The Diary of a Siege* (1900).

Another volume of short stories, *Between the Acts,* was published in 1904. James MacArthur praised it in *Harper's Weekly* (March 1904) as deserving "serious attention from those who really care for the things that matter in literature." In the preface Nevinson describes the imaginative scenes included in this book as "causal episodes and situations which I have observed or imagined in the successive acts of a life to which fortune has granted a share of variety."

This collection begins with two autobiographical sketches that later appeared in *Changes and Chances*. "A Merchant of London" describes Sunday-night prayers at his maternal grandfather's house. Though of a gentler variety, these are reminiscent of Samuel Butler's Pontifex family prayers in *The Way of All Flesh* (1903). "Sabrina Fair" reflects on Nevinson's days at his beloved Shrewsbury School on the Severn River. The twelve stories that follow include closing poems presented "in some cases to prolong the mood." "A Don's Day" vividly describes Oxford college life from the viewpoint of a Christ Church don so timid that he lives in fear of entering the dining hall late and having the high table "rake his approach with a broadside of eyes." This English don is contrasted with the puffed-up "Herr Doctor Heinrich Meyer, professor in Ordinary of Christian Ethics at the University of Jena" in "Gaudeamus Igitur."

It is not difficult to recognize Nevinson the journalist in "Sic Vos Non Vobis":

> His "stuff" was always written in a strong and concise style, always up to time, always the right length, and as easy to read as print. So editors liked him, and if sometimes he showed traces of an unaccountable depth of passion or originality, they had little difficulty in cutting all that out, as being incomprehensible to themselves and their readers.

Nevinson also portrays his feelings toward Yeats:

> Morton, as usual, felt a certain shyness in the poet's presence, partly because of his extreme admiration. In that gaunt and ascetic young face, with the unruly hair and shy but passionate eyes, he saw the thing that was lacking in himself – the sign of that inward and spiritual

grace which by one little touch would have converted his own high and serviceable talents into something rich and strange.

One fine story, "In Twenty-four Hours," relates the emotions of a young Greek boy during his first war experience. At first he feels extreme terror, but after the Greeks escape, his fear turns to shame and self-reproach at the memory of his cowardice. He then risks his life by going back to the battle area to save a baby and is hit by a "growling" bullet. Nevinson's keen perception of adolescent self-torment makes this story powerful. "Corpus Christi" is a mother's dramatic monologue of a Corpus Christi procession while in the background a line of young conscripts prepares to go to the Cuban battlefront that afternoon.

"Vae Victis" relates the return of British correspondents on a train in South Africa during the Boer War. The men joke crassly about the Pretoria Boer women. When one appears looking for a wounded Boer soldier, they crudely diminish her dignity by making her believe that one of their own is her beloved. Nevinson remarks in his autobiography that this story was received with some indignation. And in portraying British men away from home in realistic, uncomplimentary behavior, it may have met with disapproval similar to that which *In the Valley of Tophet* provoked. Other stories in *Between the Acts* include "The Relief of Eden," "Of Your Charity," "Izwa!," "A Little Honey," "The Last Rag," and "The Pinnacle of Fame."

The stories in *Between the Acts* are generally more in line with what the comfortable classes would have enjoyed reading. The collection received favorable reviews, propelling Nevinson into a higher literary standing. In *More Changes, More Chances* (1925) he recalls, "I found myself moving in new circles – new literary circles which I had long regarded with awe as inaccessible."

Nevinson's next volume was *Books and Personalities* (1905), a collection of thirty-seven essays on literary figures that he wrote as literary editor of the *Daily Chronicle*. However, he did not rest on his newfound acclaim. He traveled to Africa to witness Portuguese slave trading for the production of cocoa in Angola, a practice that he exposed in *A Modern Slavery* (1906). Back in Britain he organized a boycott against cocoa from Angola. Soon afterward he was covering the Russian Revolution. He also observed many of the sporadic rebellions preceding World War I.

In 1909 he was in London supporting the suffrage movement. He quit the *Daily News* when the editor refused to support his protest against the force-feeding of suffragists on hunger strike in a Birmingham jail. During World War I he was a correspondent on the Western front from 1914 to 1918. In 1926, at age seventy, he was a correspondent in Palestine, Syria, and Iraq for the *Manchester Guardian.* His London *Times* obituary claims that he witnessed every sight of serious world conflict from 1897 until his retirement from journalism.

As a journalist Nevinson wrote regularly for the *Daily Chronicle* (1897–1903), the *Nation* (1907–1923), the *Daily News* (1908–1909), the *New Leader* (1922–1926), and the *Manchester Guardian.* He also contributed to the *New Republic, Living Age, Literary Digest, Atlantic Monthly, Contemporary Review, Fortnightly Review, Harper's,* and *North American Review.* His journalistic essays were noted for their scrupulous fact telling, masterful style, and irony, and they were considered distinguished examples of modern prose.

Because of their deep insights into world events, these essays were often reprinted in collections. Nevinson's favorite themes — love of freedom, hatred for injustice and cruelty, and sympathy for the oppressed — mark him as a man ahead of his time. Dubbed "Knight-Errant" by S. K. Radcliffe in a review of *More Changes, More Chances* for the *New Republic* (10 February 1926), Nevinson was often referred to as a champion of lost causes. However, he was always quick to remind anyone who thought this that he never wasted an hour on a forlorn hope; his causes were all winning ones.

Nevinson's first wife died in 1932. Their son, C. R. W. Nevinson, became an artist who is remembered for his paintings of the two world wars. In 1933 Henry Woodd Nevinson married Evelyn Sharp, a fellow journalist and feminist writer.

Nevinson was handsome, popular, and acquainted with most of the important people of his time. His three autobiographical works — *Changes and Chances; More Changes, More Chances;* and *Last Changes, Last Chances* (1928) — were abridged in *Fire of Life* (1935). John Masefield wrote the introduction

to this volume, calling it "a great record, hardly equalled by any, surely not surpassed; for in his friendships and championships he has not only used voice and pen, he has run risks and suffered."

In these autobiographical works, Nevinson vividly describes friends and acquaintances, including such literary giants as Carlyle, Ruskin, Butler, Masefield, Yeats, Thomas Hardy, and Oscar Wilde. Nevinson championed the poor, working-class people living in London slums and colliery villages; slaves in Portuguese Angola; woman suffragists in Britain; and the victims of the many wars he witnessed. His autobiographies effectively describe the times, conflicts, and people of the last decade of the nineteenth century and the early part of the twentieth century. He died in 1941 after being forced into the countryside following the bombing of his London home. S. T. Ratcliffe's obituary for the *Nation* proclaimed Nevinson a "Knight without Fear."

References:

James MacArthur, "Books and Bookmen," *Harper's Weekly* (26 March 1904): 468;

John Masefield, Introduction to Nevinson's *Fire of Life* (London: Nisbet, Gollancz, 1935; New York: Harcourt, Brace, 1935);

S. T. Ratcliffe, Obituary, *Nation,* 153 (22 November 1941);

Ronald Schuchard, "An Attendant Lord: H. W. Nevinson's Friendship with W. B. Yeats," in *Yeats Annual No. 7,* edited by Warwick Gould (Atlantic Highlands, N. J.: Humanities, 1991), pp. 90–130;

J. H. Whitehouse, "Henry Nevinson," *Contemporary Review,* 161 (January 1942): 44–47.

Papers:

The largest collection of Nevinson letters, journals, and manuscripts is in the Bodleian Library, Oxford. Other collections are at the National Library of Scotland, Edinburgh; the Shrewsbury School; and the British Library.

Barry Pain

(28 September 1864 – 5 May 1928)

John D. Cloy
University of Mississippi

BOOKS: *In a Canadian Canoe, the Nine Muses Minus One, and Other Stories* (London: Henry, 1891);

Playthings and Parodies (London & New York: Cassell, 1892);

Stories and Interludes (London: Henry, 1892; New York: Harper, 1892);

Graeme and Cyril (London: Hodder & Stoughton, 1893);

The Kindness of the Celestial, and Other Stories (London: Henry, 1894);

The Octave of Claudius (London & New York: Harper, 1897);

The Romantic History of Robin Hood (London & New York: Harper, 1898);

Wilmay, and Other Stories of Women (London & New York: Harper, 1898);

Eliza (London: Bousfeld, 1900; Boston: Estes, 1904);

Another Englishwoman's Love-Letters (London: Unwin, 1901; New York: Putnam, 1901);

De Omnibus, by the Conductor (London: Unwin, 1901; New York: Dutton, 1914);

Nothing Serious (London: Black & White, 1901);

Stories in the Dark (London: Richards, 1901);

"Two": A Story of English Schoolboy Life (New York: Mershon, 1901);

The One Before (London: Richards, 1902; New York: Scribners, 1902);

Eliza's Husband (London: Chatto & Windus, 1903);

Little Entertainments (London: Unwin, 1903);

Curiosities (London: Unwin, 1904);

Deals (London: Hodder & Stoughton, 1904);

Lindley Kays (London: Methuen, 1904);

Three Fantasies (London: Methuen, 1904);

The Memoirs of Constantine Dix (London: Unwin, 1905);

Robinson Crusoe's Return (London: Hodder & Stoughton, 1906); revised and republished as *The Return of Robinson Crusoe* (London: Laurie, 1921);

Wilhelmina in London (London: Long, 1906);

Barry Pain, circa 1894

The Diary of a Baby: Being a Free Record of the Unconscious Thought of Rosalys Ysolde Smith, Aged One Year (London: Nash, 1907);

First Lessons in Story-Writing (London: Literary Correspondence College, 1907);

The Shadow of the Unseen, by Pain and James Blyth (London: Chapman & Hall, 1907);

The Luck of Norman Dale, by Pain and Blyth (London: Nash, 1908);

The Gifted Family (London: Methuen, 1909);

Proofs Before Pulping (London: Mills & Boon, 1909);

The Exiles of Faloo (London: Methuen, 1910; Leipzig: Tauchnitz, 1910);

Eliza Getting On (London & New York: Cassell, 1911);

An Exchange of Souls (London: Nash, 1911);

Here and Hereafter (London: Methuen, 1911);

Stories in Grey (London: Laurie, 1911; New York: Stokes, 1911; Leipzig: Tauchnitz, 1912);

Exit Eliza (London & New York: Cassell, 1912);

The New Gulliver, and Other Stories (London: Laurie, 1912);

Stories Without Tears (London: Mills & Boon, 1912; Leipzig: Tauchnitz, 1912; New York: Stokes, 1914);

Eliza's Son (London: Cassell, 1913);

Mrs. Murphy (London: Laurie, 1913);

Futurist Fifteen: An Old Moore or Less Accurate Forecast of Certain Events in the Year 1915 (London: Laurie, 1914);

One Kind and Another (London: Secker, 1914; New York: Stokes, 1915);

Edwards (London: Laurie, 1915);

Me and Harris (London: Laurie, 1916);

The Short Story (London: Secker, 1916; New York: Doran, 1916);

Confessions of Alphonse (London: Laurie, 1917);

Innocent Amusements (London: Laurie, 1918);

The Problem Club (London: Collins, 1919);

The Death of Maurice (London: Skeffington, 1920);

Marge Askinforit (London: Laurie, 1920; New York: Duffield, 1921);

Going Home: Being the Fantastic Romance of the Girl with Angel Eyes and the Man Who Had Wings (London: Laurie, 1921);

If Summer Don't (London: Laurie, 1922); republished as *If Winter Don't* (New York: Stokes, 1922);

Tamplin's Tales of His Family (London: Laurie, 1924);

This Charming Green Hat-Fair (London: Laurie, 1925; New York: Adelphi, 1926);

Barry Pain [selected essays] (London: Harrap, 1926);

Dumphry (London & Melbourne: Ward & Lock, 1927);

The Later Years (London: Chapman & Hall, 1927);

Forbidden Love and Other Stories (Girard, Kans.: Haldeman-Julius, 1927);

Barry Pain [selected tales] (London: Harrap, 1928);

Barry Pain [selections] (London: Methuen, 1934);

Du Sel et du Poivre (Says Mrs. Hicks) Mis en Français par Maurice Beerblock (Bruges: Desclée de Brouwer, n.d.).

Collections: *Collected Tales* (London: Secker, 1916; New York: Stokes, 1916);

Stories Barry Told Me, collected by Eva Pain (London: Longmans, 1927; New York: Longmans, 1928);

More Stories, introduction by John Head Bowden (London: Laurie, 1930);

Humorous Stories, introduction by Alfred Noyes (London: Laurie, 1930; Freeport, N.Y.: Books for Libraries, 1971);

The Eliza Books (London: Laurie, 1931);

The Eliza Stories, edited, with an introduction, by Terry Jones (London: Pavilion, 1984; New York: Beaufort, 1984);

Stories in the Dark: Tales of Terror by Jerome K. Jerome, Robert Barr and Barry Pain, selected, with an introduction, by Hugh Lamb (London: Kimber, 1989; Wellingborough: Equation, 1989).

OTHER: "Bill," in *XX Stories by XX Tellers,* edited by Leopold Wagner (London: Unwin, 1895);

Henry Louis Grin, *Grien on Rougemont,* with a pantomime sketch by Pain (London: Lloyd, 1898).

SELECTED PERIODICAL PUBLICATIONS – UNCOLLECTED:

FICTION

"The Hundred Gates," *Cornhill,* new series 13 (October 1889): 405–416;

"Sincerest Form of Flattery," *Cornhill,* new series 15 (October 1890): 367–378; *Living Age,* 187 (15 November 1890): 407–413;

"Storicules – I. The Suicide-Advertisement," *Punch,* 101 (29 August 1891): 97;

"Storicules – II. The Back-View," *Punch,* 101 (5 September 1891): 120;

"Storicules – III. The Dear Old Lady," *Punch,* 101 (12 September 1891): 132;

"Storicules – IV. A Reviewer's Confession," *Punch,* 101 (19 September 1891): 135–136;

"Storicules – V. A Born Aristocrat," *Punch,* 101 (26 September 1891): 149;

"Detected Culprits," *Cornhill,* new series 17 (September 1891): 268–276; *Living Age,* 191 (24 October 1891): 204–208;

"Storicules – VI. Budwell's Revenge," *Punch,* 101 (10 October 1891): 173;

"Storicules – VII. Gazey," *Punch,* 101 (7 November 1891): 228;

"The Portrait Painter," *Art Journal,* 54 (1892): 201–204;

"Alicia," *Bookman* (London), 2 (July–August 1892): 111–112, 146–147;

"Una at Desford," *Idler,* 2 (December 1892): 518–528;

"Cynthia's Love Affair," *English Illustrated Magazine,* 11 (February 1893): 323–329;

"Pathos of the Commonplace," *English Illustrated Magazine,* 11 (October 1893): 19–26;

"A Parochial Matter," *Black & White*, 6 (9 December 1893): 742–743;

"The Undying Thing," *Black & White*, 6 (Christmas 1893): 16–22;

"Blindfold," *Black & White*, 7 (17 February 1894): 208–209;

"In the Boudoir," *Black & White*, 7 (9 June 1894): 704;

"Faithful Fortnight," *English Illustrated Magazine*, 11 (September 1894): 1159–1164;

"The Autobiography of an Idea," *Black & White*, 8 (1 September 1894): 274–275; (8 September 1894): 306–309;

"Complete Recovery," *English Illustrated Magazine*, 13 (December 1895): 191–195;

"The Church Militant," *Idler*, 9 (April 1896): 328–333;

"Lord Ornington," *Idler*, 10 (September 1896): 146–153;

"History of Clare Tollison," *English Illustrated Magazine*, 16 (January 1897): 233–240;

"Cheevers and the Love of Beauty," *English Illustrated Magazine*, 20 (February 1898): 325–332;

"The Artistic Success," *Idler*, 17 (April 1900): 306–309;

"Language of the Dead," *Current Literature*, 30 (January 1901): 99–100;

"Lovers on an Island," *Cosmopolitan*, 34 (December 1902): 151–157;

"Interzoos," *Strand*, 25 (June 1903): 677–682;

"A Liar and an Elephant," *Strand*, 26 (September 1903): 302–304;

"The Last Chance," *Strand*, 41 (April 1911): 467–474;

"Burdon's Tomb," *Strand*, 41 (May 1911): 573–588;

"When I Was King," *Strand*, 42 (November 1911): 501–505;

"Quaint Questions," *Strand*, 45 (January 1913): 116–117; (February 1913): 221–223;

"The Journal of Aura Lovel," *Strand*, 46 (December 1913): 642–655;

"Help!," *Strand*, 48 (December 1914): 621–631;

"Celia and the Ghost," *Strand*, 52 (December 1916): 658–664;

"The Official Mind," *Strand*, 57 (April 1919): 283–286;

"The Tale of Twenty Errors," *Strand*, 60 (December 1920): 556, 573–577;

"A New Comedy of Errors," *Strand*, 61 (January 1921): 86–90; (May 1921): 412;

"A Tale with Tangles in It," *Strand*, 62 (November 1921): 452–456; (December 1921): 590;

"Bobbed Hair and Sausages," *Strand*, 69 (February 1925): 193–196;

"A New Line in Cross-Words," *Strand*, 69 (March 1925): 316–318; (April 1925): 410;

"Talent and Genius," *Strand*, 71 (March 1926): 307–311;

"James James," *Strand*, 71 (April 1926): 345–349;

"Resting," *Strand*, 71 (May 1926): 517–521.

NONFICTION

"The Humor of Mark Twain," *Bookman* (London), 38 (June 1910): 107–111;

"The Importance of the Reader," *Living Age*, 296 (9 March 1918): 629–631.

POETRY

"The Robin," *Punch*, 101 (7 December 1889): 269;

"Ænigmata," *Living Age*, 190 (11 July 1891): 66;

"Dream of the Dead World," *Blackwood's*, 179 (February 1906): 204–208; *Living Age*, 248 (24 March 1906): 747–751.

Although primarily remembered as a humorist, Barry Pain was a versatile, prolific writer and journalist whose work includes novels, detective stories, supernatural fiction, juvenile literature, parody, and poetry. His best-known works, which deal with working-class figures, offer a nonjudgmental view of lower-middle-class life, gently illustrating the foibles of human nature through a colorful cast of characters. Pain's short fiction was extremely popular during his lifetime, appearing in the popular periodicals of the day, including the *Cornhill*, the *Strand*, and the *Idler*. Most of the collections of his short pieces are taken from his voluminous magazine publications. Since his death Pain has been relegated to a position of undeserved obscurity, remaining virtually unread today except for a few anthologized short stories.

Barry Eric Odell Pain was born in Cambridge on 28 September 1864, the son of a linen draper, John Odell Pain, and his wife, Maria. Barry attended Sedbergh School from 1879 to 1883, displaying an early inclination toward literary pursuits by contributing to the school magazine. From Sedbergh he proceeded to Corpus Christi College, Cambridge, earning a scholarship in 1884. While a student at the university, Pain edited the *Cambridge Fortnightly*, an undergraduate publication that ran its course during the 1880s. He received a third-class degree in classics in 1886 and later wrote extensively for the *Granta*, another student journal, founded in 1889. While at Cambridge, Pain made friends who were to prove helpful professionally.

Upon graduation Pain obtained employment teaching classics as an army coach at Guildford, a town south of London. His introduction to the London reading public came in October 1889 with the publication of "The Hundred Gates" in the *Cornhill*. The story involves a dream in which the narrator encounters ninety-nine stock characters sitting on gates in a field. After discussing their often ludicrously predictable attributes with several of them, he finds himself the hundredth among their number as a so-called humorist who mocks things of no consequence. Pain shows considerable ingenuity in lampooning the standard fare of contemporary popular British fiction, yet without venom.

As he continued to contribute to popular magazines, Pain was invited by several editors to write for their publications, notably *Punch* and the *Speaker*. He moved to London in 1890, securing steady work from the *Daily Chronicle* and especially *Black & White*, for which he produced a regular column, "In the Smoking Room," which ran for several years during the 1890s. Peopled with characters such as the Ordinary Man, the Eminent Person, the Journalist, and the Mere Boy, this humorous feature dealt whimsically with subjects as diverse as home repairs and the abstract concept of time.

During his early days in London, Pain lived in a working-class neighborhood, gathering impressions on which he was to draw in his sketches of lower-class life. At about this time Pain and several of his contemporaries, including Jerome K. Jerome and Israel Zangwill, were given the derogatory appellation "New Humorists" by the literary establishment because of their decidedly unaristocratic approach to comic writing. Pain was undeterred by this negative attention; although advised by the poet William Ernest Henley to pursue more-serious subject matter, he continued to produce humorous material throughout his career.

Pain's first book, *In a Canadian Canoe, the Nine Muses Minus One, and Other Stories* (1891), was largely drawn from his contributions to *Granta*. This volume of short fiction was Pain's vehicle to a wider audience, bringing him almost immediate success. His reputation as a humorist was established, and an ever-increasing group of editors approached him for material.

In 1892 Pain married Amelia Lehmann, the daughter of portrait painter Rudolf Lehmann and sister of composer Liza Lehmann. Also literarily inclined, Amelia published several plays and a novel during her lifetime. The Pains had two daughters, one of whom, Eva, collected a volume of her father's short stories, *Stories Barry Told Me* (1927). Pain's output from this period was prodigious and varied. In 1893 he brought out *Graeme and Cyril*, a novel about public-school boys, which was favorably compared to Thomas Hughes's work. The

book had appeared serially in the boys' magazine *Chums* under the title "Two" in 1892.

Pain took over the editorship of *To-Day* in 1897, filling the post vacated by his close friend Jerome after a devastating lawsuit forced him to sell his interest in the publication. *To-Day* was a twopenny illustrated weekly that combined the format of a newspaper with the features of a literary journal. Pain had assisted with the editing and contributed extensively to the periodical before Jerome's departure. Pain served as its editor from 1897 until 1905, when *To-Day* was absorbed by the *London Opinion*.

Pain's *Eliza* (1900), whose stories appeared first in *To-Day*, proved to be his magnum opus. Supposedly told by a lower-middle-class clerk, the book deals with the pompous narrator, his sensible, down-to-earth wife, and their domestic adventures. Eliza's droll, masterful handling of her pretentious husband exhibits a skillful presentation of not only working-class life, but the universal shortcomings of all married couples. The stories are presented in a stilted manner utterly out of keeping with the ordinary events depicted. The incongruity between the style of delivery and the subject matter markedly increases the comic element.

"The Cards" is a prime example of Pain's ability to show harmless human folly generously. Eliza's self-important husband insists that they need calling cards in order to prove their gentility. Her disagreement on the grounds that they never make visits or receive visitors falls on deaf ears. Eliza solves the problem by leaving nearly all the newly printed cards at one house, on the pretext that there are many people resident and no one should be excluded. The reader soon becomes aware that the clerk is no match for Eliza. His ludicrous efforts to save face leave little doubt as to who is in control.

The success of *Eliza* encouraged Pain to produce, over the next thirteen years, four more volumes of short pieces concerning the entertaining couple: *Eliza's Husband* (1903), *Eliza Getting On* (1911), *Exit Eliza* (1912), and *Eliza's Son* (1913). These collections present the same type of material that made the first so popular. The unnamed husband is displayed in all his priggish absurdity. Readers could identify with the would-be martinet, whose wife easily and consistently outwits him. In "The Move" (*Eliza Getting On*) the husband is disgruntled because he is undeservedly excluded from his mother-in-law's will. Eliza receives some furniture, however, so the couple decide that they need a larger house. Preparing to relocate, Eliza manages to finagle the house she wants and has the satisfac-

People I Have Never Met.
BY SCOTT RANKIN.

BARRY PAIN.

"THE OLD HUMOUR AND THE NEW."

"The distinction between the old and the new humour is ridiculous and perfectly arbitrary."—BARRY PAIN.

*Illustration by Scott Rankin depicting Pain's observation on the lack of difference between Old Humor and New Humor (*Idler, *June 1894)*

tion of seeing her spouse's system for transporting their household goods fail. Eliza's effortless finesse in manipulating her husband is seemingly inexhaustible.

Eliza's Son, narrated by the only child of the earlier principals, offers further insights into the now-aging pair. "Introducing Ernest" shows the son to be a true limb of the paternal tree, pompous and obsessed with money and position. Ernest practices usury at school and tries to sell his birthday present from his father, whom he holds in thinly veiled contempt. A born tycoon, he reflects the mercantile fixation of the lower middle class of Pain's era, for whom commerce was the chief vehicle to prosperity. Terry Jones, in his introduction to *The Eliza Stories* (1984), sees Ernest as "a chilling epitome of a society whose only ethic is monetary gain, and of a breed of businessman that was familiar in Barry Pain's day, but had still not wrested the reins of power from the old landowning establishment."

De Omnibus, by the Conductor (1901), which originally appeared serially in *To-Day,* presents the amusing adventures of a cockney public-transport conductor. His sharp insights into human nature are gleaned from his daily transactions with a wide cross section of English society. Pain masterfully portrays the difficulties of dealing with the paying public from a tradesman's point of view. "The Last 'Bus" is the long-suffering conductor's account of the final run of the night and its attendant problems. Inebriates are his worst trial, and he recounts several unusual incidents, including that of a man who claims to be an escaped dummy from Madame Tussaud's waxworks.

Pain's dexterity at swift development and effective storytelling does not manifest itself in his novels. His ability to function well within the brief confines of the short story stands in sharp contrast to the rambling wordiness of his longer efforts. *The One Before* (1902), a tale of intrigue concerning an Oriental ring imbued with magical powers, is, however, not wholly unsuccessful. Essentially comic, the stock characters who struggle for possession of the ring provide considerable entertainment through their stereotypical behavior. The book ends on a pleasant note, with the Orientalist bachelor/scholar getting back the missing ring, while his handsome young artist nephew gets the pretty girl, after the Fagin-like Jewish villain is thwarted. The book is loosely plotted, however, and is best recommended by its presentation of characters.

Like his contemporaries Arthur Machen and Algernon Blackwood, Pain was deeply interested in occult matters and wrote stories with supernatural themes. This body of work, markedly different from his comic material, shows Pain to be equally skilled at crafting varied types of fiction. Throughout his career he could change genres with enviable facility; his supernatural fiction continued to appear until the time of his death. There is an air of shadowy unreality created in this material, leaving the reader unsure of the actual preternatural agents in the stories. Without flagrantly resorting to the use of tangible spectral entities, Pain can tantalize without overstating, presenting the possibility of supernatural elements minus the banality of visible manifestations. Thus, in this respect, he is a kindred spirit to other writers of the period who turned now and again to occult themes, such as Vernon Lee, H. D. Lowry, Ella D'Arcy, and Thomas Hardy.

"The Diary of a God" (*Stories in the Dark,* 1901) is a tale of isolation and developing madness. A clerk comes into money and decides that his profession is beneath him since he has become a gentleman. He moves to the country, gradually cuts himself off from his former connections, grows to believe himself a deity above petty human considerations, and dies insane. This pathetic story of a little man who cannot cope with his good fortune because of class-related aspirations is narrated through the unfortunate's diary, found after his death. The clerk's withdrawal is total, and, as John Clute observes in *Supernatural Fiction Writers* (1985), he "falls through the floor of his old world into a solipsistic abyss."

In "Rose Rose" (*Stories in Grey,* 1911) Sefton, an artist, believes himself victimized by the ghost of his dead model, which sits for him until he finishes a masterful painting of Aphrodite. He then commits suicide. Like the Reverend Mr. Jennings in J. S. Le Fanu's "Green Tea" (*In a Glass Darkly,* 1872), the apparition is only visible to the painter and brings on a drastic personality change. Pain demonstrates skill in psychological observation in this story, obliquely depicting the line between madness and sanity while leaving the feasibility of supernatural visitation an open question.

"The Moon-Slave" (*Stories in the Dark*) presents a case of lunar possession. Princess Viola, who lives to dance, makes a bargain with the moon, becoming its vassal in exchange for celestial music on a heady night. Every month at the full moon, Viola feels compelled to return to the same spot and cavort in the ghostly light to the eerie strains that her luminous captor provides. A strange, understated erotic element is present in the tale, and Pain handles it deftly, presenting the princess as a girl dissatisfied with her male dancing partners, whom she views as wooden and inept. She is only happy when dancing alone or with her otherworldly partner, and the sensuous movements of her performance are unmistakably sexual. Viola comes to an unpleasant end, disappearing the night before her marriage, with a cloven footprint marking the location from which she vanishes. In "The Moon-Slave" Pain can be seen as making a moral statement concerning unbridled female passion. Clute maintains that the story "tells its readers (many of them women) that to disrupt the social fabric is to merit death, that erotic abandonment on the part of a nubile female damns her."

One of Pain's most intriguing creations is the lay pastor and consummate burglar Constantine Dix. His exploits, recounted in *The Memoirs of Constantine Dix* (1905), reveal a Victorian-era Robin Hood who works continuously at the rehabilitation of lower-class criminals, many of whom unwittingly furnish the urbane thief with helpful information concerning future heists. In "Checkmate" Dix decides to steal the valuable stamp collection of a busi-

nessman who has fired a woman whom the pastor has been aiding. On learning that the man is happy about the theft, since his insurance will more than cover it (some of the stamps are forgeries), Dix sends the collection to the insurance company anonymously. Before this action is taken, however, the housebreaker, in his capacity as pastor, gives the merchant a lecture on karma after he refuses to rehire the woman. The businessman relents and takes her back into his employment. Pain shows Dix to be a complex, sardonically amusing character who fatalistically views himself as damned, although he labors for the salvation of others. His acute powers of observation and his skill at illegal entry, deduction, and disguise rival those of Sherlock Holmes. Dix eventually murders his housekeeper (who tries to blackmail him), and his last memoir states that he will not be taken alive if arrested for the crime.

In 1907 Pain collaborated with the popular fiction writer James Blyth to produce *The Shadow of the Unseen,* a novel of witchcraft set in a remote part of England. Lacking a unified plot, the book involves the return of the heiress Linda Marle to her ancestral village, where a sorceress, Judith Jennis, plans revenge against the Marle family for the drowning of one of her ancestors during a witchcraft trial. Linda is rescued by Lawrence Hebbelthwaite, a local squire whom she marries after the death of Judith. Although the book contains interesting occult lore and authentic dialect, the narrative is rambling and the denouement disappointing. Pain's inability to sustain the quality of writing that makes his short fiction outstanding is all too evident here. Another novel written with Blyth, *The Luck of Norman Dale* (1908), is no more successful.

In 1908 Pain moved with his family to Saint John's Wood from Hogarth House, Bushey, where they had resided since 1900. In 1914 he visited the United States. Pain was patriotic and, despite his age, joined an anti-aircraft section of the Royal Naval Volunteer Reserve in 1915, during World War I. He became a chief petty officer, serving at a searchlight station on Parliament Hill, but he gave up this position because of eyestrain. In 1917 he became a member of the London Appeal Tribunal, passing judgment on petitions for exemption from military duty.

In 1916 Pain's *The Short Story,* a defense of the English variety of the genre, was published. It was undertaken in response to criticism that French and Russian examples of short fiction were superior to British efforts. Pain draws on many contemporary writers in vindication of his countrymen's ability, among them George Meredith, Rudyard Kipling, and John Galsworthy. In the process of defending English literary skill, Pain also sets forth his own principles concerning the form for which he is best known.

Pain worked well within the confines of short fiction, realizing that a marked impression must be made quickly and effectively. He maintains in *The Short Story* that the author "has not the time that the novelist has to win and cajole a reader; yet never for one instant must he show a limitation of time or space." Pain also held that the audience for the short story was different from that for the novel, that they were more discriminating, mature readers who were willing to deduce rather than demand to be passively informed. As a professional writer, Pain believed in the value of prolonged effort, with a resultant increase in skill as reward. His view of effortless, inspired writing was rather dim.

Pain's knack for crafting lifelike characters is undoubtedly one of his strongest suits, and his accurate use of the vernacular speech of his lower-class creations makes them all the more believable. "Dialogue," he observes in *The Short Story,* "if it is written with art, is the briefest and best form of character-delineation – the form in which it is the most interesting. A long description of the character of a man, however well it may be done, asks the reader to believe instead of permitting him to deduct."

After his wife's death in 1920, Pain moved to Watford, where he remained for the rest of his life. His literary output during his final years did not diminish, and, despite increasingly poor health, he continued to produce a wide assortment of work. *Marge Askinforit* (1920), a burlesque of the Margot Asquith diaries, amply demonstrates Pain's skill at parody, and he continued to produce humorous stories. *Tamplin's Tales of His Family* (1924) involves a windy bore who owns a boot shop and is fond of self-importantly telling anecdotes about his household. Tamplin is an archetypal British tradesman of the period, puffed up with egotism over his accomplishments in the mercantile world. In "Egbert's Art" Pain portrays Tamplin as a true philistine who sourly recounts the story of his artist nephew's executing a satiric portrait of him gorging at mealtime. Tamplin considers this type of art immoral and unrespectable.

Pain remained to the last a man of wide interests. He enjoyed gardening and the study of gems and music, and he was an accomplished cook. A projected study of the Georgian monarchy was left unfinished at his death. He continued to attend his club, the Arts, as long as his health permitted. Pain died on 5 May 1928 after a lengthy illness. Essentially a private person, he never achieved the public recognition that probably would have been accorded a more visible figure. Alfred Noyes pointed out in the London *Bookman* (December 1927) that "Mr. Barry Pain seems to have avoided self advertisement as others have all too often sold their souls for it."

Pain's fiction flows easily, with little that is labored or contrived. His extreme readability helped contribute to his popularity among his contemporaries. There is a lyric quality to Pain's prose that enhances its fluidity. Richard Le Gallienne noted in *Harper's Weekly* (28 May 1892): "Mr. Pain is at least as much a poet as a humorist, which one need hardly say is an extremely rare combination. Such complexity was, of course, the charm of Heine." Pain's early success with light, comic material set his course. Although capable of more serious work, he returned again and again to what he knew best and evidently enjoyed writing – humorous short stories and sketches.

Perhaps the sheer volume of his output and the wide variety of his writing prevented Pain from ever producing the monumental work of which many felt he was capable. The *London Mercury* (June 1928) observed charitably: "If he never quite fulfilled his early promise, or did his gifts full justice, it was probably because of the diversity of those gifts, which never left him free to pursue a course that would have built up and consolidated the sort of reputation that has come to men of far less capacity."

References:

"Barry Pain," *Critic,* new series 18 (6 August 1892): 73–74;

John Clute, "Barry Pain," in *Supernatural Fiction Writers,* volume 1, edited by E. F. Bleiler (New York: Scribners, 1985), pp. 443–448;

Richard Le Gallienne, "Mr. Barry Pain," *Harper's Weekly,* 36 (28 May 1892): 515;

"Literary Intelligence," *London Mercury,* 18 (June 1928): 123;

Mrs. Roscoe Mullins, "Mr. Barry Pain at Home," *Sylvia's Journal,* new series 2 (February 1894): 153–157;

Alfred Noyes, "Barry Pain," *Bookman* (London), 73 (December 1927): 166–167.

Eden Phillpotts

(4 November 1862 – 29 December 1960)

John Ferns
McMaster University

See also the Phillpotts entries in *DLB 10: Modern British Dramatists, 1900–1945* and *DLB 70: British Mystery Writers, 1860–1919.*

SELECTED BOOKS: *My Adventure in the Flying Scotsman: A Romance of London and North-Western Railway Shares* (London: Hogg, 1888);

Summer Clouds and Other Stories (London, Paris & New York: Tuck, 1893);

Down Dartmoor Way (London: Osgood, McIlvaine, 1896);

Children of the Mist (London: Innes, 1898; New York & London: Putnam, 1899);

Loup-Garou! (London: Sands, 1899);

The Striking Hours (London: Methuen, 1901; New York: Stokes, 1901);

Fancy Free (London: Methuen, 1901);

The Transit of the Red Dragon and Other Tales (Bristol: Arrowsmith / London: Simpkin, Marshall, Hamilton, Kent, 1903);

The Secret Woman (London: Methuen, 1905; New York & London: Macmillan, 1905);

Knock at a Venture (London: Methuen, 1905; New York & London: Macmillan, 1905);

The Unlucky Number (London: Newnes, 1906);

The Folk Afield (London: Methuen, 1907; New York & London: Putnam, 1907);

The Fun of the Fair (London: Murray, 1909);

Tales of the Tenements (London: Murray, 1910; New York: John Lane, 1910);

The Old Time Before Them (London: Murray, 1913); revised as *Told at "The Plume"* (London: Hurst & Blackett, 1921);

The Judge's Chair (London: Murray, 1914);

The Farmer's Wife: A Play in Three Acts, by Phillpotts and Adelaide Eden Phillpotts (London: Duckworth / New York: Brentano's, 1916);

The Chronicles of St. Tid (London: Skeffington, 1917; New York: Macmillan, 1918);

Black, White, and Brindled (London: Richards, 1923; New York: Macmillan, 1923);

Eden Phillpotts

Up Hill, Down Dale: A Volume of Short Stories (London: Hutchinson, 1925; New York: Macmillan, 1925);

Peacock House and Other Mysteries (London: Hutchinson, 1926; New York: Macmillan, 1927);

Brother Man (London: Richards, 1926);

It Happened Like That: A New Volume of Short Stories (London: Hutchinson, 1927; New York: Macmillan, 1928);

The Torch and Other Tales (London: Hutchinson, 1929; New York: Macmillan, 1929);

Cherry Gambol and Other Stories (London: Hutchinson, 1930);
They Could Do No Other: A Volume of Stories (London: Hutchinson, 1932; New York: Macmillan, 1932);
Once Upon a Time: A Volume of Stories (London: Hutchinson, 1935);
The End of Count Rollo, and Other Stories (London: Polybooks, 1946);
From the Angle of 88 (London & New York: Hutchinson, 1951);
The Hidden Hand (London: Hutchinson, 1952).

Edition: *The Fun of the Fair* and *Brother Man* (London: Macmillan, 1928) — volumes 19 and 20 of the Widecombe Edition of Phillpotts's Dartmoor novels.

In a literary career that lasted seventy-one years (1888–1959), Eden Phillpotts, author of more than 250 works, produced twenty-three volumes of realistic short stories. Besides these he published eleven volumes of fairy stories and nine volumes of mystery stories. Well known as the author of *The Farmer's Wife* (1916), which ran for more than a thousand performances in London's West End, and as a catalyst in launching the career of Agatha Christie, Phillpotts is best remembered for his eighteen Dartmoor novels, published between 1898 and 1923. His realistic short stories are best seen in relation to these novels. Indeed, when Macmillan brought out the Widecombe Edition of the Dartmoor novels in twenty volumes in 1927–1928, the final two volumes, *The Fun of the Fair* and *Brother Man,* were selections of Dartmoor stories that had begun with *Down Dartmoor Way* (1896). The first Dartmoor novel, *Children of the Mist* (1898), has the same title as the final short story in *Down Dartmoor Way.*

Born on 4 November 1862 in Mount Aboo, Rajputana, India, to Capt. Henry and Adelaide Waters Phillpotts, Eden Phillpotts was the eldest of three brothers. When his father — a 15th Native Infantry officer and a political agent in Harrowtec and Rajputana — died, Eden's mother returned with her sons to England. Phillpotts was sent to Mannamead School (later Plymouth College) in Plymouth, Devon, where he first became familiar with Dartmoor, the landscape of so many of his fictional works. In 1880, at the age of seventeen, Phillpotts began work as a clerk with the Sun Fire Insurance Company in Trafalgar Square, London. He took drama lessons but felt that he could not control his legs on stage. Writing also attracted him, and by 1890 he was earning enough from this pursuit to withdraw from

insurance work and become assistant editor of *Black & White* magazine.

Phillpotts's poems and short stories appeared in such literary magazines as *London Society,* Jerome K. Jerome's *Idler, London* magazine, and *English Review,* as well as *Black & White.* His first short-story collection was *My Adventure in the Flying Scotsman: A Romance of London and North-Western Railway Shares* (1888). In 1899 Phillpotts left London to settle permanently in his beloved Devon. He lived at first in Torquay but later moved to Kerswell in the village of Broad Clyst near Exeter. In 1892 Phillpotts married Emily Topham. They had a son and a daughter, Adelaide Eden, who collaborated with her father on several plays, including *The Farmer's Wife.* As detailed in her *Reverie: An Autobiography* (1981) Adelaide's relationship with her father was incestuous. James Y. Dayananda provides further details of this relationship in *Eden Phillpotts (1862–1960): Selected Letters* (1984). Phillpotts's first wife died in 1928. The following year he married Lucy Robins Webb.

Phillpotts was a regional writer whose Dartmoor novels are to Devon what Thomas Hardy's Wessex novels are to Dorset. Indeed, Hardy was Phillpotts's favorite novelist; Emily Phillpotts once described Hardy to Arnold Bennett as her husband's "god." Phillpotts became a friend of Hardy, and they exchanged visits during Hardy's later years. Phillpotts took over the mantle of chief Devon novelist from R. D. Blackmore, in honor of whom he unveiled a memorial window in Exeter Cathedral in 1904. However, Hardy's realistic novels and short stories influenced Phillpotts more than Blackmore's romances.

In discovering Dartmoor as the setting for his realistic short stories and novels, Phillpotts fully discovered himself as a writer. "My Adventure in the Flying Scotsman" is a facile mystery story, while the stories of *Summer Clouds* (1893) are sub-Dickensian in their sentimentality. In the realistic short stories of *Down Dartmoor Way* Phillpotts hit his stride, and they led directly to his major achievement, the eighteen Dartmoor novels of 1898–1923. As he worked on his novels, Phillpotts would devote the last three or four days of each month to writing a short story. The best of his realistic short stories have Dartmoor settings.

Phillpotts wrote much less convincing stories set in the West Indies in *Loup-Garou!* (1899) and *Black, White, and Brindled* (1923), and in the Mediterranean and Middle East in *The Folk Afield* (1907). The high valuation that Phillpotts gave his Dartmoor stories is confirmed by the fact that he collected what he regarded as the best forty of them in the final two volumes of the Widecombe Edition of his Dartmoor novels. He also continued to publish collections and stories about Dartmoor into the 1930s and beyond. Indeed, one of his last "novels," *The Hidden Hand* (1952), is in fact a series of Dartmoor tales narrated by the ambiguously named "white witch," Charity Crymes.

Phillpotts's foreword to this volume casts a long light back over his efforts of fifty years:

> As in the case of similar collections, these tales reveal their cardinal figure in the teller and it is well that she should record them from her own animated angle of vision, her own life's values, and with her own gusto, self-confidence, and vainglory. Though the substance of Charity Crymes is now long sped, her shadow remains from a vanished age when such dubious spirits haunted odd corners, to win credit for their wisdom, or hatred and distrust for their malevolence. But if a witch, then this lady may fairly claim to be a white one. She resembles a waning moon, whose daylight ghost still hangs upon the blue, morning sky long after dawn has slept another night away.

Although Phillpotts was ninety years old when this foreword was published, even his earliest Dartmoor stories tend toward nostalgia. He looks at a Dartmoor of the past, cherishing local speech (many of the stories are written in Devon dialect) and memorializing local characters who draw their independence and integrity from the moor. Like Hardy, Phillpotts was a post-Darwinian deeply interested in the relationship between character and environment. Though he would likely have resented being called a naturalist – perhaps even a realist – he respected Emile Zola.

Nevertheless, in *Down Dartmoor Way*, which he calls "These Glimpses Through Moorland Mists," he criticizes "the realists" as he describes Joan West, the heroine of " 'A Curse Half Spoke' ": "Joan West was just a cottage rosebud – the sort of girl who realists will tell you is not true to nature. But while those who haunt pigsties are very unlikely at any time to find a pearl, it is nonetheless unreasonable of them to assert that pearls do not exist." Phillpotts does not eschew the realism or naturalism of the pigsty, but he also seeks the idealism of the pearl. He is perhaps better described as a regionalist than as a naturalist or even a realist, though he does wish to show his readers the reality of Dartmoor life.

" 'A Curse Half Spoke' " is a tale of love, Phillpotts's central subject. Though he wrote fairy and mystery stories (even assuming a pseudonym, Harrington Hext, for U.S. publication of his detective fiction), as a writer of realistic short stories he is principally concerned with human relationships, particularly love and family relationships, in a rural, Dartmoor setting. As Charity Crymes describes her tales of *The Hidden Hand,* "When you come to sort them out, you will find that most of the tales I have been telling are only love stories, with Nature setting her master-trap for men and women alike, and brewing gall or honey as the case may hap," so one could reasonably describe most of Phillpotts's realistic short stories.

One of his most frequent themes is "tokening" (Devon dialect for engagement) between young men and women. He admires fidelity, loyalty, and unselfishness in love while attacking selfishness and hypocrisy. A favorite term for cunning, perhaps taken from rabbit poaching, is "hookem-snivey." His Dartmoor stories are filled with fascinating characters of all ages, local lore, the vitality of Devon speech, and descriptions of Dartmoor in all seasons. His narrators, who speak with what J. C. Trewin (in *Eden Phillpotts: An Assessment and a Tribute,* edited by Waveney Girvan, 1953) calls "the red-earth vowels," are often local characters such as Tom Turtle or Johnny Rowland, landlord of the Plume of Feathers, who narrate the stories of *The Old Time Before Them* (1913). Occasionally Phillpotts withholds his narrator's identity until the end of a story in order to add mystery or heighten the sense of discovery.

In his autobiography, *From the Angle of 88* (1951), Phillpotts reflects on the importance of Dartmoor to his writing, making the interrelationship between character and environment clear. For Phillpotts, contemplating Dartmoor became like reading a palimpsest containing layers of human record: "I began to see that these chaotic wastes of earth and stone were as a palimpsest where record under record was preserved and many yet awaited deciphering eyes to read them." He continues to define his central enterprise as a regional writer:

> Thus, from being a playground for dreaming and solitude with none for company save my own imagination, Dartmoor grew full of fellow creatures and the challenges of all humanity, while my workshop, with plenty of work to be done, was fortified by their presence. Material never lacked but the need of selection from it often proved difficult. Stories harboured everywhere, now among the folk, their dwelling-place and the Moor around them, now in the chance revelations of old headstones amid their little graveyards, with brief records and inscriptions, when possible to decipher. These would often combine to complement one another and carry on some narrative, where their dates sufficed to tell of the possibilities that invention might follow into

the realms of story-telling. I never took a plot to Dartmoor for its background, but approached every new scene with empty mind, confident that a story awaited me there.

What his friend and collaborator Arnold Bennett's Five Towns of the Staffordshire Potteries were to him, Devon's tablelands and river cradles were to Phillpotts. He took an interest in Kentucky writer James Lane Allen's use of Devon vernacular in Kentucky speech. Phillpotts's admiration of Sir George Clausen's paintings clearly reveals the author's own realistic, regionalist aesthetic: "He brought no affectations to rustic life, but the sentiment and truth won of observation. He set his people in their own surroundings, but never painted anything that was not true about them, thus discovering that beauty those artists miss who only seek truth where it is garbed with ugliness." Once again, then, Phillpotts snipes at naturalism.

Considering their organic relationship to the Dartmoor novels, it is ironic that critic Waveney Girvan (in *Eden Phillpotts: An Assessment and a Tribute*) fails to mention the short stories in describing Phillpotts's diversity as a writer. Nevertheless, Girvan asserts the superiority of Phillpotts's Devon writing: "His best work has been done in and about Devon, particularly that unique and wonderful heart of it known as Dartmoor." Girvan describes Dartmoor as Phillpotts's "literary lodestone." In defining the relationship between character and environment in the Dartmoor novel *The Secret Woman* (1905), Bennett writes: "This is not a tragedy which happens to occur on Dartmoor. It is a part of Dartmoor on which a tragedy happens to occur" (*Eden Phillpotts: An Assessment and a Tribute*). The relationship between Dartmoor and Phillpotts's art is as complete in the best of his realistic short stories as it is in the best of the Dartmoor novels. Phillpotts's realism is of the kind that Eric Auerbach describes in *Mimesis* (1946; translated, 1953) as "the representation of reality." It is not surprising, then, that fellow West Country resident Isaac Foot (in *Eden Phillpotts: An Assessment and a Tribute*) suggests that *Down Dartmoor Way* should be the title of Phillpotts's whole life as well as of the book of short stories that sowed the seeds of the Dartmoor novels. Foot designates Phillpotts "the uncrowned King of Dartmoor."

In 1953 Girvan noted that "even fifty years ago Phillpotts was recognized as Devon's outstanding man of letters, a position he has occupied down to the present day." This is doubtless an accurate account of Phillpotts's importance during the first half of the twentieth century, yet he is little read

A WILD THIRST FOR NOVELTY OVERTOOK MY 'BLUE UPRIGHT'

Illustration by J. Ley Pethybridge for "A Black-Letter Day" depicting Phillpotts at one of his favorite pastimes (Badminton Magazine, February 1899)

today. Nor is there much critical evaluation of his writing. This is not to say that a judicious selection of the best twenty stories from *The Fun of the Fair*, *Brother Man*, and other related volumes might not renew critical interest in his art. His ability as a realistic short-story writer is today underrated. In an era before radio, movies, and television, Phillpotts was a popular author who was widely read. He knew that if he produced six hundred thousand words a year he could live the life of a man of letters on four hundred pounds per annum.

Phillpotts wrote unashamedly for money, often producing a half-dozen books each year. He was in every way a professional writer, but this is not to say that in his best work he was not also a true craftsman or, in his own phrase, a "creative artist." Fellow Devon writer L. A. G. Strong is right when he describes Phillpotts at his best as "a philosophical writer. A settled view of life, deeply pondered, carefully worked out, is expressed in everything he has written" (*Eden Phillpotts: An Assessment and a Tribute*).

Strong also claims that "the Dartmoor cycle ensures for him at the least a local immortality. No student of the regional novel will be able to neglect him. No one interested in English dialects will be allowed to miss the most accurate transcription of Devon, in spirit and letter, that has ever been set on paper." It is important to remember that Phillpotts selected forty of his realistic Dartmoor short stories to accompany his eighteen Dartmoor novels to complete what Strong calls "the Dartmoor cycle." The cycle would be incomplete without the tales, since they are essential to its organic life. The Dartmoor novels and short stories together form an artistic unity.

There are elements in Phillpotts's realistic short stories to reward today's reader. First, there is his preoccupation with such enduring realities of human experience as love and death, suffering, and the joy of living. He observes human nature well and renders it in direct and vital language. For example, there is the opening description of the poacher Warrender Toms in the tragic love story "Meet Me By Moonlight" (*Up Hill, Down Dale,* 1925): "He lived with his mother at Horrabridge, and said he was a plate-layer on the Great Western Railway; but it weren't many plates he'd laid, I reckon; night-lines was more to his taste, and what he didn't know of snaring game-birds and killing heavy fish weren't worth knowing. He'd larned his tricks from 'Moleskin,' a famous poacher now gone to his doubtful reward."

Toms and Alice fall in love: "It was one of them cases where like met like and woke liking. . . . Though made of sense by nature, Alice was in love and saw the world upside down just then." Alice's gamekeeper father opposes his daughter's love for Toms. On the night when he catches Toms poaching, Alice falls in the millrace behind him and drowns: "Sharp wages for sin you might say – her lost in the water and old man's fifteen stone squatted on the young man's body." Toms cannot save his beloved, and he, gamekeeper Billy, and his wife share the loss: "Billy and his wife toiled to fetch the blessed life back to their only one; but 'twas all vain; the woman had gone." Phillpotts tells the story with unsparing directness, and the effect is pure tragedy.

Phillpotts employs the direct and simple language of natural observation throughout his stories. In "The Wise Woman" (*Up Hill, Down Dale*) heather honey is described as "like amber shining through milk," while in "Grimm's Ghost" (*It Happened Like That,* 1927) Miser George is "close as wax." When "Spider" Battishill commits suicide in "The Maiden Bell" (*The Striking Hours,* 1901), he is described as

"dead as a hammer." Phillpotts moves from facts of nature to deep assessments of human character. He describes Joe Bamsey in "Hunter's Cross" (*Up Hill, Down Dale*): "His teeth were gone, and he had a little mouth like a baby; but it spoke wisdom when he opened it, and his sense was never frosty, as sense is apt to be, for he had a large understanding of human nature and a very rare knack to turn tears into laughter."

The stories are replete with perceptive observations, such as "the wages of duty will often happen to be a long sight worse than the wages of sin." Phillpotts's narrative voice speaks with a Devon folk wisdom larger than his own. In addition to accurately recorded vernacular, there is play with biblical language, as in the idea that perfect love casteth out sense as well as fear or that "true love casteth out fear of relations." Phillpotts has a wonderfully exact ear for Devon speech. Johnny, the retired gamekeeper of "Grimm's Ghost," is one of "the faithful, out-of-date sort, who used to go deeper than money in their relations with their employers." Such is the lifelong closeness of his relationship with his employer, Sir Frederick Marsden, that he addresses his master thus, "'Tis like your large heart, my dear."

The folk wisdom that Phillpotts draws from the people of "Dartymoor" is continuous and penetrating. In "The Thief" (*It Happened Like That*) the message is that "somebody has to pay, of course, but 'tis the way of great evils that often the innocent be called to suffer worse than the guilty." In contrast to the pure tragedy of "Meet Me By Moonlight," there is the comic outcome of "Silas and Anthony" (*It Happened Like That*), in which young love survives parental disapproval because "hope don't die in the young." Thus, Phillpotts depicts the full range of human experience. Although the Devon folk wisdom that he imparts shows life deeply pondered, moral reflections are not imposed on the reader. Rather, one is allowed to draw one's own conclusions. So in "The Breaker of the Law" (*Cherry Gambol,* 1930) he simply tells "a very curious tale, and when you've heard it, you can decide about the morals for yourself," while in "To Giglet Market" (*The Striking Hours*) the narrator offers "the tale, an' you can judge for yourself."

Phillpotts's admired master Hardy describes the local-color word painting that he and Phillpotts undertook as "the imaginative creation of an abiding world which shall reflect the scenes, customs, habits, thoughts and deeds of an actual and fugitive world" (*Eden Phillpotts: An Assessment and a Tribute*). The opening of "The Spring Gun" (*Down Dartmoor*

Way) shows that natural description has a dramatic function beyond simply offering a beautiful picture of Dartmoor:

> The road led downwards beneath great woods along a narrow lane which cut the forest where it extended in magnificent but gradual sweeps from the fringes of the moor above, to the confines of green valleys, silver laced with water, below. Evening filled the world with light, and the grey boughs of the March woods, broken only by masses of fir and pine – all purple under a wild sunset – glimmered gloriously with amber and ruby where water trembled on every twig. The rain had run in dark brown streaks and stains down the weather side of oak and larch, had hung twinkling beads on the briars and the dead brackens of last year, had polished the face of the ivy and gemmed the sprouting trefoils of early woodsorrel. It was a sweet-scented, soaking world.

The innocent spring setting forms a dramatically ironic contrast to the story's theme of human folly. Squire Easterbrook has set a spring gun to scare off poachers from his woods: "'Tweren't a 'appy country-zide what bristled wi' man-traps; an', tho' the poachin' weer kep down wi' 'eavy 'ands, wuss comed of it, an' the poor shawed theer dog-teeth. You see the poor's allus ready to be ferocious like if they reckons they'm bein' badly used; and wheer a 'underd'l snarl, theer's hallus wan or tu as b'ain't afeared to bite." But Squire Easterbrook bites himself, for when his son, returning home from Cambridge for Christmas, takes a shortcut through the woods described at the opening of the story, he is shot by the spring gun.

As the narrator notes, "That's 'ow the sins o' the faithers comed to be visited on the cheel. Theer 'e layed, right 'pon 'is face, wi' blood all crawlin' hout of un likes snakes, an' that black, tu, under the light of the mune." The squire realizes that his actions are like those of a figure in Greek tragedy. He "tottered like a hox arter the first blow from the pole-axe." Fortunately, his son recovers to become the present squire, who forbids hunting.

The inveterateness of human nature is revealed in the folk narrator's conclusion, in which Phillpotts allows one to draw one's own conclusions from the series of human events he has presented. What should the reader think about poaching, hunting, or human nature? The narrator ruminates on the squire: "I 'specks ole Squire rattles 'is bones mighty 'oneasy when 'e thinks 'o the lad what follered 'im; but hif he *knawed,* 'ed burrer 'is way hout, I guess, an' 'ave 'is say – jus' fur the credit of the fam'ly." In "Meet Me By Moonlight" Phillpotts presents a tragic outcome, and in "Silas and Anthony" young love wins out in a comic conclusion.

In "The Spring Gun" a potential tragedy is averted. With philosophical irony, Phillpotts would probably hold Providence responsible for all three endings.

Phillpotts's realistic short stories deserve continued currency because they are well crafted and readable, and they often provide a powerful sense of human truth. Although Phillpotts loves Dartmoor, he does not idealize Dartmoor people. He knows full well that "the Dowl be cruel busy at Plymouth half his time, and 'tis clear enough he comes and goes by way of Dartymoor." Characters can draw strength from their rural lives, but such lives can also limit them. In "Two Primitive Maids" (*Down Dartmoor Way*) the reader is told that Ben Gurney "was the nearest approach to an animated clod one might see in a year of country life. A bubble he, blown from the red bosom of his native earth – the animated, muscular reincarnation of Dartmoor mutton and beef, with just sufficient brain to control it. Few would live so long and learn so little, even in the heart of Dartmoor, as had Ben." Nevertheless, the two sisters Lizzie and Mary Rundle break their hearts over him. Yet when he disappoints both and leaves the moor farm, their father observes in a kind of double irony, "He weern't never noa true moor-man and I allus knawed it. Us be well rids of un."

A "true moor-man" or a "true moor-woman" is independent, resourceful, generous, and guided by common sense. Such a person possesses the courage of Ann Damerell in "The Little Finger" (*The Old Time Before Them*); she cuts off her own little finger in order to persuade her snake-bitten friend Susie Gay to cut off hers. The narrator notes: "Man and woman be very quick to mark a real brave thing when they see it." But there is more to it than this. As Ann's mother observes: " 'Tisn't only the bravery . . . 'tis the unselfishness; 'tis the giving up for another what she knew she could never have again. A boy will be brave enough, I grant you; a boy would jump in the river to save another; but 'twould take a girl to do what my Ann done."

Like Hardy and William Wordsworth before him, Phillpotts sought through his writing to give continuity to a rural world that he saw changing and vanishing before his eyes. At his best he preserves his rural world as well as they do theirs. Dartmoor itself, its tors and rivers, its idiom and people, their ways and lives come fully alive in Phillpotts's art. The best of his realistic Dartmoor stories deserve to be republished and read as integral parts of the literary vision in his Dartmoor novels. It is difficult to think of an early-twentieth-century writer of comparable stature who has been as severely neglected in the second half of the twentieth century as Phillpotts.

In "The Tower of the Wild Hunter" (*Down Dartmoor Way*), the narrator notes: "Board Schools stifle all imagination and kill in the bud things as well worth keeping as local idiom and the accent racy of the red soil. But older generations still detain much myth and tradition which their grandchildren scorn as shadows of a night that has passed; and to an older generation he belonged who told this tale." The story itself is characteristic of Phillpotts, "a story of two men and one woman, and the ruined theatre of it lies hid under the great pine wood that fringes Heather Tor."

The differences between twin brothers provides the turning point of the story: "The differ'nce 'tween theer hinner selves weer just as gert as theer houter likeness." But this cannot be explained: "Theer's some nowadays as 'ud 'splain the sawls hout our bodies an' God A'mighty horf 'is throne. But I bain't 'mong them as 'old wi' such wickeness." Phillpotts celebrates by dramatizing the core of mystery in human events. At his best he equals Hardy as a creative artist: "You'm young yet, an' maybe wan't be 'bove takin' a pinch o' zalt from me. 'Tes this: doan't 'e try tu 'splain tu much in this world, helse, saw like's not, you'll find yourself 'splained hout o' 'eaven, come the next."

Phillpotts's realistic short fiction provides a direct, moving encounter with imagined and dramatized human experience in a Dartmoor setting. In his best short stories, the fundamental human realities are love, relationship, joy, suffering, life itself, and death. In his most successful stories — the selections made for *The Fun of the Fair* and *Brother Man,* and for such later volumes as *Cherry Gambol* and *They Could Do No Other* (1932) — he offers the experience and wisdom of Dartmoor people immediately and powerfully realized. A careful selection of these stories should be made and published in order to bring the best of Phillpotts's creative art freshly before the contemporary reader.

Phillpotts's traditional stories move from the Victorian toward the modern tradition. If he must be categorized, he is most accurately described (as far as his realistic short stories are concerned) as a transitional regionalist short-story writer in the Wordsworth/Hardy tradition. He sees a certain arbitrariness at the heart of the mystery of human living.

Letters:

Eden Phillpotts (1862–1960): Selected Letters, edited, with an introduction, by James Y. Dayananda (Lanham, N.Y. & London: University Press of America, 1984).

Bibliography:

Percival Hinton, *Eden Phillpotts: A Bibliography of First Editions* (Birmingham, U.K.: Worthington, 1931).

References:

Waveney Girvan, ed., *Eden Phillpotts: An Assessment and a Tribute* (London: Hutchinson, 1953);

Adelaide Phillpotts Ross, *Reverie: An Autobiography* (London: Hale, 1981);

George Brandon Saul, "Phillpotts' Use of Classic Subject Matter: A Selective Consideration," *Modern British Literature,* 2 (1977): 30–43.

Papers:

The principal collections of Phillpotts's letters are in the Stevenson Library, Lock Haven University of Pennsylvania; the Falls Library, New York University; the University Research Library, University of California, Los Angeles; and the Harry Ransom Humanities Research Center, University of Texas at Austin.

Edwin William Pugh

(27 January 1874 – 5 February 1930)

Vern Lindquist
Sullivan Community College

BOOKS: *A Street in Suburbia* (London: Heinemann, 1895; New York: Appleton, 1895);

The Man of Straw (London: Heinemann, 1896);

King Circumstance (London: Heinemann, 1898; New York: Holt, 1898);

The Rogue's Paradise, by Pugh and Charles Gleig (London: Bowden, 1898);

Tony Drum: A Cockney Boy (London: Heinemann, 1898; New York: Holt, 1898);

Mother-Sister: A Tale (London: Hurst & Blackett, 1900);

The Heritage, by Pugh and Godfrey Burchett (London: Sands, 1901);

The Stumbling-Block (London: Heinemann, 1903);

The Fruit of the Vine (London: Long, 1904);

The Purple Head: A Romance of the Twentieth Century (London: Hurst & Blackett, 1905);

The Spoilers (London: Newnes, 1905);

The Shuttlecock (London: Hurst & Blackett, 1907);

The Broken Honeymoon (London: Milne, 1908);

Charles Dickens: The Apostle of the People (London: New Age, 1908);

The City of the World: A Book about London and the Londoner (London: Nelson, 1908);

The Enchantress (London: Milne, 1908);

Peter Vandy: A Biography in Outline (London: White, 1909);

The Mocking Bird: An Entertainment. Compiled by Mrs. Lorrimer Wake. With Spelling, Stops, Grammar, and Literary Graces by E. Pugh (London: Milne, 1910);

The Charles Dickens Originals (London & Edinburgh: Foulis, 1912; New York: Scribners, 1912);

Harry the Cockney (London: Laurie, 1912);

The Proof of the Pudding (London: Chapman & Hall, 1913);

Punch and Judy (London: Chapman & Hall, 1913; Indianapolis: Bobbs-Merrill, 1914);

The Cockney at Home: Stories and Studies of London Life and Character (London: Chapman & Hall, 1914);

The Phantom Peer: An Extravaganza (London: Chapman & Hall, 1914);

The Quick and the Dead: A Tragedy of Temperaments (London: Chapman & Hall, 1914);

A Book of Laughter (London: Palmer & Hayward, 1916);

Slings and Arrows (London: Chapman & Hall, 1916);

The Eyes of a Child (London: Chapman & Hall, 1917);

The Great Unborn: A Dream of To-morrow (London: Palmer & Hayward, 1918);

The Way of the Wicked (London: Cranton, 1921);

The Secret Years: Further Adventures of Tobias Morgan (London: Palmer, 1923);

The World Is My Oyster (London: Unwin, 1924);

Empty Vessels (London: Ward, Lock, 1926).

Literary historians have nearly forgotten Edwin Pugh. During the late 1890s, however, he (along with W. Pett Ridge, Arthur Morrison, and Richard Whiteing, also obscure writers today) published some well-received essays, short stories, and novels in the realist tradition, or, more specifically, in the Cockney School. Although Pugh's popularity as a writer was brief and the Cockney School's influence on later fiction is slight, his works are interesting as examples of realistic fiction as practiced by a working-class man.

Edwin William Pugh was born a Londoner, less than four years after the death of Charles Dickens, on 27 January 1874. Like Dickens, Pugh was greatly interested in working-class London, which during his youth was still (as Vincent Brome notes in *Four Realist Novelists,* 1965) "a London where the streets were gas lit, hansom cabs plied for hire, women wore skirts to the ground, men rode penny-farthing bicycles and Gladstone dominated the scene." The son of an advertising agent, Pugh attended a London boarding school, an experience to which he refers in the essay "The Mind of the Clerk" (*Slings and Arrows,* 1916):

He leaves the County Council school on the verge of fourteen, an ignorant but not an innocent child. At an age when other more fortunate boys are being initiated into the mysteries of Latin prose he is being initiated into the mysteries of the prose of existence.... There is such a vast difference between him and the public schoolboy that it is difficult to believe they are of the same race and the same clay.

After leaving school Pugh worked for eight years in a city office. In the same essay he describes one of his experiences as a clerk:

I am standing in the awful privacy of my employer's inner room. He scowls at me across the cluttered table, and says –
    "Why did you do that?"
    "I thought – " I stammered out, abashed.
    "You shouldn't think," is his retort. "I don't pay my clerks to think."
    And it is so. The clerk is paid to be an automaton. And what he is paid to be, that he becomes.

These few years of clerical experience – ten-hour days for meager pay – were enough for Pugh to learn what the working life of the London middle-class man was like and for him to decide that he wanted something more.

While still engaged in his city office job, Pugh published his first book, *A Street in Suburbia* (1895), a series of short sketches. This collection was not to prove characteristic of Pugh's literary interests, although it indicated his interest in the short-story genre. He went on to write stories for various periodicals, producing two other long volumes of short fiction. The lower-class London setting of the sketches in *A Street in Suburbia* foreshadows Pugh's interest in cockney life. Still, this collection (and his short fiction in general) is predominantly sentimental. Although it features moments of harsh reality and nearly scientific accuracy of detail, it is overlaid with maudlin phrasing and melodramatic plots.

The first three sketches detail the courtship and marriage of Jack Cotter, a denizen of the titular London street. The first, "The Courtship of Jack Cotter," comically relates his wooing of various women, which amounts to his putting the offer of matrimony to them point-blank, without any preliminaries. This odd method succeeds with Julia Canlan, whose history is related in the next sketch, "Mother-Sister Julia." Whereas the first sketch is comic and lighthearted, this one is inescapably sentimental. Julia "was the eldest daughter of a decayed gentleman" who died of alcoholism: "Mr. Canlan had been a secret drinker: than which there is nothing more horrible."

The story recounts Julia's impossibly saintly manner of raising her siblings with quiet self-sacrifice, occasionally not sleeping in order to finish her work. This laudable conduct changes when the children leave the house and Julia finds that she has "more time on her hands than she could use to advantage." She begins to read novelettes, "to neglect her household duties and to lie on sofas in greasy morning wrappers all day." Although Julia was once "clean and wholesome," the anonymous narrator states that "a year's novelette reading altered all that." Nevertheless, the narrator loves her "for what she had been and done," attributing her real degeneration to her marriage to Cotter.

The other sketches continue in much the same vein, alternating between comedy and sentimentality. "The Old School" begins with the narrator lamenting his inability to describe the title building:

No; I could as easily describe my boots or my mother as the old school. The things with which we are most familiar are always indescribable. Even the things we know best — the things we most believe in — we cannot interpret to unsympathetic others. There is an undiscovered language.

However, he does manage to describe it. The sketch concludes with similar sentimentality, the narrator being caned unjustly by an evil schoolmaster, a Dickensian grotesque with a "large and coarse" mouth, "big blue veins on his temples," and a habit of taking "his nose between his thin white fingers and handl[ing] it with grim ferocity."

The sentimentality of the series builds to the end. "Mama's Angel" concerns two unhappy adopted children who accidentally die in church on Christmas morning, just as their widowed mother, the bell ringer of the church, had died some years before. "Hiram Slike and So" features the mild, hardworking Hiram and his good wife, Tilly, whose life together is as happy as can be except that they are childless. When at long last Tilly has a baby, Hiram is so elated that he rushes outside to alter his business sign to read not "Hiram Slike," but "Hiram Slike and Son." Before

painting the final n, however, he learns that his "byeby" has "give a little grunt for all the world ez if some one ud 'it 'im on the mark" and died; thus, the sign remains unfinished.

In the final sketch, "A Cynic's Dinner," Phil Evers, who pretends to have little concern for his fellowman, gives away his dinner (when he has no prospect of securing another) to a starving street urchin (who would be satisfied, it seems, just to hear Evers talk about his food). He effects a cynical pose, however, by claiming that he only gives it to him since the child's misery has taken away his appetite.

Reviews of A Street in Suburbia were generally positive, noting the volume's "wholesomeness" (the Globe) and "healthy" pathos (the Sketch). The Daily Chronicle remarked on Pugh's similarity to and difference from another contemporary London realist, Morrison: "Mr. Pugh has more sympathy with, and consequently, perhaps, a truer insight into, the type of character he sketches than Mr. Morrison. Mr. Pugh is kindly where Mr. Morrison is only caustic." Pugh acknowledges this difference between himself and Morrison in "Real Realism" (Slings and Arrows): "Arthur Morrison is out to shock you all the time, and in every conceivable way."

Favorable reviews also accompanied the appearance of Pugh's next book, The Man of Straw (1896). At least three of them compared Pugh to Dickens rather favorably; Pall Mall called the climax of the novel "almost Zolaesque." These early successes contributed to Pugh's decision to devote himself full-time to writing.

His third book and next volume of stories, King Circumstance (1898), was one of three books by Pugh published that year. Some of the eighteen pieces collected here were previously published in such periodicals as English Illustrated Magazine, New Review, and Chapman's. Although colored throughout with sentimentality, these stories demonstrate a distinct change of outlook in Pugh's fiction. Many discuss sexual relations more openly, and the humor is not as widespread. Overall, the stories are bleaker and more in the realist mode.

The first, "The Story of Hannah Wray," takes place not in Pugh's characteristic London setting, but in the country, in the days of bold squires and meek peasants, when "Britons loved their wives sturdily, impartially thrashed their sons, and died respected in a pickle of alcohol." The title character mysteriously appears in town, takes residence in one of the squire's cottages, and builds a large stable to house her impressive black stallion, on which she is wont to ride out to observe the laborers from the local jail. When a prisoner escapes, Hannah seems distressed; but the convict turns out to be her husband. Hannah, who has been planning for this all along, smuggles him out of the country, leading his pursuers astray by riding in men's clothing. "So, this true story ends. And I would that all true stories ended as happily," concludes the anonymous narrator.

Most of the other stories do not end so happily. "The Undoing of Matty White" concerns a woman who is taken up and then abandoned by an upstart author. "Lest the reader should be inclined to sympathise unduly" with her, however, the narrator is careful to point out that she is "merely an emancipated barmaid." Matty lives with the author, Archie, for a week, at which point he leaves her. She confronts him a year later with the news that their love child was born dead ("It was better so," she says). Her pleas for Archie to take her back repulse him, but she turns down his offer of money, saying defiantly: "I will live such a life as will damn you eternally, for everything I do now I shall be doing because of you. And God will hold you responsible. I was the weaker vessel." The story concludes with Archie's relieved statement, "I'm glad she didn't make a scene."

The nobility of character that Matty displays despite rough circumstances is what distinguishes all of Pugh's cockneys from his more refined characters. In "Bettles: A Cockney Ishmael," Pugh introduces a hard-drinking, cursing, altogether repugnant bar fighter (and a bad one at that). After seeing him beaten senseless in a brawl of his own manufacture, the narrator hears nothing about him until many years later, when an army doctor recalls the name. Bettles, the reader learns, became a valiant hero in the Sudanese war, the very model of an intrepid British warrior. The story is filled with coarse details, such as Bettles slaying an Arab with half a bayonet while bleeding to death himself. This vulgarity of character got Bettles thrown out of London pubs; removed to another situation, however, Bettles distinguishes himself and, far from being a troublemaker, becomes heroic.

Bettles contrasts markedly with another type of Pugh male character, the educated dissembler. Like Archie in "The Undoing of Matty White," Arthur, the narrator of "The Little Lady," lies to a trusting, honest woman for his own purposes.

The lady, whom Arthur has never met, is convinced that he is Jack, a man Arthur does not know. She takes him home to her private room and begins pouring her heart out to him, asking him to forgive her for not marrying him many years ago. Arthur, feeling slight pangs of guilt, forgives her and leaves.

Unlike the coarse but ultimately laudable Bettles, Arthur lacks the courage to admit his mistake and cruelly lies to preserve his own honor, even at the painful cost it extracts from the innocent woman. The class propaganda inherent here is blatant; as P. J. Keating proposes in *The Working Classes in Victorian Fiction* (1971), "an extreme self-consciousness about class distinctions is still everywhere apparent" in working-class fiction of this era. Although the plots have become more starkly realistic in order to indicate some of the misery of working-class life, broad stereotyping of characters is still the rule.

The story that ends *King Circumstance*, "The First Stone," emphasizes this point: the middle-class John Arbery, in order to preserve his fragile "respectability," evicts his unwed pregnant daughter, Annie, in the middle of the night (the few coins he gives her are reminiscent of Judas's payment). As the very picture of class consciousness, John sacrifices his daughter on the altar of respectability without blinking. He is in such a rush to get her out of the house that he refuses to leave the room as she dresses. Annie — who is crying even before her father comes into her room — assents silently to his orders as though they are perfectly reasonable. Characters such as Annie, Hiram Slike, and Bettles remain noble in their poverty and misery; those who care overtly for themselves and their social positions – such as Arbery, Arthur, and Archie – are held up for derision and contempt by Pugh. The suffering or self-sacrificing cockney is laudable and entertaining; the cockney with ideas about bettering his social station is wretched and disgusting.

Many of the characters and events in these two collections of short fiction (and in many of the novels as well) run counter to some of Pugh's pronouncements about the proper form of realist fiction. In "Real Realism" he directs the writer to use "representative" characters, to keep an even hand between the lovely and the ugly so as to give an impression of reality, and to strive to maintain objectivity. Realism is not merely sordid, Pugh maintains: "One would imagine, to read current criticism, that the only real things in the world were just those things that the world would be better without." Most important, though, as Theophilus Boll states in *The Works of Edwin Pugh* (1934), the author "must not have strong opinions, lest he be invariably moved to express them, and so destroy the objective reality of his work. He must not have a purpose."

As Brome and others have discussed, this plainly contradicts Pugh's earlier praise of Dickens, the "real realist" who invented "that fine and wholly admirable thing: the Novel with a Purpose." Moreover, Pugh's novels are full of characters who cannot by any means be termed representative: Tony Drum, from the 1898 novel of the same name, is as Brome notes "the hunch-back son of an impoverished flute player" – hardly a typical Londoner. Pugh's stories are arguably closer to his ideas of realist fiction in this sense, as the characters in them are not generally as grotesque. The story collections also maintain a balance between beauty and depravity (though individual stories often relate one or the other).

Still, the ugliness and nobility are so extreme and so sentimentalized that it can hardly be said that the stories give an impression of reality. Neither the corrupt actions nor the noble deeds are really explained. Although it might be possible for a man to disown his daughter with absolutely no second thoughts or for a man to give his life unthinkingly for his fellows, these actions seem unreasonable and merely melodramatic without some accounting for motives. Finally, the notion that the author records life sensitively, objectively, and without comment is confuted by the unmistakable class prejudices that Pugh divulges in these stories.

In *The Cockney at Home: Stories and Studies of London Life and Character* (1914), Pugh does detach himself more from his subject by projecting a narrative aspect of comic criticism. In most of his fiction Pugh shows drinking in a wholly critical light, but he is more evenhanded here. As Boll notes, in this collection "there are no quarrels and no drunkenness. The humorous tone of the book is sustained in scenes of timid folk whom drink turns into boasters," but not (as in *King Circumstance*) into crude brawlers. Indeed, many of the "studies" in this collection are little more than the prompted ramblings of cockney eccentrics, drunk and otherwise, and the tone is humorous throughout. The characters (often grotesque), their concerns (generally with their class standings or financial situations), and the narrative outlook (distinctively middle class), however, are the same as in Pugh's other collections.

"The Freak" is the reminiscence (told for "the price of half a go") of a former sideshow freak, a "Two-in-One" who claimed to be both the tallest dwarf and the shortest giant on earth. When prompted further by sixpence, he claims he also has been, with differing degrees of success, a bearded lady, a dog-faced boy, a "Wild Man from Borneo," and a strong man. He claims that this last ruse "might ha' gone on for ever if there hadn't been a bit of a gale while I was performing . . . blowing my weights off the platform." But now, the freak admits, he is "only a poor old liar, sir."

Likewise, the main character of the following sketch, "The Quack," is a lying, streetwise cockney eccentric. This shabby snake-oil salesman brags good-naturedly about being "a' inspired liar," though his sad eyes belie his humor. His obvious lies are still funny and eloquent enough to sell a few of his preparations: one man buys the "Corn and Wart Elixir" after hearing that it will remove the face of its user, if not the corn. The title character sells his silver polish by touting its value as a cough medicine for one's hacking spouse; its use is also guaranteed to help one sleep soundly. The story ends as he soundly beats a rude young man in a game of insults. In his own element, it seems, the "cockney at home" is a master at witty repartee and prevarication.

The former skill is the real subject of "Afternoon Tea," which ostensibly concerns the setting up and raining out of a tea party in Oakney Terrace. Mrs. Crumm's neighbors taunt her daughter, Selina; Selina's beau, 'Erbert; and their preparations for tea on the lawn. Although Selina at first tells 'Erbert to "treat 'em wi' contempt," she soon drops this pretense of superiority and answers the neighbors' jeers with sharp insults:

> "Well, miss . . . an' what d'you think you're lookin' at, pray?"
> "Dunno," Selina replied. "But I'll soon find out. Got a zoological book indoors."
> "Suppose you mean the family album?"

Skill in retort and deception is common to the cockneys of this collection. In fact the plots of the stories are in general merely occasions for the characters to display their streetwise wit (or lack of it). When the clever retorts end, so does the plot. In "Afternoon Tea," for instance, Pugh forces the characters apart with a rainstorm. Similarly artificial contrivances bring many of the rest of these stories to a hasty conclusion: the arrival of a train ends "The Peculiarian"; a boss's reentry, "The Tender Passion"; and a crowd's dispersal, "The Phrenologist." Many other stories terminate not with the conclusion of events, but simply with the departure of one of the principals, rendering further talk impossible (such as in "The Chanter" and "The Fancier").

Because Pugh is less interested in plot than in the flurry of his characters' insults, the resulting stories often seem repetitive. The situations are changed slightly, along with the dialogue, but the characters' reactions to what happens to them become predictable. In "Change of Partners," for instance, two old married couples switch spouses for a day, with foreseeably unhappy results and a hasty return to the status quo. The same general idea is found in "Woman's Work," where a husband and wife change roles, find the reversal unacceptable, and return thankfully to their former ways. Other often-used plots include the comeuppance of a braggart, the contest between eccentric old age and impudent youth, and the attempt of a streetwise beggar to gain assistance from a wealthier man.

As Boll notes in a chapter on Pugh's "Self-Plagiarism," "the most frequently plundered author whose work reappears in Pugh is Pugh himself. He wins the distinction of being the greatest plagiarist from his own work." Boll finds one speech from a story in *King Circumstance* repeated, with only slight "improvements," in two of Pugh's other works. This kind of self-plagiarism is perhaps to be expected from an author who averaged one published book for each year of his career. Nevertheless, the constant recycling of language and plot leads Pugh's stories, especially these last ones, to be highly repetitious.

Therefore it cannot be said that Pugh developed much as a short-story writer. The author at age forty does seem slightly more detached and comic in his outlook on cockney life than he does at age twenty-one. Melodramatic situations are thus more likely to be subsumed within the general framework of humor in his later pieces. Nevertheless, the middle-class outlook on the harsh conditions of cockney London and their effects on the populace remains constant. Although Pugh continued to write novels, essays, and autobiographical pieces for twelve years after *The Cockney at Home* was published, the Cockney School was no longer in fashion, and his writing met with less and less financial success. Pugh died on 5 February 1930, four years after the publication of his last work, the autobiographical *Empty Vessels*.

References:

Theophilus Boll, *The Works of Edwin Pugh* (Philadelphia: University of Pennsylvania Press, 1934);

Vincent Brome, *Four Realist Novelists* (London: Longmans, Green, 1965);

P. J. Keating, *The Working Classes in Victorian Fiction* (London: Routledge & Kegan Paul, 1971).

Sir Arthur Quiller-Couch

(21 November 1863 – 12 May 1944)

Richard Tobias
University of Pittsburgh

BOOKS: *Athens: A Poem* (Bodmin, U.K.: Lidell, 1881);

Dead Man's Rock: A Romance (London & New York: Cassell, 1887);

The Astonishing History of Troy Town (London: Cassell, 1888; New York: Cassell, 1890);

The Splendid Spur (London & New York: Cassell, 1888);

The Blue Pavilions (London & New York: Cassell, 1891);

Noughts and Crosses: Stories, Studies, and Sketches (London: Cassell, 1891; New York: Scribners, 1898);

I Saw Three Ships, and Other Winter's Tales (London & New York: Cassell, 1892);

The Warwickshire Avon (London & New York: Osgood, McIlvaine, 1892);

Green Bays: Verses and Parodies (London: Methuen, 1893; enlarged edition, London: Milford, 1930);

The Delectable Duchy: Stories, Studies, and Sketches (London: Cassell, 1893; New York & London: Macmillan, 1893);

Wandering Heath: Stories, Studies, and Sketches (London: Cassell, 1895; New York: Scribners, 1895);

Ia: A Love Story (New York: Scribners, 1895); republished as *Ia* (London: Cassell, 1896);

Poems and Ballads (London: Methuen, 1896);

Adventures in Criticism (London: Cassell, 1896; New York: Scribners, 1896);

The Ship of Stars (London: Cassell, 1899; New York: Scribners, 1899);

Old Fires and Profitable Ghosts: A Book of Stories (London: Cassell, 1900; New York: Scribners, 1900);

The Laird's Luck and Other Fireside Tales (London: Cassell, 1901; New York: Scribners, 1901);

The White Wolf and Other Fireside Tales (London: Methuen, 1902; New York: Scribners, 1902);

The Westcotes (London: Simpkin, Marshall, Hamilton, Kent, 1902; Philadelphia: Coates, 1902);

Sir Arthur Quiller-Couch, circa 1894

The Adventures of Harry Revel (London: Cassell, 1903; New York: Scribners, 1903);

Hetty Wesley (London & New York: Harper, 1903);

Two Sides of the Face: Midwinter Tales (London: Simpkin, Marshall, Hamilton, Kent, 1903; New York: Scribners, 1903);

Fort Amity (London: Murray, 1904; New York: Scribners, 1904);

Shining Ferry (London: Hodder & Stoughton, 1905; New York: Scribners, 1905);

The Mayor of Troy (New York: Scribners, 1905; London: Methuen, 1906);

Shakespeare's Christmas and Other Stories (London: Smith, Elder, 1905; New York: Longmans, Green, 1905);

Sir John Constantine (New York: Scribners, 1905; London: Smith, Elder, 1906);

From a Cornish Window (London: Bell, 1906; New York: Dutton, 1906);

Poison Island (New York: Scribners, 1906; London: Murray, 1907);

Major Vigoureux (London: Methuen, 1907; New York: Scribners, 1907);

Merry-Garden and Other Stories (London: Methuen, 1907; Leipzig: Tauchnitz, 1907);

True Tilda (Bristol: Arrowsmith, 1909; New York: Scribners, 1909);

Lady Good-for-Nothing (London & New York: T. Nelson, 1910);

Corporal Sam and Other Stories (London: Smith, Elder, 1910);

The Roll Call of Honour: A New Book of Golden Deeds (London & New York: T. Nelson, 1911);

Brother Copas (Bristol: Arrowsmith, 1911; New York: Scribners, 1911);

Hocken and Hunkin, A Tale of Troy (Edinburgh: Blackwood, 1912; New York: Appleton, 1913);

The Vigil of Venus and Other Poems (London: Methuen, 1912);

News from the Duchy (Bristol: Arrowsmith, 1913; London: Bell, 1913);

Nicky-Nan, Reservist (Edinburgh & London: Blackwood, 1915; New York: Appleton, 1915);

On the Art of Writing: Lectures Delivered in the University of Cambridge, 1913–1914 (Cambridge: Cambridge University Press, 1916; New York: Putnam, 1916);

Mortallone and Aunt Trinidad, Tales of the Spanish Main (Bristol: Arrowsmith, 1917);

Memoir of Arthur John Butler (London: Smith, Elder, 1917);

Notes on Shakespeare's Workmanship (New York: Holt, 1917); republished as *Shakespeare's Workmanship* (London: Unwin, 1918);

Foe-Farrell (London: Collins, 1918; New York: Macmillan, 1918);

Studies in Literature, 1918–1930, 3 volumes (Cambridge: Cambridge University Press, 1918–1929; New York: Putnam, 1918–1930);

On the Art of Reading (Cambridge: University Press, 1920; New York & London: Putnam, 1920);

A Lecture on Lectures: Introductory Volume (London: Leonard & Virginia Woolf, 1923; New York: Harcourt, 1923);

Charles Dickens and Other Victorians (Cambridge: Cambridge University Press, 1925; New York & London: Putnam, 1925);

The Age of Chaucer (London: Dent, 1926; New York: AMS, 1970);

Paternity in Shakespeare: Annual Shakespeare Lecture to the British Academy (London: Milford, 1932; New York: Haskell House, n.d.);

The Poet as Citizen, and Other Papers (Cambridge: Cambridge University Press, 1934; New York: Macmillan, 1935);

Cambridge Lectures (London: Dent, 1943; New York: Dutton, 1943).

Editions and Collections: *Poetry,* edited by Mary Stratton (London: Batsford, 1914; New York: Dutton, 1914);

Selected Stories by "Q" (London: Dent, 1921; New York: Dutton, 1921);

The Duchy Edition of Tales and Romances by Q, 30 volumes (London & Toronto: Dent, 1928–1929; New York: Dutton, 1928–1929);

Poems (London: Oxford University Press, 1929);

Memories & Opinions: An Unfinished Autobiography of Q, edited, with an introduction, by S. C. Roberts (Cambridge: Cambridge University Press, 1944; New York: Macmillan, 1945);

A Q Anthology, edited by Frederick Brittain (London: Dent, 1948).

OTHER: *The Golden Pomp, A Procession of English Lyrics from Surrey to Shirley,* edited by Quiller-Couch (London: Methuen, 1895);

Fairy Tales Far and Near, edited by Quiller-Couch (London & New York: Stokes, 1895);

The Story of the Sea, 2 volumes, edited by Quiller-Couch (London: Cassell, 1895–1896);

English Sonnets, edited by Quiller-Couch (London: Chapman & Hall, 1897; enlarged edition, London: Chapman & Hall, 1935; New York: Crowell, 1936);

Historical Tales from Shakespeare, edited by Quiller-Couch (London: Arnold, 1899; New York, Scribners, 1900);

The Oxford Book of English Verse, 1250–1900, edited by Quiller-Couch (Oxford & New York: Clarendon, 1900; revised, 1939);

The World of Adventure: A Collection of Stirring and Moving Accidents, 6 volumes, edited by Quiller-Couch (London: Cassell, 1904–1905);

The Pilgrim's Way: A Little Scrip of Good Counsel for Travellers, edited by Quiller-Couch (London: Seeley, 1906; New York: Dutton, 1907);

Select English Classics, 33 volumes, edited by Quiller-Couch (Oxford: Clarendon, 1908–1912);

The Sleeping Beauty and Other Fairy Tales from the Old French, retold by Quiller-Couch (London & New York: Hodder & Stoughton, 1910);

The Oxford Book of Ballads, edited by Quiller-Couch (Oxford: Clarendon, 1910);

The Oxford Book of Victorian Verse, edited by Quiller-Couch (Oxford: Clarendon, 1912);

In Powder & Crinoline: Old Fairy Tales Retold, edited by Quiller-Couch (London: Hodder & Stoughton, 1913); republished as *The Twelve Dancing Princesses and Other Fairy Tales Retold* (New York: Doran, 1923);

The Cambridge Edition of the Works of Shakespeare: The Comedies, edited, with introductions, by Quiller-Couch and J. Dover Wilson (Cambridge: Cambridge University Press, 1921–1931; New York: Macmillan, 1921–1966);

A Bible Anthology, edited by Quiller-Couch (London: Dent, 1922; New York: Dutton, 1922);

The Oxford Book of English Prose, edited by Quiller-Couch (Oxford: Clarendon, 1925);

Felicities of Thomas Traherne, edited by Quiller-Couch (London: P. J. & A. E. Dobell, 1934).

As a student of Oxford University, Sir Arthur Quiller-Couch signed articles contributed to the *Oxford University Magazine* with the letter "Q," and he continued to use that signature all his life. Q had a remarkable, and yet dual, career: first, he published thirteen collections of short stories and nineteen novels (1887–1912); next, he became the second professor of English literature at Cambridge University and contributed to educational reform (1912–1944). This doubleness pervades his career. In London he contributed to magazines and newspapers, but he lived in Cornwall and his fiction is set almost exclusively there; in Cambridge he was in residence during term as fellow at Jesus College, but as soon as term ended, he was off to Cornwall. His Cambridge colleagues noticed only a few provincialisms in his speech, but his fiction often employs Cornish dialect speakers. He participated in local government in Cornwall (he was mayor of his town and served on educational committees), and he helped to create the English tripos (the examination for students of English literature) at Cambridge University. Oxford University Press sold a half-million copies of his *Oxford Book of English Verse* (1900), which established the canon of English poetry in the twentieth century. He wrote introductions to the Cambridge edition of Shakespeare's plays, edited schoolbooks, and attracted large numbers of students to his lectures.

Although Q threatened to "haunt and hate" any biographer, one of his cardinal principles is that literature "cannot be understood apart from the men who have made it." Because he was essentially shy and reserved, his own attempt at autobiography is bland and uninformative. He asks in the preface to the last of the thirty-volume *Duchy Edition* (1928–1929) of his tales and romances that no memoir be written, since his stories contain "all of me that is worth preserving." In the preface to his novel *Sir John Constantine* (1905) he claims that if readers "would know anything of the writer . . . [they] may find as much of him here as in any of his books." The novel is an extravagant farrago of coincidence, accident, mischance, derring-do, and high heroics in the style of Alain-René Lesage's *Gil Blas* (1715–1735), Miguel de Cervantes' *Don Quixote* (1605–1615), or Laurence Sterne's *Tristram Shandy* (1759–1767). The one clear biographical fact to be derived is that, since Q sailed yachts, the sailing lore is accurate.

In the novel a Cornish boy claims his title as King of Corsica. After sea wrecks, pirate encounters, brothel scenes, misfired executioners' rifles, and adventures with an Italian company of strolling characters, the hero walks across Europe and back to Cornwall where he dies. Q's own success as a writer of fiction might have seemed to him as surprising as becoming King of Corsica. *Sir John Constantine* is a perfect example of a boys' novel, and Q is a master of the art of boys' literature. Like Rudyard Kipling and Q's friends James M. Barrie and Kenneth Grahame, Q, on testimony of his biographer, always "retained a boy's heart."

In his fiction Q evokes the people and landscape of Cornwall, in southwest England, where he was born on 21 November 1863. His father was a physician in Bodmin, Cornwall; his paternal grandfather was a physician in a nearby coastal village, Polperro, Cornwall. Bodmin is almost equidistant from the Bristol Channel on the north and the Atlantic Ocean on the south; Polperro inhabitants subsisted on fishing and the "free trade," by which they meant smuggling. Since the Cornish profited from wrecks on that stormy coast, outsiders believed they set up false lights to insure that such accidents would occur. The Couch family had been yeoman farmers and then fishermen in the eighteenth century, but Q's grandfather, an only son, was sent to London to be trained as a physician. He married Jane Quiller, the last surviving member of her family, her brothers and her father having died at sea. Nearly all of Q's fiction contains sea adventures.

Q's mother, Mary Ford, was born in a south Devon village near Newton Abbot, on the border of the duchy of Cornwall. She was an only child, and, according to Q's autobiography, *Memories & Opinions* (1944), she had "no conception of a purse as fathomable." Q reports that "the family affluence sank or had been consumed" because of his mother's extravagance and generosity combined with his father's inattention to collecting his physician's fees. In order to obtain his education, Q had to become a "scholarship boy." As such, Q developed a keen sense of what the power structure in his world demanded. He lived in two worlds: the world of his origin and the new world that granted him the scholarship and expected him to conform to the values of the power structure that supplied the funds. In the short story "The Penance of John Emmet" (*Old Fires and Profitable Ghosts*, 1900) Q's narrator describes an experience with a tutor: "He could not teach me scholarship, which is a habit of mind; but he could, and in the end did, teach me how to win a scholarship, which is a sum of money paid annually. I have therefore a practical reason for thinking of him with gratitude." The student is grateful not for academic knowledge, but for the power to obtain an annual sum of money. For Q, especially early in his career, the sum of money was absolutely necessary. The story of John Emmet is that of a man who lives a life in disguise, just as the scholarship boy is also a person in disguise.

In his autobiography Q cites as crucial to his development as a critic an event that occurred during his first days at Clifton College, a public school (in the English sense) founded near Bristol in 1862. The headmaster, John Percival, was a man of notable skills as an educational leader. An Oxford graduate who later returned to the university as president of Trinity College, he first taught at Thomas Arnold's reformed Rugby School, where he learned of nineteenth-century England's need for reformed secondary schools. At Clifton, Q was assigned Henry Graham Dakyns's House for his lodgings. In "innocent pride" he, in conjunction with his study mate, hung up curtains given to them by one of Q's Bristol relatives. When Q came back to the house after morning classes, he found "a throng" of "grinning" fellow students gathered around the notice board. A note read: "The House is reminded that Corinthian embellishments consort ill with its tradition of Doric austerity. H.G.D." Q pulled down the curtains immediately, but with "tears of boyish impotent rage." The incident turned "the eager acolyte into an angry precocious critic." At both Trinity College, Oxford, and at Cambridge as King Edward VII Professor of English, Q read all the signs before putting up curtains, no matter how much "innocent pride" might be involved. In Q's fiction an intermediary narrator translates the manners and methods of a Cornish native's "innocent pride" to a larger audience.

The name Couch (pronounced "cooch," not like the sofa) may derive from the Cornish (a Celtic language now extinct) for *red*. Q describes himself as a child as being a "red-haired urchin," and a friend of school days reports that he "was wonderfully covered with variegated freckles." Q annoyed his grandmother by lapsing into the "rustic idiom" of Cornwall, which he learned from the outdoor servants on his grandfather's farm. Q spoke two languages: the Cornish dialect, which characters in his fiction employ, and Standard English. Q employed local speech in his many duties in Cornwall as justice of the peace, as mayor of his town, and as chair of local education committees. His most recent biographer, A. L. Rowse, also a Cornishman, documents Q's skill in conveying his native speech in his stories. Like Matthew Arnold, Q inspected schools and consulted with their governing boards. Officially he spoke Oxbridge, but his Cornish language "helped [him] to enjoy dealing with all sorts of conditions of men in local affairs, committee work, session work." Bilingualism requires a sensitive ear and may be a key factor in Q's art. He shared his life in Cornwall with only a few persons, such as Barrie and Grahame. After suffering an apparent nervous breakdown while living in London in the 1890s, Q took permanent residence in Cornwall until his death.

At first glance Q's rustic narrators belong in the realistic tradition. William Wordsworth taught writers the ideal of a countryman free of cant and fashion, direct and immediate in the expression of emotions. Wordsworth's "Matthew," however, is conveyed in Standard English, and when he does employ a bit of local speech, as in "We Were Seven," he repeats the phrase until it is defined in English. In Q's fiction an urban dweller meets a countryman to hear a story. In "The Gifts of Feodor Himkoff" (*Noughts and Crosses,* 1891), an urban hiker on the coast of Cornwall stops at a bleak cottage between the path and the sea to ask for a glass of milk, thinking such a drink would be easy to serve. The old woman in the cottage, who takes over the narrative, says it would be no trouble to make tea, for she has few troubles: "Too few by land, an' too many by sea." Her husband is lost in senility. She says to him, "Isaac, you poor deaf haddock, here's a strange body for 'ee to look at; tho' you'm past all pomp but buryin', I reckon." Not only is the narrator given a cup of tea — a kind that

Noughts and Crosses

Stories Studies and Sketches

by

Q

"*Ipsae te, Tityre, pinus,
Ipsi te fontes, ipsa haec arbusta vocabant.*"

LONDON
CASSELL AND COMPANY
LIMITED
1894

*Title page for the 1894 edition of a collection of Quiller-Couch's
short stories set in Cornwall*

he estimates would cost a working man two weeks' labor in London – but also caviar and other delicacies thoroughly out of place in a rough cottage on the Cornish shores.

In the way of folk narrators, she seems to digress. After their only son had been killed in the Battle of Inkerman during the Crimean War, the father had vowed to kill in revenge any Russian he ever met. During a stormy night in the 1870s, a Russian sailor appeared at their cottage door, asking help for his ship in distress below. The father seized a stick and beat the Russian away from his door, and the husband and wife sat in their cottage all night as the storm raged. After the storm abated, they found the sailor's body where he had fallen on rocks. They buried him and the other bodies that had washed up on the shore. Five years later the dead man's brother arrived to thank them for their care. He sent the gifts of tea and caviar.

Readers may think they have solved the mystery of the delicacies, but Q adds another twist to the story. At the end the woman announces, "He's been breaking our heads dro' the post-office wi' such-like precious balms as these here. . . . 'Tis all we can do to get rid of 'em on poor trampin' fellows same as yourself." The urban reporter and the

urban reader recognize the irony. The wife misses the point. Readers note her lack of perception and laugh. The silent husband may see his sin and in his silence recognize what his wife cannot understand.

The English-language narrator bridges the gap between Cornwall and the educated public. Q's school and Oxford experience took him out of the Cornish world of the senile husband and impercipient wife. His first instruction was with his sisters at a local school for young women. Later he was a day boy at Newton Abbot College, another of the new public schools established in the nineteenth century, where he was enrolled from age ten to nearly seventeen. His headmaster was George Townsend Warner, and Q's rival in the school was his headmaster's elder son, also George Townsend Warner, the father of Sylvia Townsend Warner, who wrote novels and books on teaching. Q then won a scholarship at Clifton College, Bristol, entering at the age of seventeen and staying for two years (1881–1883). At Clifton he won the school prize and edited the *Cliftonian,* the school magazine. His chief rival for the poetry prize was Henry Newbolt, later a minor poet and author of the Newbolt Report, the 1922 reform of secondary education in England. One of the judges for the poetry contest in

1881 was probably Thomas Edward Brown, the Manx Poet and master of the Modern Side at Clifton; Q was a student on the Classical Side.

Q did not live in Brown's House, but his fiction occupies the literary house that Brown, Robert Burns, and other dialect writers created. Q quotes Brown's "Dedication" to the *Fo'c's'le Yarns,* second series (1887), without attribution, as if the words were his own, in his preface to the 1929 edition of *News from the Duchy:*

> Dear countrymen, whate'er is left to us
> Of ancient heritage –
> Of manners, speech, of humours, polity
> The limited horizon of our stage –
> Old love, hope, fear,
> All this I fain would fix upon the page;
> That so the coming age,
> Lost in the empire's mass,
> Yet haply longing for their fathers, here
> May see, as in a glass,
> What they held dear.

Readers would assume that the words are Q's own. In both his novels and short stories Q's Cornish innocents speak the authentic human voice of his countrymen and their heritage; in *Fo'c's'le Yarns,* Brown allows his characters to speak entirely in the Manx dialect. John Addington Symonds, a minor poet and literary critic, heard Brown read his dialect poems at Clifton College in 1870 (they were first published in London in 1873 and 1881) and in a private letter suggested that Brown ought to recast them as prose stories like those of Bret Harte. Although Q could not have read Symonds's advice, he could have observed the mild critical reception of Brown's poems and taken the hint. Dialect interests readers who have just left the dialect themselves, but that audience is small. Although – as illustrated by the old woman in "The Gifts of Feodor Himkoff" – dialect is direct and vivid language, readers must be dosed carefully. Q evoked a sense of nostalgia in his middle-class audience, which was already lost in the "empire's mass." Q preserves the "innocent pride" of his native speakers, for, unlike Brown, Q wrote for a large English audience rather than Brown's small Manx audience.

In July 1882 Q went into residence at Trinity College, Oxford, where during his second year he lived in John Henry Cardinal Newman's old rooms. At Oxford he renewed ties with Charles Cannan, a Clifton alumnus and a fellow of Trinity who was four years his senior. Cannan had lived in Brown's House at Clifton, and he became editor of the *Oxford Magazine* "on the understanding that Q would

help him." Rowse estimates that Q wrote one-third of the material in the publication. His contributions included parodies, which established a mode of imitation that marks his career. Editing the *Cliftonian* had been a schoolboy's job, but assisting on the *Oxford Magazine* was professional work that trained Q to write and edit for London magazines. His career as a journalist and parodist began in his undergraduate days – the eager, anxious "scholarship boy" learning the language of the power centers and speaking confidently in language that power understood.

Q received only a second class when he sat for his final examinations, but the Trinity president and fellows "immediately appointed him to a College lectureship" rather than the fellowship "for which he had hoped." Q commented fifty years later that his examiners "pretty thoroughly understood what they were about." Since Q's father had died leaving unpaid debts and little provision for Q's mother or younger brothers and sisters, Q could not remain long as an Oxford lecturer. His mother's father had also suffered financial losses; thus a double calamity forced Q to support his family. Rowse quotes a letter from Q explaining that he had overspent "in order to keep in the running with the best men, or to have any influence.... As it was, I got this place [his lectureship] simply because I was understood to have a lot of influence with the men and to know the best of them."

Q had fallen in love with the woman he eventually married, and in the midst of these disasters he asked her to marry him. He explained to her that he was very poor and thus "heavily handicapped . . . at the start." An impecunious young man in the 1880s would have considered the market for novels as a means to earn money. During his holidays from his lectureship Q wrote *Dead Man's Rock,* which was published in 1887 by Cassell, the London firm that had published Robert Louis Stevenson's *Treasure Island* (1883) and H. Rider Haggard's *King Solomon's Mines* (1886). Soon after Q's book was brought out, his Cassell editor announced that it "had begun to sell 'like hot cakes.' " The title derives from a Cornish landmark, but the ambience is Stevenson revisited.

Q's career as a short-story writer began in his novels. *The Astonishing History of Troy Town* (1888), his second novel, includes ancillary stories that could stand alone. This new Troy is Fowey (pronounced "Foy"), his favorite Cornish seaport town, which he had discovered as a boy and where he lived as a man. The novel opens with a scene of cardplaying that invites the reader to recall Alexander Pope's *Rape of the Lock* (1714), another mock-epic. The Admiral and his lady, the Vicar, and assorted remnants of Britain's heroic past in the form of surviving maiden daughters and sisters "await the birth of fate." Their lives are all insignificant but are treated in a grand manner, as if their events moved conditions of the cosmos.

In chapter 11 of the novel, a servant, Caleb Trotter, interrupts the mock-epic action to tell an amusing story that, in the manner of epic digressions or Shakespearean subplots, amplifies the main story. A one-eyed Wesleyan preacher frightens the parents and children in his congregation, the United Free Church of Original Seceders. This preacher is, as needs must be with poor congregations that cannot pay their ministers, also a sharp businessman who mixes religion with commerce in his chapel sermon: "My pore senful flock, ef you clings to your flocks an' herds, an' tents an' dyed apparel, like onto Korah shall you be, an' like onto Dathan an' Abiram, so sure as I be sole agent for Carnaby's Bone Manure in this 'ere destrict."

Because the one eye is taken to be an evil eye, his congregation shrinks and Sunday-school children play on the beach rather than attend his classes. While he is in town on business, he sees a bowl of false eyes in a shop window and purchases the largest one. The eye enchants his congregation, for it seems to see their sins. After the eye pops out during a sermon, he buys a new one, more appropriate in size, but he keeps the old eye to use in a scarecrow. The birds, like the congregation, flee from the one-eyed scarecrow, except for a wise, old rook that falls under its charms and forms a congregation of rooks that worship the image. When the scarecrow's eye also falls out, the rook congregation dissolves. The moral is plain, as in Q's short stories: do not put on airs. There also may be an implicit personal moral that one should manage and know the world like the Oxford scholarship student. The story gently satirizes Nonconformity; Q was always a solid member of the Church of England.

The tale charms like an elaborate shaggy-dog story. Readers await the point, the climax of the joke. Caleb Trotter is clever in his fresh folk metaphors: "A kind o'shever ran through [the rook], an' hes feathers went ruffy-like, an' hes leg bowed in, and he jes' lay flat to groun' and goggled an' glazed up at that eye like a dyin' duck in a thunderstorm." The tale amplifies the main plot with its naive townspeople enchanted by the behavior and clothing of the aristocrats who are not what they seem. It recalls Aesop's fables and Geoffrey Chaucer's "Nun's Priest's Tale," the story of Chauntecleer

and Pertelote (the bold rooster and the timid hen), in *The Canterbury Tales* (circa 1387). It is both realism and fable.

When Q resigned his lectureship at Oxford and moved to London to become a journalist who could pay off his father's debts, support his mother and four siblings, and think about marriage, he contributed stories like Caleb Trotter's to the *Speaker,* a London publication identified with the Liberal party. In the late nineteenth century the Liberal party vied for power in government, and the *Speaker* supported Liberal policies. The journal has passed through various titles in its history. In 1907 it became the *Nation,* which in 1931 was incorporated in the *New Statesman,* and it continues as the present-day *New Statesman and Society.* Q was an assistant editor, and others on the staff included Barrie, George Moore, Richard Le Gallienne, and Augustine Birrell. Both William Butler Yeats and Henry James contributed.

It is difficult to estimate the desires of Q's original audience. His fiction assumes a readership familiar with Greek and Latin literature. For example, the listening English speaker interrupts Caleb Trotter's story about the one-eyed preacher to suggest that he is "like Polyphemus." Caleb responds, "Polly which?," and the story goes on. For "Psyche" (*Noughts and Crosses*) Q's audience must know the myth of the psyche – the soul – as a butterfly. Another story in this collection, "Old Aeson," revisions the Oedipus story (Rowse remarks that the story was inspired by the birth of Q's son in 1890). Members of Nonconformist churches are gently satirized, but they are generally depicted as good folk in his fiction, since the Liberals depended on Methodist, Unitarian, and Presbyterian support. Q's characters have human foibles opposite to what Nonconformists would recognize as the "true" Nonconformity. An intervening urban narrator translates rustic metaphor into familiar urban terms. The superior reader always knows more than do the rustic tellers.

Because his Oxford connections "paid off," as Rowse says, Q had friends in London to open doors. He worked as an editor for Cassell in London. Between 1887 and 1918 he published thirteen collections of short stories and twenty-one novels. In addition to the *Oxford Book of English Verse,* he edited collections of adventure fiction and anthologies of sonnets and fairy tales retold. Grub Street had fewer more-active denizens, even if Q lived mostly in Cornwall. Because he was so busy during his first years in London, it is not surprising that he had to retreat to Cornwall for eighteen months to recover his health. In 1892 he bought the house in Fowey that became his lifelong residence. He wrote his novels, short stories, and essays in Cornwall and made frequent but brief journeys to London. The railroad and the post office made his lifestyle possible. He found a gold mine in his Cornish backyard.

In 1910 Sir Harold Harmsworth (afterward Lord Rothermere), a newspaper magnate, endowed a professorship at Cambridge in honor of King Edward VII. The professor was to be nominated by the Crown, with the conditions that "the Professor . . . deliver courses on English Literature from the age of Chaucer onwards, and otherwise . . . promote, so far as may be in his power, the study in the University of the subject of English Literature." The professor was to "treat his subject on literary and critical rather than on philological and linguistic lines." Oxford appointed Sir Walter Raleigh to a chair in English literature in 1904. Both universities had taught philology and linguistics – the study of language changes and inflections – but only in the twentieth century, and then reluctantly, did they allow literature an official position on examination papers.

The appointment to the professorship was political. Q had supported the Liberal party in Cornwall and had contributed to liberal journals. His qualifications for the professorship were that he had published articles on literary topics in London journals and had edited successful anthologies. Although the grant specified that the Crown (rather than the faculty) should appoint the professor, in practice Liberal prime minister Herbert Henry Asquith recommended the candidate to the Crown. Cambridge huffed and puffed a bit. One of Q's contemporaries at Clifton, Dr. J. M. E. McTaggard, said, "A Professorship on such a subject, and to be filled up in such a manner, would not only be useless but positively harmful to the University." The *Cambridge University Reporter* summarized the arguments of another opponent; Dr. J. Mayo asked:

> What was the natural conclusion to be drawn from the position with regard to this Professorship? . . . That the University must be so ignorant of the value of English Literature that it required a bequest of £20,000 to deliver them from their state of ignorance. . . . The effect would be that it would be a professorship of English fiction, and that of a light and comic character. For that reason . . . the Professorship was a Professorship unworthy of the University.

The first professor was Arthur W. Verrall, a distinguished classical scholar who died after only sixteen months in office. Cambridge accepted Q as the

Crown's appointment, and he soon justified himself, his title, and his role in university life. Undoubtedly, Conservative party voters in Cambridge grumbled; undoubtedly, persons of no particular party grumbled. Q, however, successfully took on the manners and matter of his civilization so that criticism of him and his work became a criticism of English society. From 1912 until his death in May 1944, Q occupied the chair, and his fame as a professor may outlast and surpass his fame as a fictionist.

The one discordant event in Q's long, happy life was the death of his son. The Quiller-Couches had two children, Bevil Bryan and Foy Felicia. During World War I, Q helped enlist and train soldiers from Cornwall. He had no doubts about the war, but modern warfare impinged on his life much more than on other societies. Jane Austen kept war at a distance in her novels because warfare was at a distance. In World War I, Q's son came home from the battlefield by train and reported the horrors directly. He served in the Royal Artillery in France from 1914 until 1918. After the armistice he continued duty with his soldiers in Berlin, where he died of pneumonia on 6 February 1919, just short of thirty years old. He had been engaged to May Cannan, daughter of Charles Cannan, Q's old Oxford friend.

Q never discussed his son's death, but in a letter he tells of a fellow yachtsman who made a good end:

> His yacht foundered in the Bay of Biscay, and all took to the boats in bitter weather, and made the land somehow. But he was dead, frozen stiff, having shed his oilskin coat to wrap his small child. He was the lucky fellow after all. He could save his boy.

The reports of Q's professorship emphasize his care in his lectures and his ability to listen to students and to aid them. May Cannan, who might have become his daughter-in-law, tells how students came "at all hours, bringing him their work, the things they had written, their troubles, and he kept for them an open door." All-male Cambridge substituted, possibly, for his own dead son.

Q always addressed his Cambridge audiences as "Gentlemen." He continued this practice even during World War II, when his audience was entirely female. Q justified the practice on the theory that he was "lecturing to members of the University only; and since the women's colleges were not legally included in the University, he maintained it would be incorrect for him to include them in his form of address." Q's biographer F. Brittain, like Q a fellow at Jesus College, claims that "the women who were present understood all this and, far from resenting his manner of beginning his lectures, rather enjoyed it."

Brittain knew Q only at Cambridge. His biography is dedicated to Lady Quiller-Couch and thanks her for her full support. It is unlikely that there was an anti-Q cabal at Cambridge. He delivered his lectures and edited Shakespeare. Although he had difficulties with his eyesight in the 1920s, he edited selections from the Bible for schoolchildren and wrote introductions to books written by his friends. He never visited the United States because he disapproved of Prohibition. He bathed in cold water every morning, wrote to his wife every day, lunched at the Pitt club, dined in college, and prepared lectures in the evening. He was a good citizen who was not about to lose his scholarship because of drinking, womanizing, or indulging in any other sins that Cambridge or Fowey might have offered him. Q wrote romances, but he did not live the romantic-writer life. If he wrote Byronic adventures, he lived the life of a decent civil servant. Rowse observes that he lacked Celtic ardor and passion, but he was "a born gentleman."

Q's name seldom appears in standard annual bibliographies, and then only in connection with letters to A. E. Housman and George Moore. His two-page prefaces in the thirty-volume Duchy edition of his tales and romances are the best criticism of his work, for he is a good critic, quite conscious of his own aims as a writer. When his stories originally appeared, critics praised them. Reprintings of his collections prove that a reading public bought them, but his shifting from publisher to publisher early in the twentieth century may also suggest that he was losing his audience.

In the bewildering fecundity of his thirteen collections of short stories, the guiding principle is the duality – realistic and romantic – of his vision. Brittain praises *Noughts and Crosses* as his best, but *The Delectable Duchy* (1893) and *News from the Duchy* (1913) are also appealing. *Old Fires and Profitable Ghosts* has a central theme – all the stories are about revenants. Titles of Q's collections include words such as "winter's tales" and "fireside tales" that suggest the homelike atmosphere where they are to be read. Q's career contrasts with that of George Gissing's grim, failed novelist in *New Grub Street* (1891). From the perspective of Gissing's novel, only a philistine could have succeeded in the London literary world of the 1890s. Although Q suffered a breakdown in 1890, he went from success to

success like Gissing's Jasper Milvain, the facile, clever, and successful writer who goads Gissing's novelist hero to fury. Gissing's novelist lacks an Oxford education and a network of university friends in the publishing world. Q , unlike Gissing's novelist, wrote charming stories to please the young of all ages; he tempered the realism found in Gissing's sad, savage book with clever plotting, humor, and witty language.

Q's tales emphasize action and puzzle. His characters are stock figures – handsome young men, old sailors, and crusty countrymen. Q consciously revives the oral folk tradition of his Cornwall neighbors, who presumably have a better contact with human experience than Oxford graduates. Gerard Manley Hopkins, writing about his 1870s world, complains, "Nor can foot feel, being shod," but Q expects his country speakers to feel the ground underneath them. At the same time, romance and historical fiction charmed Q more than realism. He wrote miniature romances – in the sense that his fictional worlds are remote, his characters social ideals, and his tone optimistic. Readers' hands may sweat because of John Emmet's rowing in rough seas or his hard years as a gardener, but readers know that eventually all will be well.

In the preface to the 1928 edition of *The White Wolf,* Q explains that he desired to create "kindly worlds, if extravagant . . . in which . . . it was a privilege to live." The world of his fiction "took our span of life as companionable, humorous, on the whole making for good." Characters do not eat or drink, procreate, or flush toilets. Q wrote boys' stories, but if those words seem pejorative, one may recall that D. H. Lawrence placed classical American literature in that same category. If Q were an American writer, he might be placed with the local colorists. His best stories are vivid, efficiently structured, and witty in their language.

As befitted a scholarship boy, Q did not buck against the styles of his time. Since he consciously followed Laurence Sterne, Charles Dickens, and Stevenson, he was always, in a sense, consuming his capital. With such a great output the sheer need to provide new material (new capital) for his faithful readers meant that he had to innovate and even subvert standard values. His later stories are more enigmatic, ambivalent, and interesting. He knew his public, which he undoubtedly pleased, but, like the insecure scholarship boy, he shifted between the realistic and the romantic. He balanced between the extremes by the cleverness and the exactness of his prose.

"Te! Listen, then, to what the good father calls you!"
she shrilled, advancing on the baker and shaking a fist
under his nose; "an interloper, a scoundrel from the
Rouergue, where all are scoundrels!"

Illustration for "A Jest of Ambialet," one of Quiller-Couch's Cornish tales (London Magazine, *May 1907*)

Q wrote tales, not short stories as Edgar Allan Poe and the modernists defined the term. In his preface to the 1928 edition of *Wandering Heath,* Q remarks that, although he "admired many new-fashioned" ways of telling a story, he continued "the plain objective style, old as Boccaccio, far older" because the old style has "the advantage of being adaptable to all uses, whether tragic or comic, severe, gay, or even frankly riotous." His ideal short story is an interlude in the first book of Herodotus's *History* (fourth century B.C.), the story of the dutiful sons Cleobis and Bito. Their mother prays that they be granted "the greatest boon which could fall to man," an easy death. The boys fall asleep and never wake; "the men of Argos caused statues to be made of them . . . for a memorial of their piety and its reward." The story must have haunted Q's memory even more following Bevil's death. Q incorporates the story in "Phoebus on Halzaphron" (*The Laird's Luck,* 1901), which concerns a visit by Apollo to ancient Cornwall. His interest is the chronicle (rather than the narrative exploration of reasons for events) with a minimum of characterization. The boys take the place of oxen and draw a cart to convey their mother to a ritual. In his re-visioning of the ancient story, Q adds humorous country narrators, a touch of romance, and graceful language.

Males in Q's stories discover and understand. Women in the tales almost invariably are out of contact with reality, or else they are strong mothers who keep the house. The Wesleyan preacher's wife in *The Astonishing History of Troy Town* is "a fine, bowerly woman, but a bit ha'f-baked in her wits; put in wi' the bread, as they say, an' tuk out wi' the cakes." A woman's oral tradition exists, but in Q's stories males manage against the elements with scant help from wives or mothers. As Cambridge was a male society, so was his fictional world.

Q seems to come cautiously to a woman's oral tradition in "Ye Sexes, Give Ear!" (*News from the Duchy*). An unnamed narrator, speaking in Standard English, claims to have the story from his (or her) mother. After hearing a sermon on "Womanly Perfection" with a text from Saint Paul, the women in the community bundle the preacher in a haystack and run him out of town. When the leader of the women, Sal, hears her husband singing the ballad "Ye Sexes, Give Ear!" – a folk version of Adam and Eve in the Garden – she shouts, "Get along with 'ee, you ninth-part-of-a-man! *Me* took out of *your* side!" She challenges the males to a race at their oars over a six-mile course, which the women win. The disgruntled, defeated husband tells a press-gang (the story is set during the Napoleonic Wars) about six fine sailors celebrating their victory at a nearby public house. Because the women still have their hair braided, the press-gang seizes them and takes them aboard a warship.

The ship's captain states, "I'm sorry for you – it goes against my grain to impress men in this fashion: but the law's the law, and we're ready for sea, and if you've any complaints to make I hope you'll cut 'em short." Sal has no complaints, "except that I was born a woman. That I went on to marry that pea-green tailor yonder is my own fault, and we'll say no more about it." The officer fears that he will be the laughingstock of the fleet, but he knows that the punishment for his mistake is in good hands. He glances at Sal, who says, "You may lay to that [punishment], young man! . . . You may lay to that every night when you says your prayers." The women have won the race and reduced their husbands to ridiculous crying for their wives, but in this Cornish *Lysistrata* the victory of the women occurs offstage. These women work at "shrimping, cockling, digging [for bait] . . . bawling fish through Plymouth streets," or searching for wrecks to plunder. The New Woman would liberate women from such jobs; the six fisherwomen are neither models nor threats for middle-class women. Out in Cornwall during the Napoleonic Wars women might have had such a moment, but in Q's time the idea was cheerful and amusing nostalgia.

When Q has a situation in which women are victims, he moves away from realism to make an urban joke. "The Outlandish Ladies" (*Noughts and Crosses*) tells of two French-speaking women living on the edge of a Cornwall community during the Napoleonic Wars. Near their cottage is a field where a wildflower known as "monkey blossom" grows. When their sheep die inexplicably, farmers, wives, and children attribute their misfortune to witchcraft by the two strangers and march on the cottage. The elder woman makes a spirited speech about the men fighting Bonaparte instead of bullying poor women. So far, the tale's tone is realistic.

Because the younger woman, Madame Lucille, is a leper, the two women have isolated themselves for the sake of the community. When the Parson explains and the farmers go to the cottage to apologize, no one answers their knock. Inside is the corpse of Madame Henriette, and behind the house is a grave with a headstone reading (in French), "Here lies Lucille, in days of old so beautiful that nineteen young men, planters of Saint-Dominique, asked her hand in marriage, but she did not wish it. R. I. P." The locals remember her by calling the marsh where the monkey blossoms grow Loose Heels (Lucille's).

The story invites interpretation. Closed communities fear the strange and different, and weak country people seek easy explanations and revenge. Wartime evokes xenophobia; what appears to be reality is not reality. But the words "loose heels" are euphemistic for a prostitute. The rustics persist in their misunderstanding of the story. The women are victimized even after their deaths, and the reader smirks. Q claimed his style of short fiction merged comedy, tragedy, and the "riotous" (bawdy), as in Giovanni Boccaccio's tales. Q's realism could not go as far as the Italian's, but Q is more subtle. He tells his story quickly so that readers are not given time to ask what a Cornwall village would have thought of leprosy or known about the French in 1807.

Realism may produce a mystery to be solved and explained in a rational manner. Two stories in *Noughts and Crosses* feature the highwayman Gabriel Foot. Instead of presenting a realistic bandit, Q verges toward a romantic metaphor, remote yet safe, like that in Alfred Noyes's poem "The Highwayman," or toward the satiric figures in John Gay's *The Beggar's Opera* (1728). Q's stories neatly and efficiently present a puzzle in a few pages and then solve it satisfactorily. In the first Foot story, a clever lawyer has succeeded in obtaining Foot's acquittal for the robbery and murder of a jeweler, but as Foot leaves the court, people on the street and in taverns jeer at and curse him. Foot, to the reader's surprise, curses his lawyer. The lawyer has perceived discrepancies in the case, and he also suspects where a diamond is hidden, but he cannot use his knowledge to obtain the stolen goods. The story ends with Foot's saving the lawyer from a crime and the genuine criminals punishing one another (Chaucer's "Pardoner's Tale" comes inevitably to mind). It has the charm of escape into romantic moors, romantic outsiders and darers, and an immediate puzzle. It is entertaining in a manner established by Sir Arthur Conan Doyle, Stevenson, and Haggard. Gabriel Foot slouches off with the lawyer's assertion that he will hang within a year.

From the beginning of his career, Q was identified with Stevenson, and he identified himself as belonging to a Stevensonian school. His "determination to become a writer" dated from his reading Stevenson's *New Arabian Nights* (1882) in 1883. *Punch* advised both Stevenson and Haggard to "look to their laurels" when Q's first novel, *Dead Man's Rock,* appeared. Brittain asserts that Q's third novel, *The Splendid Spur* (1888), "shouts Stevenson's name at the reader even in its chapter headings." After Stevenson's death Q completed the last quarter of the unfinished *St. Ives* (1896). The task was easy, Q says, for he had the author's notes and he was "soaked in Stevenson." Sir Henry Newbolt, Q's old school rival from Clifton, observed that in the 1890s Q was "a writer of Stevensonian tales for the young of all ages." The crucial words are "for the young." Another early influence on Q was his first reading of Mark Twain in 1882, but Twain's sending Huck to "the territories" is much more ironic than the lawyer's dismissal of Foot to be hanged, possibly, in a year. Twain sustains his ambiguity; Q solves his.

If Q's stories master the mystery, the puzzle, and its solution, he also masters the tale as farce. He thus approaches the riotous that he admired in Boccaccio. The possibility of misunderstanding between social types (the lawyer versus the highwayman), the misunderstanding of dialect speech, the addled women, and the country dwellers remote from standard bourgeois behavior provide Q with excellent opportunities. In "Frenchman's Creek" (*Noughts and Crosses*), another story that explains a local landmark's name, Captain Bligh appears. After the mutiny on the *Bounty* and his disastrous Australian government assignment, Bligh is made an admiral and sent to the map the coast of Cornwall. When he speaks French, the wife of the local vicar takes him to be a Frenchman and goes into hysterics. Bligh purloins a gravedigger's shovel to search for Roman artifacts, and the mourners at the expected funeral transform themselves into a militia (the children come along with their fingers in their mouths) to capture the Frenchman. They find him swimming and truss him up naked. At least five different assumptions about reality conflict with each other with hilarious results.

In "Merry-Garden" (*Noughts and Crosses*) a middle-aged physician gives ancient gentlemen mud baths to restore their youthful complexions. He also wants to marry a seventeen-year-old girl who has no interest in him. In addition, a band of shore-leave sailors with female friends (who are clearly prostitutes), chaperoned schoolgirls, attractive officers, and an adolescent with pimples all manage to converge on the same tea garden. Each tries to work out an imagined future that contradicts and violates the futures imagined by the others. The maximum confusion produces many laughs. Both "Frenchman's Creek" and "Merry-Garden" involve innocents who are naked, but the nakedness does not embarrass the audience. The naked ones have logical reason to be so, and readers laugh at their embarrassment.

Q's sense of the riotous is not bawdy but innocent and naive. His tales are humorous rather than comic, since the naturalistic tradition mitigates against comedy and prefers humor. The distinction can be seen in Q's handling of the tale that may be the root story of Western comedy, the drama of spring festivals. In the late nineteenth century the Cambridge anthropologists – Sir James Frazer's *Golden Bough* (1890–1915) is the best-known work – were collecting and studying mythologies. Ritual, myth, and story become the same in communities that do not analyze themselves or their behavior. "The Mayor of Gantick" (*Noughts and Crosses*) is either an example of Q's exploiting an idea from the anthropologists or an authentic piece of West Country myth. Every year the village purges itself of evil:

> To this end the villagers prepared a huge dragon of pasteboard and marched out with it to a sandy common . . . known as Dragon's Moor. Here they would choose one of their number to be Mayor, and submit to him all questions of conscience, and such cases of notorious evil living as the law failed to provide for. Summary justice waited on all his decisions; and as the village wag was usually chosen for the post, you may guess that the horse-play was rough at times. When this was over, and the public conscience purified, the company fell on the pasteboard dragon with sticks and whacked him into small pieces, which they buried in a small hollow called Dragon Pit; and so returned gladly to their homes to start another twelve months of sin.

In 1912 Francis Cornford, one of the Cambridge anthropologists, published *The Origin of Attic Comedy*. Cornford argues that an event such as this was the basis on which the Greek comedy began. Aristophanes found, repeated, and modified the structure to start the development of Attic comedy. Since the man elected mayor in Q's story is the village innocent, who mercifully frees every person in the village from his sin, the tale also parallels the Christian Easter with its doctrine of forgiveness.

Q's realistic version illustrates his emphasis on the humorous rather than the comic. In the works of Aristophanes the village wag triumphs; in Q's version the innocent boy returns to his uncomprehending mother. The audience for Aristophanes glimpses a new society, purged of sin and error. Aristophanic comedy ends in marriage and the possibility of a new generation freed of social errors. Q's characters return "to their homes to start another twelve months of sin." English comedy from the time of Ben Jonson through Q's masters Sterne and Dickens concentrated on the social sins. Characters are caught in social habits, as in the cases of the one-eyed preacher and his business dealings, Captain Bligh's insistence on controlling his world, and the physician's belief in mud baths to restore youthful complexions.

Q seldom ends his tales in marriage. In the long story "I Saw Three Ships" (*Noughts and Crosses*) a boy wins back his girl, who has been momentarily attracted to a rescued seaman, but he wins because his opposition abandons the struggle. The marriage occurs, but the bride's first act is to clean up her kitchen. Despite his impulse for romance, Q's realistic streak – possibly his native Cornish good sense – keeps him from a grand and glorious comic fulfillment. If Q believed that life is "on the whole making for good," his males do not solve their dilemmas but escape them. They remain in their comic habit or humor, their customary and familiar behavior.

A particular word recurs in Q's autobiography: *clean*. He describes Clifton as a clean school and his grandfather's stable yards as clean. Women characters in his fiction are neat and clean in their housework. The editor of Q's *Memories & Opinions*, S. C. Roberts, states in his introduction that Q wished to be remembered by "his championship of cleanness and grace of style." In his inaugural lecture at Cambridge (published as *On the Art of Writing*, 1916) Q quotes Lucian's description of a friend:

His way was like other people's; he mounted no high horse; he was just a man and a citizen. He indulged in no Socratic irony. But his discourse was full of Attic grace; those who heard it went away neither disgusted . . . nor repelled.

The "Attic grace" saves and protects Q's audience from the raw, the dirty, and the embarrassing. Since he lectured on Aristophanes at Oxford, he would have been familiar with the bawdy and the earthy, but he avoids what might disgust or repel. His world is preadolescent in its simple, clear distinctions.

Q admired Stevenson for his ability to tell his stories "in the clean objective way." In "The Return of Joanna" (*Noughts and Crosses*) a female street singer visits her correct, proper half sisters in hope of obtaining money. They call her songs unintelligible, but since they really mean "disreputable," they refuse to give her money. At the end of the story she returns to her unsuccessful actor-husband to earn a little by singing "something pious . . . since we want our dinner. The public has still enough honesty left to pity piety." In the story the nurse who cares for the dying, respectable sisters reads a French theatrical novel at night, but she hides it inside Richard Baxter's *Saint's Everlasting Rest*, a Presbyterian manual for good conduct. Q's compulsion for cleanliness manifests itself in his fiction as order, grace, and neatness rather than the jarring, messy world of human experience. Q was always a gentleman, neat and careful in his life and fiction.

The ideals of cleanliness, grace, and romance insure Q's appeal to the young of all ages. In "The Looe Die-Hards" (*Wandering Heath*, 1895), Q writes a jolly story about the Napoleonic Wars as if they were a camping trip. The physician of a local artillery company (their village is named Looe) enlisted to protect the southern coast of England during the Napoleonic era notices that, after six years of enlistment, no member of the company has died, although statistically fifteen should have. The company has become known locally as the "Die-Hards." The captain wants to preserve the record until the company is disbanded after Napoleon's defeat at Waterloo, but Sergeant Fugler seems to be dying of cirrhosis (the local term is "hobnailed liver"). The sergeant will die in peace if he knows he will have a military funeral with a band playing the "Dead March" from George Frideric Handel's *Saul* (1739), but the artillery company has no band. In the manner of oral narrative, the story suddenly veers to a time when the soldiers run in terror after finding a Frenchman in the hut where they store ammunition. The boy who discovers the Frenchman closes his eyes because he does not want to see his "gay life whisked away in little portions" when the powder hut explodes.

The Frenchman had taught music in Dieppe before British naval forces captured him smuggling and sent him to Dartmoor Prison. He has escaped and is now in search of a "good Cornishman" – Sgt. Fugler – to smuggle him back to France. The Frenchman is given the choice of being sent back to Dartmoor or teaching the villagers the "Dead March." When the band practices in the town hall directly across from the sergeant's cottage, he is delighted: " 'Tis a beautiful tune: an' I'm ha'f ashamed to tell 'ee that I bain't a'goin' to die, this time." The narrator adds, "Nor did he." So the artillery company is disbanded without a single death. The narrator claims that the reader could look up the story in the *History of East and West Looe* and then concludes, "Still, when one comes to reflect, it does seem an odd boast for a company of warriors." The soldiers belong in a comic opera. The good war against Napoleon becomes nostalgia for a simpler, cleaner time when a boy would close his eyes in expectation of an explosion or a captain would not send his soldiers out in a rainstorm for fear of their catching cold and dying.

Q wrote so many stories that he was bound to extend his form. The Boer War disillusioned him as it did many others in Britain. In the first decade of the twentieth century he became more involved in local politics, including the establishment of school boards. In a tale written just before World War I, "The Honour of the Ship" (*News from the Duchy*), Q modifies the standard boys' story. His experience establishing and managing schools in Cornwall and his disillusion with British policy during the Boer War shape this story.

A skillful boy, Link Andrews, outwits and shames adults, but he exists outside the expected social mold. The story takes place on a training-school ship, the *Egeria*, named for the nymph who taught Numa Pompilius, the second king of Rome. The training schools were organized under the 1866 Industrial Schools Act, which required communities to create schools for delinquent, truant, and orphaned males. Link is boxing champion on the ship, and at the beginning of the story he challenges the boy, Master Bates, who is to win the Good Conduct prize. Other characters report that the atmosphere aboard the ship is "a bit off." Q may have been conscious of the *Master Bates / masturbates* pun, for his friends report that he enjoyed puns.

If Link manages to get through the public atmosphere of prize day, he will join the summer cruise on the yacht; a good sailor, he would "give his soul" to participate in the cruise. Link's speech after receiving his prize books is not overheard, and it is not typical of boys' literature:

See here – *Fights for the Flag!* And, on top of it, *Deeds What Won the Silly Empire!* And the old blighter 'oped I'd be a good boy, and grow up, and win some more. For the likes of *him*, he meant – Yuss, I *don't* think. . . . Oh, hold my little hand and check the tearful flow, for I'm to be a ship's boy at 'arf-a-crown a month, and go Empire buildin'!

The story continues after a six-year interval, when a schoolmaster arrives in a Cornish village to report that he has seen Link on the streets. When the schoolmaster insists on recognition, Link tells him to go to hell. Link had joined the cruise after the prize day. At Plymouth all the officers went ashore to view a cinematograph of a boxing match. When a storm came up and the officers did not return, Link took command and saved the ship from certain destruction. Afterward he stowed the sails and put things back in order "for the honour of the blasted ship." The officers were so drunk they could not get back to the ship. They finally located it in a distant bay the following day. Link's final speech to the officers parallels his earlier speech in its realism: "All right, my precious swine! Now step below and wash off the traces. If you behave pretty, maybe I'll not report you." Link did not report them, but word leaked out and all the officers were replaced so that now "the *Egeria* . . . is something to be proud of." Six years after the incident Link has become second gardener for Mr. Harris, a clear-thinking Cornishman. The secretary of the charity managing the trading-school ship had recommended Link as an apprentice gardener because he "had no aptitude for the sea."

In this story, which invites readers to notice that things are "a bit off," further questions arise. Is Link now in the free trade – the Cornish euphemism for smuggling? Or is the story saying that the Industrial Schools Act of 1866 was a fraud, that boys in such schools learn to violate the romantic ideal of good conduct that is taught to them? Or is Q presenting the familiar Byronic hero of boys' fiction, but this time drawing the hero from the lower class? All of these readings are possible. Q claimed that his favorite motto was from Marcus Aurelius: "The best revenge is not to be like them." In this sense the boy succeeds: he does not renege as did his teachers and officers. While they have lost their honor, he has kept his. In this late story Q trusts his realistic details possibly because of his more thorough human experience in schools and the justice system. His old battle between the realistic and the romantic (in the sense of distant and attractive) turns in this story toward the failure of human expectations.

In the preface to the 1928 edition of *I Saw Three Ships*, Q notes that since World War I "there has grown up a revulsion against the sort of plain adventurous story which engaged the young" before the war. Although he is interested in "the clash of loves, hates, strong wills and passion on the edge of that mystery which surrounds us all," he is not interested in "monkey-houses" or psychoanalysis.

By "monkey-houses" he must be referring to the animal appetites. Sex is way off his landscape – or buried beneath it. Nor is he much interested in human motives: he cares not why people act but is amazed at what they do. His stories, therefore, "simply treat men and women, with their differences, as I have been allowed their acquaintance in life."

The fairy tale resurged as a literary form in the 1890s, and Q translated classic examples and wrote his own. Oscar Wilde used the medium to escape the rigors and restraints of realism and yet to preserve that sense of ordinary reality that readers of the period demanded. Q lamented that the nineteenth century lacked fairy tales, but he never asked why. In order to fill the gap, he wrote stories that blend natural, even historical, landscapes and events with the amazement and unexpectedness of the fairy tale.

He found the germ of "The Czarina's Violet" (*Noughts and Crosses*) in a story from a diplomat's memoir. The German chancellor Otto von Bismarck, waiting in a Saint Petersburg palace to negotiate a treaty with the czar, notices a sentinel standing alone in the middle of a grassy field. Bismarck attributes his personal success to getting up early and asking questions. When he asks, "Why does the soldier stand guard?," neither the soldier nor the czar knows; nor does the soldier's sergeant, his captain, his general, or his field marshal. An old linen weaver at the top of the palace hears the czar's trumpets (she hopes "he is not declaring war against anybody") proclaiming a reward for an explanation. The old weaver remembers that the czarina, the grandmother of the present czar, had organized an archery contest for her women one spring. When she saw the first violet, she ordered a soldier to stand by it so that it would not be trampled. After the contest ended, the soldier continued to stand by the flower in order to prevent the common people from trampling it. No violet grows there now.

Q often adds a surprising coda to his stories. Years later, a young girl (her parents married after the old weaver gave them her reward for the explanation) finds that the violet has come back because the soldier no longer tramples the turf. Q adds a moral:

> Prince! your armies, horse and foot,
> Cannot kill a violet.
> Call your engineers to root it,
> Your artillery to shoot it;
> See the flower defies you yet.
> Drum, drum, fife and drum –
> Pass and let the children come!

The realistic events blend with conventions of the fairy tale to reach an unimpeachable moral that would have suited the Liberal party platform.

Q was a late Victorian undamaged by Darwinism, crude capitalism, or French realism on the model of Emile Zola. He did not attempt fiction after the disasters of World War I. The world in which "it was a privilege to live" had disappeared. The romance form that Q employed shifted to science fiction. Q's stories about Cornwall concern a world as remote as Krypton or any other fictional lost planet. In Cornwall boys dazzle adults, women exist as nonsexual beings, and readers expect surprising incidents. Readers also expect full resolution without ambiguity or irony. Q's fiction demands an audience ready to accept amazing events in an utterly distant world where heroic boys sail boats and Handel's music cures dying sergeants.

One person who has continued to praise Q is Helene Hanff, author of *84, Charing Cross Road* (1970), who credits him for her intellectual life. In *Q's Legacy* (1985) she tells of discovering a used copy of Q's Cambridge lectures. Because Hanff failed to win a scholarship, she worked as a secretary. Q's lectures, her "college of one," guided her reading of English writers "from the age of Chaucer onwards." However, Hanff never mentions having read Q's fiction. The Cambridge school of critics, which evolved in Q's time, has continued his legacy. Basil Willey's 1946 inaugural lecture, *The Tradition of Q*, is too close to its subject for a full evaluation, but it is a start and has the advantage of being from one of the beneficiaries of Q's work. Q was instrumental in F. R. Leavis's appointment to Cambridge, but he had little sympathy with Leavis's criticism or that of the *Scrutiny* school. To Q, English literature stopped in 1914. In Q's judgment T. S. Eliot never wrote a line of verse, and Eliot's politics drove him to fury. Q could not tolerate Virginia Woolf or any of the other moderns.

Q died on 12 May 1944, in his eighty-first year, in Fowey, Cornwall, where Allied forces were gathering for the invasion of France. On 4 May 1944 he had dictated a letter saying that he expected to be back in residence at Cambridge in June. Q's *Memories & Opinions* is more a memoir than an autobiography, a list of persons met and events attended. The book reveals little of his emotions and development as a writer. A recent theatrical production based on *The Wind in the Willows* (1908), by his friend Kenneth Grahame, included a scene between Grahame and Q. The realistic characters gradually slipped over into the imaginative, and Q became Badger in the story.

One of the few moments of passion in Q's autobiography is his return home from his first Latin class: he "went home as one baptised into a cult. I felt able (aged seven or so) to look my father in the face almost as initiated man to man!" He admired Sterne's *Tristram Shandy*, Wordsworth's poetry, and Sir Walter Scott's novels. He clearly learned from Dickens. At times he seems the quintessence of the Victorian spirit, but he imitates and parodies eighteenth-century styles. He was rarely out of England, but with perfect aplomb he sets tales in Colorado, Massachusetts, and Corsica – places he never visited. Usually such tales are about a Cornish pilgrim, but Q describes the landscapes. If he is most clearly to be found in his fiction, he is the anonymous London voice who meets Cornish raconteurs.

Although Q's fiction has no critical reputation at the end of the twentieth century, his works indicate much about his time, with its penchant for realism yet yearning for romance, its willingness to believe in a boy's life as the ultimate in human possibility, and its pleasure in language. Q had the audience that Gissing, Henry James, Joseph Conrad, and Ford Madox Ford did not have. His audience enjoyed Kipling, Barrie, Grahame, and Stevenson. He belonged to a school sometimes called the Victorian Activists, or the Hearties. Those authors believed in the romanticism of Scott and the early Dickens. Energy is their sign, but their energy exists best in a world remote from actual events: the empire was a fine thing, and it was a marvel to be British.

Except for his use of dialect, Q does not require exegesis. Readers either understand his jokes or they do not. Explanation enriches and expands tragic insights, but it does little for the writer of humor. Q requires a critic who can understand his delicate balance between the realistic and the farcical, between life in the country and the life of romance. Q registers one set of mind in England at the end of the nineteenth century and the beginning of the twentieth. His fictional world, in a sense, went to France and never came back from its bloody battles. Q's work awaits a critic who can demonstrate his success in the kind of short story that he chose to write and who can relate his fiction to the English mind of the period between 1880 and 1914.

References:

Frederick Brittain, *Arthur Quiller-Couch: A Biographical Study of Q* (Cambridge: Cambridge University Press, 1947);

Helene Hanff, *Q's Legacy* (Boston: Little, Brown, 1985);

A. L. Rowse, *Quiller-Couch: A Portrait of "Q"* (London: Methuen, 1988).

Papers:

Jesus College Library, Cambridge, has 150 manuscript letters and papers by Q. Trinity College, Oxford, has the bulk of his papers. His private correspondence is in the collection of G. F. Symondson, Windlesham, Surrey.

William Pett Ridge

(circa 1859 – 30 September 1930)

Mike Jasper
Kent State University

BOOKS: *Eighteen of Them: Singular Stories,* as Warwick Simpson (London: Leadenhall, 1894);

A Clever Wife (London: Bentley, 1895; New York: Harper, 1896);

Minor Dialogues (Bristol: Arrowsmith, 1895);

An Important Man and Others (London: Ward, Lock, 1896);

The Second Opportunity of Mr. Staplehurst (London: Hutchinson, 1896; New York: Harper, 1896);

Secretary to Bayne, M. P. (London: Methuen, 1897; New York & London: Harper, 1898);

Three Women and Mr. Frank Cardwell (London: Pearson, 1898);

Mord Em'ly (London: Pearson, 1899; New York: Harper, 1899);

Outside the Radius (London: Hodder & Stoughton, 1899; New York: Dodd, Mead, 1900);

A Son of the State (New York: Dodd, Mead, 1899; London: Methuen, 1900);

A Breaker of Laws (London & New York: Harper, 1900);

London Only (London: Hodder & Stoughton, 1901);

Lost Property: The Story of Maggie Cannon (London: Methuen, 1902);

Erb (New York: Appleton, 1902; London: Methuen, 1903);

Up Side Streets (London: Hodder & Stoughton, 1903);

George and the General (London: Methuen, 1904);

Next Door Neighbors (London: Hodder & Stoughton, 1904);

Mrs. Galer's Business (London: Methuen, 1905);

On Company's Service (London: Hodder & Stoughton, 1905);

The Wickhamses (London: Methuen, 1906; New York: Dutton, 1907);

Name of Garland (London: Methuen, 1907; Leipzig: Tauchnitz, 1907);

Nearly Five Million (London: Hodder & Stoughton, 1907);

Sixty-Nine Birnam Road (London: Hodder & Stoughton, 1908);

Speaking Rather Seriously (London: Hodder & Stoughton, 1908);

Splendid Brother (London: Methuen, 1909);

Thomas Henry (London: Mills & Boon, 1909);

Light Refreshment (London: Hodder & Stoughton, 1910);

Nine to Six-Thirty (London: Methuen, 1910);

Table d'hote (London & New York: Hodder & Stoughton, 1911);

Thanks to Sanderson (London: Methuen, 1911; Leipzig: Tauchnitz, 1911);

Devoted Sparkes (London: Methuen, 1912);

Love at Paddington (London & New York: Nelson, 1912);

Mixed Grill (London: Hodder & Stoughton, 1913);

The Remington Sentence (London: Methuen, 1913);

The Happy Recruit (London: Methuen, 1914; New York: Doran, 1915);

Book Here (London: Methuen, 1915);

The Kennedy People (London: Methuen, 1915);

Madame Prince (London: Methuen, 1916; New York: Doran, 1916);

On Toast (London: Methuen, 1916);

The Amazing Years (London & New York: Hodder & Stoughton, 1917);

Special Performances (London: Methuen, 1918);

Top Speed (London: Methuen, 1918);

The Bustling Hours (London: Methuen, 1919);

Just Open (London: Odhams, 1920);

Well-to-do Arthur (London: Methuen, 1920);

Bannerton's Agency (London: Methuen, 1921);

Richard Triumphant (London: Methuen, 1922);

The Lunch Basket (London: Mills & Boon, 1923; Leipzig: Tauchnitz, 1923);

Miss Mannering (London: Methuen, 1923);

A Story Teller: Forty Years in London (London: Hodder & Stoughton, 1923; New York: Doran, 1924);

Leaps and Bounds (London: Mills & Boon, 1924);

Rare Luck (London: Methuen, 1924);

I Like to Remember (London: Hodder & Stoughton, 1925);

Just Like Aunt Bertha (London: Methuen, 1925);

London Please: Four Cockney Plays (London & New York: French, 1925);

London Types (London: Methuen, 1926);

Our Mrs. Willis (London: Methuen, 1926);

Easy Distances (London: Mills & Boon, 1927);

Hayward's Flight (London: Methuen, 1927);

The Two Mackenzies (London: Methuen, 1928);

Affectionate Regards (London: Mills & Boon, 1929);

The Slippery Ladder (London: Methuen, 1929);

Eldest Miss Collingwood (London: Methuen, 1930);

Led By Westmacott (London: Methuen, 1931).

In William Pett Ridge's "The Alteration in Mr. Kershaw" (*Idler*, 1896) a cockney office boy is confronted by Mr. Kershaw, one of the senior clerks:

> "Will you be good enough to explain," demanded Mr. Kershaw, hotly, "to explain, Billing, the condition of this table? Look here! I can write my name on it."
>
> "So could I, sir," I said. "There's nothing clever in that."

This scene is typical of Ridge's fiction. He was one of the most prolific and better-known writers of the Cockney School of nineteenth-century British realism. Vincent Brome asserts in *Four Realist Novelists* (1965) that Ridge "is commonly assumed to translate the Cockney scene into more comedy than tragedy." With innate savvy and good humor, Ridge's Cockneys outwit the worst that the Fates can bring against them.

In *Mord Em'ly* (1899) the title character encounters a potential employer:

> "How old might you be?"
>
> "I *might* be a 'undred and forty-nine," said Mord Em'ly looking at herself anxiously in a square of unframed looking glass on the wall. "I *am* jest close upon thirteen."

This passage points to a flaw in Ridge's cockney fiction. As Brome puts it, "He was a writer unaware of the wider implications of what he wrote." With vivaciousness and cheek Ridge's characters are able to transcend their environment; circumstances do not matter.

There are no biographies of Ridge, and his birth date is given variously as 1857, 1859, 1860, and 1864. His London *Times* obituary (1 October 1930) lists his age as seventy-one, which would indicate 1859 (or perhaps 1860, as the day of his birth is not known) as the proper year. His autobiographical writings are of little help. *A Story Teller: Forty Years in London* (1923) and *I Like to Remember* (1925) were written in the last decade of his life, and they are scarcely more than pleasant, impressionistic meanderings through a middle-aged man's memory. Both deal exclusively with his adult life in London.

Ridge was born in the country, however – in Chartham, near Canterbury – and he was educated at Marden, Kent. Not much else is known of his life before 1880, when he came up to London. In *I Like to Remember* he shares a single childhood memory, which significantly concerns his first trip to the city:

> I could scarcely have been a pampered voluptuary at the age of ten, but I have a clear impression that, brought to town for the day, and taken in the afternoon to see the German Reed entertainment at St. George's Hall in Langham Place, I had a sense of being defrauded. And looking back now, it seems to have been little more than a glorified village schoolroom performance.

It is also significant that Ridge attended Birkbeck College, then known as Birkbeck Literary and Scientific Institute. This was the first of London's Mechanic's Institutes, the first college in England to provide for people who earned their living during the day. At the opening of the institute's lecture theater in 1823, Dr. George Birkbeck and Henry Brougham made speeches on how the education of the working classes would not subvert society. At this revolutionary college Ridge received the classical education so typical of the time, along with instruction in French. He took up "congenial social work" and became interested in a life of letters. At Birkbeck he sat in cramped desks next to the sort of working-class Londoners whom his novels would champion for most of his career.

After college Ridge supported himself as a clerk in the Railway Clearing House:

> My earliest acquaintance with the city meant a salary of a guinea a week, and hours from nine o'clock in the morning until seven at night, with no concessions for Saturday, and, now and again, Sunday duty. I sat at a desk in an office placed in a railway arch, where the sun managed to look in for a brief period only; the next arch was occupied by a wine-merchant, and this could be described as a good pull-up for carmen, for tasting went on during the day. . . .
>
> Increases in wages came – if you behaved well for twelve months – at the rate of half a crown a year, and the understanding with some appeared to be that when the sum reached thirty shillings, you were justified in getting married.

Ridge was selling his soul during the day, but he tried to buy it back at night. He became interested in writing around 1890, and his first attempts were London vignettes for the *St. James Gazette.* Borrowing a term from the pen and drawing pad, he called these "sketches." He earned his first money as a writer for a sketch (*St. James Gazette*, 1890) of a restaurant near Old Compton Street:

> Piano-organ burst into melody at every corner. The retail wine-shop has its vine-covered barrel that somehow inspires confidence in labels which not infrequently have an air of novelty to the connoisseur. There are more chateaux on bottle-labels in Soho than were ever dreamt of in Spain.

Ridge's first novel, *A Clever Wife,* was published in 1895. From that year until his death in 1930, he averaged more than one book a year, either novels or collections of short stories first published in Jerome K. Jerome's *Idler.* He also wrote theater reviews and sketches. He was as prolific as Anthony Trollope – a workmanlike writer. His eye, his imagination, and his ear for language were more like Charles Dickens's than Trollope's, however.

He knew his London, and he knew better still his Londoners.

From the first Ridge wrote about the working class, as he was moved by those he saw around him, portraying what he felt was his own social milieu. In *Mord Em'ly,* his most successful novel, he depicts the East End and its lifestyle as comedy. The title character is what he believed was a typical East End woman. She is brash and cocky, with a colorful supply of stylized cockney slang, replete with apostrophes and long *i*'s for long *a*'s (as in *Jimes* for *James*). With the popularity of *Mord Em'ly,* Ridge hit upon what was to become a major stock-in-trade: the cockney worker with charisma and an ever-sunny disposition, a self-help theme à la Samuel Smiles, and a classic comedic, happy-ending structure. Such was the social guilt of well-to-do readers of his time that they avidly sought out novels in which a working-class hero or heroine cunningly outwits the established order. By the turn of the twentieth century, Ridge found himself a member of a full-fledged school of literature.

The label "Cockney School" is typically given to writers of the 1890s who depicted East End working life. These authors constituted a specialized class of a larger trend toward realism in both British and American literature. Cockney School writers were a natural, pinpointed offshoot of that larger movement and the movement toward modernism. They were influenced by such writers as Thomas Hardy and W. E. Henley. To Ridge realism meant the world as he experienced it, through sharing cramped late-afternoon classrooms at the Birkbeck Institute and working as one clerk out of many in a downtown office.

Although Rudyard Kipling established the prototype, the first of the true Cockney School writers was Henry Woodd Nevinson, who wrote an 1893 series of short stories about working-class life, adopting the methods of what is now called the New Journalism. He buried himself in the working-class lifestyle, attending East End police courts, sailing on Thames barges, accompanying rent collectors as they made their rounds, and even picking hops in Kent. Almost without exception Cockney School writers admired Dickens and, with reservations, adopted his style. P. J. Keating states in *The Working Classes in Victorian Fiction* (1971) that "at times the influence is . . . blatant" to the point of plagiarism, citing Edwin Pugh's borrowing from Dickens's *Bleak House* (1853) for *Mother-Sister* (1900).

By early 1894 Nevinson had finished *Neighbors of Ours,* but Arthur Morrison's *Tales of Mean Streets* was published at about the same time, the result being, in Nevinson's words, "that mine was praised, and his was bought." There may have been some differences in technique between individual Cockney School writers, but what truly distinguishes them as a group is that they reject the major literary convention of the slums as a place of unattenuated horror. Jane Findlater, a contemporary of Ridge, claimed that the Cockney School presented "nearly the ultimate truth about slum dwellers. . . . There comes the truth; every slum dweller is not entirely depraved, or desperately miserable." For the first time, furthermore, East Enders were portrayed not so much sympathetically, but empathetically, by one of their own. They were no longer stock comic characters, as in early- and mid-Victorian fiction; nor were they tragic, as in George Gissing's stories.

In *Mord Em'ly* slum life is exciting and happy. The plot is simple: the title character will not be given the Pygmalion treatment. There are various attempts by individuals and institutions to "better" her, but she thwarts them all by her longing for home and home life. The novel opens with a fight between Mord Em'ly and a girl from a rival gang. This scene is emblematic of the novel as a whole. Mord Em'ly greets all attempts to separate her from her gang and the only life she has ever known with the violent resistance of an impacted molar. She leaves a position in a middle-class Peckham household. When she is later arrested for stealing a handful of cakes, she escapes from jail back to her native streets. Mord Em'ly will not be "bettered." In fact, the inescapable implication throughout Ridge's novels is that the staid, stuffy middle class ought to be bettered by taking a page from Mord Em'ly's book.

Ridge knew his devices and how to work them. More Cockney School novels followed: *Outside the Radius* (1899), *A Son of the State* (1899), and *A Breaker of Laws* (1900). But, like *Mord Em'ly,* these novels are flawed in a fundamental way. Because of his years seeing life at London's pace — seeing it in rapid-fire glimpses like passing scenery from a train — he lost his rural perspective. Someone with an urban sensibility knows that a tree grows through the sidewalk, but someone with a rural one knows why and how it grows there. This is precisely the capacity that Ridge lacked: he saw only the surface of cockney life, and even that as merely a reflection of himself. He is reminiscent of the writers of the American South before Harriet Beecher Stowe's *Uncle Tom's Cabin* (1852), writers who assumed that the slaves who were swinging their picks, hoes, and mattocks to the rhythm of up-tempo spirituals were

"Cook," I interrupted, "would you care to become my wedded wife?" "I'd sooner go," she declared, "and jolly well drown myself in the Serpentine!"

Illustration by Leonard Shields for "Trying Times" (London Magazine, *February 1915*)

happy. Perhaps this explains the popularity of his Cockney School fiction. His plucky characters absolved middle-class readers of guilt for the conditions of the East End working class. The urban conditions that might inspire that guilt simply do not exist in his fiction.

By 1909 Ridge had published almost twenty more books. That year he married Olga Hentschel, the daughter of his friend Carl Hentschel, who shared an interest in the newspaper business. Hentschel, a member of the Royal Institute and Society of Arts, was the proprietor and editor of a London theater journal, the *Playgoer,* to which Ridge occasionally contributed. Ridge and Olga had two children, a son and a daughter.

By this time his fame had come about as far as it would. He was becoming a character in literary London, one of a group of jocular but minor talents who frequented literary hangouts in London's theater district: "I have watched the progress in confidence shown by new arrivals in literature from the moment when they trembled if anyone spoke to them, to the moment (a couple of years was in one case sufficient) they started conversation at dinner table, and held control of it from the *hors d'oeuvre* to the pine-apple." His reminiscences of this time drop major and minor names: Max Beerbohm, Beerbohm Tree, George Augustus Sala, and Archibald Forbes. In *I Like to Remember* he recollects visits to

Kipling's house and describes evenings at the home of H. G. Wells:

> The authoress of *Irene Iddlesleigh* managed to add considerably to the gaity of London, and the circumstance that she lived in Ireland . . . kept her in ignorance, I hope, of the kind of reputation she was making. We used to take turns in reading chapters at H. G. Wells's house at Worcester Park. . . . "Though a man of forty summers, he never yet had entertained the thought of yielding up his bacheloric ideas to supplace them with others which eventually should coincide with those of a different sex." Nevertheless, it soon appears that Sir Hugh means business.

Ridge also implies at least partial credit for Arnold Bennett's best-known work:

> [I] mentioned that novelists had ceased to write full and complete histories, starting with the arrival of the monthly nurse and ending with the message to the undertaker . . . Arnold Bennett was there. "I'm going to take this tip," he said to me. In due course there appeared that remarkably fine book, *The Old Wives Tale.*

At the height of his popularity, Ridge received this extract from a Sydney, Australia, journal: "Pett Ridge, actor, artist, and author, present time cartoonist on London *Punch,* and a host of other things, has written a story – ." Ridge responded: "I wish the Australian reviewer had not been cramped by want of space. It would have been interesting to see an allusion to the manner in which I carried out the duties of Prime Minister."

For the most part Ridge's short stories play to his strengths: his wit, humor, and razor-eyed observations of the city and its people. In addition, his short fiction is his only work that stems from a clearly delineated literary theory, other than the "give the public what it wants" force behind his novels: "For a short story it is necessary, I think, that the period covered should be brief; if you can get all the trouble over in one day, so much the better, and *nothing like development of character is looked for*" [emphasis added]. This is the extent of his talent as a short-story writer. Any attempt at something larger fails on a critical (as opposed to a popular) sense.

Ridge was given to short stories in pseudo-dramatic form. "Presentations at Court" (*Idler,* 1898), for example, is a closet drama. It begins: "London Police Court, 10:30 a.m. One or two bareheaded policemen lounge in stalls; reporter in stage-box adjusts his carbonic paper; stout usher with pen over ear prepares to introduce applicants." This

opening is little more than a set of details that lacks a stylistic presence.

The story follows the progression of applicants before the "genial youngish" magistrate. All of them are Ridgean character types from the East End. First comes the Dusty Lady, then the Breathless Damsel, who wishes to block her landlady from evicting her:

> MAGISTRATE: What is her reason?
> BREATHLESS DAMSEL: Gaud in 'Eaven only knows, your worship, I'm sure *I* don't . . .
> MAGISTRATE (sharply): Have you paid up your rent?
> BREATHLESS DAMSEL: As a matter of fact (frankly) I *am* a bit behind'and, sir, with me rent: there's about two months and a 'alf owing – not more, I'll take me solim oath, and she ought to know the money's right enough because –
> MAGISTRATE (deliberately): If you don't pay your rent, my good woman, she can turn you out, and you deserve it. Go along.
> (BREATHLESS DAMSEL goes along grumbling. Confused man with slight hiccough enters.)

The Confused Man is followed by the Irish Lady, complete with comic spunk, *r*'s rolling like timpani; she continually shakes a slim, wiry fist. Next comes the Apologetic Man, after whom the Usher says, "That's the lot, your worship," to which the Magistrate replies (with feeling), "Thank Goodness!" Ridge's point in this inconsequential piece seems to be that he can describe a day at the bench, but for all that the reader may well ask, "So what?"

"In the Reserved Compartment" (*Idler,* 1898) is another closet drama. The setting is a train's "Ladies Only" compartment, in which "two babies [strangers] frown distantly at each other." The description of the two "babies" is excellent – the idea that they have some ingrained infant hostility toward one another – as is his ear for conversation. He succeeds here because he treats these characters with wit, sensitivity, and an eye for the true workings of the human mind. They are not just inert sources of idiosyncratic behavior and eccentric pronunciation.

Ridge approaches a permanent quality in his work only when he caps his Cockney School pen. His best-known work today is *I Like to Remember,* which does not depend on dialect or empathy for a particular social class. It is simply a human, humorous recollection of London that often causes the reader to laugh out loud. There is also an added poignance when one considers that Ridge was nearly forgotten as a literary figure when he wrote this memoir. In one amusing passage he recalls the interrogation of a defendant at the bench. The magistrate wants to bind the defendant over, and a surety is required:

"Have you any friends?" he asked.
"The Almighty is my friend," shouted the defendant.
"Yes, yes. The point is, can you give us the name of a friend living near?"
"The Almighty is everywhere."
"I know," said the magistrate patiently. "But I am afraid we shall have to think of someone of more settled habits."

Ridge wrote about the East End until the close of his long career. In his last years he grew increasingly sentimental about the area and increasingly fond of his Cockney School novels. In *I Like to Remember* he devotes an entire chapter to those he calls "Exiles," East Enders living abroad. He was obviously searching for the good in his work, for any impact that he may have had. By 1925 his popularity was sorely waning; the Cockney School had died out about twenty years before that time. He also seemed aware that he had never climbed past the third or fourth tier of British men of letters. His unassuming, self-deprecating air was now all too real: "Extravagantly prosperous folk do not seem to favour me anymore with their correspondence." So Ridge revels in a simple letter from East London, South Africa, reprinting it in its nine-page entirety in *I Like to Remember*. It begins, "As an old Cockney, I have rejoiced exceedingly at your clever and true delineation of the comedy and tragedy of the London lower-class life."

Ridge's last novel was published in 1929, wistfully titled *Affectionate Regards*. By this time his literary fame had dwindled to nearly nothing. In spite of his onetime popularity, his works lack the permanence and universality of true art. Today his oeuvre is delegated to footnotes and parenthetical asides in scholarly works dealing with a minor subset of late-Victorian realism. He was not an innovator or a major force in any literary movement. He diluted experience into a mixture that is neither tasteless nor intoxicating. Ridge thus seems doomed to remain a minor writer.

This judgment, while just, is perhaps incomplete. Ridge did possess a certain talent. While inoffensiveness kills social realism – which in some ways should be offensive in order to be effective – it may be a positive quality elsewhere. His stories are at least readable. In addition, *I Like to Remember* and *A Story Teller* are fine examples of their type: that sort of esoteric, name-dropping literary autobiography first popularized during the eighteenth century and continued during the twentieth century by such writers as Frederic Prokosch and Donald Hall.

Ridge's London *Times* obituary (1 October 1930) mourns the passing of the president of the Omar Khayyám Club. He was also active in a Charles Dickens reading club and was "an enthusiastic member of the Propaganda Committee of King Edward's Hospital Fund for London." Ridge remained loyal to the East Enders to the last. London, the *Times* stated, would miss his "kindly presence and never-failing humour."

References:

Vincent Brome, *Four Realist Novelists* (London: Longmans, Green, 1965), pp. 30–36;

P. J. Keating, *The Working Classes in Victorian Fiction* (New York: Barnes & Noble, 1971), pp. 199–222;

Sally Mitchell, ed., *Victorian Britain* (New York: Garland, 1988);

Obituary, (London) *Times,* 1 October 1930, p. 17;

William Thesing, *The London Muse: Victorian Poetic Responses to the City* (Athens: University of Georgia Press, 1982), pp. 149–151.

Clarence Rook

(1863 – 23 December 1915)

Anita Levy
University of Rochester

BOOKS: *The Hooligan Nights: Being the Life and Opinions of a Young and Unrepentant Criminal Recounted by Himself as Set Forth by Clarence Rook* (London: Richards, 1899; New York: Holt, 1899);
Switzerland: The Country and Its People (London: Chatto & Windus, 1907; New York: Putnam, 1907);
London Side-Lights (London: Arnold, 1908).

OTHER: Louis Frederic Austin, *Points of View,* edited, with prefatory notes, by Rook (London & New York: John Lane, 1906);
Selected Papers on the Social Work of the Salvation Army, edited by Rook and Hulda Friederichs (London: Salvation Army, 1907–1908).

SELECTED PERIODICAL PUBLICATIONS –
UNCOLLECTED:
FICTION
"A Moving Accident," *Idler,* 9 (December 1896): 707–710;
"A Mare's Nest," *Idler,* 15 (June 1899): 699–705.
NONFICTION
"George Bernard Shaw," *Chap-Book,* 5 (1896): 529–540.

Clarence Rook was a journalist, novelist, and writer of short, witty sketches of Edwardian London and its inhabitants. Bernard Shaw praised Rook as a "very clever fellow"; and Rook was most admired for his novel of working-class life, *The Hooligan Nights* (1899), an evocative, irreverent portrait of a young petty criminal, Alf, and his felonious and amorous adventures. As a chronicler of the slums of London's East End, Rook takes his literary and historical place among such eminent contemporaries as George Gissing, Rudyard Kipling, Arthur Morrison, and Sir Walter Besant – writers of fiction, nonfiction, and semifiction in the literature of urban life popular in Britain during the 1880s and 1890s.

It is virtually impossible to determine how Rook came to his fascination for stories of London

life. "Few authors of the period can have vanished as effectively as Rook," writes Benny Green in his introduction to the 1979 edition of *The Hooligan Nights.* "It is as though Clarence Rook had never really existed at all," he concludes with frustration. What little is known of Rook must be gleaned patiently from the glimpses into his life provided by his stories or stray anecdotes. Few details of Rook's early life remain other than his birth in an unknown town in England in 1863. Biographical facts are scarce until he became a young man – as described in *London Side-Lights* (1908), his collection of metropolitan sketches – who was fascinated by the journalist's ability "to sit somewhere in this [Fleet] street, to know all that was going on, to tell people all about it, and to tell them what to think about – that seemed an ambition that was worth cherishing."

With the publication of his first article – a "crude sketch" as he called it, describing a duel among German students in which he participated while studying in Bonn – Rook launched his writing career. From 1896 to 1908 he practiced the craft of casual journalism well enough to satisfy Shaw – one of the greatest literary figures of the period, whom Rook interviewed in 1896 for the *Chap-Book,* an American periodical – as well as the publishers of the pulp journals to which he contributed, the *Daily Chronicle* among them. Not everyone was as pleased with Rook's performance, however: Edward Verrall Lucas, Edwardian man of letters, remembers him in somewhat complimentary fashion as "a writer who never fulfilled his many talents" while Rook was contributing, around 1900, to a humorous daily column, "By the Way," which was featured in the London newspaper the *Globe.* Those who wrote for the column were well respected by their colleagues; according to another "By the Way" contributor, famed humorist P. G. Wodehouse, "There was quite a bit of prestige attached to doing it."

Finally, Rook's death certificate confirms the few solid details of his life. Entered at Saint George,

Hanover Square, in the subdistrict of Belgrave, county of London, it records his death on 23 December 1915 at age fifty-two of "paralysis, bed sores and exhaustion." The certificate also registers that he died with his wife, Clare, at his side, after suffering for twenty-six years from "locomoter ataxy" – a euphemism for a venereal disease associated with syphilis, characterized by loss of muscle control. Unfortunately, one can only speculate on the youthful indiscretion that contributed to Rook's demise.

What survives of Rook's journalistic and fictional output testifies to his diverse interests, which ranged from the East End slums depicted in *The Hooligan Nights* to the middle-class drawing rooms of his short stories to the mountains of Switzerland, the subject of his 1907 travel guide, *Switzerland: The Country and Its People*. While the quality of Rook's prose is decidedly uneven, suggesting his need to write both for love and money, common to all his work is his delight in observing and recording the minutiae of daily life. What fascinated him above all was human interaction of every kind, making him an avid student of both the famous, such as Shaw – who considered Rook's article on his youth and early manhood "one of the best things of the kind ever done about me," as he wrote in a 1905 letter to his official biographer, Archibald Henderson – and the obscure, such as the young hooligan Alf, whose "engaging personality," as Rook writes in his introduction to *The Hooligan Nights*, first attracted his attention.

In his short stories, city sketches, and longer fiction, Rook proceeds by isolating a particular event, conversation, or physical detail that then becomes the center around which his plot unfolds. This ability to "elucidate the fragmentary," which Wendell V. Harris maintains to be the hallmark of the short story, is first seen in "A Moving Accident" (*Idler*, December 1896). Unlike his later pieces dealing with the harsh, sometimes comic, realities of urban life, especially that of men, "A Moving Accident" takes the reader into the middle-class household of Celia and her unnamed, befuddled husband, who are about to change residences. "Why we were moving I cannot tell," Celia's husband complains. "In some vague way Celia had given me to understand that she was uncomfortable. . . . Celia alluded disparagingly to the stairs, the hall-porter, and finally the Higginsons." In her zeal "to drop the Higginsons" from her social circle, Celia gives her husband a list of addresses, asking him to write notes inviting her new friends to an "at home" evening at their new abode. When the long-awaited day arrives, her husband discovers that Celia's

Illustration by Ronald Gray for "A Moving Accident" (Idler, December 1896)

guests have been invited from the wrong list given him by his busy wife, as a long procession of "cooks, housemaids, and boys" winds its way through the garden to their front door.

"A Mare's Nest" (*Idler,* June 1899) describes the middle-class woman at home, her idleness and independence momentarily challenged after overhearing one of her husband's conversations. When Dollie Pakenham discovers that Gerald is secretly preparing "an empty cottage by the mill-pond" for a "charming creature" who "carries herself like a Duchess," she is sure that Gerald is preparing a love nest for an adulterous rendezvous. The joke is on her, however, when the "creature" turns out to be a magnificent horse, Gerald's birthday present to Dollie.

In their portrayal of the idle middle-class woman prey to gossip, mysterious whims, and unreasonable social responsibilities, "A Moving Accident" and "A Mare's Nest" depart from many turn-of-the-century popular short stories, such as Lucie Jackson's "Barbara Moncrieff, Typist" (*Girl's Realm,*

1904), that explore what happens when the middle-class woman goes to work. These stories belong to a historical moment in England when employment patterns for women were undergoing distinctive shifts. As the turn-of-the-century economy grew and the British Empire underwent unprecedented expansion, the tertiary sector – service, administrative, and professional jobs – grew right along with it. As a result, middle-class women entered the labor force in numbers hitherto unknown in the history of the social stratum. Rook instead imagines what happens when the middle-class woman stays home. No longer is the housewife busy baking, brewing, canning, and pickling; no longer are her visits and visitors the stuff of courtship and marriage as depicted in works by Jane Austen and in the domestic fiction of the 1840s as represented by the Brontës, Charles Dickens, and Elizabeth Gaskell. In contrast, Rook's housewife is idle, her head filled with unexplained desires, as in "A Moving Accident," or foolishness, as in "A Mare's Nest."

The Hooligan Nights marks a major departure within Rook's fiction from the domestic concerns of the late-Victorian middle class to a "study in reality," as he described his collection of tales and reminiscences of a young hooligan. As Rook writes in the introduction, his interest in the new phenomenon of hooliganism, later known as juvenile delinquency, was aroused when his publisher, Grant Richards, first showed him some manuscript sheets containing "certain confessions and revelations of a boy who professed to be a leader of Hooligans." Wishing to meet the author, Rook asked Richards to set up a meeting; a series of interviews followed between the journalist and the thief, out of which emerged *The Hooligan Nights* – purported by Rook to be the unvarnished truth. Thus he claims in the introduction that the book is "neither a novel, nor in any sense a work of imagination, whatever value or interest the following chapters possess come from the fact that their hero had a real existence."

Rook was by no means alone in his fascination with London's working class. The 1880s and 1890s brought a resurgence of middle-class interest in the laboring poor unprecedented since the midcentury, when researchers, writers, social reformers, and health inspectors invaded the slums in great numbers, eager to observe, measure, and categorize every facet of working-class life. Urban researchers and novelists as diverse as Henry Mayhew, James Kay, Friedrich Engels, Gaskell, and Dickens located the problem of the working class not in the poor conditions under which they labored but within the individuals themselves. According to this logic their uncleanliness, sexual degeneration, and laziness produced their impoverishment.

Like their earlier counterparts, late-Victorian and Edwardian fiction and nonfiction writers focused primarily on the problem of urban poverty. Their outpouring of East End tales contributed further, perhaps, to growing middle-class fears of renewed working-class political and economic power, witnessed by the prevalence of strikes, the growth in the trade-union movement, and the emergence of socialism at the turn of the century. Yet, in a clear departure from this tradition, these writers avoided the moralization of the laboring poor so common to their predecessors in favor of what they considered to be a more rigorous and detached sociological representation of East End reality of which Rook's portrayal of hooliganism is characteristic.

The "discovery" of the East End, as this resurgence has been called, took off with the publication of Besant's *All Sorts and Conditions of Men* (1882), along with Andrew Mearns and W. C. Preston's *Bitter Cry of Outcast London* (1883), both mixtures of dramatized characterization, graphic descriptions of poverty, and dubious statistics representing the East End as a city apart from London, heathen and outcast. These tracts were followed by Charles Booth's voluminous study *Life and Labour of the People in London* (1889), along with such fictional contributions as Rudyard Kipling's short story "The Record of Badalia Herodsfoot" (1890), narrating the life and brutal death of a costermonger's daughter, Morrison's *Tales of Mean Streets* (1894), and Arthur St. John Adcock's *East End Idylls* (1897).

Among the concerns preoccupying these middle-class writers and social reformers, including Rook, was the perceived irresponsibility and lack of discipline of working-class youths. Because of the lack of jobs for young boys – or their transient employment as errand boys, van boys, messenger boys, boys to hold horses' heads, and the like – they were frequently represented in newspaper accounts and police reports as quick to fight or steal when the need arose. "Street arabs," "ruffians," or "roughs," as these boys were called, were considered a foreign, un-British phenomenon in need of quick action. The word *hooligan* that Rook adopted for his account of this working-class culture first appeared in print in 1898 newspaper court reports. The term may have derived from a corruption of "Hooley's Gang" or from the followers of Patrick Hooligan, who, according to Rook, "gave laws and a name to his followers." Nevertheless, *hooligan* quickly came to stand for a general affliction among the nation's youth and a source of many ills besetting the nation and the empire at the end of the nineteenth century.

The Hooligan Nights consists of twenty-two short, descriptive sketches of the hooligan's exploits, a format that Rook perfects in *London Side-Lights*. The reader meets the hooligan Alf on the bustling streets of London's Elephant and Castle, eager to announce his "philosophy of life," which Rook transcribes in the harsh phonetics of cockney English: "If you seen a fing you want, you just go and take it wiveout any 'anging abart." From there Rook follows Alf in word and deed as he shares his life story over ginger beer in a Lambeth pub, shows Rook around his turf, and introduces him to his girlfriends and criminal associates. In the process Rook recounts such gems as "The Burglar and the Baby," a charming piece describing Alf's rescue of a choking baby in a house into which he has broken; "Jimmy," an account of Alf's first mentor in crime; and "The Course of True Love," recounting Alf's decision to marry his pregnant lover, Alice. "Holy Matrimony" finds Alf at the church after his marriage, bringing the book to a surprisingly traditional end much after the fashion of a domestic novel.

On the whole, Rook's approach to representing his working-class hero is remarkably unsanctimonious, reveling in the hooligan's felonious adventures and attempting to scandalize his middle-class readers, especially when he recounts Alf's brutal treatment of his future wife. In fact, the public was so scandalized on the publication of portions of the work in the *Daily Chronicle,* as Rook explains in the introduction, that he was accused of making too positive a portrait of criminal life. In defense Rook argues that Alf is real and that "in real life the villain does not invariably come to grief before he has come of age." He goes on to compare Alf's life favorably to that of a clerk, no doubt raising a few more eyebrows among his readers, and ends by denying responsibility for the book's contents: "If under the present conditions of life a Lambeth boy can get more fun by going sideways than by going straight, I cannot help it."

At least one contemporary, G. K. Chesterton, was openly critical of similar efforts by Morrison to chronicle working-class life. While he does not mention Rook explicitly in "Slum Novelists and the Slums" (1905), Chesterton writes stingingly, "The kind of a man who could really express the pleasures of the poor would also be the kind of man who could share them. In short these books are not a record of the psychology of poverty. They are a record of the psychology of wealth when brought

"I suppose Gerald doesn't mind your amusing yourself without him."
700

Illustration by James Greig for "A Mare's Nest" (Idler, *June 1899*)

into contact with poverty." In a similar vein P. J. Keating concludes in *The Working Classes in Victorian Fiction* (1971) that, despite their sympathy for and admiration of working-class life, cockney novelists such as Rook "finally advance an image of the working man as someone who is socially harmless if handled in the right manner."

Subsequent critics and commentators have questioned the veracity of *The Hooligan Nights,* noting that Rook's dramatic method and considerable literary skills in telling Alf's story owe more to the techniques of fiction than to journalism or sociology. He has been classified as a member of the Cockney School, a term used by historians and literary critics for novelists writing about East End working-class life. *The Hooligan Nights* has been described as part of the literature of roguery, following in the tradition of Dickens's *Oliver Twist* (1838), with Alf characterized as an updated version of the Artful Dodger.

London Side-Lights, a collection of twenty-nine sketches of London labor and leisure, may be called Rook's novel of London, if such a novel were to be written, in his words, "in snatches, as the driver with a crack of the whip on the window picks up a passenger from a side-street." Rook is indeed such a driver, and along the way he cracks his whip at "London Justice"; "Visiting Day" at Saint Bartholomew's Hospital; "Cave Dwellers," about woman caretakers of rental houses; "A Day's Work in Fleet Street," meditating on his career as a journalist; "The London Hotel"; and "Animals and Doctors," concerning the Royal Veterinary College and hospital. "To Him Who Waits" tells of Alf's fate: "Gone away and laid his bones upon a battlefield – for he enlisted in a moment of enthusiasm – and his colonel announced that he had died as a good soldier."

Rook indulges both his literary inclinations and his passion for capturing the details of modern life in *London Side-Lights*. The first sketch, "West to East," is a humorous account of "the call to the explorer, the pilgrim – the determination to go from West to East and find, if possible, the other end of London." On the way he is prone to literary lapses – "disasterous intrusions," as Benny Green calls these passages announcing Rook's literary aspirations – such as this description of a Park Lane mansion: "And the houses are elusive – most of them ... generally the house slinks behind the glass-covered approach, withdrawing itself from the vulgar gaze with a sort of impudent modesty."

Few of the accounts in *London Side-Lights* actually contain the fictional elements and plot structure characteristic of Rook's earlier short stories. In observing, describing, and commenting on an exactly realized environment and those who inhabit it, he produces what must be called sketches. These serve as a vehicle for his occasionally eccentric views on a wide range of themes, including the "schoolboy traditions" of Parliament ("Mother of Parliaments"). Thus, after observing a parliamentary debate, Rook writes with wry humor, "Three hundred and forty-seven gentlemen have spent half an hour and covered many miles to settle a question that I would leave with confidence to a kitchen-maid." And so with considerable understatement Rook deflates much parliamentary pomp and circumstance.

Despite the thoroughly delightful sketches in *London Side-Lights,* the book has failed to attract critical attention. Rook's literary legacy and critical reputation rest solely on the widely acclaimed *Hooligan Nights*. This fascinating, enduring portrait of working-class life has earned its author a permanent place in the literature and history of turn-of-the-century Britain.

References:

G. K. Chesterton, "Slum Novelists and the Slums," in his *Heretics* (New York: John Lane, 1905);

Benny Green, Introduction to Rook's *The Hooligan Nights* (Oxford: Oxford University Press, 1979);

Wendell V. Harris, *British Short Fiction in the Nineteenth Century* (Detroit: Wayne State University Press, 1979);

P. J. Keating, *The Working Classes in Victorian Fiction* (New York: Barnes & Noble, 1971);

Keating, ed., *Working-class Stories of the 1890s* (London: Routledge & Kegan Paul, 1971);

Geoffrey Pearson, *Hooligan: A History of Respectable Fears* (New York: Schocken, 1983).

George Robert Sims

(2 September 1847 – 4 September 1922)

William B. Thesing
University of South Carolina

See also the Sims entries in *DLB 35: Victorian Poets After 1850* and *DLB 70: British Mystery Writers, 1860–1919*.

BOOKS: *The Social Kaleidoscope,* first series (London: Francis, 1879);

The Dagonet Ballads (London: Francis, 1879);

The Ballads of Babylon (London: Fuller, 1880);

Zeph, and Other Stories (London: Fuller, 1880; enlarged edition, London: Chatto & Windus, 1892);

The Theatre of Life (London: Fuller, 1881);

The Social Kaleidoscope, second series (London: Francis, 1881);

Three Brass Balls (London: Fuller, 1882);

How the Poor Live (London: Chatto & Windus, 1883);

The Lifeboat, and Other Poems (London: Fuller, 1883);

Ballads and Poems (London: Fuller, 1883);

Stories in Black and White (London: Chatto & Windus, 1885);

Rogues and Vagabonds (London: Chatto & Windus, 1885; New York: Munro, 1886);

The Ring o' Bells (London: Chatto & Windus, 1886);

Mary Jane's Memoirs (London: Chatto & Windus, 1887; New York: Ivers, 1887);

Mary Jane Married: Tales of a Village Inn (London: Chatto & Windus, 1888);

The Land of Gold, and Other Poems (London: Fuller, 1888);

The Dagonet Reciter and Reader, in Prose and Verse (London: Chatto & Windus, 1888);

Tales of To-Day (London: Chatto & Windus, 1889; New York: Lovell, 1889);

How the Poor Live, and Horrible London (London: Chatto & Windus, 1889);

The Case of George Candlemas (London: Chatto & Windus, 1890);

Dramas of Life (London: Chatto & Windus, 1890; New York: United States Book Company, 1890);

A Bunch of Primroses (London & New York: Tuck, 1890);

Nellie's Prayer (London & New York: Tuck, 1890);

A Missing Husband and Other Tales (London: Chatto & Windus, 1890);

Tinkletop's Crime (London: Chatto & Windus, 1891; New York: Webster, 1891);

Dagonet Ditties (London: Chatto & Windus, 1891);

Memoirs of a Mother-in-Law (London: Newnes, 1892; New York: Waverly, 1892);

My Two Wives, and Other Stories (London: Chatto & Windus, 1894);

Memoirs of a Landlady (London: Chatto & Windus, 1894);

Dagonet on Our Islands (London: Unwin, 1894);

Scenes from the Show (London: Chatto & Windus, 1894);

Dagonet Abroad (London: Chatto & Windus, 1895);

The Ten Commandments (London: Chatto & Windus, 1896);

As It Was in the Beginning: Life Stories of To-Day (London: White, 1896);

The Coachman's Club: or, Tales Told Out of School (London: White, 1897);

Dorcas Dene, Detective: Her Adventures (London: White, 1897);

Dorcas Dene, Detective: Her Adventures, second series (London: White, 1898);

Dagonet Dramas of the Day (London: Chatto & Windus, 1898);

Once Upon a Christmastime (London: Chatto & Windus, 1898);

In London's Heart (London: Chatto & Windus, 1900; New York: Buckles, 1900);

Without the Limelight: Theatrical Life as It Is (London: Chatto & Windus, 1900);

The Small-Part Lady and Other Stories (London: Chatto & Windus, 1900);

A Blind Marriage, and Other Stories (London: Chatto & Windus, 1901);

Nat Harlowe, Mountebank (London: Cassell, 1902);

Biographs of Babylon: Life-Pictures of London's Moving Scenes (London: Chatto & Windus, 1902);

Young Mrs. Caudle (London: Chatto & Windus, 1904);

Among My Autographs (London: Chatto & Windus, 1904);

The Life We Live (London: Chatto & Windus, 1904);

The King's Pardons. The Martyrdom of Adolf Beck (London: Daily Mail, 1904);

Li Ting of London, and Other Stories (London: Chatto & Windus, 1905);

The Mysteries of Modern London (London: Pearson, 1906);

Two London Fairies (London: Greening, 1906);

For Life – and After (London: Chatto & Windus, 1906);

London by Night (London: Greening, 1906; revised, 1910);

His Wife's Revenge (London: Chatto & Windus, 1907);

Watches of the Night (London: Greening, 1907);

The Mystery of Mary Anne, and Other Stories (London: Chatto & Windus, 1907);

The Black Stain (London: Jarrolds, 1907);

Joyce Pleasantry, and Other Stories (London: Chatto & Windus, 1908);

The Devil in London (London: S. Paul, 1908; New York: Dodge, 1909);

The Death Gamble (London: S. Paul, 1909);

The Cabinet Minister's Wife (London: S. Paul, 1910);

Off the Track in London (London: Jarrolds, 1911);

Behind the Veil: True Stories of London Life (London: Greening, 1913);

The Bluebeard of the Bath (London: Pearson, 1915);

Anna of the Underworld (London: Chatto & Windus, 1916);

My Life: Sixty Years' Recollections of Bohemian London (London: Nash, 1917);

Glances Back (London: Jarrolds, 1917).

Collection: *Prepare to Shed Them Now: The Ballads of George R. Sims,* edited, with an introduction, by Arthur Calder-Marshall (London: Hutchinson, 1968).

PLAY PRODUCTIONS: *The Lights o' London,* London, Princess's Theatre, 10 September 1881; New York, Union-Square Theatre, 5 December 1881;

The Romany Rye, London, Princess's Theatre, 10 June 1882; New York, Booth's Theatre, 18 September 1882;

In the Ranks, by Sims and Henry Pettitt, New York, Standard Theatre, 1 November 1883; London, Adelphi Theatre, 6 November 1883;

Harbour Lights, by Sims and Pettitt, London, Adelphi Theatre, 23 November 1885; New York, Wallack's Theatre, 26 January 1887;

The English Rose, by Sims and Robert Buchanan, London, Adelphi Theatre, 2 August 1890; New York, Proctor's Theatre, 9 March 1892;

The Trumpet Call, by Sims and Buchanan, London, Adelphi Theatre, 1 August 1891.

OTHER: *Living London,* 3 volumes, edited by Sims (London & New York: Cassell, 1901–1903);

"The Cry of the Children," in *The Cry of the Children* (London: Tribune, 1907?), pp. 5–24.

TRANSLATION: Honoré de Balzac, *Balzac's Contes Drolatiques* (London: Chatto & Windus, 1874).

George Robert Sims was a popular, prolific writer for more than half a century. He had successes in many genres, including novels, short stories, drama, poetry, and journalism. Although his detective fiction has received some attention, he wrote many stories in the vein of social and domestic realism. His autobiography, *My Life: Sixty Years'*

Recollections of Bohemian London (1917), offers reminiscences of his work for newspapers and the theater; however, he has little to say about his efforts in fiction.

Sims was born in London on 2 September 1847. His mother came from Worcestershire; she was eighteen at the time of his birth. His father was from London; he was nineteen when G. R. was born. Sims, who spent a lifetime recording "the human panorama of the pavement," was proud to boast that "I have from my birth been a Londoner." Reportedly, the first words that he uttered as a child in the metropolis were "a bop o' tea."

The backgrounds of his parents' families contrasted. His great-grandfather Robert Sims married a Spaniard, Countess Elizabeth de Montijo. G. R.'s grandfather Robert Sims married Mary Hope, who came from a family of strict Nonconformists. G. R.'s maternal grandmother, Mary Yardley, married John Dinmore Stevenson, a leader of the Chartist movement. Only a year after Sims's birth, members of his family were on opposing sides as the Chartists threatened to use force to obtain their demands by protesting on London's streets.

Sims's father was a special constable; J. D. Stevenson was a demonstrator. Sims felt a special affinity for his grandfather, "the old Chartist," and credited him with shaping his early political views. Sims's father worked in an office in London House (formerly the palace of the bishops of London) in the historic City section. Another important early influence on Sims was his mother, an enthusiastic playgoer. From the age of six, Sims attended dramatic productions, including plays by William Shakespeare. Sims's parents were Anglicans, and he was the eldest of their six children.

Sims attended the Grove Preparatory School for Young Gentlemen in Eastbourne, Sussex. He later went to Hopley School; he recalls incidents of child abuse there, as well as a murder involving one of his schoolmates and the headmaster. In the 1860s he was trained for home defense at Hanwell Military College, where he was promoted to the rank of sergeant. In 1864 Sims went to Bonn, Germany. He pursued some studies but primarily participated in frolicsome escapades. One night he threw crab-apples at pedestrians' umbrellas in the street below. A famous German professor momentarily closed his umbrella and received a heavy shower. He furiously pursued Sims and reported him to the local chief of police. Sims was fined and had to write his father for more money. His father lost patience with these escapades and ordered him to return home to begin work as a clerk in his London office, a whole-sale and export business specializing in cabinets and plate glass. G. R. hated the drudgery of this work and soon decided that he needed to find a more satisfying career.

Sims had written "poetry of sorts" from the age of ten; however, he longed to become a journalist and an author. During these years, somewhat in the tradition of Charles Dickens, Sims walked around areas of the metropolis "to gain the knowledge of London which was to stand me in such good stead as an author in later years." During this period he met many individuals who furnished him with the material for his early stories, some of which were accepted for publication in the *Weekly Dispatch*. Throughout his life Sims enjoyed London's characters and entertainments – especially the theaters, music halls, casinos, horseracing tracks, and coffeehouses.

Sims's first real break into the world of journalism came with an arrangement negotiated at the Unity, a fashionable London club. Moving within the social circles of various London clubs, Sims was by all accounts an amiable listener, a sociable member who was known for his hard work and quick wit. In 1874 one editor, John Thomson, offered him the opportunity to take over a column called "Waifs and Strays" in the *Weekly Dispatch*. Sims started his career as a professional journalist on Fleet Street at the rate of a guinea per column. Soon he was also able to earn money contributing verses and articles to *Fun*, a popular periodical that emphasized satire and broad humor. In 1877 editor Henry Sampson started a new Sunday paper, the *Referee*, for which Sims wrote an immensely popular weekly column, "Mustard and Cress," for more than forty-five years. Besides his continuing contributions to the *Weekly Dispatch*, he published a few items in the weekly journal *Woman*.

Sims's successful melodrama *The Lights o' London* opened on 10 September 1881. In 1894 the *New York Sunday Advertiser* estimated that Sims had earned more than seventy-two thousand pounds in royalties from various productions of this popular drama. An early example of Sims's penchant for realism, the play had its origins in an early-morning walk with a working-class couple in search of employment in the capital city.

In these middle years of the 1870s, the American short-story writer Ambrose Bierce was his colleague and frequent companion. Sims remarked that Bierce's *In the Midst of Life* (1892) contained "some of the finest short stories in the English language." Two other friends of Sims in this period were Andrew Chatto (of the publishing house Chatto and

Windus) and Edmund Yates. Sims later established a friendship with Bret Harte. Sims also collaborated with poet and dramatist Robert Buchanan on several play productions. As a writer and producer of dramas, Sims maintained a frantic work pace and sometimes suffered with gout, dyspepsia, and insomnia. In a September 1896 letter he writes of his involvement in the successful production of the play *Two Little Vagabonds:* "I was so busy last week, never getting to bed till 5 o'clock in the morning, and having to be in the theatre again soon after 10, that I had no time to explain."

Sims's first collection of short stories appeared in two parts: *The Social Kaleidoscope* (1879 and 1881). As with many of his collections of short stories, the preface or introductory note provides important statements as to his artistic intentions. In "Introduction to the First Series," Sims explains the implications of his title's metaphor:

> The kaleidoscope is an optical instrument which, by an arrangement of reflecting surfaces, presents to the eye a variety of colours and symmetrical forms. Turning it now this way and now that, the fragments of variously-coloured glass which it contains fall into a succession of peculiar figures, and we have a series of perfectly dissimilar pictures, the component parts of which are in every way the same. Substitute for the fragments of coloured glass the many-hued virtues and vices, passions and peculiarities of mankind, and at every twist of the Social Kaleidoscope we get a glimpse of human nature in a varied aspect.

Sims also maintains that his purpose in the sketches is "to describe truthfully and fearlessly" the various figures of humanity that he observes. Furthermore, he describes each pattern "down to the period when the atoms have disparted and the figure is destroyed."

This last image is highly suggestive because it describes the types of people Sims often portrays in his stories. Generally, he writes about the falling fortunes of individuals who for various reasons slide down the socioeconomic scale to destruction and ruin or who suffer the consequences of deteriorating mental or physical health. The figures that he describes are selected and examined "with the keen eyes of matter of fact, and now with the dreamy orbs of fancy." Sims builds his doctrine of realism on the proverb that "The truth is always beautiful"; thus he presents heroic suffering, gallant death, and even scenes of horror. In several of the stories collected in the first series, Sims as narrator steps aside from his tale and offers commentary on the nature of his brand of realism. Accordingly, he says at the

opening of one story, "I have undertaken . . . to describe such scenes of life as may arise truthfully and fearlessly." He later states: "It does not enter into my province to raise moral or psychological discussions in these columns. In the Social Kaleidoscope I show you certain phases of life and certain people as they actually exist."

The first series includes story sequences in which up to three separately titled pieces delineate characters and develop a plot involving these individuals. This technique stems from his originally publishing these stories in the *Weekly Dispatch* on a week-by-week basis, with the carryover of serial installments building suspense for a period of weeks. Some sketches, however, stand by themselves as self-contained units. Sims labels each sketch by number: for instance, "Figure I. A Christian Sufferer."

In this exposé Sims reveals the scam operation of a wealthy urban woman, Miss Janet Gurton, who makes her living from daily begging. In a shabby, gloomy room at street level, she welcomes visitors who give her money because she appears to suffer from a crippling paralysis. At the end of the day she retires to the second-floor rooms that are never seen by the general public. These are "gorgeously furnished apartments." Her younger sister, Phoebe, tends her in her helpless, invalid state, and Janet is surrounded by dozens of religious volumes displayed as part of her scam.

Sims explains in passing how she became crippled, but his primary interest is the way she employs her deformity as a weapon of will: she "determined to use her afflictions as the weapons with which to prey upon society and make a fortune." She becomes a charity case of renown, "a London celebrity" whose name is on the lists of half the charitable institutions in England. Although the general public sees Janet Gurton as the prototype of Christian martyrdom, Sims exposes the reality of her situation through the omniscient narrator's judgment: "She is a hypocrite and an impostor, and she preys upon society. Her afflictions and her sufferings are real, but she uses them vilely and basely as a means of deception and plunder. She lives on the fat of the land." Sims regrets that she unfairly diverts charitable funds that would be more appropriately donated to "the real Christian sufferers who suffer in silence and endure in neglect, who starve and die."

Several other stories in the first series of *The Social Kaleidoscope* deal with the economic or moral decay of individuals. In "A Good Fellow" the title character, Frank Barton, lends fivers and tenners and discounts a friend's bill. However, the omniscient narrator knows that a woman holds a guilty secret of Barton's indiscretions and lets the reader see the room where the "murdered woman lies white and wan and still." In the continuation sketch, "A Little Paradise," Barton is imprisoned and soon given over to the hangman. His wife and children are outcasts for life, shunned by all as they retreat to a rural cottage. Three other linked sketches, "A Fashionable Marriage," "The Baby Heir," and "An Aristocratic Scandal," depict the decline of the aristocratic Dashton household, drained by debauchery and intemperance. Lord Dashton is found dead with a bottle in his hand; his sole heir dies; and Lady Dashton enters a convent in Belgium. A precipitous slide down the economic scale because of investment failures in shares of a Scottish bank is described in "At One Fell Swoop": "After twenty-five years of labour and thrift, they [the Dashtons] are plunged into the depths of poverty at a moment when they had expected to end their days in peace."

In sketches such as "A Brown Check Suit," Sims registers a social protest against the oppressed workers, "half-starved women and men" who produce fashionable garments in "top garrets in back slums." In "Hunting the Ghastly" he lightly satirizes the growing taste for the morbid in narratives, attributing it to American short-story pioneers, or "Edgar Allan Poe-ism." Two of the most memorable stories in the collection, however, involve murders at opposite ends of the social spectrum. Eating gourmet delicacies in "A Mayonnaise of Salmon" leads to confusion, rage, and the murder of an aristocrat; in their turn the impoverished are shown to be deliberate schemers as they murder their children for insurance-policy premiums in "A Premium for Murder." In this story Sims's re-creation of Mrs. Joyce's dialect — as she speaks of her little son Johnny drinking "his linerment" and "larkin'" with her husband — is especially effective. Stories in which Sims makes use of classical allusions, such as the myth of Sisyphus or references to Asmodeus and Alsatia, were probably less effective with his popular-reading audience.

Sims gathered more stories from his weekly journal columns and then wrote an introduction for the second series of *The Social Kaleidoscope*. He uses the introduction to establish further his commitment to the doctrine of realism. He reminds his readers that tragedies are enacted every day "in our midst with real tears, real blood, and real human agony." Thus, despite some objections from readers about the stories he had already published, he main-

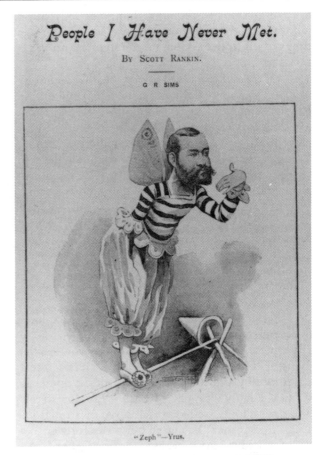

Caricature of Sims as his short-story character Zeph (Idler, November 1892)

tains that "realism is the one quality which it is necessary these sketches should possess." His scenes are from "the land of fact," and they are "painted from life." Likewise, the individuals depicted are drawn from "living, breathing models."

In the second series Sims continues to use several sketches to develop an unfolding sequence of events involving the same characters. Murder and mystery are featured even more prominently than in the first series. An eminent country gentleman and justice of the peace, Charles Greythorpe, Esq., disappears, and the family solicitor, Jeremiah Judson, is murdered over the course of the first three stories: "Not Quite Right," "Murder!," and "The Great Grafton-Street Mystery." The minute details of the case have appeared in the newspapers, and Sims reports the facts as assembled by an intelligent officer from Scotland Yard. At the end of the mystery, however, Sims advances a social-class protest. Part of the problem with the individuals involved in this case is Victorian society's treatment of the mentally ill. Sims complains that "a rich lunatic [Greythorpe] may live where he likes if his friends are not anxious to get rid of him. It is only those who are in the way, or who are poor, who are dragged off to the asylum on the slightest provocation."

Of the self-contained stories, "Father and Son" is an exceptionally tight, dramatic tale based on the prodigal-son motif. A judge unknowingly sentences his long-lost (and dissolute) son to death. In an eleventh-hour recognition/reconciliation scene, Britain's home secretary is able to commute the sentence to penal servitude for life. A slide down the economic scale – with details of domestic realism involving "broils, ill-usage, blows, and drink" – is the focus of "A Popular Actress," in which Sims portrays the rise and fall of London actress Nelly Dawson. Stretched on a straw pallet and covered with rags, she dies in obscurity in New York City. "Two Members of the Aristocracy" features a viscountess who had "come down in the world."

Besides economic misfortune Sims also explores the theme of misogyny. A preying female – a motherly type who is to be regarded with suspicion – is the focus of "Missing – A Young Lady." Here a "most strait-laced Camberwellian" with "all the domestic virtues" simply disappears from the London streets one day. The fanatic representative of a religious sect, "the mother" has lured her away forever to a life of religious retreat behind "the great gates." "An Eccentric Baronet" depicts Sir Charles Collys, "a woman-hater who is surrounded by a set of manservants at his Parkfield country seat.

The range of Sims's attention can be seen in an opposing social scene – the attics and low-life back alleys of London in the sketch "A Muslin Frock." In this tragic true story a little girl's parents argue in a public house over the purchase of a new dress for the child. The mother is killed in a drunken brawl. Sims is moved to explicit social commentary in this sketch: "They [the children] are dirty, unwashed faces, and no amount of moonlight could make them beautiful. They are the faces of London gutter children, born and bred in vice and misery and dirt, reared in squalor and the poisoned atmosphere of a London slum, beaten and starved and neglected."

Sims may very well have thought of the pieces in *The Social Kaleidoscope* as items of social commentary in the tradition of Dickens's *Sketches by Boz* (1836–1837). In the preface to *Zeph, and Other Stories* (1880) he first uses the term "stories [that] have appeared in various periodicals," and he refers to these reprinted pieces as his "first efforts in fiction," or "his firstborn." The volume is divided into four sections: "Zeph: A Story of To-day" contains eigh-

teen related parts; "Jo Powell's Pilgrimage" has six parts; "Urbain and Isette" has eight parts; and an untitled fourth section has seven stories grouped together, including the delightful tale "My Dog Pickle." The Zeph sequence is the story of various performers and families involved with Groote's circus, which travels all over the country and the Continent. Most of the pieces in the volume have several common threads: the stories are set in London; coincidence and disguise are used at key turns of the plots; and characters meet with a series of misfortunes as they slide down the economic scale in Victorian England. It was common for individuals to plunge from the top to the bottom rungs of England's social-class system; accident, misfortune, drink, or improvidence were often precipitating causes.

"Zeph: A Story of To-day" is the best series in the collection. The setting is the circus world, complete with villains and heroes. The central figure is an acrobat who assumes a variety of names: Zephaniah, Signor Zephio, Pedro, and William Eager. Zeph's wife is a flying-trapeze artist who is featured in the circus bills as the Queen of the Arena. Their young daughter, Totty, grows up throughout the narrative, and she eventually becomes an accomplished trapeze performer. The first misfortune to befall the family is a crippling accident involving Zeph's wife. Because there is no insurance, her loss of income plunges the family into debt and a cramped garret in London's slum area of Lambeth.

Toroni is an unscrupulous managing agent who has become wealthy. He conceives of a scheme to send Zeph on a circus tour to Spain and France. As a trainer Toroni plans to teach Totty acrobatic skills while Zeph is away. In Europe, Zeph has some success as a member of a performance team, the Bounding Brothers of Bagdad; however, some foreign workers betray him. He is beaten and drugged beside a roadway. Years later he makes his way back to England, where he attends a circus featuring acrobatic performances by Totty and another woman, Inez. At the climax of the spectacle the two women fall to a net that gives way, but Zeph rescues them from certain injury just in time. A recognition/reconciliation scene is then melodramatically described as Zeph is reunited with Totty. Sims steps aside from his narrative to criticize the British public's gruesome tastes in spectacle: "The British public . . . will rush in its thousands to a place of amusement on the chance of seeing women and children break their necks or dash their brains out."

The "Urbain and Isette" section includes the tale of the poor mother Marie Leslie's search for her children, Urbain and Isette, who are either lost in London or perhaps at the mercy of strangers. While the family was together, Marie was the victim of her father's violence: "He kept me locked up for weeks sometimes, and beat me till I shrieked. When I cried out, the people said, 'Listen to the mad Englishwoman; she is bad to-night.' . . . I let him abuse me and said nothing." Ten years later a good-hearted man named George Tostevor provides a home for the children and marries Marie. In a merry Christmas scene the children are depicted as "beside themselves with joy" after the dysfunctional family has suffered anguish and abuse for the past ten years.

The final section in the collection offers seven unrelated stories. One of the most effective is "One Winter Night," in which a lonely poet who spurned an attractive woman for gold and fame receives a second chance to win her hand in romance. The pair reunite at the story's end — but only after he is grotesquely disfigured in a gas explosion outside his home. Marion nurses and loves him despite his changed appearance. The story is a curious blend of realism and romance. In the 1892 edition of *Zeph*, Sims added another suspenseful story, "The Peculiar Nose; Or, The Hangman's Daughter," at the end of the collection.

The *National Press* praised Sims's "light" and "delicate" touch in *Zeph, and Other Stories*. The review claimed that Sims, like Dickens, mastered a range of emotions between farce and pathos. It also valued Sims's writing for its ability to improve conditions in the London area: to redeem "the vice-slaves" and to aid "the struggling bread-winner" through the exposure in print of suffering, oppression, and injustice.

In *The Theatre of Life* (1881) Sims gathered twenty short stories that had previously appeared in the *Weekly Dispatch*. In the prologue he advances the notion of the real world as a theater, with its tragedies, dramas, comedies, and farces. Life dramas include human joy and misery: "The plays that will be set before you shall be real and human." "Happy Jack" describes a likable vagabond of the same name who is known to workhouse masters all over the country. Sims presents the history of this handsome gentleman, Paul Royston, from his residence in a stately mansion in the north of England to a man who now has ragged clothes and empty pockets.

Years before, his father traveled and joined a Gypsy tribe, where he fell in love with Zara, the beautiful daughter of the Gypsy chief. They were married and had a son, so she was forced to give up the wild, romantic life. Through a turn in the wheel of fortune four years later, Royston suddenly became a country gentleman, the lord of one of England's stateliest homes.

Pressured to make his wife into a lady, Royston becomes embarrassed by her carefree actions. Position and wealth have led him from romance to matter-of-factness. One night he turns his rage into physical abuse of his wife, taunting "the cowering woman with her past." She offers retorts; he meets them with a blow to her face with his riding whip. She leaves the mansion but soon perishes in a great snowstorm.

A year after her death, Squire Royston remarries, this time to "a woman in his own sphere of life." Paul, his son by Zara, is still officially the heir, but he grows up wild, carefree, and neglected. He decides to leave his father's estate to sing ballads and tell tales from village to village, earning the name "Happy Jack." He enjoys leading his vagabond life and helping others until his fortieth year, when he contracts a bad cold and loses his voice forever. He dies just outside the gates of his ancestral home on a cold winter night.

The story is a pointed commentary on representations of Gypsy versus genteel life in Victorian England. Sims clearly admires the authenticity and contributions of Young Paul, the rustic bohemian, the joyful, wandering outcast: "Happy Jack! How few dramas in the great Theatre of Life are so pure and wholesome as that of which you were the vagabond hero!" Sims also reminds the reader of his groundings in realism: that this is a "true story" that first appeared in great London newspapers, but that he is providing the full details for the first time.

A mill in the village of Slocum is the setting of father-son conflicts in "The Bond of Blood," with a "dark-eyed, buxom little wench of sixteen" named Jenny as a part of the drama. The realism is too true to life in "No. 965," where Sims adds this opening footnote: "The incidents on which this story is founded actually occurred. The parties concerned are still living, and one of them is well known. For their sakes certain alterations have been made in the plot and the *denouement* in order to prevent identification." "Dead and Alive" is a haunting portrait of Charlie Pendered, a sensitive young man whose "forte was literature." He has written several stories, but their publication has brought him no more than twopence. He is forced to travel the realm by train as a "commercial traveller," a traveling salesman on commission. He is beset with problems, including a difficult wife and "ravenous creditors."

In the early 1880s Sims wrote a series of special investigative articles for the *Daily News*. These findings were published as *How the Poor Live* (1883) and *How the Poor Live, and Horrible London* (1889). Throughout the 1870s and 1880s his journalistic duties kept him in close acquaintance with London's criminal and impoverished areas. On some of his tours he received assistance from the metropolitan police. Sims continued to write short stories during the 1880s, and three more collections were published: *Stories in Black and White* (1885), *The Ring o' Bells* (1886), and *Tales of To-Day* (1889). *Stories in Black and White* includes pieces that originally appeared in the *Weekly Dispatch*. Many of these deal with society's outcasts, whether tramps, foundlings, or domestic servants.

On occasion reviewers warned readers about the possible unpopularity of Sims's subject matter. Regarding *The Ring o' Bells,* the *Daily News* wrote: "The pathos of 'The Ring o' Bells' and of 'The Doll's Secret' depends a good deal on the sufferings of children, and there are tastes to which this kind of distress does not appeal in fiction." Melodrama and gloom cast a shadow over the Christmas season in the title story, which is the name of a pub in Marshton-by-the-sea. On Christmas Eve a young woman arrives at the establishment, gives birth to a baby girl, swoons, and dies later that night. The pub manager, a widow named Van Hooten, decides to keep the child, Mary Holland. However, the widow treats her harshly, and, after a few Christmas Eves pass, the poor little drudge Mary is sent out into the snow by manipulative adult guardians who try to play revengeful games with one another.

In *Stories in Black and White* Sims adopts such techniques as the use of the first-person point of view, expanded sections of dialogue, and narratives told by characters themselves, sometimes in what he represents as cockney dialect. He also reveals details of his personal tastes and his privilege in Victorian society as an observer and writer on the London scene. Many of these stories involve complicated triangles in which a woman is in love with more than one man. Coincidence plays a large part in the plot turns. Other stories take up themes that Sims had used before, such as the prodigal-son motif and the slide down the economic scale.

The two-part tale of "The Tramp's Daughter" combines these motifs nicely. One stormy night Farmer Layton hears a loud knock at his front door, and on opening it he discovers a tramp family composed of a husband, wife, and daughter. During the night the man disappears, and the wife dies of heart disease. The abandoned daughter is taken in by the family as a household servant. The young girl, Lily Moss, grows up and falls in love with Farmer Layton's son Will. A neighbor, Frank Kettley, tries to woo her affections. In one somewhat shocking scene, he lifts her body in his arms and carries her across a "large muddy puddle." Before she can prevent him, "his lips were pressed to her cheek." A scene similar to this one was later judged to be too offensive for readers' tastes and was omitted from the periodical publication of Thomas Hardy's *Tess of the d'Urbervilles* in the early 1890s.

An enraged Will discovers the pair and shoots Frank in the chest. A detailed account is published in the local *Durtford Gazette*. All testify that it was an accident as Frank slowly recovers. He soon leaves for America for a year to give Lily time to make her decision concerning a marriage partner. At the end of a year Frank does not return, so she marries Will. Lily is able to overcome her feelings of inadequacy with regard to her social-class background when her father returns as a wealthy gentleman after a long stay in America. He had previously been reduced to ruin due to a speculation scheme. On his return he makes financial amends and sets his daughter and her new husband up in a fine estate near Durtford. Frank and his new wife even become lifelong friends of the happy couple.

Urban scam artists and scoundrels are at work in "A Noble Foundling." A young man desperately wants to believe that he was abandoned twenty-two years ago by his mother, a supposed duchess, in Saint James's Park. Martin Twiss hires a private-inquiry agent to help him with his case. The agent takes him to a splendid mansion in Eaton Square to meet his supposed long-lost father, who is in reality a butler and the brother of the agent. Twiss is defrauded of one hundred pounds, and Sims unravels the whole truth for the reader at the story's close: "It is, however, far more likely that he was left in St. James's Park by some lady's-maid in a noble house who had stolen a sheet of her mistress's paper, and who, wishing to get rid of her child, hoped to ensure it a good home by the cleverly-worded letter and the coronet."

Several other tales in *Stories in Black and White* are both realistic and entertaining. "A Coffee Stall Romance" opens with the first-person narrator complaining of chronic insomnia that causes him to walk the streets of London by night. His attention quickly focuses on a coffee stall and its owners; their personal and economic fortunes and declines are described. Part of the

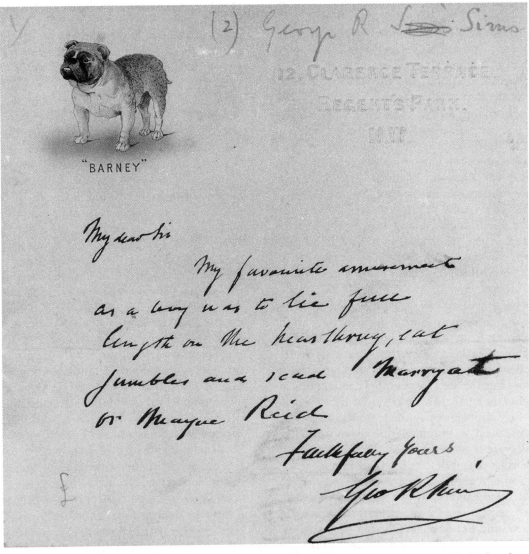

Undated letter from Sims to his friend Sidney Jousiffe. In 1896 Sims gave his bulldog, Barney, depicted at the upper left, a coming-out party (Collection of William B. Thesing).

narrative is told in Ezekiel Hart's (Zekel's), the coffee stall proprietor's, own words. He regrets that drink causes him to strike his wife with a fierce blow, but eventually they reunite and prosper enough to open a respectable shop of their own.

A first-person narrative confession from a murderer is recorded in "A Mad Revenge." Sims met the criminal at the Paris Morgue, as both men took an interest in viewing the victim's body. The setting is based on Sims's personal experiences, and it links him with such realistic writers as Emile Zola, who uses the morgue for scenes in *Thérèse Raquin* (1867; translated, 1881). Coincidence and a domestic servant's past cause problems in "The New Housemaid." Mrs. Garfoyle hires a new maid, Mary Vane, who claims that Mr.

Garfoyle was previously married to her. After a private detective is hired and there is much discussion among various characters, Mary is exposed as a liar. She departs the house "without a murmur." In stories such as "A Mad Revenge" and "The New Housemaid," Sims employs more dialect and more conversational exchanges between the characters than he usually does.

Twelve stories are collected in *Tales of To-Day*. The American edition was part of Lovell's International series, which published titles on a weekly basis. On the cover of each book Frank F. Lovell stated his policy: "Every work in this series is published by arrangement with the author to whom a royalty is paid." Most of the stories in *Tales of To-Day* involve mystery and intrigue. Many are set in

London, some in theater districts, railway stations, or even prisons. The *Scotsman* hailed the volume's accomplishment: "No one knows better than Mr. Sims how to write a short story of sensational interest, and all these tales are good examples of his skill. All the stories are good, and the book will please readers of the most varied tastes."

The opening story, "The Bloomsbury Murder," begins with a servant girl's piercing scream of "Murder!" The victim is the twenty-eight-year-old wife of George Clowbury, a commercial traveler. While he was away on business, his wife sometimes saw an Italian gentleman, Signor Moroni, who tried to swindle her into accompanying him abroad. A Sicilian girl named Margherita became entangled in the plot, and, in a mad fit of jealousy, she stabbed Mrs. Clowbury in her chambers. A note allows Scotland Yard detectives to unravel the intrigue.

Swindling plans involving the marriage mart are at work in several more stories in *Tales of To-Day*, featuring male and female villains. In "A Missing Husband" Jack Smedley goes up and down the socio-economic scale from gentility to poverty as he makes and loses money in gambling transactions involving horses and cards. To cover his losses he embezzles fifty thousand pounds from his employer. When an audit is imminent, he disappears. For years his wife is ignorant of her husband's whereabouts until a friend detects his voice in a theatrical production one night. In time Smedley marries and swindles Kate Elmore, a favorite London actress "admired everywhere for her beauty, her grace, her cleverness, and her goodness." After deserting her he flees to America, where he connives to take possession of a wealthy woman's property through marriage. However, her brother shoots him in a saloon.

In "The Lost Bride" a series of elderly gentlemen succumbs to the charms of the twenty-two-year-old Leonora, who makes a "beauteous and blushing bride." The first victim, Tobias Jones, gives his new wife five thousand pounds worth of jewelry. Bound for Paris she asks for privacy in her deck cabin for the remainder of the wedding night: "I'm going to be ill, dear . . . and I don't want you to see me ill; it isn't romantic." Jones does not hear of his wife again until he meets up with an old friend, Mr. Oldroyd, who has recently lost four thousand pounds to the same female adventuress. The French police capture her, and she is imprisoned; however, an accomplice, Mr. Moss, safely absconds with all the money she has collected. Coincidence, betrayals in relationships, and the seedy world of solicitors

make for adventure on a train bound for Scotland in "A Railway Romance." Overall, there are no significant technical improvements in this volume, although the stories are longer than those in Sims's previous volumes.

The 1890s were a high point for short-story publication in Great Britain, and Sims saw the publication of more than a half-dozen collections of his contributions to various periodicals. Throughout the 1890s readers had a constant stream of his works to entertain and instruct them; some new structural patterns and artistic innovations are also employed in these volumes. *Dramas of Life* (1890) collects sixteen stories and offers sixty illustrations by J. H. Russell. Although at the end of one story, "Why He Was Hanged," Sims again uses his basic theater metaphor — "for drama it [the story] is, as strange and as powerful as any that have been played upon the world's vast stage" — at the end of the final story, "The Last Letter," he offers a more startling and basic premise that serves as the theme of these stories: "Unhappy and ill-assorted marriages are at the bottom of half the crime and half the misery in the world, and they are the foundation of some of the most terrible Dramas of Life." Thus many of this volume's stories concern murders and betrayals involving relationships. The *Manchester Guardian* praised Sims as "a master of the art of telling short stories" and was delighted with the elements of melodrama and "ingenious surprises" in the various tales.

Sims adopted several new literary techniques in this volume. In "The Millionaire's Secret" he steps aside from the narrative and offers his own opinion on matters of crime and punishment: "Punishment is, I believe, commonly supposed to have a deterrent effect on crime. The only punishment that is absolutely deterrent is capital punishment." He also summarizes his sociological observations in the story: "After many years' careful study of the criminal classes, I have come to the conclusion that they do not object to prison life at all, especially in bad times, when good jobs are scarce." Later in this same story Sims uses light satire to render his negative opinion of Mr. Hicks's hypocritical intentions to appear respectable by ridiculing his involvement with the Vigilance Committee — "a committee which has been formed for the suppression of everything that is wicked, and for the raising of the moral tone of the Vigilance Committee's neighbours." This story also makes use of realistic observation, as Sims reports the grueling details of urban poverty in a tenement: "It was a very shaky landing at the best — for the rails were broken away, having been used as firewood by the tenants."

The penchant for sociological investigation that Sims demonstrates in his famous nonfictional accounts *How the Poor Live* and *Horrible London* (published jointly in 1889) is reflected in the opening of "Why He Was Hanged": "I had an idea that it was quite possible that a diligent explorer might discover in the East-End of London a state of things the true meaning of which the British public had as yet failed to grasp." The story concerns the fates of some Polish Jews following the discovery of a murder in a bedroom. A married Polish Jewess has been killed, apparently with a long knife found at the scene. A wounded man, Paul Narovski, is found beneath her bed. Jealousy and passion are at first supposed to be the motives for the crimes. The detective narrator has complete respect for the rational intelligence of his readers as he presents the facts of the case. He invites the reader to "form your own conclusion" and to "judge it for yourselves." Another technique used by Sims in this volume is the ending of one story with two morals: one for lady readers and one for gentleman readers ("The Last Letter").

Other characters in *Dramas of Life* move up and down the economic scale, sometimes in disguises. Most of these stories are two or three times the length of Sims's previously published stories, and their plots and characters tend to be more involved. The scoundrels do not change much, however, as various characters, both male and female, try to extort money and marry under false pretenses. In "The Suicide's Legacy" the action unfolds after a drowning, and the key element is a mysterious letter to the intended beneficiary, a young lady found lying in a lonely park. "Jim Crowe's Sister" focuses on the fates of some black people. The story's heroine, Jemima Crowe, works as a general servant; she is called Jim Crowe by her friends and associates. The main story involves Jim's sister, who lives "far away in a very hot country, where the people were all black" (the country is most probably India, since later in the story Jim receives a cable from there stating that her sister has died). In that hot country the name of Jim's sister is Mrs. God Save the Queen Jamsetjeebhoy, and she is married to a rich, dark gentleman who lives in a palace with hundreds of servants. In this land of tigers, elephants, and serpents, her husband "worshipped the Fire." The economic ups and downs of the Crowe family make up the rest of the story.

The *Daily Telegraph* had nothing but praise for *Tinkletop's Crime* (1891), describing the title tale as

Cover for Sims's 1894 collection of short stories, many of which concern marital conflicts (Special Collections, Robert W. Woodruff Library, Emory University)

"amusing" and concluding that the other tales in the collection are "full of the mingled humour and pathos for which he is renowned. . . . There could not be a better companion for a railway journey than this entertaining volume." The *Athenaeum* (30 May 1891) was indifferent in its estimation of the nineteen short stories in the volume: "In outward appearance it is unattractive, and the inward matter is neither elegant in form nor particularly exciting in kind." Perhaps the most condemnatory judgment was the reviewer's inability to find artistry in the tales: "As an example of what the short story should be, artistically speaking, the little volume is of no value." But the reviewer also notes the work's social realism, stating that the stories evince "the wish to right abuses, and with a certain knowledge of the seamy side of London life Mr. Sims may be credited." One story, "Bismarck in London," was praised as being of "another stamp" in its bright tone and amusing developments.

Swindlers, confidence men, impersonators, and mistaken identities are the hallmarks of the stories in *Tinkletop's Crime*. Three stories may be taken as lighthearted but semiserious accounts of swindles. In "Tinkletop's Crime" a sixty-year-old gentleman, Jeremiah Tinkletop, acquires a large fortune as a bookmaker, keeping "doubtful company" in the form of fighting, boxing, and racing men. After failing in his bid for a lady's hand, Tinkletop vows revenge on a competitor. His wish comes too true as he is led to believe that he must be charged for the rival's murder at the hands of a gang of young thugs on the Thames Embankment. He offers one thousand pounds to pay the fares of the three accomplices to Australia. Months later, however, he discovers that the allegedly murdered man and the woman have used his money to go jewelry shopping and that he has been the victim of a scam by some merry conspirators. The only moral of the tale is that he has become more careful of the company he keeps. He resolves to serve his church more faithfully and to spend most of his evenings at a respectable local club that serves "unimpeachable" whiskey.

In "Bismarck in London," one of Sims's best-known stories, he relates a friend's recounting of what he purports to be a true incident. Years ago in Germany, Prince Bismarck asked the narrator, "If I come to London on the extreme Q. T., will you put me up?" The plan would have involved Bismarck gathering impressions of London high society and political circles while enjoying full anonymity. A disgruntled worker overhears these remarks in the Berlin railway station, and he acts on them years later in an elaborate scheme of duplicity involving large-scale thefts. The eavesdropping railway employee, an accomplished swindler in league with a brother who plays the role of German ambassador, arrives in London disguised as a Lutheran clergyman. The two visit the homes of influential politicians, bankers, and editors. After the distinguished foreign visitor departs each home, however, valuable items of jewelry or money caches are discovered missing. Only after an interview with Kaiser Wilhelm and the real "blood and iron" prime minister, as well as a full police investigation, is the strategy behind the elaborate heist unraveled. Because "ridicule is the one thing that is most feared in German statecraft and diplomacy," Bismarck tried for years to keep the story away from public attention.

A more modest but highly whimsical story involving deception in a marital courtship is detailed in "A Prize Poem." Adolphus Jones succeeds in obtaining the hand of a former lord mayor's daughter, Adelina, on the false pretense that he is a prolific love poet. In the denouement the pair are eventually married, and the actual writer of the lyrics is awarded a huge prize: the poor poet/clerk is named heir of the millionaire former lord mayor.

My Two Wives, and Other Stories (1894) is yet another collection that caused reviewers to compare Sims's outlook to that of Zola and Dickens. The *Weekly Dispatch* observed that he combined traits of both authors, but that he was "without a peer in his peculiar line of alternate mirth and humour." The title story is a fifty-page tale divided into two sections. The narrator, William Hengist Smith, reveals his life story and the inconveniences of his being married to two wives at the same time. Smith goes through the typical Sims pattern of ups and downs on the economic wheel of fortune. Although he is the son of a prosperous city merchant, his father speculated so rashly that by the time of his death the family was penniless. Smith comments: "To pass from prosperity to comparative poverty is to most of us a great trial. The men and women who can shrug their shoulders and take a reverse of fortune with a smile are few in number."

At a boardinghouse in Bloomsbury he meets and courts a young lady, Marion Ellis. While he is at first fascinated by her, she tricks him into forging his signature on a legal letter and ultimately forces him into a hasty marriage. What follows is a realistic portrait: "It was not a happy marriage. . . . I found that she [his wife] was not truthful, and certainly not scrupulous. And she had a hard, cold way with her that disagreeably surprised me." When they eventually arrange to separate, he grows reckless and despondent. He turns to drink, loses his job, and finally flees to Australia to begin a new life.

Not many months pass before he marries again, but his second wife is the opposite of his first in that she is a loving companion. Elsewhere she is described as "a devoted wife" and a "good dutiful little woman." Since his first wife is "a daring, heartless, and unscrupulous adventuress," it comes as no surprise that she identifies a body found drowned in the Thames as that of her husband so that she is free to remarry for status. In her new role as Lady Lascelles she attends a lavish ball, where Smith and his new wife, Cora, are guests. Sims conveniently resolves the bigamous entanglements by having Lady Lascelles die unexpectedly. Smith and Cora soon become parents of a baby boy, and he enjoys his dual status – "a dead man in England" and "the happiest man alive in Australia."

Another story in this collection, "That Act of Parliament," depicts marital and political conflicts between Mr. and Mrs. Dester. In a loud voice Mr. Dester denounces the followers of William Ewart Gladstone, the well-known Victorian prime minister, as "a set o' 'owlin hatheists, who were undermin' the British Empire and knocking the marriage service into a cocked 'at." "A Young Fool" uses the popular turn-of-the-century music hall as its setting and describes Miss Daisy Delamere singing, amid rapturous applause, the ditty "Then You Jerk the Other Elbow." London's Soho district is the setting for "A Story of Soho."

The somber "A Tragic Honeymoon" deals with unrequited love. The tale's most gruesome event — the dripping of blood through a ceiling to a room below — may very well have been borrowed from the famous murder scene in *Tess of the d'Urbervilles* (1891). In his introduction to *Prepare to Shed Them Now: The Ballads of George R. Sims* (1968), Arthur Calder-Marshall claims that Sims was often "a facile adaptor" of fiction by Dickens and Hardy. Nevertheless, Sims's focus is on the male stalker who "had been in love with a young lady who had not returned his affection." With haunting determination he arranges to follow a honeymooning couple to a hotel, where he rents a room directly above theirs, commits suicide, and unnerves the bride (who has rejected him) as drops of his blood fall onto her wedding ring in the room below: "And there on her hand — the hand with the wedding-ring — was still that terrible blood-stain." This macabre scene is as chilling and melodramatic as the one described by Hardy in which Tess murders her lover, Alec, at the fashionable lodging house at Sandbourne.

The *Spectator* (8 August 1896) offered a critique of Sims's collection *The Ten Commandments* (1896), pointing to an ineffective mingling of "moral tales" with "scenes from the drama of real life." Sims uses a unique organizing device to structure the stories in this collection: each tale depicts the breaking of one commandment in melodramatic fashion. This volume is unlike any of his previous ones in its tight-knit attempt at unification. However, the *Spectator* was not impressed, finding the book "a series of disconnected tracts." The "Honour Thy Father" tale left the reviewer with a morally ambiguous message: "We gather that a man should honour his parents for fear of losing the property they may have to leave behind them." In short, the reviewer wants Sims's didacticism to be clean and clear-cut. The reviewer asserts that Sims erred fatally in assigning awards and punishment in

such a way as to leave a vague impression on the reader as to whether the characters really change for the better or actually learn from their transgressions. The reader might become weary or confused instead of edified with a clear view of moral issues. The reviewer also finds the volume's use of melodramatic devices distasteful.

The Ten Commandments and *As It Was in the Beginning: Life Stories of To-Day* (1896) are similar in two ways: both collections make use of religious principles for their fundamental organizing structure, and the settings of the stories are mainly in rural England. Nevertheless, in a few of the stories Sims returns to the well-known haunts of London, his residence for a lifetime. By the time the reader comes to "The Tenth Commandment" piece, the "street-hawkers of London" are once again shouting about a skeleton found in a cupboard. In his foreword to *As It Was in the Beginning,* Sims invokes a biblical solemnity in the proclamation that "the stories of the human passions remain the same," that through all the ages "human nature has not changed," and that "there are no new stories." Many of the twenty stories in this collection parallel contemporary characters with biblical names, such as Hagar, Delilah, Ruth, Naomi, Bathsheba, Belshazzar, and Jonah.

"The Scarlet Woman" focuses on the inhabitants of an old mansion in the Devonshire countryside. The new Lady Barston of Barston Towers is a Roman Catholic. To the local farmers and tenants she is "the foreign woman," a "Popish Jezebel," "The Scarlet Woman of Babylon." The villagers are organized into an excited mob and incited to commit outrages by one Martin Exton, an antipapist speaker who is "a religious lunatic with homicidal tendencies." The story portrays the harsh economic realities of the rural tenant system as well as recurring religious bigotry and intolerance. The story climaxes with the murder of Lord Barston: "And so it came about that . . . Lord Barston came to an untimely and violent end. Martin Exton, the mad revivalist, was tried for murder and declared to be insane, and was dragged out of the dock yelling aloud that he was the instrument of the vengeance of Heaven upon the Scarlet Woman of Babylon and the Priests of Baal."

The suffering continues, however, after Lord Barston's death as her ladyship intensifies her cruel and vindictive nature in exercising her power over the poor tenants who are her humbler neighbors. With petty tyranny and malice she strives to make her tenants as miserable as possible. In one instance of cruel rural realism that goes beyond scenes de-

*Cover for Sims's 1905 collection of short stories, many of which
involve disguises and mistaken identities (Rare Book Collection,
University of North Carolina at Chapel Hill)*

scribed by Hardy in his fiction, Lady Barston wields her imperious sway over her tenants: "One woman being feeble and ill at the time her notice to quit expired, her ladyship sent her agent to take out the windows and remove the doors." Lady Barston meets her demise in a conflagration one evening. A servant whom she has abused refuses to heed her calls for assistance when her dress catches on fire. The charred body of "The Scarlet Woman" is dragged from the wreckage the next morning, and when the news spreads through the village, "there was never an eye that shed a tear or a lip that uttered a word of pity."

Other stories of particular interest in the collection include "St. Winefred's Well," about faith healing and miraculous cures from bathing in the waters of Saint Winefred near Holywell in rural Wales, and "A Lost Eden," a nostalgic description of a young English farmer's gradual loss of the old-fashioned Worcestershire village way of life. In the end the farmer, Reuben Raybold, becomes a transplanted alien who can never return to a rural England that was once available to him: "Reuben Raybold toils to-day a labourer on another man's land in a far-off spot among stangers . . . with many a tale of the golden meadows and flowery fields of the . . . lost Eden." "The Gipsy Countess," also set in the Worcestershire region, depicts madness and customs among the Gypsies.

In *Li Ting of London, and Other Stories* (1905) Sims makes further and effective use of disguises and mistaken identities. In the title story a twenty-two-year-old man of mystery wears a pigtail and speaks Chinese – or sometimes a pidgin dialect: "Always samee, no can makee plofit." He lives in Limehouse Causeway, London's Chinese quarter; each day he goes out in the morning, wanders about London, and returns to the Causeway late at night to sleep. After a few months he moves to a single room in the house of a rag-and-bottle merchant in a back street off Walworth Road. The climactic revelation of the story is that Li Ting is a prince who once "came very near to ascending the Imperial throne of China." A similar plotline is used in "The Rescued Princess."

The volume also includes the story "A Woman's Stratagem," in which Sims makes interesting use of gender confusion. Sebastian Green tries to serve as trustee for feisty twenty-five-year-old Ulrica Dahl's recent inheritance of 250,000 pounds. The drama of relationships begins when she is attracted to young Monsieur de Revel, a Frenchman thought by some to be a fortune hunter. Weary of all the advice from financial negotiations, Ulrica cleverly disguises herself as a young man: "Her dark hair was cut short, which gave her quite a boyish appearance." In the end Ulrica laughs in triumph: " 'I was more successful as a boy than I am as a girl, then,' she said; 'nobody's fallen in love with me yet.' " In "Gilbert Hast's Housekeeper" relationships with the servants are the point of conflict at Ravenhurst, the Hast family estate since the days of Charles I. The eerie setting in an old gray mansion on a Berkshire moor makes for a domestic drama of mystery and adventure.

In the decade before the outbreak of World War I, Sims continued to write works that exposed the mistreatment of such groups as British women and children. He used graphic photographs and on-the-scene descriptions to call attention to the problem of child abuse and neglect (especially by mothers) in England's urban centers. His title piece in the pamphlet *The Cry of the Children* (1907?) was expanded into *The Black Stain* (1907). Partly as a result of his efforts an important piece of child legislation was passed by Parliament in 1908. His campaign for the national well-being also encompassed the problem of the white-slave trade in London. In the foreword to the 1910 revision of *London by Night* (1906), he reiterates his commitment to the political impact of writing in the realistic vein: "It was to present these facts [about the white-slave trade] plainly, but with due discretion, to the general reader who is such an important factor in the making of public opinion that 'London by Night' was written. That the description of 'things as they are'

was in no way exaggerated was proved by the finding of the Royal Commission and the complete exoneration of the London Police."

One of Sims's later collections of short stories is *Joyce Pleasantry, and Other Stories* (1908). The *Bookman* (London) reviewer (February 1909) welcomed it as "pleasing entertainment." The title piece is the longest of the ten tales in the volume. Its action is set in early-Victorian days and includes some of Sims's familiar characters and situations, such as a dishonest lawyer, a long-lost son, a rivalry between old and new squires, and a beautiful young woman in plight. The *Bookman* found this tale and others in the volume to be naive, genial, and idealistic in spirit. The workmanship is careful, but the mixture of tales is somewhat incompatible. Several, such as "The Motor-car of Santa Claus," "The Magic Toys," and "The Wassail Song," are in the mode of sentimental Dickensian Christmas tales, while others, such as the tale of Bridget Maguire, are powerful, pathetic, realistic sketches of working-class life and political conflicts in the slums.

Sims remained a prolific writer of short stories over a period of about five decades. However, there is only slight evidence of technical development or innovation in his many pieces. Even though he demonstrated a lack of complex aesthetic development, his stories make for highly enjoyable reading, revealing much about life during his time, especially in Victorian and Edwardian London. His best stories convey his direct knowledge of the low-life, criminal worlds of the metropolis, based on his urban observations and adventures.

Critical attention to Sims's writings has been minimal during the twentieth century, and the few scholars who have written about him have not been favorable. Mark Seltzer pairs him with Henry James in *Henry James & the Art of Power* (1984); however, Sims comes out at a disadvantage because he is portrayed as a law-and-order conservative. Seltzer claims that Sims depicts a London whose "freedom" is "guaranteed by the existence of an unlimited policing and by the dissemination of elaborate methods of police surveillance." In this light Sims seems to advocate an "intense watchfulness" in the city that verges on universal fear, with all of London becoming the network of a secret society. In short, to Seltzer, "Sims's vision of the London streets is marked by a fantastic paranoia." The purpose of Sims's works in this view is to purvey sensational entertainment and to foster police vigilance.

T. J. Binyon, in *"Murder Will Out": The Detective in Fiction* (1990), praises Sims's series of mystery stories involving a female detective named Dorcas

Dene as "readable," with "a certain freshness and liveliness." George K. Behlmer, in *Child Abuse and Moral Reform in England, 1870–1908* (1982), complains that Sims's short story "A Premium for Murder" (*The Social Kaleidoscope,* first series) sensationalizes child life-insurance policy practices in a "fanciful" way that creates "an unusually imaginative version of the road to domestic hell."

P. J. Keating is especially harsh in his judgments of Sims in *The Working Classes in Victorian Fiction* (1971). Keating believes that Sims was not successful in using his considerable knowledge of working-class life to write authentic, convincing working-class fiction. Too often he "superimposed middle-class sentiment." For Keating, Sims's "vicarious" and "ambiguous attitudes" in many of his short stories undercut their interest. He is especially impatient with Sims's use of "the sentimental-melodramatic mixture." In the final analysis Keating believes that Sims made no original contribution to working-class fiction because he lacked "profound social understanding" and was too rooted in "literary conventions." Because of Sims's close association with the theater, Keating argues, he tended to deal with "a kind of lower-class limbo land where few social distinctions are made between chorus girls, clowns, coachmen, ragamuffins and maidservants." Keating also finds Sims's reproduction of cockney dialect and use of phonetics inconsistent, "harsh and arbitrary." He reproduces a sentence from Sims's *How the Poor Live* (1883) and concludes: "The speech does not flow, the alternative spellings do not contribute to the rhythm of the sentences, and the use and misuse of aspirates is nonsensical."

On a more positive note, Frederick Rogers, in *Labour, Life and Literature: Some Memories of Sixty Years* (1973), recalls the effect of reading Sims's fiction as a young man. In his chapter "Social Ideals," Rogers begins: "Among the popular writers who, in days now entirely passed, have exercised a great influence on the mind of the working classes is Mr. George R. Sims." He especially praises Sims's light-hearted outlook: "His gift of humour was spontaneous, abounding, and clean, and he was full of a manly straightforwardness which went right home to the heart of the workshop." Rogers believes that the stories in *The Social Kaleidoscope* were "powerful" in influencing social reform. He recalls how crowds of workmen heard his lecture on "George R. Sims as a Public Teacher." Rogers's evaluation of working-class reading habits is interesting because it suggests that Sims's stories were read by this section of the British public: "The average workman, as I knew him, was not capable of sustained reading, and the short story and crisp paragraph inaugurated by G. R. Sims were much more to his palate than the long stories." Clearly, a comprehensive assessment of Sims's life and varied writing forms needs to be written as the centenary of his death approaches.

References:

George K. Behlmer, *Child Abuse and Moral Reform in England, 1870–1908* (Stanford: Stanford University Press, 1982);

T. J. Binyon, *"Murder Will Out": The Detective in Fiction* (New York: Oxford University Press, 1990);

P. J. Keating, *The Working Classes in Victorian Fiction* (New York: Barnes & Noble, 1971);

Frederick Rogers, *Labour, Life and Literature: Some Memories of Sixty Years* (Brighton, U.K.: Harvester, 1973);

Mark Seltzer, *Henry James & the Art of Power* (Ithaca, N.Y.: Cornell University Press, 1984);

Judith R. Walkowitz, *City of Dreadful Delight: Narratives of Sexual Danger in Late-Victorian London* (Chicago: University of Chicago Press, 1992).

Papers:

Sims's correspondence is held in some private collections as well as at the Harry Ransom Humanities Research Center, University of Texas at Austin; the Lilly Library, Indiana University; and the Bodleian Library, Oxford.

May Sinclair

(24 August 1863 – 14 November 1946)

Catherine E. Hoyser
Saint Joseph College

See also the Sinclair entry in *DLB 36: British Novelists, 1890–1929: Modernists.*

BOOKS: *Nakiketas and Other Poems,* as Julian Sinclair (London: Kegan Paul, 1886);

Essays in Verse (London: Kegan Paul, Trench & Trübner, 1891);

Audrey Craven (London: Blackwood, 1897; New York: Holt, 1906);

Mr. and Mrs. Nevill Tyson (Edinburgh & London: Blackwood, 1898); republished as *The Tysons* (New York: Dodge, 1906);

Two Sides of a Question (London: Constable, 1901; New York: Taylor, 1901);

The Divine Fire (London: Constable, 1904; New York: Holt, 1904);

Superseded (New York: Holt, 1906);

The Helpmate (London: Constable, 1907; New York: Holt, 1907);

The Judgment of Eve (London & New York: Harper, 1908);

Kitty Tailleur (London: Constable, 1908); republished as *The Immortal Moment: The Story of Kitty Tailleur* (New York: Doubleday, Page, 1908);

The Creators: A Comedy (London: Constable, 1910; New York: Century, 1910);

The Flaw in the Crystal (New York: Dutton, 1912);

The Three Brontës (London: Hutchinson, 1912; Boston & New York: Houghton Mifflin, 1912);

Feminism (London: Woman Writers' Suffrage League, 1912);

The Combined Maze (London: Hutchinson, 1913; New York & London: Harper, 1913);

The Judgment of Eve and Other Stories (London: Hutchinson, 1914);

The Return of the Prodigal and Other Stories (New York: Macmillan, 1914);

The Three Sisters (London: Hutchinson, 1914; New York: Macmillan, 1914);

May Sinclair

A Journal of Impressions in Belgium (London: Hutchinson, 1915; New York: Macmillan, 1915);

America's Part in the War (New York: Commission for Relief in Belgium, 1915);

Tasker Jevons: The Real Story (London: Hutchinson, 1916); republished as *The Belfry* (New York: Macmillan, 1916);

The Tree of Heaven (London & New York: Cassell, 1917; New York: Macmillan, 1917);

A Defence of Idealism: Some Questions and Conclusions (London: Macmillan, 1917; New York: Macmillan, 1917);

Mary Olivier: A Life (London & New York: Cassell, 1919; New York: Macmillan, 1919);

The Romantic (London: Collins, 1920; New York: Macmillan, 1920);

Mr. Waddington of Wyck (London: Cassell, 1921; New York: Macmillan, 1921);

The New Idealism (London & New York: Macmillan, 1922);

Life and Death of Harriett Frean (London: Collins, 1922; New York: Macmillan, 1922);

Anne Severn and the Fieldings (London: Hutchinson, 1922; New York: Macmillan, 1922);

Uncanny Stories (London: Hutchinson, 1923; New York: Macmillan, 1923);

A Cure of Souls (London: Hutchinson, 1923; New York: Macmillan, 1924);

The Dark Night: A Novel in Verse (London: Cape, 1924; New York: Macmillan, 1924);

Arnold Waterlow: A Life (London: Hutchinson, 1924; New York: Macmillan, 1924);

The Rector of Wyck (London: Hutchinson, 1925; New York: Macmillan, 1925);

Far End (London: Hutchinson, 1926; New York: Macmillan, 1926);

The Allinghams (London: Hutchinson, 1927; New York: Macmillan, 1927);

History of Anthony Waring (London: Hutchinson, 1927; New York: Macmillan, 1927);

Fame (London: Elkin Mathews & Marrot, 1929);

Tales Told by Simpson (London: Hutchinson, 1930; New York: Macmillan, 1930);

The Intercessor and Other Stories (London: Hutchinson, 1931; New York: Macmillan, 1932).

OTHER: Emily Brontë, *Wuthering Heights,* introduction by Sinclair (London: Dent, 1907);

Charlotte Brontë, *Jane Eyre,* introduction by Sinclair (London: Dent, 1908);

Elizabeth Cleghorn Gaskell, *The Life of Charlotte Brontë,* introduction by Sinclair (London: Dent, 1908);

Charlotte Brontë, *Shirley,* introduction by Sinclair (London: Dent, 1908);

Charlotte Brontë, *Villette,* introduction by Sinclair (London: Dent, 1909);

Charlotte Brontë, *The Professor,* introduction by Sinclair (London: Dent, 1910);

Anne Brontë, *The Tenant of Wildfell Hall,* introduction by Sinclair (London: Dent, 1914);

Jean de Bosschere, *The Closed Door,* introduction by Sinclair (London: John Lane, 1917);

Dorothy Richardson, *Pilgrimage,* introduction by Sinclair (New York: Knopf, 1919).

TRANSLATIONS: Rudolf Sohm, *Outlines of Church History* (London: Macmillan, 1895; Boston: Beacon Press, 1958);

Theodore von Sosnosky, *England's Danger: The Future of British Army Reform* (London: Chapman & Hall, 1901).

SELECTED PERIODICAL PUBLICATIONS –
UNCOLLECTED: "The Ethical and Religious Import of Idealism," *New World,* 2 (December 1893): 694–708;

"A Study from Life," *Black & White,* 10 (2 November 1895): 570;

"A Friendly Critic," anonymous, *Macmillan's,* 74 (October 1896): 435–443;

"Not Made in Germany," anonymous, *Macmillan's,* 75 (January 1897): 201–209;

"A Hero of Fiction," *Temple Bar,* 38 (September 1898): 135–153;

"Man and Superman: A Symposium," *New York Times,* Holiday Book Number, Literary Section, 1 December 1905, pp. 813–814;

"Three American Poets of Today: Edwin Arlington Robinson, William Vaughan Moody and Ridgely Torrence," *Atlantic Monthly,* 98 (September 1906): 325–335;

"How It Strikes a Mere Novelist," *Votes for Women,* 2 (24 December 1908): 211;

"The Novels of George Meredith," *Outlook,* 92 (June 1909): 413–418;

"The Gitanjali: Or Song Offerings of Rabindra Nath Tagore," *North American Review,* 197 (May 1913): 659–676;

"The New Brontë Letters," *Dial,* 60 (November 1913): 343–346;

"Red Tape," *Queen* (14 November 1914): 802–803;

"Two Notes: I 'On H. D.' II 'On Imagism,' " *Egoist,* 2 (June 1915): 88–89;

"Symbolism and Sublimation I," *Medical Press & Circular,* 153 (9 August 1916): 118–122;

"Symbolism and Sublimation II," *Medical Press & Circular,* 153 (16 August 1916): 142–145;

"Prufrock and Other Observations," *Little Review,* 4 (December 1917): 8–14;

"The Novels of Dorothy Richardson," *Egoist,* 5 (April 1918): 57–59; *Little Review,* 5 (April 1918): 3–11;

"The Reputation of Ezra Pound," *English Review,* 30 (April 1920): 326–335; *North American Review,* 211 (May 1920): 658–668;

"Worse Than War," *English Review,* 31 (August 1920): 147–153;

"The Poems of F. S. Flint," *English Review,* 32 (January 1921): 6–18;

"The Future of the Novel," *Pall Mall Gazette,* 10 January 1921, p. 7;

"The Poems of Richard Aldington," *English Review,* 32 (May 1921): 397–410;

"The Return," *Harper's,* 142 (May 1921): 693–703;

"The Novels of Violet Hunt," *English Review,* 34 (February 1922): 106–118;

"The Poems of H. D.," *Dial,* 72 (February 1922): 203–207;

"The Man From Main Street," *New York Times Book Review,* 24 September 1922, p. 1;

"Psychological Types," *English Review,* 36 (May 1923): 436–439;

"Primary and Secondary Consciousness," *Proceedings of the Aristotelian Society,* new series 23, no. 7 (1923): 111–120.

In 1923 Lewis Mumford wrote in a review (*Nation,* 24 January) of May Sinclair's novel *Anne Severn and the Fieldings* (1922): "Saving perhaps Mr. D. H. Lawrence, who in England can keep [Sinclair] company?" The equation of Lawrence and Sinclair seems most appropriate because both wrote scathing critiques of families; both came from the nonelite, nonuniversity middle class; and both studied and wrote about the new field of psychoanalysis. Although not well known today, Sinclair's *Mary Olivier: A Life* (1919) was controversial in its time for blending psychoanalysis and fiction. Some reviewers praised the novel, but others were dubious as to its value. E. M. Forster questioned whether it was art; Katherine Mansfield, notorious for her negative reviews, wondered whether the material (the development of a girl) warranted attention. But by 1923 the novel's reputation was established enough that Mumford declared: " 'Mary Olivier,' it seems to me, is not merely Miss Sinclair's masterpiece: it is one of the outstanding novels of the century."

Sinclair did not begin as a novelist. Poetry and short fiction served as her apprentice genres, but she continued to write short stories despite her fame as a novelist, enjoying the challenge of concise writing that they required. In a review (*Nation,* 10 December 1930) of Sinclair's *Tales Told by Simpson* (1930), Florence Codman declared that Sinclair was an expert in handling the short-fiction genre. Her stories excel at subtle examinations of social situations and gender relations, exploring the subtleties of sexuality in daily commerce. Her short fiction

moved the genre into new territory, introducing new techniques.

By the time *Mary Olivier* came out, Dorothy Richardson's first four parts of *Pilgrimage* (1915–1967), D. H. Lawrence's *Sons and Lovers* (1913), James Joyce's *A Portrait of the Artist as a Young Man* (1916), and Virginia Woolf's *The Voyage Out* (1915) and *Night and Day* (1919) had been published. Sinclair had published eleven novels, two short-story collections, two books of verse, and several essays before her breakthrough 1919 novel using the psychoanalytic-narrative form. She had experimented all along with narrative technique, focusing particularly on the shortcomings of the traditional narrator. Sinclair was writing during the turmoil of literary experimentation that filled the early twentieth century, and she was a leader of its spirit.

Mary Amelia St. Clair Sinclair was born on 24 August 1863, the youngest of seven children of a Liverpool shipowner, William Sinclair, and Amelia Hind Sinclair, the daughter of a Belfast merchant. They had been married in Belfast on 26 September 1850 when William was twenty-one and Amelia was twenty-eight or twenty-nine. May was the only surviving female child in the family. In 1854 the Sinclairs had suffered the death of a one-year-old daughter.

William Sinclair's ships sailed from the base port of Belfast from 1850 to 1870, although his business offices were in Liverpool. During this time the family was upwardly mobile. May was born in a villa at the Rock Park estate of Rock Ferry, in the neighborhood where Nathaniel Hawthorne had lived when he served as consul in Liverpool from 1853 to 1857. However, William went bankrupt when May was seven. Mother and daughter left him to live with relatives in Ilford, Essex, and Fairford, Gloucestershire, while William spent the rest of his life as an alcoholic, dying from alcohol-related diseases in 1881.

Like so many mothers of the nineteenth century and earlier, Sinclair's sacrificed everything so that her sons could live like gentlemen. She expected them to believe themselves entitled to gentlemanly pursuits. William, the oldest, was in business in London and owned a yacht; he died of heart disease in 1896 at age forty-four. Another brother, Harold, died of Bright's disease and heart problems at age twenty-eight. Reginald, who was two years older than May, died of heart-valve disease in 1891 at age thirty. Francis Edwin, or Frank, entered the Royal Military Academy, Woolwich, as a gentleman cadet in 1874. His career took him to India, where he became a lieutenant, then a captain of the

Sinclair's home near Sidmouth, South Devon (May Sinclair Collection, Special Collections Department, Van Pelt Library, University of Pennsylvania)

Royal Artillery. He died of heart failure in Poona in 1889 at the end of his second five-year tour of duty.

By 1896 only May, her one remaining brother, Joseph, and her mother were left of the immediate family. Joseph volunteered in the first Boer War, immigrated to British Columbia, and died in 1905. May supported and cared for her mother until Amelia's death in 1901, which freed May to pursue her dreams of travel. Amelia had been a strictly religious woman, both rigid and demanding. May never married.

The details of Sinclair's education remain unclear. She lived at home until she attended Cheltenham Ladies College in 1881 for one year. Before she arrived at Cheltenham, she had learned German, Greek, and French. She had also read widely in the books available in her father's extensive library. In a letter to Marc Loge, Sinclair pointed to portions of *Mary Olivier* that are based on events in her life, including a list of the reading she had done before 1881: classical Greek tragedies and comedies as well as works by William Shakespeare, John Milton, Samuel Pepys, Alexander Pope, Immanuel Kant, Thomas Babington Macaulay, and Percy Bysshe Shelley. Because Sinclair was such an informed, able student, it seems logical that Dorothea

Beale, the school principal, befriended her, encouraging her interest in philosophy and writing.

Sinclair's first publication was an article on the philosopher René Descartes in the school's *Cheltenham Magazine* (1882). Her first book, *Nakiketas and Other Poems,* was published in 1886. Eleven years later William Blackwood, George Eliot's publisher, brought out Sinclair's first novel, *Audrey Craven* (1897). It was well received, and the first edition sold out in a few months. Early in her career she regarded herself as a poet, although she also wrote essays, novels, and verse plays.

Before the publication of *Audrey Craven,* Sinclair saw several short stories into print. The first, "A Study from Life" (*Black & White,* 2 November 1895), was signed M. A. St. C. Sinclair. This piece captures the nature of Sinclair's shorter writings, which always focus on the dynamics of personality, the ironies of life, and the conflict of the artist between life and art. Her female protagonist is a writer who loses a lover because she uses his character in her work. However, she chooses art over love with only a flash of regret. In this first published story the narrator reports the thoughts of the female's mind; in subsequent stories Sinclair focuses on male narrator/participants who ruminate about people's motives and feelings.

Sinclair explores characters as seen by others, yet her narrators often reveal more about themselves than about other people. In pursuit of realism she exhibits the boundaries of traditional limited-omniscient third-person narration. The observing character can never report the interior life of the observed: he can only speculate on others' motivations and reactions. Sinclair simultaneously turns the tables on the narrator by revealing that character's interior life more than the character would like to believe he is doing.

During this time Sinclair became a friend of Richard Garnett, keeper of the printed book at the British Museum from 1890 to 1899, and asked his advice about publishing her various poems in one volume. In the meantime she was developing as a writer of prose fiction, publishing the stories "A Friendly Critic" (*Macmillan's,* October 1896), "Not Made in Germany" (*Macmillan's,* January 1897), and "A Hero of Fiction" (*Temple Bar,* September 1898). The stories in *Macmillan's,* a popular magazine, were published anonymously at editorial request. Sinclair based "A Friendly Critic" on her friend Anthony Charles Deane, who met her when she was living with her mother in Sidmouth. He was in his third year at Cambridge (1892) when he experienced a spiritual calling that convinced him he was meant for the ministry. Sinclair's biographer T. E. M. Boll speculates that she may have been at the root of his awakening.

Sinclair and Deane were intellectual companions, and much of their correspondence survives. Sinclair seems to have destroyed some letters from the early period of their relationship. Deane published a volume of poetry, *Frivolous Verse,* during this crisis year, and the London *Daily News* carried an article by Andrew Lang about it. Lang's recommendation led to Deane's becoming a regular contributor to *Punch,* an association that lasted fifteen years. Later in his career Deane became a canon of the Church of England, but he continued writing and editing.

Deane was also a contributor to *Black & White,* which published Sinclair's first short fiction, and he expressed his admiration for her ability to push the editor into finally printing her story. Deane encouraged her writing, particularly the switch from poetry to prose. He advised her that "A Hero of Fiction" needed a lighter touch, and she adhered to his editorial suggestions when she revised this story. He pressured her to finish a fifteen-chapter story that she had begun, and he encouraged her to join the Society of Authors, an organization that represented writers who had problems with editors and publishers. She joined the society with Deane's

sponsorship in 1897. "Not Made in Germany" evoked mixed responses from her friendly critics Deane and Beale. Deane praised the story, but Beale felt it was too frivolous, although well written.

Throughout her career transition from poetry to prose writer, Sinclair was poor, supporting herself and her mother by selling her work to periodicals. Her self-taught German was strong enough to qualify her for translating. Her reputation as a writer and thinker created many literary friendships that continued during her life. Gwendoline (Zack) Keats, a short-story writer and novelist, became a good friend of Sinclair during the 1890s. They began an extended correspondence in 1898.

In Sinclair's stories sensitive observation of details reveals the nuances of relationships between people. Edward Garnett – manuscripts reader for several major British publishing houses and a promoter of such writers as Lawrence – noticed a similarity between her main young-man narrator and Henry James's. She admitted James's influence in a 1914 letter to her friend Charlotte Mew. Sinclair knew James, and she met his brother William during a trip to the United States. In fact, William's positivist philosophy encouraged much of Sinclair's analyses of idealism. She continued to write about philosophy throughout her career, including several essays and two books on idealism, and was a member of the Aristotelian Society. She lectured to this group, among whom was the philosopher/thinker Bertrand Russell.

Garnett praised Sinclair's *Two Sides of a Question* (1901), which contains two long stories, "The Cosmopolitan" and "Superseded." He also advised her to send him any work she felt worthy of publishing. In fact, *Two Sides of a Question* and her third novel, *The Divine Fire* (1904), were so well received that several publishing houses from both sides of the Atlantic sent letters soliciting manuscripts from her. Henry Holt served as her American publisher, but she ignored his editorial suggestions. Holt disliked compact style, which Sinclair favored as her career advanced. Of the two stories in *Two Sides of a Question,* "Superseded" received the highest praise from reviewers. Deane and Keats considered it a masterpiece, and Holt published it separately in 1906 because of his fondness for it.

After her mother's death in 1901 Sinclair traveled to Europe and America, championed the Imagist poets, became a founder of the first psychoanalytic clinic in London, and worked with an ambulance corps in Belgium during World War I. She participated in the woman-suffrage movement, writing pamphlets and articles for the cause, serving as vice-president of the National Union of Women's Suffrage Societies of Tunbridge Wells, and marching for the female vote. She was sympathetic to many other social causes.

Sinclair was at the center of literary activity in England and America during the early twentieth century. In 1905 she toured the United States to promote her third novel, *The Divine Fire*. President Theodore Roosevelt introduced her to automobile touring, a pleasure that she enjoyed for the rest of her life, and she was among the literary celebrities at Mark Twain's seventieth birthday celebration. In 1921 she was among the writers invited to sign a presentation in honor of the eighty-first birthday of Thomas Hardy. She aided many young writers, including Ezra Pound, H. D. (Hilda Doolittle), Dorothy Richardson, Ford Madox Ford, Violet Hunt, Mew, Richard Aldington, and T. S. Eliot, providing them with important introductions to editors and famous writers, reviewing their books before others had noticed their writing, and giving them money. Her review (*Little Review*, April 1918) of Richardson's *Pointed Roofs*, the first novel-chapter in Richardson's *Pilgrimage*, coined the term *stream of consciousness* as a literary form. William James developed the expression in his philosophical and psychological theories.

Sinclair was also friends with Sarah Orne Jewett, Annie Fields, H. G. Wells, Katharine Tynan, G. B. Stern, Netta Syrett, Arnold Bennett, Alice Meynell, Rosamond Lehmann, Rebecca West, Hugh Walpole, and Rose Macaulay. She defied Henry James's social ban on Ford and Hunt, often inviting them to her home despite their notoriety as unmarried lovers. Harriet Monroe, editor of the American journal *Poetry*, met with Sinclair in England, declaring her "a wholly adorable person." Sinclair gave Monroe two volumes by Pound, which helped to launch his reputation with American audiences because Monroe responded enthusiastically to his work. Whatever her good fortune as a writer, she shared the benefits, often to her financial peril.

Sinclair was active in philosophical circles as well. She and Bernard Shaw were the only fiction writers to be elected members of the Aristotelian Society. Sinclair also embraced the new theories of psychoanalysis developed by Sigmund Freud and Carl Jung, writing on them as early as 1916. Her fiction depicts characters who are depressed, motivated by guilt, and sacrificed to others' needs. Freud's writings, some of which had appeared in England by 1911, examine the uncomfortable feelings of the child toward the parents. This aspect of

human development she left primarily to her novels. In her short stories she focuses mainly on adults who are trying to live creative lives and according to society's demand that people marry and bear children. Because Sinclair translated German texts, Freud's writings were accessible to her in their original language. Furthermore, she was friends with Dr. Jessie Murray, who had trained with Pierre Janet in Paris and who, with Sinclair, was instrumental in founding the first psychoanalytic clinic in Great Britain. Sinclair probably received news of Freud and Jung from Murray. In a two-part lecture on Freud and Jung, "Symbolism and Sublimation" (*Medical Press & Circular*, 9 and 16 August 1916), she discusses the importance of religion in crushing the human spirit. In part 2 she confirms her support for Freud and Jung despite what she regards as their shortcomings, believing that they have not gone far enough in their analysis of the impact of repression and that they both lack a necessary synthesis of symbol, theory, and life.

With her interest in human psychology and emotion, Sinclair was fascinated by the writings of the Brontë sisters. She wrote introductions to their novels for the Everyman series published by Dent. Sinclair also wrote a book on the Brontës and a novel based on their lives. The short stories that Sinclair published in periodicals during her Brontë period (1907–1914) were collected in two volumes, *The Judgment of Eve and Other Stories* (1914) and *The Return of the Prodigal and Other Stories* (1914). Sinclair dedicated the first collection to the staff of the psychoanalytic clinic that she helped to found and to finance. The *Independent* (7 May 1908) described the title story as "an analyst's portrayal of the subjective phases of two egoists' married life." The stories in these collections do not, however, rely heavily on psychoanalytic clichés but focus on the methods of interpretation available to observers of individuals and relationships.

In the introduction to *The Judgment of Eve and Other Stories*, Sinclair felt compelled to answer criticisms about her innovations in short fiction. She declares her intention as an author: to condense the story to its "simplest possible expression." Each scene in the title story represents several scenes of the same nature being repeated relentlessly in the characters' lives. This technique renders "the effect of disillusionment and retribution more vividly and more intensely than any long and lingering record of the seven years in between" their courtship, their marriage, and the wife's demise.

Another story in the collection, "The Wrackham Memoirs," is almost a novella. In the introduction she defends its length by asserting that it "would have made a thin and ineffectual novel, [but] their [the characters'] subject would have burst the bounds of the short story." She bewails the "ghastly mutilations" that *Harper's* made to "The Wrackham Memoirs" in order to fit it into the December 1913 issue. The version in this volume maintains nearly all of the "lost passages" removed by *Harper's*. Sinclair claims that presenting her material in an "oblique narrative" focuses the story on "*how* certain things and certain people appeared to the teller of the tale."

The stories in these collections investigate male and female relationships, with emphasis on the egoism of both genders. Some of the females are destructive of male artistic talent, while some sacrifice themselves or their reputations for the sake of men. Sinclair seems fascinated with the nature of marriage when one of the partners is an artist. She also examines family dynamics. The mother and sisters in "The Return of the Prodigal" make sacrifices for the title figure but spend the rest of their days complaining about him and fearing more demands from him. Their hatred is bitter, revealing the price of "proper" female behavior. As proper females, however, their feelings are not directly presented to the "prodigal," but he accidentally overhears them as he sentimentally peeks in the house before ringing the bell to announce his return as a wealthy Chicago meat packer.

The male characters in these stories possess enormous egos and demand extraordinary sacrifices from the women in their lives. "The Cosmopolitan" (*Two Sides of a Question*) also features such a man. His daughter, however, escapes his tyranny after several years of sacrifice and much planning for his needs. After she successfully manages his marriage to a second wife, who will replace her as organizer of his papers and life, the daughter leaves the country to live on a yacht with her female cousin. The teller of this tale is the artist Maurice Durant. Sinclair dropped him as a narrator in favor of the artist Roland Simpson, whom she develops in "The Wrackham Memoirs" and uses in the stories in *Tales Told by Simpson*.

"The Wrackham Memoirs" concerns a pompous writer who sacrifices his daughter – nicknamed Antigone by the narrator and his friend – in order to further his career and perpetuate his fame. He is a mediocre author of great popularity who maintains his reputation by keeping up appearances. He seeks an able editor to shape his memoirs into a work that will ensure his literary reputation. The daughter realizes her father's absurdity and releases

A little cup of water

Illustration by Jean de Bosschere for the title story in The Intercessor and Other Stories *(1931)*

her fiancé, the perfect editor for the task, from his pledge to work on the memoirs. By switching her affections from her father to her fiancé, the daughter gains the critical perspective to evaluate her father's career and to free her fiancé from a task that would ruin his credibility as a serious editor and biographer. Sinclair's housekeeper, Florence Bartrop, believed that Wrackham was modeled on Hall Caine (Sir Thomas Henry), a friend of Dante Gabriel Rossetti. Caine was an editor and novelist who wrote popular, somewhat sensational novels from 1885 to 1913. Sinclair introduces characters in "The Wrackham Memoirs" who reappear in later tales. The story's narrator is Roland Simpson, who discusses his friends and fellow writers Grevill Burton and Furnival.

The reviews of *The Return of the Prodigal and Other Stories* were both receptive and critical. Two reviewers focused on Sinclair's portraits of the male mind, while another compared her insights to Edith Wharton's. This same reviewer (*Boston Transcript,* 17 June 1914) wrote that Sinclair "has always had a most uncanny skill at the prying into hidden masculine secrets." Another reviewer (*Athenaeum,* 23 May 1914) singled out Sinclair's men as "examples of the incomplete and the ill working of the masculine intellect." Other positive praise focused on her writing ability. Frederick T. Cooper (London *Bookman,* 14 August 1914) declared that "this volume gives new evidence of this author's fine artistry, deep insight and unwavering adherence to her own high standard." Cooper includes a chapter on Sinclair in his *Some English Story Tellers: A Book of the Younger Novelists* (1912).

Two stories noted particularly in reviews were "The Fault" and "The Gift." Sinclair expresses her fondness for "The Gift" in the defense of her short-story narrative technique. Its primary female character is a writer whose belief that a male friend has liberated her talents destroys their relationship and her life. The story is significant for several reasons, most importantly for the protagonist's being a female writer. Boll observes that the male master/inspirer in "The Gift" is patterned after Henry James, whom Sinclair admired for his aesthetic and artistic passion for narrative.

One story from this period remains uncollected. "Red Tape" (*Queen,* 14 November 1914) focuses on World War I. Like most British civilians, Sinclair wanted to help in the war effort. She went to Belgium to serve in the first non-Belgian ambulance corps from 25 September to 13 October 1914. As a consequence of her war work, she published *A Journal of Impressions in Belgium* (1915).

In 1915 Sinclair joined Bennett in protesting the banning of Lawrence's *The Rainbow.* A year later she was elected to membership in the Royal Society of Literature. Sinclair was a founding member of the International Association of Poets, Playwrights, Editors, Essayists and Novelists (P.E.N.). In 1924 she was the English delegate to the second International P.E.N. Conference in New York City.

Sinclair was a strong supporter and contributor to major avant-garde journals such as the *Egoist,* the *Criterion,* the *Little Review,* and the *English Review.* Between 1914 and 1930 Sinclair concentrated on novelistic technique, publishing fourteen novels in sixteen years. *The Tree of Heaven* (1917) advocates a less violent approach to the pursuit of woman's rights and was quite popular with younger readers.

Her philosophical work *A Defence of Idealism: Some Questions and Conclusions* (1917) was highly praised. Two psychoanalytic novels, *Mary Olivier* and *Life and Death of Harriett Frean* (1922), are most often studied today as early examples of narrative style fused with psychoanalytic theory. These last three novels, along with *The Divine Fire* and *The Three Sisters* (1914), are regarded by the novelist and critic Margaret Drabble as Sinclair's most important works.

As did many writers of this time, Sinclair wrote stories featuring ghosts and supernatural events. Most of these tales were collected in *Uncanny Stories* (1923), illustrated by Flemish artist Jean de Bosschere. A few of the remaining stories were placed in *The Intercessor and Other Stories* (1931). Mary Ross (*New York Herald Tribune Books,* 6 March 1932) compared the tales in *The Intercessor and Other Stories* to the best early stories of Rudyard Kipling. "The Intercessor" is a moving piece about child abuse and neglect. The ghost of a rejected child haunts a house until reunited with her parents by the intercession of a historian boarding at the house. Its Yorkshire setting evokes Sinclair's residencies at Reeth and the works of the Brontë sisters. The *Saturday Review of Literature* (23 April 1932) praised the title story but found the remainder of the volume lacking.

The story "Jones's Karma" apparently influenced T. S. Eliot's poem "Little Gidding" (*New English Weekly,* 1942). The character Jones receives the chance to relive events of his life, correcting faulty behavior; however, his karma is such that he will repeat his bad behavior. "The Mahatma" and "The Mahatma's Story" explore free will, destiny, and innate character. The title character invokes Buddhism and caste to explain events in these stories.

The stories in *Tales Told by Simpson* further develop the narrator, successful bachelor artist Roland Simpson. The collection does not include the Simpson-narrated "The Return" (*Harper's,* May 1921). It is not clear why this story was omitted; Boll considers "The Return" one of Sinclair's best tales. The first story in the collection, "Khaki," centers on Simpson and his artist friends, who tease Miles Dickinson about his inventions and his fascination with the Boer War. They essentially drive Dickinson, nicknamed "Khaki," to enlist. The story examines the senselessness and tragedy of war as well as Simpson's blindness regarding females in general and especially his fiancée, artist Frances Archdale. The characters Simpson, Archdale, Furnival, and Burton appear throughout these stories. The narrative tone is that of a cozy chat at

Simpson's club. He addresses the reader as "you," invoking memories of events as though the reader already knew them. The variety of moods among the stories keeps the reader alert for farce, tragedy, and irony.

The thirteen stories in this collection received substantially positive reviews. Gilbert Thomas (*Spectator,* 17 May 1930) wrote that Sinclair's stories "contain some of her best work." He continued: "She has the marvelous capacity for probing in a few pages to the very roots of character, and, while often caustic in her exposure of human foibles, she is merciless only when confronted with the poison of jealousy." The *New York Times* (14 September 1930) declared the collection "fastidious" and "of the school of Henry James." The *New York World* (19 October 1930) praised the stories for their "technical brilliance" and "acrobatic dexterity." The *Boston Transcript* (24 September 1930) declared: "No one could possibly sit down and read these stories all at once, with satisfaction. To assimilate their flavor and appreciate the beauty of Miss Sinclair's style, one must have leisure and a deep respect for the finer shadings of personality." The *New Statesman* (7 June 1930) appreciated the humor in the stories, especially in "Miss Tarrant's Temperament," which recalls the intricacies of social life in the world of Henry James and Edith Wharton. This collection was the last book by Sinclair to earn significant attention.

From 1931 until her death on 14 November 1946, Sinclair lived a reclusive life in the country, cared for by her housekeeper, Bartrop, and her chauffeur, Ernest Williams. Bartrop worked for her for twenty-seven years. Bartrop and Williams dressed in evening clothes whenever they attended her to a formal event. A passionate cat fancier, Sinclair gave up her will to live after the death of her cat Jerry in 1927. Bartrop told the story that Sinclair had sworn she would never adopt another pet after the death of her cat Tommy. Shortly afterward, though, a stray cat came into the yard and up the stairs to her writing desk, where she was working. The cat carried a kitten in her mouth and dropped it onto Sinclair's writing pad. She immediately adopted this kitten, which she named Jerry.

The illnesses that had been creeping up on her took over after Jerry's demise. He had replaced in her affections the younger writers whom she had encouraged and who no longer had use for her. Bartrop found a house in Buckinghamshire near medical facilities but too far from London for quick trips there. Sinclair did not realize or admit the ex-

tent of her illness. Her doctor advised the avoidance of the London dinners, meetings, and parties that she enjoyed. She had always alternated between the excitement of the capital and the quiet of the country. She worked most efficiently in the country and at different times lived in Yorkshire, Cornwall (next door to Richardson and her husband, Alan Odle), and the Cotswolds before moving to Buckinghamshire.

Because of her degenerative illness and lengthy seclusion from the public sphere, Sinclair's obituaries and tributes were not as voluminous as they would have been had she passed on in 1931. The *New York Times* (15 November 1946) revealed only a vague knowledge of her writing career, stating that she "amazed the literary critics in somewhat the same way as the Brontë sisters had done before her, by writing of a side of life of which she had had no practical experience." The London *Times* obituary (15 November 1946) was more informed about her work, eloquently praising her writing talent and career. It declared her "a novelist of keenly analytical intellect, a careful and finished stylist, and the possessor of a comprehensive imaginative grasp of character." It stated further that "her style did not obtrude itself, but her prose was evocative, well-wrought, and distinguished."

According to the London *Times,* her novels *The Creators: A Comedy* (1910), *The Flaw in the Crystal* (1912), and *Life and Death of Harriett Frean,* plus several short stories, consolidated her reputation as a superb writer. Her later novels received highest praise from this writer because they are "more subtle in character drawing," "more finely contrived," and "surer in delineation" than her previous works.

The London *Times* obituary invokes the 1916 evaluation of William Lyon Phelps, who declared Sinclair "the foremost living writer among English-speaking women." In his *The Advance of the English Novel* (1923), Phelps praises Sinclair as a "reincarnation of Charlotte Brontë." Ford reports in *Thus to Revisit: Some Reminiscences* (1921) that an important scholarly publication in the United States asked him to write an essay on the contemporary British literary scene. Sinclair was one of the sixteen writers he included in the piece. Furthermore, Ford believed that Sinclair and G. B. Stern were two of three writers who would lead the arts to innovation.

Like many woman writers who passed into obscurity only to be resurrected by the feminist Virago Press in the 1980s, Sinclair received quiet but steady recognition as a secondary writer. Sinclair criticized the Victorian family and writing style. She recognized the importance of psychoanalysis before the Bloomsbury Group began its translations of Freud. She was in the vanguard of those who experimented with point of view and subject matter. She championed social causes such as feminism and freedom of expression. Boll recognizes Sinclair's talent and importance in his 1973 biography. In his estimation Sinclair should be ranked above Lawrence and on a level with Virginia Woolf and Arnold Bennett.

In volume eleven of *The History of the English Novel* (1967), Lionel Stevenson asserts that Sinclair "knew more about modern psychology" than Dorothy Richardson and Woolf. Sinclair is discussed in Elaine Showalter's landmark study *A Literature of Their Own: British Women Novelists from Brontë to Lessing* (1977). Susan Gubar and Sandra Gilbert include Sinclair's story "The Bambino" (*Tales Told by Simpson*) in *The Norton Anthology of Literature by Women* (1985), thereby cementing her place among woman writers.

Interviews:

Willis Steell, "May Sinclair Tells Why She Isn't a Poet," *Literary Digest International Book Review*, 2 (June 1924): 513, 559;

Burton Rascoe, "Contemporary Reminiscences – Two Important English Visitors – May Sinclair and Bertrand Russell," *Arts & Decoration*, 21 (July 1924): 25, 56.

Bibliographies:

Corrine Y. Taylor, "A Study of May Sinclair – Woman and Writer, 1863–1946 – with an Annotated Bibliography," Ph.D. dissertation, Washington State University, 1969;

T. E. M. Boll, "May Sinclair: A Check List," *Bulletin of the New York Public Library*, 74 (September 1970): 459–467;

Kenneth Robb, "May Sinclair: An Annotated Bibliography of Writings About Her," *English Literature in Transition*, 16, no. 3 (1973): 177–231.

Biographies:

T. E. M. Boll, *Miss May Sinclair: Novelist. A Biographical and Critical Introduction* (Rutherford, N. J.: Fairleigh Dickinson University Press, 1973);

Hrisey Dimitrakis Zegger, *May Sinclair* (Boston: G. K. Hall, 1976).

References:

Sydney Janet Kaplan, *Feminine Consciousness in the Modern British Novel* (Urbana: University of Illinois Press, 1975);

Jean Radford, Introductions to Sinclair's *Mary Olivier: A Life*, *Life and Death of Harriett Frean*, and *The Three Sisters* (London: Virago, 1980, 1980, 1982);

Elaine Showalter, *A Literature of Their Own: British Women Novelists from Brontë to Lessing* (Princeton: Princeton University Press, 1977);

Lionel Stevenson, *The History of the English Novel*, volume 11: *Yesterday and Today* (New York: Barnes & Noble, 1967).

Papers:

A collection of Sinclair's papers is in the University of Pennsylvania Library. See T. E. M. Boll, "On the May Sinclair Collection," *Library Chronicle*, 27 (Winter 1961): 1–15.

Edith Œnone Somerville
(2 May 1858 – 8 October 1949)

and

Martin Ross
(Violet Florence Martin)
(11 June 1862 – 21 December 1915)

Claire Denelle Cowart
Southeastern Louisiana University

BOOKS: *Mark Twain Birthday Book,* by Somerville (London: Remington, 1885);

An Irish Cousin, by Somerville as Geilles Herring and Ross (London: Bentley, 1889; revised edition, London: Longmans, Green, 1903);

The Kerry Recruit, by Somerville (London: Perry, 1889);

Naboth's Vineyard, by Somerville and Ross (London: Blackett, 1891);

Through Connemara in a Governess Cart, by Somerville and Ross (London: Allen, 1893);

In the Vine Country, by Somerville and Ross (London: Allen, 1893);

The Real Charlotte, by Somerville and Ross (London: Ward & Downey, 1894);

Beggars on Horseback, by Somerville and Ross (London & Edinburgh: Blackwood, 1895);

The Silver Fox, by Somerville and Ross (London: Lawrence & Bullen, 1898);

Some Experiences of an Irish R.M., by Somerville and Ross (London: Longmans, Green, 1899; New York: Longmans, Green, 1929);

A Patrick's Day Hunt, by Somerville and Ross (London: Constable, 1902);

Slipper's ABC of Foxhunting, by Somerville and Ross (London: Longmans, Green, 1903);

All on the Irish Shore, by Somerville and Ross (London: Longmans, Green, 1903);

Some Irish Yesterdays, by Somerville and Ross (London & New York: Longmans, Green, 1906);

Further Experiences of an Irish R.M., by Somerville and Ross (London: Longmans, Green, 1908);

Dan Russel the Fox, by Somerville and Ross (London: Methuen, 1911);

The Story of the Discontented Little Elephant, by Somerville (London: Longmans, Green, 1912);

In Mr. Knox's Country, by Somerville and Ross (London: Longmans, Green, 1915);

Irish Memories, by Somerville and Ross (London: Longmans, Green, 1917; New York: Longmans, Green, 1918);

Mount Music, by Somerville and Ross (London: Longmans, Green, 1919; New York: Longmans, Green, 1920);

Stray-Aways, by Somerville and Ross (London: Longmans, Green, 1920);

An Enthusiast, by Somerville (London & New York: Longmans, Green, 1921);

Wheel-Tracks, by Somerville and Ross (London: Longmans, Green, 1923);

The Big House of Inver, by Somerville and Ross (London: Heinemann, 1925; Garden City, N.Y.: Doubleday, Page, 1925);

French Leave, by Somerville and Ross (London: Heinemann, 1928; Boston: Houghton Mifflin, 1928);

The States Through Irish Eyes, by Somerville (Boston: Houghton Mifflin, 1930; London: Heinemann, 1930);

An Incorruptible Irishman, by Somerville and Ross (London: Ivor Nicholson & Watson, 1932; Boston: Houghton Mifflin, 1932);

The Smile and the Tear, by Somerville and Ross (London: Methuen, 1933);

The Sweet Cry of Hounds, by Somerville and Ross (London: Methuen, 1936);

Sarah's Youth, by Somerville and Ross (London: Longmans, Green, 1938);

Edith Œnone Somerville and Martin Ross, 1894

Records of the Somerville Family, 1174–1940, by Somerville and Boyle Townshend Somerville (Cork: Guy, 1940);

Notions in Garrison, by Somerville and Ross (London: Methuen, 1941).

Collections: *The Irish R.M. and His Experiences,* by Somerville and Ross (London: Faber & Gwyer, 1928);

Happy Days, by Somerville and Ross (London: Longmans, Green, 1946);

Maria, & Some Other Dogs, by Somerville and Ross (London: Methuen, 1949).

OTHER: Somerville and Ross, "A Betrayal of Confidence," in *The Funny-Bone,* edited by Lady Cynthia Asquith (London: Jarrolds, 1928).

SELECTED PERIODICAL PUBLICATIONS – UNCOLLECTED: Somerville, "Slide No. 42," *Lady's Pictorial* (Christmas 1890);

Somerville and Ross, "A Regrettable Incident," *Nash's* (November 1909).

The Irish writers Edith Œnone Somerville and Violet Florence Martin, who wrote under the pseu-

donym Martin Ross, collaborated on many novels, short stories, travel books, memoirs, and essays during the last decade of the nineteenth century and the early part of the twentieth century. From the time they published their first novel, *An Irish Cousin* (1889), the authors enjoyed great popularity. Their most critically acclaimed work is the novel *The Real Charlotte* (1894), but they are best known for three volumes of humorous stories – *Some Experiences of an Irish R.M.* (1899), *Further Experiences of an Irish R.M.* (1908), and *In Mr. Knox's Country* (1915), which were later collected as *The Irish R.M. and His Experiences* (1928).

The two women, who were second cousins, were born into the Anglo-Irish Ascendancy, at that time the ruling class of Ireland. Their families, although originally English, had lived in Ireland for generations as part of the group that governed the country from its Big Houses, the family seats at the center of each estate. The cousins' short stories and novels reflect the Ireland they knew from this vantage point.

Born in Corfu on 2 May 1858 to Col. T. Henry Somerville and Adelaide Coghill Somerville, Edith was raised in the Somerville family home, Drishane, in the village of Castletownshend on the southern coast of West Cork. Drishane was built by her great-grandfather Thomas Somerville during the Georgian period and is described by Thomas Flanagan in "The Big House of Ross-Drishane" (*Kenyon Review,* January 1966) as a "masculine" house, whose "true life lay out of doors . . . a life of dogs and guns, tenants and estate agents, stables and kennels." During Edith's youth her grandfather, known as "The Big Master," headed the household, and he kept a firm hold on the estate until his death in 1882. As the eldest of six children, Edith took over the daily running of Drishane after her mother's death in 1895. Edith was a woman of many activities: a serious painter and an enthusiastic hunter (becoming first female master of the West Carbery Hunt), as well as an organist at Castletownshend church for seventy-five years. She also helped support herself and her family with the proceeds from her writing, imported the first Friesian cattle into Cork, and in her later years raised horses and sold them in America. This busy, productive life at Castletownshend echoes throughout many of the works on which Somerville collaborated with Violet Martin.

Violet Florence Martin was born on 11 June 1862 at her family home, Ross, in West Galway. Her mother, Anna Selina Fox Martin, was the second wife of Richard Martin, and Violet was the youngest of fourteen children. Like the Somerville family, the Martin family is of Norman origin, but because the Martins settled in Ireland many centuries before the Somervilles, their history as Anglo-Irish is much longer and more complex. The founder of the Irish branch, Oliver Martin, had come to Ireland in the twelfth century with the army headed by Strongbow and acquired the land near Galway where the family eventually settled. Originally Catholics, the Martins suffered religious persecution during Oliver Cromwell's invasion. Partly in response to the eighteenth-century penal laws, which prevented Catholics from owning property, and partly because Violet's great-grandfather wished to marry a Protestant woman, the family elected to become Anglican and thus saved their land.

By the time Violet was born, the family had lost much of its wealth and power. The Great Famine of 1847 had weakened the Martins' hold on Ross; in the election of 1872 the Ross tenants voted against the interest of Richard Martin. This particular reversal hit the family hard, and despondency may have contributed to Richard's death later that year. Violet's bitterness at what she considered a betrayal and a personal injury to her father contributed to her conservative political views. The misfortunes of the Ross estate multiplied in the fol-

lowing years. The crops failed in 1879, and a land commission later took over the estate. After her husband's death Anna Martin and her unmarried daughters, including ten-year-old Violet, moved to Dublin and stayed there for sixteen years, interspersing their residence in the city with extended visits to relatives. When Violet and her mother returned to Ross, they were tenants rather than owners. Violet's brother Robert, heir to Ross, elected to live in England, where he gained fame as a songwriter and went by the name "Ballyhooely," the title of his best-known work. He was also a journalist, and his connections to various periodicals later proved helpful to his sister.

Somerville and Ross did not set out to become serious authors. When the cousins first met, in January 1886, they were well into adulthood; Somerville was twenty-seven and Ross was twenty-three. Neither woman had had much formal schooling. Each had been taught to some degree by a succession of governesses, and each had taken some classes in Dublin at Alexandra College, a school for women founded in 1886. Both had also read extensively on their own. Somerville up to this time had concentrated most of her energies on painting; she had studied art in Düsseldorf in 1881 and in Paris in 1884. Before they began their joint writing career, each had published some of her own work, primarily as a means of generating much-needed income. Ross had placed some articles, mostly political, in various periodicals, especially in the *World.* Edmund Yates, editor of the *World,* became a great supporter of Somerville and Ross; Major Yeates, the narrator of the *Irish R.M.* stories, was named in his honor. As an outgrowth of her painting career, Somerville had been illustrating texts since the age of eighteen. She had published comic-strip stories, with the emphasis on pictures rather than text, in the *Graphic* and other journals.

In *Irish Memories* (1917), written the year after Ross's death, Somerville explains that the cousins' initial intention in collaborating on a novel had been to write a "shilling shocker," partly as a lark, partly as a way to make money. Although their gift for writing would probably have raised the level of their endeavor in any case, Somerville recalls a visit they paid to an old house near Drishane as sparking both their interest and talent. They called on a distant cousin living in isolated circumstances. Somerville describes in detail the moment when they turned to leave and the effect that the scene had on Ross and herself:

The sunset was red in the west when our horses were brought around to the door, and it was at that precise moment that into the Irish Cousin some thrill of genuineness was breathed. In the darkened facade of the long gray house, a window, just above the hall door, caught our attention. In it, for an instant, was a white face. . . . The shock of it was what we needed, and with it "the Shocker" started into life, or, if that is too much to say for it, its authors, at least, felt that conviction had come to them – the insincere ambition of the "Penny Dreadful" faded, realities asserted themselves, and the faked "thrills" that were to make our fortunes were repudiated for ever.

According to Maurice Collis in *Somerville and Ross: A Biography* (1968), the cousins believed that the face in the window was that of "some half-witted relative, a living ghost that haunted the house." In *The Selected Letters of Somerville and Ross* (1989) Gifford Lewis maintains that only Somerville actually made that visit and saw that face, which she described to her cousin in a letter. Somerville's experience did have a marked effect on the cousins' work, however. In the decline of the Big House, a topic suggested by the old woman's face, they found a subject to which they could turn their insights and skills – one that would preoccupy them and serve as the unifying theme of their work. Rapidly changing economic and political circumstances brought about radical changes in the authors' lifetimes, and they took account of these in their fiction. In *Shadowy Heroes: Irish Literature of the 1890's* (1980) Wayne Hall claims that "their combined experiences brought to their collaboration an epic breadth that depicts the Protestant Ascendancy in relation to every other major social force in Ireland."

The comic stories of Somerville and Ross have too often been dismissed as unimportant; the stories, however, reveal the authors' understanding of and attitude toward Ireland. And even when considered simply as entertainment, the short fiction is superb. The Irish poet Katharine Tynan pays tribute to the skill of Somerville and Ross in mastering humor as well as drama. As she puts it in an article for the London *Bookman* (June 1916): "In very few writers can there have been such a true proportion between the tragedy and comedy of life." The world of their humorous stories is on its surface secure and carefree. Beneath that surface, however, are signs that unrest and transition in the outside world are making themselves felt.

Before they began the *Irish R.M.* stories, the cousins had written four novels and several travel books, which were previously serialized in magazines such as the *Lady's Pictorial*. This was predominantly a fashion magazine, but Somerville and Ross, at this point in their careers were more con-

cerned with finances than literary credibility. They submitted their works to various periodicals in search of the best possible pay and were elated when a publication agreed to take Somerville's drawings along with their writing. Of the magazines that published their work, *Black & White* and the *Graphic* were both heavily illustrated weeklies. They also published stories in *Longman's,* a monthly with no illustrations, which was an offshoot of Longmans, Green and Company, a firm that published many works by Somerville and Ross.

The cousins achieved particular success with stories featuring hunting, a sport they both loved and at which they excelled. They proved more than equal to the task of transferring their enthusiasm into print. Many of these early hunting and hunt-related stories appeared in *Badminton Magazine of Sports and Pastimes,* a monthly with stories and articles designed to amuse men and women with sporting interests. As a result of the public's demand for their stories, the authors' literary agent, J. B. Pinker, urged them to produce more stories with hunting themes. In an 1897 letter to Ross, Somerville describes a visit she and Pinker paid to Hedley Peek, an art editor for *Badminton* who also worked for the publishing firm Lawrence and Bullen's. She writes that Peek and Arthur Henry Bullen "raved of the Bad Mag stories . . . especially the Grand Filly [later collected in *All on the Irish Shore,* 1903]. . . . They then all . . . swore that we had got hold of a very good thing in this serio-comic hunting business . . . said Pinker, 'this is *your own stuff* and no one else does anything like it.'"

Pinker, Peek, and Bullen urged Somerville to stay true to the style of "A Grand Filly," which is told from the point of view of an Englishman visiting Ireland. His host's aunt is eccentric, and the story centers around comic hunting mishaps. All these elements appear in the first group of *Irish R.M.* stories, for which Pinker arranged exclusive serialization with *Badminton*. Major Yeates, the narrator of the stories and the R.M. (Resident Magistrate) of the first volume's title, is an Anglo-Irishman who has been living for some time in England and who returns to Ireland with an English wife. His neighbor, Flurry Knox, is reminiscent of the host of "A Grand Filly," and Flurry's grandmother far outdoes the aunt of that story in eccentricity. Somerville and Ross connected some of these early stories by continuing characters and situations from one to another; they pursued this unifying technique with great success throughout the *Irish R.M.* stories.

The first *Irish R.M.* story, "Great Uncle Mc-Carthy's Ghost," appeared in *Badminton* in October 1898, and the monthly series concluded in September of the following year. These stories were then collected in *Some Experiences of an Irish R.M.* The stories in the second volume, *Further Experiences of an Irish R.M.*, first appeared in various periodicals, while the stories in the third volume, *In Mr. Knox's Country,* seem to have been written specifically for that volume. In 1928 the series was collected in one volume, *The Irish R.M. and His Experiences,* and the stories have not been out of print since. Some of them were adapted for a British television series, *The Irish R.M.,* which was shown in the United States on *Masterpiece Theatre* (1984). In all of their incarnations these tales of an R.M. in Ireland at the turn of the century have been wildly popular. They helped to establish the cousins as successful authors and contributed handsomely to their incomes.

During the time that they were writing the first series of stories in 1898, Ross took a bad fall while hunting. The accident left her in great physical distress for several years, and she did not hunt again until 1909. She somehow managed to put aside her pain in order to conjure up, with her cousin, the entertaining world of the *Irish R.M.* stories, but she was too weak to take on the task of writing another novel with Somerville.

Not all readers were pleased with the *Irish R.M.* stories, however. To some the tales seemed to consist of stereotypical representations of Irish "types." Some readers and critics, then and now, have focused on the minor players in the stories. In a 1968 article for *Eire-Ireland,* Sean McMahon says that "the jolly, childlike servants of the R.M. stories – Mrs. Cadogan, Slipper and the rest – smack of white Uncle-Tomism." But the authors are much more likely to zero in on the jolly, childlike behavior often exhibited by the servants' masters and to direct their barbed comments toward the gentry.

In fact, Ross criticized English audiences for expecting to meet "the Stage Irishman" in Irish literature. While acknowledging this fact, Ann Power writes in a 1964 article for the *Dubliner* that although Somerville and Ross do show great sympathy and admiration for the Irish, they are unable to keep "that deadly touch of condescension . . . the fatal sense of displaying the Irish to an English reader . . . from their work." In response to charges that Somerville and Ross wrote primarily for an English audience, Conor Cruse O'Brien comes to their defense in *Writers and Politics* (1965):

They exaggerate, obviously, as every comic writer does, but their exaggeration is firmly based on Irish ground which they knew well and which in their own way they loved deeply. They lived in Ireland for almost all their writing lives and they had, as a writing team, a sensitive ear and a penetrating, humorous eye. If their writing is not part of the literature of Ireland, then Ireland is a poorer place than many of us believe it to be.

In a 1945 article for the *Irish Times,* Frank O'Connor points out that the cousins' connection to England has more to do with literary technique than with subject matter. He observes that their "intellectual centre is rather London than Paris" and emphasizes that their writing is in the realistic mode favored by English writers of the time, while Irish writers such as James Joyce preferred naturalism and symbolism, which were prevalent on the Continent.

Even their exaggerated characters must have been rooted in truth, for as Somerville notes in the preface to the 1928 edition of the stories, many readers believed that they knew the original persons on whom the authors had based characters in the *Irish R.M.* stories. Somerville claims that "of them all, Slipper and Maria alone had prototypes in the world as Martin Ross and I knew it." Maria is a dog, while Slipper is a canny resident of the Castletownshend area with a special affinity for horses. On another occasion she admitted that some characters should indeed be thought of as types – not types of Stage Irishmen, but "composite photographs of the people of an Ireland that has not yet lost its originality and its sense of humour." Despite the disclaimer, letters of the time show that the character Flurry Knox was to some degree based on Somerville's brother Aylmer. Somerville herself shared characteristics with Bobbie Bennett, an attractive hunting enthusiast frequently encountered by the R.M., and the traits of other family members also can be recognized in the stories.

In addition to using the characters of their native land to create much of the humor in the stories, Somerville and Ross reproduce the speech of the Irish of all classes. In 1902 they published a picture book, *A Patrick's Day Hunt,* with a story written primarily by Ross and illustrations by Somerville. The narrator speaks in an Irish, rather than an Anglo-Irish, voice – a rare departure for the authors. This book was well received, contributing to the demand for more hunting stories. For the most part, however, both women believed that idiom rather than dialect was the defining characteristic of Irish speech, and they were preoccupied with recording it as precisely as possible. Somerville carried a sketchbook and a notebook at all times so that she could record what she saw and heard. Ross had the ability to remember conversations word for word, and she held on to the memory until she could write them down.

This interest in language and research among the Irish people is also characteristic of the writers associated with the Irish Literary Revival, which was contemporaneous with the writing careers of Somerville and Ross. In most ways, however, Somerville and Ross operated outside the revival. Although Ross was a cousin to Lady Isabella Augusta Gregory and occasionally socialized with William Butler Yeats, she and Somerville did not share Yeats's romantic view of Ireland, nor did they share his politics. Their focus on the Big House was aimed at a much different audience from that targeted by those involved in the revival. Ross was once invited to write a play for the Abbey Theatre, but the comical, good-natured peasant often found in Somerville and Ross works would not have been welcome there, nor would the authors' darker visions of the crumbling Anglo-Irish life. The "Celtic twilight" did not hover over their world.

The authors impart a subtle, pervasively humorous slant to the *Irish R.M.* stories by using the device of a detached narrator. When the first volume begins, Major Yeates has just arrived in Ireland to take up the post of resident magistrate. Although he is Irish by birth, Yeates has been living in England and has married an Englishwoman. Consequently, he views his new home in the west of Ireland from the perspective of an outsider; behavior and conditions that the natives take for granted as normal seem outlandish and amusing to him. Yeates's point of view may at first seem to lend credence to the criticism that Somerville and Ross were playing to an English audience. But the freshness of the major's perceptions has its own charm. He sees things in a way that the natives do not; his nearsightedness corresponds to his apprehension of the world he inhabits. Many times Yeates is the butt of the humor in the stories. Because he is not an insider in the fairly closed society of Skebawn and its environs, he is often in the dark about events that are well known to the natives. In addition, Yeates would be an innocent in any society; he is eminently dupable, a characteristic his neighbors often recognize.

In "Holy Island" (*Some Experiences of an Irish R.M.*), the entire populace save Yeates seems to know about a ruse to smuggle liquor from a shipwrecked vessel. And in the preceding story, "A Misdeal," Yeates and another outsider, Bernard Shute, mistakenly exchange horses — an error that knowl-

edgeable natives, such as the Knoxes, would never make. Despite or perhaps because of his naiveté, though, the R.M. seems sympathetic both to the reader and to the other characters in the stories. In addition, Yeates is the only character in these stories who really develops. As the volumes progress, he becomes more informed about his environs and more adept at reading both character and situation. He also comes to be accepted as friend and compatriot by those who once regarded him as an outsider. As these changes occur, the source of the humor in the stories also alters so that the laughs more often come to depend on character than on situation. In the early stories Yeates is often taken advantage of and made fun of by the native Irish, but gradually, as he gains understanding and trust, he moves to a position of conspirator rather than dupe. In many of these instances, moreover, Yeates as narrator laughs at himself. Rarely are the Irish of the lower or servant classes the main targets of his amusement; more often, the Anglo-Irish are given that distinction.

If any social class or group can be described as stereotyped or consistently made fun of in the *Irish R.M.* stories, that group must be the English visitor. Although the R.M.'s wife, Philippa, comes to have a fairly good understanding of her neighbors and seems eventually to feel at home in a foreign environment, her early misadventures provide much mirth. Somerville and Ross, however, always portray casual English visitors as totally on the outside; they are unable to understand the Irish way of life or to adapt themselves to it. For instance, in "Lisheen Races, Second-Hand" (*Some Experiences of an Irish R.M.*), Yeates's point of view has already changed enough so that he can regard his English visitor, Leigh Kelway, with disapproval because Kelway views the Irish as a subject for study. His college friend's new profession of politician has made him much less amusing than in earlier days, and Yeates concludes that Kelway's "society, when combined with a notebook and a thirst for statistics, was not what I used to find it at Oxford." Such a staid Englishman is a convenient butt for humor, but the role in which Somerville and Ross cast Kelway also reveals something of the authors' negative attitude toward the English and their treatment of Ireland. Although Ireland's problems do not play an overt role in the R.M. stories, they often have a place in the background.

Just as elements of comedy sometimes find their way into the more-dramatic works of Somerville and Ross, however, so do more-serious elements find their way into the *Irish R.M.* stories. Many critics believe that the gradual unraveling of

COUNTRY RACES OF A TYPICAL SORT

*Illustration by Somerville for "Lisheen Races, Second-Hand" (*Badminton Magazine, *February 1899)*

the Anglo-Irish glory days, the subject of so many novels by Somerville and Ross, simply does not appear in their stories. Today's reader should keep in mind that the authors compiled the *Irish R.M.* volumes from individual stories. It may be tempting, especially when reading them straight through, to think that the authors intended the atmosphere they created for these tales to re-create completely the atmosphere of everyday life in the Ireland of their time. The reader of Somerville and Ross novels, however, knows that the authors were well aware of, and were well able to convey, a much bleaker picture of Irish life.

That bleaker Ireland is not entirely absent from the *Irish R.M.* stories. It lives below the surface and sometimes at the edges of the stories. The reader should not assume that the characters in the stories are unaware of the realities of Irish life. In some ways, in fact, the Anglo-Irish of the stories may have a more realistic, more balanced view of Irish life than the Anglo-Irish of the novels, who are apt to deny reality until it overtakes them. The humor of the stories does not invalidate them as a portrait of Irish life; indeed, humor is probably essential to such a portrait. But, because the stories

concentrate primarily on funny episodes in the lives of the characters, every moment of their lives need not be funny. After all, Flurry Knox does go to war, his mother does live in reduced circumstances, and Major Yeates, as a magistrate, must certainly have to deal with serious affairs. Because the emphasis in the stories is not on these circumstances but on humor, the reader must look to the details that provide the backdrop for the action in order to see that some of the same themes that inform the tragic fiction of Somerville and Ross are also present, though not predominant, in their comic work.

In the first story of the series, "Great Uncle McCarthy's Ghost," Somerville and Ross demonstrate the wide range of status that can exist within one family. An elderly couple is discovered living in Yeates's attic, from which they have been engaged in the disreputable business of selling foxes and stealing from the major. Yeates's neighbor Flurry Knox, who is slightly down-at-the-heels but nevertheless a true member of the gentry, is embarrassed when he realizes that the woman who has been squatting at Shreelane is his relation. She, however, seems to believe that her bloodlines have kept her actions from being disgraceful: "And is it you,

Flurry Knox, that's calling me a disgrace! Disgrace, indeed, am I? Me that was your poor mother's own uncle's daughter and as good a McCarthy as ever stood in Shreelane!"

Flurry's cousin disappears fairly early from the *Irish R.M.* stories, but many other members of this far-flung family make up for her absence. Flurry is one of the most engaging, memorable characters in the stories, and Yeates initially appraises him, in a line that has become well known, as one "who looked like a stableboy among gentlemen, and a gentleman among stableboys." Yeates further describes the Knoxes as "a clan that cropped up in every grade of society in the country, from Sir Valentine Knox of Castle Knox down to the auctioneer Knox, who bore the attractive title of Larry the Liar." Flurry, he feels, "occupied a shifting position about midway in the tribe."

Although Sir Valentine lives at Castle Knox in an atmosphere nostalgically reminiscent of better days, the main characters of the *Irish R.M.* stories rarely experience that luxury. Castle Knox serves in some ways as a counterpoint to the ordinary lives of people such as the Yeateses and Flurry Knox and in other ways as a standard by which the reader can judge the extent of change in the lives of the Anglo-Irish. The most obvious example of such change is Flurry's grandmother, Mrs. Knox of Aussolas Castle, succinctly described by Lady Knox in a late story as "a rag bag held together by diamond brooches." In "Trinket's Colt" (*Some Experiences of an Irish R.M.*) at his first glimpse of her Yeates declares:

> She looked as if she had robbed a scarecrow. Her face was small and incongruously refined, the hand that she extended to me had the grubby tan that bespoke the professional gardener, and was decorated with a magnificent diamond ring.

The dinner she serves likewise indicates Mrs. Knox's unconventional ways: "There was detestable soup in a splendid old silver tureen . . . a perfect salmon, perfectly cooked, on a chipped kitchen dish . . . a bottle of port, draped in immemorial cobwebs, wan with age, and probably priceless."

But the incongruity of the dinner and the hostess does not express mere eccentricity; it also demonstrates the rate and the kinds of changes that have occurred at Aussolas Castle. The silver tureen, priceless bottle of port, and dazzling jewelry all bespeak better times, while the cobwebs, chipped dish, and uneven quality of both the supper and her attire attest to a much sorrier state of affairs in the present. Mrs. Knox is clearly not starving, nor is she totally without means. She has made her own peculiar

adjustment to changing times. Although she cannot entertain grandly like Sir Valentine and Lady Knox, she does not settle for smooth mediocrity; instead, she lays on a dinner of uneven grandeur and dresses in startlingly uneven fashion, mixing diamonds with an ancient bonnet. Aussolas is an establishment that Yeates sees as "vast, dilapidated, and of unknown age"; nevertheless, Aussolas is and always has been Mrs. Knox's home, which she will retain regardless of its condition.

From Mrs. Knox's point of view, politics bears some of the blame for her estate's condition. When a former tenant comes to her for help in a sticky situation, she snaps, "I have no tenants . . . the Government is your landlord now, and I wish you joy of each other!" She does relent and help the man, but she is unhappy about continuing to be held responsible for those who no longer have real ties to her. Politics is not often a topic of conversation with her or with the other characters in the *Irish R.M.* stories, however, and her conduct throughout the stories indicates that she has made an essentially peaceful adjustment to her new circumstances. Occasionally she ventures out to do battle in the new world, as when coaxed by her former tenant, but on the whole she rejects the new rules and simply lives by her own lights.

In some of these ways Flurry Knox is like his grandmother. While he is not by any means the eccentric she is, he is just as strong-willed and just as sure of himself. In time he will inherit Aussolas, and after he marries he gradually makes himself more and more at home there, as he and his wife pay extended visits. In "The Aussolas Martin Cat" (*In Mr. Knox's Country*), Mrs. Knox puts up a brief resistance by planning to lease the house while she takes a long vacation, but Flurry contrives to scare off a potential lessee by simulating a supernatural invasion. In so doing he demonstrates his intention to keep the estate firmly in the hands of the family; there is little reason to believe that once he inherits Aussolas things will be different. Although Flurry is not at the head of the Knox family nor completely secure financially, he seems destined to survive difficulty because he is shrewd, determined, and confident.

An example of Somerville and Ross's ability to recognize social change comes with the entrance of the McRory family, first mentioned in "The Pug-Nosed Fox" (*Further Experiences of an Irish R.M.*). Yeates refers to the head of the family as "old McRory . . . a retired Dublin coal merchant, with an enormous family, and a reputation for great riches." The McRorys are social climbers who buy a dilapidated Big House, Temple Braney, and restore it. Mr. McRory also manages to obtain, "by strenuous efforts, that dubious honor, Commission of the Peace," which brings him in contact with Yeates and other members of the gentry. While the McRorys participate in the social life of the gentry to some degree, they are not truly perceived as equals. As Yeates puts it, "The family had worn its way, unequally and in patches, into the tolerance of the neighborhood" by virtue of their talents at dancing and sports, as well as their generosity and participation in local events. Yeates even speaks of De Lacey "Curly" McRory as "the pioneer of his family in their advance to cross what has been usefully called 'the bounder-y line.'" The encroachment of the McRorys into upper-class society clearly occasions some concern among Yeates's circle. They have allowed the intrusion, however, and indeed seem powerless to stop such an exuberant clan. In this respect their stories show a link to their novels, where so often the listless aristocracy simply gives way before the vital middle class.

Although the social superiors of the McRorys do nothing to stop the latter's rise, they display some insecurity and poor taste of their own when the McRorys first begin affecting their lives. Much of "Sharper Than A Ferret's Tooth" (*Further Experiences of an Irish R.M.*) makes fun of the McRorys by showing their vulgarity. Yeates, Philippa, Sally Knox, Bernard and Cecilia Shute, and Sybil Hervey suffer from the effects of a boating accident and a rainstorm near Temple Braney, the McRorys' home. They are rescued and provided with clothing and lunch by that family. But rather than feeling properly grateful for these ministrations, Yeates and his party, while mouthing thanks to their hosts, make fun among themselves of the expensive garments and lavish food that the McRorys have pressed on them. They regret the prospect of eating with the family, and after the meal Yeates even makes a point of ignoring his host, expressing the foolish belief that this will make "old McRory" feel more comfortable. As John Cronin points out in *Somerville and Ross* (1972), by sneering at their hosts the major and his friends seem vulgar. Rather than finding the story amusing, today's reader is more likely to think of the Anglo-Irish behavior as a lapse in taste.

"The Bosom of the McRory's" (*In Mr. Knox's Country*) also contains some sniping comments about the McRorys' taste and manners. Again, Yeates and his wife socialize only grudgingly, out of a sense of obligation, with the family. Although Yeates suffers some mortification as a result of a prank by the younger McRorys and resolves never to visit Temple Braney again, Philippa actually enjoys dancing with Curly McRory after some initial distress at finding the head of the family as her dinner partner. In addition, the major makes closer acquaintance with the mischievous Larkie McRory, who figures prominently in the following two stories.

In "Put Down One and Carry Two" and "The Comte des Pralines," Larkie's high spirits and friendliness soften Yeates's attitude toward her and, by extension, toward her family. Both stories center around a hunt. The first, which is set the morning after the dinner party with the McRorys, marks a change in the way the narrator regards Larkie. When she attaches herself to him for the duration of the hunt, the burden of her presence at first irks him. But he is gradually won over by her willingness to take chances and by her charm. As the story nears its end, the major is enjoying Larkie's company. His new way of thinking about her continues into the next story, "The Comte des Pralines." Here Larkie shows herself a good sport in more ways than one. When she realizes that Yeates and a few others are playing a practical joke on the other members of the hunt, she willingly becomes a co-conspirator. Then, when the hunt becomes serious, she demonstrates great staying power for one with so little experience. By the story's end, which is also almost the end of the series, Yeates accepts Larkie into the world of the hunt, a world dear to him and to both Somerville and Ross.

Many years after the stories were written, the comte de Suzannet offered Somerville a substantial sum for the original manuscripts. The practical Somerville opined that the papers were a "collection of rubbish," but she nevertheless sold them and used the money for her farm overdraft. To the many readers who have enjoyed the stories, the manuscripts are far from rubbish. Few books have inspired so much devotion and appreciation over so many years, and few collections of comic tales have won such critical praise. Flanagan observes that "the *Irish R.M.*" stories are . . . miracles of comic exuberance and improvisation in which great literary economy and craft are concealed by an air of infinite leisure." In *The Heart Grown Brutal: The Irish Revolution in Literature from Parnell to the Death of Yeats* (1977) Peter Costello sets the stories in their proper place: "Somerville and Ross have caught the whole flavor of Ireland in their tales, a light laugh at death's door."

Because Somerville and Ross formed an unusually close relationship both as writers and as friends, many readers and critics have wondered about the nature of their partnership. Within a year of their first meeting, the cousins had embarked on the writing career that would become their main pursuit. Neither woman ever married or became involved in any serious romance with a man, although there is some evidence that, as a nineteen-year-old, Edith was in love with her cousin Hewitt Poole; another cousin, Herbert Greene, proposed to her on a regular basis. Because Ross lived for many years at Drishane, her collaborator's home, and because their correspondence often takes an affectionate tone, some observers have concluded that Somerville and Ross were lovers. But, while the two women were obviously emotionally close and did in some way love each other, there is no concrete evidence that their relationship ever took a sexual form. In fact, Somerville's family and friends believed that during her friendship with Ross she was, in Lady Violet Powell's words, "unenlightened on the subject of sexual inversion."

Collis, in his 1968 biography of Somerville and Ross, concludes that Somerville felt a "profound distaste" for men and directed her most heartfelt feelings toward women, but he maintains that her emotions were sublimated. Collis indicates that Ross, unlike Somerville, would probably have been able to marry successfully. However, he thinks that her emotional and creative partnership with her cousin took the place of any such relationship and had the additional benefit of giving her "an outlet for her genius." In *Somerville and Ross: The World of the Irish R.M.* (1987), as well as in her 1989 edition of Somerville and Ross's letters, Lewis takes issue with Collis's position, asserting that Collis has misread much of the evidence. Lewis believes that there was no such romantic feeling whatsoever between the cousins and that their avoidance of marriage stemmed from seeing many arranged marriages in which the women were unhappy. In addition, she shows that Somerville was much more of a social being than her cousin, never turning down an invitation to a dance and seeming to enjoy the company of men more than did Ross.

Whatever the depth of feeling between the cousins, their writing clearly benefited from their closeness. In their prose, which C. L. Graves ("The Lighter Side of Irish Life," 1913) calls "the most brilliantly successful example of creative collaboration in our times," no seams are ever apparent. Somerville and Ross often found themselves confronted with questions about how they wrote in partnership, and Somerville's irritation at these queries emerges in a letter to her brother Cameron; it

also provides some clues as to why the collaboration was so successful:

> The whole "secret" lay in community of tastes, and sympathy as to the point of view and, of course, a certain diversity of gifts and of stock in trade, so that one could and did supplement the other. I am sick of being asked for the key to the mystery, etc. etc. *ad nauseam*.... Why don't they ask me how I write by myself? I could assure them that it is much harder than writing with Martin and much more of a "mystery" to me how I do it.

After Ross's death from a brain tumor on 21 December 1915, Somerville had different questions to answer about collaboration. She and other members of her family had become interested in spiritualism before Ross's death. In September 1912 Jem Barlow, an amateur medium, visited Drishane. She took up residence in Castletownshend the following year, and soon Somerville's Uncle Kendal and cousin Egerton Coghill were joining her for séances. Somerville took a lively interest in the results, but she did not become actively involved until 1916, the year after Ross died. On the evening of 16 June Somerville went to dine with Barlow and took part in a séance designed to communicate with a Colonel Isherwood. When Somerville and Barlow began the process of automatic writing, however, the author of the script claimed to be Ross, writing: "You and I have not finished our work. Dear, we shall. Be comforted. V.M." Understandably doubtful, Somerville wrote in her diary that night: "Received communication of which I hardly know what to think."

She set aside her initial doubts, however, and came to believe strongly that she could not only communicate but also collaborate with the spirit of her cousin. Because of her grief over Ross's death, Somerville had not attempted to do any writing of her own and had indeed worried that she was not equal to the task. She found encouragement and promises of help in the supposed messages from Martin. With Barlow always acting as medium, she engaged almost daily in "communication" with Martin's spirit. The book that Somerville wrote as a result of this experience, *Irish Memories,* was not a novel or a collection of stories but a selection of essays and remembrances, some written by herself and some by Ross before her death. Somerville continued to demonstrate her faith in the automatic writing by listing Ross as co-author in almost every book she published until her death in 1949.

Yet whether Somerville completely believed in this form of spiritualism is open to some doubt. In a letter to her brother Cameron at the time she was writing *Irish Memories,* she seems to be trying to convince herself of the communication's validity:

> She [Ross] is helping me. I am quite sure of it. By suggestion, not by direct writing. Yet I cannot be mistaken and when we are writing (the daily talk that I am now able to have with her), she has often confirmed my own feeling as to which bits she inspired and which originated with me and were touched up by her. Just as always was our practice. It is a very wonderful thing and becomes more so. Anyhow it has changed the world for me.

In any event, the automatic writing helped Somerville move forward. Furthermore, believing that she was in touch with Ross's spirit allayed her grief, allowing her to concentrate on her work. Although she took time to discover her own voice, Somerville went on to produce a daunting quantity of literature. She wrote five novels, the most notable of which is *The Big House of Inver* (1925). *Maria, & Some Other Dogs* (1949), Somerville's last published work, features some slight pieces reminiscent of the *Irish R.M.* stories; Maria is Major Yeates's dog in that series.

Partly from a desire to preserve her cousin's work and partly from the need to generate income, Somerville began to gather articles that she and Ross had written separately for various periodicals, along with unpublished pieces. Sometimes she combined these with new pieces or reminiscences of her own. The first volume of this sort was *Irish Memories.* She followed it with *Stray-Aways* (1920), which is chiefly notable for several short stories that were separately authored. Among these is Ross's "The Dog from Doone," which features a supernatural element. This is an interest more usually attributed to Somerville, but for most of her life she was a realistic, practical person. Only after her cousin's death did she become interested in phenomena such as automatic writing.

Somerville also wrote several other volumes of reminiscences as well as more travel books. In 1929, when she was seventy-one, she traveled to the United States to sell some horses. Ever one to combine business with not only pleasure but more business, Somerville managed to do some hunting (from a buggy, not on a horse) and to write a series of articles for *Vogue* describing her experiences. She then worked the pieces into book form, *The States Through Irish Eyes* (1930).

Somerville also remained actively involved with the politics of her day. She had been the first president of the Munster Women's Franchise League, a suffrage group that she and Ross had joined in 1910, and she continued to work for woman's rights after Ross's

death. Somerville's position on the Irish political situation was more complex. While Ross had been a staunch unionist, Somerville favored nationalism. Her beliefs frequently put her at odds with others of her class and even with members of her family, so that she often felt torn. In a 1921 letter to Ethel Smyth, Somerville refers to herself as "half-rebel and a Miss-Facing-both-ways." Her brother Boyle shared her Nationalist beliefs, and when he was murdered in 1936 for helping local boys join the English navy, Edith was understandably shaken. She did not blame the local villagers, however, and maintained an optimistic outlook for Ireland's future.

In other respects the 1930s were a source of great satisfaction for Somerville. In 1932 Trinity College, Dublin, offered her an honorary doctorate, which she accepted on condition that Ross's name be included along with hers. In that year Yeats founded the Irish Academy of Letters, which he invited her to join. She attended an academy dinner in 1933, an occasion that heralded a sense of fellowship with other Irish writers; in her own words, "All was peace and love." She gained further recognition in 1941, when the academy awarded her the Gregory Gold Medal for literary excellence. Somerville died on 8 October 1949, having reached the great age of ninety-one. She is buried in the cemetery of Saint Barrahane's Church, Castletownshend, next to her collaborator, cousin, and dearest companion.

Letters:
The Selected Letters of Somerville and Ross, edited by Gifford Lewis (London: Faber & Faber, 1989).

Bibliography:
Elizabeth Hudson, *A Bibliography of the First Editions of the Works of E. Œ. Somerville and Martin Ross,* with notes by Somerville (New York: Sporting Gallery & Bookshop, 1942).

Biographies:
Geraldine Cummins, *Dr. E. Œ. Somerville: A Biography* (London: Dakers, 1952);

Maurice Collis, *Somerville and Ross: A Biography* (London: Faber & Faber, 1968);

Violet Powell, *The Irish Cousins* (London: Heinemann, 1970);

Gifford Lewis, *Somerville and Ross: The World of the Irish R.M.* (Middlesex, U.K.: Penguin, 1987).

References:
Sir Patrick Coghill, "Opening Address," in *Somerville and Ross: A Symposium* (Belfast: Queen's University of Belfast, 1968), pp. 5–7;

Coghill, "Somerville and Ross," *Hermathena,* no. 79 (May 1952): 47–60;

Peter Costello, *The Heart Grown Brutal: The Irish Revolution in Literature from Parnell to the Death of Yeats* (Totowa, N. J.: Roman & Littlefield, 1977);

John Cronin, *Somerville and Ross* (Lewisburg, Pa.: Bucknell University Press, 1972);

Thomas Flanagan, "The Big House of Ross-Drishane," *Kenyon Review,* 28 (January 1966): 54–78;

C. L. Graves, "The Lighter Side of Irish Life," *Quarterly Review,* 219, no. 436 (1913): 26–47;

Wayne Hall, *Shadowy Heroes: Irish Literature of the 1890's* (Syracuse, N.Y.: Syracuse University Press, 1980);

B. G. MacCarthy, "E. Œ. Somerville and Martin Ross," *Studies,* 34 (June 1945): 183–194;

Roger McHugh and Maurice Harmon, *A Short History of Anglo-Irish Literature* (Totowa, N. J.: Barnes & Noble, 1982);

Sean McMahon, "John Bull's Other Island: A Consideration of *The Real Charlotte* by Somerville & Ross," *Eire-Ireland,* 3 (Winter 1968): 119–135;

Hilary Mitchell, "Somerville and Ross: Amateur to Professional," in *Somerville and Ross: A Symposium,* pp. 20–37;

Conor Cruse O'Brien, *Writers and Politics* (New York: Pantheon, 1965);

Frank O'Connor, "Somerville and Ross," *Irish Times,* 15 December 1945, p. 4;

Donal O'Donnell, "The Novels and Stories of Somerville and Ross," *Irish Writing,* no. 30 (March 1955): 7–15;

Harold Orel, "Some Elements of Truth in the Short Stories of Somerville and Ross: An Appreciation," *English Literature in Transition, 1880–1920,* 30, no. 1 (1987): 17–25;

Ann Power, "The Big House of Somerville and Ross," *Dubliner,* 3 (Spring 1964): 43–53;

V. S. Pritchett, "The Irish R.M.," in his *The Living Novel* (London: Chatto & Windus, 1966), pp. 267–291;

Hilary Robinson, *Somerville and Ross: A Critical Appreciation* (New York: St. Martin's Press, 1980);

Katharine Tynan, "Violet Martin (Martin Ross) and E. Œ. Somerville," *Bookman* (London), 50 (June 1916): 65–66;

Cresap Watson, "The Collaboration of Edith Somerville and Violet Martin," Ph.D. dissertation, Trinity College, Dublin, 1953;

Ann Owens Weekes, *Irish Women Writers: An Uncharted Tradition* (Lexington: University of Kentucky Press, 1990).

Papers:

Trinity University, Dublin, holds the manuscripts for works by Somerville and Ross (formerly the Suzannet Collection); their correspondence with their literary agent, J. B. Pinker, and publishers; sketches by Somerville; her correspondence with the comte de Suzannet; and her papers dealing with the Hunt Club of West Carbery, county Cork. Many other Somerville and Ross papers are in the Queen's University of Belfast Library, which has the diaries of both, notebooks, miscellaneous papers, and some of Somerville's correspondence with Ethel Smyth. The mutual correspondence of Somerville and Ross and Ross's correspondence with Lady Augusta Gregory are in the Berg Collection, New York Public Library. Various branches of the family also hold some of the correspondence and miscellaneous papers, including a collection at Drishane.

G. S. Street

(18 July 1867 – 31 October 1936)

Linda Anne Julian
Furman University

BOOKS: *Miniatures and Moods* (London: Nutt, 1893);

The Autobiography of a Boy: Passages Selected by His Friend, G. S. Street (London: Elkin Mathews / John Lane, 1894; Philadelphia: Lippincott, 1894);

Episodes (London: Heinemann, 1895; New York: Merriam, 1895);

Quales Ego: A Few Remarks in Particular and at Large by G. S. Street (London: John Lane, 1896; New York: Merriam, 1896);

The Wise and the Wayward (London & New York: John Lane, 1896);

Some Notes of a Struggling Genius (London & New York: John Lane, 1898);

The Trials of the Bantocks (London & New York: John Lane, 1900);

A Book of Essays (Westminster [London]: Constable, 1902; New York: Dutton, 1903);

A Book of Stories (Westminster [London]: Constable, 1902);

The Views of an Angry Man (London: Bullen, 1902);

Books and Things: A Collection of Stray Remarks (London: Duckworth, 1905);

The Ghosts of Piccadilly (London: Constable, 1907; New York: Dutton, 1907?);

People and Questions (London: Secker, 1910; New York: Kennerley, 1910);

On Money and Other Essays (London: Constable, 1914);

At Home in the War (London: Heinemann, 1918);

The London Assurance, 1720–1920 (London: Privately printed, 1920).

PLAY PRODUCTIONS: *Miss Bramshott's Engagement,* London, Prince of Wales Theatre, 30 April 1902;

Great Friends, London, Court Theatre, 29 January 1905;

The Anonymous Letter [revised as *Enterprising Helen*], London, Vaudeville Theatre, 18 June 1907.

G. S. Street (portrait by Francis Howard; Yellow Book, October 1896)

OTHER: *The Comedies of William Congreve,* edited, with an introduction, by Street (London: Methuen, 1895);

George Warrington Steevens, *Things Seen: Impressions of Men, Cities, and Books,* edited by Street, with a memoir by W. E. Henley (Indianapolis: Bowen-Merrill, 1900).

SELECTED PERIODICAL PUBLICATIONS – UNCOLLECTED:

DRAMA

"Noctes Ambrosianoe," anonymous [by Street and J. H. Millis], *Blackwood's,* 165 (February 1899): 167–192.

NONFICTION

"Sheridan and Mr. Shaw," *Blackwood's,* 167 (June 1900): 832–836;

"The Betting Book at Brooks's," *North American Review,* 173 (July 1901): 44–55;

"The Great Duchess," *Living Age,* 232 (15 February 1902): 436–439;

"The Early Victorians: A Twentieth-Century English View," *Putnam's Monthly,* 1 (November 1906): 173–179;

"Lord Randolph Churchill," *Quarterly Review,* 206 (January 1907): 236–249;

"To Honor a Pilgrimage," *Living Age,* 271 (28 October 1911): 236–238;

"Young and Old," *Nineteenth Century and After,* 87 (June 1920): 1132–1138;

" 'Society' Once More," *Nineteenth Century and After,* 88 (December 1920): 1037–1041;

"Oxford: A Thought or Two," *Nineteenth Century and After,* 89 (May 1921): 819–824;

"Thoughts on Success," *Nineteenth Century and After,* 94 (July 1923): 68–71;

"Censorship of Plays," *Fortnightly Review,* 124 (September 1925): 348–357.

Whimsy, detachment, sympathy, tenderness, satire, humor, and occasionally cynicism – these are the lenses through which George Slythe Street viewed the late-Victorian and Edwardian periods in stories, novels, essays, and plays. His distinctive style propelled him to the forefront of the literary world during the 1890s and the first decade of the twentieth century, but his fame had diminished greatly by 1936, the year of his death. For most of the twentieth century Street's work has been neglected, which is both unfortunate and surprising, given his skill and association with other writers, especially W. E. Henley and Max Beerbohm.

Street deftly satirized his age, attacking snobbery, hypocrisy, vulgarity, and pretentiousness at all levels of society, especially among the aesthetes and the upper class. As he decried the encroaching noisiness, crassness, and mediocrity of his own day, he idealized the past, particularly the eighteenth century, in elegantly restrained prose. Many of his keen observations seem equally relevant to a society on the verge of the twenty-first century. However, the decline of Street's reputation may have resulted largely from his greatest strength: the brief narrative. He seems to have superimposed his desire to write essays, novels, and plays over his singular talent as a short-story writer so that his work has a kind of sameness no matter what the genre. His essays are narrative, and his novels are compilations of episodes. Also contributing to his declining popularity was the rise of literary modernism, which passed him by. Street's leisurely style was superseded by a modern style that relied on such techniques as oblique symbolism, stream of consciousness, and fragmentation. The late-Victorian and Edwardian themes that Street explored were left in the wake of darker modern concerns.

Street was born in Wimbledon on 18 July 1867, the son of Samuel Philip Street, who was distantly related to G. E. Street, a well-known architect. G. S. Street attended school at Temple Grove, East Sheen, and went to Charterhouse at the same time as Beerbohm, although they did not know each other there. Street entered Exeter College, Oxford, taking a first class in Classical Moderations in 1888 and a second class in literature and humanities in 1890.

Street produced six books during the 1890s, most of them collections of essays first published in periodicals, but after the turn of the century he slowed his pace, publishing one book every three or four years until 1920, when his last book appeared. As he explains in the essay "Censorship of Plays" (*Fortnightly Review,* September 1925), his slower pace after 1900 resulted from his growing interest in the theater. At the end of the 1890s he reviewed London play productions. In the early 1900s he wrote several plays that were produced but not published. In 1913 he was named an examiner of plays in the Lord Chamberlain's Department, succeeding Charles Brookfield, who died that year. When his coexaminer, Ernest Bendall, died in 1920, Street assumed the full responsibility of examining plays, reading about four hundred each year. His job was not to censor but to make recommendations about censorship to the lord chamberlain. In his essay on that topic Street defends the role of the censor, claiming that the office maintained an "enlightened balance," not only protecting the public from salacious work but also protecting playwrights, actors, and theater managers from unfair protest.

Street's last years were plagued with health problems, including the loss of vision in one eye. When Street died, Beerbohm wrote in the London *Times* obituary (2 November 1936) that "no account of George Street could be sufficient without some reference to the charm of his unusual personality, conversation, and wit: and that charm is indeed difficult to define. . . . He had an extraordinary power in talk of illuminating commonplace things of the day with his humour: and another quality that peeps out from his books was a capacity for laughing at himself, and his wit was never unkind." Another friend, R. Ellis Roberts, wrote in the *Saturday Review* (5 December 1936) that Street was "one of the kindliest and most modest of men." In 1924 he was awarded the M.V.O. (Member of the Victorian Order). He was a member of the Athenaeum Club, the United University Club, and the Savile Club, where he could be found nearly every day for forty years. He never married.

Despite Street's modesty, Beerbohm drew more than twenty-five caricatures of him, and in *A Christmas Garland* (1912) he parodies Street's style, along with the styles of such writers as Thomas Hardy, H. G. Wells, Bernard Shaw, Rudyard Kipling, Henry James, and Joseph Conrad. Beerbohm promoted Street's books, trying to persuade his friends to buy them, and his letters applaud Street's work and express hope for its success. In the early 1890s Beerbohm and Street met for the first time at Solferino's Restaurant on Rupert Street as part of Henley's literary group, which Beerbohm dubbed "the Henley Regatta." They became friends, but not until each had tried to outdandy the other with aloofness.

Street's association with Henley, which also began in the early 1890s, thrust him into a group of fin-de-siècle writers imbued with the spirit of all that was novel, outrageous, and modern. Henley's group, which debated literary matters regularly at Solferino's, included Kipling, George Steevens, Charles Whibley, George Wyndham, and W. B. Yeats. As editor of the *National Observer* (formerly the *Scots Observer*) from 1888 to 1894, Henley published the work of these writers, including stories, essays, and play reviews by Street. Once Henley became editor of the *New Review* in 1894, he attracted to his journal such writers as Conrad, James, Wells, Kenneth Grahame, Paul Valéry, Arthur Symons, and Stephen Crane.

Many of these writers were also major contributors to the *Yellow Book,* published by the Bodley Head, which was at the forefront of the Decadent movement, bringing out books by such writers as Street, Beerbohm, Grahame, Oscar Wilde, Lionel Johnson, and Alice Meynell. Street's essays, stories, and reviews were also published in *Blackwood's, North American Review, Cornhill* magazine, *Fortnightly Review, Putnam's Monthly, Quarterly Review, Nineteenth Century and After,* and *Pall Mall* magazine.

Street's first book, *Miniatures and Moods* (1893), is a compilation of essays first published in the *National Observer.* The ten "miniatures" and nine "moods" explore seventeenth-century figures such as the Comte Pilibert de Gramont, whose memoirs were written by his brother-in-law, Anthony Hamilton, and edited by Horace Walpole; George Villiers, second Duke of Buckingham, a minister to Charles II; and John Wilmot, second Earl of Rochester, a poet at the court of Charles II. Although most of the essays require a reader with more than superficial knowledge of the seventeenth century, several are more accessible ("The Portrait on the Stairs," "Insomnia," "Cruelty," and "The Curse of Cleverness"). "Etheridge" shows Street's early bent toward theater and his particular interest in William Congreve, whose works he edited in 1895.

One of these essays that is likely to appeal to modern readers is "The Atalantis," which discusses Mary Manley, the political novelist who wrote *The New Atalantis* (1701). Street identifies Manley as the second Englishwoman, after Aphra Behn, to earn a living as a writer competing with men. He is intrigued with the question of whether or not Manley reveals through her style that she is a woman, ultimately deciding that for the most part she writes like a man. Revealing the dominant attitude of his day toward women, Street laments that Manley is not "to know alive; for than a strong intellect in a woman's weak nature there is no more interesting thing under heaven."

The review of *Miniatures and Moods* in the London *Bookman* (September 1893) identified it as belonging to a new school of literature, which was "shared by a considerable number of young men and a few women, all ready to back each other up, and joyfully full of scorn of the rest of the world. The mark of the school is, let us say, a freedom from the opinions current outside its borders, and from the usual prejudices, and a conscious pride in this freedom, a revolt, of a decorous kind, from Puritanic traditions, and a distaste for the main tendencies of the present age." The review states that Street's theme is "whatever is elegant is right." Generally acknowledging the truth and beauty of the essays, it ends by suggesting that "all that is wanted to make Mr. Street and some of his elegant fellow writers really a wholesome power, is a little less elegant observation of life, which is, after all, more fatiguing to eyes and brain than a sturdy participation in some of life's struggles, campaigns, and compromises."

Street's skill as a satirist was widely applauded on publication of his second and most famous book, *The Autobiography of a Boy* (1894), which, like its predecessor, had been published in installments in the

Title page for Street's best-known book, about a dandy who is sent by his father to work in Canada

National Observer. Although only 450 copies of the first edition were printed, within three years the book had gone into its sixth edition. This novel is a collection of episodes chosen by the editor (Street) to represent the life of his friend "Tubby," an irrepressible dandy who is being sent to Canada by his well-to-do father to work in a bank and stop wasting his life. Street shows remarkable talent in making Tubby both compelling in his naiveté and amusing in his posing: he is both aware of manipulating those around him with his dramatic flair and wonderfully unaware of the true nature of the situations in which he finds himself or the ridiculousness of his behavior. Tubby was recognized at once as a parody of Wilde and an attack on the aesthete who devoted his energies to crafting witty barbs and worshiping at the shrine of art and truth.

The episodes that constitute the novel report the state of Tubby's love for Gwendolen, who is married; detail the growing unpleasantness with his father, who wants him to have a job; and chronicle Tubby's egotistical observations of various friends and acquaintances. In describing his relationship to "those frank young barbarians who were some of my comrades at school and at Oxford," Tubby remarks:

> In truth, I find it restful to listen to their simple, homely talk, even to share their kindly, honest pleasures. I like to see their fresh young faces sparkle with merriment, as I suit some piece of simple irony to their comprehension, to watch their pathetic (is it not?) appreciation of their little successes in love and sport. Yet often, as I sit listening to their prattle, I feel wistful, thinking of what I have lost to gain my difference from them, wistful and almost regretful; I feel old, so old, sad, and very weary.

In the same episode Tubby is visited by one of these "barbaric" friends just as "it struck me that my new rug matched ill with my smoking suit. The better to test it I had sat down on the floor." When the friend says he wants to take him racing, Tubby shows him "my Ballad of Shameful Kisses" so that "you may know what a gulf there is between us."

Tubby hates philanthropists and is interested in only the ritual of the church, from "a purely aesthetic point of view" ("I love to sit in some old cathedral and fancy myself a knight of the middle ages, ready to die – dear foolish fellow – for his simple faith"). He denigrates middle-class propriety and philistine values. As he faces expulsion to Canada, he concludes that "I have tried to compromise between the imperfect civilisation I found and my own nature, and the compromise has failed." He contemplates Canada as a place where "my nature will expand," even though "I have avoided, so far as I could, learning anything about it, that my impressions might be absolutely free." He surmises that "it is of no use to take my evening clothes to Canada."

The London *Bookman* (July 1894) remarked that "the pictures of him [the 'Cad Aesthetic'] are timely, happy, and humorously wise." The *Athenaeum* (15 September 1894) praised the book: "There is no disguising it that here is a new vein of wit and satire, of literary tact and dexterity. It is, indeed, a vein so original that to hit off its proper quality aright is impossible, and even an approximate description is not an easy matter." This reviewer imagines that Jonathan Swift would have been happy to sign his name to this satire, concluding that "there is more observation and art of presentment in this little book than in a wilderness of three-volume novels, even by eminent hands, and from Mr. Street we should have something big in fiction."

Street's next book, *Episodes* (1895), was not the "something big in fiction" predicted by the *Athe-*

naeum, but a subtle, restrained collection of sketches that realistically portrays thwarted passion, avaricious manipulation, and lost idealism. This volume was less well received than Street's first two books. The *Critic* (10 August 1895) observed that the book has "such an array of ugly and unlovable characters, that no *raison d'être* can be conceived for these sketches, except it be Mr. Street's anxiety to display his ingenuity in the line mentioned." The review accuses Street of treating serious situations with "mockery," and it dismisses *Episodes* as "the kind a dissipated club habitué might chuckle over a half hour or so, and then throw aside, with a little less faith in mankind than he possessed the hour before." The London *Bookman* (February 1895) was kinder, stating that the very "excellence of *The Autobiography of a Boy* . . . is the chief reason of our slight discontent with this volume of clever, keen-sighted, and various studies of modern life." The review remarks that Street's "coldness is in accord with the manner he has chosen; and he has done what he purposed to do very well. Only it is a thin-blooded kind of writing at the best."

The sketches in *Episodes* are peopled with actors, journalists, schoolboys, orphaned young women, clerks, dilettantes, and others, mostly of the middle class. These characters present a dark view of middle-class marriages. The stories derive their power from the irony inherent in their dramatic form: they are developed mostly by dialogue. In fact, one of the stories, "In a Man's Life," is written as a play whose dialogue alternates between *M* (man) and *W* (woman), who are ending a love affair because the man has found someone else "feminine and frivolous and that sort of thing." In another story, "The Episode of Johnson," Street writes about the thoughtless cruelty of the well-to-do Geraldine, whose cat-and-mouse game of love with Johnson, socially inferior to her but morally superior, drives him to suicide. In a cynical tone the narrator says that he considers her story an episode, "for though it was a climax to the other person concerned [Johnson], it was but an episode to her and she was by far the more important and useful member of society."

One of the strongest stories, "Peter Sanderson's Passion," continues the attack on the aesthetes. The first paragraph defines Sanderson, twenty-eight, as a dilettante:

That is to say, although he dressed well, had a charming flat in Park Place, and went occasionally to race meetings, he did not keep racers; although he haunted theatres and was seen at dress rehearsals, he did not finance an actress or write a play; although a critic of books and pictures, of wide and miscellaneous knowledge and happy phrases, he had never painted a picture or published a line. A century and a half ago he would have been called a wit.... His own opinion was that there were too many people doing things in the world, and that being a rich man he willed a not altogether useless place in the scheme of things as an intelligent idler.

Nevertheless, Sanderson becomes a brilliant chemist, jarred from his idle life by desire for a woman who ultimately marries someone else and dies an early death.

This collection of stories was followed by a collection of essays, *Quales Ego* (1896), which "represents Mr. Street not quite at his best," according to the London *Bookman* (April 1896). One of the most interesting of these essays is "Mr. Meredith in Little," a review of George Meredith's *The Tale of Chloe; The House on the Beach; The Case of General Ople and Lady Camper* (1894) that acknowledges Street's intellectual debt to Meredith. Street says he was first attracted to the author because Meredith was considered obscure:

It was his very obscurity – another name, so often, for a higher intelligence – that was the stimulating force in him for such as myself.... Mr. Meredith was sometimes an affectation in us, and sometimes the most powerful educator we had. In the passage of years, as we grew from conceit of intelligence into appreciation, in our degrees, of things artistic, we perceived that he was also a great artist, and sympathy was merged in admiration.

Street rates the title story highly, though he complains of the stories overall that the prose "does not satisfy my ideal" because its "ease and rhythm" are flawed.

Of the fifteen essays, two others, "An Appreciation of Ouida" and "In Arcady," have literary interest. The first is a spirited defense of the work of Marie Louise de la Ramée, whose pen name was Ouida. She wrote forty-five novels as well as critical and social commentary for periodicals. Street praises the "genuine and passionate love of beauty" and the "genuine and passionate hatred of injustice and oppression" in her work. In "In Arcady," Street reviews Grahame's *The Golden Age* (1895), calling it "an achievement of art of a rare quality."

Street's second novel, *The Wise and the Wayward,* was also published in 1896. The London *Bookman* (January 1897) was lukewarm, applauding the "naturalness of the man and the woman" whose marriage disintegrates and stating that Street "has handled it [the deteriorating marriage] with such composure, deliberation, and reserve as render it nearly impressive." A harsher review in the *Critic* (April 1898) describes the characters as "bloodless and singularly lacking in reality," and it complains:

> We are so often threatened with the direful consequences of a hand-pressure or a cousinly kiss upon the cheek, that we are almost tempted to wish for a consistently outrageous situation worked out to a crisis. But Mr. Street's risky situations dissolve untimely, serving only to heighten the sense of artificiality of the book. The manner of the present volume gives no evidence of the admirable humor which pervaded "The Autobiography of a Boy."

The truth lies somewhere between these two reviews. Although the marriage of George Ashton, a landed aristocrat, to Nelly Canover, daughter of a disreputable major, is doomed and the outcome predictable, the book is compelling nevertheless in its realistic presentation of the gossipy, backbiting, manipulative interference that besets the newlyweds from well-intentioned friends and relatives. Particularly well drawn are Jack and Mildred Ashton, George's cousins, whose greed for the family estate motivates their despicable behavior. Like *The Autobiography of a Boy,* this novel is developed by episodes, but unlike those in *The Autobiography,* which are the narrator's reflections, the episodes in *The Wise and the Wayward* are filled with dialogue and distinguished by the shift in point of view from episode to episode. The multiple points of view are skillfully used to advance the plot.

Some Notes of a Struggling Genius (1898) was published two years later, and another novel, *The Trials of the Bantocks,* appeared in 1900. Both show a revival of the humor that enlivens *The Autobiography of a Boy.* The London *Bookman* (September 1898) considered *Some Notes of a Struggling Genius* "nearly as amusing as his 'Boy,' whose bland autobiography opened our eyes very wide a few years ago." The review states, "The fooling is light and pleasant; and Mr. Street knows when to stop." The eleven brief reflections are the whimsical musings of a first-person narrator, who, Street writes in the preface, is a fictional character not to be confused with the author. The essays' titles clearly indicate the narrator's worries: "He Pawns a Watch," "His Annoying Reputation," "On the Folly of Being Poor," "On the Joys of Borrowing," "On Hard Work," and "On Writing an Article."

The Trials of the Bantocks also uses a first-person narrator. This brief novel is a collection of stories about the naive young narrator who – unbeknownst to him – is humiliated and abused by the great aristocratic family whom he serves as a clerk-errand-boy-companion. This book is at least as funny as *The Autobiography of a Boy,* partly because its scope is wider. Whereas *The Autobiography of a Boy* employs a first-person narrator to satirize the narrator's behavior as an aesthete, *The Trials of the Bantocks* uses the naive narrator to attack each of several institutions represented by various members of the Bantock family.

For example, he skewers the ignorant stubbornness of the upper class when Miss Clavering, hired as a governess for thirteen-year-old Ethel Bantock, is fired after four days because she dares to argue with Mrs. Bantock about literature. Mrs. Bantock says with authority that William Makepeace Thackeray is a cynic; the governess argues that he is a sentimentalist. Mrs. Bantock says that Dickens is vulgar; Miss Clavering argues that he is a realist. Mrs. Bantock expresses relief that Henrik Ibsen is gone from the London stage for the season; Miss Clavering defends him as a talented dramatist. In another episode Russell Bantock, twenty-six years old, impresses the narrator with his "selectiveness" in choosing the right friends while he impresses the reader as a thoroughgoing snob. His younger brother, Tom, is criticized by their mother for giving dinners "to people whom he professed to like, but who could be of no use to him socially." In other episodes Street criticizes the gluttony, hypocrisy, and social machinations of the rich. In one of the most amusing episodes, he has the sixteen-year-old daughter become a rabid socialist.

In 1902 *A Book of Essays, A Book of Stories,* and *The Views of an Angry Man* were published. Previously published in periodicals, *A Book of Essays* has three parts: "London," which gives a view of such places as the Strand, Piccadilly, Kensington, and Hammersmith, and some of their history; "Books and Men," which includes two essays defending George Gordon, Lord Byron's life and work as well as essays on such figures as Charles Fox, George Selwyn, and Anthony Trollope; and "Various," a miscellany that includes the most interesting essays in the book.

One essay from this section, "The Paradox of the Jew," expresses Street's ambivalent feelings about Jews. He cannot understand why so many English Jews hide their heritage and adopt English names and customs:

> Then why should any English Jew be ashamed of his birth? Professed and recognized Jews are to be found in both our Houses of Parliament, and ... in our Law Courts. Their native love of the theatre is invaluable to

our stage, in front of it and on it. They are not yet on the whole such good citizens as we hope they will be, since there is too much of them money-lending and financing, too little manufacturing, doctoring, soldiering, policing, but we understand the historical reason, and hope confidently for an improvement. But why should any of them wish to be – superficially even – merged in the English middle-classes?

Another interesting essay in this last section is "Twenty Years Since," in which Street prophesies the demise of individuality: "We cannot afford our cherished stupidity; we must seek for and use our brains. And in the future it is plain we shall have to act strongly and together, that our indifferentism and individualism must go by the board." He also attacks Matthew Arnold's attitudes about the philistines and his notion of educating them about culture:

If you wish to improve the manners of an ill-mannered man, and by way of doing so first call him opprobrious names and then draw his attention to your own superiority, he can make a tolerably obvious retort, and whether he makes it or not, he is hardly likely to be impressed, to tremble and turn and be changed. To express a plain disgust for the mass of your fellow-countrymen, and claim for an infinitesimal minority a monopoly of social merits, is not likely either to convert the former or to improve the latter. And, in fact, the effect has been nothing.

A Book of Stories contains seven stories ranging from eighteen to a hundred pages. Except for "Two Sorts of Life," all had been previously published in periodicals. This novella traces the fortunes of Hubert Dane, who has returned to London from India, where he has been awarded the Victoria Cross. The title not only applies to his two sorts of life – that of the soldier and that of the leisurely man-about-town – but also refers to the lifestyle of the flashy but disreputable group Dane falls in with in London as opposed to that of well-respected General Brook and his virtuous daughter, Alice, whom Dane loves. The plot involves the machinations of Mrs. Davis to make Dane a correspondent in a divorce case.

All the stories are amusing. "Saved" is a brief, humorous tale about a married woman who tries to ensnare her friend Percy Gunting into taking her away from her brutish husband, but she stands him up when her husband suddenly turns kind. "The Good Baronet" tells the story of Arthur Whittleworth, a baronet who has no money and no means of earning any, except by marriage. As a tutor he is manipulated by Mabel, the daughter of the house, into asking for her hand in marriage –

not because she loves him but because she is sure that in the face of this outlandish proposal her parents will let her marry the man she loves. Mabel is Jewish, and her family has assumed the name of Lessiter instead of Levi.

One of the two best stories in the collection is "The Hero and the Burglars," a brief, funny tale that turns on the irony of the narrator's misunderstanding of his hosts' reaction to a robbery. The strongest story, "Like to Like: A Trivial Romance," displays Street's sense of humor as well as his sense of tenderness. It also reflects his interest in the seventeenth century and his cynical view of vulgarity, especially that of the nouveau riche. The story concerns Herbert Mardon and Lady Betty Mereworth, childhood friends who are almost kept from the marriage they both want by Lady Betty's willingness to marry the vulgar Arthur Fairbrother, son of a wealthy manufacturer, in order to save her family from financial problems. Herbert, reared by the Mereworths after his parents' deaths, is the son of a socialist whom Arthur's father recalls as a man who "tried to set the working classes against their natural superiors – and their best friends. He had the impudence to put me in a pamphlet."

The Views of an Angry Man is a series of satiric essays by a misanthropic narrator who rages against a wide range of topics: clothes, food, editors, doctors, money, work, and even civilization itself. In "The Problem of the Rich" the narrator proposes a solution to the pretentiousness and idleness of this class:

My idea is to start a Government Department with a staff of social missionaries, who should be imposed on the plutocrats whether they like it or not . . . . The missionary, who would take the place of the existing parasite, and indeed be a kind of good, independent parasite, would instil honesty and modesty into the plutocrat, accompany the plutocrat's wife on her shopping, and teach her to be polite to the shop people, lead the conversation at meals to cultivated topics, and so on. There would be a periodical examination for the plutocrat and all his family, and fines from unsuccessful plutocrats would be handed over to successful missionaries. What good might not be done by a highly-educated, nicely-mannered, and kind but firm missionary!

The first production of Street's *Miss Bramshott's Engagement* took place in April 1902. The play was a warm-up for Frank Stayton's musical *The President.* The London *Times* (1 May 1902) wrote that Street was "well known to all people of taste as novelist and critic" and complimented him for handling a common plot "in a fresh and diverting way." The review expressed hope that the play's warm reception would "encourage Mr. Street to attempt a more serious contribution to the stage." *Miss Bramshott's Engagement* was revived in June 1905 at the Avenue Theatre, London.

Street's other plays did not live up to the expectation of the *Times* review. *Great Friends,* produced at the Court Theatre in January 1905, was not well received. The *Athenaeum* (4 February 1905) observed that "the interest it stirred in a friendly audience was the mildest conceivable." Street's third play, *The Anonymous Letter* (revised as *Enterprising Helen*), opened in June 1907 as a forepiece to F. C. Burnand's *Mrs. Ponderbury's Past.* The London *Times* (19 June 1907) noted that the play was "a delicate trifle written with Mr. G. S. Street's finest pen-nib, but not handled quite lightly enough by the players."

Street's most famous late work, *The Ghosts of Piccadilly* (1907), is another volume of previously published essays. The seventeen in this collection are charming, gossipy visits to places in Piccadilly. They give a sense of the place as it was in Street's day, but mostly they give a sense of the history of each stop, especially famous inhabitants of the houses and shops thereabouts. For example, in "The Ghosts of Albany" Street explains that the Albany is an amalgamation of three houses on the site. He then goes into famous people who have lived there, including Byron, Henry Luttrell, Edward Bulwer-Lytton, Thomas Babington Macaulay, and Matthew "Monk" Lewis, who aside from Byron is Street's favorite of the Albany's ghosts. Street's least favorite ghost is Macaulay, and his remarks about him give a sense of the flavor of the work: "I do not pretend to believe, personally, for a moment, that Macaulay's ghost wastes time in haunting any scene of his labour on earth. Wherever he is, I am sure he is talking hard, or writing earnestly, for the instruction of his companions, and has no leisure to muse on the accidents of his past." At the close of the essay Street ends his unfavorable treatment of Macaulay in the same vein:

> I notice with regret that I have not written of Macaulay so genially as I am wont to write. His personality does not attract me, I fear; and then he was a partisan in history, and in my own little reading I incline to be a partisan on the other side. Well, we all have our prejudices, and Macaulay's memory can afford mine. Besides, as I said, I am in no fear of meeting his ghost.

Other essays discuss Burlington House; Cambridge House; Charles Douglas, third Duke of Queensberry; Emma Hamilton; and Harriot Mellon.

Of Street's final four books, three are collections of essays, and his last book, *The London Assurance, 1720–1920* (1920), which was privately printed, is a lively history of the insurance company in the title. *People and Questions* (1910), *On Money and Other Essays* (1914), and *At Home in the War* (1918) offer Street's views on a wide range of topics. The review of *On Money and Other Essays* in the London *Bookman* (May 1914) summarized well the attraction of Street's essays:

> Blessed with a happy indolency that has prevented him from using his ideas and observations as fast as he has gathered them, Mr. Street has now a rich background of thought and reflection that gives a fine suggestiveness to all his remarks on life. He writes from the fulness of experience, in the manner of the great essayists, and his early vein of satirical observation is lost in a wistful sort of kindly interest in all the pleasant aspects of human activities.

The "pleasant aspects of human activities," however, do not extend to Street's thoughts about World War I and its effects on youth, on literature and the theater, and on science. The essay "War and Science" is particularly interesting in light of his predictions about the uses of technology in battle.

Street's large body of work is worth reclamation from obscurity. His skillful, witty, urbane short stories and novels suggest the world of Edith Wharton and Henry James, to whom Beerbohm compared Street. Street's essays reveal both his virtuosity and wisdom, and they provide valuable insights into an age that was a bridge from the Victorians to the twentieth century.

References:

Max Beerbohm, "Mr. George Street," London *Times,* 2 November 1936;

Stuart P. B. Mais, "G. S. Street," in his *Some Modern Authors* (Freeport, N.Y.: Books for Libraries Press, 1970), pp. 345–355;

R. Ellis Roberts, "A London Letter," *Saturday Review,* 15 (5 December 1936): 50.

Papers:

A file of Street's contracts with the Bodley Head and twenty-nine of his letters are in the archives of the Bodley Head at the University of Reading Library.

Netta Syrett
(17 March 1865 – 15 December 1943)

Bonnie J. Robinson
University of Miami

BOOKS: *Nobody's Fault* (London: John Lane, 1896;
    Boston: Roberts, 1896);
The Tree of Life (London & New York: John Lane,
    1897);
The Garden of Delight: Fairy Tales (London: Hurst &
    Blackett, 1898);
Rosanne (London: Hurst & Blackett, 1902);
The Magic City and Other Fairy Tales (London: Law-
    rence & Bullen, 1903);
Six Fairy Plays for Children (London & New York:
    John Lane, 1904);
The Day's Journey (London: Chapman & Hall, 1905;
    Chicago: McClurg, 1906);
Women and Circumstance (London: Chapman & Hall,
    1906);
The Child of Promise (London: Chapman & Hall,
    1907);
Anne Page (London: Chatto & Windus, 1908; New
    York: John Lane, 1909);
A Castle of Dreams (London: Chatto & Windus, 1909;
    Chicago: McClurg, 1909);
The Castle of Four Towers (London: Duckworth,
    1909);
The Vanishing Princess (London: Nutt, 1910);
The Story of Saint Catherine of Siena (London:
    Mowbray, 1910);
Olivia L. Carew (London: Chatto & Windus, 1910);
The Old Miracle Plays of England (London: Mowbray,
    1911; Milwaukee: Young Churchman Co.,
    1911);
Drender's Daughter (New York: John Lane, 1911;
    London: Chatto & Windus, 1911);
The Endless Journey and Other Stories (London: Chatto
    & Windus, 1912);
Three Women (London: Chatto & Windus, 1912);
Stories from Medieval Romance (Oxford: Clarendon,
    1913);
Barbara of the Thorn (London: Chatto & Windus,
    1913);
The Jam Queen (London: Methuen, 1914);

Miss Netta Syrett

London Magazine, October 1906

The Victorians (London: Unwin, 1915); republished
    as *Rose Cottingham* (Chicago: Academy Press,
    1978);
Rose Cottingham Married (London: Unwin, 1916);
Troublers of the Peace (London: Chatto & Windus,
    1917);
Godmother's Garden (London: Blackie, 1918);
Robin Goodfellow and Other Fairy Plays for Children
    (London & New York: John Lane, 1918);
The Wife of a Hero (London: Skeffington, 1918);

The God of Chance (London: Skeffington, 1920);

One of Three (London: Hurst & Blackett, 1921);

Toby and the Odd Beasts (London: Royal Road Library, 1921; New York: Stokes, 1922);

Rachel and the Seven Wonders (London: Royal Road Library, 1921; New York: Stokes, 1922);

Two Domestics: A Play for Women in One Act (London & New York: French, 1922);

Magic London (London: Butterworth, 1922);

The Fairy Doll and Other Plays for Children (New York: Dodd, Mead, 1922; London: John Lane, 1922);

Tinkelly Winkle (London: John Lane, 1923);

The Path to the Sun (London: Hutchinson, 1923);

Lady Jem (London: Hutchinson, 1923); republished as *Cupid and Mr. Pepys: A Romance of the Days of the Great Diarist* (New York: Stokes, 1923);

Two Elizabeths (London: Stage Play Publishing Bureau, 1924);

The House in Garden Square (London: Hutchinson, 1924);

As the Stars Come Out (London: Hutchinson, 1925);

The Mystery of Jenifer (London: Hutchinson, 1926);

Julian Carroll (London: Hutchinson, 1928);

The Shuttles of Eternity (London: Bles, 1928);

Portrait of a Rebel (London: Bles, 1929; New York: Dodd, Mead, 1930);

Strange Marriage (London: Bles, 1930; New York: Dodd, Mead, 1931);

Sketches of European History (London: Murray, 1931);

The Manor House (London: Bles, 1932); republished as *Moon out of the Sky* (New York: Dodd, Mead, 1932);

Who Was Florriemay? (London: Benn, 1932);

Aunt Elizabeth (London: Bles, 1933);

The House That Was (London: Rich & Cowan, 1933);

Girls of the Sixth Form (London: Mellifont Press, 1934);

Judgment Withheld (London: Bles, 1934);

Linda (London: Bles, 1935);

Angel Unawares (London: Bles, 1936);

The Farm on the Downs (London: Bles, 1936);

Fulfilment (London: Bles, 1938);

As Dreams Are Made On (London: Bles, 1939);

The Sheltering Tree (London: Bles, 1939);

Gemini (London: Bles, 1940).

PLAY PRODUCTION: *The Finding of Nancy,* London, Saint James's Theatre, 8 May 1902.

OTHER: "A School Year," in *The Little Blue Books for Children,* edited by E. V. Lucas (London: Methuen, 1902);

The Dream Garden, edited by Syrett (London: Bailie, 1905).

SELECTED PERIODICAL PUBLICATIONS – UNCOLLECTED:

DRAMA

"The Song That No One Knows," *Acorn,* no. 2 (1906): 235–258.

FICTION

"That Dance at the Robson's," *Longman's,* 15 (April 1890): 630–649;

"Sylvia," *Macmillan's,* 64 (June 1891): 134–146;

"A Birthday," *Longman's,* 19 (1892): 512–527;

"Thy Heart's Desire," *Yellow Book,* 2 (July 1894): 228–255;

"A Correspondence," *Yellow Book,* 7 (October 1895): 150–173;

"Fairy-Gold," *Temple Bar,* 109 (October 1896): 218–241;

"Her Wedding Day," *Quarto,* 1 (1896): 67–84;

"Far Above Rubies," *Yellow Book,* 12 (January 1897): 250–272;

"Chiffon," *Pall Mall,* 22 (1900): 70–76;

"A Revelation in Arcadia," *Harper's Monthly,* 105 (August 1902): 327–334;

"An Idealist," *Harper's Monthly,* 106 (May 1903): 923–928;

"Poor Little Mrs. Villiers," *Venture,* 1 (1903): 53–73;

"A Common Occurrence," *Harper's Monthly,* 108 (February 1904): 345–357;

"The Disenchanted Squirrel: A Strictly Grown-Up Story," *Longman's,* 43 (1904): 82–88;

"The Last Journey," *Venture,* 2 (1905): 42–52;

"Madame de Meline," *Acorn,* 1 (October 1905): 91–111;

"The Fascination of the Dolls' House," *Temple Bar,* 133 (February 1906): 109–116.

NONFICTION

"On the Right Choice of Books for Children," *Academy* (5 December 1903): 641.

Netta Syrett – author of thirty-eight novels, twenty-seven short stories, four plays, and twenty children's books – received contemporary accolades from such notable figures as Henry Harland, John Lane, Max Beerbohm, and W. Somerset Maugham. Her novel *Portrait of a Rebel* (1929) became the 1936 movie *A Woman Rebels* starring Katharine Hepburn. *The Victorians* (1915) was republished as *Rose Cottingham* by the Chicago Academy Press in 1978. Many of her novels, such as *Three Women* (1912) and *Rose Cottingham Married* (1916), are gaining attention as New Woman efforts.

Current critical notice of Syrett, however, mainly clusters around her participation in the 1890s *Yellow Book* milieu, which she recorded in her autobiography, *The Sheltering Tree* (1939), and the novel *Strange Marriage* (1930). In the *Yellow Book* section of *British Short Fiction in the Nineteenth Century* (1979), Wendell V. Harris commends Syrett as a realist writer of the 1890s whose short stories are "worth preserving." A. Brisau places Syrett with the *Yellow Book* contributors whose work is "characterized by objectivity, a tendency towards psychological analysis, and a vivid, sometimes acid style." In the introduction to his 1974 anthology of the *Yellow Book*, Fraser Harrison states that Syrett was one of that publication's female contributors who "led vigorous, passionate lives, wrote prolifically and successfully and survived to ripe old age." Katherine Lyon Mix, whose *A Study in Yellow: The Yellow Book and Its Contributors* (1960) recounts the social and literary circles surrounding the *Yellow Book,* describes Syrett as a successful, realist writer whose novels draw on her early experiences.

Both Mix and Karl Beckson use Syrett's autobiography for information about such *Yellow Book* figures as Henry and Aline Harland, Aubrey and Mabel Beardsley, Beerbohm, and Oscar Wilde. One of the most frequently cited reminiscences from this memoir concerns the publication's inception:

> I happened to be at the Harlands when the idea of the *Yellow Book* was first suggested, I think by Henry Harland himself, as we sat round the fire in the drawing-room of the Cromwell House. I remember Harland's excited talk about starting a magazine that should represent the "new movement." "Aubrey" was to be art editor. "Johnny Lane" was to be roped in and persuaded to publish it from the Bodley Head.

In 1897 Arthur Waugh placed Syrett in the *Yellow Book* milieu: "Miss Syrett, who is very young, is practically a product of *The Yellow Book*." He commended her "merry laugh, contempt for Ibsen, and busy bicycle. She can talk of an infinity of subjects, and gathers the materials for her fiction largely from the observation which accompanies her own conversation."

Syrett's contempt for Henrik Ibsen seems not to have prevented her from taking up such New Woman traits as riding her bicycle; earning her own living (first as a teacher, then as a writer); repudiating marriage as a woman's only career; maintaining her own apartment (in such places as Saint John's Wood, Battersea, and Chelsea); traveling in Italy, France, and Switzerland; and remaining independent throughout her life. She thus proves that the Victorian woman's life was far less restricted or tyrannically oppressed than is commonly believed. As she points out in the introduction to her autobiography, by the 1890s the woman's movement was in full swing, its participants asserting their "right to independence if they could prove themselves capable of earning their own living."

This last caveat exemplifies both Syrett's common sense and her realism. No iconoclast, no "housebreaker" (as she calls Bernard Shaw), Syrett readily remained within fields, such as governessing and teaching, then available to women. Yet she moved beyond the common ground by unflinchingly facing the realities of a woman's life in the late-Victorian and early-Modern era. As Jill T. Owens notes in a 1988 bibliography, these realities included the labor movement, socialism, educational reform, aestheticism, psychic phenomena, and psychoanalysis as well as the Woman Question. Indeed, the sheer bulk of her work attests to Syrett's large grasp of issues: she grapples with Renaissance and medieval history, fairy tales, and the occult as well as with woman's issues.

But Syrett's work is best characterized by its realism, which counters stereotypical or sentimental views and social prejudices concerning the Victorian woman in particular. Syrett thus participated in the New Realism of the 1890s, the critical phase to which the body of her short fiction belongs. Syrett was exposed early to this phase through the work and conversation of her relative Grant Allen, the immensely popular author of *The Woman Who Did* (1891), which was branded as "sexually-degenerate." Through Allen's literary connections Syrett met such important writers as George Meredith and Algernon Charles Swinburne and received help in placing an early short story, "That Dance at the Robson's," with *Longman's* magazine (April 1890).

Like Allen's, Syrett's immediate family seems to have been singularly free from prejudice, limitations, and intolerance (qualities against which the New Realism pitted itself). This liberal-mindedness appears in the education she received. In 1877, at the age of eleven, Janet Syrett, daughter of silk mercer Ernest Syrett, left what she described as a financially privileged home in Landsgate, Kent — where she and her four sisters and one brother were educated by an advanced mother and a German governess — to attend England's first high school for girls, the famous London North Collegiate. She stayed there for four years, then went on to the Cambridge Higher Local, where she prepared for a teaching career by cramming into one year the three years' course work necessary for a full teaching certificate.

After finishing her training, Syrett took a post at the London Polytechnic School for Girls. There she met fellow teacher Mabel Beardsley, sister of the artist Aubrey Beardsley, who introduced her to the "Beardsley set," which included such writers as Beerbohm, Robert Ross, and Kenneth Grahame. On the strength of Syrett's few published stories, Mabel Beardsley introduced her to another member of this set, Henry Harland, as a "brilliant young writer." Harland then included Syrett in his circle of friends and helped her to his publishing connections with the Bodley Head. He eventually published three of her short stories in the *Yellow Book*. Her first novel, *Nobody's Fault* (1896), became part of the Bodley Head's prestigious Keynote series.

For a time Syrett's writing and teaching careers coincided. Yet in 1902 she was forced to relinquish a lucrative teaching post when her play *The Finding of Nancy* (1902) received unpleasant notoriety. This drama, which won the Playgoers' competition for new dramatists, was produced at the St. James's Theatre with Beerbohm Tree and George Alexander in the cast. It concerns a young woman who "lives in sin" with a man who loves her, but is not free to marry. Clement Scott, writing for the *Daily Telegraph* (9 May 1902), damaged Syrett's reputation by insinuating that the play was thinly disguised autobiography, costing Syrett her teaching post.

Except for children's plays, *The Finding of Nancy* was Syrett's only produced drama. In pursuing her writing career she turned from drama to fiction not out of fear for her reputation but for practical reasons: she was unable, as she put it, to "indulge in the gamble of play-writing" after the death of her father, which resulted in the loss of the comfortable financial background she had previously known. By 1902 novel writing had become for her "a sure thing." And so, maintaining a regular schedule of writing every morning, Syrett produced approximately one novel a year for her gradually acquired but "very faithful" public until, by the year 1939, she reached that "dull eminence known as the 'established.' " She maintained this "eminence" until her death in a London nursing home on 15 December 1943.

Despite her renown Syrett made only modest claims for her writing, declaring that "circumstances have forced me to write too much . . . though I have always wished to write as well as I could." In writing as well as she could, Syrett espoused the neutrality of the artistic mind that im-

partially explores "forbidden" and "vicious" aspects of life in order to portray it with psychological validity and breadth of vision. Her short fiction in particular investigates the true, rather than socially sanctioned, nature of women. Countering the Victorian view of the ideal woman – the "angel in the house" – Syrett thus presents positive views of adulterous women, "fallen" women who bear illegitimate children, and women who choose personal fulfillment through careers in the public sphere rather than in the private sphere of the home. All of these views appear in such novels as *Nobody's Fault*, *Strange Marriage*, and *Three Women* (1912).

In her first *Yellow Book* story (July 1894), for example, Syrett sympathetically depicts a woman who is adulterous-minded because she is unhappily married. The reader of "Thy Heart's Desire" learns that Kathleen Drayton has married her dull, oafish husband for the same reasons that thousands of "ignorant girls" marry: "My home wasn't a happy one, I was miserable, and oh, – restless." In the barren, desolate Indian landscape where she and her husband lead lonely lives, Kathleen learns the painful truth that women should never marry without love because "I have come to know that there are things one owes to oneself. Self-respect is one of them." Such loveless marriages as hers destroy both partners: Mr. Drayton deliberately takes insufficient precautions against the heat when he realizes that his wife loves another man. Upon her husband's death from exposure, however, Kathleen does not marry the other man, Broomhurst. Instead, her sense of guilt causes her, and the reader, to question the viability of marriage for women.

Several of Syrett's stories deal with the similar theme of women who marry unhappily in order to escape censure, penury, and loneliness. In "A Correspondence," her second story to appear in the *Yellow Book* (October 1895), Syrett presents the plight of Cecily Armstrong, a beautiful but unintelligent girl who asks a modern Cyrano de Bergerac, her governess Gretchen Verrol, to help her keep the love of her erudite, worldly fiancé, Margrave. Gretchen assists Cecily by wittily corresponding with Margrave under Cecily's name because she knows that Cecily's beauty will make her mental deficiencies "of no consequence." When Cecily realizes the shame and wretchedness she would endure in such an unsuitable marriage, she breaks the engagement by revealing Gretchen as the letters' author. However, Cecily's mother forces her to marry the rich Margrave, who wants her anyway because he looks upon her merely as an objet d'art. Cecily continues to hide her real self

ANNE STOOD AT THE FURTHER END IN FRONT OF THE SHELF, FILLING BOXES WITH FLOWERS

Illustration for "A Revelation in Arcadia" (Harper's Monthly Magazine, August 1902)

in the marriage, the false basis of which appears in the constant presence of Gretchen, with whom Margrave maintains "friendly" relations.

A later story, "One Solution" (*The Endless Journey and Other Stories,* 1912), depicts the poverty-stricken life of an artist, Jean, who early in life rejects marriage with Stephen Knowles in order to pursue her career. Though respected and admired as an artist, Jean receives so few material rewards from her painting that by late middle age she faces the possibility of starving to death in her bare studio in Paris's Latin Quarter. When a neighbor is found dead in a studio where "there was no fire, and no food in the place," Jean accepts Knowles's renewed marriage proposal in order to escape a similar fate. She is thus forced to accept the conventional view of marriage as a woman's only suitable career.

Men also suffer from such superficial, materialistic marriages in Syrett's fiction. In "Far Above Rubies," her third story to appear in the *Yellow Book* (January 1897), Syrett presents Mrs. Gilman, a woman who remains in an unhappy marriage in order to enjoy its "material advantages." She reveals herself as little better than a prostitute when she attempts, out of boredom, to seduce her young physician, Dr. Strong. Though enthralled by her sexual allure, Dr. Strong rejects her. She reacts to

this by falsely accusing him of attacking her; consequently, he loses his reputation, his practice, his fiancée, and even his father, who dies of a heart attack on learning of his son's "disgrace."

Other stories dismantle conventions and sentiments that foster false relations between the sexes. "Her Wedding Day" (*Quarto,* 1896) reveals how marriage with Jack cannot "consummate" and perfect young Effie's life. Instead of offering her a romantic love that exists beyond death, Jack offers the transient, superficial love of an "average" man, from whom "you cannot expect too much." He forsakes Effie for Lizzie Randall when Effie becomes too weak from consumption to accompany him to parks and church, to flirt with him, and to wear pretty hats. This betrayal causes Effie's early death, which might have been postponed had she possessed a more realistic view of men and marriage. "Chiffon" (*Pall Mall,* 1900) rejects the very idea of an ideal man when its heroine, Roseanne, describes her ideal husband as attractive, well-dressed, silly, and clever. She marries Mr. Arnstruther, a gentleman who not only embodies this "ideal" but also proves to be its prototype. A later story, "Poor Little Mrs. Villiers" (*Venture,* 1903), explodes the ideal of the pure Victorian woman — a fresh, innocent, childlike beauty — when the title character deliberately uses these traits to trap a rich husband.

The hero of "A Revelation in Arcadia" (*Harper's Monthly,* August 1902) relinquishes his illusions concerning the pure woman when he falls in love with Anne. Though intellectually avid and strong-minded, Anne has led a secluded, restricted life on her father's vineyard. Her life contrasts completely with that of the tourist Knowles: "Tomorrow, if he so wished, he could go down into the world, take his part in the strenuous life of men, spend his energy in a thousand directions." Because she is a woman, Anne has none of these opportunities. When Knowles offers her the conventional means for a woman's escape by asking her to marry him, he learns that she has had an affair with the vineyard's only previous visitor, a poet Knowles earlier describes as "the sort of man women would do well to avoid." Knowles virtuously rejects Anne – only to reach a more realistic understanding of her character when he acknowledges the lack of restraint in his own life, and then when he puts himself in her place. He comes to appreciate how a woman with no outlet for her talents and abilities could have been seduced by a man of the world, justifying her decision as "the lesser evil in the last resort."

Many of Syrett's stories have narrators who, like Knowles, reach a more realistic understanding of so-called impure women by relinquishing their own hypocrisy. In "Madame de Meline" (*Acorn,* October 1905), Mrs. Sylvester learns to see the human being beneath the stereotype of the "loose" woman when she befriends the title character, who is mourning the recent death of her little girl. Mrs. Sylvester continues to sympathize with this woman, even when she learns her identity as the prostitute Clothilde de Saffrey, mother of an illegitimate child, and even when this "fallen" woman is hounded out of their "decent" hotel. For this sympathy Madame de Meline thanks Mrs. Sylvester "*de tout mon cœur*" (with all my heart).

Mrs. Sylvester thus laughs at the ironic behavior of her charge, a puritanical vicar's daughter who feels defiled by her unconscious contact with Madame de Meline, but who deliberately accepts a proposal of marriage from Mr. Wotton, a man she does not love who is more than twice her age, "for the sake of his balance at the bank." The irony is further developed when Mrs. Sylvester learns that Mr. Wotton, who has enjoyed commerce with Madame de Meline, is especially vociferous in hounding the woman from their hotel. A later story, "Miss Cordelia" (*The Endless Journey and Other Stories*), takes the point of view of Tony Devereaux, who learns on the death of Miss Cordelia that she was not his guardian, as he had always thought, but his

unwed mother. The small village in which they lived quickly forgets Miss Cordelia's piety, charity, and kindness in shock and condemnation at her "sinfulness." But Tony rejoices to learn that the "best and wisest" woman he has ever known was "the mother that bore him."

Syrett also realistically investigates the conflicts and troubles of women who, though unmarried, support themselves "respectably." In "A Common Occurrence" (*Harper's Monthly,* February 1904), Avice metes out her fifty-pound-a-year salary from typewriting to satisfy both her bodily and spiritual appetites: she buys tea and toast for her body and a beautifully furnished apartment, filled with Italian-art prints and joined to a lovely garden, for her artistic soul. Despite these "comforts," Avice longs for all the "normal experiences of womanhood – love, home, children." Her loneliness makes her willing to marry any man, even fatuous Col. Ridley, who believes women should concern themselves not with such serious matters as politics but with such suitable matters (that is, matters suitable to their capacities) as a husband's conversation and preparing perfect dinners. Avice is dissuaded from accepting Col. Ridley's marriage proposal by the urgings of Mr. Wetherby, an artist whom she loves, himself unhappily married to a wealthy woman. He advises Avice to avoid his mistake of confusing material with spiritual happiness: "Life has infinite possibilities for misery. At least now you are free to think your own thoughts, to love what seems to you beautiful, to struggle after its happy expression." The story ends with Avice accepting a journalistic post at the *Comet.*

"An Idealist" (*Harper's Monthly,* May 1903) exposes the "barren" life of Margaret Ferris, a lecturer who fires her students with a love for literature and inspires them to seek beauty in their lives. When Nancy Felton takes Margaret's teaching to heart and follows the literary examples of Aucassin and Nicollette, Tristram and Isolde, and Romeo and Juliet by finding happiness in love and romance, she thanks Margaret for her guidance and then inquires about her past lovers. Margaret confesses to having never even been kissed by a man. Her position as a lecturer, which just meets her economic needs, has forced her into the narrowest of lives: "I have never had any opportunity of meeting men. I know all about love, and no man has ever so much as looked at me." Even within the labor force, women have limited lives. The narrator points out that "there must be something very wrong" with a society that leads women to expect fulfillment only in romance and marriage and that therefore offers no reward to women whose need to earn their own living frustrates their fulfillment: "Many modern women in a complex, unrestful age, [are driven by fate] in ever-increasing numbers into the backwaters of life."

In "The Passing of a Hero" (*The Endless Journey and Other Stories*), Miss Blantyre escapes these backwaters when an eccentric relative on her deathbed makes over "all her worldly goods to 'Elizabeth Blantyre, the only one of my great-nieces who has had the sense to remain unmarried.'" A lack of opportunities in her life as a governess, not good sense, has prevented Elizabeth from marrying. With her inheritance, however, she escapes drudgery and seeks a fulfillment that seems achieved when she meets Captain Forrest, a simple, homely, and nice man who proposes marriage. He thus offers her the "normal experiences of womanhood." However, the narrator realistically suggests that these "experiences" may be crippling illusions fostered by a fraudulent society that systematically denies women equal opportunities. The story ends with the revelation, on Captain Forrest's unexpected death, that he was a confidence man who seduced women for their money. Through exposing hypocrisies, inequalities, prejudices, and lies, Syrett's realistic writing illuminates not only the true life of her age but also the true nature of women stifled and repressed by the conventions and expectations of this age.

Bibliography:

Jill T. Owens, "Netta Syrett: A Chronological, Annotated Bibliography of Her Works, 1890–1940," *Bulletin of Bibliography,* 45 (March 1988): 8–14.

References:

Ann Ardis, *New Women, New Novels: Feminism and Early Modernism* (New Brunswick, N. J.: Rutgers University Press, 1990);

Karl Beckson, *Henry Harland: His Life and Work* (London: Eighteen-Nineties Society, 1978);

A. Brisau, "*The Yellow Book* and Its Place in the Eighteen-Nineties," *Studia Germanica Gandensia,* 8 (1966): 140–162;

Wendell V. Harris, *British Short Fiction in the Nineteenth Century* (Detroit: Wayne State University Press, 1979);

Fraser Harrison, *The Yellow Book; An Illustrated Quarterly: An Anthology* (New York: St. Martin's Press, 1974);

Katherine Lyon Mix, *A Study in Yellow: The Yellow Book and Its Contributors* (Lawrence: University of Kansas Press, 1960);

Arthur Waugh, "London Letter," *Critic,* 30 (2 January 1897): 11;

Harold Williams, *Modern English Writers: Being a Study of Imaginative Literature, 1890–1914* (London: Sidgwick & Jackson, 1918).

Papers:

Syrett's papers are at the Bodleian Library, Oxford; the Merton College Library, Oxford; and the National Library of Scotland, Edinburgh.

Israel Zangwill

(21 January 1864 – 1 August 1926)

Meri-Jane Rochelson
Florida International University

See also the Zangwill entry in *DLB 10: Modern British Dramatists, 1900–1945.*

BOOKS: *Motza Kleis,* anonymous, by Zangwill and a Jews' Free School colleague (London: Privately printed, 1882);

The Premier and the Painter, by Zangwill and Louis Cowen, as J. Freeman Bell (London: Blackett, 1888; Chicago & New York: Rand McNally, 1896);

"A Doll's House" Repaired, by Zangwill and Eleanor Marx Aveling (London: Privately printed, 1891);

The Bachelors' Club (London: Henry, 1891; New York: Brentano's, 1891);

The Big Bow Mystery (London: Henry, 1892; Chicago & New York: Rand McNally, 1895);

The Old Maids' Club (London: Heinemann, 1892; New York: Tait, 1892);

Children of the Ghetto (3 volumes, London: Heinemann, 1892; 2 volumes, Philadelphia: Jewish Publication Society of America, 1892);

Ghetto Tragedies (London: McClure/Simpkin, Marshall, 1893);

The Great Demonstration, by Zangwill and Cowen (London: Capper & Newton, 1893);

Merely Mary Ann (London, Paris & New York: Tuck, 1893);

The King of Schnorrers: Grotesques and Fantasies (London: Heinemann, 1894; New York & London: Macmillan, 1894);

Joseph the Dreamer: A Tale (London: Heinemann, 1895);

The Master (London: Heinemann, 1895; New York: Harper, 1895);

Without Prejudice (London: Unwin, 1896; New York: Century, 1896);

The Celibates' Club, Being the United Stories of The Bachelors' Club and The Old Maids' Club (London: Heinemann, 1898; New York & London: Macmillan, 1905);

Dreamers of the Ghetto (London: Heinemann, 1898; New York & London: Harper, 1898);

The People's Saviour (New York & London: Harper, 1898);

"They That Walk in Darkness": Ghetto Tragedies (London: Heinemann, 1899; New York & London: Macmillan, 1899);

The Mantle of Elijah: A Novel (New York & London: Harper, 1900; London: Heinemann, 1900);

Blind Children (London: Heinemann, 1903; New York: Funk & Wagnalls, 1903);

The Grey Wig: Stories and Novelettes (London: Heinemann, 1903; New York & London: Macmillan, 1903);

Merely Mary Ann [play] (New York & London: Macmillan, 1904; London: Heinemann, 1904);

The Serio-Comic Governess [play] (New York & London: Macmillan, 1904; London: Heinemann, 1904);

Ghetto Comedies (London: Heinemann, 1907; New York: Macmillan, 1907);

The Melting Pot: Drama in Four Acts (New York: Macmillan, 1909; revised, 1914; London: Heinemann, 1914);

Italian Fantasies (London: Heinemann, 1910; New York: Macmillan, 1910);

The War God, A Tragedy in Five Acts (London: Heinemann, 1911);

The Next Religion, A Play in Three Acts (London: Heinemann, 1912; New York: Macmillan, 1912);

Plaster Saints: A High Comedy in Three Movements (London: Heinemann, 1914; New York: Macmillan, 1915);

The War for the World (London: Heinemann, 1916; New York: Macmillan, 1916);

Chosen Peoples: The Hebraic Ideal "Versus" the Teutonic (London: Allen & Unwin, 1918; New York: Macmillan, 1919);

Jinny the Carrier (London: Heinemann, 1919; New York: Macmillan, 1919);

The Voice of Jerusalem (London: Heinemann, 1920; New York: Macmillan, 1921);

The Cockpit, Romantic Drama in Three Acts (London: Heinemann, 1921; New York: Macmillan, 1921);

The Forcing House, or The Cockpit Continued: Tragicomedy in Four Acts (London: Heinemann, 1922; New York: Macmillan, 1923);

Watchman, What of the Night? (New York: American Jewish Congress, 1923);

Too Much Money, A Farcical Comedy in Three Acts (London: Heinemann, 1924; New York: Macmillan, 1925);

We Moderns, A Post-War Comedy in Three Movements (London: Heinemann, 1925; New York: Macmillan, 1926).

Collection: *Speeches, Articles and Letters of Israel Zangwill,* edited by Maurice Simon (London: Soncino Press, 1937).

OTHER: "My First Book," in *My First Book,* edited by Jerome K. Jerome (London: Chatto & Windus, 1897);

Mary Antin, *From Plotzk to Boston,* foreword by Zangwill (Boston: Clarke, 1899).

TRANSLATIONS: *The Service of the Synagogue,* 3 volumes, translated by Zangwill, Nina Salaman, and Elsie Davis (New York: Hebrew Publishing Co., 1917);

Selected Religious Poems of Solomon Ibn Gabirol, translated into English verse by Zangwill from a critical text edited by Israel Davidson (Philadelphia: Jewish Publication Society of America, 1923).

SELECTED PERIODICAL PUBLICATIONS – UNCOLLECTED:
FICTION
"Professor Grimmer," *Society,* 5 (November 1881): 133–135;

"Under Sentence of Marriage," as J. Freeman Bell, *Myer's Calendar & Diary* (1888–1889): 54–79.
NONFICTION
"English Judaism: A Criticism and a Classification," *Jewish Quarterly Review,* 1 (April 1889): 376–407;

"Growth of Respectability," *Jewish Chronicle,* Special Jubilee Number, 13 November 1891, pp. 19–20;

"That Telephone," as Z., *To-Day,* 1 (23 December 1893): 13;

"The Tree of Knowledge" [symposium to which Zangwill contributed], *New Review,* 10 (1894): 675–690;

"The Drama as a Fine Art," *Werner's Magazine* (November 1898): 159–166;

"Fiction as the Highest Form of Truth," *Bookman* (New York), 9 (April 1899): 100–101;

"Zionism and Territorialism," *Fortnightly Review,* 87 (1 April 1910): 645–655; *Living Age,* 265 (11 June 1910): 663–671.

To characterize Israel Zangwill as an outstanding and prolific writer of short fiction at the end of the nineteenth century is to be accurate but incomplete. Zangwill gained his greatest literary reputation with such novels as *Children of the Ghetto* (1892) and *The Master* (1895); his play *The Melting Pot* (1909; performed, 1908) established a new phrase in American cultural discourse, while another, *Merely Mary Ann* (1904), brought him his greatest financial success. Early in the twentieth century Zangwill became active in the Zionist movement and was the leading spokesman for English Jewry on the international scene. He was also an active literary and political journalist and, after the turn of the century, a vocal supporter of pacifism and women's rights. Still, the short fiction that Zangwill published in all phases of his career – from the satiric humor of *The Bachelors' Club* (1891) to the bitter reflectiveness of *Dreamers of the Ghetto* (1898) to the sentimental artistry of *The Grey Wig* (1903) – contains his best and most widely remembered work and reflects the preoccupations of the man and his times.

Zangwill was born in London to Jewish immigrants from Latvia and Poland, Moses and Ellen Marks Zangwill. He was the second of five children and the eldest son; his younger brothers Louis ("Z. Z.") and Mark became, respectively, a novelist and an artist, but neither achieved his elder brother's success. Like many Jewish immigrants Moses Zangwill earned his living as an old-clothes peddler who traveled around the countryside. The family actually resided in Plymouth at the time of Israel's birth and later moved to Bristol, where he received his early education. When the Zangwills finally settled in London, Israel attended the Jews' Free School and then London University, where he studied at night and in 1884 received a degree with honors in French, English, and Mental and Moral Science. Zangwill's biographers point out a spiritual incompatibility between his parents, depicting Ellen Marks Zangwill as the more assertive and freethinking of the two, impatient with her husband's quiet piety. Maurice Wohlgelernter writes that Israel inherited her "fearless feminine independence," a characteristic that reveals itself in Zangwill's political activism as well as in his often-controversial writings on religious themes. Still, the nostalgic longing for tradition and the pathos with which the older generation of Jews is often represented in Zangwill's work suggest his father's legacy.

Although Zangwill gained his most enduring reputation as a writer on Jewish themes, his contemporaries recognized the excellence of a more diverse literary productivity. His literary career began while he was a university student and a pupil-teacher at the Jews' Free School. In the essay "My First Book" (*Idler,* 1893; reprinted in Jerome K. Jerome's 1897 collection of the same title), Zangwill writes that after "contributing verses and virtuous essays to various juvenile organs," at the age of sixteen he came upon a literary contest in the newspaper *Society* and submitted a short novel – a "comedietta" – and, almost as an afterthought, a humorous story, "Professor Grimmer." The latter won the prize of five pounds and was published serially in three issues in November 1881. Joseph H. Udelson notes affinities in style and details of subject matter

between this early work – a comic love story involving the search by a professor of evolution for the missing (cuff) link – and much of Zangwill's later short fiction. Udelson is the only writer on Zangwill to list the date of publication for this story as 1881; elsewhere it is cited as 1882. However, the earlier date makes more sense in the light of Zangwill's own chronology of the contest.

After this early success Zangwill published an anonymous pamphlet, *Motza Kleis* (Matzo Balls, 1882), with a fellow pupil-teacher. Here again accounts differ, as most commentators have identified Zangwill's collaborator as Louis Cowen, with whom he wrote other works. However, Joseph Leftwich names Meyer Breslar as Zangwill's partner in this early effort, and Bernard Winehouse cites persuasive evidence in support. Zangwill himself takes pains to identify this first collaborator as "Y." in "My First Book," where Cowen is specifically referred to as co-author of *The Premier and the Painter* (1888). Zangwill records how *Motza Kleis* (later incorporated into *Children of the Ghetto*), a sketch of market day in the Jewish East End, was hugely popular with its Jewish readership, "who were afterwards to explain . . . their horror and disgust at its illiteracy and vulgarity," referring to the author's use of Yiddish expressions and dialect. Apparently Lord Rothschild, the president of the board of the Jews' Free School, also objected to a representation he considered undignified. Zangwill and Cowen, left with the choice of submitting all future manuscripts to the censorship of the board or ceasing to publish, elected the latter. This choice did not, however, prevent Zangwill from editing and writing for a Jewish annual, *Purim,* between 1883 and 1885.

By June 1888 Zangwill had resigned his teaching position. An 1898 interview with the *Bookman* (London) traces the cause to Zangwill's opposition to the Free School's policy of corporal punishment. Udelson sees it as the result of Cowen and Zangwill's publication in that year of *The Premier and the Painter,* under the pseudonym J. Freeman Bell. The lengthy novel, in a "prince and the pauper" format, was written for the most part by Zangwill. In recent times the book has been praised for its far-reaching and trenchant political satire, but at first publication its critical and popular receptions were unenthusiastic. It did, however, go into three editions by the end of the 1890s, when Zangwill had achieved greater fame. Later in 1888 J. Freeman Bell published a short story, "Under Sentence of Marriage," in *Myer's Calendar & Diary,* a Jewish publication. Accounts differ as to whether this, too, was a collaboration; Leftwich claims it is Zangwill's alone. This story details the plight of a rabbi hired by a congregation on the condition that he marry within a year, and Udelson sees it as prefiguring central preoccupations of Zangwill's later work: marriage for love over marriage for convenience, and the competing values of beauty and intellect.

In 1888 Zangwill also began his humor column "Morour and Charoseth" in the *Jewish Standard,* a weekly newspaper for which he also served as subeditor during its short run until 1891. Writing under the pseudonym "Marshallik" (fool or jester), Zangwill poked fun at news events, gossip, trends, and current literature affecting the Jewish community. The writing is filled with Zangwill's characteristic puns and clever literary allusions, and in many ways it anticipates his style in his humorous fiction. A lead-in (15 June 1888) regarding news of a Jewish celibates' club in New York suggests a possible source for *The Bachelors' Club* and *The Old Maids' Club* (1892), later united as *The Celibates' Club* (1898). A poem (25 May 1888) on catholicity of belief taken to the extreme – originally in derisive response to Jewish converts to Christianity – finds its way, with only slight revision, into *The Old Maids' Club,* where a comic poem is presented in nearly every chapter. The satire in "Morour and Charoseth" is aimed both at the foibles of the Anglo-Jewish community (and occasionally at its American counterpart) and at the anti-Semitism that perpetually surrounded it. In his "humorous" attacks on anti-Semites and their views, both the bittersweetness and essential seriousness of Zangwill's Jewish fiction are apparent.

In 1889 Zangwill was asked to contribute a serious article to a newly established intellectual periodical, the *Jewish Quarterly Review.* This essay, "English Judaism, a Criticism and a Classification," led to his ultimately gaining the commission from the Jewish Publication Society of America to write *Children of the Ghetto.* But before that, in 1889 and 1890, Zangwill published two more short stories in *Myer's Calendar & Diary* (this time alone and under the pseudonym "Baroness von S.") that marked a departure from his habitual comic tone. "Satan Mekatrig" is the mystical, disturbing tale of a woman's struggle against the forces of evil for the soul of her husband. He is saved and gains peace at the moment of death, but the last image of the story is of the hunchback, the representation of the devil, who, although in agony, still stands at the door. "Diary of a Meshumad" deals with evil in its human and political forms. Anti-Semitism forces a Russian Jew to convert in order to make a living. Although

*Illustration of Zangwill from his essay "My First Book" (*Idler, *1893)*

the Meshumad (apostate) never sincerely embraces his new faith, his son grows up as a believing Christian. Distraught when the parents of the Jewish woman he loves will not let her marry him, Paul, the son, becomes an anti-Semite, writing articles for an anti-Jewish newspaper that ultimately incite a pogrom in his father's town. The story ends as the repentant Meshumad decides to cast his fate openly with his own people by joining the struggle against the pogrom, most probably going to his own death.

These stories, reprinted in *Ghetto Tragedies* and again in the expanded collection *They That Walk in Darkness* (1899), reveal the pessimism that often characterizes Zangwill's fiction on Jewish subjects. While the otherworldliness of "Satan Mekatrig" is unusual in his writing, the story's depiction of suffering and family sacrifice is not. Similarly, "Diary of a Meshumad" prefigures a concern with hidden identity that recent critics have related to his own anxieties as a modern Jew inhabiting both the Jewish and secular worlds. The story's emphasis on the ironies of life reappears throughout Zangwill's fiction. That one's best efforts can lead directly to one's downfall, that one can make major decisions based on assumptions that turn out to be false, form the basis of a great many of Zangwill's short stories, both comic and tragic. Indeed, as he writes in an introductory note to *Ghetto Comedies* (1907), "In the old definition a comedy could be distinguished from a tragedy by its happy ending. . . . This is a crude conception of the distinction between Tragedy and Comedy, which I have ventured to disregard."

As these early tragic stories were being published, Zangwill also took up the editorship of a comic magazine, *Puck* – soon renamed *Ariel, or the London Puck* – for which he continued to edit and write during the next two years. Here he worked with George Hutchinson, who was to provide illustrations for much of Zangwill's subsequent short fiction, including the novella *The King of Schnorrers* (*Idler,* 1893) and *The Bachelors' Club.* Most of *The Old Maids' Club* was serialized in the last issues of *Ariel,* until the periodical ceased publication in February 1892.

"My First Book" recounts how J. T. Grein solicited a story by Zangwill for his *Playgoers' Review* and went on to refer Zangwill to the editor of a new Library of Wit and Humour that ended up publishing *The Bachelors' Club.* Zangwill notes that from that point on he never wrote "a line anywhere that has not been purchased before it was written." Additionally significant is the role of Grein in this episode. He is best known as the man who founded the Independent Theatre in order to bring Henrik Ibsen's *Ghosts* (1881) to London in 1891, using the "subscription only" method of ticket sales in an attempt to circumvent the censor. Zangwill allied himself with the Ibsenists when in March 1891 he published "A Doll's House Repaired," co-authored with Eleanor Marx Aveling, in *Time* (London). This "revision" of the ending of *A Doll's House* (1879), purportedly to make the play more acceptable to the British public, is a funny, pointed satire of those who would deny women independence of thought and action. Clearly both Grein and Zangwill saw no incompatibility between the more recently disparaged, light New Humor and humor used for social ends.

The stories in *The Bachelors' Club* and *The Old Maids' Club* exemplify the New Humor as they incorporate contemporary satire with romantic comedy and, especially in the first book, verbal gymnastics. *The Bachelors' Club* takes as its starting point the all-male club life that was a turn-of-the-century institution and that Zangwill himself enjoyed as a habitué of the Vagabonds and other clubs. (The Playgoers' Club, which Zangwill also frequented, was one of the few at that time to admit women.) The Bachelors' Club's rooms are located in Leicester Square, with easy access to the music halls, and "all the Bachelors were members of the Anti-Anti-Tobacco League." The larger, less frequented

room is decorated with texts deploring marriage, the organization's "articles of faith." Although the chapters of *The Bachelor's Club* (and even more so those of its successor) are linked to create the appearance of a novel, individually they are sufficiently self-contained to suggest short stories gathered together. Their inventiveness, topicality, and sentimentality make them characteristic of the lighter side of Zangwill as a short-fiction writer.

The book details, chapter by chapter, the ways in which each member of the Bachelors' Club succumbs to matrimony. In "The Second Ticket," for example, Osmund, a theater critic, marries to make use of the extra ticket he is customarily sent by theater managers to review their plays. As soon as he marries, however, the reputation of his newspaper coincidentally goes down, and he is from then on sent only one ticket. Similarly, in "A Novel Advertisement" the woman who answers O'Roherty's ad for someone well versed in all areas of knowledge – so that she can provide the factual background for the popular novels O'Roherty writes – turns out to be a "lady novelist" herself, and O'Roherty retires from the field to provide her with information. Even in this small sampling one observes the collection's concerns with irony, mistaken identity, and the more laughable realities of the popular art world. "Hamlet Up to Date," one of the longest stories in the book, ends with a rather lame ironic twist. Much more compelling, however, is the story's satire of a publishing world that makes ghostwriting epidemic.

The Bachelors' Club was a popular success; Winehouse writes that of nearly forty contemporary reviews of *The Bachelors' Club* and *The Old Maids' Club,* only one or two give less than enthusiastic praise. Reviews in 1905 of the combined collection, *The Celibates' Club,* present a more mixed evaluation. While the cleverness and invention of the stories are highly praised, they are also seen as excessive. Frances Duncan, who on many points liked the book, writes in the New York *Critic* that "[a] very battledore and shuttlecock of words and phrases, quips and cranks is kept up, staid and sober quotations are jostled into frivolousness, epigram follows epigram with a tirelessness which suggests a boy's firecracker enthusiasm and the Fourth of July – until one's wits weary of the perpetual *bang* and *fizz.*" Today's reader is likely to have a similar reaction, although staying with the stories brings unexpected rewards. Once Zangwill's international reputation was established by more-serious books, such as *Children of the Ghetto,* even these light works were translated and read outside the English-speaking world. But in reviews of his later work as well, they are often referred to disparagingly as light entertainment, in contrast to art. *The Bachelors' Club* won Zangwill the attention of Jerome, who made him one of the *Idler* writers and also published his work in a subsequent periodical, *To-day*. Jerome and Zangwill remained loyal friends and associates whose correspondence continued until at least 1925, the year before Zangwill's death.

Among modern critics, Udelson begins by calling *The Bachelors' Club* and *The Old Maids' Club* "literary fluff meant for amusement" but adds that they introduce such "Zangwillian motifs [as] the irony of life, the fragility of idealism, and the utility of even delusive ideals." Wohlgelernter notes that "inward laughter" is directed at the central characters in these stories, while Elsie Bonita Adams points to the critiques of contemporary society that abound. The element of social satire, in fact, is what allows these books to be considered part of the realist tradition at all, for the plots of the tales themselves defy probability. The stories in *The Old Maids' Club* are more varied in structure than those in its predecessor; notable among them is the modern quest fairy tale "The Princess of Portman Square." There is also a significant decrease in overingenious wordplay: as the character Lillie Dulcimer notes, "I hate puns. . . . They spoiled the Bachelors' Club."

The theme of celibacy versus marriage in both these books – and of course the misogyny of the texts in the Bachelors' Club's larger room – raises the question of Zangwill's attitude toward women at this early stage in his career. Udelson believes "the future feminist campaigner's suspicion of women" is evident in both books; the *Public Opinion* review of *The Celibates' Club* quotes the Old Maids' bylaws in a way that suggests Zangwill ridicules the more advanced women of his day. In order to bring about "the depolarization of the term 'Old Maid' " – that is, to eliminate its less agreeable associations – members are required, among other things, "not to have any ideals or to take part in Woman's Rights Movements, Charity Concerts, or other Platform Demonstrations. . . . Not to wear caps, curls, or similar articles of attire. . . . Not to kiss females."

The New Woman's activism is apparently trivialized when placed among other "spinsterish" characteristics, and there is no denying that Zangwill is cautious in his early fiction, reiterating familiar stereotypes and jokes. However, "The Logic of Love" (*The Bachelors' Club*) tells the story of a man whose ideal woman is a sweet, unspoiled country maiden; instead he falls in love with a witty, satiric urbanite whom the reader sees as far more attractive than the imagined beloved. In *The Old Maids' Club* the one real New Woman, Nelly Nimrod, is masculine in appearance and dress. She is also intelligent, lively, and interesting, and she remains so even after the obligatory marriage and change of attire. Woman writers and critics are presented as facts of literary life, and they meet with no more particular satire than do their male counterparts. When a true old maid – an elderly woman childishly dressed, her mind wandering – appears at the end of the book, Zangwill takes the opportunity to chastise society, as Lillie Dulcimer, the would-be founder of the club, is chastised by her soon-to-be husband, Lord Silverdale: "Life is a cruel tragedy for many – never crueller than when its remorseless laws condemn gentle loving women to a crabbed and solitary old age." While it is unlikely that Zangwill conceived these entertainments as a protest, neither was he able to keep his social conscience entirely separate from them.

In the same year that *The Bachelors' Club* was published, *The Big Bow Mystery,* a detective novella, appeared in the London *Star*. It was published serially each day from 22 August to 4 September 1891. Though some accounts state that Zangwill wrote the story all in one sitting, the more credible statement is Zangwill's own, in a prefatory note, that it "was written in a fortnight – day by day – to meet a sudden demand from the *Star*." The story attracted enormous interest as it appeared, with so many readers suggesting solutions that Zangwill jokingly wrote, in his own letter to the editor, that the one he ultimately adopted was simply the one no one else had guessed. Later he felt obliged to point out the joke, noting that "the mystery-story is just the one species of story that can not be told impromptu or altered at the last moment." In tribute to the public's general enthusiasm for participating in periodical debates, he included some in the novella as an important plot device. The *Star* was a daily newspaper written for the masses; in its early years (1888–1891) it had had a socialist orientation, though this soon subsided into a liberal stance. The paper's politics may account at least in part for the working-class setting and activist characters in *The Big Bow Mystery*. Zangwill's association with the *Star* went beyond this one story; Winehouse notes that he (like others in the New Humor group) used his literary column in the paper to praise his associates' writing.

The twist at the end of *The Big Bow Mystery* is one of Zangwill's most effective, and the story remains powerful and satisfying to readers of detective fiction. Its contemporary popularity is evident from the fact that it was published in book form almost immediately and went into several editions. It is still in print, and the story has formed the basis of three feature films, the most recent and truest to the original being *The Verdict* (1946), the last feature starring Sydney Greenstreet and Peter Lorre and the first directed by Don Siegel. If one does not count Poe's "The Murders in the Rue Morgue" (1841), with its nonhuman perpetrator, *The Big Bow Mystery* can be and often is considered the first locked-room murder mystery. Writers on Zangwill from Hamlin Garland to Udelson have tended to treat it as a simple entertainment, though Meri-Jane Rochelson has more recently seen in it affinities to the plots of identity in Zangwill's Jewish fiction.

In 1892 Zangwill continued his prolific, varied journalistic career. Two stories that were reprinted in *The King of Schnorrers: Grotesques and Fantasies* (1894) – "Mated by a Waiter" and "A Double-Barrelled Ghost" – appeared in Arrowsmith's and Phil May's summer annuals shortly before the publication of *The Old Maids' Club*. The first of these stories successfully carries out a plot of multiple mistaken identities reminiscent of those in the *Club* books but on a grand scale. The second takes up the ghostwriter theme of "Hamlet Up to Date," with an actual specter doing the writing. Most notably at this time, however, Zangwill became a regular contributor to Jerome's *Idler,* starting with the first issue. He was a frequent participant in its roundtable discussion feature, "The Idlers' Club," and between 1892 and 1895 contributed five short stories: "The English Shakespeare," expanded and reprinted in *The Old Maids' Club*; "The Memory Clearing House"; "The Queen's Triplets"; and "Cheating the Gallows" (a crime story with resemblances to Sir Arthur Conan Doyle's "The Man with the Twisted Lip" [*The Adventures of Sherlock Holmes,* 1892]), all reprinted in *The King of Schnorrers: Grotesques and Fantasies;* and "The Abolition of Money," more essay than story, pointing out that once a standard medium of exchange is abolished and barter becomes the rule, it becomes clear what society does and does not value. As might be expected, the writers and artists suffer. During the second half of 1893 the *Idler* serialized *The King of Schnorrers* itself, an episodic novella of eighteenth-century Anglo-Jewish life about a beggar who outsmarts his economic superiors.

The *Idler* brought Zangwill into the circle of New Humorists, which included Jerome, Robert Barr, G. B. Burgin, Barry Pain, and William Pett Ridge, none of whom is well known today. But frequent contributors to the periodical also included Doyle, Bret Harte, Rudyard Kipling, and J. M. Barrie, as well as woman writers – Marie Corelli, Ella Hepworth Dixon, Edith Nesbit, and others – who are only now being rediscovered. Mark Twain's *The American Claimant* was serialized in the first volume. Thus the *Idler* brought Zangwill into contact, both on paper and in person, with some of the most prominent writers of the day, both in England and America, and in contemporary periodicals and literary studies he is reviewed as one of them. The diversity of writing presented in the *Idler* is also worth noting in relation to Zangwill's subsequent reputation. Contributions ranged from the rather silly ethnic humor of W. L. Alden's "Jewseppy" in volume 1 (about an Italian organ-grinder, told by a stereotypical American) to Sophie Wassilieff's searing report of the Russian prison system in "Memoirs of a Female Nihilist," serialized in volumes three and four. It is therefore not entirely strange that Zangwill published both "Jewish" and "non-Jewish" fiction in this periodical; indeed, a story about Jews and Jewish religious practice ("Adventures in Search of the Pole") appears in *The Old Maids' Club.* Udelson is thus not exact when he states that Zangwill "wrote 'Jewish stories' for one set of readers and 'non-Jewish literature' for another." The cross-publication went in both directions, too. The *Jewish Chronicle* (17 June 1892), for example, advertised Zangwill's summer annual pieces, and Israel Abrahams, coeditor of the *Jewish Quarterly Review,* praised *The Bachelors' Club* and *The Big Bow Mystery* in letters to their author.

The major event of 1892 for Zangwill, however, was the publication of *Children of the Ghetto,* first in London in September of that year, then in Philadelphia in December. The British edition was published by Heinemann, who was to become Zangwill's major British publisher from then on. The early arrival of the British edition was a cause of annoyance for the Jewish Publication Society of America, which had commissioned the novel from Zangwill in the first place, but the book was a great success on both sides of the Atlantic.

In its portrayal of life in the East End Jewish ghetto and the generational conflict felt by modern Jews, *Children of the Ghetto* incorporates many of the themes and techniques – the irony, pathos, social satire, and verbal humor – that characterize Zangwill's short fiction. Many of the chapters, in fact, can stand on their own as vignettes of ghetto life. Zangwill's goal in *Children of the Ghetto* was to paint a realistic picture of Jews in their diversity, neither idealizing nor falling into negative stereotypes. By most accounts, contemporary and subsequent, he succeeded. Although the book was commissioned, Zangwill insisted on and received complete authorial freedom. As a result he was criticized by some Jewish readers who objected that his realism was more like airing dirty linen. For the most part, however, the book was much admired and widely read, and it established Zangwill's position as interpreter of the Jews to the English-speaking world.

Zangwill's interest in theater is apparent throughout his fiction, and in the early 1890s he was an avid theatergoer. He was a frequent associate of actor-managers Henry Irving and Beerbohm Tree and of actresses such as Olga Brandon and Elizabeth Robins. His first play, *The Great Demonstration,* a political satire cowritten with Cowen, was produced at the Royalty Theatre, London, in September 1892. *Aladdin at Sea,* a short play about a traveling theater company lost on the way to an engagement, was performed in Camborne in January 1893. *Six Persons,* a drama about a relationship in which two characters appear in several different aspects, was performed at London's Theatre Royal, Haymarket, at the end of that year.

In May 1893 Zangwill began to write a column for *Pall Mall Magazine,* "Without Prejudice" – a legal term that of course had additional associations for Zangwill and that he took every opportunity to quote. The column ran until October 1896 and featured reviews, general literary and social criticism, and much miscellaneous ephemera. Most of these columns, except for the reviews, were collected and published as a book in 1896, along with other miscellaneous pieces including a mildly satiric story, "The Choice of Parents," which had appeared in the Christmas number of *Chapman's Magazine* in 1895. Zangwill's prefatory note to *Without Prejudice* indicates he had a subsequent volume of reviews in mind, but this never materialized. During much of the period when he was writing the *Pall Mall Magazine* column (1894–1896), Zangwill also published a column called "Men, Women, and Books" in the *Critic* (New York). There is considerable overlap in content between the two.

All this critical and dramatic activity took place in a year in which Zangwill wrote some of his most important short fiction. *Merely Mary Ann,* which with a revised happy ending became Zangwill's most successful play, was published as the first number of R. Tuck and Sons' Breezy Library Series. Zangwill's diary notes that his brother Mark provided the illustrations, though Tuck decreed that "the men must be made taller." The short novel, subsequently collected in *The Grey Wig,* re-

Caricature of Zangwill based on a passage from his 1892 novel Children of the Ghetto (Idler, *1892*)

counts a young composer's reluctant attraction to the serving maid of the rooming house where he lives. At the same time he struggles against prostituting his talents by writing popular rather than serious music. He succumbs to both temptations but priggishly stops short of marrying Mary Ann. When she becomes an heiress at the end of the story, honor prevents him from doing so. The ending, with Mary Ann leaving Lancelot and returning his gifts and her canary as a reminder, incorporates typical Zangwillian irony as it punishes the snobbish, shortsighted suitor. The bitterness of the irony that appears in later stories, however, especially those on Jewish themes, is blunted here, as Lancelot accepts his fate and proceeds to care for the canary.

The short novel was a popular success, although reviews were mixed. Some critics objected to what now seem fairly conventional adaptations of modernist technique – the opening of the story in the midst of the action and the relative open-endedness of the conclusion. The *Nation* (13 July 1893) remarked that, rather than "breezy," *Merely Mary Ann* was "a gloomy, indeed sordid and morbid, tale," pointing out that Zangwill was capable of satisfying a more discriminating novel-reading public than that to which this work appealed. In 1903 reviews of *The Grey Wig* as a whole were mixed, although *Merely Mary Ann* tended not to be singled out for comment. Recent writers on Zangwill also deal with it only briefly and generally in relation to the 1904 play; Adams emphasizes its avoidance of the sentimentality that pervades the dramatic adaptation. All in all, though, *Merely Mary Ann* is readable, and it demonstrates the persistence of Zangwill's interests in the life of the artist and the social pressures that affect both career and romantic life. The story was written in three weeks; Wohlgelernter states that the play brought Zangwill more money "than all the ghetto books put together."

Ghetto Tragedies (1893) collects "Satan Mekatrig" and "Diary of a Meshumad" with two new, shorter stories, "Incurable" and "The Sabbath-Breaker," both set in a home for the terminally ill and severely disabled. These form the last four stories in the much-expanded volume *"They That Walk in Darkness"*. *Ghetto Tragedies* was on the whole favorably received by critics, although some (for example, the London *Bookman* [September 1893]) were reluctant to accept a change in theme and tone from the author of *The Bachelors' Club* and *The Old Maids' Club* without reminding him of his "earlier literary sins."

Both the *Bookman* and the *Athenaeum* gave high praise to "Diary of a Meshumad" but found fault with "Satan Mekatrig," whose dark mysticism is more compelling to a later generation. Udelson observes that in this story "Zangwill is at his artistic best and also closest to the heart of Jewish thought." "The Sabbath-Breaker" is a highly sentimental tale of a woman who breaks the Sabbath to walk thirty-seven miles to her dying son, only to learn, upon arrival, that he died and was buried just before the Sabbath began. The *Athenaeum* singled it out as the best of the four, though readers would be unlikely to do so today. "Incurable" is a disturbing, painful story about a terminally ill institutionalized woman whose husband has begun to live with another woman. She grants him a divorce so that he can remarry and then, kindly but miserably, gives the new wife her blessing. The story ends with an explicit allusion to her Christ-like sacrifice, one of the earliest references in Zangwill's fiction to the idea that Judaism and Christianity, at their best, share a common nobility.

At about the same time *Ghetto Tragedies* was published (August), *The King of Schnorrers* began to appear serially in the *Idler*. It continued in six parts until January 1894, although apparently Zangwill wanted to stop publication sometime in the middle of the run but, fortunately, was dissuaded. It became the most well known and enduring of Zangwill's works, republished many times throughout the twentieth century. Its episodic nature leads one to classify it as short fiction; even allowing for the plot threads that join the episodes, it is at most a short novel. Set in eighteenth-century London, *The King of Schnorrers* recounts the adventures of Manasseh Bueno Barzillai Azevedo da Costa, a Sephardic Jew who uses his wit and Talmudic learning to make himself king of the Jewish beggars. Zangwill draws on Jewish folklore and traditional humor to show how class distinctions are meaningless when the clever can place themselves above the wealthy. Among other things, Manasseh uses his begging income to buy an expensive salmon and contrives to have a wealthy man carry it home for him, brings another beggar (his habitual Sabbath guest) to the rich man's home for dinner, and talks his way into a stage box at the theater. The reader cheers him along each step of the way.

When *The King of Schnorrers* appeared in volume form in 1894, it was widely reviewed in the literary magazines. On the whole the book was highly praised, with the *Athenaeum* (10 March 1894) calling Manassah "a stupendous hero." There is "no more delightful personage in fiction," noted the *Outlook* (3 March 1894). The other stories in the collection were also reviewed favorably, particularly those with Jewish themes. In the distinctions made between the two types, however, a disturbing current in Zangwill criticism appears. For example, the reviewer for the *Nation* (26 July 1894) writes, "As a delineator of Jewish character and customs, Mr. Zangwill is an author to be cherished, but when he goes prancing among the end-of-the-century London gentiles, he is an author whose existence is not necessary for the perpetuation of the tradition of polite letters." Zangwill's publication of *The King of Schnorrers* in the *Idler*, with Jerome's encouragement, is an indication that the exclusionary view was not universally shared, while the mixture of stories in the rest of the 1894 volume, reprinted with their original magazine illustrations, may suggest Zangwill's insistence on presenting both kinds of writing as valuable.

The additional stories in *The King of Schnorrers: Grotesques and Fantasies* include "The Semi-

Sentimental Dragon" and "The Principal Boy," both romantic comedies that reflect Zangwill's intimate knowledge of the popular theater. The title character of the second work is actually a young woman, since the "principal boy," a stock figure of Victorian pantomime, was always played in cross-dress. The first of these stories was singled out for praise in several reviews; both were mentioned by the *Outlook.* The remaining stories on non-Jewish themes are not very memorable and tend to be based on one-note (though occasionally ingenious) conceits. Among these are "An Honest Log-Roller," about an author who loses the manuscript of his novel and then, years later, finds himself reviewing it as the work of another. In "An Odd Life" a man who has lived all the odd-numbered years of his life finds himself dying at age two, at the start of what he thought would be a long second chance. Similarly distressing is the end of "A Successful Operation," in which a young wife, after caring lovingly for her father-in-law through an operation that restores his sight, gives birth to a baby who is blind. Zangwill presents this finale without comment. These and other bleak stories jar in the company of the fine comic fiction in the collection, but in tone and outlook they are in keeping with the later stories collected in *"They That Walk in Darkness"* and *Dreamers of the Ghetto.*

The three Jewish stories, apart from the title novella, are "A Tragi-Comedy of Creeds," in which a rabbi finds himself giving humanistic "last rites" to a devout Christian woman (this piece first appeared in the *Bohemian* in 1893); "A Rose of the Ghetto," a comedy of marriage manners featuring Sugarman the Shadchan, the matchmaker introduced in *Children of the Ghetto*; and "Flutter-Duck: A Ghetto Grotesque," a story in several chapters about a Jewish mother, a misunderstanding, and a reconciliation. "Flutter-Duck" was praised in some initial reviews and is singled out by Udelson as "the most truthful and effective piece in the book." Its depiction of the Jewish mother's excesses is stereotyped, however, and her ending in senility is less moving than pathetic. An obituary article on Zangwill in the *Outlook* records that "A Tragi-Comedy of Creeds" was reprinted in that magazine's short-story series in September 1894, some months after the book's publication. The title given retrospectively (and probably inadvertently) is "A Tragedy of Creeds," which ignores the subtle commingling on which Zangwill insisted, emphasizing instead his frequently melancholy tone.

One week after this story was published in the *Outlook,* a new story, "The Silent Sisters," appeared

Illustration for The King of Schnorrers (Idler, *1893*)

there. Once again Zangwill takes the reader into realms of (this time non-Jewish) sentimentality, with the story of two sisters who stubbornly adhere until death to a vow of silence taken in childhood for a silly, ephemeral reason. It is a tribute to Zangwill's skill as a writer that this basically maudlin story turns out, by the end, to be somewhat affecting. It is collected in *The Grey Wig.*

In June 1894 Zangwill participated in a *New Review* symposium on sex education, "The Tree of Knowledge." That he was asked to contribute along with Thomas Hardy, Sir Walter Besant, the Chief Rabbi, and several other well-known figures indicates the place he had attained by this point in the literary world. His brief, satiric response — essentially that young girls already knew as much as their parents, through reading modern novels — suggests that he placed himself in the modern, forward-looking camp, though perhaps somewhat ambivalently.

At about the same time *The King of Schnorrers: Grotesques and Fantasies* was published in March 1894, Zangwill finished writing his novel *The Master.* This study of a young Nova Scotian painter in conflict between the demands of the artist's life and the moral values in which he was raised to believe was published between May and November in *Harper's* in the United States, and in Jerome's *To-day* in England. Brought out in book form in 1895, *The Master* helped establish Zangwill as a writer of serious fiction beyond the Jewish context.

The year 1895 was significant in Zangwill's personal and political life as well as his literary career. At the home of a friend, Cecile Hartog, he first met Mr. and Mrs. William Ayrton, the father and stepmother of Edith Ayrton, whom Zangwill married in 1903. Hertha Marks Ayrton was a Jewish woman who as a teenager was taken under the wing of the feminist Barbara Leigh Smith Bodichon. Bodichon and George Eliot were friends at the time, and for some time legend ran that Hertha Marks was the original of Mirah in *Daniel Deronda* (1876). Presumably, Zangwill met his future wife at around this time, too, although Leftwich dates their first meeting at 1901. Edith Ayrton Zangwill, who was herself a writer and feminist, was not Jewish, but clearly Jews and Judaism were part of her environment. Zangwill often commented on the similarity of their religious philosophies.

Zangwill's career as a Zionist began in 1895 when, through Max Nordau, he met Theodor Herzl. Herzl visited Zangwill in Kilburn on 21 November and described in his diary how "in his book-lined study Zangwill sits before a huge writing-table, his back to the fireplace. Also close to the fire, his brother [Louis] – reading.... The disorder in his room and on his desk leaves me the inference that he is a man who lives in his inner life." Zangwill sponsored and introduced Herzl's first address on Zionism to an English-speaking audience at the Maccabeans Club on 24 November. From that point until late in his life, Zangwill was the chief spokesman on Zionism for Anglo-Jewry, and the chief representative of English Jews at international Zionist conferences.

Zangwill attended the first World Zionist Congress, at Basel, Switzerland, in February 1897. His continued travels, which ended in mid May, took him through France, Switzerland, Italy, Egypt, Palestine, Syria, Lebanon, Turkey, and Greece. Throughout most of the year he was also working on the biographical stories that form *Dreamers of the Ghetto*. Some of these, including "Joseph the Dreamer" and "Maimon the Fool and Nathan the Wise," were first published as early as 1895. "Uriel Acosta" and "Chad Gadya" appeared in 1896, and "The Palestine Pilgrim," "A Child of the Ghetto," "The Turkish Messiah," "The Conciliator of Christendom," "From a Mattress Grave," "The Joyous Comrade," and "Dreamers in Congress" (about the Zionist meeting that August in Paris) appeared in 1897; "The Maker of Lenses" and "The People's Saviour" were first published in 1898. These thirteen stories (out of sixteen in the volume) were first printed in periodicals as diverse as *Cosmopolis, Cosmopolitan, Atlantic, Outlook, Review of Reviews,* and *Illustrated London News.* Only one, "Maimon the Fool

and Nathan the Wise," appeared in a specifically Jewish publication, the *Jewish World.*

Dreamers of the Ghetto is often considered Zangwill's best and most important literary work. It is also his most difficult to interpret. Each story relates a crucial episode in the life of a Jewish idealist, frequently one who has looked beyond the faith and faced persecution in a search for meaning. Zangwill's subjects include Benedict de Spinoza, Heinrich Heine, Sabbatai Zevi, the Baal Shem Tov, Moses Mendelssohn, Benjamin Disraeli, and Ferdinand Lassalle, along with lesser-known seekers of truth. Udelson notes that most of these figures would have been familiar to contemporary readers through recent historical and literary works. A few of the stories, including the framing tales, "A Child of the Ghetto" and "Chad Gadya," are frankly fictional. In virtually every case the search for truth ends in failure, ridicule, disappointment, or death – or, as in the case of the Baal Shem Tov, founder of Hasidism, in a distortion of the original message. The opening poem, "Moses and Jesus," makes clear that Zangwill's lament for the distance between religious truth and organized religion extends to Christianity as well as Judaism. The Christian parallel is explored again in the book's epilogue, "A Modern Scribe in Jerusalem."

Some contemporary reviewers of *Dreamers of the Ghetto* saw it as a continuation of Zangwill's work in educating the English public about the Jews, and these writers tended to fault the book for not answering their own questions about Jews in modern society. Others praised the work as giving valuable insight into previously unknown or unexplored sides of Jewish character and history. Some reviewers, such as the one for the *Critic,* felt compelled to note the disparity between this high-minded, idealistic book and that side of Zangwill's career perceived as responding solely to publishers' demands. But William Morton Payne, in the *Dial* (1 August 1898), found *Dreamers of the Ghetto* "deeply significant, both as a richly sympathetic and imaginative interpretation of the Jewish ideal, and as an altogether unexpected revelation of the powers hitherto latent in its author."

The book was widely translated, both in its own time and in the 1920s and 1930s. In 1950 Philip Rubin, in the American Jewish *Congress Weekly* (16 October), recommended it for "dusting off the bookshelf," pointing out that it was "regarded more highly in Hebrew literary circles in Israel than any other of Zangwill's books." Adams devotes a full chapter to its unique content and skillful execution, and Wohlgelernter discusses the book as

Zangwill's profound contribution to exploring the Arnoldian conflict between Hellenism and Hebraism. Like Wohlgelernter, Udelson sees the book as a reflection of Zangwill's conflicts as a Jew in modern society; he even titles his study of Zangwill *Dreamer of the Ghetto*. To a greater extent than other recent writers, Udelson attributes the failure of Zangwill's dream to his efforts at reconciling Judaism and Christianity, and, in light of this sympathy toward Christian ideals, expresses surprise at its wide acceptance by Jewish readers and critics in 1898 and later.

In fact, the sources of disillusionment in Zangwill's historical "heretics" and fictional truth-seekers are not easy to define. At the much-quoted end of his preface to *Dreamers of the Ghetto,* Zangwill calls his book "the story of a Dream that has not come true." Joseph Jacobs, a Jewish writer and an associate of Zangwill, reviewing the book for the *Bookman* (New York) in 1898, admired it greatly while admitting "it is somewhat difficult even from the inside to gather the exact nature of the Dream which occurs in so many forms." The conflicts between tradition and assimilation for the modern Jew that are explored most intensely in the frame stories are the same as those related in *Children of the Ghetto,* although they are resolved more pessimistically here. Several of the stories criticize the failure of religious practice to embody religious ideals. In "Dreamers in Congress," Zangwill extols the political idealism of the early Zionists, but at the same time he suggests doubt about whether their goal can be achieved.

The book as a whole is extremely ambitious, and, though the common mode is fictionalized biography, Zangwill employs different narrative strategies and personas. The stories vary in power and interest, but most are individually affecting. *Dreamers of the Ghetto* reflects the scope of Zangwill's imagination, his energy as a writer, and the combination of high standards and pessimism with which he confronted the idea of religious belief and idealism in all forms. It is unlikely ever to be the best known of Zangwill's works, but it represents some of his most serious thought. The mixed nature of Zangwill's career in fiction was underscored by the publication of *The Celibates' Club* in the same year.

That year ended with a three-month lecture tour of the United States that took Zangwill from the Northeast to the Midwest, as far west as Chicago and as far south as Nashville. It was presumably during this visit that he met Mary Antin, the young Russian immigrant to Boston whose *The Promised Land* was to become a major work in Jewish-American literature. Zangwill wrote the foreword to her first book, *From Plotzk to Boston* (1899), an account of the immigrant's crossing. At the end of 1899 the London production of his play *Children of the Ghetto* closed after a week's performances; it was somewhat more successful in American cities. But the major literary achievement for Zangwill in 1899 was the publication of the expanded collection *"They That Walk in Darkness": Ghetto Tragedies.*

To the four original stories of 1893 were added seven others, all further developing themes Zangwill explores in *Children of the Ghetto* and *Dreamers of the Ghetto.* As in previous collections, some of these stories originated in periodicals: "Transitional" and "Bethulah" appeared in the July and October issues of *Harper's,* respectively. The *Ghetto Tragedies* vary in treatment and mode, but all are set in the nineteenth century and confront the conflict between tradition and modernity in a variety of contexts. "Bethulah" reintroduces the mysticism of "Satan Mekatrig," this time in the setting of central European Hasidism; "Noah's Ark" presents Peloni, a "dreamer of the ghetto" who waits in vain near Niagara Falls for the arrival of the charlatan Mordecai Noah and his promised Jewish homeland.

Several of the stories recount the sacrifices of parents and children for each other, sacrifices often made in vain. In "They That Walk in Darkness" a faithful Jewish woman takes her son to see the pope, having heard he can cure blindness; the son regains his sight and immediately dies. "Transitional" relates the love of a young Jewish woman in London for a Christian man and her ultimate rejection of him for the sake of her father. This story, like "To Die in Jerusalem," combines generational conflict with mutual self-sacrifice and an unexpected, ironic ending. The irony in "The Keeper of Conscience" is more bitter, as Salvina, who sacrifices her own happiness for her greedy, unappreciative family, dies at twenty-five, her sacrifices unrecognized. Here, as in earlier works, the Christian parallel is implicit. "The Land of Promise" tells of disillusionment even in America, which Zangwill proposes as the answer for Jews at least as early as *Children of the Ghetto.* He was also always aware of its shortcomings as a promised land. In this story a Russian Jew goes to America so that he can practice his religion, and he waits there for his fiancée. When she finally arrives, he has abandoned his piety and is married to her younger sister.

"They That Walk in Darkness": Ghetto Tragedies was well received on its first publication, and it continues to be admired. Udelson justly states that it "displays Zangwill's artistic gifts at their finest"; he

adds that "no answers are suggested, no solutions proferred; only questions pleading for responses." In this collection, as in *Children of the Ghetto* and *Ghetto Comedies,* Zangwill's profound enunciation and exploration of the questions are impressive. The three works were published in one volume by the Jewish Publication Society of America in 1938 and form what should remain the most enduring body of Zangwill's fiction.

By 1899 Zangwill had become a widely acclaimed literary celebrity. He began to be frequently interviewed and mentioned in the "comment" sections of such periodicals as the *Bookman;* this has led later critics to see him as something of a self-promoter. Garland, in *Roadside Meetings of a Literary Nomad* (serialized in the *Bookman* [London] in 1930), recalls Zangwill's reputation at the time when the English author visited Chicago: "No recent visitor had so deeply stirred our literary circles. His wit, his brilliant comment and his humor quite won the reporters and paragraphers, and long accounts of him filled the daily press. Naturally the Jews of the city took intense pride in his success." Garland describes, as did many contemporaries, Zangwill's striking, somewhat "ugly" appearance, his "thick, black, curly hair," and his physical clumsiness. He reports a conversation between the two in which Zangwill convinced the American to purchase a swallowtail coat, saying, "It is the most democratic of garments. When you are encased in one you will be indistinguishable from an earl or a waiter." In recounting his own subsequent visit to London, Garland places Zangwill as "a growing figure" along with Hardy, James, Barrie, Shaw, and Kipling – in his view the "outstanding English writers at this time."

Around 1900 Zangwill's writing and his activity in general became more political. His novel *The Mantle of Elijah* (1900) first appeared serially in *Harper's.* Published in the midst of the Boer War, it embodies Zangwill's pacifist as well as feminist values. Wohlgelernter remarks that although *The Mantle of Elijah* is not a bad novel (he finds it in some respects better than *The Master*), interest in the novel declined after the Boer War ended. It was not a critical success in its day, and its lasting reputation has been mixed at best.

In the early years of the twentieth century Zangwill became a more active dramatist, with *The Moment of Death* (also called *The Moment Before*) produced in New York in 1900 and *The Revolted Daughter* produced in London the following year. Both are what Udelson calls "didactic satires," and, like many of Zangwill's plays, neither was a commercial

or critical success. In 1901 Zangwill represented the English Zionist Federation at the Fifth World Zionist Congress. By 1902 he was already criticizing various branches of the Zionist movement for diffusing resettlement efforts when the need to remove Russian Jews from violent persecution was dire. In 1905 he split from mainstream Zionism to form the Jewish Territorial Organization, whose goal was a Jewish homeland wherever one was attainable. His support for the Uganda Plan in 1903 prefigured this rift.

But as Zangwill was becoming a more controversial figure in Zionist politics, he was settling down in his personal life, with marriage to Edith Ayrton on 26 November 1903. In the same year he began serialization of *Italian Fantasies,* a collection of essays on social, religious, and artistic themes; it was published in book form in 1910. *Blind Children,* a collection of virtually all the serious poetry Zangwill had been publishing in periodicals and in his books, appeared in 1903. It includes translations of Hebrew verse from the synagogue service (still used in bilingual prayer books today), poetry about Jewish life and on religious themes, and a good deal of other poetry – romantic, philosophical, lyrical – more difficult to characterize. Zangwill's poetry has been generally dismissed, but he was a prolific poet, if not a great one, throughout his literary career. Many of the poems in this large output are worth reading.

The Grey Wig: Stories and Novelettes collects *The Big Bow Mystery, Merely Mary Ann,* and a new novelette, *The Serio-Comic Governess,* with five short stories in what is "mainly a study of woman," as Zangwill's dedication to his mother and sisters points out. When one considers that Zangwill was shortly to begin his active campaigning for woman suffrage, the presentation of women in some of these stories is curious. "The Grey Wig" and "The Silent Sisters" are both effective and affecting stories of women's friendships, particularly in old age. The feud in "The Silent Sisters" seems rather overdone, although no more so than such schematic relationships in many of Zangwill's works. The title story's Parisian setting and conclusion in the morgue are reminiscent of Guy de Maupassant and French realism. "Chassé-Croisé," "The Woman Beater," and "The Eternal Feminine" are disappointing, however, each striking too much of one note.

The Serio-Comic Governess is more effective, delineating more complexly the life and adventures of Eileen O'Keeffe/Nelly O'Neill – "respectable governess" by day, risqué comic singer at a music hall by night. Adams finds that the "central character . . . does not engage one's sympathies," but she is alone in her estimation. Udelson praises the story, seeing in it, once again, a reflection of Zangwill's anxieties about being a Jew and an Englishman. But, despite the heroine's more reflective and even despairing moments, *The Serio-Comic Governess* is not essentially an anguished work. The music-hall material makes enlightening, entertaining use of Zangwill's love for the theater, and Eileen/Nelly has an energy and exuberance that make her a winning protagonist. The conclusion of the story, in which she rejects a loving suitor and enters a convent, suggests independence as well as resignation. Zangwill's theatrical version of this story was produced in New York in 1904.

The Grey Wig received mixed to poor reviews. The *Athenaeum* (28 March 1903) criticized the artificiality of many of the stories, including *The Big Bow Mystery,* and, alluding to the ghetto fiction, commented: "Mr. Zangwill does much better work . . . when he writes on a subject in which he feels a sympathetic interest and is not ashamed to forget the brilliancy of his own gifts in the sorrows of other people." Even Abraham Cahan, who could usually be counted on to praise Zangwill's writing, lamented the effects of epigram on it in a review for the London *Bookman.* On the other hand, Cahan generally expressed admiration for *The Serio-Comic Governess,* seeing in it the mixture of tragic and comic that characterized Zangwill's outlook as reflected in his writing.

In 1904 Zangwill's dramatic versions of *The Serio-Comic Governess* and *Merely Mary Ann* were produced; the following year *Jinny the Carrier* was performed in Boston. This love story of a young woman who works as a carter in mid-nineteenth-century rural England became the subject of Zangwill's last novel, published in 1919. While praising the technique of the novel, Adams notes that it is "an anachronism, showing no evidence of having been written in the twentieth century." Yet, at the time of its composition as a play, Zangwill was very much involved in twentieth-century politics. In 1905, after Herzl had died and the Uganda Plan had been rejected by the Seventh Zionist Congress, Zangwill founded the Jewish Territorial Organization. The following year his organization accepted Jacob Schiff's Galveston Plan, which, while it did not found an American Zion, succeeded in rescuing many Jews from Russian pogroms and repatriating them in the United States.

Zangwill published his last collection of short fiction, *Ghetto Comedies,* in 1907. It may be said to close the circle of Zangwill's ghetto writings at the

Zangwill, circa 1911

same time as it reflects his increasing pessimism and the increasing urgency of the situation of European Jewry. More unified than *Ghetto Tragedies, Ghetto Comedies* interweaves its stories of Jewish life in Europe, America, and Russia through the repetition of characters, including several who first appear in *Children of the Ghetto.* Reading the collection is, in fact, reminiscent of reading that first ghetto work, with its turns given to rich and poor, shop and synagogue, and politics and theatrics.

Some of the stories – in particular "The Red Mark," "The Luftmensch," "The Tug of Love," "The Yiddish 'Hamlet,'" and "Holy Wedlock" – are nostalgic portraits of ghetto life and institutions: the board school, the true believer living on charity and faith, the matchmaker, the Yiddish theater, and the old couple in love, reminiscent of the Hyamses in *Children of the Ghetto.* "Anglicization," "The Jewish Trinity," and "The Sabbath Question in Sudminster" all deal with the collision of Judaism and English life, and the ultimate loss to Judaism in the contact. In "Anglicization" (originally published in *Cosmopolitan* as "S. Cohn & Son"), the son of an English Jew who has dropped his orthodoxy is honored by his country for service in the Boer War, but still his fiancée decides she cannot marry him because he is a Jew. "The Sabbath Question in Sudminster" relates how the efforts of Jewish merchants to stop a newcomer from staying open on the

Sabbath ends in their all conforming to his practice. And "The Jewish Trinity" is defined as "the Briton, the Jew, and the anti-Semite — three-in-one and one-in-three" when a wealthy English Jew rejects a prospective son-in-law because the young man is a Zionist. In his portrayal of Sir Asher Aaronsberg, Zangwill expresses his frustration with those who would use religious arguments to oppose the building of a Jewish homeland and who would hide behind privileged positions to avoid rescuing poor Jews in Russia.

In "The Hirelings," Zangwill treats critically a situation with affinities to his own. Rozenoffski, a Jewish pianist who resents anti-Semites, is reluctant to identify himself as a Jew until he falls in love with a beautiful Jewish activist. Before he can reveal himself to her, however, a wealthy woman who has refused to hear him in the past is enraptured by an original composition she hears him play, a medley of synagogue-inspired melodies. Rozenoffski accepts her offer of patronage without identifying himself as a Jew, taking refuge in a universal ideal of brotherhood. In the remaining stories, "The Converts" finds a Jew who has abandoned his family denied forgiveness but obtaining solace and material sustenance as an apostate minister; "The Bearer of Burdens" (like the "Tragi-Comedy of Creeds") shows the reconciliation of Jew and Christian in a personal context; and "Elijah's Goblet" is a story of hope in which the actions of a repentant apostate save a Russian Jewish community from destruction in a pogrom.

The first and last stories in *Ghetto Comedies* are also the longest, and they frame the collection with two different kinds of critiques of contemporary Jewish life. In "The Model of Sorrows" a Christian artist thinks he has found the model for his painting of Christ in a suffering Jewish immigrant. As the painting progresses and he learns more about his subject, he keeps changing its conception until finally he is forced to admit that his noble sufferer is a con artist. He completes the painting, however, saying, "For surely here at last was the true tragedy of the people of Christ — to have persisted sublimely, and to be as sordidly perverted; to be king and knave in one." In "Samooborona" (Self-Defense) the proliferation of Jewish political groups, treated comically in *Children of the Ghetto,* is shown to have a darker side, as is the preference for thought over action, also treated comically in "The Yiddish 'Hamlet.'" A young man seeking recruits for weapons training in self-defense against pogroms is rebuffed by one representative after another of religious, Zionist, socialist, antireligious, anti-Zionist,

and antisocialist organizations, each person differing only minutely from the other and each finding a different reason to avoid joining together to fight. As a result, the entire community is destroyed by Russian artillery, and the idealistic recruiter kills himself as he witnesses the destruction.

Ghetto Comedies was widely reviewed and widely admired. Some of the reviewers commented on Zangwill's leading role in the Zionist movement, and these tended to find some of the stories polemical, but on the whole the book was seen as giving assured, humane, and knowing portrayals of Jews and Jewish life. Whether implicitly or explicitly, the maturity of Zangwill's style was noted, including the absence of his earlier strained witticisms and verbal gymnastics. The subtleties of such stories as "The Jewish Trinity" and "Hirelings" were understood and appreciated, as were the political realities satirized so bleakly in "Samooborona." Zangwill's predominance among writers about the Jews was confirmed, as was the superiority of his Jewish fiction over the non-Jewish. The stories were praised, most significantly, for their realism.

In the decade following *Ghetto Comedies,* Zangwill's three children, Ayrton, Margaret, and Oliver, were born. Edith Zangwill published several short works in periodicals, notably *Lippincott's*; her six novels appeared between 1904 and 1928. Zangwill continued his work for the Jewish Territorial Organization and became active in the woman-suffrage movement as a speaker and writer. Many of his papers on feminism, as well as on other political subjects, are collected in *The War for the World* (1916). He continued to write plays, most of them polemical works on universalism and pacifism, and most of them unsuccessful.

In 1911, the year his play *The War God* was produced in London, he also addressed the Universal Races Congress meeting there. The one great exception to Zangwill's dramatic failures in this period is *The Melting Pot* (1909; performed, 1908), which attained great popularity in the United States. Its theme of the melding of the races in the American crucible won cheers from President Theodore Roosevelt at its premiere, though its promotion of intermarriage has continued to trouble Jews. The play's title gave a name to an American ideal that, as Zangwill's experience with idealism might have predicted, never came to pass. In 1914, the year of the first London production of *The Melting Pot, Plaster Saints* was published and performed.

In 1918 Zangwill gave the Arthur Davis Memorial Lecture for the Jewish Historical Society of England, an organization that he had helped to found and of which he served a term as president; the lecture was published as *Chosen Peoples: The Hebraic Ideal "Versus" the Teutonic* (1918). In 1919 the novel *Jinny the Carrier* appeared. The following year he published *The Voice of Jerusalem,* a collection of essays on Judaism and the world situation of the Jews. His translation *Selected Religious Poems of Ibn Gabirol* was published in 1923 by the JPSA as the first volume in the Schiff Library of Jewish Classics.

During this period Zangwill became increasingly frustrated with the slowness of organized Zionism to respond to the immediate need for resettlement of persecuted Jews in Russia and elsewhere. In October 1923, invited to address the American Jewish Congress in Carnegie Hall, he antagonized his audience and essentially severed his ties to the movement by declaring political Zionism dead. Hostility followed him for the rest of his American tour. The speech was published as *Watchman, What of the Night?* (1923). In 1923 Zangwill began a novel, "The Baron of Offenbach," which he was never to finish. His plays of this period continued to fail, culminating in the disaster of his own production of *We Moderns* in 1925. He resigned his leadership of the Jewish Territorial Organization, which was then dissolved, and his health, emotional as well as physical, continued to deteriorate. Zangwill died in a nursing home at Midhurst, Sussex, on 1 August 1926.

The damage to Zangwill's reputation caused by the 1923 address was not lasting, and he was eulogized, in speech and in print, by many of the leading Jewish figures of the day. In 1937 his selected *Speeches, Articles and Letters* became the first book published by the Soncino Jewish Publication Society, the British analogue to the JPSA. The JPSA's own publication of the *Selected Works* in 1938 attests to Zangwill's continued prominence at that time. Soon, however, he faded into literary obscurity, though John Gross reports that he was fondly remembered in the East End "a full generation after his death." A small revival of interest in Zangwill came about in the 1950s and 1960s with the republication of *The King of Schnorrers* and the centennial of Zangwill's birth in 1964. But much of the commentary at this time tempered praise of his goals and his depictions of Jewish life with criticism of what Harold Fisch called, in a 1966 *Judaism* review, "his sentimentality, his extravagance, his frequent shallowness." In short, while the New Criticism reigned, Zangwill was not seen as a very good writer, and predictions were that his reputation would fade once again.

More-sympathetic portrayals of Zangwill's artistry, however, appeared in the studies by Wohl-

gelernter and Adams, each of whom argues for taking Zangwill's writings seriously as literature. A major theme of Wohlgelernter's work is the idea of Zangwill's self-division, as Jew and modern Englishman. Udelson has taken the discussion further by finding evidence of identity conflicts in the secular as well as the Jewish fiction; he also emphasizes (and criticizes) Zangwill's universalist ideology, particularly in his attempts to show the common sources of Judaism and Christianity. Bryan Cheyette places Zangwill in a larger turn-of-the-century tradition of Anglo-Jewish fiction, as both an apologist for the Jews and a universalist in presenting them to the rest of the world.

In a 1954 *Commentary* review, "Does Zangwill Still Live?," Milton Hindus questions the depth of Zangwill's Jewish learning, as Udelson has done more recently. The implication is that although Zangwill was well regarded in his time, he does not fully deserve a high place in Jewish letters. But the evidence of scholarship one hundred years after the first publication of *Children of the Ghetto* suggests that the dilemmas Zangwill faced and described still strike a chord with Jewish readers. The continued publication of such works as *The Big Bow Mystery* and the renewed appearance of Zangwill's short stories in teaching anthologies (such as "The Woman Beater" in Everyman's *Victorian Short Stories: The Trials of Love,* 1990) indicate that Zangwill's work is very much alive. He remains, insistently, a fascinating, controversial figure in literary and Jewish studies, a "minor" writer who will not disappear and whose fiction still has the power to provoke strong feeling and thought.

Interviews:

Raymond Blathwayt, "A Talk with Mr. Zangwill," *Great Thoughts,* 9 (1893): 302;

Isidore Harris, "Mr. Israel Zangwill Interviewed," *Bookman* (London), 13 (February 1898): 145–148; reprinted as "Mr. Israel Zangwill: An Interview," *Bookman* (New York), 7 (April 1898): 104–107;

Patricia Hoey, "Zangwill: An Aggressive, Vivid Factor Among Modern Intellectuals," *Nash's Magazine* (June 1912): 304–308;

Edward Price Bell, "Israel Zangwill on the Ku Klux Klan: A Reply to 'Imperial Wizard' Dr. H. W. Evans," *Landmark,* 4, no. 6 (1924): 411–418.

Bibliographies:

Annamarie Peterson, "Israel Zangwill (1864–1926): A Selected Bibliography," *Bulletin of Bibliogra-*

phy, 23, no. 6 (September–December 1961): 136–140;

Elsie Bonita Adams, "Israel Zangwill: An Annotated Bibliography of Writings About Him," *English Literature in Transition, 1880–1920,* 13, no. 3 (1970): 209–244.

Biographies:

Joseph Leftwich, *Israel Zangwill* (London: Clarke, 1957);

Joseph H. Udelson, *Dreamer of the Ghetto: The Life and Works of Israel Zangwill* (Tuscaloosa: University of Alabama Press, 1990).

References:

Elsie Bonita Adams, *Israel Zangwill* (New York: Twayne, 1971);

J. C. Benjamin, "Israel Zangwill (1864–1926): A Revaluation," *Jewish Quarterly,* 24, no. 3 (1976): 3–5;

Edward N. Calisch, *The Jew in English Literature, as Author and Subject* (Richmond, Va.: Bell Book & Stationery Co., 1909);

Bryan Cheyette, "The Other Self: Anglo-Jewish Fiction and the Representation of Jews in England, 1875–1905," in *The Making of Modern Anglo-Jewry,* edited by David Cesarani (London: Blackwell, 1990);

Harold Fisch, "Israel Zangwill: Prophet of the Ghetto," *Judaism,* 13 (1964): 407–421;

Hamlin Garland, "Roadside Meetings of a Literary Nomad," *Bookman* (London), 71 (June 1930): 302–313;

John Gross, "Zangwill in Retrospect," *Commentary,* 38 (December 1964): 54–57;

Jacques Ben Guigui, *Israel Zangwill, penseur et écrivain (1864–1926)* (Toulouse: Imprimerie Toulousaine–R. Lion, 1975);

Holbrook Jackson, "Israel Zangwill," *Bookman* (London), 46 (May 1914): 67–73; *Living Age,* 282 (26 September 1914): 790–797;

Montagu Frank Modder, *The Jew in the Literature of England: To the End of the Nineteenth Century* (Philadelphia: Jewish Publication Society of America, 1939);

Meri-Jane Rochelson, "*The Big Bow Mystery:* Jewish Identity and the English Detective Novel," *Victorian Review,* 17 (Winter 1991): 11–20;

Rochelson, "Language, Gender, and Ethnic Anxiety in Zangwill's *Children of the Ghetto,*" *English Literature in Transition, 1880–1920,* 31 (1988): 399–412;

Bernard Winehouse, "Israel Zangwill's *Children of the Ghetto:* A Literary History of the First Anglo-Jewish Best-Seller," *English Literature in Transition, 1880–1920,* 16, no. 2 (1973): 93–117;

Winehouse, "The Literary Career of Israel Zangwill from Its Beginnings Until 1898," Ph.D. dissertation, University of London, 1970;

Maurice Wohlgelernter, *Israel Zangwill: A Study* (New York: Columbia University Press, 1964);

Linda Gertner Zatlin, *The Nineteenth-Century Anglo-Jewish Novel* (Boston: Twayne, 1981).

Papers:

The largest collection of Zangwill's letters, diaries, photographs, clippings, manuscripts, and other papers is at the Central Zionist Archives in Jerusalem, file A120. Material on Zangwill also appears in the Archives' files on Zionism and the Jewish Territorial Organization. Significant collections of letters can be found at the American Jewish Archives, Cincinnati; the Brotherton Collection, University of Leeds Library; the Jewish Theological Seminary of America; the New York Public Library; the University of California at Los Angeles; Columbia University; the Yivo Institute for Jewish Research, New York; and in the private collections of Dr. M. H. Salaman and R. A. Salaman of England. Zangwill's manuscripts are at the British Library; the Moccata Library of University College, London; and the University of London Library.

Books for Further Reading

Allen, Walter. *The Short Story in English*. Oxford: Clarendon, 1981.

Altick, Richard D. *The English Common Reader: A Social History of the Mass Reading Public, 1800–1900*. Chicago: University of Chicago Press, 1957.

Altick. *Victorian People and Ideas: A Companion for the Modern Reader of Victorian Literature*. New York: Norton, 1973.

Beachcroft, Thomas Owen. *The English Short Story*, volumes 1 and 2. London: Longmans, Green, 1964.

Beachcroft. *The Modest Art: A Survey of the Short Story in English*. London: Oxford University Press, 1968.

Beckson, Karl. *London in the 1890s: A Cultural History*. New York: Norton, 1992.

Bernstein, Carol L. *The Celebration of Scandal: Toward the Sublime in Victorian Urban Fiction*. University Park: Pennsylvania State University Press, 1991.

Brantlinger, Patrick. *The Spirit of Reform: British Literature and Politics, 1832–1867*. Cambridge, Mass.: Harvard University Press, 1977.

Brown, Julia Prewitt. *A Reader's Guide to the Nineteenth-Century English Novel*. New York: Macmillan, 1985.

Cevasco, G. A., ed. *The 1890s: An Encyclopedia of British Literature, Art, and Culture*. New York: Garland, 1993.

Cross, Nigel. *The Common Writer: Life in Nineteenth-Century Grub Street*. Cambridge: Cambridge University Press, 1985.

Fletcher, Ian, ed. *Selections from British Fiction: 1880–1900*. New York: Signet/New American Library, 1972.

Flora, Joseph M., ed. *The English Short Story, 1880–1945: A Critical History*. Boston: Twayne, 1985.

Hanson, Clare. *Short Stories and Short Fictions, 1880–1980*. London: Macmillan, 1985.

Harris, Wendell V. *British Short Fiction in the Nineteenth Century: A Literary and Bibliographic Guide*. Detroit: Wayne State University Press, 1979.

Hewitt, Douglas. *English Fiction of the Early Modern Period, 1890–1940*. London: Longmans, 1988.

Jackson, Holbrook. *The Eighteen Nineties: A Review of Art and Ideas at the Close of the Nineteenth Century*. New York: Kennerly, 1914.

Jones, Phyllis M., ed. *English Short Stories, 1888–1937*. London: Oxford University Press, 1973.

Keating, Peter. *The Working Classes in Victorian Fiction*. New York: Barnes & Noble, 1971.

Keating, ed. *Into Unknown England, 1866–1913: Selections from the Social Explorers*. Manchester, U.K.: Manchester University Press, 1976.

Keating, ed. *Working-class Stories of the 1890s*. London: Routledge & Kegan Paul, 1971.

Levine, George. *The Realistic Imagination: English Fiction from Frankenstein to Lady Chatterley*. Chicago: University of Chicago Press, 1981.

Lohafer, Susan, and Jo Ellyn Clarey, eds. *Short Story Theory at a Crossroads*. Baton Rouge: Louisiana State University Press, 1989.

Orel, Harold. *The Victorian Short Story: Development and Triumph of a Literary Genre*. Cambridge: Cambridge University Press, 1986.

Orel, ed. *Victorian Short Stories,* volume 2: *The Trials of Love*. London: Dent, 1990.

Pittock, Murray G. H. *Spectrum of Decadence: The Literature of the 1890s*. New York: Routledge, 1993.

Rose, Jonathan. *The Edwardian Temperament, 1895–1919*. Athens: Ohio University Press, 1986.

Showalter, Elaine, ed. *Daughters of Decadence: Women Writers of the 'Fin de Siècle'*. London: Virago, 1993.

Siebenschuh, William R. *Fictional Techniques and Factual Works*. Athens: University of Georgia Press, 1983.

Stanford, Derek. *Short Stories of the 'Nineties: A Biographical Anthology*. London: Baker, 1968.

Stokes, John, ed. *Fin De Siècle, Fin Du Globe: Fears and Fantasies of the Late Nineteenth Century*. New York: St. Martin's Press, 1992.

Stott, Rebecca. *The Fabrication of the Late-Victorian Femme Fatale: The Kiss of Death*. London: Macmillan, 1992.

Sutherland, John. *The Stanford Companion to Victorian Fiction*. Stanford: Stanford University Press, 1989.

Swindells, Julia. *Victorian Writing and Working Women: The Other Side of Silence*. Minneapolis: University of Minnesota Press, 1985.

Vannatta, Dennis, ed. *The English Short Story, 1945–1980: A Critical History*. Boston: Twayne, 1985.

Walkowitz, Judith R. *City of Dreadful Delight: Narratives of Sexual Danger in Late-Victorian London*. Chicago: University of Chicago Press, 1992.

White, Robert B., Jr. *The English Literary Journal to 1900: A Guide to Information Sources*. Detroit: Gale, 1977.

Wolff, Michael, ed. *The Victorian Perodical Press: Samplings and Soundings*. Leicester: Leicester University Press, 1982.

Wright, Anne. *Literature of Crisis, 1910–22*. London: Macmillan, 1984.

Yelling, J. A. *Slums and Slum Clearance in Victorian London*. London: Allen & Unwin, 1986.

Contributors

Ann L. Ardis ....*University of Delaware*
Lee Baker ....*High Point University*
Marilyn Bonnell..*Susquehanna University*
Olga R. R. Broomfield ....*Mount Saint Vincent University*
Glenn S. Burne....................................*University of North Carolina at Charlotte*
John D. Cloy ....*University of Mississippi*
Claire Denelle Cowart...................................*Southeastern Louisiana University*
Barry Faulk..*University of Illinois*
John Ferns..*McMaster University*
Benjamin Franklin Fisher IV.......................................*University of Mississippi*
Hal W. French ....*University of South Carolina*
John R. Greenfield ....*McKendree College*
Donald E. Hall ....*California State University, Northridge*
Catherine E. Hoyser ....*Saint Joseph College*
Mike Jasper ....*Kent State University*
Linda Anne Julian ....*Furman University*
Catherine Jurča ....*Johns Hopkins University*
Shoshana Milgram Knapp ....*Virginia Polytechnic Institute and State University*
Dale Kramer ....*University of Illinois*
Jil Larson..*Western Michigan University*
Anita Levy ....*University of Rochester*
Becky W. Lewis ....*University of South Carolina*
Vern Lindquist..*Sullivan Community College*
Clinton Machann...*Texas A&M University*
Kathleen McCormack.......................................*Florida International University*
Anita Moss.......................................*University of North Carolina at Charlotte*
Jill Tedford Owens.....................................*Southwestern Oklahoma State University*
Bonnie J. Robinson ....*University of Miami*
Meri-Jane Rochelson.......................................*Florida International University*
William B. Thesing..*University of South Carolina*
R. K. R. Thornton ....*University of Birmingham*
Richard Tobias...*University of Pittsburgh*
Jack W. Weaver...*Winthrop University*
Saundra Segan Wheeler ....*Yeshiva University*
Anne M. Windholz ....*Roanoke College*
Jonathan Wike ....*North Carolina A&T State University*

Cumulative Index

Dictionary of Literary Biography, Volumes 1-135
Dictionary of Literary Biography Yearbook, 1980-1992
Dictionary of Literary Biography Documentary Series, Volumes 1-11

Cumulative Index

DLB before number: *Dictionary of Literary Biography*, Volumes 1-135
Y before number: *Dictionary of Literary Biography Yearbook*, 1980-1992
DS before number: *Dictionary of Literary Biography Documentary Series*, Volumes 1-11

A

E

M

O

O'Dell, Scott 1903-1989 .... DLB-52

Odets, Clifford 1906-1963 .... DLB-7, 26

Odhams Press Limited DLB-112

O'Donnell, Peter 1920- DLB-87

O'Faolain, Julia 1932- DLB-14

O'Faolain, Sean 1900- DLB-15

Off Broadway and Off-Off
    Broadway DLB-7

Off-Loop Theatres DLB-7

Offord, Carl Ruthven 1910- DLB-76

O'Flaherty, Liam 1896-1984 ... DLB-36; Y-84

Ogilvie, J. S., and Company DLB-49

Ogot, Grace 1930- DLB-125

O'Grady, Desmond 1935- DLB-40

O'Hagan, Howard 1902-1982 ...... DLB-68

O'Hara, Frank 1926-1966 .... DLB-5, 16

O'Hara, John 1905-1970 .... DLB-9, 86; DS-2

Okara, Christopher 1930-1967 ..... DLB-125

O'Keeffe, John 1747-1833 .... DLB-89

Okigbo, Christopher 1930-1967 .... DLB-125

Okot p'Bitek 1931-1982 .... DLB-125

Olaudah Equiano and Unfinished Journeys:
    The Slave-Narrative Tradition and
    Twentieth-Century Continuities, by
    Paul Edwards and Pauline T.
    Wangman DLB-117

Old Franklin Publishing House DLB-49

Older, Fremont 1856-1935 .... DLB-25

Oldham, John 1653-1683 .... DLB-131

Olds, Sharon 1942- DLB-120

Oliphant, Laurence 1829?-1888 ..... DLB-18

Oliphant, Margaret 1828-1897 ...... DLB-18

Oliver, Chad 1928- DLB-8

Oliver, Mary 1935- DLB-5

Ollier, Claude 1922- DLB-83

Olsen, Tillie 1913?- DLB-28; Y-80

Olson, Charles 1910-1970 .... DLB-5, 16

Olson, Elder 1909- DLB-48, 63

Omotoso, Kole 1943- DLB-125

"On Art in Fiction "(1838),
    by Edward Bulwer DLB-21

On Learning to Write Y-88

On Some of the Characteristics of Modern
    Poetry and On the Lyrical Poems of
    Alfred Tennyson (1831), by Arthur
    Henry Hallam DLB-32

"On Style in English Prose" (1898), by
    Frederic Harrison DLB-57

"On Style in Literature: Its Technical
    Elements" (1885), by Robert Louis
    Stevenson DLB-57

"On the Writing of Essays" (1862),
    by Alexander Smith DLB-57

Ondaatje, Michael 1943- DLB-60

O'Neill, Eugene 1888-1953 .... DLB-7

Onetti, Juan Carlos 1909- DLB-113

Onofri, Arturo 1885-1928 .... DLB-114

Opie, Amelia 1769-1853 .... DLB-116

Oppen, George 1908-1984 .... DLB-5

Oppenheim, E. Phillips 1866-1946 ... DLB-70

Oppenheim, James 1882-1932 .... DLB-28

Oppenheimer, Joel 1930- DLB-5

Optic, Oliver (see Adams, William Taylor)

Orczy, Emma, Baroness
    1865-1947 .... DLB-70

Orlovitz, Gil 1918-1973 .... DLB-2, 5

Orlovsky, Peter 1933- DLB-16

Ormond, John 1923- DLB-27

Ornitz, Samuel 1890-1957 .... DLB-28, 44

Ortiz, Simon 1941- DLB-120

Orton, Joe 1933-1967 .... DLB-13

Orwell, George 1903-1950 ...... DLB-15, 98

The Orwell Year Y-84

Ory, Carlos Edmundo de
    1923- DLB-134

Osbey, Brenda Marie 1957- DLB-120

Osbon, B. S. 1827-1912 .... DLB-43

Osborne, John 1929- DLB-13

Osgood, Herbert L. 1855-1918 ...... DLB-47

Osgood, James R., and
    Company DLB-49

Osgood, McIlvaine and
    Company DLB-112

O'Shaughnessy, Arthur
    1844-1881 .... DLB-35

O'Shea, Patrick
    [publishing house] DLB-49

Osofisan, Femi 1946- DLB-125

Ostenso, Martha 1900-1963 .... DLB-92

Ostriker, Alicia 1937- DLB-120

Oswald, Eleazer 1755-1795 .... DLB-43

Otero, Blas de 1916-1979 .... DLB-134

Otero, Miguel Antonio
    1859-1944 .... DLB-82

Otis, James (see Kaler, James Otis)

Otis, James, Jr. 1725-1783 .... DLB-31

Otis, Broaders and Company DLB-49

Ottaway, James 1911- DLB-127

Ottendorfer, Oswald 1826-1900 ..... DLB-23

Otto-Peters, Louise 1819-1895 ..... DLB-129

Otway, Thomas 1652-1685 .... DLB-80

Ouellette, Fernand 1930- DLB-60

Ouida 1839-1908 .... DLB-18

Outing Publishing Company DLB-46

Outlaw Days, by Joyce Johnson DLB-16

The Overlook Press DLB-46

Overview of U.S. Book Publishing,
    1910-1945 .... DLB-9

Owen, Guy 1925- DLB-5

Owen, John 1564-1622 .... DLB-121

Owen, John [publishing house] DLB-49

Owen, Robert 1771-1858 .... DLB-107

Owen, Wilfred 1893-1918 .... DLB-20

Owen, Peter, Limited DLB-112

Owsley, Frank L. 1890-1956 .... DLB-17

Ozick, Cynthia 1928- DLB-28; Y-82

P

Pacey, Desmond 1917-1975 .... DLB-88

Pack, Robert 1929- DLB-5

Packaging Papa: The Garden of Eden Y-86

Padell Publishing Company DLB-46

Padgett, Ron 1942- DLB-5

Padilla, Ernesto Chávez 1944- ... DLB-122

Page, L. C., and Company DLB-49

Page, P. K. 1916- DLB-68

Page, Thomas Nelson
    1853-1922 .... DLB-12, 78

Page, Walter Hines 1855-1918 ... DLB-71, 91

Paget, Violet (see Lee, Vernon)

Pagliarani, Elio 1927- DLB-128

Pain, Barry 1864–1928 .... DLB-135

Pain, Philip ?-circa 1666 .... DLB-24

Paine, Robert Treat, Jr. 1773-1811 ... DLB-37

Paine, Thomas 1737-1809 ... DLB-31, 43, 73

Palazzeschi, Aldo 1885-1974 .... DLB-114

Paley, Grace 1922- DLB-28

Palfrey, John Gorham
    1796-1881 .... DLB-1, 30

Palgrave, Francis Turner
    1824-1897 .... DLB-35

ISBN 0-8103-5394-6

90000

9 780810 353947

(Continued from front endsheets)

Documentary Series

Yearbooks